A NEW
WITNESS
FOR THE
ARTICLES
OF FAITH

A NEW WITNESS
FOR THE
ARTICLES OF FAITH

BRUCE R. M^cCONKIE

Deseret Book

Salt Lake City, Utah

No part of this book may be reproduced in any
form or by any means without permission in writing
from the publisher, Deseret Book Company,
P.O. Box 30178, Salt Lake City, Utah 84130

First printing August 1985
Second printing September 1985
Third printing December 1985

Library of Congress Cataloging in Publication Data

McConkie, Bruce R.
    A new witness for the Articles of Faith.

    Includes index.
    1. Church of Jesus Christ of Latter-day Saints.
Articles of Faith. 2. Church of Jesus Christ of Latter-
day Saints—Creeds. 3. Mormon Church—Creeds.
I. Title.
BX8649.M35   1985   238'.9332   85-12888
ISBN 0-87747-872-4

Contents

ARTICLE 1

*We believe in God, the Eternal
Father, and in His Son, Jesus Christ,
and in the Holy Ghost.*

ARTICLE 2

*We believe that men will be
punished for their own sins, and
not for Adam's transgression.*

72012

ARTICLE 3

*We believe that through the
Atonement of Christ, all mankind
may be saved, by obedience to the
laws and ordinances of the Gospel.*

ARTICLE 4

*We believe that the first principles
and ordinances of the Gospel are:
first, Faith in the Lord Jesus Christ;
second, Repentance; third, Baptism
by immersion for the remission of
sins; fourth, Laying on of hands for
the gift of the Holy Ghost.*

ARTICLE 5

*We believe that a man must be
called of God, by prophecy, and by
the laying on of hands by those
who are in authority, to preach the
Gospel and administer in the
ordinances thereof.*

ARTICLE 6

*We believe in the same
organization that existed in the
Primitive Church, namely, apostles,
prophets, pastors, teachers,
evangelists, and so forth.*

ARTICLE 7

*We believe in the gift of tongues,
prophecy, revelation, visions,
healing, interpretation of tongues,
and so forth.*

ARTICLE 8

*We believe the Bible to be the word
of God as far as it is translated
correctly; we also believe the Book
of Mormon to be the word of God.*

ARTICLE 9

*We believe all that God has
revealed, all that He does now
reveal, and we believe that He will
yet reveal many great and
important things pertaining to the
Kingdom of God.*

ARTICLE 10

*We believe in the literal gathering
of Israel and in the restoration
of the Ten Tribes; that Zion (the New
Jerusalem) will be built upon the
American continent; that Christ will
reign personally upon the earth;
and, that the earth will be renewed and
receive its paradisiacal glory.*

ARTICLE 11

*We claim the privilege of
worshiping Almighty God according
to the dictates of our own
conscience, and allow all men the
same privilege, let them worship
how, where, or what they may.*

ARTICLE 12

*We believe in being subject to kings,
presidents, rulers, and magistrates,
in obeying, honoring, and
sustaining the law.*

ARTICLE 13

*We believe in being honest, true,
chaste, benevolent, virtuous, and in
doing good to all men; indeed, we
may say that we follow the
admonition of Paul—We believe all
things, we hope all things, we have
endured many things, and hope to
be able to endure all things. If there
is anything virtuous, lovely, or of
good report or praiseworthy, we
seek after these things.*

Publisher's Preface

Only the scriptures, official statements, and other publications written under assignment from the First Presidency and the Council of the Twelve Apostles are considered authorized publications of the Church. Other books, including those written by General Authorities, such as this one, are the responsibility of the author.

This work is the final written contribution of Elder Bruce R. McConkie. He served as a General Authority for over forty years, the concluding thirteen years as a member of the Quorum of the Twelve Apostles. He was trained in the field of law and was a powerful preacher and a gifted writer. His written and spoken testimony, always on the restored gospel of Jesus Christ, has been and will remain an inspiration to the Church.

Elder McConkie regarded this book as something of a benediction to his ministry. The first draft of the manuscript was delivered to the publisher shortly before he passed away, and he did not have the opportunity to review the text in the several stages of the publication, as was his custom. With his other published works he had the opportunity to provide a detailed reference to every quotation, to read and polish, to reorganize and clarify up to the day that the finished work was "locked up" and the press would roll to set upon the printed page once more the testimony and counsel of this gifted gospel scholar, this modern-day apostle of the Lord.

So that you may begin at the very point where he concluded his ministry, his final testimony delivered at general conference is given here as a preface. It was delivered on April 6, 1985, just thirteen days before he passed away.

Preface

I feel, and the Spirit seems to accord, that the most important doctrine I can declare, and the most powerful testimony I can bear, is of the atoning sacrifice of the Lord Jesus Christ.

His atonement is the most transcendent event that ever has occurred or ever will occur from Creation's dawn through all the ages of a never-ending eternity. It is the supreme act of goodness and grace that only a god could perform.

Through it, all of the terms and conditions of the Father's eternal plan of salvation became operative. Through it are brought to pass the immortality and eternal life of man. Through it, all men are saved from death, hell, the devil, and endless torment. And through it, all who believe and obey the glorious gospel of God, all who are true and faithful and overcome the world, all who suffer for Christ and his word, all who are chastened and scourged in the cause of him whose we are —all shall become as their Maker and sit with him on his throne and reign with him forever in everlasting glory.

In speaking of these wondrous things I shall use my own words, though you may think they are the words of scripture, words spoken by other apostles and prophets.

True it is they were first proclaimed by others, but they are now mine, for the Holy Spirit of God has borne witness to me that they are true, and it is now as though the Lord had revealed them to me in the first instance. I have thereby heard his voice and know his word.

Two thousand years ago, outside Jerusalem's walls, there was a pleasant garden spot, Gethsemane by name, where Jesus and his intimate friends were wont to retire for pondering and prayer.

There Jesus taught his disciples the doctrines of the kingdom, and all of them communed with Him who is the Father of us all, in whose ministry they were engaged, and on whose errand they served.

This sacred spot, like Eden where Adam dwelt, like Sinai whence Jehovah gave his laws, like Calvary where the Son of God gave his life a ransom for many, this holy ground is where the Sinless Son of the Everlasting Father took upon himself the sins of all men on condition of repentance.

We do not know, we cannot tell, no mortal mind can conceive, the full import of what Christ did in Gethsemane.

We know that he sweat great gouts of blood from every pore as he drained the dregs of that bitter cup his Father had given him.

We know that he suffered, both body and spirit, more than it is possible for man to suffer, except it be unto death.

We know that in some way, incomprehensible to us, his suffering satisfied the demands of justice, ransomed penitent souls from the pains and penalties of sin, and made mercy available to those who believe in his holy name.

We know that he lay prostrate upon the ground as the pains and agonies of an infinite burden caused him to tremble, and would that he might not drink the bitter cup.

We know that an angel came from the courts of glory to strengthen him in his ordeal, and we suppose it was mighty Michael who foremost fell that mortal man might be.

As near as we can judge, these infinite agonies—this suffering beyond compare—continued for some three or four hours. After this, his body then wrenched and drained of strength, he confronted Judas and the other incarnate devils, some from the very Sanhedrin itself; and he was led away with a rope around his neck, as a common criminal, to be judged by the archcriminals who as Jews sat in Aaron's seat and who as Romans wielded Caesar's power.

They took him to Annas, to Caiaphas, to Pilate, to Herod, and back to Pilate. He was accused, cursed, and smitten. Their foul saliva ran down his face as vicious blows further weakened his pain-engulfed body. With reeds of wrath they rained blows upon his back. Blood ran down his face as a crown of thorns pierced his trembling brow. But above it all he was scourged, scourged with forty stripes save one, scourged with a multithonged whip into whose leather strands sharp bones and cutting metals were woven.

Many died from scourging alone, but he rose from the sufferings of the scourge that he might die an ignominious death upon the cruel cross of Calvary. Then he carried his own cross until he collapsed from the weight and pain and mounting agony of it all.

Finally, on a hill called Calvary—again, it was outside Jerusalem's walls—while helpless disciples looked on and felt the agonies of near death in their own bodies, the Roman soldiers laid him upon the cross. With great mallets they drove spikes of iron through his feet and hands and wrists. Truly he was wounded for our transgressions and bruised for our iniquities.

Then the cross was raised that all might see and gape and curse and deride. This they did, with evil venom, for three hours from 9 A.M. to noon. Then the heavens grew black. Darkness covered the land for the space of three hours, as it did among the Nephites. There was a mighty storm, as though the very God of Nature was in agony. And truly he was, for while he was hanging on the cross for another three hours, from noon to 3 P.M., all the infinite agonies and merciless pains of Gethsemane recurred. And, finally, when the atoning agonies had taken their toll—when the victory had been won, when the Son of God had fulfilled the will of his Father in all things— then he said, "It is finished" (John 19:30), and he voluntarily gave up the ghost.

As the peace and comfort of a merciful death freed him from the pains and sorrows of mortality, he entered the paradise of God. When he had made his soul an offering for sin, he was prepared to see his seed, according to the messianic word. These, consisting of all the holy prophets and faithful Saints from ages past; these, comprising all who had taken upon them his name, and who, being spiritually begotten by him, had become his sons and his daughters, even as it is with us; all these were assembled in the spirit world, there to see his face and hear his voice.

After some thirty-eight or forty hours—three days as the Jews measured time—our Blessed Lord came to the Arimathaean's tomb, where his partially embalmed body had been placed by Nicodemus and Joseph of Arimathaea. Then, in a way incomprehensible to us, he took up that body which had not yet seen corruption and arose in that glorious immortality which made him like his resurrected Father. He then received all power in heaven and on earth, obtained eternal exaltation, appeared unto Mary Magdalene and many others, and ascended into heaven, there to sit down on the right hand of God the Father Almighty and to reign forever in eternal glory.

His rising from death on the third day crowned the atonement. Again, in some way incomprehensible to us, the effects of his resurrection pass upon all men so that all shall rise from the grave. As Adam brought death, so Christ brought life; as Adam is the father of mortality, so Christ is the father of immortality. And without both mortality and immortality, man cannot work out his salvation and ascend to those heights beyond the skies where gods and angels dwell forever in eternal glory.

Now, the atonement of Christ is the most basic and fundamental doctrine of the gospel, and it is the least understood of all our revealed truths. Many of us have a superficial knowledge and rely upon the Lord and his goodness to see us through the trials and perils of life. But if we are to have faith like that of Enoch and Elijah, we must believe what they believed, know what they knew, and live as they lived.

May I invite you to join with me in gaining a sound and sure knowledge of the atonement. We must cast aside the philosophies of men and the wisdom of the wise and hearken to that Spirit which is given to us to guide us into all truth. We must search the scriptures, accepting them as the mind and will and voice of the Lord and the very power of God unto salvation.

As we read, ponder, and pray, there will come into our minds a view of the three gardens of God—the Garden of Eden, the garden of Gethsemane, and the garden of the empty tomb, where Jesus appeared to Mary Magdalene.

In Eden we will see all things created in a paradisiacal state —without death, without procreation, without probationary experiences. We will come to know that such a creation, now unknown to man, was the only way to provide for the Fall. We will then see Adam and Eve, the first man and the first woman, step down from their state of immortal and paradisiacal glory to become the first mortal flesh on earth. Mortality, including as it does procreation and death, will enter the world. And because of transgression, a probationary estate of trial and testing will begin.

Then in Gethsemane we will see the Son of God ransom man from the temporal and spiritual death that came to us because of the Fall. And finally, before an empty tomb, we will come to know that Christ our Lord has burst the bands of death and stands forever triumphant over the grave.

Thus, Creation is father to the Fall; and by the Fall came mortality and death; and by Christ came immortality and eternal life. If there had been no fall of Adam, by which cometh death, there could have been no atonement of Christ, by which cometh life.

And now, as pertaining to this perfect atonement, wrought by the shedding of the blood of God, I testify that it took place in Gethsemane and at Golgotha; and as pertaining to Jesus Christ, I testify that he is the son of the Living God and was crucified for the sins of the world. He is our Lord, our God, and our King. This I know of myself, independent of any other person. I am one of his witnesses, and in a coming day I shall feel the nail marks in his hands and in his feet and shall wet his feet with my tears. But I shall not know any better then than I know now that he is God's Almighty Son, that he is our Savior and Redeemer, and that salvation comes in and through his atoning blood and in no other way.

God grant that all of us may walk in the light as God our Father is in the light so that, according to the promises, the blood of Jesus Christ his Son will cleanse us from all sin. In the name of the Lord Jesus Christ. Amen.

CHAPTER 1

Joseph Smith— Prophet and Seer

Jesus and Joseph—Blessed Names

Salvation—blessed, hallowed, wondrous word—*salvation* is available to men on earth today because of Joseph Smith, the prophet and seer of the latter days. He is the one to whom the Lord revealed anew the fulness of the everlasting gospel in the dispensation of the fulness of times. He is the one who received anew the keys of the kingdom of heaven so that mortal men might have power once again to bind and loose on earth and in heaven. He is a new witness for the Lord Jesus Christ and His gospel.

The Lord and his prophets are one. They are united in the same mind and in the same judgment. Light and truth and righteousness come from God and are revealed and bestowed by him upon chosen servants who wear the prophetic mantle. They in turn proclaim the Lord's word and his righteousness to the residue of men. Accordingly, salvation is in Christ and comes because of his infinite and eternal atonement. It is through his gospel that all men are raised in immortality, with those who believe and obey gaining the added glory of eternal life. But the word of salvation is preached and the plan of salvation is offered to men by prophets and apostles and holy men who are called of God, who are endowed with power from on high, and who go forth in the Lord's name and power to lead their fellowmen to eternal salvation. Joseph Smith is the chief and foremost of these prophets in this final gospel dispensation.

Thus it is that we link the names of Jesus Christ and Joseph Smith together, and, in the same breath and by the power of the same Spirit, bear testimony of the wondrous works of each of them. And in so doing we simply follow the patterns of the past. The names of the Lord Jehovah and of Michael our Prince are forever revered because Michael, under Jehovah, led the armies of heaven when Lucifer rebelled and was cast like lightning from the Divine Presence. They are linked together also because Michael became Adam, the first man of all men and the father of the human race; because he chose to fall so that mortal man might be; and because he was the one unto whom Christ first revealed on earth the eternal plan of redemption. The names of Mary and Christ are spoken together in tones of reverent awe because she was overshadowed by the Holy Ghost and conceived in her womb and brought forth God's own Son and called his name Jesus.

And so it is with the great prophet and seer of the latter days. His name is everlastingly linked with the name of that Lord whose servant he was and is. Jesus and Joseph—blessed, sacred, holy names; names of wondrous glory; names recorded forever along with those of Adam and Enoch and Noah and Abraham and Moses in the Lamb's Book of Life! The Lord and his prophets in all ages go together. Every prophet is a witness of the Lord; every prophet teaches the plan of salvation in his appointed day; every prophet is a legal administrator who is endowed with holy power sent down from heavenly realms. The Lord rejoices in them and they in him, and Joseph Smith is no exception.

As we begin this work, there must be no misunderstanding relative to the foundation upon which we shall build. Salvation comes because of Christ. He is our Lord, our King, and our God. He is the Redeemer of men and the Savior of the world; he alone worked out the infinite and eternal atonement. He is the One who died on the cross of Calvary that we might live. His is the only name given under heaven whereby men may be saved. He "made himself of no reputation, and took upon him the form of a servant, and was made in the likeness of men: And being found in fashion as a man, he humbled himself, and became obedient unto death, even the death of the cross. Wherefore God also hath highly exalted him, and given him a name which is above every name: that at the name of Jesus every knee should bow, of things in heaven, and things in earth, and things under the earth; and that every tongue should confess that Jesus Christ is Lord, to the glory of God the Father." (Philippians 2:7-11.)

But neither must there be any misunderstanding as to the position of Joseph Smith in the eternal scheme of things. He is the restorer of the knowledge of Christ and of salvation for our day. He is the one to whom Christ revealed anew the pure and perfect plan of salvation. He is the legal administrator to whom the keys of the kingdom of God were given in modern times so that once again men would have power to bind on earth and have their acts sealed eternally in the heavens. He is the head of the dispensation of the fulness of times in which the Lord will yet gather together all things in Christ. He is the chief apostle of the latter days, the one whose witness of the Lord Jesus must be accepted by all who will save themselves in the presence of that blessed Lord.

Joseph Smith—His Prophetic Foreordination

Joseph Smith was foreordained in the councils of eternity, before the foundations of the earth were laid, to be a prophet of God in the last days and to preside over the dispensation of the fulness of times. This call to come into mortality and stand as a revealer of truth and a witness of Christ came because of his valiance and devotion in the premortal first estate. He is numbered with those who were "called and prepared from the foundation of the world according to the foreknowledge of God, on account of their exceeding faith and good works" (Alma 13:3), as these works were manifest during the long ages they dwelt in the Divine Presence.

Indeed, all of the prophets of all the ages; all of the Lord's witnesses who have held apostolic power; all of the holy and righteous men who have been commissioned to carry the message of salvation to the world; all who have been appointed to minister for the spiritual needs of the sons of men—all were foreordained. The Lord Jesus himself set the pattern. He came into mortality as "a lamb without blemish and without spot: who verily was foreordained before the foundation of the world, but was manifest" (1 Peter 1:19-20) at the appointed time.

Jeremiah is the classical illustration among the prophets of one who was foreordained. To him the Lord said: "Before I formed thee in the belly I knew thee; and before thou camest forth out of the womb I sanctified thee, and I ordained thee a prophet unto the nations." (Jeremiah 1:5.) Nearly six hundred years before their mortal birth, Nephi saw in vision the Lamb of God, the Twelve Apostles who should stand at his side, and the Virgin of Nazareth of Galilee in whose womb the Lord's mortal body would be formed. Each of these noble and great ones was foreordained for the work he or she would do as a mortal.

Abraham, in one of the grandest visions ever vouchsafed to man, saw "the intelligences that were organized before the world was; and among all these there were many of the noble and great ones," he said. "And God saw these souls that they were good, and he stood in the midst of them, and he said: These I will make my rulers; for he stood among those that were spirits, and he saw that they were good." All of the prophets and apostles and preachers of righteousness of all the ages were present in that mighty congregation. And to the Father of the Faithful the great God then said: "Abraham, thou art one of them; thou wast chosen before thou wast born." (Abraham 3:22-23.)

As it was with Abraham, so it was with Joseph Smith. Each was foreordained to preside over a great gospel dispensation. This very pre-choice by an All-wise God bears testimony of their exceedingly high prophetic status. There have been many prophets and numerous apostles, but there have been few heads of dispensations. Those prophetic souls who minister in the various dispensations are but echoes and witnesses of the one chosen to head the dispensation in which they live. Thus, Joseph Smith ranks with the dozen or score of the mightiest spiritual giants who have so far dwelt upon our earth.

Joseph Smith—A Modern Prophet

This modern man, with a most ordinary name, our revered and honored Prophet Joseph Smith, began his mortal life on December 23, 1805, in Sharon, Windsor County, Vermont. He was born with all of the scriptural talents and capacities he had acquired through long ages of obedience and progression among his fellow prophets. Men are not born equal in talents and capacities; mortality commences where preexistence ends, and the talents earned in the life that went before are available for use in this mortal life.

In the spring of 1820, while yet in his fifteenth year, young Joseph, who was living near Palmyra, New York, in a frontier area, found himself in the midst of a violent, almost fanatical, religious revival that ignited the flames of passion and oratory in all the churches of the area.

Young Joseph heard a sermon that dwelt upon these blessed words: "If any of you lack wisdom, let him ask of God, that giveth to all men liberally, and upbraideth not; and it shall be given him." (James 1:5.) A single sentence, twenty-six plain and simple words—these Spirit-authored words have had a great impact upon religion and all that appertains to it. Though they present a divine concept of universal application and were written for the guidance of all men, though they chart the course all must follow in their search for that religion which is pure and undefiled, and though they are a guide for all who seek the Lord and his saving truths—yet they were preserved through the ages for the especial guidance of that prophet who should usher in the dispensation of the fulness of times.

This was the hour when the man and the time came together. This was the set time, in the providences of that Lord who knows all things, to open the heavens and begin as in days of old to rain righteousness upon his children. And Joseph Smith was the noble and great one who had been prepared from all eternity to receive the heaven-sent word. "Never did any passage of scripture come with more power to the heart of man," he said, "than this did at this time to mine." (Joseph Smith – History 1:12.) The Spirit of God rested mightily upon him. Not even Enoch and Abraham and Moses and the ancient prophets had been overpowered by such yearnings for truth and salvation as then filled Joseph's soul. As guided from on high, he retired to the place before appointed by the Lord of heaven and there began to offer up to God the desires of his heart.

What followed has no parallel of which we know. Joseph asked of God, and God gave liberally. The heavens were rent; revelation commenced anew. The great God, who created the very universe of which this earth is but a small part, came down; at his side, in glorious immortality and in the exact image of his person, appeared the Lord Jesus Christ. The Father and the Son, the supreme rulers of the universe, came personally to mortal man on earth!

"I saw a pillar of light exactly over my head, above the brightness of the sun, which descended gradually until it fell upon me," Joseph said. "When the light rested upon me I saw two Personages, whose brightness and glory defy all description, standing above me in the air. One of them spake unto me, calling me by name, and said, pointing to the other—*This is My Beloved Son. Hear Him!*" Have more blessed words ever saluted human ears? Is it not again as it was at Bethabara when John baptized the Lamb of God who takes away the sin of the world? Is it not once more as it was when the Son of God was transfigured before the chief of his ancient apostles? The voice of God is heard again! The Father bears witness of the Son and introduces him to the world!

"My object in going to inquire of the Lord was to know which of all the sects was right, that I might know which to join," the Prophet continues. "No sooner, therefore, did I get possession of myself, so as to be able to speak, than I asked the Personages who stood above me in the light, which of all the sects was right (for at this time it had never entered into my heart that all were wrong)—and which I should join." How natural it was that an unlearned youth—one unschooled in creeds and doctrines of Christendom—should hope that somewhere on earth there was a true church that taught true doctrines that would save men.

But, alas, such was not the case. Unbeknown to the yet spiritually inexperienced youth, darkness covered the earth and gross darkness the minds of the people. The reply he received was earthshaking. Seldom have such words been spoken to doomed and fallen man. "I was answered that I must join none of them, for they were all wrong," the Prophet said, "and the Personage who addressed me said that all their creeds were an abomination in his sight; that those professors were all corrupt; that: 'they draw near to me with their lips, but their hearts are far from me, they teach for doctrines the commandments of men, having a form of godliness, but they deny the power thereof.' " (JS-H 1:16-19.) "I was expressly commanded 'to go not after them,' at the same time receiving a promise that the fullness of the Gospel should at some future time be made known unto me," he later said in a letter to John Wentworth. (*History of the Church* [HC] 4:536.)

In due course and in the providences of Him who holds all things in his hands and who wants all men to believe and obey his saving truths, the Lord of Heaven restored the fulness of his everlasting gospel to Joseph Smith. The Book of Mormon came forth; in it the doctrines of Christ are set forth in purity and perfection. Angelic ministrants descended from the courts of glory and conferred upon Joseph Smith and Oliver Cowdery priesthoods and keys and powers. Revelations containing the mind and will of the Lord for men in modern times were poured out upon the faithful. By revelation and commandment, the church and kingdom of God was again established among men. The Lord's law was made known line upon line and precept upon precept until, once again, mortals knew the truths and possessed the powers whereby they might gain eternal life.

When the Lord's purposes had been accomplished in full; when the Latter-day Saints had received the same gifts and powers enjoyed by the ancients; when in literal reality the grand plan of salvation was once again on earth—then the newly called Prophet of God on earth had but one thing more to do as a mortal. It was then his destiny to seal his testimony with his own blood. This he did on June 27, 1844, in Carthage Jail. His eternal spirit then went on into the realms ahead, there to continue his prophetic labors among the departed souls, while his innocent blood was mingled "with the innocent blood of all the martyrs under the altar that John saw, [to] cry unto the Lord of hosts till he avenges that blood on the earth." (D&C 135:7.)

CHAPTER 2

Was Joseph Smith Called of God?

"Beware of False Prophets"

Whenever the servants of the Lord in our day teach and testify that Joseph Smith is a prophet of God, Satan's ministers immediately spew forth a stream of venomous evil and falsehood, belittling, defaming, and opposing that prophet whom the Lord appointed to bring to pass his strange act in the last days. It is their wont to wrest the scriptures, falsify history, and give a false color to the spoken word. Not infrequently the Saints themselves are unwise in casting pearls before swine—in telling the spiritually immature more than their unenlightened minds can receive—with the result that those who receive the pearls turn again and rend them.

Those who oppose the Church and the gospel it administers cry out: Delusion, fantasy, false prophets, beware! But all of this is one of the great evidences of the divinity of the Lord's great latter-day work. Those in all sects, parties, and denominations find it easy to put aside their differences when the seeming need arises to unite on the one point that Joseph Smith is a false prophet. It seems that men may believe any doctrine and follow any practice—except one—and still be in good standing in the Christian community. Everything is acceptable except to believe in the divine mission of Joseph Smith.

"It seems as though the adversary was aware, at a very early period of my life, that I was destined to prove a disturber and an annoyer of his kingdom," the Prophet said, "else why should the powers of darkness combine against me? Why the opposition and persecution that arose against me, almost in my infancy?" (JS-H 1:20.) Why indeed? Why should so many religionists unite against an unknown youth of no renown or standing in the community? Would the whole sectarian world shiver and shake and call for a sword if some other unknown fourteen-year-old youth in an obscure frontier village should claim that he was visited by angels and that he saw the Lord? The problem when Joseph Smith announced such a claim was that it was true and that Lucifer knew of its verity.

Joseph Smith told an unnamed minister about the vision in which the Father and the Son appeared to usher in the new dispensation. "I was greatly surprised at his behavior," the Prophet said. "He treated my communication not only lightly, but with great contempt, saying it was all of the devil, that there were no such things as visions or revelations in these days; that all such things had ceased with the apostles, and that there would never be any more of them." (HC 1:21.) Such was and is the benighted state of modern Christendom. Even its leaders—those who are assumed to have read the holy word that says God is no respecter of persons; who are supposed to know that the scriptures testify of a God who is the same yesterday, today, and forever; who are expected to believe and teach that a soul is just as precious in the sight of heaven today as it ever was—even the shepherds of the flocks did and do deny visions and revelations.

This innocent act of a guileless lad in telling what the Lord had done for him soon reaped awful consequences. Hatred from religionists who preached love and brotherhood, and persecution from those who professed allegiance to the Prince of Peace, became the order of the day. "Though I was an obscure boy, only between fourteen and fifteen years of age, and my circumstances in life such as to make a boy of no consequence in the world, yet men of high standing would take notice sufficient to excite the public mind against me, and create a bitter persecution; and this was common among all the sects—all united to persecute me." (JS-H 1:22.) Would they have pursued such a course for any other country lad? Is not the persecution itself a witness of the reality of the First Vision? Or if it were not true, would the worldly wise and the intellectual religionists today devote their talents and means to defaming Joseph Smith and the work that bears his imprint? What is it to anyone else what we believe unless they in their unbelief fear lest our doctrines are true and our practices may have divine approval?

"It caused me serious reflection then, and often has since," the Prophet said, "how very strange it was that an obscure boy, of a little over fourteen years of age, and one, too, who was doomed to the necessity of obtaining a scanty maintenance by his daily labor, should be thought a character of sufficient importance to attract the attention of the great ones of the most popular sects of the day, and in a manner to create in them a spirit of the most bitter persecution and reviling." (JS-H 1:23.)

What Jesus had actually said about false prophets on the hillside above Capernaum was this: "Beware of false prophets, which come to you in sheep's clothing, but inwardly they are ravening wolves." His warning was directed against the Sanhedrinists, and the scribes and priests and rabbis, who rejected him and exhorted the people to do likewise. But the principle is one of universal application. It prevails in every age and applies in all situations in which false doctrines are taught. Beware of prophets and teachers and ministers who teach any other gospel than that which is ordained and established by the Lord. Beware of those who proclaim a plan of salvation different from the one taught by the apostles and prophets of old.

That we and all persons might be left without excuse in choosing those prophets and teachers to whom we give heed, Jesus said: "Ye shall know them"—the prophets, those who are true and those who are false—"by their fruits." Prophets are known by their works! All men who hear their message must choose for themselves. They must choose whether to believe or to disbelieve, whether to accept or to reject the prophetic word, whether to join with the true prophets and become the friends of God or to follow false prophets and be numbered with his enemies. Such is the purpose of life. This mortality is a probationary estate. In it we take the test that will determine our place in the kingdoms that lie beyond the veil.

And so Jesus asks: "Do men gather grapes of thorns, or figs of thistles?" The answer is so obvious that it is assumed. "Even so every good tree bringeth forth good fruit; but a corrupt tree bringeth forth evil fruit. A good tree cannot bring forth evil fruit, neither can a corrupt tree bring forth good fruit." True prophets, true teachers, and true ministers (having as they do the true gospel!)—all these bring forth good fruit that nourishes the soul. False prophets, false teachers, and false ministers (having a corrupt and false system of supposed salvation!)—all these bring forth evil fruit, fruit without eternal nourishment, fruit that lets the soul die.

As to the fate of false prophets, false teachers, and false ministers, Jesus said: "Every tree that bringeth not forth good fruit is hewn down, and cast into the fire." Conversely, those who bring forth good fruit will abide the day of burning and have joy forever with the Lord of the Harvest. "Wherefore by their fruits ye shall know them." (Matthew 7:15-20.) Prophets are known by their fruits. The divine command is twofold: (1) Beware of false prophets; shun them; flee from them; reject their doctrines; turn from their practices; rid yourselves of every evil thing. (2) Cleave unto true prophets; believe their words; take their counsel; receive the ordinances of salvation under their hands; do as they do, so as to be as they are.

Follow Joseph Smith—A True Prophet

In every age when the Lord has a people on earth, the great question confronting all mankind is whether they will believe and obey the prophet who presides over their dispensation. He is the one sent of God to reveal the truths of salvation to people on earth and to perform with heavenly power the ordinances that seal them up unto eternal life. Salvation is always in Christ. He alone is the Savior and Redeemer. But Christ is revealed to and made manifest by his prophets. And the dispensation heads are, for the times in which they live, the ones to whom the heavens are opened and who gain the truths of salvation direct from their Divine Author.

Thus, in the day of Adam, mankind could be saved through Christ and his doctrine as it was revealed by Adam. And Adam was the one who held the keys and who could perform for his children the ordinances of salvation so they would be binding on earth and in heaven. It was not possible to accept Christ and his gospel and reject Adam's prophetic calling, because this first man of all men was the source through which gospel

11

knowledge and gospel power were relayed to mortal men in that day. Thus the pattern was set. Those in the days of Enoch and Noah and Abraham and Moses who gained salvation did so by accepting the truth as it was revealed by those dispensation heads.

In the meridian of time, Jesus proclaimed himself to be the Son of God. In his day the great issue was whether Jesus of Nazareth was the son of Joseph or the Son of God; whether he was the promised Messiah or just another itinerant rabbi; whether he was the Son of the living God, as Peter testified, or a fraud and blasphemer, as Annas and Caiaphas claimed. In that dispensation it was not possible to accept Christ and the salvation made available by him without accepting Peter, James, and John and all those whom Jesus called and sent forth to proclaim his gospel to perform, for and in his stead, the ordinances of salvation.

For our day and dispensation the issue facing all men is clearly set. It is this: *Is Jesus Christ the Son of the living God, and was Joseph Smith called of God?* None need say or pretend that we are centering all our attention in Joseph Smith, or lavishing praise upon him that should be reserved for the Lord Jesus. Joseph Smith is the messenger, not the Master; but the servant, as in all dispensations past, is the one who has brought the message.

Joseph Smith is the one through whom the fulness of the everlasting gospel—the gospel of the Lord Jesus Christ, not of any man—has been restored for the last and final time on earth. He is not the Savior, but he is the revealer of saving truths and of the knowledge of the One who saves and redeems. Joseph Smith is not the source of divine or almighty power, nor is any man, but he is the one who was called of God and endowed with power from on high. He is the one who received the priesthood and the keys from angelic ministrants so that he could preach the gospel and perform the ordinances of salvation with authority from on high. He is thus a legal administrator whose lawful acts, as were Peter's, were binding on earth and in heaven.

Now, if these things are true, if the Prophet Joseph Smith was called of God, then the fulness of the everlasting gospel has been restored for the salvation of all who will believe and obey. If he was called by the Lord as a prophet, a seer, and a revelator, then once again all can learn the truths of salvation and find their way back to the Eternal Presence. If he was the Lord's anointed for our day, then there are legal administrators again on earth who have power to seal themselves and their fellow beings up unto eternal life. If Joseph Smith received power from on high, then The Church of Jesus Christ of Latter-day Saints is the kingdom of God on earth and the one place where salvation is found. If Joseph Smith was a prophet, then revelation has commenced anew, angelic ministrants again descend from the courts of glory, and the saints on earth, as with their ancient counterparts, work miracles and enjoy all of the gifts of the Spirit.

Conversely, if Joseph Smith was not called of God, if he was a fraud and an imposter, if he was a false prophet—then Mormonism, as the restored gospel is often called, is itself a fraud and a delusion. In that event we as a people are in as dark, as benighted, and as fallen a state as the rest of mankind. And thus the issue is squarely put. Joseph Smith either was a prophet or he was not. He was either a revealer of Christ and God and their saving truths or he was not. His work on earth was either for good or for ill. There is no middle ground, no gray area, no room for compromise.

Moroni, a holy angel descending from celestial heights in resurrected glory, told Joseph Smith on that memorable night in September 1823 that Joseph's name "should be had for good and evil among all nations, kindreds, and tongues, or that it should be both good and evil spoken of among all people." (JS-H 1:33.) This unknown farm lad—then only seventeen years of age, without renown, without scholastic standing, without ministerial training—this backwoods boy from Palmyra would, in due course, be hailed as either a true or a false prophet by people in all nations. Some would say he was called of God as were Abraham and Moses, others that Beelzebub was his brother and friend.

Fifteen and a half years later, in March of 1839, while the Prophet from Palmyra was imprisoned in a Missouri dungeon for his testimony of Jesus and the witness of truth that was his, that Lord whose servant he was spoke these consoling words to him: "The ends of the earth shall inquire after thy name, and fools shall have thee in derision, and hell shall rage against thee; while the pure in heart, and the wise, and the noble, and the virtuous, shall seek counsel, and authority, and blessings constantly from under thy hand." (D&C 122:1-2.)

Men always have and, until the Millennial day dawns, will continue to treat the prophets of God as they treated the Son of Man himself. Those today and in the coming days who love the Lord and live as he commands will cleave unto the true prophet who heads our dispensation. Those who love darkness rather than light because their deeds are evil; those who draw near to the Lord with their lips but have removed their hearts far from him; those who have been deceived by men and devils so as to believe false doctrines—all these will rise up in derision to chant: "Crucify him, crucify him! He is a false prophet—beware of false prophets."

Amid it all, those who are wise and who have taken the Holy Spirit for their guide will remember the word of the Lord to Joseph Smith: "This generation shall have my word through you." (D&C 5:10.) They will know that there is no other way for mankind to gain the knowledge that saves except as it has come from the lips and pen of the Lord's latter-day seer. They will remember and rejoice in the divine word which announces that Joseph Smith was called of God to be "a seer, a translator, a prophet, an apostle of Jesus Christ, an elder of the church through the will of God the Father, and the grace of [the] Lord Jesus Christ," that he was "inspired of the Holy Ghost to lay the foundation" of the Church, "and to build it up unto the most holy faith." And their hearts will burn within them as they hear anew the Divine Voice command: "Wherefore, meaning the church, thou shalt give heed unto all his words"—his inspired utterances, his Spirit-guided words, his prophetic utterances—"and commandments which he shall give unto you as he receiveth them, walking in all holiness before me; for his word ye shall receive, as if from mine own mouth," saith the Lord, "in all patience and faith." (D&C 21:1-5.)

The Articles of Faith—Fruits of Joseph Smith

As it is with belief in Christ; as it is with accepting him as the Son of God, whose atoning sacrifice makes salvation possible; as it is with believing all that the prophets and apostles have taught in days gone by—so it is with accepting Joseph

Smith as the prophet of the latter days. All spiritual things must be accepted by faith. But in the process of gaining faith, those who are wise will taste the fruits of those who profess prophetic insight. Those who partake of the fruits of true prophets will find them sweet, full of flavor, delicious to the taste, and desirable to the soul, while those who seek nourishment from the fruits of false prophets will remain unrefreshed spiritually. The fruit they eat will be bitter to the taste; it will be as wormwood in their bellies, and from it they will gain none of the sustenance needed for the long journey back to the presence of the Lord.

The prophetic fruits of Joseph Smith are many and varied. All are as delicious as manna and as overflowing with goodness as the fruits of Eden. Volumes have been and will yet be written about them. They have not grown in secret nor been harvested in the night. In this work, however, it will be our purpose, in large measure, to feast upon but one of his prophetic fruits—the doctrines he taught relative to the basic beliefs of true Christians as these are summarized in the Articles of Faith.

In his now famous Wentworth Letter, written in March 1842, the Prophet Joseph Smith gave an account "of the rise, progress, persecution, and faith of the Latter-day Saints," of which he had "the honor, under God, of being the founder." (HC 4:535.) As the climax of this inspired historical account, he uttered these prophetic words: "No unhallowed hand can stop the work from progressing; persecutions may rage, mobs may combine, armies may assemble, calumny may defame, but the truth of God will go forth boldly, nobly, and independent, till it has penetrated every continent, visited every clime, swept every country, and sounded in every ear, till the purposes of God shall be accomplished, and the Great Jehovah shall say the work is done." He then listed the thirteen Articles of Faith in almost the verbatim language they now contain. (HC 4:540-41.)

"These Articles of Faith were not produced by the labored efforts and harmonized contentions of scholastics, but were struck off by one inspired mind at a single effort to make a declaration of that which is most assuredly believed by the Church. . . . The combined directness, perspicuity, simplicity and comprehensiveness of this statement of the principles of our religion may be relied upon as strong evidence of a divine inspiration resting upon the Prophet, Joseph Smith." (HC 4:535n.) The Articles of Faith are part of an eternal fulness of everlasting truth that was then and is now in process of being revealed by the Lord to his people. They did not, when first given, mention all of the basic doctrines then known, and since then added light and knowledge have been revealed relative to many things, as the Articles of Faith themselves said would be the case.

We might with utmost propriety adopt such declarations as the following: We believe that God has restored in these last days the fulness of his everlasting gospel to prepare a people for the coming of the Son of Man, and that this gospel shall be preached in all the world, for a witness unto all people, and then shall the end come. We believe in a premortal life, in eternal marriage, in salvation for the dead, in the resurrection of the just and of the unjust, in eternal judgment, and in kingdoms of glory in the eternal worlds. These statements are simply illustrations of what might be. And as to the future, who knows what glories and wonders will come forth and be received by the Saints as the mind and will of the Lord.

To the Latter-day Saints, no creed transcends the creed of revelation. We are not circumscribed by fiats set forth by men in uninspired councils. The gospel we have received is the gospel of God, and in the full and eternal sense it includes all truth, most of which has yet to be revealed or discovered. Providentially we have received the saving truths and ordinances, but an eternal fulness yet remains to come forth as soon as we are able spiritually to receive it.

As we approach our study of what has been revealed so far, we would do well to heed Paul's counsel to his Galatian friends: "There be some that trouble you, and would pervert the gospel of Christ," he said. "But though we, or an angel from heaven, preach any other gospel unto you than that which we have preached unto you, let him be accursed." Then, because repetition is one of a teacher's best tools, he said: "If any man preach any other gospel unto you than that ye have received, let him be accursed." (Galatians 1:7-9.)

If what came through Joseph Smith is true, if it is scriptural, if the wisdom and glory of God shine forth in it—then he was called of God and wore the prophetic mantle. If his teachings were false, then he was a false prophet. We would be remiss in our duty if we did not say to all persons everywhere: Come and see. Learn about Joseph Smith, and ask God, in faith, whether this latter-day mortal, with foibles and weaknesses like our own, was not a true prophet. Those of us who have already paid the investigator's price know and testify of his divine calling.

Our inspired writings testify: "Joseph Smith, the Prophet and Seer of the Lord, has done more, save Jesus only, for the salvation of men in this world, than any other man that ever lived in it." (D&C 135:3.) In harmony with this revealed word, those of us who have felt the promptings of the Holy Spirit bear witness of Joseph Smith along the following lines:

We announce, in words of soberness and of doctrine and of testimony, that God has in these last days restored the fulness of his everlasting gospel for the salvation of all who will believe and obey its eternal truths.

We say boldly and calmly, knowing with surety whereof we speak, that the angelic ministrant seen by John has flown through the midst of heaven, bringing again the everlasting gospel, for the benefit and blessing of all who dwell on the earth, including those of every nation, and kindred, and tongue, and people. (See Revelation 14:6.)

We proclaim with the sound of a trump, and invite all persons everywhere to hear our words, that the promised restoration has commenced. We now live in "the times of restitution of all things, which God hath spoken by the mouth of all his holy prophets since the world began." (Acts 3:21.)

And we testify—hear it, O ye heavens, and give ear, O earth—that Joseph Smith was called of God to restore the gospel, to establish anew the church and kingdom of God on earth, and to send the message of salvation to all men.

ARTICLE 1

We believe
in God,
the Eternal Father,
and in His Son,
Jesus Christ,
and in the Holy Ghost.

CHAPTER 3

The Doctrine
of Belief

Belief and Faith Are One

Belief, humble belief, is the foundation of all righteousness and the beginning of spiritual progression. It goes before good works, opens the door to an eternal store of heavenly truth, and charts the course to eternal life.

Belief is the brilliant beacon that marks the course through the waves and woes of the world to that celestial harbor where rest and safety are found. It is implanted, as we shall see, by divine decree to some extent in every human heart; it is the guiding light that determines the course each mortal pursues.

Belief in its full glory and beauty comes from God and is a divine gift bestowed upon all mankind. It is a heaven-sent boon of infinite worth that, in the full and true sense, is nothing more nor less than faith itself.

We must, therefore, of necessity and as a prelude to any rightly guided study of cardinal beliefs, set forth certain basic concepts relative to belief itself. Belief, as commonly defined, is the state or habit of mind of one who believes, that is, of one who has faith or confidence in some person or thing. It is defined as faith, confidence, or trust in a divine being; or, in a lesser sense, as a conviction or persuasion, or even a mere intellectual assent, to some truth or supposed truth. It is thus said to embrace a mere passive agreement to or acceptance of some truth as differentiated from the dynamic miracle performing power that is faith itself.

There is a limited scriptural warrant for defining belief in this passive and worldly sense. It is found in the writings of James. This ancient and inspired author taught that faith was dead and fruitless and without saving power unless attended by good works. In the course of his exhortation, he said that even the devils believe, though they are, of course, totally devoid of faith. (JST, James 2:14-25.) This is a special usage of words for the particular purpose involved. The great body of revealed writ uses belief and faith as synonymous terms, and this is the course we shall follow.

Belief, in the sense of intellectual assent to the existence of various truths, is the common inheritance of all mankind. Every normal and accountable person believes something. Such is a part of the natural heritage that goes with existence itself. Each human being has a mind, given of God, that believes and knows certain things without reference to revelation. The thought process is inherent in life itself, and we cannot exist without believing something. Belief in this sense has no relationship to gaining salvation.

Belief, in the sense of accepting or adhering to certain standards or principles of goodness, is also the common inheritance of all mankind. All are in a position to know the difference between good and evil. This knowledge comes to each person from his conscience. It is a divine endowment. It is the light of Christ, the light that enlightens every soul born into mortality. Thus all persons know instinctively that murder is evil, and "the Gentiles, which have not the law, do by nature the things contained in the law." In a sense and to a degree "the law [is] written in their hearts, [and] their conscience" bears witness to them of what they should do. (Romans 2:14-15.) In this connection, belief is related to salvation only in the sense that those who heed the voice of conscience and follow the promptings of the light of Christ prepare their souls to receive the gospel. When the gospel is accepted by them, they then become heirs of salvation.

Belief, in the true gospel sense and as commonly used in the scriptures, means faith. And faith is a gift of God reserved for those who abide the law entitling them to receive a boon so beneficent and a gift so great. Thus, to gain salvation, mankind must believe in Christ, or in other words, have faith in him. Such scriptural pronouncements as "It is by faith that miracles are wrought" (Moroni 7:37), and "All things are possible to him that believeth" (Mark 9:23), are kindred truths. They mean essentially the same thing; they equate belief in the Lord Jesus Christ with faith in his holy name. It is in this sense that we shall speak when we tell what the saints believe as these beliefs are summarized in the Articles of Faith and elsewhere. This belief is essential to salvation, and without it no accountable person can enter the kingdom of God.

Belief Brings Salvation

Belief brings salvation and belief brings damnation. Men are saved or damned, depending upon what they believe. If they believe in Christ and his saving truths, they are heirs of salvation. If they believe in a false system of salvation, they will be damned. It is one thing to worship the living Lord and quite another to worship dead deities that have been graven by art and man's device. It is one thing to believe God is a personal being in whose image man is made, as the scriptures attest, and quite another to believe he is a spirit nothingness that fills the immensity of space, as the creeds of Christendom aver. What men believe is the governing force in their lives. If they truly believe the truth, they will be saved in the kingdom of God; if they truly believe a lie, they will fail to gain this high reward.

Salvation comes to those who believe the gospel of the Lord Jesus Christ. Rejection of his gospel closes the door to salvation. Men believe his gospel, are seeking to believe, or do not believe; and if they do not, they must of necessity believe something else. Men do not and cannot live in a vacuum; they believe one thing or another. Disbelief in the gospel consists of belief in other things that do not lead to salvation.

There are degrees of belief, degrees of salvation, and degrees of damnation. To believe all the saving truths of the gospel is to gain full salvation; it is to become a son or daughter of God who inherits exaltation and rules and reigns forever in the highest heaven. To reject and oppose all divine truth, in the complete sense, is to gain full damnation; it is to become a son of perdition who dwells with Lucifer in hell forever. In between the glorious height of eternal life in God's kingdom and the abysmal depth of eternal damnation in the kingdom of the devil, there are many degrees of salvation. The one each person obtains depends upon how much of the truth he chooses to believe and obey.

Jesus said with reference to himself and his gospel: "He that believeth and is baptized shall be saved; but he that believeth not shall be damned." Then to identify what he meant by belief and who the true believers are, he added: "And these signs shall follow them that believe; in my name" shall they perform miracles and receive the gifts of the Spirit. (Mark 16:16-17.) Such was but a reaffirmation of the message he had given his disciples: "He that believeth on me, the works that I do shall he do also." (John 14:12.)

Thus God's holy word calls for a belief in Christ that is infinite and eternal. It is not a mere lip-service declaration that he is the Savior nor a mere confessing with idle lips that he is Lord of all. To believe in Christ in the sense of gaining eternal life is to believe his words and accept his messengers. It is to honor his prophets and take counsel from his apostles. It is to have "the mind of Christ" (1 Corinthians 2:16), to believe what he believes, and to say what he would say in all situations. It is to abide in the truth and keep the commandments. It is to enjoy the gifts of the Spirit, to work the works of righteousness, and to perform miracles as he did.

There are degrees of belief in Christ and his gospel, and it is for this very reason that there are degrees of salvation. Those who believe in him, as Paul did, and who as a consequence keep the commandments and are valiant in the testimony of Jesus, shall gain eternal life. They shall dwell forever in celestial glory. Those who know he is the Son of God but who do not put first in their lives the things of his kingdom, and "who are not valiant in the testimony of Jesus" (D&C 76:79), shall go to the terrestrial kingdom. And those who believe in Christ and in such of his gospel as is taught in the churches of the world, and who themselves continue as a consequence to live after the manner of the world, shall go to a telestial kingdom. "For these are they who are of Paul, and of Apollos, and of Cephas," the revealed word testifies. "These are they who say they are some of one and some of another—some of Christ and some of John, and some of Moses, and some of Elias, and some of Esaias, and some of Isaiah, and some of Enoch; but [who] received not the gospel, neither the testimony of Jesus, neither the prophets, neither the everlasting covenant." (D&C 76:98-101.)

It matters not that people simply say they believe in Christ or think they are followers of Moses, Peter, Paul, or any of the ancients. What counts is the reality. If they truly believe in Christ and correctly understand the revealed word that has come down from them of old, they will believe the restored gospel, gain the testimony of Jesus by revelation from the Holy Ghost, and abide in the everlasting covenant.

Men Are Judged According to Their Beliefs

All persons will be judged according to the deeds done in the flesh; as their works have been here in mortality, so shall their rewards be in immortality. This means they will be judged for their beliefs, or in other words for their thoughts, their words, and their acts. Beliefs are born of thoughts; they are then expressed in words; and, finally, they are manifest before mankind in works. Speaking of that great day when we will stand "before the bar of God, to be judged according to our works," Alma says: "Then if our hearts have been hardened, yea, if we have hardened our hearts against the word, insomuch that it has not been found in us, then will our state be awful, for then we shall be condemned." If we have not believed in Christ, if we have not accepted his holy gospel, if we have not believed the truths of salvation, a decree of damnation will be forthcoming. "For our words will condemn us, yea, all our works will condemn us; we shall not be found spotless; and our thoughts will also condemn us." (Alma 12:12-14.)

Jesus spoke similarly in these words: "Out of the abundance of the heart the mouth speaketh. A good man out of the good treasure of the heart bringeth forth good things: and an evil man out of the evil treasure bringeth forth evil things. But I say unto you, That every idle word that men shall speak, they shall give account thereof in the day of judgment. For by thy words thou shalt be justified, and by thy words thou shalt be condemned." (Matthew 12:34-36.)

We conclude, therefore, that salvation depends upon belief. If we believe in God and feel in our hearts that he is a Holy Man; if we believe we are his children, endowed with power to become like him; if we believe that by godly conduct we can so obtain—then we will do the things whereby salvation comes. On the other hand, if we believe that the Supreme Being is simply a congeries of laws floating like a fog in the universe, what incentive is there to be like him?

If we believe in the divine creation and the fall of man; if we believe that Adam fell that mortal men might be and that his fall brought temporal and spiritual death into the world; and if we believe that the atonement of Christ ransoms fallen man by bringing life and immortality to light through the gospel—if we believe these things, surely we will be in a position to love and serve him and will want to keep his commandments. On the other hand, if we believe that the creation was happenstance, that death has always held sway on earth and there was no fall of man, and that Christ therefore could not have redeemed us from death and brought immortality and eternal life into being, what is left of the gospel system?

Questions of this sort might be multiplied until they fill volumes. But these suffice, and the concept is clear. Truly, belief is basic, belief is fundamental, belief is the foundation of all righteousness. Let us, then, take Moroni's inspired counsel: "Doubt not, but be believing, and begin as in times of old, and come unto the Lord with all your heart, and work out your own salvation with fear and trembling before him." (Mormon 9:27.)

The Oneness of Gospel Beliefs

True doctrines, true beliefs, the truths of salvation, the doctrines of the everlasting gospel are perfectly united together. They are welded as one; they bear testimony of each other.

For instance: If Jesus is the Son of God, then God is his Father, and to believe in one is to believe in the other. Jesus said: "Whosoever shall receive me receiveth him that sent me." (Luke 9:48.) It could not be otherwise. "And no man knoweth the Son, but the Father; neither knoweth any man the Father, save the Son, and he to whomsoever the Son will reveal him." (Matthew 11:27.) And also: "I am the way, the truth, and the life: no man cometh unto the Father, but by me." (John 14:6.) Thus, if we believe in Christ, we believe also in the Father; and if we do not believe in Christ, we do not believe in that God whose Son he is.

This same principle applies also to the acceptance of Jesus' disciples and their message, which is his message. They are as he is and he is as they are. Could the Roman jailer believe on the Lord Jesus Christ and be saved without accepting Paul and Silas as the disciples of that Lord? Was it possible for anyone in the meridian of time to believe in Christ, as he was proclaimed by Peter, James, and John, without also believing that those preachers were his apostles? Who in Galatia could accept Jesus as the Son of God without honoring Paul, who declared the doctrine of the divine Sonship unto them? And so we hear Jesus say: "He that receiveth whomsoever I send receiveth me; and he that receiveth me receiveth him that sent me." (John 13:20.) And also: "He that heareth you heareth me; and he that despiseth you despiseth me; and he that despiseth me despiseth him that sent me." (Luke 10:16.) To his latter-day disciples this same Lord Jesus said: "Whoso receiveth you receiveth me." (D&C 84:89.)

True ministers speak by the power of the Holy Ghost; they speak the words of Christ and say what he would say if he personally were ministering in their stead. It follows that to receive the gospel from those appointed to preach it is to receive Christ. "And verily, verily, I say unto you, he that receiveth my gospel," saith the Lord, "receiveth me; and he that receiveth not my gospel receiveth not me." (D&C 39:5.)

Those in the sects of Christendom have the Bible and believe some of the doctrines of salvation. Much of what they believe is commingled with the philosophies of men. As we are aware, partial belief brings partial salvation. A twinkling ray from a distant star does not compare with the blazing brilliance of the noonday sun. Any truth that any person believes is all to the good. A little light is better than no light at all. But the fulness of salvation is for those who believe and obey the fulness of the Lord's holy word.

Believe the Revelations Given in Your Day

The real test of one's beliefs is not how much he purports to believe of what the dead prophets have said, but what he accepts from the lips of the living oracles of the same God who inspired those of old. Salvation comes through belief in the doctrines taught by the true disciples sent as legal administrators in our day. Needless to say, their teachings conform to those of their ancient fellowservants; in addition, modern disciples have the present power to perform the ordinances of salvation so they will be binding on earth and in heaven.

All persons who now live on earth, in order to be saved, must believe what God has revealed in this day. To gain salvation today, they must believe the doctrines revealed through the Prophet Joseph Smith and his successors, who are the apostles and prophets sent to reveal Christ to the world in this day. To believe them is to believe in Christ, and to reject them is to reject the Lord by whom salvation comes. "Whosoever receiveth my word receiveth me, and whosoever receiveth me, receiveth those, the First Presidency, whom I have sent." (D&C 112:20.)

Speaking of that portion of his word which is in the Book of Mormon, and also of all those things seen by the brother of Jared, which shall be revealed to others of like faith in a future day, the Lord Jesus Christ said: "He that believeth not my words believeth not my disciples." His words, his holy gospel, his everlasting truths—these and his disciples always go together; they cannot be separated. "But he that believeth these things which I have spoken, him will I visit with the manifestations of my Spirit, and he shall know and bear record. For because of my Spirit he shall know that these things are true." (Ether 4:10-11.) Converting belief comes to true believers with complete certainty. Once they truly believe in Christ, and in his disciples, and in his word as found in the scriptures, then they receive the Holy Ghost. This Holy Spirit bears witness to the spirit within them of the eternal verity of the things they have chosen to believe.

And "he that will not believe my words," the Lord Jesus continues, "will not believe me—that I am." Christ lives; he is; he exists; he is the Eternal One. And those who do not believe his words as he speaks them by the mouths of his servants the prophets—and his voice is their voice and their voice is his voice—do not believe that he is the living God. They may suppose he exists and is God's Son, but to believe in him with the surety required to gain eternal life—such a belief comes only to those who believe his words as he speaks them by his own mouth and by the mouths of his ministers.

"And he that will not believe me will not believe the Father

28

who sent me." (Ether 4:12.) Those who think they believe in God but who reject Christ are living in a realm of fantasy and delusion. No one can choose which of the sun's rays will fall upon him. He cannot rejoice in some and turn the others into darkness. Nor can anyone walk in the light shed forth from the Father without also being engulfed in the same light as it shines forth from the Son. True believers do not and cannot pick and choose which gospel truths they will believe.

After testifying of Christ and after expounding the doctrines of Christ, Nephi said: "The words which I have spoken shall stand as a testimony against you; for they are sufficient to teach any man the right way; for the right way is to believe in Christ and deny him not; for by denying him ye also deny the prophets and the law." (2 Nephi 25:23-28.) This was the very thing that the Jews did in the day when the Lord Jesus, as a mortal, ministered among them. We have Abraham and the prophets to guide us, and we keep the law of Moses, they reasoned, but as for this Nazarene, his words are false and his miracles are wrought by the power of Beelzebub; we will have nothing to do with him and his system of religion. Indeed, Nephi equated belief in his words with belief in the very Being whose witness he was. "No man will be angry at the words which I have written save he shall be of the spirit of the devil," he said. And further: "Hearken unto these words and believe in Christ. . . . And if ye shall believe in Christ ye will believe in these words, for they are the words of Christ, and he hath given them unto me." (2 Nephi 33:5, 10.) What he says of his own words applies also to the whole Book of Mormon.

Nearly a thousand years later Mormon preached this same doctrine. In a proclamation to the latter-day Lamanites he calls: "Believe in Jesus Christ"; believe that "he is the Son of God"; believe that "he was slain by the Jews"; believe that "by the power of the Father he hath risen again"; believe that "he hath gained the victory over the grave"; believe that "in him is the sting of death swallowed up." Believe that "he bringeth to pass the resurrection of the dead"; believe that all men "must be raised to stand before his judgment-seat." Believe that "he hath brought to pass the redemption of the world"; believe that any man who "is found guiltless before him at the judgment day hath it given unto him to dwell in the presence of God in his kingdom," and that all such shall "sing ceaseless praises with the choirs above, unto the Father, and unto the Son, and unto the Holy Ghost, which are one God, in a state of happiness which hath no end."

Having tied all these doctrines together, and knowing that to believe any one of them is to believe them all, Mormon commands: "Repent, and be baptized in the name of Jesus, and lay hold upon the gospel of Christ." (Mormon 7:5-8.) And, be it known, true believers always seek to be baptized. Unless they lay hold upon the gospel and believe its doctrines and join the true church, any sprouting seeds of true belief die aborning. True belief is the father of repentance; it is the power that moves sin-forsaking souls to the "waters of Mormon" on whose shores the gift of the Holy Ghost is conferred.

Saving Belief Comes Through the Book of Mormon

As to the gospel of Christ, Mormon says, it "shall be set before you, not only in this record [the Book of Mormon] but also in the record [the Bible] which shall come unto the Gentiles from the Jews. . . . For behold, this is written for the intent that ye may believe that; and if ye believe that ye will believe this also." (Mormon 7:8-9.) Every living soul on earth to whom the Book of Mormon comes, who truly believes the Bible, also believes the Book of Mormon. And conversely, it is belief in the Book of Mormon that causes men to believe the Bible. One of the very purposes of the coming forth of this latter-day volume of scripture is to cause men to believe the truths written in the Bible.

When the Lord commanded his servants to organize his church and kingdom again on earth, of necessity, in the very nature of things—it could not have been otherwise—he had to tell them what to believe and how to learn all of his true doctrines. He could not tell them all things at that time, for his words are endless and his doctrines are eternal. But he could and did tell them certain basic verities and gave them the key whereby they could continue to learn his mind and will. This he did in the Doctrine and Covenants in section 20, which is the constitutional document of the Church, as well as in some of the other early revelations.

In this section we learn that the Lord gave Joseph Smith "power from on high . . . to translate the Book of Mormon," which is a record of God's dealings with a people who had the fulness of the gospel. In it is recorded a summary of the plan of salvation and of the basic doctrines men must believe as they start out on the course leading to eternal life. This book "was given by inspiration" to Nephi, Alma, Mormon, and other prophetic leaders of the ancient Americans. What they wrote was the mind and will of the Lord; it was addressed to people in their day and in our day. The Book of Mormon "is confirmed to others by the ministering of angels," meaning that angelic ministrants, sent of God, delivered the ancient record to Joseph Smith and testified to him and to other witnesses that it was true and had been translated correctly. And it "is declared unto the world by them." That is, those who stood in the angelic presence and who heard the voice of God bear witness to the eternal verity of the book have themselves, in turn, borne that same witness to the world.

All this is the foundation for the divine pronouncement that the Book of Mormon came forth, "proving to the world that the holy scriptures are true, and that God does inspire men and call them to his holy work in this age and generation, as well as in generations of old." In other words, the Book of Mormon came forth to prove the Bible is true and also to prove that Joseph Smith was called of God in the same sense as were the ancient prophets. The Book of Mormon is a new witness for Christ. It proves his divine Sonship and sets forth his doctrines—the doctrines of salvation—in plainness and perfection. It is that portion of the Lord's eternal word which starts modern men out in the direction of eternal salvation.

"Therefore, having so great witnesses"—the Book of Mormon, the Bible, and the prophets of our day—"by them shall the world be judged, even as many as shall hereafter come to a knowledge of this work." Among the books out of which men will be judged at the bar of the great Jehovah will be the Book of Mormon and the Bible, for in them is recorded what men must believe and how they must live to return to the Eternal Presence.

"And those who receive it in faith"—who receive this work; who receive the true church; who hearken to the voices of the living prophets—"and [who] work righteousness, shall receive a crown of eternal life; but those who harden their hearts in unbelief, and reject it, it shall turn to their own condemnation." Why? Because "the Lord God has spoken it." It is his word. And "the elders of the church, have heard and bear witness to the words of the glorious Majesty on high."

At this point the revelation says: "By these things we know" certain great and eternal verities. What are these things? They include the call of Joseph Smith and Oliver Cowdery to be the first and second elders in the new kingdom; they include the ministry of Moroni to the youthful Joseph and to others; they include the translation of the Book of Mormon by the gift and power of God; they include the sure witness it bears of the truthfulness of the Bible; and they include, therefore, the verity of the glorious gospel as its doctrines are recited in both volumes of holy scripture. If the Saints know of the truthfulness of this latter-day work, they automatically believe all that is found in all of the prophetic records of all the ages.

Among the things we know because of the coming forth of the Book of Mormon and all that attended it, the revelation lists these: the very existence of the infinite God; the creation of the heavens and the earth and all things that in them are; the creation of man in the image of God; the revelation of the holy gospel to our first parents; the foreordained fall of Adam; the atonement of the Lord Jesus Christ and the redemption of man; the plan of salvation, including faith, repentance, baptism, the receipt of the Holy Ghost, and the keeping of the commandments of God; the law of justification; the law of sanctification; and so on and so on. (D&C 20:1-36.) We believe and know spiritual and eternal truths—truths and doctrines without number—once we gain testimonies of the truth and divinity of the Lord's latter-day work, and as rapidly as our spiritual capacity enables us to drink from the eternal fountains.

CHAPTER 4

The Talent
to Believe

Belief—A Gift from Preexistence

Why is it easy for some people to believe in Christ, in his prophets, and in his gospel? Why do others reject the gospel, persecute the prophets, and even deny the divinity of Him whose gospel it is? Jesus said: "I am the good shepherd, and know my sheep, and am known of mine. . . . My sheep hear my voice, and I know them, and they follow me." (John 10:14, 27.) Interwoven through Paul's epistles are numerous statements about chosen people being predestined—we would say foreordained—to gain full salvation. They are described as becoming "joint-heirs with Christ," and of thus conforming to "the image" of God's Son. (Romans 8:17, 29.) Paul speaks of "the purpose of God according to election," as a result of which some men are saved and others are damned. (Romans 9:11.) He says of the saints: "[God] hath chosen us in him before the foundation of the world, that we should be holy and without blame before him in love." (Ephesians 1:4.)

From these and a host of other passages, it is clear that people do not all have the same talent for recognizing truth and believing the doctrines of salvation. Some heed the warning voice and believe the gospel; others do not. Some would give all they possess if they could but touch the hem of the garment of him who is the Way, the Truth, and the Life; others find fault with every word that falls from prophetic lips. Some forsake lands and riches, friends and families, to gather with the true saints; others choose to walk in the ways of the world and to deride the humble followers of Christ. Why? Why this difference in people?

To this problem there is no easy answer. Every person

stands alone in choosing his beliefs and electing the course he will pursue. No two persons are born with the same talents and capacities; no two are rooted in the same soil of circumstances; each is unique. The cares of this world, gold and honor and power and renown, the lusts of the flesh, the chains of past sins, and a thousand other things—all exert their influence upon us. But in the final sense the answer stems back to premortality. We all lived as spirit beings, as children of the Eternal Father, for an infinitely long period of time in the premortal existence. There we developed talents, gifts, and aptitudes; there our capacities and abilities took form; there, by obedience to law, we were endowed with the power, in one degree or another, to believe the truth and follow the promptings of the Spirit. And the talent of greatest worth was that of spirituality, for it enables us to hearken to the Holy Spirit and accept that gospel which prepares us for eternal life.

Men are not born equal. They enter this life with the talents and capacities developed in preexistence. Abraham saw in vision the spirit hosts of men before they were born, "and among all these there were many of the noble and great ones." It was of that select and talented group that the Lord said: "These I will make my rulers." And to Abraham, the Father of the Faithful, one of the greatest of the Lord's earthly rulers, the comforting word came: "Thou art one of them; thou wast chosen before thou wast born." (Abraham 3:22-23.) Alma tells us that those who are faithful high priests in this life were in fact "called and prepared from the foundation of the world according to the foreknowledge of God, on account of their exceeding faith and good works" while they yet dwelt in his presence. (Alma 13:3.) To Jeremiah the Lord said: "Before I formed thee in the belly I knew thee; and before thou camest forth out of the womb I sanctified thee, and I ordained thee a prophet unto the nations." (Jeremiah 1:5.)

And as it is with the prophets, so is it with all the chosen seed. "God's elect," as Paul calls them (Romans 8:33), are especially endowed at birth with spiritual talents. It is easier for them to believe the gospel than it is for the generality of mankind. Every living soul comes into this world with sufficient talent to believe and be saved, but the Lord's sheep, as a reward for their devotion when they dwelt in his presence, enjoy greater spiritual endowments than their fellows.

Belief—Found in Favored Families

When and where and under what circumstances are "the noble and great ones" sent to earth? What of "God's elect," what of those who are foreordained and chosen to join the Church and "be holy and without blame" before the Lord— under what circumstances will they receive their mortal probations? Again there are no simple answers. Our finite limitations and our lack of knowledge of the innate capacities of all men do not let us envision the complexities of the Lord's system for sending his children to mortality. But we do know one great and eternal principle. We know that the Lord operates through families. He himself lives in the family unit; it is his eternal system of government in heaven and on earth, and he always offers as much of his own system to men as they are willing to receive.

Adam, our father, the first man, is the presiding high priest over the earth for all ages. The government the Lord gave him was patriarchal, and from the expulsion from Eden to the cleansing of the earth by water in the day of Noah, the righteous portion of mankind were blessed and governed by a patriarchal theocracy.

This theocratic system, patterned after the order and system that prevailed in heaven, was the government of God. He himself, though dwelling in heaven, was the Lawgiver, Judge, and King. He gave direction in all things both civil and ecclesiastical; there was no separation of church and state as we now know it. All governmental affairs were directed, controlled, and regulated from on high. The Lord's legal administrators on earth served by virtue of their callings and ordinations in the Holy Priesthood and as they were guided by the power of the Holy Ghost.

"This order was instituted in the days of Adam, and came down by lineage." It was designed "to be handed down from father to son." It came down in succession; it is priesthood government; it is the government of God both on earth and in heaven. And even today, it "rightly belongs to the literal descendants of the chosen seed, to whom the promises were made." (D&C 107:40-41.) That it is not now in full operation simply means that fallen men have departed from the ancient ways and are now governing each other as they choose.

But in the beginning the Lord's true system prevailed. The

successive sons who held rulership of one kind or another in the original earthly kingdom were Adam, Seth, Enos, Cainan, Mahalaleel, Jared, Enoch, Methuselah, Lamech, and Noah. In their respective days there were, of course, apostate peoples who set up governments of their own. But those who believed the gospel and sought salvation remained subject to the patriarchal order revealed and established by the Eternal Patriarch. And into their immediate families the Father of Spirits sent those of his primeval children who, through faith and devotion in preexistence, had earned the right to be born in the households of faith.

After the flood, Shem and Melchizedek and others unknown to us continued to exercise divine power among the righteous in the Old World through the patriarchal order. In the New World the Jaredite prophets held similar sway. Abraham received from Melchizedek the power to perpetuate the patriarchal system, a system that would make him the Father of the Faithful from that day onward as long as the earth should stand. He was called by the Lord to "be a father of many nations." To him the Lord said: "I will establish my covenant [the gospel covenant] between me and thee and thy seed after thee in their generations for an everlasting covenant, to be a God unto thee, and to thy seed after thee." (Genesis 17:4, 7.) "And in thy seed shall all the nations of the earth be blessed" (Genesis 22:18), meaning that all who thereafter believed what Abraham believed and lived as Abraham lived would bless themselves through the everlasting gospel covenant.

"Thou shalt be a blessing unto thy seed after thee," the Lord promised Abraham, "that in their hands they shall bear this ministry and Priesthood unto all nations." This is the very thing the seed of Abraham is commencing to do in these last days. "I will bless them [all nations] through thy name," the Lord continues, "for as many as receive this Gospel shall be called after thy name, and shall be accounted thy seed, and shall rise up and bless thee, as their father." Even the believing Gentiles shall cleave unto Abraham, account him as their father, and be adopted into his family. "And I will bless them that bless thee," saith the Lord, "and curse them that curse thee; and in thee (that is, in thy Priesthood) and in thy seed (that is, thy Priesthood), for I give unto thee a promise that this right shall continue in thee, and in thy seed after thee (that is to say, the literal seed, or the seed of the body) shall all the families of the earth be blessed, even with the blessings of the Gospel, which are the blessings of salvation, even of life eternal." (Abraham 2:9-11.)

How glorious is the promise! The seed of Abraham shall take the gospel and the priesthood to all nations, and those who accept the divine word shall become as though they too were the chosen seed. And also: The literal seed of Abraham's body, his natural descendants, those born with his blood flowing in their veins—though they be scattered and scourged and lost in all nations—yet they have a right to certain blessings. They have a *right* to hear the *gospel*, and if they accept it, to receive the *priesthood*, to have their own family units continue everlastingly so that they with Abraham shall have *eternal life*. If they believe, they have the right to the gospel, the priesthood, and eternal life because they are the seed of Abraham. The Lord operates through families; in general he sends his choice spirits to earth in the lineage of Abraham.

All of the promises given to Abraham were centered in due course in Sarah's son. "My covenant will I establish with Isaac," the Lord said. (Genesis 17:21.) And also: "In Isaac shall thy seed be called." (Genesis 21:12.) Why Isaac? Because he kept the commandments and did everything he was counseled to do by his father. And so, in due course the Lord came also to Isaac and renewed upon his head all the promises given to Abraham. "I will make thy seed to multiply as the stars of heaven," was the divine word to Abraham's son, "and in thy seed shall all the nations of the earth be blessed." (Genesis 26:4.) And as it was with Isaac, so with Jacob. "Thy seed shall be as the dust of the earth," the Lord promised Jacob, who would be the father of all Israel; "in thee and in thy seed shall all the families of the earth be blessed." (Genesis 28:14.)

Abraham, Isaac, and Jacob—our patriarchal fathers—are the patterns and types for all their seed. The tribes of Israel were the Lord's ancient chosen and covenant people. In one of them the Lord Jesus himself was born. Those among them who served Jehovah with Abrahamic zeal received the same blessings bestowed upon their fathers. Israel is now scattered in all nations upon all the face of the earth. Her latter-day gathering, to the ancient and everlasting covenant, is in process. And almost all of those who accept the gospel in this day are the literal seed of Abraham.

Thus we hear the voice of the Lord say to Joseph Smith: "Abraham received promises concerning his seed, and of the fruit of his loins—from whose loins ye are, namely, my servant Joseph—which were to continue so long as they were in the world; and as touching Abraham and his seed, out of the world they should continue; both in the world and out of the world should they continue as innumerable as the stars; or, if ye were to count the sand upon the seashore ye could not number them. This promise is yours also, because ye are of Abraham, and the promise was made unto Abraham." (D&C 132:30-31.) In the full sense this promise is fulfilled for those only who enter into the new and everlasting covenant of marriage and thereby gain a continuation of the family unit in eternity. Abraham's seed is promised eternal life, and eternal life comes to those who live everlastingly in the same kind of a family unit as does the great Elohim.

Thus also we see Elias come to Joseph Smith and Oliver Cowdery and commit unto them "the dispensation of the gospel of Abraham, saying that in us and our seed all generations after us should be blessed." (D&C 110:12.) As with the ancient patriarchs, so with all of their seed who enter into eternal marriage covenants. By doing the works of Abraham, they inherit for themselves the same blessings he received.

And thus also we read in the revealed word that those who redeem Israel and build up Zion in the last days have a right to the priesthood "by lineage." (D&C 113:8.) They are identified as "lawful heirs, according to the flesh," and are the ones "with whom the priesthood hath continued through the lineage of [their] fathers." They have the promise that this same priesthood will remain with them and descend through their "lineage until the restoration of all things spoken by the mouths of all the holy prophets since the world began" (D&C 86:8-10), until all things have come to pass in their eternal fulness.

What Is Believing Blood?

What then is believing blood? It is the blood that flows in the veins of those who are the literal seed of Abraham—not that the blood itself believes, but that those born in that lineage have both the right and a special spiritual capacity to recognize, receive, and believe the truth. The term is simply a beautiful, a poetic, and a symbolic way of referring to the seed of Abraham to whom the promises were made. It identifies those who developed in preexistence the talent to recognize the truth and to desire righteousness.

Do all of Abraham's seed believe the truth and pursue the course he charted? Not by any means. "Abraham shall surely become a great and mighty nation," the Lord said, "for I know him, that he will command his children and his household after him, and they shall keep the way of the Lord, to do justice and judgment." (Genesis 18:18-19.) That he commanded them all so to believe, so to walk, and so to live, we cannot doubt. But Ishmael fell by the wayside, and though Abraham himself prayed unto God, "O that Ishmael might live before thee!", yet God told him, Nay. Rather the promise came: "Sarah thy wife shall bear thee a son indeed; and thou shalt call his name Isaac: and I will establish my covenant with him for an everlasting covenant, and with his seed after him." (Genesis 17:18-19.) The birthright fell to Isaac, and he remained true and faithful all his days.

Through their long history, portions of Israel were faithful and portions were disobedient. The righteous in Israel became as Isaac, the wicked as Ishmael. Some of those who came from the loins of Abraham lost their promised blessings because they rejected the gospel. When certain of the Jews boasted, "Abraham is our father," Jesus replied: "If ye were Abraham's children, ye would do the works of Abraham. But now ye seek to kill me, a man that hath told you the truth, which I have heard of God: this did not Abraham. . . . Ye are of your father the devil, and the lusts of your father ye will do." (John 8:39-40, 44.)

Rebellious members of the house of Israel are disinherited. They are no longer numbered with the chosen seed; their lot is to have another inheritance with a worldly people. "The rebellious are not of the blood of Ephraim," saith the Lord, "wherefore they shall be plucked out." (D&C 64:36.) Those who reject the gospel and who persecute the saints, though the blood of the prophets flows in their veins, are nonetheless cast off. As it is written: "They shall not have right to the priesthood, nor their posterity after them from generation to generation." (D&C 121:21.)

Speaking of Israel—"my kinsmen according to the flesh," he calls them—Paul says: "They are not all Israel, which are of Israel: Neither, because they are the seed of Abraham, are they all children: but, In Isaac shall thy seed be called. That is, They which are the children of the flesh, these are not the children of God: but the children of the promise are counted for the seed." (Romans 9:3, 6-8.) There is, thus, no substitute for personal righteousness. Abraham's seed have the blessed privilege to believe and obey. It is easier for them to do so than for the aliens and Gentiles, though in the providences of a just God, all may believe and become, through faith, the children of God and the seed of Abraham.

What the Latter-day Saints Believe

Each of the Articles of Faith except one begins with the simple yet solemn affirmation, "We believe." In each instance these two ordinary words sound a call—a clarion call both loud and clear—bearing witness that the verities they introduce come from the Lord of Truth and have his all-wise approval. Who, then, are "we," and what truths do we "believe"? What verities have come to us that are worthy of acceptance and canonization and analysis?

We are the chosen people, the elect of God, those in whose veins flows believing blood. Abraham is our father. We are the children of the prophets and have been born in the house of Israel. Isaac and Jacob are our forebears. We are the children of the covenant God made with Abraham, that Abraham's seed should have the right to the gospel and the priesthood and eternal life. There is no blessing ever offered to the ancients that is not ours to obtain. "If God be for us, who can be against us? . . . Who shall lay any thing to the charge of God's elect?" (Romans 8:31, 33.)

We are the true saints, the saints of latter days, the saints of the Most High. We have come out of darkness into the marvelous light of Christ. We believe in Christ with a fixed purpose that defies earth and hell; we are Christians in the true, full, literal, and complete sense of the word. We are members of The Church of Jesus Christ of Latter-day Saints—Mormons, if you will—and as such we have power to become the sons and daughters of God by faith. We are all these things and much, much more because we believe the truth and have a hope of eternal life.

But this is not all. There is another aspect to the problem of our identity. Though we are many things and have much reason to rejoice in the goodness of God to us both individually and collectively, there are some things we are *not*. And—need we say it?—it is just as important *not* to be numbered with the wicked and ungodly as it is to be gathered *with* the true believers. We cannot be all things to all men. We cannot both worship and curse God in the same breath; we cannot be both hot and cold, both righteous and wicked, at one and the same time.

We are *not* of the world. We are commanded to be neither carnal, sensual, nor devilish; our hearts are set on eternal values. We march to the beat of a divine drum; ours is a Godly and upright course. Do other men love money and set their hearts on wealth and power? Our treasure is laid up in heaven where neither moth nor rust doth corrupt. Do others steal from the weak and slay with the sword? Our course is one of honesty and peace. Are others unclean, indecent, immoral? We seek to sanctify our souls so as to be fit associates for gods, angels, and the saints of ages past. We are a peculiar people.

And in no way is our peculiarity dramatized more pointedly than by reference to our beliefs. We believe, for instance, in God the Creator, God the Redeemer, and God the Testator, whose proclaimed plan of salvation will enable all who conform and obey to be one with them. We believe the gospel of God and have received power to gain a knowledge of all truth by revelation from the Holy Spirit. We are not bound by any restrictive creeds; no limiting barrier decrees that we may go thus far and no farther in our pursuit of eternal truth. Taking the scriptures as our guide and the Holy Ghost as our companion, we are in process of learning and believing all things, with the full expectancy of becoming omniscient ourselves as is the all-wise One whom we worship.

We believe what the ancient saints believed. We have received by revelation some, at least, of the same everlasting truths that lighted their souls. Our views accord with those of Abraham, Moses, Paul, and all of the prophets and apostles of old. Indeed, Jesus himself is our pattern. We have the mind of Christ and believe what he believed insofar as it has come to us by an outpouring of heavenly grace.

We do *not,* of course, believe all that our enemies, for their purposes, ascribe to us. Those in the sects of the world whose delight it is to expose us, as they suppose, and to warn all mankind against the menace of Mormonism, do not know and do not want to know what we really believe. Their self-assigned mission is to say that we believe this or that absurdity and then to warn others against us and our supposed doctrines. So be it. All must choose for themselves what they will believe; and true beliefs save, while false beliefs damn.

In truth and in verity our doctrines are the doctrines of salvation. We believe those things which all must believe to gain an eternal inheritance in the kingdom of God. Obviously the Articles of Faith are a basic statement of the beginnings of our beliefs. When we have mastered what is in them, we will be in a position to go forward in the University of the Universe, studying and believing until we believe and know all things.

Belief—pure, blessed belief! How wondrous it is! "All things are possible to him that believeth." (Mark 9:23.) "Doubt not, but be believing, and begin as in times of old, and come unto the Lord with all your heart, and work out your own salvation with fear and trembling before him." (Mormon 9:27.)

The Lord Our God

God and Salvation

God is the center of all things. By him all things are, and from him all things flow. He is the Creator of the sidereal heavens; this earth is the work of his hands, and man is his crowning creation. He is the author of all life, the source of all power, the supreme governor of the universe. He is the Eternal Father of us all, and our Blessed Lord is his Only Begotten in the flesh.

No words are known to man and no language is spoken by angels that can fully express the glory and honor and renown properly ascribed unto the Father and the Son. The names and titles by which they are known are the most sacred and holy words that can be spoken on earth or in heaven. In the Song of the Redeemed the heavenly choir, composed of every creature on earth and in heaven, joins in this grand accolade of eternal praise: "Blessing, and honour, and glory, and power, be unto him that sitteth upon the throne, and unto the Lamb for ever and ever." (Revelation 5:13.)

Life itself comes from God and has a purpose. This mortal sphere is the appointed time for men to work out their salvation. The Lord's own work and glory is "to bring to pass the immortality and eternal life of man." (Moses 1:39.) And eternal life—salvation in the full and supreme sense—is reserved for those who worship the true God and who keep his commandments. True religion is the system he ordained to enable his children to worship him in such a way as to gain full salvation.

Thus, a knowledge of God and of his laws is essential to salvation. No one can be saved in ignorance of God, of Christ, and of their everlasting gospel. All are saved as rapidly as they gain a knowledge of God and of his laws. And thus we find these words of Jesus in his great Intercessory Prayer: "This is life eternal, that they might know thee the only true God, and Jesus Christ, whom thou hast sent." (John 17:3.)

Man was created to be saved, and salvation comes to those who worship the true God. Deity is revealed to mankind through the gospel, which is the plan of salvation, and all are commanded to believe its truths and live its laws. Jesus stated the eternal law of worship in these words: "Thou shalt worship the Lord thy God, and him only shalt thou serve." (Luke 4:8.) There is no other course leading to eternal life. In our day the divine word commands: "Thou shalt love the Lord thy God with all thy heart, with all thy might, mind, and strength; and in the name of Jesus Christ thou shalt serve him." (D&C 59:5.)

When the woman of Samaria asked Jesus whether men should worship according to the Samaritan way on Mount Gerizim or according to the Jewish way in the temple in Jerusalem, our Lord said: "Ye worship ye know not what; we know what we worship; and salvation is of the Jews." True religion, true worship, and a hope of salvation are all based on a knowledge of the truth about God. There is no salvation in worshipping a false god. "The hour cometh, and now is," Jesus continued, "when the true worshippers shall worship the Father in spirit and in truth; for the Father seeketh such to worship him. For unto such hath God promised his Spirit. And they who worship him, must worship in spirit and in truth." (JST, John 4:24-26.)

Salvation comes to those who worship the Father, in the name of the Son, by the power of the Holy Ghost. How, then, could anything be more important than to know God and to be enlightened by the power of his Spirit?

How God Is Known

There is no question as to the existence of God. Such is one of the eternal verities. It is as clear and certain as life itself; it is not a subject open to debate. There are questions as to who or what he is, what his powers are, and the nature of his character, perfections, and attributes. There are questions as to whether he has a body of flesh and bones, whether he is a spirit essence that fills the immensity of space, or whether he is a congeries of laws floating like a fog in the universe. But there neither is nor can be any question about his existence.

Those who profess to be atheists do no more than deny a belief in some traditional concept of God. Knowing there is a creature, it is not philosophically possible to deny the existence of a Creator. All things have a source or origin, a point in time when they are organized as at present constituted. God is the First Great Cause. It is instructive, however, to note the evidences men have of the existence of a Supreme Being. These are four in number:

1. *God is known by instinct.*

All men are spirit children of God the Eternal Father. In the premortal life we all dwelt in his presence, saw his face, and heard his voice. We were as well acquainted with him in that day as we are with our earthly fathers in this. The spirit within us is the offspring of God. Now housed in a tabernacle of clay, it is the intelligent, sentient, believing, knowing part of the human personality. The mind of man is in the spirit.

The probationary nature of our mortal estate calls for us to forget the life we lived and the experiences we had when we dwelt in the courts of the Eternal King. But it does not divest us of the spiritual and mental talents we acquired while in that eternal world. We are born into mortality with every innate capacity, every instinct to believe truth and cleave unto light, every faculty and ability with which we were then endowed.

Further, as part of life itself, all mortals are endowed with a heavenly gift called the light of Christ. This divine endowment manifests to us the difference between good and evil. We do not need to be taught what is right and wrong. This knowledge is bred in our bones; it is hereditary; it is innate, inborn, and intuitional in nature. Call it conscience, if you will; say that it is a divine inheritance from a Divine Parent; identify it as a spark of divinity sent by Deity to fire the soul with the flames of righteousness; call it the Spirit of Christ—it has many names. But what counts is that it is real. It is "the true light that lighteth every man that cometh into the world." (D&C 93:2.) Of it Mormon said: "The Spirit of Christ is given to every man, that he may know good from evil." (Moroni 7:16.) In a revelation to Joseph Smith the Lord called it "the Spirit of Jesus Christ, and the Spirit giveth light to every man that cometh into the world." All receive a divine inheritance at birth. It is a free gift as far as any act performed in mortality is concerned. "The Spirit enlighteneth every man through the world, that hearkeneth to the voice of the Spirit. And every one that hearkeneth to the voice of the Spirit cometh unto God, even the Father." (D&C 84:45-47.)

All persons are thus placed by their Creator in a position to believe. The seeds of faith are sown at birth. They must hearken to the voice of the Spirit in order to gain the true knowledge of God that leads to salvation. But they know by instinct that there is a god of some sort and that it is right for them to worship and serve some divine being or power. And this same instinct, running in their blood, tells them the difference between good and evil. The issue is not whether there is a god or whether there is good and evil, but who or what god is, and what is good and what is evil. It is good to believe in the true and living God.

2. *God is known by reason.*

Man's instinctive belief in God and his inborn desire to worship a Supreme Being is strengthened by reason. The seeds of belief are watered from the wells of reason, and the tree of faith soon sprouts in the believing soul. And the more man learns about himself and all the mysteries and marvels of the human body; the more he knows about life in all its forms and varieties; the greater his knowledge becomes about the planets and suns that sweep through the starry heavens—the more he knows about all things, the clearer it becomes to him that there is a divine hand, an omnipotent power, a supreme person, a ruling law that first created and now governs all that is. Truly, all things attest that there is an Almighty God. "All things denote there is a God," Alma said, "yea, even the earth, and all things that are upon the face of it, yea, and its motion, yea, and also all the planets which move in their regular form do witness there is a Supreme Creator." (Alma 30:44.)

But seeking God by reason alone and through intellectual processes without more is fraught with peril. It is easy for a rational mind to see order in the system of creation and to learn of the laws by which worlds and galaxies are controlled. There are evidences of design on every hand; cause and effect operate in the animal and vegetable kingdoms as well as with the rocks and the rains. The peril lies in assuming that the laws and powers are God, in worshipping and serving "the creature more than the Creator." (Romans 1:25.)

Neither instinct nor reason, nor the two combined, sets forth the nature and kind of being whom men must worship to gain salvation. Both simply lay a foundation and chart a course leading to a knowledge of the true and living God. Every rational person knows there is some supreme power, some first great cause, some omnipotent force in the universe. The reasoning step that follows this recognition is that the design is not the designer, the contrivance is not the contriver, the law and power are not the being by whom these came. The existence of created things simply bears witness that there is a Creator. The laws of nature are not God, but their existence bears witness that above and beyond nature and presiding over all her laws is nature's God. "For every house is builded by some man; but he that built all things is God." (Hebrews 3:4.) "[God] who sitteth upon the throne and governeth and executeth all things . . . hath given a law unto all things, by which they move in their times and their seasons." (D&C 88:40, 42.) The Creator governeth his creations, for he is their God.

3. *God is known through history and tradition.*

Because God created man in his own image and likeness and placed him on earth as an essential requirement for gaining salvation, because salvation is gained through a knowledge of God and an obedience to the laws of his gospel, and because eternal life itself consists of knowing the Father and the Son, it follows that God must in necessity reveal himself and his laws to man. This he did. Adam our father, the first man of all men, the primal parent of the human race, received a knowledge of God by revelation. God the Eternal Father walked and talked with him in the Garden of Eden; the Lord Jehovah appeared to him after the fall; and from angelic ministrants and by the gift of the Holy Ghost he learned the saving truths of the gospel. This was the beginning of the knowledge of the true God among man. "And Adam and Eve blessed the name of God, and they made all things known unto their sons and their daughters." (Moses 5:12.)

Adam is the pattern. He stands as earth's first prophet, and among his righteous descendants a host of prophets are numbered. At least eight generations of descendants lived to hear his teachings. Presiding high priests representing seven of these generations (Seth, Enos, Cainan, Mahalaleel, Jared, Enoch, and Methuselah) were all with him at Adam-ondi-Ahman when the Lord Jehovah appeared and ministered among them. (D&C 107:53-55.) To see and commune with either the Father or the Son is to know them both, for they are in the express image of each other and are one in all they do.

Noah, who stands next to Adam in the eternal priestly hierarchy, also knew the Lord and was a witness of his holy name. Enos, Cainan, Mahalaleel, Jared, Methuselah, and Lamech were all acquainted with both Adam and Noah, and by them was the knowledge of God spread forth among men. Noah himself taught several generations of his descendants. Abraham, who was born two years after the death of Noah, saw the Lord face to face and received from him the saving truths of the gospel by direct revelation. Isaac, Jacob, and a host of prophets in Israel all saw and knew the Lord, the chief among them being the great lawgiver Moses. Thus it is perfectly clear how the knowledge of God was preserved among men from the creation of Adam on down from generation to generation. And even among those, such as Cain, who departed from the faith, the fact of the existence of a god was continued from father to son, as a matter of tradition.

4. *God is known by revelation.*

Though every man in his inner being, by instinct and in the very marrow of his soul, knows there is a God; though logic and sense and reason, and the persuasive voice of nature, and the thunderous trumpet of creation, all bear witness that there is a God; though the voice of our fathers, carried to us by history and tradition, speaks the common consensus of all men that there is a God—yet, in the final and supreme sense, there is only one way to know God. That way is by revelation. Where religion and divine beings are concerned, we are in the realm not of the mind and of the human senses, but of the Spirit. God stands revealed or he remains forever unknown. The Holy Ghost is a revelator. His mission is to reveal truth and to bear witness of the Father and the Son. There is no other way to gain knowledge of the true and living God; revelation alone is the source of that perfect wisdom.

Joseph Smith, by the spirit of prophecy and revelation, wrote the constitutional document of the Church. In it the revealed word speaks of authoritative calls to the ministry in modern times, including calls to the holy apostleship; of angelic ministrations to mortal men, in which glorious truths were revealed; of the truth and verity of both the Book of Mormon and the Bible, and how they set forth the fulness of the everlasting gospel; of the witness of the truth borne to the world in these volumes of holy writ; and of the elders in modern Israel hearing the voice of "the glorious Majesty on high." And then, after reciting all these things, the revealed word attests: "By these things we know that there is a God in heaven, who is infinite and eternal, from everlasting to everlasting the same unchangeable God, the framer of heaven and earth, and all things which are in them." (D&C 20:1-17.) The knowledge of God is found in the holy scriptures, but it is revealed only to those who attune themselves to the promptings of the Holy Spirit and who heed the witness of the legal administrators sent of God in their day. All others fall short of gaining the pure and perfect knowledge promised the faithful.

Joseph Smith said: "After any portion of the human family are made acquainted with the important fact that there is a God, who has created and does uphold all things, the extent of their knowledge respecting his character and glory will depend upon their diligence and faithfulness in seeking after him, until, like Enoch, the brother of Jared, and Moses, they shall obtain faith in God, and power with him to behold him face to face." (*Lectures on Faith* 2:55.) This is the ultimate aim and hope of faithful mortal men: to see the face of God while they dwell in the flesh. After they have gained a knowledge of him by the power of the Holy Ghost, if they are true and faithful in all things and because he is no respecter of persons, they have power to see his face as have prophets in all ages. "And it shall be in his own time, and in his own way, and according to his own will." (D&C 88:68.)

"How do men obtain a knowledge of the glory of God, his perfections and attributes?" the Prophet asked. His answer: "By devoting themselves to his service, through prayer and supplication incessantly strengthening their faith in him, until, like Enoch, the brother of Jared, and Moses, they obtain a manifestation of God to themselves." (*Lectures on Faith* 2, Questions and Answers.) "Verily, thus saith the Lord: It shall come to pass that every soul who forsaketh his sins and cometh unto me, and calleth on my name, and obeyeth my voice, and keepeth my commandments, shall see my face and know that I am." (D&C 93:1.)

CHAPTER 6

True and False Gods

The True and Living God

In the ultimate and final sense of the word, there is only one true and living God. He is the Father, the Almighty Elohim, the Supreme Being, the Creator and Ruler of the universe. Paul said: "There is none other God but one. For though there be [others] that are called gods, whether in heaven or in earth, (as there be gods many, and lords many,) but to us there is but one God, the Father, of whom are all things, and we in him; and one Lord Jesus Christ, by whom are all things, and we by him. Howbeit there is not in every man that knowledge." (1 Corinthians 8:4-7.)

Christ is God; he alone is the Savior. The Holy Ghost is God; he is one with the Father and the Son. But these two are the second and third members of the Godhead. The Father is God above all, and is, in fact, the God of the Son. Indeed, the resurrected Christ said to Mary Magdalene: "I ascend unto my Father, and your Father; and to my God, and your God." (John 20:17.) And also: "I go unto the Father: for my Father is greater than I." (John 14:28.) And yet again: "My Father . . . is greater than all." (John 10:29.)

Thus Paul is saying that the Father is the one God who is supreme; that he is thus the God even of the Lord Jesus Christ, who himself also is God; that many others bear the name of Deity, including all exalted beings and even all false gods, but that none of them is our God; and that Jesus, under the Father, is Lord and Creator of all things. The Prophet Joseph Smith, in discussing the object upon which faith rests, bears this concordant witness: "God is the only supreme governor and independent being in whom all fullness and perfection dwell; who is omnipotent, omnipresent, and omniscient; without beginning of days or end of life; and . . . in him every good gift and every good principle dwell; and . . . he is the Father of lights; in him the principle of faith dwells independently; and he is the object in whom the faith of all other rational and accountable beings centers for life and salvation." (*Lectures on Faith* 2:2.) This includes the fact that the faith of Christ, who is God, is centered in his God, who is the Father.

We shall speak more particularly of the Father, the Son, and the Holy Ghost as we consider the Godhead. And we shall set forth the character, perfections, and attributes of Deity as an essential part of our discussion on faith. At this point we need only explain the three ways in which God is Almighty.

1. *God is omnipotent.*

He has all power, all might, and all dominion; he is the Almighty. He has power to do all that he wills to do. He is the Creator of worlds without number. If it were possible to number the particles of millions of earths like ours, the sum obtained would not be a beginning to the number of his creations; and the whole sidereal heavens, all of which are the works of his hands, move through the midst of immensity at his word. Truly he is infinite and eternal, without limits or bounds. His power is immeasurable, his might is without end, and his ways cannot be fathomed. There is no power yet to be gained that he does not now possess. If it were otherwise, our faith in him could not be other than limited and partial.

2. *God is omniscient.*

He has all wisdom, all knowledge, and all understanding; he is the All-Wise One, the All-Knowing One. There is no truth he does not know, no wisdom hidden from his view, no laws or powers or facts for him to discover in some distant eternity. His wisdom and knowledge are absolute and have neither bounds nor limitations. He knows all things now; he is not progressing in knowledge; he is not discovering new truths; there are no higher spheres than the one in which he now walks. His mind is infinite; his knowledge comprehends all things, and he is in fact the source and author of all truth. Were it otherwise, he could not be the Creator of galaxies unnumbered; were it otherwise, he could not hold the universe in his hands and govern and control all things. Indeed, his glory and greatness and goodness exist and are because he knows all things and is the source of all truth. And if such were not the case, men could not exercise faith in him unto life and salvation, for they would know that he might someday discover some truth that would destroy immortality, or eternal life, or the whole scheme and system of things.

3. *God is omnipresent.*

By the power of his Spirit, God is everywhere present at one and the same time. There is no place on earth or in heaven or through all the broad expanse of boundless space where his presence is not felt. Though he is a personage of tabernacle who created man "in the image of his own body" (Moses 6:9); though he has a material, tangible, corporeal body of flesh and bones; though as a person he can be in only one place at one time—yet Paul says, "In him we live, and move, and have our being." (Acts 17:28.) Though he is an individual set apart from all others, a person separated from all other persons, yet his senses are infinite and there is no limit to the power of his mind. He can hear and see and know all things at one and the same time—all by the power of his Spirit. "He is above all things, and in all things, and is through all things, and is round about all things; and all things are by him, and of him, even God, forever and ever." (D&C 88:41.) This Spirit that is everywhere present is also called the light of Christ; it is the light which "proceedeth forth from the presence of God to fill the immensity of space." It is "the light which is in all things, which giveth life to all things, which is the law by which all things are governed, even the power of God who sitteth upon his throne, who is in the bosom of eternity, who is in the midst of all things." (D&C 88:12-13.)

We know very little of the false gods before the flood. The Mosaic account simply says that in the days of Adam, Satan came among the children of Adam, saying: "I am also a son of God," and commanded them not to believe the teachings of their parents. "And they believed it not," the account says of the true gospel taught by Adam and Eve, "and they loved Satan more than God. And men began from that time forth to be carnal, sensual, and devilish." (Moses 5:13.) Of the people in Enoch's day, the Lord said: "Ever since the day that I created them, have they gone astray, and have denied me, and have sought their own counsels in the dark." (Moses 6:28.) We suppose they worshipped and served whatever gods seemed to suit their fancies.

In more recent historical times, however, we know something of the worship of many nations and peoples. Idols made of wood and stone, and of ores from the earth, all crafted by man's hand, have reared their marred and ugly visages on every hand. Cows and crocodiles from the animal kingdom; the sun, moon, and stars in the sidereal heavens; rivers and mountains, fires and volcanoes, and many of the forces of nature—all have been objects of veneration.

Sad as it may be, almost the entire history of mankind is an account of false worship, false gods, and all the ills that attend such a course. For instance, the gods of the Greeks, and those gods that the Romans copied from them, were mere men and women in whom were seen the vices and virtues of the people. These deities were involved in acts of lust, war, and depravity. The Romans adopted the gods of all the nations they conquered and even formally deified many of their emperors. Among the Moslems, the creed or formula of Islamic worship was and is that there is no god but Allah, and Mohammed is his prophet. Shintoism is the cultish religion of the Japanese in which reverence is shown to the spirits of imperial ancestors, to historical personages, and to some deities of nature. Buddhism is the religion of central and eastern Asia that first deified and now worships its founder, and that seeks to free men, through nirvana, from the necessity of future transmigration of their souls. Communism is in reality a form of religion in which men deny the God of the Bible and worship the gods of compulsion and power and war. Philosophy in all its forms and varieties is a way of worship. It is an attempt by reason and without revelation to explain existence, ethical principles in general, and the whence, why, and whither of life. Hedonism is the worship of pleasure and the doctrine that man's sole duty in life is to gratify his pleasure-seeking instincts.

True religion and the worship of the true and living God have been the exception rather than the rule during all the weary years of this earth's temporal continuance. Since the fall, most of mankind have chosen darkness rather than light because their deeds were evil. The gods of power and wealth and worldliness have always been the favorite deities of fallen man. They are the religion of the natural man, of fallen man, of man in his carnal, sensual, and devilish state. They corrupt the moral sense and open the door to every vice. And nowhere is this more clearly seen than among the idolatrous peoples who made human sacrifices—religious murders!—a way of worship. So it was with the slaughter of human beings under the Druidical tyranny, and with the unnumbered human sacrifices among the Aztecs, and with the sacrificing of children to Moloch and, among the Hindus, to the Ganges.

The false gods of Christendom bear the same names as the true Gods of the Bible. Beyond this they have little resemblance. They are described in the creeds that the Lord told Joseph Smith were "an abomination in his sight." (JS-H 1:19.)

False Gods Bring Damnation

Worship of the true and living God leads to salvation; the worship of false and dead deities does not. Perfect worship is manifest by living in such a manner as to be like the Venerated One. Thus, the extent of man's knowledge of God determines the excellence of his worship and the progress he makes toward salvation. If God is known to be a Holy Man, those who worship him can seek to be holy as he is holy. "Ye shall be holy: for I the Lord your God am holy." (Leviticus 19:2.) When men worship false gods, their way of life degenerates; they live after the manner of the world, and they do not do all that is needed to save themselves.

In writing to the Romans, Paul set forth the relationship between the knowledge of God and man's manner of living with a clarity and plainness seldom found in holy writ. "The wrath of God is revealed from heaven against all ungodliness and unrighteousness of men, who hold the truth in unrighteousness," he said. Why? "Because that which may be known of God is manifest in them; for God hath shewed it unto them." Man himself is a manifestation of God; if we know we are the children of God, we know something about what our Father is like—and God has revealed this Parent-child relationship to us.

"For the invisible things of him [God] from the creation of the world are clearly seen, being understood by the things that are made, even his eternal power and Godhead." God, who is unseen, is understood and known by the things he has made; and, particularly, we know what he is like because we are made in his image and likeness. We also know his eternal power and Godhead because he created all things.

"So that they are without excuse: because that, when they knew God, they glorified him not as God, neither were thankful; but became vain in their imaginations, and their foolish heart was darkened." The sons of Adam knew God and were taught the truth, but they did not appreciate the wonder of the knowledge that was theirs. In their vanity they turned from the gospel light to the darkness of the world.

"Professing themselves to be wise, they became fools, and changed the glory of the uncorruptible God into an image made like to corruptible man, and to birds, and fourfooted beasts, and creeping things." They apostatized from the truth, they made gods to their own liking, and they worshipped idols and all the vagaries that have existed and do exist.

"Wherefore"—meaning because they forsook him and his laws—"God also gave them up to uncleanness through the lusts of their own hearts, to dishonour their own bodies between themselves." Lust and passion ruled in their lives. Why? Because they "changed the truth of God into a lie, and worshipped and served the creature more than the Creator, who is blessed for ever."

Men forsook the Lord and made gods of their own; they worshipped and served the works of their own hands; their hearts were set upon false gods. And so, "For this cause God gave them up unto vile affections: for even their women did change the natural use into that which is against nature: And likewise also the men, leaving the natural use of the woman, burned in their lust one toward another; men with men working that which is unseemly, and receiving in themselves that recompence of their error which was meet." Paul is using the most evil abominations he can in order to show how low men can sink when they make and worship their own gods. He is speaking of homosexual perversions.

"And even as they did not like to retain God in their knowledge," Paul continues, "God gave them over to a reprobate mind, to do those things which are not convenient; being filled with all unrighteousness, fornication, wickedness, covetousness, maliciousness; full of envy, murder, debate, deceit, malignity; whisperers, backbiters, haters of God, despiteful, proud, boasters, inventors of evil things, disobedient to parents, without understanding, covenantbreakers, without natural affection, implacable, unmerciful: who knowing the judgment of God, that they which commit such things are worthy of death, not only do the same, but have pleasure in them that do them." (Romans 1:18-32.)

Such was the state of an apostate world in Paul's day, and such is the state of affairs in the world today. And the reason for all this evil—let it be written with a pen of iron on tablets of granite; let it be sounded in every ear; let all men know that it is the divine word—the reason for all this evil is that men no longer worship the true and living God.

CHAPTER 7

God the Father

Nature of the Godhead

Three glorious persons comprise the Godhead or supreme presidency of the universe. They are the Father, the Son, and the Holy Ghost. Each one possesses the same divine nature, knows all things, and has all power. Each one has the same character, the same perfections, and the same attributes. In Christ, Paul says, "dwelleth all the fulness of the Godhead bodily." (Colossians 2:9.) Because of this perfect unity, they are spoken of as being one God. "Hear, O Israel," Moses proclaimed, "the Lord our God is one Lord: And thou shalt love the Lord thy God with all thine heart, and with all thy soul, and with all thy might." (Deuteronomy 6:4-5.) This unity and oneness is the perfect pattern for all who seek salvation, for salvation consists in being one with the Lord our God. Thus Jesus prayed for all true believers, "that they all may be one; as thou, Father, art in me, and I in thee, that they also may be one in us." (John 17:21.)

This divine doctrine that the three persons in the Godhead are one is as clear and as plain and as easy to understand as any of the basic doctrines of the gospel. There is little excuse for the vagaries and contradictions found in the creeds of Christendom. These three divine beings comprise what has come to be called, in the sectarian world, the Holy Trinity. The sacred name-titles they bear are not simply different manifestations of the same divine essence or power or being. The living Gods are individuals who can and do come and go throughout the universe as the needs of their eternal ministries require. Men cannot worship the true God with that faith and devotion which brings salvation unless they distinguish between the members of the Godhead and know the place and functions of each.

Our faith is centered in the Son of God, and through him in the Father, and the Holy Ghost is their minister. It is of their diverse yet coordinated functions that Joseph Smith said: "Everlasting covenant was made between three personages before the organization of this earth, and relates to their dispensation of things to men on the earth; these personages, according to Abraham's record, are called God the first, the Creator; God the second, the Redeemer; and God the third, the witness or Testator." (*Teachings of the Prophet Joseph Smith,* p. 190.) Creation, redemption, and testification are thus the chief and paramount labors of the respective members of the Godhead. These are separate and identifiable pursuits, each as distinct from the others as the Gods of heaven are separate in being from each other. And yet the three are inseparably woven together as the essential parts of one eternal plan of salvation; they unite as one, as do those Gods whose work they are. We shall consider these separable yet united labors along with others that relate to them, each in due order and in its proper place.

Ministry of the Father

There are four ways in which the labors and ministry and status of "God the first," who is the Father, are distinct and separate from the other members of the Godhead. These are:

1. *The Father is a Holy Man; he is Ahman, the Almighty Elohim.*

The profound truth concerning God is that he is a Holy Man, a personage of tabernacle, a being in whose image and likeness mortal man was made. His work and his glory are to bring to pass the immortality and eternal life of man. Eternal life is the name of the kind of life he lives, and until men know that he is a Holy Man, they will never have the desire and the incentive to become like him and to be inheritors of eternal life.

The whole body of revealed writ attests to the eternal verity that the Supreme God is a Holy Man. "In the language of Adam," the Mosaic account recites, "Man of Holiness is his name, and the name of his Only Begotten is the Son of Man, even Jesus Christ." (Moses 6:57.) Thus, when Jesus asked the ancient disciples, "Whom do men say that I the Son of man am?" (Matthew 16:13), it was as though he asked: "Who do men say that I am? I testify that I am the Son of Man of Holiness, which is to say, the Son of that Holy Man who is God, but who do men say that I am?" In this same vein, one of the early revelations given in this dispensation asks: "What is the name of God in the pure language?" The answer: *"Ahman."* Question: "What is the name of the Son of God?" Answer: *"Son Ahman."* (Orson Pratt, cited in *Mormon Doctrine*, 2nd ed., p. 29.) And to Enoch the Lord identified himself by saying: "Behold, I am God; Man of Holiness is my name; Man of Counsel is my name; and Endless and Eternal is my name, also." (Moses 7:35.)

Properly understood, the four Gospels (Matthew, Mark, Luke, and John) contain the purest and most expansive accounts of the nature and kind of being that God is that can be found anywhere in the revealed word. All Christians are assumed to know that God, in the meridian day, was in Christ manifesting himself to the world. We know what Christ was like as a mortal, and we know the kind of body he now possesses in glorious immortality. Thus, we are not left in darkness nor in doubt as to the character, perfections, and attributes of the Father, nor as to the kind of body now possessed by the Father of the Son of Man.

The resurrected Lord Jesus invited great hosts of Nephites to feel the nail marks in his hands and feet and to thrust their hands into his riven side. His disciples in Jerusalem, assembled in the Upper Room on the very day of his resurrection, had a similar privilege. To them he said: "Behold my hands and my feet, that it is I myself: handle me, and see; for a spirit hath not flesh and bones, as ye see me have." And then in their presence he ate "a piece of a broiled fish, and of an honeycomb," that they might know and bear witness that his body was real and tangible and personal, one that could eat and digest food, even as is the case with mortal bodies. (Luke 24:39-43.) These solemn scenes give meaning and light and life to Paul's words: "God, who at sundry times and in divers manners spake in time past unto the fathers by the prophets, hath in these last days spoken unto us by his Son, whom he hath appointed heir of all things, by whom also he made the worlds; who being the brightness of his glory, and the express image of his person, and upholding all things by the word of his power, when he had by himself purged our sins, sat down on the right hand of the Majesty on high." (Hebrews 1:1-3.) And these scenes, coupled with Paul's words, are but the foundation for Joseph Smith's revealed pronouncement: "The Father has a body of flesh and bones as tangible as man's; the Son also; but the Holy Ghost has not a body of flesh and bones, but is a personage of Spirit." (D&C 130:22.)

Perhaps no single verse of scripture has spread greater spiritual confusion or led more people to build their houses of worship on the sands of false doctrine than John 4:24. It contains the words "God is a Spirit," which are interpreted by the Christian world to mean that God is a spirit essence that fills all space, has no form or substance, and dwells in human hearts. It might properly be said that "God is a Spirit" if by that is meant that he has a spiritual or resurrected body in harmony with Paul's statement relative to the resurrection that the body "is sown a natural body; it is raised a spiritual body. There is a natural [mortal] body, and there is a spiritual [resurrected] body." (1 Corinthians 15:44.) But the fact is that John 4:24 is mistranslated. It is part of a passage in which Jesus is teaching that the Father seeks true worshippers who will worship him in spirit and in truth. "For unto such," he says, "hath God promised his Spirit." (JST, John 4:26.)

2. *Elohim is the Father of spirits.*

As we view the starry heavens with their endless orbs, all spinning in assigned spheres; as we marvel at the wonders of life in all its varieties, as it is found on this and endless other earths; as we think of the miracles of creation, of redemption, and of everlasting life, all operating by the will and at the word of the Creator of the universe, we are led to exclaim: How can we conceive of such an Omnipotent God? how can mere man ever hope to know him whom it is eternal life to know? Can man comprehend God?

Strangely, marvelously, wondrously, the answer is found in the simple declaration that God is our Father. Our finite minds cannot comprehend his infinite laws. But we can envision him as a Father, as a personal, loving being filled with tenderness and compassion. He is more than the Father of the

Firstborn; more than the Father of the Only Begotten in the flesh; more than the Father in the sense that he created the first mortal man. He is, in deed and in fact, the Father of the spirits of all men in the literal and full sense of the word. Each of us was begotten by him in the premortal life. We are his spirit children.

Holy writ abounds in statements about the preexistent life of man. To Adam the divine voice said: "I am God; I made the world, and men before they were in the flesh." (Moses 6:51.) Enoch, in vision, "beheld the spirits that God had created." (Moses 6:36.) To Moses, the great Creator said: "I, the Lord God, had created all the children of men; and not yet a man to till the ground; for in heaven created I them." (Moses 3:5.) Abraham saw all the hosts of spirits in their preexistent home. They were identified as "the intelligences that were organized before the world was." They were called "souls" and "spirits," and the "noble and great ones" among them were foreordained to perform prophetic labors in mortality. Abraham saw that "there stood one among them that was like unto God." This one, under the Father, became the Creator, and was chosen and foreordained to be the Redeemer. Those spirits who kept their first estate were then assured of a mortal probation, while those who rebelled were cast out of heaven. (Abraham 3:22-28.) Isaiah and John and Jude, in their biblical accounts, tell us of the casting out of the rebels from their heavenly home. (Isaiah 14:12-20; Revelation 12:7-9; Jude 1:6.) Lehi records the same event in the Book of Mormon. (2 Nephi 2:17.) All of Paul's teachings about election and the special blessings given the house of Israel presuppose an understanding of the premortal life and the foreordination of the faithful spirits. And one of Paul's most compelling exhortations to keep the commandments is couched in these words: "We have had fathers of our flesh which corrected us, and we gave them reverence: shall we not much rather be in subjection unto the Father of spirits, and live?" (Hebrews 12:9.)

There are hundreds of scriptural passages that speak of the Father and his relationship to mortals. Implicit in all of them is the eternal verity that we are his children. After his resurrection, Jesus said to Mary Magdalene: "I ascend unto my Father, and your Father" (John 20:17), thus attesting that God both had a Son in mortality and was the Father of all men in the spirit. Ancient Israel prayed: "O God, the God of the spirits of all flesh." (Numbers 16:22.) Jesus taught the people to pray: "Our Father which art in heaven." (Matthew 6:9.) How better could he have taught us our relationship to the Father of us all?

3. *The Father is the Creator.*

In the ultimate and final sense of the word, the Father is the Creator of all things. That he used the Son and others to perform many of the creative acts, delegating to them his creative powers, does not make these others creators in their own right, independent of him. He is the source of all creative power, and he simply chooses others to act for him in many of his creative enterprises. But there are two creative events that are his and his alone. First, he is the Father of all spirits, Christ's included; none were fathered or created by anyone else. Second, he is the Creator of the physical body of man. Though Jehovah and Michael and many of the noble and great ones played their assigned roles in the various creative events, yet when it came time to place man on earth, the Lord God himself performed the creative acts. "I, God, created man in mine own image, in the image of mine Only Begotten created I him; male and female created I them." (Moses 2:27.)

4. *The Father is the author of the plan of salvation.*

Only the Father is or could be the author of the plan of salvation. He alone was in a position to ordain the laws and establish the system whereby his spirit children (Christ included!) could be saved. Others might perform labors for a portion or for all of the family of God, but only he could create salvation and specify how it might be gained. This concept becomes clear when we learn how God came to be God, how he gained his exaltation, and how he made provision for his spirit children to go and do likewise.

As to God's high status as an exalted man, as to how he attained this position of supreme eminence, and as to how we may pursue the same course to the same eternal destiny, the Prophet Joseph Smith proclaimed: "God himself was once as we are now, and is an exalted man, and sits enthroned in yonder heavens! That is the great secret." Let all the saints ponder these words in their hearts; let them plead for enlightenment from the Holy Spirit; let them know that the concept involved opens the door to an understanding of the plan of salvation.

"If the veil were rent today, and the great God who holds this world in its orbit, and who upholds all worlds and all things by His power, was to make himself visible,—I say, if you were to see him today, you would see him like a man in form—like yourselves in all the person, image, and very form as a man; for Adam was created in the very fashion, image and likeness of God, and received instruction from, and walked, talked and conversed with Him, as one man talks and communes with another." Oh, how great the importance to make these things known unto all men so that they no longer worship gods of their own creating!

"It is the first principle of the gospel to know for a certainty the character of God," the inspired word continues, "and to know that we may converse with Him as one man converses with another, and that He was once a man like us; yea, that God himself, the Father of us all, dwelt on an earth, the same as Jesus Christ Himself did." The Father is a glorified, perfected, resurrected, exalted man who worked out his salvation by obedience to the same laws he has given to us so that we may do the same.

"Here, then, is eternal life—to know the only wise and true God; and you have got to learn how to be gods yourselves, and to be kings and priests to God, the same as all gods have done before you, namely, by going from one small degree to another, and from a small capacity to a great one; from grace to grace, from exaltation to exaltation, until you attain to the resurrection of the dead, and are able to dwell in everlasting burnings, and to sit in glory, as do those who sit enthroned in everlasting power." (King Follett Address in *History of the Church* 6:305-6.)

In the light of this infinite and eternal perspective of the everlasting system of salvation, how could anyone but the Father create a plan of salvation for his spirit children? And so we read in the inspired word: "God himself, finding he was in the midst of spirits and glory, because he was more intelligent, saw proper to institute laws whereby the rest could have a privilege to advance like himself. The relationship we have with God places us in a situation to advance in knowledge. He has power to institute laws to instruct the weaker intelligences, that they may be exalted with Himself, so that they might have one glory upon another, and all that knowledge, power, glory, and intelligence, which is requisite in order to save them in the world of spirits." (Ibid., p. 312.)

After the plan of salvation had been taught to all the spirit children of the Father; after the nature of this mortal probation had been explained; after the need for a Redeemer had been set forth—then the Lord God, who is the Father, sent forth a great cry in the grand council. "Whom shall I send?" he asked. 'Whom shall I send to be my Son, to be the Savior and Redeemer, to work out the infinite and eternal atonement? Whom shall I send to put into full operation all the terms and conditions of my plan of salvation?'

There were two volunteers. The Lord Jehovah said: "Here am I, send me." (Abraham 3:27.) And also: "Father, thy will be done, and the glory be thine forever." That is to say: 'Send me and I will follow thy plan, Father; men shall have their agency, and all things will be done as thou wilt.' The second volunteer, who was Lucifer, said: "Behold, here am I, send me, I will be thy son, and I will redeem all mankind, that one soul shall not be lost, and surely I will do it; wherefore give me thine honor." (Moses 4:1-2.) Thus Satan sought to amend the plan of the Father and to take the glory in all things unto himself. And then "the Lord," who is the Father, said, "I will send the first." (Abraham 3:27.)

The plan of salvation is known to us as the gospel of Jesus Christ. In the ultimate sense, as Paul says, it is "the gospel of God . . . concerning his Son Jesus Christ our Lord." (Romans 1:1-3.) We, properly, call it after the Son of God to show that all of its terms and conditions are put into operation because of his atoning sacrifice. But the plan is the Father's; he is its author. It is Christ's by adoption, even as it is ours by adoption if we believe and obey its laws and ordinances.

CHAPTER 8

The Son and the Holy Spirit

Ministry of the Son

There are numerous ways in which the labors and ministry and status of "God the second," who is the Son, are distinct and separate from the other members of the Godhead. Chief among them are these:

1. *He is the Firstborn.*

Our Blessed Lord is the firstborn spirit child of the Father of Spirits; all others are junior to him. His is the eternal birthright and the everlasting right of presidency. "I was in the beginning with the Father," he says, "and am the Firstborn." (D&C 93:21.) Paul says he is "the image of the invisible God, the firstborn of every creature." (Colossians 1:15.) The body he then possessed was a spirit body, a body made of spirit element, a body like those of all the spirit hosts of heaven. Appearing to the brother of Jared, he said: "This body, which ye now behold, is the body of my spirit." (Ether 3:16.) In that spirit state he advanced and progressed until, in power, dominion, and intelligence, he became "like unto God." (Abraham 3:24.) It was then that he created all things and was foreordained to be the Savior and Redeemer.

2. *He is the Creator.*

Under the Father, Christ is the Creator of this earth, of worlds without number, of all things. Paul says: "By him were all things created, that are in heaven, and that are in earth, visible and invisible, whether they be thrones, or dominions, or principalities, or powers: all things were created by him, and for him: and he is before all things, and by him all things consist." (Colossians 1:16-17.) Being "like unto God," he became and was the GREAT I AM, the I AM THAT I AM, the Eternal

One, the Lord Jehovah. He operated and ministered in his Father's name and by his Father's power.

3. *He is the Promised Messiah.*

The ancient prophets testified that God would send his Son into the world to save and deliver his people, to save them from the temporal and spiritual death brought upon all mankind through the fall, to be their Deliverer and Redeemer. The prophetic word acclaimed him as the Messiah, the Anointed One, the Son of David, who would reign on the throne of his Father.

All of the ordinances of the gospel and the whole Mosaic system were established in such a way as to bear record of the Son and the atonement he would make. Many of the faithful saints of old knew about him and his atonement and messiahship.

4. *He is the God of our Fathers.*

Because God is known only by revelation, because the knowledge of God and of salvation was revealed to our fathers, and because there is only one God and one plan of salvation for all men in all ages, how appropriate it is to call Christ (by whom salvation comes) the God of our fathers. He was their God and he is our God. "All the holy prophets," the Nephite Jacob said, ". . . believed in Christ and worshiped the Father in his name." (Jacob 4:4-5.) As the Lord Jehovah, he appeared to Abraham and the ancient patriarchs, and he bears their name to signify to their descendants that they worship that same blessed person who guided their forebears. He is the God of Abraham, Isaac, and Jacob, the God of Israel, the Holy One of Israel. "I am the God of Israel, and the God of the whole earth, and have been slain for the sins of the world" (3 Nephi 11:14), he told the Nephites after his resurrection.

5. *He is the Son of God.*

All men (Christ included) were born as the sons of God in the spirit; one man (Christ only) was born as the Son of God in this mortal world. He is the Only Begotten in the flesh. God was his Father; Mary was his mother. His Father was an immortal man; his mother was a mortal woman. He is the Son of God in the same literal, full, and complete sense in which he is the son of Mary. There is nothing symbolic or figurative about it. He is God's Almighty Son and as such is distinguished from the

Father in the same way any son is a separate person from his father.

6. *He is our Redeemer, Savior, Mediator, Intercessor, and Advocate.*

Salvation comes because of Christ and his atoning sacrifice. He is the Redeemer who ransoms men from the effects of Adam's fall. He brings immortality to all men, thus redeeming them from temporal death through the resurrection. Those who believe and obey his laws are redeemed from spiritual death and have eternal life. In like manner he is the Savior. He came "to save that which was lost" (Matthew 18:11), not to save fallen man in his sins but from his sins.

"God was in Christ, reconciling the world unto himself," Paul says, "not imputing their trespasses unto them." That is, through the gospel, fallen man may be ransomed from a state of sin and spiritual darkness and restored to one of harmony and unity with Deity. The gospel is "the ministry of reconciliation." (2 Corinthians 5:18-19.) Our Lord's ministry is one of mediation. He interposes himself between the immortal Man of Holiness and mortal men who are sinners; he intercedes on their behalf and pleads their cause in the courts above. "There is one God, and one mediator between God and men, the man Christ Jesus." (1 Timothy 2:5.) "He shall make intercession for all the children of men; and they that believe in him shall be saved." (2 Nephi 2:9.) As our Advocate with the Father, he pleads: "Father, behold the sufferings and death of him who did no sin, in whom thou wast well pleased; behold the blood of thy Son which was shed, the blood of him whom thou gavest that thyself might be glorified; wherefore, Father, spare these my brethren that believe on my name, that they may come unto me and have everlasting life." (D&C 45:3-5.)

7. *He manifests and reveals the Father.*

There are two concepts here. First, God was in Christ manifesting himself to the world. That is, because the Son was in the express image and likeness of the Father, and because he was one with the Father in all things, insomuch that he did and said what the Father would do and say in like circumstances, anyone who saw the Son saw also the Father. To know the Son is to know the Father. Second, Christ reveals the Father to the faithful, as it is written, "Neither knoweth any man the Father, save the Son, and he to whomsoever the Son will reveal him." (Matthew 11:27.) Christ is the Way—the way to the Father. "No man shall come unto the Father but by me or by my word, which is my law," he says. (D&C 132:12.)

8. *He is the Eternal Judge.*

"The Father judgeth no man, but hath committed all judgment unto the Son: that all men should honour the Son, even as they honour the Father." (John 5:22-23.) And this Son of Man, in a not far-distant day, shall come again, in all the glory of his Father's kingdom, to take vengeance upon the ungodly and to give glory and honor to the righteous.

9. *He is the Father.*

There are three ways in which Christ the Son is properly called the Father. First, he is "the Father of the heavens and of the earth, and all things that in them are." (Ether 4:7.) That is, he is the Maker, Organizer, and Creator of all things; he fathered them in this sense. Second, he is the Father of all who believe and obey his law. Those who receive the gospel have "power to become [his] sons." (D&C 39:4.) They thus become "the children of Christ, his sons, and his daughters"; they are "spiritually begotten" by him; they take upon them "the name of Christ." (Mosiah 5:7-8.) They are born again and have a new Father. Third, he is the Father by divine investiture of authority. "In all His dealings with the human family Jesus the Son has represented and yet represents Elohim His Father in power and authority." The Father, accordingly, places his own name upon the Son so the Son can speak in the first person as though he were the Father. "And so far as power, authority and Godship are concerned His words and acts were and are those of the Father." ("The Father and the Son," exposition of the First Presidency, June 30, 1916.)

Ministry of the Holy Ghost

There are several ways in which the labors and ministry and status of "God the third," who is the Holy Ghost, are separate from the other members of the Godhead. Chief among them are these:

1. *He is a personage of spirit.*

The Father and the Son have tangible bodies of flesh and bones, while "the Holy Ghost has not a body of flesh and bones, but is a personage of Spirit." That is, he is a spirit person, a spirit entity, a spirit man. He is the Holy Spirit, the Spirit of the Lord. Why this difference between him and the other two members of the Godhead? With reference to his status as "a personage of Spirit," the scripture says: "Were it not so, the Holy Ghost could not dwell in us." (D&C 130:22.) That is to say, according to the eternal laws ordained by the Father, there are certain separate and distinct things to be done by a spirit member of the Godhead. He is to dwell, figuratively, in the faithful, and he is to speak to their spirits in a special and particular way, which he can do because he himself is a spirit.

    2. *He is the Testator, Revelator, Comforter.*

    The Holy Ghost is God's minister; he is appointed to teach and testify, to bear witness of the Father and the Son, and to reveal all needful things to men. As the Testator, he bequeaths salvation, through an eternal testament, to the heirs of God. The Holy Ghost is a Revelator. Almost always the first great revelation received by any person is a testimony of the truth and divinity of the Lord's work on earth. "And by the power of the Holy Ghost ye may know the truth of all things." (Moroni 10:5.) He is the Comforter. Those who enjoy his companionship find their whole souls are filled with comfort and joy. And the very reason men are commanded to repent and be baptized is so they "may be sanctified by the reception of the Holy Ghost, that [they] may stand spotless before [the Lord] at the last day." (3 Nephi 27:20.)

    3. *He uses the light of Christ in his ministry.*

    The light of Christ (also called the Spirit of Christ and the Spirit of the Lord) is a light, a power, and an influence that proceeds forth from the presence of God to fill the immensity of space. It is everywhere present and accounts for the omnipresence of God. It is the agency of God's power and the law by which all things are governed. It is also the agency used by the Holy Ghost to manifest truth and dispense spiritual gifts to many people at one and the same time. For instance, it is as though the Holy Ghost, who is a personage of spirit, was broadcasting all truth throughout the whole universe all the time, using the light of Christ as the agency by which the message is delivered. But only those who attune their souls to the Holy Spirit receive the available revelation. It is in this way that the person of the Holy Ghost makes his influence felt in the heart of every righteous person at one and the same time.

CHAPTER 9

The Eternal Godhead

The Mystery of Godliness

We have set forth the true doctrine relative to those Gods whose witnesses and servants we are. It is the same doctrine that those holy beings have always revealed to their servants the prophets, and it has come anew to us in these last days by the opening of the heavens. The scriptures, both ancient and modern, contain as much about the members of the Eternal Godhead as the members of that Holy Presidency, in their infinite wisdom, feel that we as mortals should have before us in our present state of spiritual progression. But in the final and ultimate sense they are known only by personal revelation, revelation that comes to those separate individuals who attune their souls to the Infinite. To the faithful, the Holy Ghost bears witness of the Father and the Son. Then those who receive this divine witness have power, through faith and righteousness, to progress in spiritual things until the heavens are rent and they see and know for themselves.

Those desiring to know the only true God and Jesus Christ, whom he sent into the world, must of necessity turn for help and guidance to others who have already gained that knowledge. Truth seekers must heed the voices of the legal administrators sent to teach the truth in their day, and they must search the scriptures and ponder the inspired writings of the apostles and prophets of all ages. The light and truth they receive from the spoken word and from the written record will depend on their own spiritual status. Each pronouncement in the holy scriptures, for instance, is so written as to reveal little or much, depending on the spiritual capacity of the student. To a carnal person, a passage of scripture may mean nothing; to an honest though uninformed truth seeker, it may shed forth only a few rays of heavenly light; but to one who has the mind of Christ, the same passage may blaze forth an effulgence of celestial light. That which is a mystery to one is plain and simple to another. The things of the Spirit can be understood only by the power of the Spirit.

Using the holy scriptures as the recorded source of the knowledge of God, knowing what the Lord has revealed to them of old in visions and by the power of the Spirit, and writing as guided by that same Spirit, Joseph Smith and the early brethren of this dispensation prepared a creedal statement on the Godhead. It is without question the most excellent summary of revealed and eternal truth relative to the Godhead that is now extant in mortal language. In it is set forth the mystery of Godliness; that is, it sets forth the personalities, missions, and ministries of those holy beings who comprise the supreme presidency of the universe. To spiritually illiterate persons, it may seem hard and confusing; to those whose souls are aflame with heavenly light, it is a nearly perfect summary of those things which must be believed to gain salvation.

"There are two personages [of tabernacle] who constitute the great, matchless, governing, and supreme, power over all things, by whom all things were created and made, that are created and made, whether visible or invisible; whether in heaven, on earth, or in the earth, under the earth, or throughout the immensity of space." (Lectures on Faith 5:2.)

These two, standing alone, are not the Godhead. But they are God the first and God the second. They are personages, individuals, persons, holy men. They created and they have power over all things. Their power is supreme and their wisdom infinite; there is no power they do not possess, no truth they do not know. From eternity to eternity they are the same; they are omnipotent, omniscient, and omnipresent.

"They are the Father and the Son—the Father being a personage of spirit, glory, and power, possessing all perfection and fullness, the Son, who was in the bosom of the Father, a personage of tabernacle." (Lectures on Faith 5:2.)

They are the two personages who came to Joseph Smith in the spring of 1820 in a grove of trees in western New York. They are exalted men. Each is a personage of spirit; each is a personage of tabernacle. Both of them have bodies, tangible bodies of flesh and bones. They are resurrected beings. Words, with their finite connotations, cannot fully describe them. A personage of tabernacle, as here used, is one whose body and spirit are inseparably connected and for whom there can be no death. A personage of spirit, as here used and as distinguished from the spirit children of the Father, is a resurrected personage. Resurrected bodies, as contrasted with mortal bodies, are in fact spiritual bodies. With reference to the change of our bodies from mortality to immortality, Paul says: "It is sown a natural body; it is raised a spiritual body. There is a natural body, and there is a spiritual body." (1 Corinthians 15:44.) "For notwithstanding they [the saints] die, they also shall rise again, a spiritual body." (D&C 88:27.)

"The Son, who was in the bosom of the Father, a personage of tabernacle, made or fashioned like unto man, or being in the form and likeness of man, or rather man was formed after his likeness and in his image; he is also the express image and likeness of the personage of the Father, possessing all the fullness of the Father, or the same fullness with the Father." (Lectures on Faith 5:2.)

Christ as the Firstborn, the firstborn spirit child of the Father, was in the bosom of the Father before the world was. Though he was then "in the form of God" and was "equal with God," as Paul expresses it—equal in knowledge and truth and all of the attributes of godliness—yet he "made himself of no reputation, and took upon him the form of a servant, and was made in the likeness of men." Thus he was "found in fashion as a man." (Philippians 2:6-8.) After the days of his flesh and when he had been raised from mortality to immortality by the power of the Father, he was able to say: "All power is given unto me in heaven and in earth." (Matthew 28:18.) Thus, the Son, as Paul tells us, now possesses "the brightness of his [Father's] glory, and the express image of his person." (Hebrews 1:3.) From all of this it follows that the Son possesses the same fulness with the Father, that is, the same glory, the same power, the same perfection, the same holiness, the same eternal life.

"The Son, . . . being begotten of him, and ordained from before the foundation of the world to be a propitiation for the sins of all those who should believe on his name, . . . is called the Son because of the flesh, and descended in suffering below that which man can suffer; or, in other words, suffered

greater sufferings, and was exposed to more powerful contradictions than any man can be." (*Lectures on Faith* 5:2.)

As with all men, Christ was *a* spirit son in preexistence. In that premortal sphere he was chosen and ordained to be the Redeemer and Savior and to make a propitiation for the sins of all who believe and obey. But he is *the* Son because he alone was begotten in the flesh, in mortality, in this probationary sphere, where, as a man, he would "suffer temptations, and pain of body, hunger, thirst, and fatigue, even more than man can suffer, except it be unto death." (Mosiah 3:7.) The greatest suffering ever endured by man or God was in Gethsemane, where the Son, in agony, sweat great drops of blood from every pore. Truly, "in bringing many sons unto glory," it pleased God "to make the captain of their salvation perfect through sufferings." (Hebrews 2:10.)

"But, notwithstanding all this, he kept the law of God, and remained without sin, showing thereby that it is in the power of man to keep the law and remain also without sin; and also, that by him a righteous judgment might come upon all flesh, and that all who walk not in the law of God may justly be condemned by the law, and have no excuse for their sins." (*Lectures on Faith* 5:2..)

Jesus was and is the Sinless One; he kept the whole law of the whole gospel. His every thought and word and deed conformed to a divine and perfect standard. Before his birth, during mortality, and now in exalted immortality, he was and is the Holy One. Because he was sinless and perfect, he is both our Exemplar and our Judge. Being himself perfect—without taint of sin and under no personal condemnation—he can sit in judgment upon all others without having his judgments colored by any untoward thought, word, or deed. Thus, speaking of himself as both our Exemplar and our Judge, he said to the Nephite Twelve: "Ye shall be judges of this people, according to the judgment which I shall give unto you, which shall be just. Therefore, what manner of men ought ye to be? Verily I say unto you, even as I am." (3 Nephi 27:27.)

"And he being the Only Begotten of the Father, full of grace and truth, and having overcome, received a fullness of the glory of the Father, possessing the same mind with the Father, which mind is the Holy Spirit, that bears record of the Father and the Son." (*Lectures on Faith* 5:2.)

The mortal Jesus, as a man among men, had both a father and a mother. God was his Father, and Mary was his mother. He was begotten by a Holy Man, by that God whose name is Man of Holiness; and he was conceived in the womb of a mortal woman. Mary, a virgin of Nazareth in Galilee, was "the mother of the Son of God, after the manner of the flesh." (1 Nephi 11:18.) She was overshadowed by the Holy Ghost; "she was carried away in the Spirit" (1 Nephi 11:19); she conceived "by the power of the Holy Ghost," and she brought forth a son, "even the Son of God" (Alma 7:10). That Son, who is called Christ, is the Only Begotten, the only offspring of the Father born into mortality. As a man, as God's only Son, his only mortal Son, he overcame the world. He overcame the world of evil and carnality and devilishness, and then, having died, he rose again in glorious immortality to receive all power both on earth and in heaven, which power is the fulness of the glory of the Father. He thus possesses the same mind with the Father, knowing and believing and speaking and doing as though he were the Father. This mind is theirs by the power of the Holy Ghost. That is, the Holy Ghost, who is a personage of spirit (a spirit man!), using the light of Christ, can give the same mind to all men, whether mortal or immortal. The saints who are true and faithful in all things have, as Paul said, "the mind of Christ" (1 Corinthians 2:16), which means also that they have the mind of the Father. It is to the faithful saints that the Holy Spirit bears witness of the Father and the Son, and it is to them that he reveals all things.

"And these three are one; or, in other words, these three constitute the great, matchless, governing and supreme power over all things; by whom all things were created and made that were created and made." (Lectures on Faith 5:2.)

In what way are the Father, the Son, and the Holy Ghost one God? Though three persons are involved, they are one supreme presidency, one in creating all things, one in governing the universe with almighty power.

"And these three constitute the Godhead, and are one; the Father and the Son possessing the same mind, the same wisdom, glory, power, and fullness—filling all in all; the Son being filled with the fullness of the mind, glory, and power; or, in other words, the spirit, glory, and power, of the Father, possessing all knowledge and glory, and the same kingdom,

sitting at the right hand of power, in the express image and likeness of the Father, mediator for man, being filled with the fullness of the mind of the Father; or, in other words, the Spirit of the Father, which Spirit is shed forth upon all who believe on his name and keep his commandments. (*Lectures on Faith* 5:2.)

One Godhead! Three persons possessing the same mind, power, and glory! Three individuals actuated by the same spirit, knowing all things, and working together in perfect unity! God the Creator united in all things with God the Redeemer, who mediates between the Great Creator and his fallen creatures! And—wonder of wonders—the same spirit which unites the Gods of heaven is shed forth on the righteous, that they may be one as the Gods themselves are one.

"And all those who keep his commandments shall grow up from grace to grace, and become heirs of the heavenly kingdom, and joint heirs with Jesus Christ; possessing the same mind, being transformed into the same image or likeness, even the express image of him who fills all in all; being filled with the fullness of his glory, and become one in him, even as the Father, Son, and Holy Spirit are one." (*Lectures on Faith* 5:2.)

Thus is set forth in the creedal document the doctrine—later to be endorsed and expounded in even plainer language—that as God now is, man may become.

"From the foregoing account of the Godhead, which is given in his revelations, the saints have a sure foundation laid for the exercise of faith unto life and salvation, through the atonement and mediation of Jesus Christ; by whose blood they have a forgiveness of sins, and also a sure reward laid up for them in heaven, even that of partaking of the fullness of the Father and the Son through the spirit. As the Son partakes of the fullness of the Father through the Spirit, so the saints are, by the same Spirit, to be partakers of the same fullness, to enjoy the same glory; for as the Father and the Son are one, so, in like manner, the saints are to be one in them. Through the love of the Father, the mediation of Jesus Christ, and the gift of the Holy Spirit, they are to be heirs of God, and joint heirs with Jesus Christ." (*Lectures on Faith* 5:3.)

Such is the course whereby the saints gain eternal life, the greatest of all the gifts of God. And how could Deity give anything greater to any man than the glory, power, and dominion that he himself possesses? The name of the kind of life he lives is eternal life, and all those who know him in the full and complete sense shall have eternal life.

"Behold, the mystery of godliness, how great is it!" (D&C 19:10.)

ARTICLE 2

*We believe
that men will be punished
for their own sins,
and not for Adam's transgression.*

CHAPTER 10

The Fall of Adam

The Three Pillars of Eternity

The three greatest events that ever have occurred or ever will occur in all eternity are these:

1. The creation of the heavens and the earth, of man, and of all forms of life;

2. The fall of man, of all forms of life, and of the earth itself from their primeval and paradisiacal state to their present mortal state; and

3. The infinite and eternal atonement, which ransoms man, all living things, and the earth also from their fallen state so that the salvation of the earth and of all living things may be completed.

These three divine events—the three pillars of eternity— are inseparably woven together into one grand tapestry known as the eternal plan of salvation. We view the atonement of the Lord Jesus Christ as the center and core and heart of revealed religion. It brings to pass the immortality and eternal life of man. Salvation is in Christ.

But had there been no fall, there could have been no atonement. The fall of Adam brought temporal and spiritual death into the world, and it is from these deaths that man and all forms of life are ransomed through the atonement wrought by the Lord Jesus Christ. Adam brought mortality; Christ brought immortality. Salvation comes because of the fall and the atonement.

But if the earth and man and all living things had not been created in their physical and paradisiacal state, in a state of deathlessness, there could have been no fall. The fall, with its resultant probationary estate, is the child of the original and primeval creation, and the atonement is the child of the fall.

Hence salvation was made available in and through and be-cause of the creation of the heavens and the earth and all that in and on them are. Salvation comes because of the creation, the fall, and the atonement; these three are each part of one divine plan.

It is not possible to believe in Christ and his atoning sacri-fice, in the true and full sense required to gain salvation, with-out at the same time believing and accepting the true doctrine of the fall. If there had been no fall, there would have been no need for a Redeemer or Savior. And it is not possible to believe in the fall, out of which immortality and eternal life come, without at the same time believing and accepting the true doc-trine of the creation. If there had been no creation of all things in a deathless or immortal state, there could have been no fall, and hence no atonement and no salvation. The Father's eternal plan called for the creation, for the fall, and for the atonement, all woven together into one united whole.

In connection with the second Article of Faith, we shall consider· the creation and the fall and man's probationary estate so as to lay the necessary foundation for our study of the atonement as set forth in the third Article of Faith.

The Creation of All Things

Mankind's knowledge of the creation of the heavens and the earth, and of life in all its forms and varieties, comes by revelation from the Creator himself. The Lord has revealed only that portion of eternal truth relative to the creation of all things that finite minds are capable of understanding. He has given man only what he needs to know to comprehend the true doctrine of the fall, and thus to gain that salvation which comes because of the fall. There are various man-made, specu-lative theories about the creation. That these theories do not accord with the revealed word and that they change with every wind that blows is well known. All of this is part of the divine design. Each person is free to choose his beliefs with reference to all things, the creation included. Proper choices enable him to build a house of faith that will shelter him from every wind of false doctrine that may chance to blow in his day.

To create is to organize. In the beginning the Lord Jehovah, in obedience to the direction of the Father, declared: "We will go down, for there is space there, and we will take of these materials, and we will make an earth whereon these may dwell; and we will prove them herewith, to see if they will do all things whatsoever the Lord their God shall command them." (Abraham 3:24-25.) Thus, the spirit children of the Father were to undergo a mortal probation. And the purpose of the creation was to provide the way and means whereby man might be saved.

The creative events took place during six periods of time, called days. Divine laws and powers governed all that transpired. As set forth in holy writ, the work was accomplished as follows:

First Day: God organized and formed the atmospheric heavens and the physical earth. The earth was without form and void; that is, it was empty and desolate. Darkness reigned. A divine decree brought forth light, and as the newly created planet rotated on its axis, day and night came into being.

Second Day: A firmament or expanse called heaven was created so as to divide the waters on the earth from those in the atmospheric heavens.

Third Day: The waters on the earth were gathered into one place called the sea, and dry land appeared. The earth was prepared to bring forth grass, herbs, trees, and foliage. Seeds were planted, and all forms of plant life grew. Each variety then brought forth its own seed; this seed could reproduce only its own kind.

Fourth Day: The earth was given its relationship to the sun, moon, and stars. These lights in the firmament were so organized as to be for signs and for seasons, for days and for years.

Fifth Day: Fishes and great whales and every living creature that dwells in water came forth. Winged fowls in all their varieties were created. All these were commanded to multiply and fill the waters and the earth, each bringing forth after his own kind.

Sixth Day: This was the creative day of days. On it animal life, cattle, beasts, living creatures of all sorts, everything that creepeth upon the earth—all these came forth. Then the Eternal Father created man in his own image and likeness, both male and female. They were given dominion over all other created things and were commanded to multiply and fill the earth with those of their own race. (Genesis 1; Moses 2; Abraham 4.)

At this point the holy word says: "Thus the heaven and the earth were finished, and all the host of them." (Moses 3:1.) The creation was accomplished; it was done. This earth, and man, and life in all its forms and varieties existed in physical form. But none of these had the same nature they now possess. The great Creator had created a paradisiacal earth, an edenic earth, an earth of the kind and nature that will exist during the Millennium, when it will be renewed and receive again its paradisiacal glory. There was as yet neither procreation nor death. These would enter the scheme of things only after the fall. The earth, man, and all created things were in a deathless state of immortality, but they were so organized that they could become mortal through the fall.

And so the Lord, in the Mosaic account, makes the needed interpolative explanations to enable us to understand the nature of the original creation, the paradisiacal creation, the creation that antedated the fall. There is no revealed account of the spirit creation, simply an explanation that all things were created in heaven before they were created naturally on earth. And although all things had been created physically, "there was not yet flesh upon the earth, neither in the water, neither in the air." That is, there was no flesh as we know it, no mortal flesh, no mortality. All forms of fish and fowl and animal life existed physically before man was placed on earth, and yet Adam is described as "the first flesh upon the earth, the first man also." (Moses 3:2-7.) Through his fall, Adam became mortal. He took upon himself mortal flesh and became the first mortal flesh on earth, and the effects of his fall then passed upon the earth and all created things.

The Universal Fall

After the creation came the fall; after all things had been created, all things fell. The fall was as universal as the creation. It included man, the earth, and all forms of life. Through the fall, all things passed downward to a lower status; they lost the station and dignity that once was theirs and were changed from the primeval and paradisiacal state to their present mortal state. This change from a deathless to a mortal state brought with it all things that appertain to mortality, including pro-creation, disease, suffering, and death. None of these existed on this earth prior to the fall.

This change of status for all created things is plainly set forth in the revealed word. "Because that Adam fell, we are," Enoch said; "and by his fall came death; and we are made partakers of misery and woe." (Moses 6:48.) We live on earth, we shall die, and we are subject to all of the ills of the flesh—all because of the fall.

"Were it not for our transgression we never should have had seed," said Eve, the mother of all living, "and never should have known good and evil, and the joy of our redemption, and the eternal life which God giveth unto all the obedient." (Moses 5:11.) Except for the fall, the earth would not be peopled; we would still be in the preexistence living as spirits, and that agency and those trials we now possess would not be. There would be no redemption from death, no immortality, no eternal life, no salvation of any sort. The purposes of God would thus be frustrated and come to naught.

In expounding the true doctrine of the fall, as it grew out of the creation, Lehi said: "If Adam had not transgressed he would not have fallen, but he would have remained in the garden of Eden." He would be there now, fresh and vibrant, with all the strength and beauty of youth, for there was no death. "And all things which were created must have remained in the same state in which they were after they were created; and they must have remained forever, and had no end." All created things—the earth; plants, herbs, and trees; fishes, fowls, animals, and beasts; that which creepeth upon the earth, or swimmeth in waters, or flieth in the air—all things would have retained their paradisiacal state. They would not be mortal and therefore not subject to death.

Speaking of our first parents, Lehi testified: "And they would have had no children; wherefore they would have remained in a state of innocence, having no joy, for they knew no misery; doing no good, for they knew no sin." (2 Nephi 2:22-23.) Mortality, procreation, and a probationary estate, with all its woes and miseries—all these came because of the fall.

We do not know how the fall was accomplished any more than we know how the Lord caused the earth to come into being and to spin through the heavens in its paradisiacal state. We have been given only enough information about the creation and the fall to enable us to understand the purposes of the Lord, to exercise faith in him, and to gain our salvation.

As to the fall, the scriptures set forth that there were in the Garden of Eden two trees. One was the tree of life, which figuratively refers to eternal life; the other was the tree of knowledge of good and evil, which figuratively refers to how and why and in what manner mortality and all that appertains to it came into being. "Of every tree of the garden thou mayest freely eat," the Lord told our first parents, "but of the tree of the knowledge of good and evil, thou shalt not eat of it, nevertheless, thou mayest choose for thyself, for it is given unto thee; but, remember that I forbid it, for in the day thou eatest thereof thou shalt surely die." (Moses 3:16-17.)

Eve partook without full understanding; Adam partook knowing that unless he did so, he and Eve could not have children and fulfill the commandment they had received to multiply and replenish the earth. After they had thus complied with whatever the law was that brought mortality into being, the Lord said to Eve: "I will greatly multiply thy sorrow and thy conception. In sorrow thou shalt bring forth children, and thy desire shall be to thy husband, and he shall rule over thee." To Adam the decree came: "Cursed shall be the ground for thy sake; in sorrow shalt thou eat of it all the days of thy life. Thorns also, and thistles shall it bring forth to thee." Thus the paradisiacal earth was cursed; thus it fell; and thus it became as it now is.

Adam was then told that he would surely die, returning through death to the dust whence his physical body had come. And then the Lord said to his Only Begotten: "Behold, the man is become as one of us to know good and evil; and now lest he put forth his hand and partake also of the tree of life, and eat and live forever [in his sins!], therefore I, the Lord God, will send him forth from the Garden of Eden, to till the ground from whence he was taken." (Moses 4:22-29.) Such is the ancient account of the fall.

The fall of Adam brought temporal and spiritual death into the world. Temporal death is the natural death; it occurs when body and spirit separate, thus leaving the body to return to the dust whence it came. Spiritual death is to be cast out of the presence of the Lord and to die as pertaining to the things of righteousness. Adam died spiritually when he was cast out of the heavenly presence found in the garden, and he remained spiritually dead until he repented and was born again through baptism and the receipt of the Holy Spirit. Having thus the companionship of the Holy Ghost, he became alive in Christ and was again guided and directed from on high. He was again in the presence of the Lord. Adam died temporally when his spirit separated from his mortal body.

Man's Probationary Estate

The effects of Adam's fall pass upon all mankind; that is, all are mortal and all die temporally. Also, all accountable persons are dead spiritually until they repent and receive the gift of the Holy Ghost. Thus, this life becomes a probationary estate in which all are commanded to repent and reconcile themselves to God through the cleansing blood of his Son.

Properly understood, it becomes apparent that the fall of Adam is one of the greatest blessings ever given of God to mankind. It is the way and the means whereby the spirit children of the Father go forth from their celestial home to gain mortal and then immortal bodies. And it provides the way for the experiences, tests, and trials that prepare the faithful for eternal life. Is it any wonder, then, that Michael himself—who stood next to the Lord Jehovah in power, might, and dominion, when they both dwelt in the presence of the Father—is it any wonder that Michael was the one chosen to come here as Adam to make such glorious blessings available to the billions of his descendants who should be born on earth?

Alma recited the account of Adam's fall and told how Adam was cast out of the garden lest he partake of the tree of life and live forever in his sins. To live forever in one's sins is to be damned; to live forever free from sin is to be saved. And so, Alma concluded, "there was a time granted unto man to repent, yea, a probationary time, a time to repent and serve God. For behold, if Adam had put forth his hand immediately, and partaken of the tree of life, he would have lived forever, according to the word of God, having no space for repentance."

If this had happened, Alma said, "the word of God would have been void, and the great plan of salvation would have been frustrated." Adam must fall; Adam must die spiritually; Adam must repent and keep the commandments and live again spiritually; Adam must die temporally; Adam must be raised in the resurrection—all this must be or he could not be saved.

Because Adam and Eve were cut off both temporally and spiritually, "they had become carnal, sensual, and devilish, by nature, [and] this probationary state became a state for them to prepare; it became a preparatory state." Such being the case, and if there were no plan of redemption, their souls would have been "miserable, being cut off from the presence of the Lord" forever. Man could not redeem himself from that which befell him "because of his own disobedience," Alma said. "Therefore, according to justice, the plan of redemption could not be brought about, only on conditions of repentance of men in this probationary state, yea, this preparatory state." And the plan of mercy, the plan of redemption, called for God himself to atone "for the sins of the world." (Alma 42:1-15.)

CHAPTER 11

The Agency of Man

Agency—Essential to Salvation

Inherent in the whole system of salvation that grows out of the fall of man; inherent in the great and eternal plan that makes of this life a preparatory and a probationary state; inherent in the very atoning sacrifice of God himself—inherent in the whole eternal plan of salvation is the eternal law of agency. All of the terms and conditions of the Lord's eternal plan operate because man has his agency, and none of it would have efficacy, virtue, or force if there were no agency. Agency requires opposites; agency demands freedom of choice; agency decrees personal accountability for sin. Every person must forsake his own sins. Repentance is a personal matter. Men will be punished for their own sins, not for Adam's transgression.

Speaking of the fall, Lehi said: "All things have been done in the wisdom of him who knoweth all things." The fall was part of the Lord's eternal plan and purpose. Then the ancient prophet gave forth the grand pronouncement: "Adam fell that men might be; and men are, that they might have joy." Only those who gain eternal life will receive a fulness of joy. "And the Messiah cometh in the fulness of time, that he may redeem the children of men from the fall." The fall and the atonement are two parts of one doctrine. "And because that they are redeemed from the fall they have become free forever, knowing good from evil; to act for themselves and not to be acted upon, save it be by the punishment of the law at the great and last day, according to the commandments which God hath given." Then in exalting tones our ancient Nephite friend concluded: "Wherefore, men are free according to the flesh; and all things are given them which are expedient unto man. And they are

89

free to choose liberty and eternal life, through the great Mediator of all men, or to choose captivity and death, according to the captivity and power of the devil; for he seeketh that all men might be miserable like unto himself." (2 Nephi 2:24-27.)

Agency underlies all things—all advancement, all progression, even existence itself. It is based on the presence of opposites between which a choice must be made. If there were no opposites, there would be nothing. "It must needs be, that there is an opposition in all things," Lehi said. "If not so . . . righteousness could not be brought to pass, neither wickedness, neither holiness nor misery, neither good nor bad." Then, to show why all this is so, Lehi reasoned, with divine insight and logic, in this way: If there were no opposites, and thus no agency, "all things must needs be a compound in one." That is, things would be both good and bad, hot and cold, light and dark at one and the same time, a thing that is impossible, as Lehi will show. "Wherefore, if it should be one body it must needs remain as dead," he continues, "having no life neither death, nor corruption nor incorruption, happiness nor misery, neither sense nor insensibility." Again, this is something that could not be. But assuming it to be so, Lehi reaches this conclusion: "Wherefore, it must needs have been created for a thing of naught; wherefore there would have been no purpose in the end of its creation. Wherefore, this thing must needs destroy the wisdom of God and his eternal purposes, and also the power, and the mercy, and the justice of God."

Thus, if men were not accountable for their own sins, if they were not agents unto themselves, the very purpose of creation and existence would vanish away and the plans and designs of God would fail. "And if ye shall say there is no law, ye shall also say there is no sin," the divine reasoning continues. "If ye shall say there is no sin, ye shall also say there is no righteousness. And if there be no righteousness there be no happiness. And if there be no righteousness nor happiness there be no punishment nor misery. And if these things are not there is no God. And if there is no God we are not, neither the earth; for there could have been no creation of things, neither to act nor to be acted upon; wherefore, all things must have vanished away." Such is the logic and reasoning of heaven. Opposites, agency, justice, rewards and punishments—all these are and must be part of the eternal plan. Without them, nothing would or could exist.

Having thus shown why men must be endowed with agency, Lehi bears his own witness that such is, in fact, the case. "There is a God," he says, "and he hath created all things, both the heavens and the earth, and all things that in them are, both things to act and things to be acted upon. And to bring about his eternal purposes in the end of man, after he had created our first parents, and the beasts of the field and the fowls of the air, and in fine, all things which are created, it must needs be that there was an opposition; even the forbidden fruit in opposition to the tree of life; the one being sweet and the other bitter. Wherefore, the Lord God gave unto man that he should act for himself. Wherefore, man could not act for himself save it should be that he was enticed by the one or the other." (2 Nephi 2:11-16.)

Thus we see why the Lord gave two conflicting commandments—one to become mortal and have children, the other to not eat of the tree of knowledge of good and evil out of which mortality and children and death would result. The issue is one of choosing between opposites. Adam must choose to become mortal so he could have children, on the one hand; on the other hand, he must choose to remain forever in the garden in a state of innocence. He chose to partake of the forbidden fruit so that the purposes of God might be accomplished by providing a probationary estate for his spirit children. Adam must needs fall so that he would know good from evil, virtue from vice, righteousness from wickedness. He could not have done this without breaking a law and becoming subject to sin. He chose the Lord's way; there was no other way whereby salvation might come unto the children of men.

Agency—An Eternal Principle

Agency is an eternal principle and has existed with God from eternity to eternity. When the Father presented the plan of salvation in the councils of eternity; when all his spirit children had been taught that through a mortal probation they could gain immortality and eternal life; when they all knew that to gain salvation they must choose good rather than evil while in mortality—then the Lord asked whom he should send to earth to be his Son and to put all the terms and conditions of his plan into operation. Lucifer, who is Satan, offered his services, but he did so on his own terms. "Behold, here am I, send me," he said. "I will be thy son, and I will redeem all mankind, that one soul shall not be lost, and surely I will do it; wherefore give me thine honor." As we have seen, this would have been a philosophical impossibility. Opposites must exist in every department of creation and in all phases of life. There could be no salvation unless there was also damnation.

After rejecting Lucifer's offer to deny men their agency and thus to save them without reference to any choice of either good or evil on their part, the Lord said: "Because that Satan rebelled against me, and sought to destroy the agency of man, which I, the Lord God, had given him, and also, that I should give unto him mine own power; by the power of mine Only Begotten, I caused that he should be cast down." (Moses 4:1-3.) That is the day when there was war in heaven—a war fought to preserve the agency of man, a war in which one-third of the spirit host followed Lucifer "because of their agency."

And thus it is that the Lord God "gave unto" Adam "that he should be an agent unto himself," while he yet dwelt in the garden of Eden. Thus it is that the devil and his angels came out in opposition to all righteousness and were cast out of heaven. "And it must needs be," the Lord says, "that the devil should tempt the children of men, or they could not be agents unto themselves; for if they never should have bitter they could not know the sweet—wherefore, it came to pass that the devil tempted Adam, and he partook of the forbidden fruit and transgressed the commandment, wherein he became subject to the will of the devil, because he yielded unto temptation. Wherefore, I, the Lord God, caused that he should be cast out from the Garden of Eden, from my presence, because of his transgression, wherein he became spiritually dead." Thus was the scene set for repentance, for choosing good rather than evil while in mortality, and for all of the trials and tests needed to qualify a human soul for eternal life.

"But . . . I, the Lord God, gave unto Adam and unto his seed, that they should not die as to the temporal death, until I, the Lord God, should send forth angels to declare unto them repentance and redemption, through faith on the name of mine Only Begotten Son. And thus did I, the Lord God, appoint unto man the days of his probation—that by his natural death he might be raised in immortality unto eternal life, even as many as would believe; and they that believe not unto eternal damnation; for they cannot be redeemed from their spiritual fall, because they repent not." (D&C 29:35-44.)

Punishment for Sin

Punishment for sin is part of the divine plan. Indeed, according to the law of agency, which is the law of opposites and of an opposition in all things, there could be no rewards unless there were also punishments. And yet many people are troubled in their minds, as was Corianton, "concerning the justice of God in the punishment of the sinner"; they "try to suppose that it is injustice that the sinner should be consigned to a state of misery." (Alma 42:1.) They choose to believe that God so abounds in mercy and is such a being of love and kindness that he will not impose eternal misery and woe upon any of his children.

The reason why punishments must be imposed is found in a correct understanding of the plan of salvation, with particular reference to the fall of Adam and the probationary way of life thereby created. Endowed with agency, having power in himself to obey or disobey, Adam was commanded not to partake of the tree of the knowledge of good and evil. The penalty for eating the forbidden fruit was that he would die spiritually and temporally. He chose to partake. Having partaken, could the Lord in justice do other than impose the penalty? Can the word of God return unto him void? Adam transgressed and Adam paid the penalty for his transgression; he died spiritually and he died temporally.

And as with Adam, so with his seed. "By one man sin entered into the world, and death by sin; and so death passed upon all men, for that all have sinned." (Romans 5:12.) In this mortal probation men have agency; they can choose for themselves. While here they are subject to laws—the laws of God, the laws of nature, the laws of men. And every law carries its own penalty. All men commit sin. "All have sinned, and come short of the glory of God." (Romans 3:23.) "If we say that we have no sin, we deceive ourselves, and the truth is not in us. . . . If we say that we have not sinned, we make him [God] a liar, and his word is not in us." (1 John 1:8, 10.) And as with Adam, so with all men; the justice of God requires that they pay the penalty for their disobedience. That penalty is to die spiritually, to die as to things of righteousness, to be cast out of the presence of God.

If there were no resurrection, all men would remain subject to temporal death forever; if there were no eternal life, all men would remain spiritually dead forever; all would continue to suffer for their sins everlastingly. Hence the divine plan called for a Redeemer, for a Savior, for one who could ransom men from their fallen state, for one who could pay the penalty for their sins. Thus, Alma tells his wayward son Corianton: "As the soul [spirit] could never die, and the fall had brought upon all mankind a spiritual death as well as a temporal, that is, they were cut off from the presence of the Lord, it was expedient that mankind should be reclaimed from this spiritual death." Otherwise men, having become "carnal, sensual, and devilish, by nature," and being subject to sin, would, after their temporal death, remain "miserable, being cut off from the presence of the Lord."

Because man could not redeem himself (that is, because he could not resurrect himself), and because he could not ransom himself from spiritual death (that is, because he could not, in the justice of God, return to the Divine Presence while in his sins), there must needs be a plan of redemption. Arrangements must be made whereby man could be redeemed from death, hell, the devil, and endless torment. "Therefore, according to justice, the plan of redemption could not be brought about, only on conditions of repentance of men in this probationary state, yea, this preparatory state; for except it were for these conditions, mercy could not take effect except it should destroy the work of justice. Now the work of justice could not be destroyed; if so, God would cease to be God. And thus we see that all mankind were fallen, and they were in the grasp of justice; yea, the justice of God, which consigned them forever to be cut off from his presence." Thanks be to God that there was a fall so there could be a plan of mercy and of redemption!

"And now, the plan of mercy could not be brought about except an atonement should be made; therefore God himself atoneth for the sins of the world, to bring about the plan of mercy, to appease the demands of justice, that God might be a perfect, just God, and a merciful God also." (Alma 42:9-15.) How great and wondrous are the ways of God whereby he made the fall the father of the atonement and of salvation!

Having so testified, Alma proceeds to reason about justice and mercy with the divine logic of a Lehi or a Paul. "Now, repentance could not come unto men," he continues, "except there were a punishment, which also was eternal as the life of the soul should be, affixed opposite to the plan of happiness, which was as eternal also as the life of the soul." Repentance and punishment go together. If there were no punishment, what need would there be for repentance?

"Now, how could a man repent except he should sin? How could he sin if there was no law? How could there be a law save there was a punishment?" The reasoning is perfect. "Now, there was a punishment affixed, and a just law given, which brought remorse of conscience unto man." The damnation of hell is in large measure nothing more than remorse of conscience.

"Now, if there was no law given—if a man murdered he should die—would he be afraid he would die if he should murder? And also, if there was no law given against sin men would not be afraid to sin. And if there was no law given, if men sinned what could justice do, or mercy either, for they would have no claim upon the creature?" Good questions these, philosophically sound, questions that prepare the mind for the declaration to follow.

"But there is a law given, and a punishment affixed, and a repentance granted; which repentance mercy claimeth; otherwise, justice claimeth the creature and executeth the law, and the law inflicteth the punishment; if not so, the works of justice would be destroyed, and God would cease to be God." All men are sinners; those who repent gain mercy from the Lord; upon those who do not, a just God inflicts the punishment decreed for their disobedience.

"But God ceaseth not to be God, and mercy claimeth the penitent, and mercy cometh because of the atonement; and the atonement bringeth to pass the resurrection of the dead; and the resurrection of the dead bringeth back men into the presence of God; and thus they are restored into his presence, to be judged according to their works, according to the law and justice. For behold, justice exerciseth all his demands, and also mercy claimeth all which is her own; and thus, none but the truly penitent are saved." Alma is giving, as no other prophet whose words have been preserved for us has ever done, the divine solution to the whole problem of punishment and rewards, of sin and of repentance, of justice and mercy, and of salvation for the penitent.

"What, do ye suppose that mercy can rob justice? I say unto you, Nay; not one whit. If so, God would cease to be God. And thus God bringeth about his great and eternal purposes, which were prepared from the foundation of the world. And thus cometh about the salvation and the redemption of men, and also their destruction and misery." (Alma 42:16-26.)

Thus, agency, which is the law of choosing between opposites, requires both rewards and punishments. But both of these come in varying degrees. The better man's works, the higher his reward will be; and the more evil his deeds, the greater his punishment. The highest reward is eternal life for the sons of God, and the greatest condemnation is eternal damnation for the sons of perdition. Speaking of what shall be in the day of judgment, Alma says: "Then shall the righteous shine forth in the kingdom of God." These are they who shall inherit eternal life. "But behold, an awful death cometh upon the wicked; for they die as to things pertaining to things of righteousness; for they are unclean, and no unclean thing can inherit the kingdom of God; but they are cast out, and consigned to partake of the fruits of their labors or their works, which have been evil; and they drink the dregs of a bitter cup." (Alma 40:25-26.) Between these two extremes are many degrees of both salvation and damnation. All men will be judged according to their works. The wicked go to hell, there to remain in anguish and torment until the day of their resurrection. All men, eventually, except the sons of perdition, will inherit a place in either the celestial, terrestrial, or telestial kingdom.

The extent of one's punishment depends upon the degree of his disobedience. Even hell shall deliver up the dead which are in it, so that the once buffeted souls may attain a telestial inheritance. The nature of eternal punishment is set forth by the Lord in these words: "Surely every man must repent or suffer, for I, God, am endless." These are the alternatives that face mankind; repentance begets mercy, otherwise the law inflicts a just penalty. "I revoke not the judgments which I shall pass," saith the Lord, "but woes shall go forth, weeping, wailing and gnashing of teeth, yea, to those who are found on my left hand." The judgments of the Lord are sure; justice will always prevail where the wicked and ungodly are concerned. "Nevertheless, it is not written that there shall be no end to this torment, but it is written *endless torment*. Again, it is written *eternal damnation;* wherefore it is more express than other scriptures, that it might work upon the hearts of the children of men, altogether for my name's glory. . . . For, behold, I am endless, and the punishment which is given from my hand is endless punishment, for Endless is my name. Wherefore— Eternal punishment is God's punishment. Endless punishment is God's punishment. . . . Therefore I command you to repent —repent, lest I smite you by the rod of my mouth, and by my wrath, and by my anger, and your sufferings be sore—how sore you know not, how exquisite you know not, yea, how hard to bear you know not. For behold, I, God, have suffered these things for all, that they might not suffer if they would repent; but if they would not repent they must suffer even as I." (D&C 19:4-17.)

CHAPTER 12

False Doctrines about the Fall

Heresies Concerning Adam and the Fall

It is not generally recognized how far man may go astray if he does not understand the true doctrine about Adam and the fall. The fall of man is one of the great foundations upon which salvation rests. Unless and until it is placed in its proper relationship to all things, almost unbelievable heresies will rise to plague and curse mankind. From among the many that have so risen, and as a means of dramatizing the need to learn the truth about Adam and his fall, we shall now list several of the current heresies. It should be noted that these heresies, though often formally espoused by the same church or group of believers, disagree with and contradict each other, as one would expect the case to be in the realms of error.

Heresy 1: There is no Christian God, no Adam in the sense of his being created as the first man, and no Christ in the sense of Jesus being the Son of God.

Commentary: This is the atheistic, agnostic, worldly view held by hosts of people who assume the creation came by chance and that life developed through evolutionary processes. It prevails among many who worship at the altars of science, and who espouse that godless communism which calls religion the opiate of the people. Such unbelievers pretend to find no need for divine guidance and intervention in the lives of men.

Heresy 2: There is no such thing as a fall of Adam and an atonement of Christ.

Commentary: This is the view of all pagan and heathen people who have no knowledge of the true God and the plan of salvation he ordained and established. It is, for instance, the false Islamic view. Their Koran teaches that there is no God but

Allah and that he had no need for a son. Allah, it says, has but to speak and his will is done. It considers Jesus to be in the same class as Moses or one of the prophets, denies the doctrine of the divine Sonship, and claims to know nothing about the fall of man.

Heresy 3: Organic evolution is the process whereby all life on earth came into being, and man, as now constituted, is the end product of this process.

Commentary: This is the false view of many self-designated scientists. The tendency among them is to present Darwinian theories as established realities. These theories postulate the evolvement of all forms of life from lower orders over astronomically long periods of time. They assume death has always been present and that there never was a fall, and they make no provision for a plan of redemption and a resurrection of all forms of life.

Heresy 4: Evolution is the process God used to create all forms of life except Adam, who came by special creation; or Adam was the end product of an evolutionary system used by the Lord for his own purposes.

Commentary: These false notions, together with whatever variations of them happen to be in vogue at any given time, are simply an attempt, on the part of those whose faith falls short of the divine standard, to harmonize the specious theories of men with the revelations of the Lord. They pledge a superficial allegiance to religious truth and allow for a form of divine worship without forsaking the theories of men. They, of necessity, assume that death has always existed on earth, that it did not have its beginning with the fall of Adam, and that there must be some other explanation for all the revelations which say that the atonement ransoms man from the effects of the fall. When those who espouse this view talk of a fall and an atonement, they falsely assume such applies only to man rather than to the earth and all forms of life, as the scriptures attest.

Heresy 5: Salvation comes by grace alone, without works, through the blood of Christ, and is given only to those who confess the Lord Jesus with their lips.

Commentary: Christ did it all, so this heresy supposes, and all that man must do is believe. This heresy maintains that good works are as nothing; it is grace, and grace alone, that counts. The concept of a probationary estate, of a preparatory state, of being baptized for the remission of sins, of keeping the commandments and overcoming the world, of obedience to all of the laws and ordinances of the whole gospel, of pressing forward with a steadfastness in Christ, of living by every word that proceedeth from the mouth of God—all of these are foreign to this saved-by-grace fantasy.

Heresy 6: Men will be punished for Adam's transgression. All are subject to original guilt or birth-sin, and they will automatically be damned because Adam fell. To gain salvation, they must repent of Adam's transgression and be baptized, infants included.

Commentary: If there was ever a false doctrine that runs counter to the whole concept of the fall and the atonement, this is it. Personal accountability for sin lies at the very root of the plan of salvation. Every man is accountable for his own sins, not for those of another. Men are judged for the deeds they do in the flesh, not for those of another. Men work out their own salvation, not the salvation of another. This is what the plan of salvation is all about—every man being judged according to his own works and every man being awarded his own place in the kingdoms that are prepared.

Thus, Adam asked the Lord: "Why is it that men must repent and be baptized in water?" The answer he received was dual in nature. First it announced the redemption of all men from original guilt, for which they were in no sense accountable, and then it proclaimed the need for repentance for all men from their own personal sins.

As to man's freedom from the transgression of Adam, the Lord said to the first man: "Behold I have forgiven thee thy transgression in the Garden of Eden." Adam himself was forgiven of this transgression; it no longer rested upon him, let alone upon any of his posterity. "Hence came the saying abroad among the people," the scripture continues, "that the Son of God hath atoned for original guilt, wherein the sins of the parents cannot be answered upon the heads of the children, for they are whole from the foundation of the world." (Moses 6:53-54.) This accords with the revealed word to the Prophet Joseph Smith: "Behold, I say unto you," saith the Lord, "that little children are redeemed from the foundation of the world through mine Only Begotten; wherefore, they cannot sin, for power is not given unto Satan to tempt little chil-

dren, until they begin to become accountable before me."
(D&C 29:46-47.)

As to man's personal sins, forgiveness comes only by repentance. To Adam the Lord said: "Inasmuch as thy children
are conceived in sin"—meaning born into a world of sin—
"even so when they begin to grow up, sin conceiveth in their
hearts, and they taste the bitter, that they may know to prize
the good. And it is given unto them to know good from evil;
wherefore they are agents unto themselves." Agency is a divine boon conferred upon all men. All are subject to the law of
opposites; all are free to flee from evil and to cleave unto good.
"Teach it unto your children," the Lord commanded Adam,
"that all men, everywhere, must repent, or they can in nowise
inherit the kingdom of God." And further: "I give unto you a
commandment," the Lord said, "to teach these things freely
unto your children, saying: That by reason of transgression
cometh the fall, which fall bringeth death, and inasmuch as ye
were born into the world by water, and blood, and the spirit,
which I have made, and so became of dust a living soul, even
so ye must be born again into the kingdom of heaven." (Moses
6:55-59.) Salvation grows out of the fall and comes to those
who repent, who are baptized, and who keep the commandments.

Heresy 7: Everyone, infants included, must be baptized to
rid themselves of the guilt of Adam's fall; otherwise, they
cannot be saved.

Commentary: Few heresies have been more firmly lodged
in the minds of large segments of fallen man than that of infant
baptism. Some even say that because original sin begins not
with birth but at conception itself, baptism is required not only
for every aborted fetus, but even for a blood clot that has yet
to take upon itself an embryonic form. The traditional sectarian phrase in many of the sermons of the past was that the road
to hell was paved with the skulls of unbaptized infants not a
span long. And upon few heresies, as the Book of Mormon
attests, has there been such an outpouring of divine condemnation as upon this practice of infant baptism. (Moroni 8.)

Heresy 8: Man cannot of his own free will—that is, by the
exercise of his own agency—turn to the Lord and pursue a
course of righteousness; such, rather, is reserved only for those
who are called or elected to be blessed and saved.

Commentary: It is the formal doctrine of many churches that man by his own power and agency cannot turn to righteousness and begin the process of working out his own salvation. Unless he is elected to be saved, he will be damned, as they suppose. The true doctrine is that all mankind, in and through and because of the atoning sacrifice of the Lord Jesus Christ, may be saved by obedience to the laws and ordinances of the gospel. Such is implicit in the whole eternal scheme of things and is abundantly set forth in the whole body of revealed writ, as we shall see throughout this whole work.

Heresy 9: The elect are justified by faith only, without reference to good works; indeed, if they perform any good works before they are justified, such works are accounted the same as sin and accrue not to their benefit but to their condemnation.

Commentary: Justification is the placing of a divine seal of approval upon the course of conduct pursued by righteous people. It is the approval of the Holy Spirit of the lives being lived by members of the Church. It is a divine ratification of the way of life of the true saints. It is being sealed by the Holy Spirit of Promise.

How far the Christendom of the day has departed from this true doctrine! They even say that any good works done outside their definition of justification have the nature of sin. It is as though their goal was to set forth as doctrine the very opposite of divine reality! How little the professors of religion know of the true meaning of the doctrine that men are justified by faith alone!

Heresy 10: All men are predestined to be saved or damned, as the case may be, and there is nothing they of themselves can do about it one way or the other.

Commentary: Underlying this heresy is the same philosophy that prompted Satan to offer to save all mankind without reference to any personal merit or righteousness on their part. It is a doctrine that denies men their agency, negates the whole probationary nature of this mortal estate, and withdraws from man the need to strive and labor in the cause of righteousness. If the elect are to be saved regardless of earth or hell, of good or evil, of the lives they live or the deeds they do, and if those not so elected are predestined to be damned without reference to any choice or labors on their part, has not God's eternal plan of salvation been completely negated?

Truly, if ever there was a doctrine that runs counter to the whole plan of salvation and to every principle growing out of both the fall and the atonement, predestination to eternal life or eternal damnation, according to the whimsy of a god who thus becomes a respecter of persons, is that doctrine.

Heresy 11: There will be a final harmony of all souls with God; that is, all will be saved because of the infinite love and mercy of the Divine Being.

Commentary: Clearly the hope implicit in this heresy is one born of desperation; it is one that springs up in the hearts of those who dare not face the trials of life with any real expectancy of overcoming; it is akin to and a substitute for what Lucifer proposed with reference to the salvation of all men. That this hope of erring souls is false is apparent from all that we have already said about justice and mercy. Mercy cannot rob justice; otherwise God would cease to be God, as we have already seen.

Heresy 12: There cannot be a God, at least a just God, who would permit so many of his children to suffer severe pain and disease and affliction, a God who would permit the desolation of war and plague to cover the earth.

Commentary: This view is not suggested as the official doctrine of any given organization, but it is something that is commonly expressed by many would-be worshippers in divers sects and cults. That it runs counter to the whole purpose and plan of Deity goes almost without saying. This life is a probationary estate; it never was intended to be easy. Men are here gaining experiences that could not be gained in any other way. Disease, pain, suffering, war, and death—even as it was with the Son of Man himself, all these are needed. A gracious God allows them as part of the trials and tests of mortality.

Heresy 13: Adam is our father and our god and the only god with whom we have to do; he is the father of our eternal spirits and our mortal bodies, and as such he presides over and is superior to the Lord Jesus Christ.

Commentary: This so-called Adam–God theory is false. We are bound by the truths set forth in the Standard Works, and the Book of Moses in the Pearl of Great Price sets forth the true and proper relationship between Elohim (the Father), Jehovah (the Son), and Michael, who is Adam. Truly, "the Lord God, the Holy One of Zion, . . . hath appointed Michael your prince, and established his feet, and set him upon high, and given unto him the keys of salvation under the counsel and direction of the Holy One, who is without beginning of days or end of life." (D&C 78:15-16.)

Heresy 14: There is no resurrection, no life as conscious identities after death, nothing but the grave. Death ends all.

Commentary: This was the view of the Sadducees in ancient Jewry; it is also the view of many religionists in many sects today. That it is contrary to the whole plan of salvation, including particularly the fall and the atonement, is apparent.

Other heresies will occur to the minds of many, and in each instance a true understanding of the fall and the atonement will constitute their complete refutation. Salvation comes because of the fall, and until this truth is known, men will never be able to do the things that will enable them to gain so great a gift.

ARTICLE 3

*We believe
that through the
Atonement of Christ,
all mankind may be saved,
by obedience to the laws and ordinances
of the Gospel.*

CHAPTER 13

The Atonement of Christ

What Is the Atonement?

The atonement of the Lord Jesus Christ is the third of the three infinite events that comprise the eternal plan of salvation. The other two are the physical creation of all things and then their subsequent fall to their present mortal state. As the paradisiacal creation was the precursor of the fall, so the universal fall, first of Adam and then of all created things, is the foundation upon which the atonement rests. The creation, the fall, and the atonement, these three, are the divine and eternal events through which the purposes of the Supreme God are accomplished.

The atonement is the most transcendent event that ever has occurred or ever will occur from creation's morn through all the endless ages of eternity. It is the occasion on which a God paid the ransom to reclaim fallen man, and all created things, from the effects of Adam's fall. In it, Jesus Christ, who became the first immortal flesh, paid the penalty for the transgression of the First Adam, who was the first mortal flesh. In it, the Only Begotten made amends for a broken law, satisfied the demands of justice, and took upon himself the sins of all men on conditions of repentance. Through it, all men are raised in immortality while those who believe and obey are raised also unto eternal life in the kingdom of the Father. The atonement makes possible a reconciliation between God and man; it provides a Savior and a Redeemer for mortals; it gives man an advocate and an intercessor in the courts above. The atonement is the great and eternal plan of redemption.

Moroni, addressing himself to unbelievers—to those who do not believe the true doctrine of the creation, the fall, and the atonement—bore this witness: God "created Adam, and by Adam came the fall of man. And because of the fall of man came Jesus Christ." If there had been no fall, there would have been no need for an atonement. "And because of Jesus Christ came the redemption of man." (Mormon 9:12.) Spiritual and temporal death entered the world because Adam fell. Spiritual death is to be cast out of the presence of the Lord and to die as pertaining to the things of the Spirit, which are the things of righteousness. Temporal death is the natural death in which the body returns to the dust and the spirit enters its disembodied state, there to await the resurrection. Spiritual life and temporal life come because of Christ. Spiritual life is eternal life; it is life in the presence of God; it is to be alive as to the things of God, to the things of righteousness, to the things of the Spirit. Temporal life is immortality, the reuniting of body and spirit in a never-ending state of physical perfection.

And so, Moroni continues, "Because of the redemption of man, which came by Jesus Christ, they are brought back into the presence of the Lord; yea, this is wherein all men are redeemed, because the death of Christ bringeth to pass the resurrection, which bringeth to pass a redemption from an endless sleep, from which sleep all men shall be awakened by the power of God when the trump shall sound; and they shall come forth, both small and great, and all shall stand before his bar, being redeemed and loosed from this eternal band of death, which death is a temporal death." The resurrection is universal; it is as universal as death; all men will be raised in immortality because of the atonement. "And then cometh the judgment of the Holy One upon them." (Mormon 9:13-14.) Then those who gain immortality only will be awarded their places in the kingdoms that are prepared, while those who merit eternal life will go on to eternal exaltation in the highest heaven.

Salvation, meaning eternal life, is reserved for the faithful. It is offered to all men in all ages on the same terms and conditions. "The Spirit is the same, yesterday, today, and forever," Lehi says, "and the way is prepared from the fall of man, and salvation is free." It is offered to man without money and without price; it is available to all because of the atonement. "And men are instructed sufficiently that they know good from evil." The light of Christ is given to all men; all are guided by the still, small voice of conscience. "And the law is given unto men. And by the law no flesh is justified; or, by the law men are cut off." Obedience and good works would count for nothing if there were no atonement. "Yea, by the temporal law they were cut off; and also, by the spiritual law they perish from that which is good, and become miserable forever." Temporal and spiritual death would reign forever if there were no atonement. "Wherefore, redemption cometh in and through the Holy Messiah; for he is full of grace and truth. Behold, he offereth himself a sacrifice for sin, to answer the ends of the law, unto all those who have a broken heart and a contrite spirit; and unto none else can the ends of the law be answered." Salvation is for the obedient; it is their sins that are borne by Christ.

"Wherefore, how great the importance to make these things known unto the inhabitants of the earth, that they may know that there is no flesh that can dwell in the presence of God, save it be through the merits, and mercy, and grace of the Holy Messiah, who layeth down his life according to the flesh, and taketh it again by the power of the Spirit, that he may bring to pass the resurrection of the dead, being the first that should rise." (2 Nephi 2:4-8.) Thus, salvation of every sort, kind, and degree—whether it is resurrection only, on the one hand, or eternal exaltation, on the other—comes by the grace of God. There is no other way; salvation is in Christ, and it comes because of his atoning sacrifice.

This sacrifice, which only a God could make, took place in Gethsemane when he sweat great gouts of blood from every pore, "which suffering caused myself, even God, the greatest of all," he says, "to tremble because of pain, and to bleed at every pore, and to suffer both body and spirit—and would that I might not drink the bitter cup, and shrink." (D&C 19:18.) And it also took place as he hung on the cruel cross of Calvary. During the last three hours of that agonizing ordeal, while darkness overspread the land, all the pains and suffering of Gethsemane returned. He came into the world, not alone to suffer in Gethsemane, but also at Golgotha. "I came into the world to do the will of my Father, because my Father sent me," he said. "And my Father sent me that I might be lifted up upon the cross." (3 Nephi 27:13-14.)

We can no more comprehend the atonement than we can understand the creation or the fall. It suffices, in our present state of probation, and subject to our present finite limitations, to know that we exist, to know that there was a fall, and to know that Christ is the Redeemer. It makes no more sense to reject the fall and the atonement than to reject the creation. The fact is, all three are realities; all three are the means whereby salvation comes.

The Divine Sonship

Our Lord's infinite and eternal atonement, than which there neither has been, nor is, nor ever shall be anything more wondrous and great, rests on two foundations. One is the fall of Adam; the other is Christ's divine Sonship. Christ atoned because Adam fell; the fall created the need for the atonement; and unless and until spiritual and temporal death came into being, there neither was nor could be a ransom from their dire effects. But our Lord was able to perform the atoning sacrifice, itself an act of infinite love, of endless mercy, and of supreme condescension, because he was God's Son and had inherited from his immortal Father the power of immortality.

All of this was part of the divine plan. When this plan, this gospel of God, was presented by the Father to all his spirit children in the councils of eternity, the need for a Savior and Redeemer was set forth in full. After the doctrine of the fall and the plan of redemption had been set forth in all their wonder and glory, the Father sent forth a great proclamation to this effect: 'Whom shall I send to be my Son; who will be the Only Begotten in the flesh; who of all my spirit sons shall dwell among mortals with the divine power to atone for their sins; who will go down as the Savior and Redeemer?' (See Abraham 3:27-28; Moses 4:1-4.)

The choice fell upon the Firstborn. He who was beloved and chosen from the beginning then became the Lamb slain from the foundation of the world; he was then chosen and foreordained to be the One who would work out the infinite and eternal atonement. "Behold, I am he who was prepared from the foundation of the world to redeem my people," he said to the brother of Jared. "Behold, I am Jesus Christ." (Ether 3:14.) And so before mortal men were, before Adam fell that men might be, before there was mortality and procreation and death—before all this, provision was made for the redemption. Then it was decreed that "the Lord Omnipotent who reigneth, who was, and is from all eternity to all eternity," should go "down from heaven among the children of men, and . . . dwell in a tabernacle of clay." Then the decree went forth that he should be "the Son of God," and "his mother" should be Mary; that he would bring "salvation . . . unto the children of men even through faith on his name"; that he would be scourged and crucified and "rise the third day from the dead"—all to the end that "a righteous judgment might come upon the children of men." (Mosiah 3:5-10.)

For Christ to be the Son of God means that God was his Father in the literal and true sense of the word; for our Lord to be the Only Begotten in the flesh means that he was begotten by God, who is a Holy Man. "The condescension of God," of which the scriptures speak, means that the Immortal Father— the glorified, exalted, enthroned ruler of the universe—came down from his station of dominion and power to become the Father of a Son who would be born of Mary, "after the manner of the flesh." (1 Nephi 11:16-18.) Thus, God, an immortal man, was his Father; and Mary, a mortal woman, was his mother. He was begotten; he was conceived; he was born. From his immortal Father he inherited the power of immortality, which is the power to live; from his mortal mother he inherited the power of mortality, which is the power to die; and being thus dual in nature, being able to choose life or death, according to the will of the Father, he was able to work out the infinite and eternal atonement. Having chosen to die, as he did because he had the power of mortality, he could choose to live again because he had the power of immortality.

This, then, is the doctrine of the divine Sonship. It took our Lord's mortal and his immortal powers to work out the atonement, for that supreme sacrifice required both death and resurrection. There is no salvation without death, even as there is no salvation without resurrection. Thus Amulek, speaking of this "great and last sacrifice," says it could not be "a human sacrifice; but it must be an infinite and eternal sacrifice. Now there is not any man that can sacrifice his own blood which will atone for the sins of another." (Alma 34:10-11.) Man cannot resurrect himself; man cannot save himself; human power cannot save another; human power cannot atone for the sins of another. The work of redemption must be infinite and eternal; it must be done by an infinite being; God himself must atone for the sins of the world.

Because Jesus was the Son of God and had divine power, he was able to say: "I am the good shepherd: the good shepherd giveth his life for the sheep. . . . I lay down my life for the sheep." The atonement was a voluntary act on his part; he had power to live or to die—the choice was his. "Therefore doth my Father love me, because I lay down my life, that I might take it again. No man taketh it from me, but I lay it down of myself. I have power to lay it down, and I have power to take it again. This commandment have I received of my Father." (John 10:11-18.) Truly, truly is it written: "God so loved the world, that he gave his only begotten Son, that whosoever believeth in him should not perish, but have everlasting life. For God sent not his Son into the world to condemn the world; but that the world through him might be saved." (John 3:16-17.)

The Blood of Christ

Salvation comes because of the shedding of the blood of Christ, which, as we have seen, took place in the garden of Gethsemane and on the cross of Calvary. His voluntary death was itself an atoning sacrifice; as with the prefiguring sacrifices, made through the ages from the flocks and herds of the faithful, his blood also must be shed—for the remission of sin.

John the Baptist, putting a seal on the sacrificial dispensation of Moses and preparing the way for the divine sacrifice that was soon to be, introduced the Lord Jesus to Jewish Israel with this perfectly framed declaration: "Behold the Lamb of God, which taketh away the sin of the world." (John 1:29.) Great numbers of lambs had already been offered on the altars of Israel, all in similitude of the great offering that was to be, that of the Lamb of God. And with reference to every proper sacrifice offered during the whole Mosaic period, these words from the mouth of Jehovah himself applied: "For the life of the flesh is in the blood: and I have given it to you upon the altar to make an atonement for your souls: for it is the blood that maketh an atonement for the soul." (Leviticus 17:11.)

And as with all the types and shadows, so with the great event toward which they pointed—the blood of the Lamb would atone for the sins of the faithful. "There can be nothing which is short of an infinite atonement which will suffice for the sins of the world," Amulek reasoned. "Therefore, it is expedient that there should be a great and last sacrifice; and then shall there be, or it is expedient there should be, a stop to the shedding of blood; then shall the law of Moses be fulfilled; yea, it shall be all fulfilled, every jot and tittle, and none shall have passed away." This, of course, is precisely what did take place. Why was it thus? Because, as Amulek expounded, "this is the whole meaning of the law, every whit pointing to that great and last sacrifice; and that great and last sacrifice will be the Son of God, yea, infinite and eternal." (Alma 34:12-14.)

That there are degrees of salvation and differing rewards for men is implicit in the concept that they will be judged and rewarded according to their works. In the Sermon on the Atonement, preached by an angel to King Benjamin, we read: "His [Christ's] blood atoneth for the sins of those who have fallen by the transgression of Adam, who have died not knowing the will of God concerning them, or who have ignorantly sinned." Their state will be tolerable; they will not be numbered with those who have overcome the world; neither will they be cast out eternally with the damned. "But, wo, wo unto him who knoweth that he rebelleth against God!" the angelic word continues. "For salvation cometh to none such except it be through repentance and faith on the Lord Jesus Christ."

As to those who kept the law of Moses, the angelic witness affirmed: "The law of Moses availeth nothing except it were through the atonement of his blood." And the same applies even to the salvation of children. "Even if it were possible that little children could sin they could not be saved [except through the atonement]; but I say unto you they are blessed; for behold, as in Adam, or by nature, they fall, even so the blood of Christ atoneth for their sins."

"And moreover, I say unto you, that there shall be no other name given nor any other way nor means whereby salvation can come unto the children of men, only in and through the name of Christ, the Lord Omnipotent." How often is it repeated in the divine word—salvation is in Christ! "For behold he judgeth, and his judgment is just; and the infant perisheth not that dieth in his infancy; but men drink damnation to their own souls except they humble themselves and become as little children, and believe that salvation was, and is, and is to come, in and through the atoning blood of Christ, the Lord Omnipotent." (Mosiah 3:11-12, 15-18.) Those who live the whole law of the whole gospel shall gain eternal life in and through and because of the shedding of the blood of Christ.

The Atonement: Its Symbols and Types

It is the design and the purpose of Deity to keep man's attention everlastingly centered in the atoning sacrifice of the Lord Jesus Christ. The more man knows about God and Christ and the fall and the eternal plan of redemption, the greater will be his desire to be reconciled to God and to receive the blessings offered by the great Mediator. It follows that all of the prophets prophesy of Christ; all of the inspired teachers proclaim the truths of his gospel; all of the doctrines of salvation center in Christ; and all of the rites and ordinances of his holy gospel are designed in such a way as to center our attention in him and in his atoning sacrifice. Reference to the following ordinances, rites, and performances illustrates this.

1. *Animal sacrifices testified of Christ.*

As far as we know, the first gospel ordinances revealed to Adam involved the offering of sacrifices. After our first parents were shut out from the presence of the Lord, "he gave unto them commandments, that they should worship the Lord their God, and should offer the firstlings of their flocks, for an offering unto the Lord." These commandments obviously included instructions as to how and in what manner the sacrifices should be made. Adam obeyed. In due course—"after many days"—an angel appeared unto him and asked: "Why dost thou offer sacrifices unto the Lord?" The great underlying reason for the sacrificial system had not then been made known. Adam replied: "I know not, save the Lord commanded me." Then, because Adam was obedient and prepared spiritually to understand the great concept involved, the angel poured forth a wondrous flood of new light. He said: "This thing is a similitude of the sacrifice of the Only Begotten of the Father, which is full of grace and truth. Wherefore, thou shalt do all that thou doest in the name of the Son, and thou shalt repent and call upon God in the name of the Son forevermore." (Moses 5:4-8.)

From Adam to Moses, and from Moses to the coming of the

Lord Jesus Christ in the flesh, either as part of the gospel or of the Mosaic law, as the cases might be, all of the saints offered sacrifices in similitude of the sacrifice of the Lamb of God. Always they offered the firstlings of their flocks; always the sacrificial animals were without spot and blemish; always their blood was shed; always it was an occasion to renew the covenants, made in the waters of baptism, to serve God and keep his commandments; and always those who worshipped in spirit and in truth received a remission of their sins and were hastened along the course leading to eternal life. For a pastoral people whose lives depended on their flocks and herds, there could have been no better similitude than this.

2. *The law of Moses testified of Christ.*

Though the law of Moses was given of God to his people; though it was of divine origin and had divine approval in all its parts and ramifications; though it was the highest system of worship ever had on earth, except the fulness of the gospel itself—yet salvation did not come by the law alone. Salvation then and now and always is in Christ and his atoning sacrifice. The whole purpose of the Mosaic system was to testify of Christ and his atonement and to prepare men to receive the fulness of the gospel.

Abinadi said: "Salvation doth not come by the law alone; and were it not for the atonement, which God himself shall make for the sins and iniquities of his people, . . . they must unavoidably perish, notwithstanding the law of Moses." The law of Moses, as with all things in the gospel itself, had efficacy, virtue, and force because of the atonement.

Why was the law given? Abinadi answers: "It was expedient that there should be a law given to the children of Israel, yea, even a very strict law; for they were a stiffnecked people, quick to do iniquity, and slow to remember the Lord their God; therefore there was a law given them, yea, a law of performances and of ordinances, a law which they were to observe strictly from day to day, to keep them in remembrance of God and their duty towards him. But behold, I say unto you, that all these things were types of things to come." Only part of the people understood this; only part knew that "there could not any man be saved except it were through the redemption of God." (Mosiah 13:28-32.) Truly, the Lord gave his people "many signs, and wonders, and types, and shadows

. . . concerning his coming," and taught them "that the law of Moses availeth nothing except it were through the atonement of his blood." (Mosiah 3:15.)

Of all the Mosaic performances, none typified the atonement better than their sacrificial offerings. These were of four general kinds: (1) *Burnt offerings* symbolized the entire surrender of the Lord's people to him and his laws. They were sacrifices in which a covenant of service and devotion was made. (2) *Sin offerings* were the means whereby the whole congregation of Israel, based on repentance, was freed from sin. The same thing happens to the faithful saints in this day when they partake worthily of the sacramental emblems. (3) *Trespass offerings* were designed to cleanse individuals from particular sins, especially those committed through ignorance. This forgiveness was predicated upon repentance. (4) *Peace offerings* were sacrifices of worship and adoration and gratitude to the Lord for the fellowship that existed between him and his people.

Once each year, on the Day of Atonement, the high priest entered the Holy of Holies, entered, as it were, the presence of God, to signify that all Israel would enter the divine presence if true and faithful. This was a day for sin offerings in particular. On it also, two goats were selected; one was named "la-Jehovah," and the other "la-Azazel." The sins of the people were placed upon "la-Azazel," the scapegoat, and he bore them away into a wilderness area. The goat named "la-Jehovah" was sacrificed as Jehovah himself would be at the appointed time.

Such, among much else, was the law of the Lord until He came who said: "I am he that gave the law, and I am he who covenanted with my people Israel; therefore, the law in me is fulfilled. . . . Behold, I am the law, and the light. Look unto me, and endure to the end, and ye shall live; for unto him that endureth to the end will I give eternal life." (3 Nephi 15:5, 9.) After he came and offered himself as the Lamb of God, other similitudes and types were to be used to center our attention in his atoning sacrifice and the blessings that flow therefrom.

3. *The sacramental emblems testify of Christ.*

When Jesus ate the Paschal Supper with the Twelve in the Upper Room, he instituted a new ordinance, the Sacrament of the Lord's Supper. That feast of the Passover was the last such legal celebration of the Mosaic order. The day after the apostolic group ate the Paschal Supper, the Lamb of God, the True Paschal Lamb, was himself sacrificed for the sins of the world. That night in the Upper Room, he blessed and brake bread and blessed wine—all as part of the Jewish ritual—but as he did so, he gave the emblems a new meaning. Of the broken bread he said: "Take, eat; this is in remembrance of my body which I give a ransom for you." Of the wine, he said: "Drink ye all of it. For this is in remembrance of my blood of the new testament, which is shed for as many as shall believe on my name, for the remission of their sins." (JST, Matthew 26:22-24.)

Paul said: "For as often as ye eat this bread, and drink this cup, ye do shew the Lord's death till he come." (1 Corinthians 11:26.) And as it was among the ancient saints, so it is with us today. As the Lord's people eat the bread and drink the cup, they do so in remembrance of the broken flesh and spilt blood of Him who died that they might live. They express anew their willingness to bear his name, and they covenant anew to always remember him and to keep his commandments, all to the end that they may have his Spirit to be with them. And when they receive that Spirit, their sins are remitted, for the Spirit will not dwell in an unclean tabernacle.

4. *Baptism testifies of Christ.*

Baptism by immersion for the remission of sins; baptism in water and of the Spirit; baptism whereby men are born again into the kingdom of heaven; baptism which places fallen man on the path leading to eternal life—baptism is the ordinance of the ages. No accountable person can be saved without it. It is efficacious because of the atonement, and it is designed in such a way as to center our attention in that infinite sacrifice.

Baptisms are performed in similitude of the death, burial, and resurrection of Christ. "Know ye not, that so many of us as were baptized into Jesus Christ were baptized into his death," Paul wrote to the Romans. "Therefore we are buried with him by baptism into death: that like as Christ was raised up from the dead by the glory of the Father, even so we also should walk in newness of life. For if we have been planted together in the likeness of his death, we shall be also in the likeness of his resurrection." (Romans 6:3-5.)

The essential elements of every baptism are the same as those in the atoning sacrifice, thus reminding us that because of the atonement and through baptism, men may be saved. These elements are water, blood, and spirit. Jesus permitted his spirit to leave his body, and soon thereafter a Roman spear pierced his side, "and forthwith came there out blood and water." (John 19:34.) The atonement came by water, blood, and spirit. Similarly, men are "born again into the kingdom of heaven, of water, and of the Spirit," and are "cleansed by blood," the spilt blood of Christ. (Moses 6:59.)

5. *Abraham and his only begotten son testify of Christ.*

Among all the similitudes arranged by the Lord to testify of him, none is more dramatic, none sinks with deeper feeling into the hearts of men, than the call of Abraham to offer Isaac in sacrifice. Nothing dramatizes better the sacrificial death of the Only Begotten of the Father than Abraham's willingness to sacrifice his son Isaac—his "only son," as pertaining to the royal lineage. (Genesis 22:1-14.) How often this story was used in ancient Israel as a text to teach and testify about the sacrifice of the Lamb of God, we can only guess. That such usage prevailed among the Nephites, we know from Jacob's statement that "it was accounted unto Abraham in the wilderness to be obedient unto the commands of God in offering up his son Isaac, which is a similitude of God and his Only Begotten Son." (Jacob 4:5.)

No other would be trusted in this way. There would henceforth be no need for a similar sacrifice because of "the offering of the body of Jesus Christ once for all." Christ had "offered one sacrifice for sins for ever, . . . for by one offering he [had] perfected for ever them that are sanctified." (Hebrews 10:10-14.) Truly, "all things which have been given of God from the beginning of the world, unto man, are the typifying of [Christ]." (2 Nephi 11:4.)

CHAPTER 14

Mediation
and Atonement

The Plan of Redemption

As there was a *temporal fall* and a *spiritual fall,* so there is a *temporal redemption* and a *spiritual redemption.* The temporal redemption is the resurrection; it comes as a free gift to all men by the grace of God. All men are resurrected; there are no exceptions. "As in Adam all die, even so in Christ shall all be made alive." (1 Corinthians 15:22.) It is of this temporal redemption that the Lord said: "Through the redemption which is made for you is brought to pass the resurrection from the dead. And the spirit and the body are the soul of man. And the resurrection from the dead is the redemption of the soul." (D&C 88:14-16.)

Except for the sons of perdition, the resurrection alone, without more, is a degree and kind of salvation. It delivers men "from that awful monster, death and hell, and the devil, and the lake of fire and brimstone, which is endless torment." (2 Nephi 9:26.) The sons of perdition—those evil and defiant rebels who, having a perfect knowledge that Jesus is the Lord, yet fight against God and Christ and the holy gospel— having been resurrected, will yet remain as though there had been no redemption made. They are "the only ones who shall not be redeemed in the due time of the Lord, after the sufferings of his wrath." (D&C 76:38.) Their fate is to be cast out eternally with the devil and his angels; the true blessings of immortality will never be theirs. They alone shall suffer eternal damnation in the sense of endless torment. "Their torments shall be as a lake of fire and brimstone, whose flame ascendeth up forever and ever; and then is the time that they shall be chained down to an everlasting destruction, according to the power and captivity of Satan, he having

119

subjected them according to his will. Then . . . they shall be as though there had been no redemption made; for they cannot be redeemed according to God's justice; and they cannot die, seeing there is no more corruption." (Alma 12:17-18.)

The spiritual redemption is to regain spiritual life; it is to die as to all that is evil and live in the Spirit; it is to return to the presence of God; it is, in the full and complete sense of the word, to have eternal life. Those who gain eternal life are the ones who believe and obey the Lord's eternal gospel. As to the disobedient, the holy word says: "They that believe not" shall be raised in immortality "unto eternal damnation; for they cannot be redeemed from their spiritual fall, because they repent not; for they love darkness rather than light, and their deeds are evil, and they receive their wages of whom they list to obey." (D&C 29:44-45.) All these, after having paid the penalty for their own sins, and having been judged according to the deeds done in the flesh, will receive an inheritance in one of the lesser kingdoms.

The redeemed of the Lord are those, such as Abraham, who now have eternal life in his kingdom. But it is also the design and intent and purpose of the Lord to redeem men spiritually while they yet remain in the flesh. For instance: after the brother of Jared parted the veil by faith; after he had seen the finger of the Lord; after he had learned that Christ would take upon himself flesh and blood; after he had borne witness that God was a God of truth who could not lie —then the Lord said unto him: "Because thou knowest these things ye are redeemed from the fall; therefore ye are brought back into my presence; therefore I show myself unto you." (Ether 3:13.)

Thus redemption is for the faithful. Thus Amulek said that Christ would "come to redeem his people, but that he should not come to redeem them in their sins, but to redeem them from their sins." (Helaman 5:10.) And thus Alma said: "He cometh to redeem those who will be baptized unto repentance, through faith on his name." (Alma 9:27.) "And thus he shall bring salvation to all those who shall believe on his name; this being the intent of this last sacrifice, to bring about the bowels of mercy, which overpowereth justice, and bringeth about means unto men that they may have faith unto repentance. And thus mercy can satisfy the demands of justice, and encircles them in the arms of safety, while he that exercises no faith unto repentance is exposed to the whole law of the demands of justice; therefore only unto him that has faith unto repentance is brought about the great and eternal plan of redemption." (Alma 34:15-16.)

Redemption is wrought by the Redeemer. He is the one "in whom we have redemption through his blood," Paul says, "even the forgiveness of sins." (Colossians 1:14.) And he himself, after the atoning sacrifice had been made, said: "Behold, I am Jesus Christ the Son of God. . . . And as many as have received me, to them have I given to become the sons of God; and even so will I to as many as shall believe on my name, for behold, by me redemption cometh." (3 Nephi 9:15, 17.) Those who exercise the gospel power to become the sons of God, to gain membership in the family of the Lord Jesus Christ, and to be his sons and his daughters—these are they who are redeemed from the spiritual fall here and now, and if they endure to the end, they shall have eternal redemption in the eternal kingdom among those who have eternal life.

The Doctrine of the Atonement

What is the true doctrine of the atonement? What is the finite rationale relative to this infinite act? Can we explain by reason and logic how even a God could bring to pass the immortality and eternal life of men, thus redeeming them from temporal and spiritual death?

We can no more explain the whole doctrine of the atonement than we can set forth a fulness of knowledge concerning the creation and the fall. But enough truth has been revealed about each of these great and eternal verities to enable us to work out our salvation. Such truths as have been revealed can be understood and explained, and we are duty-bound to believe and conform to every word that proceedeth forth from the mouth of God.

We know that Adam and Eve in their Edenic garden were without sin; that they lived in innocence, without any taint of evil; that theirs was then a deathless state; and that they were in perfect harmony with God and his laws. Sin and mortality and death had their beginnings with the fall. Because of transgression, man died spiritually and was cast out of the Divine Presence. Christ came to ransom men from the temporal and spiritual death that came into the world through the fall. In some way incomprehensible to us, his death and resurrection bring to pass the resurrection of all men, thus redeeming them from the temporal fall. In some way equally incomprehensible to us, he bore the sins of all men on conditions of repentance, so that men may be redeemed from the spiritual fall. That these concepts might be known and understood by us mortals, they are set forth in the revealed word under five separate headings, all of which are interwoven together and are in fact teaching the same truths in different ways. These are:

1. *The Law of Propitiation.*

The revealed word speaks of a propitiation for sins; of a ministry of reconciliation; of intercession being made for the faithful; of One who advocates the cause of his people in the courts above; of the labors and work of the great Mediator; and of what man must do to put off the natural man and be numbered with the redeemed. It is in connection with all of these divine pronouncements that we will find the rationale that explains, so far as can be, the infinite and eternal atonement.

Neither Adam nor any man has power to save himself. Man cannot create a state of eternal life, nor can he resurrect himself. Having fallen, man is subject to sin, and no unclean thing can enter the Divine Presence. Sinful man, having transgressed the law, is subject to the law of justice unless someone intervenes on his behalf.

And so, according to the law of propitiation, Christ came to appease the demands of divine justice and effect a reconciliation between God and man. Thus John taught: "Jesus Christ the righteous . . . is the propitiation for our sins: and not for ours only, but also [on conditions of repentance] for the sins of the whole world." (1 John 2:1-2.) Our theological friend Paul expounds this doctrine by saying, "All have sinned, and come short of the glory of God." Indeed, the natural man is an enemy to God and has been cast out of his presence. But the saints, Paul continues, are "justified freely by [God's] grace through the redemption that is in Christ Jesus." How is it that the saints are justified? It is because "God hath set forth [his Son] to be a propitiation through faith in his blood, to declare his righteousness for the remission of sins that are past, through the forbearance of God; to declare . . . his righteousness: that he might be just, and the justifier of him which believeth in Jesus." (Romans 3:23-26.)

2. *The Law of Reconciliation.*

Salvation comes to those fallen men who reconcile themselves to God. Through Christ and by faith, men may be ransomed from their state of sin and spiritual darkness and be restored to one of harmony and unity with their Maker. Paul expounded this theological concept in this manner: "If any man be in Christ, he is a new creature." That is, he has been born again. "And all things are of God, who hath reconciled us to himself by Jesus Christ." Christ is the Reconciler; his atoning sacrifice opened the door so that men could return to God. And the Lord "hath given to us the ministry of reconciliation." That ministry and doctrine is "that God was in Christ, reconciling the world unto himself, not imputing their trespasses unto them."

And what is the responsibility of those who have been reconciled? The Lord "hath committed unto us the word of reconciliation." We are to preach the gospel of reconciliation to the world, inviting all men to return to the Lord and be one with him. "Now then we are ambassadors for Christ, as though God did beseech you by us: we pray you in Christ's stead, be ye reconciled to God." (2 Corinthians 5:17-20.)

Paul also taught that "while we were yet sinners, Christ died for us"; that the saints are "justified by his blood"; and that, accordingly, "we shall be saved from wrath through him." Mercy shall overpower justice in that Christ pays the penalty for our sins. "When we were enemies, we were reconciled to God by the death of his Son," and "being reconciled, we shall be saved." Therefore, "we also joy in God through our Lord Jesus Christ, by whom we have now received the atonement." (Romans 5:8-11.)

Such is the law of reconciliation. And because of it, the prophetic call to all men is: "Reconcile yourselves to the will of God, and not to the will of the devil and the flesh; and remember, after ye are reconciled unto God, that it is only in and through the grace of God that ye are saved." (2 Nephi 10:24; 25:23; 33:9.) Yea, "be reconciled unto him through the atonement of Christ, his Only Begotten Son." In this way, in the resurrection, ye shall "be presented as the first-fruits of Christ unto God, having faith, and [having] obtained a good hope of glory in him." (Jacob 4:11.)

    3. *The Law of Mediation.*

It was God our Father who made the law of mediation; he established it as one of the chief provisions of his eternal plan of salvation. He is the one who appointed his Only Begotten Son to stand as the Mediator between himself and fallen men. Christ is our Mediator; he intervenes between God and man to effect a reconciliation; he interposes himself between parties at variance. He who committed no sin invites his mortal brethren to forsake their sins and thus place themselves in harmony and unity with the Sinless Son and the Sinless Father.

Jesus is called the Mediator of the new covenant, to distinguish him from Moses, the mediator of the old covenant. The blessings of the old covenant, of the old testament, of the law of carnal commandments, came to Israel through Moses; he was the great lawgiver who stood between the Lord and the people in administering to their needs. The blessings of the new covenant, of the new testament, of the everlasting gospel, come to all men through Jesus Christ. He is the Eternal Lawgiver who stands between God and all men; he invites men to cleanse themselves from sin and receive salvation with him in the kingdom of his Father. Thus it is written that "the law was given through Moses, but life and truth came through Jesus Christ. For the law was after a carnal commandment, to the administration of death; but the gospel was after the power of an endless life, through Jesus Christ, the Only Begotten Son, who is in the bosom of the Father." (JST, John 1:17-18.)

Thus, life, meaning eternal life, comes by the mediating power of Christ. If there had been no atonement, the law of Moses, standing alone, would have been "the administration of death." In this connection Paul says: "Moses . . . was ordained by the hand of angels to be a mediator of this first covenant, (the law). Now this mediator was not a mediator of the new covenant; but there is one mediator of the new covenant, who is Christ, as it is written in the law concerning the promises made to Abraham and his seed. Now Christ is the mediator of life; for this is the promise which God made unto Abraham." (JST, Galatians 3:19-20.)

Those who turn to the Mediator of life become heirs of eternal salvation. Paul invites men to come unto Christ and accept the ministry of mediation: "Come unto the knowledge of the truth which is in Christ Jesus, who is the Only Begotten Son of God, and ordained to be a Mediator between God and man; who is One God, and hath power over all men. For there is one God, and one mediator between God and men, the man Christ Jesus; who gave himself a ransom for all." (JST, 1 Timothy 2:4-6.) Lehi says: "Men are free according to the flesh. . . . They are free to choose liberty and eternal life, through the great Mediator of all men, or to choose captivity and death, according to the captivity and power of the devil." Accordingly, Lehi issues this prophetic invitation: "Look to the great Mediator, and hearken unto his great commandments; and be faithful unto his words, and choose eternal life, according to the will of his Holy Spirit." (2 Nephi 2:27-28.) All those who heed the call and live the law become "just men made perfect through Jesus the mediator of the new covenant, who wrought out this perfect atonement through the shedding of his own blood." (D&C 76:69.)

4. *The Law of Intercession.*

Because the propitiation of Christ appeased the demands of divine justice; because he paid the penalty for the sins of all who repent, thus enabling men to be reconciled to God; because he mediates between God and man—because of all this, he becomes the Intercessor and the Advocate for all who believe in him.

According to the law of intercession, as ordained and established by the Father, the Lord Jesus has "power to make intercession for the children of men." (Mosiah 15:8.) That is to say, he has the role of interceding, of mediating, of praying, petitioning, and entreating the Father to grant mercy and blessings to men. One of Isaiah's great Messianic prophecies says: "He bare the sins of many, and made intercession for the transgressors." (Isaiah 53:12.) Of this ministry of intercession, Paul affirms: "It is Christ that died, yea rather, that is risen again, who is even at the right hand of God, who also maketh intercession for us." (Romans 8:34.) And it is Lehi who tells us: Christ "is the firstfruits unto God, inasmuch as he shall make intercession for all the children of men; and they that believe in him shall be saved. And because of the intercession for all, all men come unto God; wherefore, they stand in the presence of him, to be judged of him according to the truth and holiness which is in him." (2 Nephi 2:9-10.)

    5. *The Law of Advocacy.*

According to the law of advocacy, our Lord intercedes for the faithful saints and pleads their cause in the courts above. "He claimeth all those who have faith in him," Mormon says, "and they who have faith in him will cleave unto every good thing; wherefore he advocateth the cause of the children of men; and he dwelleth eternally in the heavens." (Moroni 7:28.) "If any man sin, we have an advocate with the Father," John tells us, who is "Jesus Christ the righteous." (1 John 2:1.) And in a revelation to the Prophet Joseph Smith, the Lord Jesus said: "Listen to him who is the advocate with the Father, who is pleading your cause before him—saying: Father, behold the sufferings and death of him who did no sin, in whom thou wast well pleased; behold the blood of thy Son which was shed, the blood of him whom thou gavest that thyself might be glorified; wherefore, Father, spare these my brethren that believe on my name, that they may come unto me and have everlasting life." (D&C 45:3-5.)

Thus we see that Christ appeaseth the demands of justice according to the law of propitiation; that his ministry was one of reconciling sinful man with the Sinless Father; that he interposed himself as a mediator between God and man, so that fallen man might regain his pristine innocent and sinless state; that he intercedes for repentant souls before the Father; and that he advocates the cause of all who believe in his name, pleading that they may be freed from sin and have fellowship with Gods and angels. All of this is the rationale that underlies the atonement. All of it is needed because of the fall of Adam. Christ has served and is serving in all of the indicated ways. His comforting labors will not cease. And each man must choose for himself whether to accept or reject the proffered blessings. Truly, as the angelic ministrant said to King Benjamin: "The natural man is an enemy to God, and has been from the fall of

Adam, and will be, forever and ever, unless he yields to the enticings of the Holy Spirit, and putteth off the natural man and becometh a saint through the atonement of Christ the Lord, and becometh as a child, submissive, meek, humble, patient, full of love, willing to submit to all things which the Lord seeth fit to inflict upon him, even as a child doth submit to his father." (Mosiah 3:19.)

CHAPTER 15

The Atonement: Infinite and Eternal

If There Were No Atonement—What?

If there had been no physical creation of this earth, of man, and of all forms of life, the purposes of God would have come to naught. All forms of life would yet be in preexistence, and man would never become like his Maker and have eternal life.

If there had been no fall of Adam, with its consequent effect upon the earth and all forms of life, there would have been no mortality, no procreation, no death. And the purposes of God would have been frustrated. Adam and all forms of life would be living in a deathless state in the Garden of Eden. There would have been no probationary estate, and man would never gain the glorious gift of eternal life.

But there has been a creation, and there was a fall. Under these circumstances, suppose there had been no atonement of Christ—what then? The answer is obvious, and it is one to which the Book of Mormon prophets make frequent reference. It is that death would have triumphed; that there would be no victory over the grave; that there would be no resurrection, no immortal souls, no living forever with bodies of flesh and bones. Further, there would be no spiritual life, no eternal life, no return to the presence of God, no glory and honor and exaltation in the kingdom of heaven. And thus the purposes of the Almighty would fail, and if such were the case, he would cease to be God.

"Salvation [comes] through the atonement which was prepared from the foundation of the world for all mankind, which ever were since the fall of Adam, or who are, or who ever shall be even unto the end of the world." (Mosiah 4:7.) If there were no atonement, there would be no salvation. But "it is expedient that an atonement should be made," Amulek

128

explains, "for according to the great plan of the Eternal God there must be an atonement made, or else all mankind must unavoidably perish; yea, all are hardened; yea, all are fallen and lost, and must perish except it be through the atonement which it is expedient should be made." (Alma 34:9; Mosiah 15:19.)

If there were no atonement, there could have been no redemption. "Thus all mankind were lost; and behold, they would have been endlessly lost were it not that God redeemed his people from their lost and fallen state. . . . And now if Christ had not come into the world, . . . there could have been no redemption. And if Christ had not risen from the dead, or have broken the bands of death that the grave should have no victory, and that death should have no sting, there could have been no resurrection." (Mosiah 16:4-7.) Thus, "If it had not been for the plan of redemption, which was laid from the foundation of the world, there could have been no resurrection of the dead." (Alma 12:25.) And further: "If it were not for the plan of redemption, (laying it aside) as soon as they were dead their souls were miserable, being cut off from the presence of God." (Alma 42:11.)

In a passage of great spiritual insight, the Nephite Jacob says: "For as death hath passed upon all men, to fulfil the merciful plan of the great Creator, there must needs be a power of resurrection." Both death and the resurrection are essential parts of the eternal plan; without either, there would be no purpose in life. "And the resurrection must needs come unto man by reason of the fall." Had there been no fall, there would be no resurrection. "And the fall came by reason of transgression." Adam had to transgress and become subject to sin and undergo a consequent probationary experience to be saved. "And because man became fallen they were cut off from the presence of the Lord." Never in their fallen state could they return to their celestial home and find peace and joy in the Eternal Presence.

"Wherefore," meaning in the light of all this, "it must needs be an infinite atonement—save it should be an infinite atonement this corruption could not put on incorruption." There would have been no resurrection and no immortal glory. "Wherefore, the first judgment which came upon man must needs have remained to an endless duration." Temporal and spiritual death would have endured forever without end. "And if so, this flesh must have laid down to rot and to crumble to its mother earth, to rise no more." There would have been no victory over the grave. "O the wisdom of God, his mercy and grace! For behold, if the flesh should rise no more our spirits must become subject to that angel who fell from before the presence of the Eternal God, and became the devil, to rise no more." Our spirits, stained with sin, unable to cleanse themselves, would be subject to the author of sin ever-lastingly; we would be followers of Satan; we would be sons of perdition. "And our spirits must have become like unto him, and we become devils, angels to a devil, to be shut out from the presence of our God, and to remain with the father of lies, in misery, like unto himself." We would suffer eternal damnation, eternal torments, anguish and sorrow that in intensity is described as being like a lake of fire and brimstone. We would never be redeemed from "death and hell, and the devil, and the lake of fire and brimstone, which is endless torment." (2 Nephi 9:6-9, 26.)

How the Atonement Is Infinite and Eternal

The atonement is eternal—as eternal as the gospel, as eternal as the plan of salvation—because its saving and redeeming powers have always been manifest. It is the means by which Adam and all the ancient saints were saved. Through it they had the fulness of the everlasting gospel with all its gifts and glories. Baptism and celestial marriage had eternal efficacy and everlasting virtue for four thousand years before the Lord Jesus was even born in the flesh. The plan of salvation is always the same, and souls in those days were just as precious in the sight of the Lord as are souls today. All that was ever done by the ancient saints looked forward to and was built upon the foundation of the atonement that was to be. All was done in anticipation of an act that is eternal in nature. And the blessings of the atonement will continue to be manifest as long as there are men on earth —and, for that matter, everlastingly thereafter. It is truly an eternal, an everlasting, a perpetual thing that, like God, is to us without beginning and without end.

Speaking of the infinite scope of the atonement on this earth, the early brethren of this dispensation published these words: "As effected by Jesus Christ, it signifies the deliverance, through his death and resurrection, of the earth and everything pertaining to it, from the power which death has obtained over them through the transgression of Adam. . . . Redemption from death, through the sufferings of Christ, is for all men, both the righteous and the wicked; for this earth, and for all things created upon it." (*Compendium*, pp. 8-9.

As to the effect of the atonement on other worlds, we must note, first, that all those who receive Christ and his gospel have "power to become [his] sons." (D&C 39:4.) Through faith, they are born again. They become "the children of Christ, his sons, and his daughters." They are "spiritually begotten"; Christ becomes their Father; they are members of his family. (Mosiah 5:7.) All of this is made possible because of his atoning sacrifice. Also, as Paul tells us, "as many as are led by the Spirit of God, they are the sons of God." They become "heirs; heirs of God, and joint-heirs with Christ." (Romans 8:14, 17.) They receive an "adoption" into the family of the Father. All of this, of course, is in addition to the fact that they are the spirit children, as all men are, of that Father who dwells in the heavens.

Next, we turn to these words of testimony and doctrine as recorded in the vision of the degrees of glory. "[We] saw the holy angels, and them who are sanctified before his throne, worshiping God, and the Lamb, who worship him forever and ever. And now, after the many testimonies which have been given of him, this is the testimony, last of all, which we give of him: That he lives! For we saw him, even on the right hand of God; and we heard the voice bearing record that he is the Only Begotten of the Father—That by him, and through him, and of him, the worlds are and were created, and the inhabitants thereof are begotten sons and daughters unto God." (D&C 76:21-24.) That is to say: Christ created worlds without number whose inhabitants are adopted into the family of God by the atoning sacrifice wrought on our earth. The faithful on all worlds are spiritually begotten in the same way as on our earth; they are begotten sons and daughters *unto,* not *of,* God.

How wondrous is the holy word! How glorious are the saving truths! How infinite is the power of God! And how much we have yet to learn of the wonders of eternity!

CHAPTER 16

The Holy Gospel

The Gospel of God

What is the gospel? In the full and eternal sense, it is the plan of salvation, ordained and established by the Father, to enable his spirit children (Christ included!) to advance and progress and become like him. Thus, it includes all things both temporal and spiritual and is as eternal as God himself. Every truth, every eternal verity, every law and power— whether on earth, in heaven, or throughout a boundless universe—all of these are part of the gospel of God. He is their source and author, and all that *is* has been created for the benefit and blessing of man.

In the eternal sense, all things are part of the plan of salvation; all play their part in making eternal life available to the children of the Father. The three supreme events that comprise the system that makes salvation possible are the creation, the fall, and the atonement. The creation and the fall—so intertwined together as to constitute one divine enterprise—are the means whereby spirit children are housed in tabernacles of clay and subjected to the trials and sorrows of a mortal probation. The atonement is the divine ransom that raises man from mortality to immortality, from spiritual death to eternal life.

To us, the central thing in the plan of salvation is the atoning sacrifice of Christ. The blessings of the creation and the fall have passed upon all mankind. Those who kept their first estate earned the right to a mortal probation. But only those who believe and obey will gain the full blessings of the atonement. Accordingly, we speak of the gospel of Jesus Christ— he adopted his Father's plan—to center our attention everlastingly in the One by whom salvation comes. Thus Paul writes of "the gospel of God . . . concerning his Son Jesus

Christ our Lord, which was made of the seed of David according to the flesh; and declared to be the Son of God with power, according to the spirit of holiness, by the resurrection from the dead." (Romans 1:1-4.) It is God's gospel and it is Christ's gospel, and if we believe and obey its truths and laws and play our assigned parts in the divine system, it becomes our gospel also.

Those things which men must do to gain the full blessings of the gospel were revealed to Adam, for himself and for all mankind, in these words: "If thou wilt turn unto me, and hearken unto my voice," the Lord said, "and believe, and repent of all thy transgressions, and be baptized, even in water, in the name of mine Only Begotten Son, who is full of grace and truth, which is Jesus Christ, the only name which shall be given under heaven, whereby salvation shall come unto the children of men, ye shall receive the gift of the Holy Ghost, asking all things in his name, and whatsoever ye shall ask, it shall be given you."

Then the ancient record speaks of forgiveness of sins through the atonement, of an inheritance in the kingdom of God for those who are clean and pure, and of the spiritual rebirth that is theirs, a new birth that comes by water, and of the Spirit, and because of the atoning blood of Christ. "For by the water ye keep the commandment; by the Spirit ye are justified, and by the blood ye are sanctified," the Lord says. "Therefore"—that is, because of faith and righteousness— "it is given to abide in you; the record of heaven; the Comforter; the peaceable things of immortal glory; the truth of all things; that which quickeneth all things, which maketh alive all things; that which knoweth all things, and hath all power according to wisdom, mercy, truth, justice, and judgment." The mortal mind cannot conceive of greater blessings coming to fallen man than those conferred by the Holy Ghost upon the saints of God! Truly, they are Christ's, and Christ is God's, and they, having had peace and joy in this world, will go on to eternal life in the world to come. "And now, behold, I say unto you," the Lord continues, "this is the plan of salvation unto all men, through the blood of mine Only Begotten, who shall come in the meridian of time." (Moses 6:52-62.) Such is the nature and scope and power of the gospel of God, which has become the gospel of Christ.

The Gospel of Jesus Christ

Viewed from our mortal position, the gospel is all that is required to take us back to the Eternal Presence, there to be crowned with glory and honor, immortality and eternal life. To gain these greatest of all rewards, two things are required. The first is the atonement by which all men are raised in immortality, with those who believe and obey ascending also unto eternal life. This atoning sacrifice was the work of our Blessed Lord, and he has done his work. The second requisite is obedience on our part to the laws and ordinances of the gospel. Thus the gospel is, in effect, the atonement. But the gospel is also all of the laws, principles, doctrines, rites, ordinances, acts, powers, authorities, and keys needed to save and exalt fallen man in the highest heaven hereafter.

Speaking of the gospel as a virtual synonym for the atoning sacrifice, the inspired writings say: "And this is the gospel, the glad tidings, which the voice out of the heavens bore record unto us—That he came into the world, even Jesus, to be crucified for the world, and to bear the sins of the world, and to sanctify the world, and to cleanse it from all un-righteousness; that through him all might be saved whom the Father had put into his power and made by him." That is to say, salvation in the celestial kingdom is available to all because Christ bore their sins on conditions of repentance. But that is not all. The Savior "glorifies the Father, and saves all the works of his hands, except those sons of perdition who deny the Son after the Father has revealed him." (D&C 76:40-43.) Even those who do not believe the gospel; even those who have lived after the manner of the world; even the wicked and ungodly—even these shall receive a degree and kind of salvation. They shall be judged according to their works and receive a place in a terrestrial or a telestial kingdom.

Speaking of the gospel as the atonement, and also as the plan of salvation to which men must conform to be saved, Jesus said to the Nephites: "I have given unto you my gospel, and this is the gospel which I have given unto you—that I came into the world to do the will of my Father, because my Father sent me. And my Father sent me that I might be lifted up upon the cross; and after that I had been lifted up upon the cross, that I might draw all men unto me, that as I have been lifted up by men even so should men be lifted up by the Father, to stand before me, to be judged of their works, whether they be good or whether they be evil." Next he spoke of faith and repentance, of enduring to the end, of the wicked being cast into the fire, and of the need for the saints to wash their garments in his blood and be faithful all their days. And then came the great commandment: "Repent, all ye ends of the earth, and come unto me and be baptized in my name, that ye may be sanctified by the reception of the Holy Ghost, that ye may stand spotless before me at the last day. Verily, verily, I say unto you, this is my gospel." (3 Nephi 27:13-21; D&C 39:6.)

Thus, as pertaining to mankind, the gospel is faith, repentance, and baptism; it is receiving the gift of the Holy Ghost and being born again; it is keeping the commandments of God and enduring to the end; it is working out our salvation with fear and trembling before the Lord. We cannot be saved by the good works of others, not even those of the Lord Jesus himself.

Dispensations of the Gospel

The gospel is infinite in scope, eternal in nature, and everlasting in duration. It is the system that saves men on this world and all of the worlds of the Lord's creating. It is like unto God in beauty, glory, and perfection. It has existed from all eternity and will continue through all ages without end. But the Lord has given us an account of its operation on this earth only.

God alone can give the gospel to man. It comes by revelation and in no other way, and when it comes, it is always the same. Its truths and laws and doctrines never vary. Each new revelation of the plan of salvation is referred to as a dispensation of the gospel; it is an occasion on which the Lord dispenses anew his saving truths to man on earth. In the days of Adam, men were commanded: "Believe on his Only Begotten Son, even him whom he declared should come in the meridian of time, who was prepared from before the foundation of the world." It is of this teaching that the scripture says: "And thus the Gospel began to be preached, from the beginning, being declared by holy angels sent forth from the presence of God, and by his own voice, and by the gift of the Holy Ghost." These three ways of dispensing the gospel to men set the pattern for all subsequent dispensations. In each succeeding day of grace the voice of God was heard anew, angels parted the veil and communed with their fellow laborers, and the wondrous gift of the Holy Ghost enlightened the minds of men. "And thus all things were confirmed unto Adam, by an holy ordinance, and the Gospel preached, and a decree sent forth, that it should be in the world [in a series of dispensations], until the end thereof." (Moses 5:57-59.)

Enoch and Noah each presided over a gospel dispensation in his day. In both cases their powers and keys came down from Adam, but their ministries involved works of such magnitude and import that they were in constant communion with that Lord whose gospel they proclaimed. Under the direction of Enoch, the ancient saints built a City of Holiness and were all translated and taken up into heaven without tasting death. Noah's ministry involved the building of the ark, the universal flood, and the repeopling of the earth with his seed.

Though they each ministered under unique and singular circumstances, the gospel message they taught was the same. It is written: "The Lord ordained Noah after his own order, and commanded him that he should go forth and declare his Gospel unto the children of men, even as it was given unto Enoch." His declaration of the gospel included these words: "Believe and repent of your sins and be baptized in the name of Jesus Christ, the Son of God, even as our fathers, and ye shall receive the Holy Ghost, that ye may have all things made manifest; and if ye do not this, the floods will come in upon you." (Moses 8:19, 24.)

Abraham and Moses stand as heads of two great dispensations. Both held the Melchizedek Priesthood and the keys of the kingdom in their days. Paul says, "God . . . preached before the gospel unto Abraham." (Galatians 3:8.) Of the gospel given to Moses, the ancient apostle says: "Unto us [the meridian saints] was the gospel preached, as well as unto them [Israel in the day of Moses]: but the word preached did not profit them, not being mixed with faith in them that heard it." (Hebrews 4:2.) Having rejected the fulness of the gospel, ancient Israel was given "the preparatory gospel; which gospel is the gospel of repentance and of baptism, and the remission of sins, and the law of carnal commandments." (D&C 84:26-27.) This system, called the law of Moses, was the governing order in Israel until the coming of Christ, which caused Paul to say, "The law was our schoolmaster to bring us unto Christ." (Galatians 3:24.) As to Abraham, so great was his standing and so righteous were his doings that the Lord made him the father of the faithful of his own and all future ages. All who receive the gospel, from his day on to the end of the earth, "shall be accounted [his] seed, and shall rise up and bless [him], as their father." (Abraham 2:10.)

Jesus and his ancient apostles brought in a new dispensation. In their day the Mosaic law was fulfilled; their message of salvation was identical with that preached in all previous dispensations. After his own baptism, "Jesus came into Galilee, preaching the gospel of the kingdom of God, and saying, The time is fulfilled, and the kingdom of God is at hand: repent ye, and believe the gospel." (Mark 1:14-15.) Jesus was a restorer. He preached the same gospel proclaimed by Adam, Enoch, Noah, Abraham, Moses, and all of the ancient prophets and patriarchs. It is the everlasting gospel. Jesus invited men to worship the Father in spirit and in truth; to have faith in the Son, who then ministered among them; to repent and be baptized by him and his apostolic witnesses; to receive the Holy Ghost so that they might have all things made manifest unto them; and then to endure in righteousness and truth unto the end.

How many dispensations there have been, we do not know. The Jaredites, Nephites, and lost tribes of Israel all had their dispensations, perhaps a number of them. It suffices, for the moment, for us to know that always and everlastingly, in all dispensations and among all peoples, the saving truths are the same. There is one Lord and one gospel, which, in the providences of Him whose gospel it is, has been restored in our day, never to be lost again, but to remain among men and to prepare a people for the second coming of the Son of Man. Our dispensation is the one into which all the powers and glories of past ages will flow in due course. It is the dispensation of the fulness of times.

The Church and the Gospel

The plan of salvation (the gospel of God) in the eternal sense—meaning the creation, the fall, and the atonement; meaning the system ordained of God whereby his spirit children might be saved—the gospel in this sense stands independent of all things. It operates without reference to anything man has done or can or will do. All that appertains to it has been done by others for and on behalf of man.

But the plan of salvation (the gospel of Christ) as it operates in the lives of men—meaning faith, repentance, baptism, the gift of the Holy Ghost, and enduring to the end; meaning all of the truths, powers, ordinances, and laws by obedience to which mortals may be saved—the gospel in this sense operates through an organized body of believers. That organization is the Church; it is the kingdom of God on earth. In our day it is The Church of Jesus Christ of Latter-day Saints. It is composed of congregations of true believers who have come unto Christ and made covenant with him to keep his commandments and live his laws. This church is built upon the gospel; this gospel is administered by the Melchizedek Priesthood; this priesthood is the power and authority of the Lord; and those who hold it stand in the place and stead of Deity in administering salvation to men.

If there were no true church on earth, if mortal men were without the power and authority of the greater priesthood, if the legal administrators of God's earthly kingdom were not performing their various ministerial services, there would be no true gospel on earth and no way for men to work out their salvation. The Lord's house is a house of order and not a house of confusion. He does not personally teach and baptize and ordain and guide each person to salvation. Rather, he sends his ministers to act for him, to act in an organized and intelligent way, and those who receive the servants of the Lord receive him; they believe his gospel; and they join his church.

"Ye shall call the church in my name," Jesus said to the Nephites, "and ye shall call upon the Father in my name that he will bless the church for my sake." The gospel standing alone, independent of the Church, does not suffice; it must be administered and its blessings offered to men through a divine institution. And so, Jesus continues, "if it be called in my name then it is my church, if it so be that they are built upon my gospel. . . . And if it so be that the church is built upon my gospel then will the Father show forth his own works in it." Signs always follow true believers; miracles always abound in the true church; the power of God is always manifest in the congregations of the saints. "But if it be not built upon my gospel, and is built upon the works of men, or upon the works of the devil, verily I say unto you they have joy in their works for a season, and by and by the end cometh, and they are hewn down and cast into the fire, from whence there is no return." (3 Nephi 27:7-11.) The Church and the gospel always go together; they cannot be separated; they are one.

Similarly, the "priesthood continueth in the church of God in all generations. . . . And this greater priesthood administereth the gospel." (D&C 84:17, 19.) Thus, where the true church is, there is the gospel of Jesus Christ, and there is the Melchizedek Priesthood; and where the true church is not, there is no gospel, no priesthood, no salvation.

Restoration of the Gospel

God has given the gospel to men in our day. By his own voice, by the ministering of holy angels sent from his presence, and by the gift of the Holy Ghost, once again the power that saves is found on earth. The heavens, long sealed, have been opened, and the heavens are raining down righteousness again. As it was anciently, believing souls may be sanctified by the power of the Holy Ghost, and those who believe and obey the whole law may be sealed up unto eternal life. Ours is, indeed, the great day of restoration, the day in which all the truths and powers ever possessed in any dispensation of the past either have been or will be given to men. This restoration is the greatest and grandest event that has happened on earth since the Son of God worked out the infinite and eternal atonement.

John the Revelator, seeing in vision that which was destined to be in a day subsequent to his, said: "And I saw another angel fly in the midst of heaven, having the everlasting gospel to preach unto them that dwell on the earth, and to every nation, and kindred, and tongue, and people." The angelic message was that men should worship and glorify the true God, the Creator, the one "that made heaven, and earth, and the sea, and the fountains of waters." (Revelation 14:6-7.) That is, through the gospel, men once again would receive the saving truths; they would again come to a knowledge of those Holy Beings whom it is life eternal to know. And all this, the angelic voice acclaimed, would take place when the hour of God's judgment—which occurs at the time of the second coming of the Son of Man—was imminent.

What is it that has been restored by the heavenly voice, by angelic ministration, and by the power of the Holy Ghost? We have received all of the keys and powers needed to perform every saving ordinance. We have all of the truths and laws by obedience to which salvation comes. New scripture, confirming and upholding the ancient word, has come forth. The Book of Mormon, which contains a record of God's dealings with a people who had the fulness of the gospel, has been translated by the gift and power of God and is now published to the world. This holy book teaches the doctrines of salvation and testifies of the Divine Sonship of that Lord whose doctrines they are. Revelations, visions, and commandments have come from God in heaven to man on earth as it was in days of old. The Doctrine and Covenants, a book of commandments, contains the mind and will and voice of the Lord to men in modern times. Revelation has commenced and will not cease until man knows all that is in the mind of his Maker.

What glorious things have happened in this our day? The heavens have been opened, and the great God who upholds all things by his own power, accompanied by his Beloved Son, has appeared to mortal man. An ancient American prophet, ministering in resurrected glory, has given the gold plates from which the Book of Mormon was translated. John, who baptized Jesus, came and conferred the Aaronic Priesthood upon Joseph Smith and Oliver Cowdery. Peter, James, and John—the holy three who were with Jesus in his ministry— have given their keys and powers to mortals, as have Moses, Elias, Elijah, Gabriel, Raphael, and divers angels. The true church has been organized; apostles and prophets once more speak the mind and will of the Lord; and scattered Israel is returning to the sheepfold of the Good Shepherd. Temples have risen in many nations, Israel is gathering, and the saints are in process of building up Zion and preparing for the return of the Lord. The gifts of the Spirit are being poured out upon the faithful, oftentimes almost without measure. Truly, there are no words to describe, nor can any tongue tell, the glory and marvel of all that has come anew in our day as part of the promised restoration of all things.

False Gospels

There is and can be only one Supreme God, one true gospel, one divine church, one plan of salvation, that can give eternal life to the faithful. God cannot be both a spirit essence, diffused as an immaterial nothingness through all immensity, and also a corporeal being having a tangible body of flesh and bones. Salvation cannot come by grace alone, without works and without obedience to the laws and ordinances of the gospel. There are, of course, many churches, many supposed systems of salvation, many gospels, as it were. But it is an obvious and inescapable truism that all churches may be false, but only one can be true.

If the everlasting gospel taught by Jesus and his apostles was destined to be restored in the last days, it follows that both true religion and the pure gospel would be lost in the intervening years. If in the last days an angelic ministrant was to come from God in heaven to man on earth to bring the everlasting gospel, it follows that mortal men would not already have the gospel so restored. If that restored gospel was to be preached to every nation, kindred, tongue, and people—to all men without exception—it follows that no single person on earth already had the gospel. If these things are true—and they are—it follows that universal apostasy fell upon men between Jesus' day and our day. And the conclusive proof of a universal apostasy is the very fact that there was a restoration.

Churches built on false gospels are false churches. They have no saving power. They may, as Jesus said, be "built upon the works of men, or upon the works of the devil." (3 Nephi 27:11.) They may have "a form of godliness," as Paul said, but their followers are "ever learning, and never able to come to the knowledge of the truth." (2 Timothy 3:5-7.) The way to find the true religion and the pure gospel is to find what Jesus and the ancient apostles taught. It is, however, universally recognized by all professors of religion in all churches that such a system no longer exists either in any one sect or in all the sects of Christendom combined.

Even in his day, Paul had occasion to warn against "some that . . . would pervert the gospel of Christ." Apostasy had its roots even in the apostolic era. "But though we, or an angel from heaven, preach any other gospel unto you than that which we have preached unto you, let him be accursed." Then he said: "The gospel which was preached of me is not after man. For I neither received it of man, neither was I taught it, but by the revelation of Jesus Christ." (Galatians 1:7-8, 11-12.) That, of course, is the grand secret, the great key: no man ever receives true religion and the pure gospel except by revelation. He must gain a personal testimony by the power of the Holy Ghost. Indeed, the very possession of the fulness of the everlasting gospel consists in having the Melchizedek Priesthood and the gift of the Holy Ghost. Where these are, there is the gospel, and where these are not, there the gospel is not.

Paul also tells us that the gospel comes both in *word* and in *power*. "The gospel of Christ," he says, "is the power of God unto salvation to every one that believeth." (Romans 1:16.) "For our gospel came not unto you [the saints] in word only, but also in power, and in the Holy Ghost, and in much assurance." (1 Thessalonians 1:5.) The word of the gospel is found in the holy scriptures. They, as Paul also says, "are able to make [men] wise unto salvation through faith which is in Christ Jesus." (2 Timothy 3:15.) But they of themselves only chart the course that men must follow to gain salvation. They record the doctrines of salvation; they teach true principles; they tell us what the Lord expects of us. But in the true and eternal sense, the gospel is *power.* It is the power that saves; it is the power that raises a dead man from the grave and gives him eternal life; it is the power of God. And this power is and can be found only in the one true church.

How fearful, how solemn are the words of Jesus, spoken that spring morning in 1820, when he said that all the professors of religion in the world were corrupt and that "all their creeds were an abomination in his sight." "They draw near to me with their lips," he said, "but their hearts are far from me, they teach for doctrines the commandments of men, having a form of godliness, but they deny the power thereof." (JS–H 1:19.)

CHAPTER 17

Salvation

Salvation Universal

Salvation and damnation are poles apart; they are opposites; one is white and the other is black. One is to dwell with God in the kingdom of heaven; the other is to dwell with Lucifer in the kingdom of hell.

Full salvation, often called eternal life or exaltation, is to be like God, to be a son of God, a joint-heir with Christ, receiving, inheriting, and possessing, as he does, the fulness of the kingdom of the Father. Full damnation, often called eternal damnation, is to be like Lucifer, to be a son of perdition, an inheritor of eternal misery forever in the kingdom of the devil. Between these two extremes are many hues and tones, many degrees and types, of both salvation and damnation.

Few men now living will gain eternal life, and fewer still will receive eternal death, meaning eternal spiritual death. In the Father's house are many mansions, many kingdoms, many degrees of glory and honor, many types and kinds of salvation. Jesus "saves all the works of his hands, except those sons of perdition who deny the Son after the Father has revealed him." These rebels are damned souls; these traitors become devils, angels to a devil, to dwell forever in misery in his kingdom. "They shall go away into everlasting punishment, which is endless punishment, which is eternal punishment, to reign with the devil and his angels in eternity, where their worm dieth not, and the fire is not quenched, which is their torment." They are "the only ones on whom the second death shall have any power" after the resurrection; they are the only ones who shall not be "redeemed" from spiritual death "in the due time of the Lord, [and] after the sufferings of his wrath." (D&C 76:37-44.) As Alma expressed it: "They shall be as though there had been no redemption made; for they cannot be redeemed according to God's justice; and they cannot die, seeing there is no more corruption." (Alma 12:18.)

There are three kingdoms of glory in which resurrected men will be saved: the celestial, the terrestrial, and the telestial. "In the celestial glory there are three heavens or degrees." The highest of these is reserved for those who gain eternal life. All others are damned in the sense that their progress is limited. There are restrictions placed upon them; they have reached the "end of [their] kingdom"; they "cannot have an increase." (D&C 131:1, 4.)

The celestial kingdom is reserved for those who sanctify their souls by obedience to the laws and ordinances of the gospel. They are the ones whose sins Christ bore. Because of the atonement, all men, except the sons of perdition, are saved from "death and hell, and the devil, and the lake of fire and brimstone, which is endless torment." (2 Nephi 9:26.) This salvation takes place when they are resurrected; until that day they suffer with the damned.

They are saved from death, meaning the natural death or the death of the body, by the fact of resurrection. They are saved from hell—from the spirit prison where the souls of the wicked await the day of their resurrection—when their spirits enter again the physical tenement that once was theirs. They are saved from the devil because he no longer has power over them; they have paid the penalty for their sins, and these sins no longer weigh them down. After much sorrow and misery they are prepared to live as resurrected beings and find their places in one of the lower kingdoms. They are saved from endless torment, for, according to the law of justice, they have paid the penalty for all their evil deeds, and Satan no longer has any claim upon them. As John of old saw in vision: "The sea gave up the dead which were in it; and death and hell delivered up the dead which were in them." There is thus an end to death and hell. "And they were judged every man according to their works." It is this judgment that awards them their place in the kingdoms of glory. "And death and hell were cast into the lake of fire. This is the second death." (Revelation 20:13-14.) That is, death and hell and eternal torment remain for the sons of perdition.

It is a glorious and wondrous thing to be saved, even in

the telestial kingdom; but oh! what a course of sorrow and suffering one must travel to gain this lowest of all glories. "These are they who are liars, and sorcerers, and adulterers, and whoremongers, and whosoever loves and makes a lie. These are they who suffer the wrath of God on earth. These are they who suffer the vengeance of eternal fire. These are they who are cast down to hell and suffer the wrath of Almighty God, until the fulness of times, when Christ shall have subdued all enemies under his feet, and shall have perfected his work." (D&C 76:103-106.) And yet again: "These are they who shall not be redeemed from the devil until the last resurrection, until the Lord, even Christ the Lamb, shall have finished his work." (D&C 76:85.) They suffer the second death until the day of their resurrection. They are the ones of whom it is written: "The fearful, and the unbelieving, and all liars, and whosoever loveth and maketh a lie, and the whoremonger, and the sorcerer, shall have their part in that lake which burneth with fire and brimstone, which is the second death." They are the ones of whom it is decreed: "They shall not have part in the first resurrection." (D&C 63:17-18.) And when they finally come forth in the resurrection of damnation, their inheritance is not to be compared with that found in a terrestrial or a celestial kingdom.

Those destined to inherit the terrestrial kingdom are: (1) those who died "without law"—those heathen and pagan people who do not hear the gospel in this life, and who would not accept it with all their hearts should they hear it; (2) those who hear and reject the gospel in this life and then accept it in the spirit world; (3) those "who are honorable men of the earth, who [are] blinded by the craftiness of men"; and (4) those who are lukewarm members of the true church and who have testimonies, but who are not true and faithful in all things. (See D&C 76:71-80.)

Salvation for the Saints

However pleasing it may be to know that there is a general, a universal, and an unconditional salvation for all men; a salvation that comes by the grace of God alone, without faith, without repentance, without baptism, without the works of righteousness; a redeeming power that brings all men forth in immortality; a divine mercy and a holy compassion that rewards even the wicked and ungodly—yet this is not the salvation sought by the saints. The true saints seek salvation in the kingdom of God. Their desire is to gain an inheritance in the celestial kingdom. And almost every reference to salvation in holy writ equates such a celestial inheritance with eternal life.

"The living God," Paul says, "is the Saviour of all men, specially of those that believe." (1 Timothy 4:10.) Jesus said: "Whoso believeth in me, and is baptized, the same shall be saved; and they are they who shall inherit the kingdom of God. And whoso believeth not in me, and is not baptized, shall be damned." (3 Nephi 11:33-34.) Thus, salvation is for the faithful, and all who do not so obtain are damned. They cannot go where God and Christ are; they will not gain the eternal fulness that would have been theirs if they had filled the full measure of their creation.

Gaining salvation is a process, and those so obtaining must sanctify their souls and become fit companions for Gods and angels. And so Amulek says: "No unclean thing can inherit the kingdom of heaven; therefore, how can ye be saved, except ye inherit the kingdom of heaven? Therefore, ye cannot be saved in your sins." Freedom from sin is salvation, a freedom that no mortal ever fully obtains. All men sin daily, either in deed or word or thought. Christ "shall come into the world to redeem his people," Amulek continues, "and he shall take upon him the transgressions of those who believe on his name; and these are they that shall have eternal life, and salvation cometh to none else." As far as the saints are concerned, there is only one salvation that men ought to seek. "Therefore the wicked remain as though there had been no redemption made, except it be the loosing of the bands of death; for behold, the day cometh that all shall rise from the dead and stand before God, and be judged according to their works." (Alma 11:37-41.)

As Amulek equated salvation and eternal life, which is exaltation, so do the revelations given in our day. "If thou wilt do good, yea, and hold out faithful to the end, thou shalt be saved in the kingdom of God, which is the greatest of all the gifts of God; for there is no gift greater than the gift of salvation." (D&C 6:13.) "And, if you keep my commandments and endure to the end you shall have eternal life, which gift is the greatest of all the gifts of God." (D&C 14:7.)

In the writings that have come down to us, we find this reasoning of the Prophet Joseph Smith relative to what salvation is and who will obtain it: "Where shall we find a prototype into whose likeness we may be assimilated, in order that we may be made partakers of life and salvation? or, in other words, where shall we find a saved being?" What better starting point could there be than this—find a saved being and then seek to be like him.

"For if we can find a saved being, we may ascertain, without much difficulty, what all others must be, in order to be saved." They must be like that individual or they cannot be saved. "We think that it will not be a matter of dispute, that two beings who are unlike each other cannot both be saved; for whatever constitutes the salvation of one will constitute the salvation of every creature which will be saved; and if we find one saved being in all existence, we may see what all others must be, or else not be saved." The reasoning is sound; the logic is perfect; and the foundation is laid to introduce a Saved Being.

"We ask, then, where is the prototype? or where is the saved being? We conclude, as to the answer of this question, there will be no dispute among those who believe the bible, that it is Christ: all will agree in this, that he is the prototype or standard of salvation, or, in other words, that he is a saved being." The Lord Jesus set the pattern in all things. He is the great Exemplar. His command is that we should be as he is. If he gained salvation by treading the strait and narrow path, so must it be with us.

"And if we should continue our interrogation, and ask how it is that he is saved? the answer would be—because he is a just and holy being; and if he were anything different from what he is he would not be saved; for his salvation depends on his being precisely what he is and nothing else; for if it were possible for him to change, in the least degree, so sure he would fail of salvation and lose all his dominion, power, authority and glory, which constitute salvation; for salvation consists in the glory, authority, majesty, power, and dominion which Jehovah possesses and in nothing else; and no being can possess it but himself or one like him." (*Lectures on Faith* 7:9.)

Salvation by Grace

Salvation of every sort, kind, type, and nature comes by the grace of God; that is, it comes because of the mercy, love, and condescension of God. If it were not for the grace of God, there would be nothing—no creation, no fall, no mortal probation, no atonement, no redemption, no immortality, no eternal life. It is God's grace that underlies all things, that causes all things to be, that makes all things possible. Without it there would be nothing; with it there is everything.

And as with the Father, so with the Son—their goodness and grace redound to the benefit and blessing of all men. The Messianic promise of the Father himself attests: "Mine Only Begotten is and shall be the Savior, for he is full of grace and truth." (Moses 1:6.) The Son came. He came to atone for the sins of the world; he came to bring to pass the immortality and eternal life of man—and all that he did in his ministry was because of his goodness and grace.

Thus, as Paul so ably teaches, "God, who is rich in mercy, for his great love wherewith he loved us, even when we were dead, in sins, hath quickened us together with Christ, (by grace ye are saved;) and hath raised us up together, and made us sit together in heavenly places in Christ Jesus." That is to say, even when we were dead spiritually; even when we lived after the manner of the world, and were carnal, sensual, and devilish; even when we lived in the bondage of sin—yet God saved us because of his grace. Because of his love, his mercy, and his condescension, he redeemed us spiritually; because of his grace, he has raised us from spiritual death to spiritual life through the gospel. We have been born again and are alive to the things of the Spirit. We have become clean by the sanctifying power of the Holy Ghost, and we shall stand spotless before the Lord at the last day. Thus we shall sit down with Christ and the holy angels in the kingdom of God. And all of this comes by the grace of God. It is by his grace that we are saved. There is no other way. And all this God hath done "that in the ages to come he might shew the exceeding riches of his grace in his kindness toward us through Christ Jesus."

Building on the foundation so laid, Paul proclaims: "By grace are ye saved through faith; and that not of yourselves: it is the gift of God: not of works, lest any man should boast. For we are his workmanship, created in Christ Jesus unto good works, which God hath before ordained that we should walk in them." (Ephesians 2:4-10.) Salvation comes by faith. Jesus said it was for "those who have washed their garments in my blood, because of their faith, and the repentance of all their sins, and their faithfulness unto the end." (3 Nephi 27:19.) But it is available because of the grace of God.

Man cannot save himself. He cannot be saved by the works of the Mosaic law; he cannot be saved by the works of the gospel. Man cannot resurrect himself; neither Mosaic works nor gospel works can bring him forth from the grave. The resurrection comes by the grace of God; all men are resurrected, and in that sense all are saved by grace alone. And further: No man can raise himself unto eternal life; he cannot create a state of salvation and provide the means to obtain it. Man cannot create the kingdom of God, nor can he save himself in such a kingdom. If it were not for the grace of God, as shown forth in the redemption of his Son, there would be no eternal life. Neither the works of the Mosaic law nor the works of Christian righteousness, standing alone, without the grace of God as manifest in the sacrifice of his Son, could save a man. Salvation does not come into being by the works of men; it comes because of Christ and his atonement. Because there was such an atonement, man can have faith, perform the works of righteousness, endure to the end, and "work out [his] own salvation with fear and trembling." (Philippians 2:12.)

Nephi's teachings accord with Paul's. "Believe in Christ," the American Hebrew exhorts, "and . . . be reconciled to God; for we know that it is by grace that we are saved, after all we can do." (2 Nephi 25:23.) His brother Jacob also accords: "Reconcile yourselves to the will of God, and not to the will of the devil and the flesh; and remember, after ye are reconciled unto God, that it is only in and through the grace of God that ye are saved." (2 Nephi 10:24.) But perhaps no one has ever expounded the doctrine of salvation by grace better than Moroni did in these words: "Come unto Christ, and be perfected in him, and deny yourselves of all ungodliness; and if ye shall deny yourselves of all ungodliness, and love God with all your might, mind and strength, then is his grace sufficient for you, that by his grace ye may be perfect in Christ." Hear it, O all men: the grace of God, in the full sense, in the sense of salvation, is manifest only to those who, through righteousness, become perfect in Christ. "And if by the grace of God ye are perfect in Christ," Moroni continues, "ye can in nowise deny the power of God. And again, if ye by the grace of God are perfect in Christ, and deny not his power, then are ye sanctified in Christ by the grace of God, through the shedding of the blood of Christ, which is in the covenant of the Father unto the remission of your sins, that ye become holy, without spot." (Moroni 10:32-33.) God be thanked and God be praised for his goodness and grace unto the children of men.

CHAPTER 18

Exaltation

Immortality—for All Men

Immortality is one thing, eternal life another. Immortality is to live forever in a resurrected state; it is to have a tangible body of flesh and bones. After the judgment, immortal beings are assigned their places in the celestial, terrestrial, and telestial kingdoms. Eternal life is the name of the kind of life possessed by the Eternal One, by the Eternal Father. It is reserved for those immortal beings who gain an inheritance in the highest heaven of the celestial realm.

Both immortality and eternal life come because of the atonement; both are part of the gospel. Immortality is for all men, both the righteous and the wicked; eternal life is for those who believe and obey the whole law of the whole gospel. Immortality is for the disobedient; eternal life is for the obedient. "Jesus Christ . . . hath abolished death, and hath brought life and immortality to light through the gospel," Paul said. (2 Timothy 1:10.) Immortality is the ransom from temporal death; eternal life is the ransom from spiritual death. Both come by the grace of God. One comes as a free gift; the other is earned by obedience to the laws and ordinances of the gospel.

The whole purpose of the plan of salvation is to provide immortality for all men and to make eternal life available for those who overcome the world and qualify for such a high exaltation. "For behold, this is my work and my glory," saith God, "to bring to pass the immortality and eternal life of man." (Moses 1:39.) This is accomplished through the redemption of Christ, by virtue of which all men are "raised in immortality," thus being redeemed from the temporal fall, and by virtue of which the saints are "raised [also] unto eternal life," thus being "redeemed from their spiritual fall." (D&C 29:43-44.)

Salvation is in Christ. Immortality comes through him; his resurrection brings to pass the resurrection of all men. Eternal life is his gift to those whose sins he has borne. "I am the resurrection, and the life," he said. 'Both immortality and eternal life come because of my atoning sacrifice.' "He that believeth in me, though he were dead, yet shall he live." Temporal death and spiritual death are both swallowed up in Christ. "And whosoever liveth and believeth in me shall never die." (John 11:25-26.) Those who are alive in Christ because they have the companionship of the Holy Spirit shall never die. They are alive spiritually in this sphere, and they shall have eternal life in the realms ahead.

As to immortality coming to all men, the scriptures say: "Behold, the day cometh that all shall rise from the dead and stand before God, and be judged according to their works." These are the words of Amulek. "Now, there is a death which is called a temporal death," he continues. "And the death of Christ shall loose the bands of this temporal death, that all shall be raised from this temporal death. The spirit and the body shall be reunited again in its perfect form." There will be no physical imperfections in the resurrection, no disease, no corruption, nothing to impair the proper functioning of every organ of the body. "Both limb and joint shall be restored to its proper frame, even as we now are at this time; and we shall be brought to stand before God, knowing even as we know now, and have a bright recollection of all our guilt." The resurrection will not erase either the remembrance of sin or the anguish of conscience as a result of a wasted life.

"Now, this restoration shall come to all, both old and young, both bond and free, both male and female, both the wicked and the righteous." Men can no more escape the fact of resurrection than they can choose to go out of existence and cease to be. The resurrection will be so literal and so real that "even there shall not so much as a hair of their heads be lost; but every thing shall be restored to its perfect frame, as it is now, or in the body, and shall be brought and be arraigned before the bar of Christ the Son, and God the Father, and the Holy Spirit, which is one Eternal God, to be judged according to their works, whether they be good or whether they be evil.

. . . I say unto you that this mortal body is raised to an immortal body, that is from death, even from the first death unto life, that they can die no more; their spirits uniting with their bodies, never to be divided; thus the whole becoming spiritual and immortal, that they can no more see corruption." (Alma 11:41-45.)

Eternal Life—for the Saints

Immortality is for all men; eternal life is for a favored few. Eternal life is available to all, for God is no respecter of persons, but few will pay the price in service, in obedience, and in personal righteousness to gain so great a gift. In its very nature and by definition, eternal life consists of two things: (1) the continuation of the family unit in eternity, and (2) receiving the fulness of the glory and power of the Father.

God also has all power, all might, and all dominion. He knows all things, has all wisdom, and is the embodiment of all truth. Those who receive a like state of glory and exaltation become like him; they become one with the Father and the Son. They are the ones of whom Jesus said: "Ye shall be even as I am, and I am even as the Father; and the Father and I are one." (3 Nephi 28:10.) And it is of them that the revealed word recites: "They shall pass by the angels, and the gods, which are set there, to their exaltation and glory in all things, as hath been sealed upon their heads, which glory shall be a fulness and a continuation of the seeds forever and ever. Then shall they be gods, because they have no end; therefore shall they be from everlasting to everlasting, because they continue; then shall they be above all, because all things are subject unto them. Then shall they be gods, because they have all power, and the angels are subject unto them." (D&C 132:19-20.)

"They are they who are the church of the Firstborn. They are they into whose hands the Father has given all things— they are they who are priests and kings, who have received of his fulness, and of his glory; and are priests of the Most High, after the order of Melchizedek, which was after the order of Enoch, which was after the order of the Only Begotten Son. Wherefore, as it is written, they are gods, even the sons of God—wherefore, all things are theirs, whether life or death, or things present, or things to come, all are theirs and they are

Christ's, and Christ is God's. And they shall overcome all things. These shall dwell in the presence of God and his Christ forever and ever. . . . These are they whose names are written in heaven, where God and Christ are the judge of all. These are they who are just men made perfect through Jesus the mediator of the new covenant, who wrought out this perfect atonement through the shedding of his own blood." (D&C 76:54-60, 68-69.)

Salvation for the Dead

If it is the design and purpose and work of the Lord to bring to pass the immortality and eternal life of man; if eternal life comes by obedience to the laws and ordinances of the gospel and in no other way; if this gospel has been given of God to a select few among the masses of men—if these things are true, what hope is there for the generality of mankind? Are they to be damned because they never had a chance to hear the true gospel preached by messengers sent of God? Would a just God damn whole races and nations and kingdoms because their municipals did not accept a gospel that he himself did not even make available to them? Will men be saved in a celestial heaven or damned in an endless hell simply on the basis of whim or chance or happenstance? Would a just God damn men for not believing a message that he did not send to them? How can God be other than a respecter of persons if he offers his saving truths to some and denies them to others?

Every thoughtful person should know by instinct that a just God will treat all his children with divine impartiality. Some truths are self-evident. They are bred in our bones; they are ingrained in our souls. For instance, Jesus said: "In my Father's house are many mansions: if it were not so, I would have told you." (John 14:2.) That is to say, the Lord expects men to believe in degrees of glory in the eternal world. Otherwise there could be no judgment according to works. If there were no levels and degrees of reward in eternity, the Lord would have to reveal such to us, lest our instincts lead us astray. So it is also with respect to making salvation available to all men through the gospel.

Unless men have closed their minds and bound their sense of reason with the heresies of a fallen world, they know in their hearts that a just God could not do other than make salvation available to all his children on the same terms and conditions. Such is, of course, the case. The gospel is offered to some while they yet dwell in mortality; it comes to others as they abide in the spirit world, awaiting the day of their resurrection. The living and the dead are all alike unto God; all are alive unto him whether, for the moment, they dwell in a mortal or a spirit sphere.

In the day when the Lord Jesus dwelt among men, he said: "The hour is coming, and now is, when the dead shall hear the voice of the Son of God: and they that hear shall live." (John 5:25.) He was then preaching to mortals; soon he would go to the world of spirits, there to preach to the dead. Those in the spirit world who accepted the gospel would live. They would be born again and live as pertaining to the things of the Spirit; they would gain spiritual life as contrasted with spiritual death; and they would be heirs of eternal life.

Peter recounts the fulfillment of Jesus' promise. In speaking of the false accusations heaped upon the saints, he says, "It is better . . . that ye suffer for well doing, than for evil doing," as will be the case with their persecutors. "For Christ also hath once suffered for sins," he says, "the just for the unjust," the Sinless One for us sinners, "that he might bring us to God, being put to death in the flesh, but quickened by the Spirit; by which also he went and preached unto the spirits in prison." For the forty or so hours that his body lay in the Arimathean's tomb, the Spirit Lord proclaimed liberty to the captives in the paradise of God. As an illustration of those spirits to whom he offered the gospel, Peter names those who "were disobedient . . . in the days of Noah." (1 Peter 3:17-20.) For two thousand years they had been shut up in a spirit prison; now some hope was offered to them through the gospel.

Why preach the gospel in the spirit world unless believing souls in that realm can repent and be saved? Truly, as Peter says, all men "shall give account to him that is ready to judge the quick and the dead." All men are alive in the sight of God; to him there is no death and there are no dead. Accordingly, "for this cause was the gospel preached also to them that are dead, that they might be judged according to men in the flesh, but live according to God in the spirit." (1 Peter 4:5-6.) The judgments of God are just because of salvation for the dead. If the dead could not be saved on the same basis as the living, God would be neither just nor merciful, and thus would cease to be God.

Baptism is an ordinance of salvation; it opens the door to celestial salvation, and without it, no man can be saved. Unless a man is born of water and of the Spirit, he can neither see nor enter the kingdom of heaven. Baptism in water can only be performed where there is water. It is an earthly ordinance. Hence, provision is found in the gospel for this ordinance to be performed by mortals for and on behalf of the dead. We are privileged to act on a vicarious basis for our deceased brethren even as the Lord Jesus vicariously atoned for our sins. If the dead, on their part, believe and obey, then our acts in their behalf are efficacious; otherwise, they confer no blessings upon them. Similarly, if we believe and obey, the atoning sacrifice of Christ cleanses us from sin; otherwise, we are not redeemed from our spiritual fall. In the light of all this, the true saints understand Paul's statement: "Else what shall they do which are baptized for the dead, if the dead rise not at all? why are they then baptized for the dead?" (1 Corinthians 15:29.) And as with baptism for the dead, so with respect to all of the ordinances of salvation and exaltation: all are performed in holy places for and on behalf of the dead. What work is a greater manifestation of love for our fellowmen than this?

If men reject the gospel in this life and then accept it in the spirit world, are they heirs of eternal life? Will those who lived in Noah's day and who rejected him and his word be heirs of the celestial kingdom? If they repent and receive the gospel in the spirit world, is not their final destiny a place in the terrestrial kingdom? In one of the great revelations of our day, the Lord said to Joseph Smith: "All who have died without a knowledge of this gospel, who would have received it if they had been permitted to tarry, shall be heirs of the celestial kingdom of God; also all that shall die henceforth without a knowledge of it, who would have received it with all their hearts, shall be heirs of that kingdom; for I, the Lord, will judge all men according to their works, according to the desire of their hearts." (D&C 137:7-9.)

President Joseph F. Smith saw in vision the visit of the Lord Jesus Christ in the spirit world. He saw that the Lord appeared to the righteous; that among the wicked and ungodly he did not go; and that he organized the work there and sent messengers to preach to all the spirits in prison. "The Son of God appeared, declaring liberty to the captives who had been faithful," the scriptural account says, "and there he preached to them the everlasting gospel, the doctrine of the resurrection and the redemption of mankind from the fall, and from individual sins on conditions of repentance."

Christ preached to the righteous; others proclaimed the word to the wicked who were not entitled to see his face. "But behold, from among the righteous, he organized his forces and appointed messengers, clothed with power and authority, and commissioned them to go forth and carry the light of the gospel to them that were in darkness, even to all the spirits of men; and thus was the gospel preached to the dead. And the chosen messengers went forth to declare the acceptable day of the Lord and proclaim liberty to the captives who were bound, even unto all who would repent of their sins and receive the gospel. Thus was the gospel preached to those who had died in their sins, without a knowledge of the truth, or in transgression, having rejected the prophets. These were taught faith in God, repentance from sin, vicarious baptism for the remission of sins, the gift of the Holy Ghost by the laying on of hands, and all other principles of the gospel that were necessary for them to know in order to qualify themselves that they might be judged according to men in the flesh, but live according to God in the spirit. And so it was made known among the dead, both small and great, the unrighteous as well as the faithful, that redemption had been wrought through the sacrifice of the Son of God upon the cross."

The close relationship between the work of the Lord's kingdom here and that in the spirit world is shown from these words of President Joseph F. Smith: "The Prophet Joseph Smith, and my father, Hyrum Smith, Brigham Young, John Taylor, Wilford Woodruff, and other choice spirits who were reserved to come forth in the fulness of times to take part in laying the foundations of the great latter-day work, including the building of the temples and the performance of ordinances therein for the redemption of the dead, were also in the spirit world. I observed that they were also among the noble and great ones who were chosen in the beginning to be rulers in the Church of God. . . . I beheld that the faithful elders of this dispensation, when they depart from mortal life, continue their labors in the preaching of the gospel of repentance and redemption, through the sacrifice of the Only Begotten Son of God, among those who are in darkness and under the bondage of sin in the great world of the spirits of the dead. The dead who repent will be redeemed, through obedience to the ordinances of the house of God." (D&C 138:18-19, 30-35, 53-58.)

ARTICLE 4

We believe
that the first principles
and ordinances
of the Gospel are:
first, Faith in the Lord Jesus Christ;
second, Repentance;
third, Baptism by immersion
for the remission of sins;
fourth, Laying on of hands
for the gift of the Holy Ghost.

CHAPTER 19

Faith in God

What Is Faith?

Faith bringeth salvation; miracles are wrought by faith; by faith the worlds were made. God is God because faith dwells in him independently; and faith is power, the very power of God himself. Any man who has faith in the Lord Jesus Christ, in the full and true sense, will sit down with him on his throne in the kingdom of his Father. All who do not gain this saving faith will fall short of that inheritance which might have been theirs had they believed and obeyed the word of faith. Oh, how great the importance to make these things known unto all men, that they may learn what faith is, how it may be gained, and the eternal rewards reserved for all who gain this blessed boon.

"In presenting the subject of faith," the Prophet Joseph Smith said, "we shall observe the following order—First, faith itself—what it is. Secondly, the object on which it rests. And, Thirdly, the effects which flow from it." (*Lectures on Faith* 1:2-5.) We shall build our house of faith on the foundation he laid. Our desire is to know and feel and be as he was.

What, then, is faith? In the broad, generic, and universal sense of the word, having no particular reference to religion and salvation, the Prophet tells us that faith "is the moving cause of all action . . . in all intelligent beings." All accountable and intelligent beings have faith in this sense. Such is part of life itself. Because this faith dwells in the hearts of all mankind, they sow with the assurance of reaping; they plant with the hope of harvesting; they exert themselves in the pursuit of knowledge, wisdom, and intelligence because they believe they can obtain them. Without this faith, "both mind and body would be in a state of inactivity, and all their exertions would cease, both physical and mental."

Faith as so defined is not saving faith; it does not lead to life and salvation; an assurance that crops will grow is not an assurance of a celestial inheritance. Saving faith centers in the Lord Jesus Christ and through him in the Father. "As faith is the moving cause of all action in temporal concerns," the Prophet continues, "so it is in spiritual. . . . As we receive by faith all temporal blessings that we do receive, so we in like manner receive by faith all spiritual blessings that we do receive." (*Lectures on Faith* 1:10-13.) Paul's statement that "faith is the substance [confidence or assurance] of things hoped for, the evidence [the demonstration or proof] of things not seen" (Hebrews 11:1), applies to both temporal and spiritual concerns.

But faith in its true signification is more than the moving cause pursuant to which men and angels act. It is also a principle of power. Faith is power. And where there is power, there is faith; and where there is no power, there is no faith. Thus, Joseph Smith continues: "Faith is not only the principle of action, but of power also, in all intelligent beings, whether in heaven or on earth." Faith applies in all spheres. All intelligent beings—be they gods, angels, spirits, or men—all operate by its power.

Thus, " 'Through faith we understand that the worlds were framed by the word of God, so that things which are seen were not made of things which do appear.' [Hebrews 11:3.] By this we understand that the principle of power which existed in the bosom of God, by which the worlds were framed, was faith; and that it is by reason of this principle of power existing in the Deity, that all created things exist; so that all things in heaven, on earth, or under the earth, exist by reason of faith as it existed in HIM." How came this earth into being? Whence came the sidereal heavens? the universe? and created things in all their varieties? The power that organizes chaotic matter; the power that sends worlds without number into governed orbits; the power that gives order and system, location and appointment, to worlds and life—that power is named faith. It is the power of God; it is the faith of God, the faith that dwells in him independently. "Had it not been for the principle of faith the worlds would never have been framed, neither would man have been formed of the dust." Nor, without faith, would any other form of life have been created.

What if there were no faith? That would mean no power would exist to create or to control. Faith "is the principle by which Jehovah works, and through which he exercises power over all temporal as well as eternal things. Take this principle or attribute—for it is an attribute—from the Deity, and he would cease to exist." Thus, if there is no faith, there is no power; if there is no power, there was no creation; if nothing exists, there is no God; or, conversely, if there is no God, there is nothing. And thus all things rest on the foundation of faith, and without faith there would be nothing.

"Who cannot see," the Prophet asks, "that if God framed the worlds by faith, that it is by faith that he exercises power over them, and that faith is the principle of power? And if the principle of power, it must be so in man as well as in the Deity?" (*Lectures on Faith* 1:13-17.) Truly, if all of God's acts are righteous, if his work is to bring to pass the immortality and eternal life of man, and if all of his works are performed by faith, it follows that whatever man does, in righteousness, to gain salvation must also be done by faith, "for whatsoever is not of faith is sin." (Romans 14:23.)

Thus: "It was by faith that the worlds were framed—God spake, chaos heard, and worlds came into order by reason of the faith there was in HIM. So with man also; he spake by faith in the name of God, and the sun stood still, the moon obeyed, mountains removed, prisons fell, lions' mouths were closed, the human heart lost its enmity, fire its violence, armies their power, the sword its terror, and death its dominion; and all this by reason of the faith which was in him. Had it not been for the faith which was in men, they might have spoken to the sun, the moon, the mountains, prisons, the human heart, fire, armies, the sword, or to death in vain!" What miracles and marvels are wrought by faith. And it is the same whether they are done by men or angels or gods; the same faith (power!) always brings to pass the same eventuality.

How, then, shall we define faith? Joseph Smith answers: "Faith [is] the first principle in revealed religion, and the foundation of all righteousness." "Faith . . . is the first great governing principle which has power, dominion, and authority over all things; by it they exist, by it they are upheld, by it they are changed, or by it they remain, agreeable to the will of God. Without it there is no power, and without power there could be no creation nor existence!" (*Lectures on Faith* 1:1, 22-24.)

Knowledge Precedes Faith

Queries: Which comes first, faith or knowledge? Is faith a vague and uncertain hope in something unseen that, as a sprouting seed, may grow into knowledge? Or is faith based on truth and knowledge? Is faith something that grows out of and comes because of a prior knowledge of the truth?

Answers: Faith is the child of knowledge. It is reserved for those only who first have knowledge; there neither is nor can be any faith until there is knowledge. No one can have faith in a God of whom he knows nothing. Faith is founded on truth; it is the offspring of truth; it can never exist alone and apart from the truth. No one can have faith unto life and salvation in a false god; no idol ever had power to raise the dead or stop the sun. And faith is power. It is true that faith in some doctrine or on some theological point may be imperfect; it is true that sproutings of either faith or knowledge can become perfect relative to that doctrine or concept. But faith itself—the great and eternal power that creates and governs and saves, faith unto life and salvation—saving faith grows out of knowledge and cannot come in any other way.

"Faith cometh by hearing," Paul says, "and hearing the word of God" taught by the power of the Holy Ghost. (Romans 10:17.) Faith comes to those only who receive the word of truth. Hence the gospel truism that "it pleased God by the foolishness of preaching to save them that believe." (1 Corinthians 1:21.) The gospel embraces all truth, and truth —nothing else—can bring salvation. Thus Alma says, "If ye have faith ye hope for things which are not seen, which are true." (Alma 32:21.) Indeed, faith is a hope in that which is not seen that is true, and there can be no faith in an unseen thing that is false. There is no power in falsehood. No one can have faith unto life and salvation in a god who is believed to be a spirit nothingness, or in a doctrine that denies the resurrection, or in a philosophy that postulates man's evolutionary evolvement from lower forms of life, or in anything that is not true.

Truth, diamond truth, is the rock foundation upon which faith rests, and no one can have faith in God or in any gospel truth unless and until he comes to a knowledge of whatever truth is involved.

With reference to saving faith, to faith in that God whose we are, to the faith by which the worlds were made and miracles are wrought, the Prophet taught: "Three things are necessary in order that any rational and intelligent being may exercise faith in God unto life and salvation. First, the idea that he actually exists. Secondly, a *correct* idea of his character, perfections, and attributes. Thirdly, an actual knowledge that the course of life which he is pursuing is according to his will."

That is to say: (1) There is a true and living God, the very being who created all things. (2) He has a certain character; he possesses specified attributes; he is the embodiment of all perfections. (3) Man may so live as to have an actual knowledge that he is conforming to the mind and will of the Lord. Faith comes to those who know these truths and who keep the commandments. Those who meet this standard gain faith unto life and salvation. Where there is a deficiency, in part or in whole, there faith is either weak or entirely wanting. "Without an acquaintance with these three important facts," the blessed word continues, "the faith of every rational being must be imperfect and unproductive; but with this understanding it can become perfect and fruitful, abounding in righteousness, unto the praise and glory of God the Father, and the Lord Jesus Christ." (*Lectures on Faith* 3:2-5.)

Knowing, then, that knowledge precedes faith, that faith is founded on truth, and that falsehood and error do not and cannot exercise any saving power, we are led to the inevitable conclusion that faith cannot be exercised contrary to the order of heaven. It takes the power of God (which is faith!) to bring to pass the immortality and eternal life of man. All progress, all science, all religion, even life itself, exist and are because of truth. And faith can only be exercised in conformity with true principles.

For instance: The Prophet, discoursing upon the great plan of redemption and the sacrifices offered to typify the atoning sacrifice of our Lord, explained that Abel's sacrifice was accepted because it conformed to the true pattern. Then he said: "Cain offered of the fruit of the ground, and was not accepted, because he could not do it in faith, he could have no faith, or could not exercise faith contrary to the plan of heaven. . . . As the sacrifice was instituted for a type, by which man was to discern the great Sacrifice which God had prepared, to offer a sacrifice contrary to that, no faith could be exercised, because redemption was not purchased in that way, nor the power of the atonement instituted after that order; consequently, Cain could have no faith; and whatsoever is not of faith, is sin." (*Teachings of the Prophet Joseph Smith,* p. 58.)

Similarly, no faith unto life and salvation can be exercised in any false doctrine, in any false ordinance, or in any false system of religion. If a man believes with all his heart that there will be no resurrection; if every hope in his heart cries out in favor of annihilation of both soul and body at death; if he believes with every fiber of his being and every thought of his mind that death ends all—it does not matter one particle in the eternal sense. He cannot have faith in a doctrine that denies the resurrection. The fact, the reality, the truth is, there will be a resurrection, and there is nothing any of us can do about it one way or the other. A hope in an unseen expectancy that is false does not bring into being a single scintilla of faith. There is no such thing as faith unto life and salvation in a false doctrine. No man can exercise the slightest faith in infant baptism, or in baptism by sprinkling, or in a sacramental ordinance that has departed from the primitive similitude established by the Lord Jesus. All such are contrary to the order of heaven. They are not based and grounded on eternal truth. And faith is a hope in that which is not seen which is true.

Faith and the Knowledge of God

God the Father, in the ultimate and final sense, is the Creator of all things. He is the creator of spirit men, of mortal men, and of immortal men. He created life and death and immortality and eternal life. He made the laws whereby spirit men gain mortality, and mortal men gain immortality, and faithful men gain eternal life. The power he uses in these and in all things is faith. Faith is power, and the power of God is the faith of God. "In him the principle of faith dwells independently, and he is the object in whom the faith of all other rational and accountable beings center for life and salvation." (*Lectures on Faith* 2:2.)

God the Father is an eternal being. The very name of the kind of life he lives is eternal life, and thus eternal life consists in living and being as he is. In other words, eternal life is to gain the power of God, which power is faith, and thus to be able to do what he does and to live as he lives. And the great and eternal plan of salvation that he has ordained and established consists of those laws, ordinances, and powers whereby faith is acquired and perfected until it is possessed in the same degree and to the same extent that it exists in Deity. Faith will thus dwell independently in every person who gains eternal life.

It follows that to gain eternal life, men must know God. They must believe in the true and living God and do the things that will enable them to become like him. Knowledge of God is the foundation upon which a house of faith is built. This knowledge begins with the assurance that he actually is, that he exists and is indeed the Self-Existent One, and that Deity is as real and literal and actual as any of the common verities of life. As we have seen, "the knowledge of the existence of God came into the world" when he revealed himself to Adam and the ancients. And "it was by reason of the knowledge of his existence that there was a foundation laid for the exercise of faith in him, as the only Being in whom faith could center for life and salvation; for faith could not center in a Being of whose existence we have no idea, because the idea of his existence in the first instance is essential to the exercise of faith in him." (*Lectures on Faith* 3:1.)

But by the knowledge of God is meant not simply that he exists and is a personal being in whose image man is made; not merely that he is a resurrected, glorified, and perfected man who has all power, all might, and all dominion; not the mere fact that he is the Father of spirits and as such lives in the family unit; rather, in addition to all this, by the knowledge of God is meant the very nature and kind of being that he is. The knowledge of God includes an understanding of his character, perfections, and attributes. If men are to become like him, they must know what his characteristics and attributes are so that they can begin the process of obtaining these very acquirements, endowments, and personality traits. As the Prophet taught: "God became an object of faith among men after the fall," in consequence of which multitudes were "stirred up . . .

to search after a knowledge of his character, perfections and attributes, until they became extensively acquainted with him," so that they could "not only commune with him and behold his glory, but [also] be partakers of his power and stand in his presence." (*Lectures on Faith* 2:34.)

Accordingly, as the Prophet expressed it, "We shall proceed to examine his character, perfections, and attributes, in order that [we] may see, not only the just grounds which they [the ancient saints] have for the exercise of faith in him for life and salvation, but the reasons that all the world, also, as far as the idea of his existence extends, may have to exercise faith in him, the Father of all living." (*Lectures on Faith* 3:6.)

CHAPTER 20

Faith and the
Nature of God

The Character of God

What is the nature and character of God? What kind and sort of being is he? What is his position, rank, and status, and as the Supreme Being, what qualities does he possess? His character as set forth in the revealed word is summarized by the Prophet under six headings:

1. *God is an eternal being.*

"He was God before the world was created, and the same God that he was after it was created." (*Lectures on Faith* 3:17.) "Before the mountains were brought forth, or ever thou hadst formed the earth and the world, even from everlasting to everlasting, thou art God." (Psalm 90:2.)

This attribute of the divine character is the basic foundation upon which faith rests, "for if [man] did not, in the first instance, believe him to be God, that is, the Creator and upholder of all things, he could not *center* his faith in him for life and salvation, for fear there should be greater than he who would thwart all his plans, and he, like the gods of the heathen, would be unable to fulfill his promises; but seeing he is God over all, from everlasting to everlasting, the Creator and upholder of all things, no such fear can exist in the minds of those who put their trust in him, so that in this respect their faith can be without wavering." (*Lectures on Faith* 3:19.)

2. *God is merciful and gracious.*

Joseph Smith taught: "He is merciful and gracious, slow to anger, abundant in goodness, and . . . he was so from everlasting, and will be to everlasting." (*Lectures on Faith* 3:14.) To Moses Deity said of himself: "The Lord, the Lord God, merciful and gracious, longsuffering, and abundant in goodness and truth." (Exodus 34:6.) In the Psalmic word we read: "The Lord executeth righteousness and judgment for all that are oppressed. . . . The Lord is merciful and gracious, slow to anger, and plenteous in mercy. . . . The mercy of the Lord is from everlasting to everlasting upon them that fear him, and his righteousness unto children's children; to such as keep his covenant, and to those that remember his commandments to do them." (Psalm 103:6, 8, 17-18.)

The relationship of these elements in the character of Deity to faith and the salvation that flows therefrom is set forth in these words: "Unless he was merciful and gracious, slow to anger, long-suffering and full of goodness, such is the weakness of human nature, and so great the frailties and imperfections of men, that unless they believed that these excellencies existed in the divine character, the faith necessary to salvation could not exist; for doubt would take the place of faith, and those who know their weakness and liability to sin would be in constant doubt of salvation if it were not for the idea which they have of the excellency of the character of God, that he is slow to anger and long-suffering, and of a forgiving disposition, and does forgive iniquity, transgression, and sin. An idea of these facts does away doubt, and makes faith exceedingly strong." (*Lectures on Faith* 3:20.)

3. *God is an unchangeable being.*

The teaching proclaimed in the School of the Prophets was: "He changes not, neither is there variableness with him; but . . . he is the same from everlasting to everlasting, being the same yesterday, to-day, and for ever; and . . . his course is one eternal round, without variation." (*Lectures on Faith* 3:15.) To this, the concurring voice of scripture attests: "God doth not walk in crooked paths, neither doth he turn to the right hand nor to the left, neither doth he vary from that which he hath said, therefore his paths are straight, and his course is one eternal round." (D&C 3:2.) The scriptures acclaim that he is a being "with whom is no variableness, neither shadow of turning" (James 1:17) and that his "course is one eternal round, the same today as yesterday, and forever" (D&C 35:1).

From these basic gospel truisms, our prophet-prepared source material concludes: "It is equally as necessary that men should have the idea that he is a God who changes not, in order to have faith in him, as it is to have the idea that he is gracious and long-suffering; for without the idea of unchangeableness in the character of the Deity, doubt would take the place of faith. But with the idea that he changes not, faith lays hold upon the excellencies in his character with unshaken confidence, believing he is the same yesterday, to-day, and forever, and that his course is one eternal round." (*Lectures on Faith* 3:21.)

4. *God is truthful.*

What a simple yet wondrous truth this is. "God is not a man, that he should lie." (Numbers 23:19.) "He is a God of truth and cannot lie." (*Lectures on Faith* 3:22.) God tells the truth! "Thy word," O God, "is truth." (John 17:17.)

And from this basic verity comes this conclusion relative to faith: "The idea that he is a God of truth and cannot lie, is equally as necessary to the exercise of faith in him as the idea of his unchangeableness. For without the idea that he was a God of truth and could not lie, the confidence necessary to be placed in his word in order to the exercise of faith in him could not exist. But having the idea that he is not man, that he cannot lie, it gives power to the minds of men to exercise faith in him." (*Lectures on Faith* 3:22.)

5. *God is impartial.*

"He is no respecter of persons; but in every nation he that fears God and works righteousness is accepted of him." (*Lectures on Faith* 3:17.) These words are but a restatement of what Peter said in the house of Cornelius. (Acts 10:34-35.) And Paul said simply: "There is no respect of persons with God." (Romans 2:11.)

As to gaining faith in God, the conclusion is: In addition to all other aspects of his character, "it is also necessary that men should have an idea that he is no respecter of persons, for with the idea of all the other excellencies in his character, and this one wanting, men could not exercise faith in him; because if he were a respecter of persons, they could not tell what their privileges were, nor how far they were authorized to exercise faith in him, or whether they were authorized to do it at all, but all must be confusion; but no sooner are the minds of men made acquainted with the truth on this point, that he is no respecter of persons, than they see that they have authority by faith to lay hold on eternal life, the richest boon of heaven, because God is no respecter of persons, and that every man in every nation has an equal privilege." (*Lectures on Faith* 3:23.)

6. *God is a loving being.*

"He is love." (*Lectures on Faith* 3:18.) As to this attribute in his character, John says: "He that loveth not knoweth not God; for God is love." (1 John 4:8.)

And in setting forth the relationship between this element of his character and the acquiring of faith in Deity, the Prophet taught: "Not less important to the exercise of faith in God," than all the other attributes in his character, "is the idea that he is love; for with all the other excellencies in his character, without this one to influence them, they could not have such powerful dominion over the minds of men; but when the idea is planted in the mind that he is love, who cannot see the just ground that men of every nation, kindred, and tongue have to exercise faith in God so as to obtain eternal life?" (*Lectures on Faith* 3:24.)

Having thus summarized the teachings of God's greatest latter-day prophet relative to the character of God, we need only set forth his general conclusion with reference thereto. It is: "An acquaintance with these attributes in the divine character, is essentially necessary, in order that the faith of any rational being can center in him for life and salvation." And further: A knowledge "of the character of the Deity," as thus set forth, "is a sure foundation for the exercise of faith in him among every people, nation, and kindred, from age to age, and from generation to generation." (*Lectures on Faith* 3:19, 25.)

The Attributes of God

The character of God and his attributes are all interwoven to form one grand tapestry. His attributes are the qualities of his character. They are the elements of character that are attributed or ascribed to him in the revealed word; they are the elements that are inherent in his person, as, for instance, that he is merciful.

After teaching the true doctrine as to the character of God, and by way of introduction to his teachings about the attributes of Deity, the Prophet Joseph Smith laid this foundation: "Having shown . . . that correct ideas of the character of God are necessary in order to the exercise of faith in him unto life and salvation," he said, "and that without correct ideas of his character the minds of men could not have sufficient power with God to the exercise of faith necessary to the enjoyment of eternal life; and that correct ideas of his character lay a foundation, as far as his character is concerned, for the exercise of faith, so as to enjoy the fulness of the blessing of the gospel of Jesus Christ, even that of eternal glory; we shall now proceed to show the connection there is between correct ideas of the attributes of God, and the exercise of faith in him unto eternal life."

A *correct* understanding of the attributes of God—how eternally important this is to the gaining of faith and salvation! "Let us here observe," the powerful word continues, "that the real design which the God of heaven had in view in making the human family acquainted with his attributes, was, that they, through the ideas of the existence of his attributes, might be enabled to exercise faith in him, and, through the exercise of faith in him, might obtain eternal life; for without the idea of the existence of the attributes which belong to God the minds of men could not have power to exercise faith on him so as to lay hold upon eternal life."

Such wondrous gifts as faith and eternal life are not bestowed upon unworthy recipients. Man must prepare and qualify himself to receive them. "The God of heaven, understanding most perfectly the constitution of human nature, and the weakness of man, knew what was necessary to be revealed, and what ideas must be planted in their minds in order that they might be enabled to exercise faith in him unto eternal life. Having said so much, we shall proceed to examine the attributes of God, as set forth in his revelations to the human family," the Prophet continues, "and to show how necessary correct ideas of his attributes are to enable men to exercise faith in him; for without these ideas being planted in the minds of men it would be out of the power of any person or persons to exercise faith in God so as to obtain eternal life. So that the divine communications made to men in the first instance were designed to establish in their minds the ideas necessary to enable them to exercise faith in God, and through this means to be partakers of his glory." (*Lectures on Faith* 4:1-3.)

The chief attributes of God are many; they include every godly and uplifting quality. The Prophet Joseph Smith chose the six chief ones to show the relationship between faith and a knowledge of the attributes of God. We shall name these six and show how and why a correct understanding of each one must be gained in order to have faith unto life and salvation. They are:

1. *Knowledge.*

Does God know all things? He does. Is there anything he does not know? There is not. Is he progressing in knowledge and learning new truths? He is not. He is not a student God. His knowledge and supremacy are *not* limited to a sphere or realm beyond which there are higher spheres and greater realms. He is an Eternal God, an infinite being, an omniscient man, one in whose person all knowledge, all power, and all truth center.

Be it remembered: He created the universe; the sidereal heavens are the works of his hands; all things, animate and inanimate, life in all its forms and varieties, life on all worlds, all things exist and are governed by him. Envision worlds without number; think of earths more numerous than the particles of dust on this planet and on millions of other like spheres: all this is but a beginning to the number of his creations. And he has given a law unto all things. Need anyone be foolish enough to suppose that such a being does not know all things and have all power?

A belief that there is or might be another being greater and more powerful than God of itself precludes the exercise of full faith in him. And so Joseph Smith taught: "Without the knowledge of all things God would not be able to save any portion of his creatures; for it is by reason of the knowledge which he has of all things, from the beginning to the end, that enables him to give that understanding to his creatures by which they are made partakers of eternal life; and if it were not for the idea existing in the minds of men that God had all knowledge it would be impossible for them to exercise faith in him." (*Lectures on Faith* 4:11.)

2. *Faith or power.*

It is with faith or power as it is with knowledge. God himself is the very embodiment of this attribute. His infinite knowledge gives him infinite power. None can stay his hand.

There is nothing greater to create than one universe upon another with all the forms of life found in them. What laws require more power than those that govern worlds and spheres and all forms of life? God himself is the Author of it all. Unless men know that God has all power (which power is itself faith), it is not possible for them to exercise faith in him unto life and salvation. The reasoning is as follows: "Unless God had power over all things, and was able by his power to control all things, and thereby deliver his creatures who put their trust in him from the power of all beings that might seek their destruction, whether in heaven, on earth, or in hell, men could not be saved." Salvation comes by power; it is the power of God that brings to pass the immortality and eternal life of man, and the very gospel of salvation is defined as the power of God unto salvation. "But with the idea of the existence of this attribute [power or faith] planted in the mind, men feel as though they had nothing to fear who put their trust in God, believing that he has power to save all who come to him to the very uttermost." (*Lectures on Faith* 4:12.)

3. *Justice.*

"It is also necessary, in order to the exercise of faith in God unto life and salvation, that men should have the idea of the existence of the attribute justice in him." That which is just is right and proper. It is true; it conforms to spiritual law; it is righteous before God. Justice is the administration and the maintenance of that which is just and right. Justice, therefore, deals with the unbending, invariable results that always and ever flow from the same causes. Fairness, impartiality, perfect rectitude, complete integrity, righteousness itself— all of these are inherent in justice. The whole tenor of the scriptures is that God is just and that justice and judgment are the habitation of his throne.

And "without the idea of the existence of the attribute justice in the Deity men could not have confidence sufficient to place themselves under his guidance and direction; for they would be filled with fear and doubt lest the judge of all the earth would not do right, and thus fear or doubt, existing in the mind, would preclude the possibility of the exercise of faith in him for life and salvation. But when the idea of the existence of the attribute justice in the Deity is fairly planted in the mind, it leaves no room for doubt to get into the heart, and the mind is enabled to cast itself upon the Almighty without fear and without doubt, and with most unshaken confidence, believing that the Judge of all the earth will do right." (*Lectures on Faith* 4:13.)

4. *Judgment.*

"It is also of equal importance that men should have the idea of the existence of the attribute of judgment in God, in order that they may exercise faith in him for life and salvation." As with justice, so with judgment, the whole tone and tenor of holy writ attests that "the Lord is a God of judgment." (Isaiah 30:18.) Judgment consists in the power to arrive at a wise and righteous decision and in the execution of that decision, to the blessing of the righteous and the condemnation of the wicked. In its perfect form, judgment is the very decree and mandate and sentence of that God who is judge of all.

And "without the idea of the existence of this attribute in the Deity, it would be impossible for men to exercise faith in him for life and salvation, seeing that it is through the exercise of this attribute that the faithful in Christ Jesus are delivered out of the hands of those who seek their destruction; for if God were not to come out in swift judgment against the workers of iniquity and the powers of darkness, his saints could not be saved; for it is by judgment that the Lord delivers his saints out of the hands of all their enemies, and those who reject the gospel of our Lord Jesus Christ." How perfect the Prophet's reasoning is!

What effect does it have on the minds and acts of men when they come to know that judgment is an attribute of God? "No sooner is the idea of the existence of this attribute planted in the minds of men," the reasoning continues, "than it gives power to the mind for the exercise of faith and confidence in God, and they are enabled by faith to lay hold on the promises which are set before them, and wade through all the tribulations and afflictions to which they are subjected by reason of the persecution from those who know not God, and obey not the gospel of our Lord Jesus Christ, believing that in due time the Lord will come out in swift judgment against their enemies, and they shall be cut off from before him, and that in his own

due time he will bear them off conquerors, and more than conquerors, in all things." (*Lectures on Faith* 4:14.)

5. *Mercy.*

Along with the other attributes of his character, "it is
equally important that men should have the idea of the existence of the attribute mercy in the Deity, in order to exercise
faith in him for life and salvation." God is merciful. "His mercy
endureth for ever." (Psalm 106:1.) He is compassionate. His
compassion knows no bounds. His mercy is manifest in a
divine forbearance, on certain specified conditions, from
imposing punishments that, except for his goodness and grace,
would be the just reward of man.

All men have sinned; all must pay the penalty for their sins.
Punishment always follows sin; otherwise there would be no
sin. Thus, all men are subject to justice, and all must pay the
price for their wayward works. That is, all men would pay the
penalty for their own sins, all would suffer a just punishment
for their transgressions, all would be subject to the law of
justice, if it were not for the law of mercy.

Mercy is a gift of God bestowed bounteously upon the
penitent. It is reserved for those who repent. In their case,
mercy appeases the demands of justice; it frees men from the
penalty of sin. Thus saith the Lord: "If ye will repent, and
harden not your hearts, then will I have mercy upon you,
through mine Only Begotten Son; therefore, whosoever
repenteth, and hardeneth not his heart, he shall have claim on
mercy through mine Only Begotten Son, unto a remission of
his sins; and these shall enter into my rest." (Alma 12:33-34.)
Thus the great and eternal plan of redemption operates in the
lives of men, on conditions of repentance and because of the
mercy of God.

And thus, the Prophet reasons: "Without the idea of the
existence of this attribute [mercy!] in the Deity, the spirits of
the saints would faint in the midst of the tribulations, afflictions, and persecutions which they have to endure for righteousness' sake. But when the idea of the existence of this
attribute is once established in the mind it gives life and energy
to the spirits of the saints, believing that the mercy of God will
be poured out upon them in the midst of their afflictions, and
that he will compassionate them in their sufferings, and that

the mercy of God will lay hold of them and secure them in the arms of his love, so that they will receive a full reward for all their sufferings." (*Lectures on Faith* 4:15.)

6. *Truth.*

We have heretofore set forth the great and eternal verity that faith is a hope in that which is not seen which is true; that faith is founded and grounded on the bedrock of truth, and upon nothing else; and that men must come to a knowledge of the truth about God and his laws before they can have faith in him. Now we shall see that men must believe that truth is an attribute of God before they can have faith in him. "Not less important to the exercise of faith in God," than all the other attributes we have considered, "is the idea of the existence of the attribute truth in him," our account recites.

The Lord is a God of truth. He is the "Lord God of truth." (Psalm 31:5.) His law, his commandments, his word, his scriptures—all are truth. Truth is that which really is. It includes a knowledge of things as they are, as they were, and as they shall be; it is absolute and eternal; it endures forever. It is not relative; it does not vary; it never changes. What is true in one eternity is true in the next. All progress, all enlightenment, all salvation—everything that is good and right grows out of and comes because of truth. If there were no invariable truths, if truth changed from age to age, or from world to world, or from universe to universe, all would be confusion and chaos and disorganization. Life and matter themselves would be without form and void, and God, no longer controlling all things, would cease to be God.

"For without the idea of the existence of this attribute [in God] the mind of man could have nothing upon which it could rest with certainty—all would be confusion and doubt. But with the idea of the existence of this attribute in the Deity in the mind, all the teachings, instructions, promises, and blessings, become realities, and the mind is enabled to lay hold of them with certainty and confidence, believing that these things, and all that the Lord has said, shall be fulfilled in their time; and that all the cursings, denunciations, and judgments, pronounced upon the heads of the unrighteous, will also be executed in the due time of the Lord; and, by reason of the truth and veracity of him, the mind beholds its deliverance and salvation as being certain." (*Lectures on Faith* 4:16.)

The Perfections of God

The perfections of God—what are they? And what must we know relative to them in order to have faith unto life and salvation? Our exposition as to the nature and kind of being in whom our faith centers has already shown that God is the only supreme governor and independent being, in whom all fulness and perfection dwell; that he is omnipotent, omniscient, and omnipresent; and that in him every good gift and every good principle dwell independently. Having set forth the character and attributes of God, the inspired account we are now studying says: "What we mean by perfections is, the perfections which belong to all the attributes of [God]." (*Lectures on Faith* 5:1.)

Thus, by the perfections of God is meant that he is the embodiment—totally, completely, and perfectly—of every good thing. He is the possessor of every good gift, of all uplifting attributes, of all edifying graces, all in their eternal fulness. We speak thus in the infinite and unlimited sense. All of the attributes of godliness are resident in the person of Deity in their entirety, in their transcendence, in their holiness. His is the totality, the wholeness, the completeness of every attribute. God does not fall short and is not wanting in anything.

After setting forth the six chief attributes of God, as we have listed them, the Prophet Joseph Smith counseled: "Let the mind once reflect sincerely and candidly upon the ideas of the existence of the before-mentioned attributes in the Deity, and it will be seen that, as far as his attributes are concerned, there is a sure foundation laid for the exercise of faith in him for life and salvation." By way of summary and recapitulation, he continues:

1. *As to knowledge:*

"For inasmuch as God possesses the attribute knowledge, he can make all things known to his saints necessary for their salvation." But be it known, the attribute of knowledge must exist in Deity in perfection, and he must be recognized as knowing all things. Unless men conceive of God as knowing all things, they cannot have faith in him to a sufficient degree to gain eternal life.

2. *As to power:*

"And as he possesses the attribute power, he is able

thereby to deliver them from the power of all enemies." The power is omnipotence; it is the power that made man and all things, and that upholds, preserves, and maintains the endless worlds and all that in them are. How could man have infinite faith in anything less than an infinite being? God's perfection in this field consists in having all power, all might, and all dominion.

3. *As to justice:*

"And seeing, also, that justice is an attribute of the Deity, he will deal with them upon the principles of righteousness and equity, and a just reward will be granted unto them for all their afflictions and sufferings for the truth's sake." Again the issue is whether Deity enjoys the named attribute in all its glory and perfection. Does he fall short with reference to charity, love, honesty, integrity, benevolence, or any good thing? Is there some degree of any of these that he has not yet obtained? Who will contend that the Judge of all the earth falls short in the field of justice? Will the Almighty act capriciously by dealing justly with his saints in one age and failing to reward others in another age for like sufferings and afflictions? The answers are self-evident.

4. *As to judgment:*

"And as judgment is an attribute of the Deity also, his saints can have the most unshaken confidence that they will, in due time, obtain a perfect deliverance out of the hands of all their enemies, and a complete victory over all those who have sought their hurt and destruction." To question the righteousness and rectitude of the judgments of God is to deny his divinity. If he were deficient in judgment, if his judgments were less than perfect, if he dealt capriciously and without sense and reason—how could he be a divine being? God is God because of the perfections existing in all of the attributes of his nature.

5. *As to mercy:*

"And as mercy is also an attribute of the Deity, his saints can have confidence that it will be exercised towards them, and through the exercise of that attribute towards them comfort and consolation will be administered unto them abundantly, amid all their afflictions and tribulations." Salvation is the child of mercy. It is because of the great plan of mercy that sinful men become clean and are fit candidates to go where God and Christ are. Mercy tempers justice to claim penitent persons; if it were not so, all men would be lost, for all have sinned. Suppose God did not possess all mercy, or that men did not know he was a merciful being; would they then turn to him for remission of their sins, relying wholly on the merits of Him who is mighty to save? Truly, unless men know that mercy is in God in all its glory, fulness, and perfection, they would not and could not exercise faith in him unto life and salvation.

6. *As to truth:*

"And, lastly, realizing that truth is an attribute of the Deity, the mind is led to rejoice amid all its trials and temptations, in hope of that glory which is to be brought at the revelation of Jesus Christ, and in view of that crown which is to be placed upon the heads of the saints in the day when the Lord shall distribute rewards unto them, and in prospect of that eternal weight of glory which the Lord has promised to bestow upon them, when he shall bring them into the midst of his throne to dwell in his presence eternally." Truth, glorious, pure, diamond truth; truth, the eternal foundation upon which all things rest; truth, the eternal verity that controls and governs in time and in eternity—take truth away and what would remain? All would be chaos; anarchy would rule; chance and happenstance would replace the Father and the Son. And unless fallen man can turn to a God in whom all fulness and perfection dwell and who is the possessor of all truth, how can he be expected to have faith? If Deity does not possess all truth, how long will it be before he learns a new truth that will lead to the death of all life and the end of an organized universe?

"In view, then, of the existence of these attributes"—*they being present in their eternal fulness and perfection*—"the faith of the saints can become exceedingly strong, abounding in righteousness unto the praise and glory of God." Such faith, faith like that possessed by the ancients, "can exert its mighty influence in searching after wisdom and understanding, until it has obtained a knowledge of all things that pertain to life and salvation."

Can man gain faith unto life and salvation without an understanding of the character, perfections, and attributes of God? The answer is, No. Such knowledge "is the foundation which is laid, through the revelation of the attributes of God, for the exercise of faith in him for life and salvation; and seeing that these are the attributes of the Deity, they are unchangeable—being the same yesterday, to-day, and for ever—which gives to the minds of the Latter-day Saints the same power and authority to exercise faith in God which the Former-day saints had; so that all the saints, in this respect, have been, are, and will be, alike until the end of time; for God never changes, therefore his attributes and character remain forever the same. And as it is through the revelation of these that a foundation is laid for the exercise of faith in God unto life and salvation, the foundation, therefore, for the exercise of faith was, is, and ever will be, the same; so that all men have had, and will have, an equal privilege." (*Lectures on Faith* 4:17-19.)

CHAPTER 21

Faith in the Lord Jesus Christ

Faith Centers in Christ

Thus far in our analysis of faith we have spoken primarily of faith in God without differentiating between the Father and the Son. Nor has it been necessary so to do, for faith in one is faith in the other. Joseph Smith taught that the Father is the author of the plan of salvation and of the law of faith that is part of this great and eternal plan. This plan has become Christ's by adoption, and he has put all its terms and conditions into full operation through his infinite and eternal atonement.

To gain salvation, men must come unto the Father, attain the faith that he exercises, and be as he is. Christ has done so; he is both a saved being and the perfect and only illustration of what others must do to gain like inheritances and be joint-heirs with him. He is thus the way to the Father; no man cometh unto the Father but by him and by his word. He is our Mediator, Advocate, and Intercessor, all because he wrought out the perfect atonement through the shedding of his own blood. Through him, and through him only, fallen men may be reconciled to God if they repent and work righteousness.

Christ and his Father are one. They possess the same powers, are of the same character, embody the same attributes, and stand as beacons to all others with reference to the same eternal perfections. The words and acts of one are the words and acts of the other. The Father was in Christ manifesting himself to the world. Hence, faith in the Son is faith in the Father. And as Christ is the way to the Father, faith centers in him and in his redeeming sacrifice and goes thereby to the Father, who is the Creator.

We do not single Christ out and set him apart from the

Father; our prayers do not go through him to the Father; he does not stand alone as a person with whom we do or should have some special relationship that excludes the other members of the Godhead. We are commanded in the revealed word to worship the Father, in the name of the Son, by the power of the Holy Ghost. We are the spirit children of the Father, as is Christ, and our objective is to do what Christ did and thus become like the Father. Elohim is our God and he is Christ's God. The Son worships the Father, as we are commanded to do; if there is any being with whom we should feel a special kinship, it is with the Father. But Christ as the Only Begotten in the flesh, as the Redeemer, as the Savior, has made salvation possible and has become one with the Father. Thus salvation is in Christ; faith centers in him; and faithful saints have power to become like him and be as he is, even as he is as his Father.

Growing in Faith

One man and one man only had perfect faith. He was the Lord Jesus, and his faith was perfect because he lived a life of perfection. None others have ever done so. He alone knew no sin. His every word and act conformed to a divine standard; from Bethlehem to Calvary, the light of heaven guided his deeds and placed words in his mouth. None of the residue of men have ever walked in such an upright course. But all faithful people have the desire, born of the Spirit, to grow in faith and be more like him. All the saints desire to increase in faith and godliness. His ancient apostles, for instance, said to him: "Increase our faith." Such of his reply as is recorded tells them not how to increase their faith, but the power that will be theirs if they do so. "If ye had faith as a grain of mustard seed," Jesus responded, "ye might say unto this sycamine tree, Be thou plucked up by the root, and be thou planted in the sea; and it should obey you." (Luke 17:5-6.)

These ancient apostles had faith. They knew Jesus was the Son of God, and they had already preached and would yet preach the gospel and work miracles. Faith was theirs because they worshipped the true God and had a knowledge of his character, attributes, and perfections. We also stand where they stood. We have forsaken the creeds of Christendom and believe in those Holy Beings who appeared to Joseph Smith in the spring of 1820. We have proper views as to their character, attributes, and perfections. What must we yet do to gain faith unto life and salvation? The answer is found in these words of the Prophet Joseph Smith: "An actual knowledge to any person, that the course of life which he pursues is according to the will of God, is essentially necessary to enable him to have that confidence in God without which no person can obtain eternal life." (*Lectures on Faith* 6:2.)

Faith is born of knowledge. It first breathes the breath of life in the hearts of those who believe in God and who know what kind of a being he is. Then, as a newborn baby, it begins to grow by obedience to the laws of the Lord. It reaches full maturity when its possessor, through righteousness, gains the assurance that his way of life conforms to the divine will.

Faith in its full and pure form requires an unshakable assurance and an absolute confidence that Deity will hear our pleas and grant our petitions. It requires a mental guarantee, sealed with surety in the soul, that what we ask is right and will be granted. Only then can we "come boldly unto the throne of grace," there to "obtain mercy, and find grace to help in time of need." (Hebrews 4:16.) And it scarcely needs stating that no person can have this confidence and assurance when he knows he is not living in the way the Lord wants him to live.

According to the Prophet, it was this knowledge of conformity to divine standards, and the resultant oneness it created between man and his Maker, "that enabled the ancient saints to endure all their afflictions and persecutions, and to take joyfully the spoiling of their goods, knowing (not believing merely) that they had a more enduring substance. (Hebrews 10:34.) Having the assurance that they were pursuing a course which was agreeable to the will of God, they were enabled to take, not only the spoiling of their goods, and the wasting of their substance, joyfully, but also to suffer death in its most horrid forms; knowing (not merely believing) that when this earthly house of their tabernacle was dissolved, they had a building of God, a house not made with hands, eternal in the heavens. (2 Corinthians 5:1.)"

And if it was thus among the ancients, whom we so highly revere, should it not be the same among us? In answer, the

Prophet's account attests: "Such was, and always will be, the situation of the saints of God, that unless they have an actual knowledge that the course they are pursuing is according to the will of God they will grow weary in their minds, and faint; for such has been, and always will be, the opposition in the hearts of unbelievers and those that know not God against the pure and unadulterated religion of heaven (the only thing which insures eternal life), that they will persecute to the uttermost all that worship God according to his revelations, receive the truth in the love of it, and submit themselves to be guided and directed by his will; and drive them to such extremities that nothing short of an actual knowledge of their being the favorites of heaven, and of their having embraced that order of things which God has established for the redemption of man, will enable them to exercise that confidence in him, necessary for them to overcome the world, and obtain that crown of glory which is laid up for them that fear God." (*Lectures on Faith* 6:2-4.)

Sacrificing to Gain Faith

In this mortal probation, as pilgrims far from their heavenly home, the saints are called upon to put first in their lives the things of God's kingdom and to let the things of this world sink into a place of relative insignificance. If their hearts are set upon worldly things, including lands and money and power, their reward will come in the currency of the world. It is only when men's hearts are set on heavenly things, when they lay up treasures in heaven, where neither moth nor rust doth corrupt and where thieves do not break through and steal, that they are paid in the currency of heaven.

The trials and tests of mortality are designed to determine whether men will use their time and talents in worldly or spiritual pursuits. The crowning test in this field is the test of sacrifice. The Lord's saints must be willing, if called upon to do so, to sacrifice all that they have, including life itself, in their pursuit of eternal life. It is to them that this promise of Jesus applies: "Every one that hath forsaken houses, or brethren, or sisters, or father, or mother, or wife, or children, or lands, for my name's sake, shall receive an hundredfold, and shall inherit everlasting life." (Matthew 19:29.)

Nowhere in all our literature is the law of sacrifice set forth with such clarity and power as is found in these words of Joseph Smith: "For a man to lay down his all, his character and reputation, his honor, and applause, his good name among men, his houses, his lands, his brothers and sisters, his wife and children, and even his own life also—counting all things but filth and dross for the excellency of the knowledge of Jesus Christ—requires more than mere belief or supposition that he is doing the will of God; but actual knowledge, realizing that, when these sufferings are ended, he will enter into eternal rest, and be a partaker of the glory of God. For unless a person does know that he is walking according to the will of God, it would be offering an insult to the dignity of the Creator were he to say that he would be a partaker of his glory when he should be done with the things of this life. But when he has this knowledge, and most assuredly knows that he is doing the will of God, his confidence can be equally strong that he will be a partaker of the glory of God."

Faith and sacrifice go hand in hand. Those who have faith sacrifice freely for the Lord's work, and their acts of sacrifice increase their faith. "Let us here observe," the Prophet continues, "that a religion that does not require the sacrifice of all things never has power sufficient to produce the faith necessary unto life and salvation; for, from the first existence of man, the faith necessary unto the enjoyment of life and salvation never could be obtained without the sacrifice of all earthly things. It was through this sacrifice, and this only, that God has ordained that men should enjoy eternal life; and it is through the medium of the sacrifice of all earthly things that men do actually know that they are doing the things that are well pleasing in the sight of God."

We do not say that no person will gain eternal life unless and until he sacrifices all things, life included. If such were the case, there would be no saved beings except the martyrs whose blood is spilt in the cause of truth and righteousness. But we do say that all who receive so great a reward must be willing to forsake their all if called upon to do so. "When a man has offered in sacrifice all that he has for the truth's sake, not even withholding his life," our account continues, "and believing before God that he has been called to make this sacrifice because he seeks to do his will, he does know, most assuredly, that God does and will accept his sacrifice and offering, and that he has not, nor will not seek his face in vain. Under these circumstances, then, he can obtain the faith necessary for him to lay hold on eternal life."

To gain the same faith and inherit the same reward enjoyed by the saints of old, we must live and sacrifice as they did. "It is vain for persons to fancy to themselves that they are heirs with those, or can be heirs with them, who have offered their all in sacrifice, and by this means obtained faith in God and favor with him so as to obtain eternal life, unless they, in like manner, offer unto him the same sacrifice, and through that offering obtain the knowledge that they are accepted of him."

Addressing himself to the Latter-day Saints, who in holy places "have made a covenant" of sacrifice with the Lord, the Prophet continues: "Those, then, who make the sacrifice, will have the testimony that their course is pleasing in the sight of God; and those who have this testimony will have faith to lay hold on eternal life, and will be enabled, through faith, to endure unto the end, and receive the crown that is laid up for them that love the appearing of our Lord Jesus Christ. But those who do not make the sacrifice cannot enjoy this faith, because men are dependent upon this sacrifice in order to obtain this faith: therefore, they cannot lay hold upon eternal life, because the revelations of God do not guarantee unto them the authority so to do, and without this guarantee faith could not exist."

Thus, it is with the true believers today as it has been with their counterparts in former days. "All the saints of whom we have account, in all the revelations of God which are extant, obtained the knowledge which they had of their acceptance in his sight through the sacrifice which they offered unto him; and through the knowledge thus obtained their faith became sufficiently strong to lay hold upon the promise of eternal life, and to endure as seeing him who is invisible; and were enabled, through faith, to combat the powers of darkness, contend against the wiles of the adversary, overcome the world, and obtain the end of their faith, even the salvation of their souls."

What of the saints, no matter what age they live in, who are not willing to offer their all upon the Lord's altar? "Those who have not made this sacrifice to God do not know that the course which they pursue is well pleasing in his sight; for whatever may be their belief or their opinion, it is a matter of doubt and uncertainty in their mind; and where doubt and uncertainty are there faith is not, nor can it be. For doubt and faith do not exist in the same person at the same time; so that persons whose minds are under doubts and fears cannot have unshaken confidence; and where unshaken confidence is not there faith is weak; and where faith is weak the persons will not be able to contend against all the opposition, tribulations, and afflictions which they will have to encounter in order to be heirs of God, and joint heirs with Christ Jesus; and they will grow weary in their minds, and the adversary will have power over them and destroy them." (*Lectures on Faith* 6:5-12.)

Working by Faith

How do men exercise faith? If they have an occasion to heal the sick, raise the dead, or move mountains, how is it done? Faith is power, but what causes the power to flow forth and accomplish the desired result? As an introductory explanation, the account we are studying asks: "What are we to understand by a man's working by faith?"

By way of answer, the account says: "We understand that when a man works by faith he works by mental exertion instead of physical force. It is by words, instead of exerting his physical powers, with which every being works when he works by faith. God said, 'Let there be light: and there was light.' Joshua spake and the great lights which God had created stood still. Elijah commanded, and the heavens were stayed for the space of three years and six months, so that it did not rain: he again commanded and the heavens gave forth rain. All this was done by faith. And the Saviour says: 'If you have faith as a grain of mustard seed, say to this mountain, "Remove," and it will remove; or say to that sycamine tree, "Be ye plucked up, and planted in the midst of the sea," and it shall obey you.' Faith, then, works by words; and with these its mightiest works have been, and will be performed." (*Lectures on Faith* 7:3.)

But working by faith is not the mere speaking of a few well-

191

chosen words; anyone with the power of speech could have commanded the rotting corpse of Lazarus to come forth, but only one whose power was greater than death could bring life again to the brother of Mary and Martha. Nor is working by faith merely a mental desire, however strong, that some eventuality should occur. There may be those whose mental powers and thought processes are greater than any of the saints, but only persons who are in tune with the Infinite can exercise the spiritual forces and powers that come from him.

Those who work by faith must first have faith; no one can use a power that he does not possess, and the faith or power must be gained by obedience to those laws upon which its receipt is predicated. These we have set forth. Those who work by faith must believe in the Lord Jesus Christ and in his Father. They must accept at face value what the revealed word teaches as to the character, attributes, and perfections of the Father and the Son. They must then work the works of righteousness until they know within themselves that their way of life conforms to the divine will, and they must be willing to lay their all on the altar of the Almighty.

And then—when the day is at hand and the hour has arrived for the miracle to be wrought—then they must be in tune with the Holy Spirit of God. He who is the Author of faith, he whose power faith is, he whose works are the embodiment of justice and judgment and wisdom and all good things, even he must approve the use of his power in the case at hand. Faith cannot be exercised contrary to the order of heaven or contrary to the will and purposes of him whose power it is. Men work by faith when they are in tune with the Spirit and when what they seek to do by mental exertion and by the spoken word is the mind and will of the Lord.

CHAPTER 22

The Fruits of Faith

The Eternal Fruits of Faith

Faith is known by its fruits—on earth, in heaven, everywhere. Where the fruits of faith are found, there is faith; where there are no fruits, there is no faith. It is an eternal law of the universe that like begets like, that every tree brings forth after its own kind, and that the tree of faith bears, always and everlastingly, the fruit of faith. It is no more possible to pick the fruit of faith from the tree of unbelief than it is to harvest grapes from bramble bushes or figs from thistles.

There is no better way to envision the infinite and eternal nature of faith than to see its infinite and eternal fruits, the fruits that transcend the bounds of our lone earth. Thus we find the Prophet Joseph Smith saying that the effects of faith "embrace all things in heaven and on earth, and encompass all the creations of God, with all their endless varieties." How, we ask, can faith have such immanent, indwelling, ever-present, omnipotent power? We hear the answer: "No world has yet been framed that was not framed by faith, neither has there been an intelligent being on any of God's creations who did not get there by reason of faith as it existed in himself or in some other being"—worlds are created and men are saved by faith!—"nor has there been a change or a revolution in any of the creations of God, but it has been effected by faith; neither will there be a change or a revolution, unless it is effected in the same way, in any of the vast creations of the Almighty, for it is by faith that the Deity works."

Thus, faith precedes and accompanies all things. It is as near to being the First Great Cause of which philosophers speak as anything can be. Let the wise and the learned speak of the laws of nature or of the universe; in reality, as the weak and the simple know, they are viewing the effects of faith, the faith that dwells independently in the Supreme Being. And thus the fruits of faith include this earth and all earths, our atmospheric heavens and the sidereal heavens, and all forms of life that have existed and do exist in every sphere of life, whether temporal or spiritual.

"It surely will not be required of us to prove that this [faith] is the principle upon which all eternity has acted and will act," the Prophet reasons, "for every reflecting mind must know that it is by reason of this power that all the hosts of heaven perform their works of wonder, majesty, and glory. Angels move from place to place by virtue of this power; it is by reason of it that they are enabled to descend from heaven to earth; and were it not for the power of faith they never could be ministering spirits to them who should be heirs of salvation, neither could they act as heavenly messengers, for they would be destitute of the power necessary to enable them to do the will of God." Thus, it is by faith that gods and angels live and move and have their being. It is by faith that the Lord God Omnipotent operates and performs his wondrous works. It is by faith that the universe was created and is upheld and preserved.

"It is only necessary for us to say that the whole visible creation, as it now exists, is the effect of faith. It was faith by which it was framed, and it is by the power of faith that it continues in its organized form, and by which the planets move round their orbits and sparkle forth their glory." All that God does is done by the power of faith. "So, then, faith is truly the first principle in the science of THEOLOGY, and, when understood, leads the mind back to the beginning, and carries it forward to the end; or, in other words, from eternity to eternity." (*Lectures on Faith* 7:2, 4-5.)

Faith Among Mortals

"As faith, then, is the principle by which the heavenly hosts perform their works, and by which they enjoy all their felicity," our account continues, "we might expect to find it set forth in a revelation from God as the principle upon which his creatures here below must act in order to obtain the felicities enjoyed by the saints in the eternal world." How can

mortals become either gods or angels unless they obtain the
same powers, the same attributes, and the same holiness that
such eternal beings now possess? God is God and angels are
angels because they possess the powers and perfections that
now are theirs. If men gain these same states of glory and
exaltation, can they do it without becoming like those who already have so inherited? *implied answer "yes"*

God created all men in his own image—physically, men-
tally, morally, spiritually. His offspring inherited from him the
power and ability to become like him. Men are patterned after
their Eternal Father, and if they ever become as their Maker,
they must gain the same faith or power embodied in the Deity.
To the extent that fallen men gain faith, they become like God
and exercise his power. To the extent that they live in unbelief,
they are without God in the world, do not exercise his power,
are not in process of becoming like him, and cannot and will
not be saved.

"Therefore it is said, and appropriately too, that 'Without
faith it is impossible to please God.' If it should be
asked—Why is it impossible to please God without faith? The
answer would be—Because without faith it is impossible for
men to be saved; and as God desires the salvation of men, he
must, of course, desire that they should have faith; and he
could not be pleased unless they had, or else he could be
pleased with their destruction. From this we learn that the
many exhortations which have been given by inspired men, to
those who had received the word of the Lord to have faith in
him, were not mere common-place matters, but were for the
best of all reasons, and that was—because without it there was
no salvation, neither in this world nor in that which is to
come." The two alternatives that face all men are salvation or
damnation. Though there are degrees of each, any who fall
short of becoming as God is fail to inherit eternal life, which
status is the fulness of salvation.

"When men begin to live by faith they begin to draw near
to God; and when faith is perfected they are like him; and
because he is saved they are saved also; for they will be in the
same situation he is in, because they have come to him; and
when he appears they shall be like him, for they will see him as
he is. As all the visible creation is an effect of faith, so is
salvation also." Manifestly there neither is nor can be anything

greater than God. If men become like him, they ascend the throne of eternal power, are exalted to the highest state that exists in all the endless expanse of created things, and are themselves gods. Thus salvation is not only the greatest of all the gifts of God, it is also the chief and most glorious of all the fruits of faith.

At this point our account asks: "What situation must a person be in in order to be saved? or what is the difference between a saved man and one who is not saved?" In describing saved beings, the Prophet's words attest: "They must be persons who can work by faith and who are able, by faith, to be ministering spirits to them who shall be heirs of salvation; and they must have faith to enable them to act in the presence of the Lord, otherwise they cannot be saved. And what constitutes the real difference between a saved person and one not saved is—the difference in the degree of their faith—one's faith has become perfect enough to lay hold upon eternal life, and the other's has not." (*Lectures on Faith* 7:6-9.)

Here on earth we are far removed from our heavenly home and can know only by revelation of the laws that prevail in that holy place. To the extent that we accept and obey the divine laws that prevail in that realm whence we came, we gain faith and thus prepare ourselves to return to the presence of Him whose we are. And salvation, as we have and shall set forth, is to be like Christ and inherit, receive, and possess as he does in the kingdom of the Father.

Faith Like the Ancients

Faith unto life and salvation has dwelt in the hearts of righteous men from the days of Adam to the present moment. They have overcome the world, and amid suffering and sorrow, and even death, they have pursued the one and only course back to the presence of Him by whom faith comes. Indeed, as it is written: "Through the whole history of the scheme of life and salvation, it is a matter of faith." It is faith, and faith alone, that opens the door to peace in this life and eternal life in the world to come. Beginning with father Adam and continuing down through all succeeding generations, "every man [has] received according to his faith—according as his faith was, so were his blessings and privileges; and nothing was withheld from him when his faith was sufficient to receive it." How could it be otherwise when faith is the power of God?

Thus, of all and any who had faith, it is written: "He could stop the mouths of lions, quench the violence of fire, escape the edge of the sword, wax valiant in fight, and put to flight the armies of the aliens; women could, by their faith, receive their dead children to life again; in a word, there was nothing impossible with them who had faith. All things were in subjection to the Former-day Saints, according as their faith was. By their faith they could obtain heavenly visions, the ministering of angels, have knowledge of the spirits of just men made perfect, of the general assembly and church of the first born, whose names are written in heaven, of God the judge of all, of Jesus the Mediator of the new covenant, and become familiar with the third heavens, see and hear things which were not only unutterable, but were unlawful to utter." (*Lectures on Faith* 7:17.)

An account of the faith of the ancients has been preserved in holy writ to serve as a pattern for us. What God did for them, he will do for us; in like circumstances and when importuned with like faith, the same unchangeable God will always respond in the same way. A miracle today need be no different than a miracle anciently. A soul is just as precious in the sight of the Lord today as it has ever been. And what matter the perils of the present and the future if we have faith in God? His power can and will preserve the faithful now as in days gone by, all in harmony with his will and purposes. Let us, then, bring into holy remembrance the faith of the ancients.

By faith, Adam, dwelling in the peace and serenity of Eden, chose to fall that mortal man might be; this he did knowing that such a course opened the door to immortality and eternal life. By faith, he offered sacrifices, received revelations, entertained angels, and learned of the great plan of redemption. By faith, he assembled his righteous posterity in the valley of Adam-ondi-Ahman, where the Lord appeared unto them all, and where Adam "being full of the Holy Ghost, predicted whatsoever should befall his posterity unto the latest generation." (D&C 107:56.)

By faith, Enoch walked with God, founded a City of Holiness called Zion, and with his whole city was translated and taken up into heaven without tasting death. "And so great was the faith of Enoch, that he led the people of God, and their enemies came to battle against them; and he spake the word of the Lord, and the earth trembled, and the mountains fled, even according to his command; and the rivers of water were turned out of their course; and the roar of the lions was heard out of the wilderness; and all nations feared greatly, so powerful was the word of Enoch, and so great was the power of the language which God had given him." (Moses 7:13.)

By faith, Noah preached the gospel, prepared an ark, and saved seed through the flood. And as to Melchizedek, he was like unto Enoch. Of him the holy word says: "Now Melchizedek was a man of faith, who wrought righteousness; and when a child he feared God, and stopped the mouths of lions, and quenched the violence of fire. And thus, having been approved of God, he was ordained an high priest after the order of the covenant which God made with Enoch, it being after the order of the Son of God; which order came, not by man, nor the will of man; neither by father nor mother; neither by beginning of days nor end of years; but of God; and it was delivered unto men by the calling of his own voice, according to his own will, unto as many as believed on his name." The priesthood here spoken of is called the *Holy Priesthood, after the Order of the Son of God,* which we and the ancient saints call the *Melchizedek Priesthood,* to avoid the too frequent repetition of the name of Deity.

It is of this Melchizedek Priesthood and of all the faithful ones who hold it that the scripture attests: "For God having sworn unto Enoch and unto his seed with an oath by himself; that every one being ordained after this order and calling should have power, by faith, to break mountains, to divide the seas, to dry up waters, to turn them out of their course; to put at defiance the armies of nations, to divide the earth, to break every band, to stand in the presence of God; to do all things according to his will, according to his command, subdue principalities and powers; and this by the will of the Son of God which was from before the foundations of the world. And men having this faith, coming up unto this order of God, were translated and taken up into heaven." (JST, Genesis 14:26-32.)

By faith, Abraham "looked forth and saw the days of the Son of Man, and was glad, and his soul found rest, and he believed in the Lord; and the Lord counted it unto him for righteousness." (JST, Genesis 15:12.) Through faith, Abraham, Isaac, and Jacob, each in turn, received promises concerning their seed. With them Jehovah covenanted that their seed, the fruit of their loins, should continue, both in the world and out of the world, as many as the stars in the sky or innumerable as the sand upon the seashore. Each of them, by faith, gained the divine promise that in them and in their seed all generations should be blessed and that their seed after them should have the right to the priesthood and to the gospel and to eternal life.

By faith, Moses caused the waters of the Red Sea to part, to congeal, and to form a wall of water on the right hand and on the left, that the fleeing Israelites might escape the chariots of Pharaoh. By faith, he fed the chosen seed with manna from heaven for forty years, during all of which time their clothes did not wear out and their shoes did not wax old. By faith, and to prepare them to receive their Messiah, he gave them the law that bears his name, and finally, like Enoch and those whose faith moved mountains, Moses the man of God was translated and taken into heaven without tasting death.

All of these things and other miracles without number have been wrought by faith by the prophets and saints of all dispensations. And always faith precedes the miracle; always the power of faith performs the miracle; always the miracle proves that faith was present and in active operation. For instance: "The brother of Jared said unto the mountain Zerin, Remove—and it was removed." Those few words tell all we know about what must have been a mighty struggle of one of earth's greatest prophets. To them Moroni appends the rather wry understatement: "And if he had not had faith it would not have moved." (Ether 12:30.)

"Faith is things which are hoped for and not seen," Moroni says; "wherefore, dispute not because ye see not, for ye receive no witness until after the trial of your faith." Some may suppose that the various miracles and historical events recorded in the scriptures took place simply because of some divine providence being shown forth in the lives of men. True it is that divine providence controls the destinies of men and nations, but behind each miracle is divine power, and that power is named faith. "For it was by faith that Christ showed himself unto our fathers, after he had risen from the dead,"

Moroni continues; "and he showed not himself unto them until after they had faith in him." That is, the Risen Lord came to the Nephites because they had faith, not simply to fulfill a divine providence that called, for instance, for his teachings to be preserved for us in the Book of Mormon.

After his resurrection "he showed himself *not* unto the world" in general, only to those who were prepared by faith to feel the nail marks in his hands and in his feet and to thrust their hands into his riven side. "But because of the faith of men he has shown himself unto the world," that is, unto those in the world who had faith, and he has "glorified the name of the Father, and prepared a way that thereby others might be partakers of the heavenly gift, that they might hope for those things which they have not seen. Wherefore, ye [meaning us and all men] may also have hope, and be partakers of the gift, if ye will but have faith."

As to faith among the ancients, our inspired author continues: "Behold it was by faith that they of old were called after the holy order of God. Wherefore, by faith was the law of Moses given. But in the gift of his Son hath God prepared a more excellent way; and it is by faith that it hath been fulfilled. For if there be no faith among the children of men God can do no miracle among them; wherefore, he showed not himself until after their faith."

Moroni speaks of the faith of Alma and Amulek "that caused the prison to tumble to the earth"; of the faith of Nephi and Lehi "that wrought the change upon the Lamanites, that they were baptized with fire and with the Holy Ghost"; of the faith of Ammon and his brethren "which wrought so great a miracle among the Lamanites." Then he makes this all-comprehensive, prophetic declaration: "Yea, and even all they who wrought miracles wrought them by faith, even those who were before Christ and also those who were after." There neither has been, nor is, nor ever shall be an exception to this eternal law. God never changes, and his laws are everlastingly the same.

As his crowning illustration of faith among mortals, Moroni names the translation of the Three Nephites. "And it was by faith that the three disciples obtained a promise that they should not taste of death," he says, "and they obtained not the promise until after their faith." What greater miracle could there be among us mortals than the miracle of translation? What power but the power of God can extend the life of mortal man on earth for thousands of added years? And what power does Deity possess except the power of faith?

And out of it all, our inspired author reaches this grand conclusion: "And neither at any time hath any wrought miracles until after their faith; wherefore they first believed in the Son of God." (Ether 12:6-18.) Truly, as the Lord Jesus said: "All things are possible to him that believeth." (Mark 9:23.)

CHAPTER 23

Faith and Salvation

Faith and Miracles

Faith and salvation are linked together everlastingly. They attend and strengthen each other and are perfectly united in all things. By faith, salvation comes, and salvation is nothing more and nothing less than perfect faith in active operation. God is a saved being because faith dwells in him independently, and men will be saved when they become like God and faith dwells in them independently. Hence, mortals who are in process of gaining salvation are in process of perfecting their faith. The gospel is the law and system whereby men grow in faith until they gain salvation. And thus, where the gospel is, there is faith; and where faith is, there will be the fruits of faith. Hence, signs and miracles always attend, identify, and bless true believers.

"When faith comes," the Prophet Joseph Smith taught, "it brings its train of attendants with it—apostles, prophets, evangelists, pastors, teachers, gifts, wisdom, knowledge, miracles, healings, tongues, interpretation of tongues, etc. All these appear when faith appears on the earth, and disappear when it disappears from the earth; for these are the effects of faith, and always have attended, and always will, attend it. For where faith is, there will the knowledge of God be also, with all things which pertain thereto—revelations, visions, and dreams, as well as every necessary thing, in order that the possessors of faith may be perfected, and obtain salvation; for God must change, otherwise faith will prevail with him. And he who possesses it will, through it, obtain all necessary knowledge and wisdom, until he shall know God, and the Lord Jesus Christ, whom he has sent—whom to know is eternal life." (*Lectures on Faith* 7:20.)

Our Blessed Lord, ministering to the Nephites in resurrected glory, gave this divine promise: "Whatsoever ye shall ask the Father in my name, which is right, believing that ye shall receive, behold it shall be given unto you." (3 Nephi 18:20.) Nearly four hundred years later Mormon gave this rendition of Jesus' promise: "Whatsoever thing ye shall ask the Father in my name, which is good, in faith believing that ye shall receive, behold, it shall be done unto you." Thus, all true believers, in all ages, who ask the Father, in the name of Christ, in faith, for anything that is *right* and *good* shall receive that which they desire. In this connection the inspired account of Mormon preserves for us these words of Christ: "If ye will have faith in me ye shall have power to do whatsoever thing is expedient in me."

What, then, is the destiny of those who have faith? It is to work miracles while in this mortal probation and to gain eternal life in the estate ahead. Of them the scripture says, Christ "claimeth all those who have faith in him." None such shall be lost; all who have faith will be saved.

How may those who have faith be known? What witness do they bear that sets them apart from the masses of men? "They who have faith in him [Christ] will cleave unto every good thing," Mormon says. Signs will attend their mortal ministries and angels will minister unto them while they yet dwell on earth.

Faith and angels go together. "Angels," according to the Book of Mormon account, show "themselves unto them of strong faith and a firm mind in every form of godliness." Why do they minister unto men? "The office of their ministry is to call men unto repentance, and to fulfill and to do the work of the covenants of the Father, which he hath made unto the children of men, to prepare the way among the children of men, by declaring the word of Christ unto the chosen vessels of the Lord, that they may bear testimony of him. And by so doing, the Lord God prepareth the way that the residue of men may have faith in Christ, that the Holy Ghost may have place in their hearts, according to the power thereof; and after this manner bringeth to pass the Father, the covenants which he hath made unto the children of men."

Mormon, whose words we are quoting, viewing the decadent and fallen religions of an apostate world, breaks forth with these words of doctrine and of warning: "It is by faith that miracles are wrought." There is no other way. "And it is by faith that angels appear and minister unto men." Without faith they remain hidden from mortal eyes. "Wherefore, if these things have ceased wo be unto the children of men, for it is because of unbelief, and all is vain. For no man can be saved, according to the words of Christ, save they shall have faith in his name." Faith and salvation go together. "Wherefore, if these things"—the working of miracles and the ministering of angels—"have ceased, then has faith ceased also; and awful is the state of man, for they are as though there had been no redemption made." Without faith they cannot be redeemed from their spiritual fall and they remain forever cast out of the presence of the Lord. Such is Mormon's evaluation of apostate peoples and of those who belong to other churches than the Lord's. And having so stated, he says of those who have forsaken the world and taken upon themselves the name of Christ: "If ye have not faith in him then ye are not fit to be numbered among the people of his church." (Moroni 7:26-39.)

"Miracles are the fruits of faith," the Prophet said. "Faith comes by hearing the word of God. If a man has not faith enough to do one thing, he may have faith to do another: if he cannot remove a mountain, he may heal the sick. Where faith is there will be some of the fruits: all gifts and power which were sent from heaven, were poured out on the heads of those who had faith." (*History of the Church* 5:355.) Also: "Because faith is wanting, the fruits are. No man since the world was had faith without having something along with it. The ancients quenched the violence of fire, escaped the edge of the sword, women received their dead, etc. By faith the worlds were made. A man who has none of the gifts has no faith; and he deceives himself, if he supposes he has. Faith has been wanting, not only among the heathen, but in professed Christendom also, so that tongues, healings, prophecy, and prophets and apostles, and all the gifts and blessings have been wanting." (*History of the Church* 5:218.)

Signs Attend True Believers

Moroni raises his voice alongside that of his father, Mormon, in proclaiming the gospel truths relative to faith, miracles, and signs. As "an unchangeable Being," by whose power miracles have been wrought from the beginning, Deity is "a God of miracles," he says. "And the reason why he ceaseth to do miracles among the children of men is because that they dwindle in unbelief, and depart from the right way, and know not the God in whom they should trust." There is no such thing as faith unto life and salvation in a false god. Either men believe in the true and living God or they wear out their lives in faithless unbelief.

"Behold, I say unto you," Moroni continues, "that whoso believeth in Christ, doubting nothing, whatsoever he shall ask the Father in the name of Christ it shall be granted him; and this promise is unto all, even unto the ends of the earth. For behold, thus said Jesus Christ, the Son of God, unto his disciples who should tarry [the Three Nephites who were translated], yea, and also to all his disciples, in the hearing of the multitude: Go ye into all the world, and preach the gospel to every creature; and he that believeth and is baptized shall be saved, but he that believeth not shall be damned." This is the same commission given the apostles who were with Jesus in Jerusalem. The message to all men was and is and ever shall be that salvation is in Christ and his holy gospel. Believe the true gospel and be saved; believe a false gospel and receive a lesser reward.

But how is the true gospel to be known? One voice cries out that Christ and salvation are here; another affirms they are there. There is unending discord and division among men, including those who profess to be Christians. To his legal administrators on both continents Jesus said: "And these signs shall follow them that believe—in my name shall they cast out devils; they shall speak with new tongues; they shall take up serpents; and if they drink any deadly thing it shall not hurt them; they shall lay hands on the sick and they shall recover; and whosoever shall believe in my name, doubting nothing, unto him will I confirm all my words, even unto the ends of the earth." (Mormon 9:19-25; Mark 16:14-20.)

Signs follow true believers! Miracles are the fruits of faith! Healings and gifts of the Spirit are always found in the true church! Where these are, there is the gospel that saves; where these are not, any supposed system of salvation has no saving power. Faith and signs are inseparably connected. There is no such thing as having one without the other.

The law governing faith and signs is eternal and everlasting; it is the same in all ages and among all peoples, and it has been given to us in our day in these words: "It shall come to pass that he that hath faith in me to be healed," saith the Lord, "and is not appointed unto death, shall be healed." The exercise of faith is always subject to the overriding providences of the Lord. If it is the will of the Lord to take one of his children from this life to the next, then the Lord's will prevails. Faith cannot be exercised contrary to the order and will of heaven. Nevertheless, "he who hath faith to see shall see. He who hath faith to hear shall hear. The lame who hath faith to leap shall leap. And they who have not faith to do these things, but believe in me"—the Lord is speaking— "have power to become my sons; and inasmuch as they break not my laws thou shalt bear their infirmities." (D&C 42:48-52.)

To his people in these last days, the Lord has promised that signs shall follow those who truly believe. "But a commandment I give unto them," he cautions and warns, "that they shall not boast themselves of these things, neither speak them before the world; for these things are given unto you for your profit and for salvation." (D&C 84:73.)

As faith *precedes* the miracle, so signs *follow* those who believe. Belief comes first; then its fruits are shown forth. Hence the saints seek faith, not signs. "Faith cometh not by signs, but signs follow those that believe. Yea, signs come by faith, not by the will of men, nor as they please, but by the will of God. Yea, signs come by faith, unto mighty works, for without faith no man pleaseth God; and with whom God is angry he is not well pleased; wherefore, unto such he showeth no signs, only in wrath unto their condemnation." (D&C 63:9-11.)

Being One with Christ

To be saved is to be like Christ, inheriting, receiving, and possessing as he does. To gain salvation is to grow in faith until we have the faith of Christ and thus are like him. Our nearness to him and to salvation is measured by the degree of our faith. To gain faith is to attain the power of Christ, which is God's power. To believe in Christ in the full and true sense is to "have the mind of Christ" (1 Corinthians 2:16), that is, to believe what he believes, think what he thinks, say what he says, and do what he does. It is to be one with him by the power of the Holy Ghost.

What say the scriptures about being one with Christ? "By faith," Mormon says, we "become the sons of God." (Moroni 7:26.) Speaking of true believers, John says: "Now are we the sons of God, and it doth not yet appear what we shall be: but we know that, when he shall appear, we shall be like him; for we shall see him as he is. And every man that hath this hope in him purifieth himself, even as he is pure." (1 John 3:2-3.) "Ye shall be holy," the Lord says to his saints, "for I the Lord your God am holy." (Leviticus 19:2.) As Christ "which hath called you is holy," Peter pleads with the saints, "so be ye holy." (1 Peter 1:15.) And the great exhortation of the Lord Jesus himself is: "I would that ye should be perfect even as I, or your Father who is in heaven is perfect." (3 Nephi 12:48.)

Why must those who seek salvation pursue the course charted in these scriptures? Because if they do not, they cannot be like Christ. If they are not pure as he is pure, "holy, as he is holy, and perfect, as he is perfect, they cannot be like him; for no being can enjoy his glory without possessing his perfections and holiness, no more than they could reign in his kingdom without his power." (*Lectures on Faith* 7:10.)

It is on the basis of these principles that men are able to do the works of Christ. "He that believeth on me," Jesus said, "the works that I do shall he do also; and greater works than these shall he do; because I go unto my Father." (John 14:12.) When and why and how can men do greater works than the Lord Jesus did when he ministered among men? The answers are found in his great Intercessory Prayer. "Holy Father, keep through thine own name those whom thou hast given me," Jesus prayed, "that they may be one, as we are." The apostles are to be one with the Father and the Son. "Neither pray I for these alone," the Lord continued, "but for them also which shall believe on me through their word; that they all may be one; as thou, Father, art in me, and I in thee, that they also may be one in us: that the world may believe that thou hast sent me." All true believers, all who have faith, all the saints, all the righteous of all the ages are to be one with the Father and the Son.

Then of the Twelve, Jesus prayed: "And the glory which

thou gavest me I have given them; that they may be one, even as we are one: I in them, and thou in me, that they may be made perfect in one; and that the world may know that thou hast sent me, and hast loved them, as thou hast loved me. Father, I will that they also, whom thou hast given me, be with me where I am; that they may behold my glory, which thou hast given me: for thou lovedst me before the foundation of the world." (John 17:11, 20-24.)

After quoting the scriptures that we have quoted, the Prophet Joseph Smith said: "All these sayings put together give as clear an account of the state of the glorified saints as language could give—the works that Jesus had done they were to do, and greater works than those which he had done among them should they do, and that because he went to the Father. He does not say that they should do these works in time; but they should do greater works, because he went to the Father." That is to say: "The greater works which those that believed on his name were to do were to be done in eternity, where he was going and where they should behold his glory." They were to be done by those who were one with him and his Father. "For he declares to his Father, in language not to be easily mistaken, that he wanted his disciples, even all of them, to be as himself and the Father, for as he and the Father were one so they might be one with them."

Jesus is thus saying "that unless they have the glory which the Father had given him they could not be one with them; for he says he had given them the glory that the Father had given him that they might be one; or, in other words, to make them one. . . . They were to be partakers with him in all things, not even his glory excepted."

What is this New Testament doctrine but a proclamation that as God now is, man may become? Continuing his exposition of such a transcendent and glorious concept, Joseph Smith says that "the glory which the Father and the Son have is because they are just and holy beings; and that if they were lacking in one attribute or perfection which they have, the glory which they have never could be enjoyed by them, for it requires them to be precisely what they are in order to enjoy it; and if the Saviour gives this glory to any others, he must do it in the very way set forth in his prayer to his Father—by making them one with him as he and the Father are one. In so doing he would give them the glory which the Father has given him; and when his disciples are made one with the Father and Son, as the Father and the Son are one, who cannot see the propriety of the Saviour's saying—The works that I do shall he do also; and greater works than these shall he do; because I go to my Father."

What, then, is the relationship between faith and salvation? "These teachings of the Saviour most clearly show unto us the nature of salvation," the Prophet continues, "and what he proposed unto the human family when he proposed to save them—that he proposed to make them like unto himself, and he was like the Father, the great prototype of all saved beings; and for any portion of the human family to be assimilated into their likeness is to be saved; and to be unlike them is to be destroyed; and on this hinge turns the door of salvation. Who cannot see, then, that salvation is the effect of faith? for, as we have previously observed, all the heavenly beings work by this principle; and it is because they are able so to do that they are saved, for nothing but this could save them. And this is the lesson which the God of heaven, by the mouth of all his holy prophets, has been endeavouring to teach to the world."

Thus, we see "the light in which the Saviour, as well as the Former-day Saints, viewed the plan of salvation. That it was a system of faith—it begins with faith, and continues by faith; and every blessing which is obtained in relation to it is the effect of faith, whether it pertains to this life or that which is to come. To this all the revelations of God bear witness. If there were children of promise, they were the effects of faith, not even the Saviour of the world excepted." (*Lectures on Faith* 7:12-17.)

Faith and Knowledge

In the eternal sense, because faith is the power of God himself, it embraces within its fold a knowledge of all things. This measure of faith, the faith by which the worlds are and were created and which sustains and upholds all things, is found only among resurrected persons. It is the faith of saved beings. But mortals are in process, through faith, of gaining eternal salvation. Their faith is based on a knowledge of the truth, within the meaning of Alma's statement that "faith is not to have a perfect knowledge of things," but that men have faith when they "hope for things which are not seen, which are true." In this sense faith is both preceded and supplanted by knowledge, and when any person gains a perfect knowledge on any given matter, then, as pertaining to that thing, he has faith no longer; or, rather, his faith is dormant; it has been supplanted by pure knowledge. (See Alma 32:21-34.)

Once the saints gain faith, because they have believed in the true and living God, their assured hope in the unseen is the basis by which they may acquire knowledge; that is, they gain knowledge by faith. Thus, Peter said to those saints who had "obtained like precious faith" with the apostles: "Grace and peace be multiplied unto you through the knowledge of God, and of Jesus our Lord, according as his divine power hath given unto us all things that pertain unto life and godliness, through the knowledge of him that hath called us to glory and virtue." (2 Peter 1:1-3.)

Thus, for those who desire to gain all things that pertain to life and godliness, the great issue is one of coming to know God in the full and true sense of the word. In expounding upon this, our modern prophet said: "How were they to obtain the knowledge of God? (for there is a great difference between believing in God and knowing him—knowledge implies more than faith. And notice, that all things that pertain to life and godliness were given through the knowledge of God) the answer is given—through faith they were to obtain this knowledge; and, having power by faith to obtain the knowledge of God, they could with it obtain all other things which pertain to life and godliness. By these sayings of the apostle, we learn that it was by obtaining a knowledge of God that men got the knowledge of all things which pertain to life and godliness, and this knowledge was the effect of faith; so that all things which pertain to life and godliness are the effects of faith."

Building, then, on this foundation, the Prophet set forth this concept: "From this we may extend as far as any circumstances may require, whether on earth or in heaven, and we will find it the testimony of all inspired men, or heavenly messengers, that all things that pertain to life and godliness are the effects of faith and nothing else; all learning, wisdom and prudence fail, and every thing else as a means of salvation but faith. . . . This is the reason that the Former-day Saints knew more, and understood more, of heaven and of heavenly things than all others beside, because this information is the effect of faith—to be obtained by no other means. And this is the reason that men, as soon as they lose their faith, run into strifes, contentions, darkness, and difficulties; for the knowledge which tends to life disappears with faith, but returns when faith returns." (*Lectures on Faith* 7:20.)

The brother of Jared stands out as a good illustration of how the knowledge of God is gained by faith, and also of how that perfect knowledge, from a mortal perspective, replaces faith. He received the most complete revelation of the Lord Jesus Christ that had been given down to his day. After recording some of the details of this incomparable outpouring of divine truth, Moroni says: "And because of the knowledge of this man he could not be kept from beholding within the veil; and he saw . . . the finger of the Lord; and he had faith no longer, for he knew, nothing doubting. Wherefore, having this perfect knowledge of God, he could not be kept from within the veil; therefore he saw Jesus; and he did minister unto him." And further: "The Lord . . . showed unto the brother of Jared all the inhabitants of the earth which had been, and also all that would be; and he withheld them not from his sight, even unto the ends of the earth. For he had said unto him in times before, that if he would believe in him that he could show unto him all things—it should be shown unto him; therefore the Lord could not withhold anything from him, for he knew that the Lord could show him all things." (Ether 3:19-20, 25-26.)

"And there were many whose faith was so exceedingly strong, even before Christ came, who could not be kept from within the veil, but truly saw with their eyes the things which they had beheld with an eye of faith, and they were glad." (Ether 12:19.)

CHAPTER 24

The Doctrine of Repentance

The Philosophy of Repentance

How and in what manner does repentance fit into the eternal scheme of things? What part does it play in the plan of salvation? Why did the Lord provide a system of salvation under which men must forsake their sins if they are to be reconciled to him? Is repentance something to be shunned and avoided because it would curtail the seeming delicacies of a carnal way of life? Or is it a heaven-sent boon—greatly to be desired, ardently to be sought—that will enable us to escape the sorrows of the world and find peace and joy with Christ? What is the doctrine of repentance?

Before sinners can repent and gain the inestimable blessings that flow therefrom, they must come to a knowledge of the plan of salvation. Before they can free themselves from the bondage of sin and rejoice in the liberty of the Lord, they must know the part repentance plays in the gospel plan.

God is a holy and pure being who is entirely free from sin. As such, he is a saved being; and because he is saved, he has a fulness of joy and is a being in whom all fulness and perfection dwell. Man, created in the image of God, has been given power to become like his Maker. But in his present state man is carnal, sensual, and devilish by nature; in his fallen state he is subject to the world. In order to gain salvation he must triumph over the fall; he must rise above the carnality of the world; he must free himself from sin. Then and then only can he become like God and be saved as God is saved. And repentance is the process and means and way whereby this freedom from sin and this eternal salvation may be gained. Hence, repentance is essential to salvation, and without repentance there can be no salvation.

There are two things that come, universally and without exception, to all accountable beings. These are sin and death. Paul said: "As by one man sin entered into the world, and death by sin; and so death passed upon all men, for that all have sinned." (Romans 5:12.) Also: "There is none righteous, no, not one." (Romans 3:10.) And one of the ancient preachers of righteousness said: "There is not a just man upon earth, that doeth good, and sinneth not." (Ecclesiastes 7:20.) Because of the atoning sacrifice of the Lord Jesus, all men will be raised in immortality, thus overcoming death. Those who believe and obey will also be raised "unto eternal life." But "they that believe not" shall be raised "unto eternal damnation; for they cannot be redeemed from their spiritual fall, because they repent not." (D&C 29:43-44.) That God who "cannot look upon sin with the least degree of allowance" (Alma 45:16) will not bear the sins of the unrepentant.

To Adam, by whom sin and death entered the world, the Lord said: "Inasmuch as thy children are conceived in sin," that is, are born into a world where sin and death reign, "even so when they begin to grow up, sin conceiveth in their hearts, and they taste the bitter, that they may know to prize the good. And it is given unto them to know good from evil; wherefore they are agents unto themselves, and I have given unto you another law and commandment. Wherefore teach it unto your children, that all men, everywhere, must repent, or they can in nowise inherit the kingdom of God, for no unclean thing can dwell there, or dwell in his presence." (Moses 6:55-57.)

Thus, to enable men to escape the bondage of sin, God provided a plan of redemption, a plan of mercy, a plan of repentance. In expounding how this plan operates, Alma says that "Adam did fall," and that "by his fall, all mankind became a lost and fallen people." He says that through the fall "death comes upon mankind," meaning that all men die a natural or a temporal death. However, "there was a space granted unto man in which he might repent; therefore this life became a probationary state; a time to prepare to meet God; a time to prepare for that endless state which . . . is after the resurrection of the dead." Mortality, he says, thus becomes a "preparatory state," a day of trial and testing, a day for repentance. And thus "God did call on men, in the name of his

Son, (this being the plan of redemption which was laid) saying: If ye will repent, and harden not your hearts, then will I have mercy upon you, through mine Only Begotten Son; therefore, whosoever repenteth, and hardeneth not his heart, he shall have claim on mercy through mine Only Begotten Son, unto a remission of his sins; and these shall enter into my rest." (Alma 12:22-34.) Thus the doctrine and philosophy underlying the prophetic calls to repentance invite men to be reconciled to God, through Christ, by repentance.

The Atonement and Repentance

Repentance is made available to men through the atoning sacrifice of the Lord Jesus Christ. It is granted (Acts 11:18) or given as a gift from God to those who believe in Christ and who seek to live in harmony with the laws of the gospel. "The goodness of God leadeth [men] to repentance." (Romans 2:4.) The gift itself is reserved for those who abide the law that entitles them to receive it. How foolish it is to suppose that God would give so great a boon—repentance, salvation, becoming as he is!—except to those who obey the laws which entitle them so to inherit!

Of himself Jesus said: "The Son of man is come to seek and to save that which was lost." (Luke 19:10.) Paul said: "Christ Jesus came into the world to save sinners." (1 Timothy 1:15.) Salvation is in Christ; his is the only name given under heaven whereby salvation comes, and salvation is available through "the gospel of repentance" (D&C 13) and through obedience to all his holy laws. "For, behold, the Lord your Redeemer suffered death in the flesh; wherefore he suffered the pain of all men, that all men might repent and come unto him. And he hath risen again from the dead, that he might bring all men unto him, on conditions of repentance. And how great is his joy in the soul that repenteth!" (D&C 18:11-13.) Such pronouncements as these have been the burden of the prophetic word from the beginning—all showing that salvation comes because of the atonement and through repentance.

After offering sacrifices in "similitude of the sacrifice of the Only Begotten of the Father," Adam received these divine words from an angel: "Thou shalt do all that thou doest in the name of the Son, and thou shalt repent and call upon God in the name of the Son forevermore." (Moses 5:7-8.) After reminding his sons that Christ "should come to redeem his people, but that he should not come to redeem them in their sins, but to redeem them from their sins," Helaman said: "And he hath power given unto him from the Father to redeem them from their sins because of repentance." Without repentance there can be no redemption from the spiritual fall. "Therefore he hath sent his angels to declare the tidings of the conditions of repentance." Those conditions we have and shall set forth. By complying with them, men are brought "unto the power of the Redeemer, unto the salvation of their souls." (Helaman 5:10-11.)

Amulek said that because of the atonement, mercy could overpower justice and enable men to "have faith unto repentance." Accordingly, he continued, "mercy can satisfy the demands of justice, and encircles them in the arms of safety, while he that exercises no faith unto repentance is exposed to the whole law of the demands of justice; therefore only unto him that has faith unto repentance is brought about the great and eternal plan of redemption." (Alma 34:15-16.) Alma spoke similarly: "According to justice," he said, "the plan of redemption could not be brought about, only on conditions of repentance of men in this probationary state, yea, this preparatory state; for except it were for these conditions, mercy could not take effect except it should destroy the work of justice. Now the work of justice could not be destroyed; if so, God would cease to be God. . . . And now, the plan of mercy could not be brought about except an atonement should be made; therefore God himself atoneth for the sins of the world, to bring about the plan of mercy, to appease the demands of justice, that God might be a perfect, just God, and a merciful God also." (Alma 42:13-15.) Again the divine message is one of salvation through Christ on conditions of repentance.

With these truths before us, we are prepared to rejoice in the many hard things written by Paul about Adam and Christ, through whom came sin and righteousness, sin coming by the fall and righteousness by the redemption. "For all have sinned, and come short of the glory of God," the ancient apostle said. But those who repent are "justified freely by his grace through the redemption that is in Christ Jesus: whom God hath set forth to be a propitiation through faith in his blood, to declare his righteousness for the remission of sins that are past, through the forbearance of God." (Romans 3:23-25.) God forbears to subject repentant souls to the law of justice; sins are mercifully remitted for the penitent. "For as by one man's disobedience [Adam's!] many were made sinners, so by the obedience of one [Christ!] shall many be made righteous." Though "sin abounded" because of Adam, "grace did much more abound" because of Christ: "That as sin hath reigned unto death, even so might grace reign through righteousness unto eternal life by Jesus Christ our Lord." (Romans 5:19-21.)

Continuing his inspired discourse, our apostolic friend asks the saints: "Know ye not, that to whom ye yield yourselves servants to obey, his servants ye are to whom ye obey; whether of sin unto death, or of obedience unto righteousness?" Serve Satan and die; serve Christ and live. Remain in your sins and be damned; repent of your sins and be saved. "But God be thanked, that ye were the servants of sin, but ye have obeyed from the heart that form of doctrine which was delivered you." The doctrine delivered to them was the gospel of repentance and of obedience. "Being then made free from sin, ye became the servants of righteousness." When the saints repent, their sins flee away; they then become righteous, pure, holy, fit candidates to go where God and Christ are and to inherit eternal life. "Now being made free from sin, and become servants to God, ye have your fruit unto holiness, and the end [for all such is an inheritance of] everlasting life. For the wages of sin is death; but the gift of God is eternal life through Jesus Christ our Lord." (Romans 6:16-23.)

The Nature of Repentance

Repentance means many things and has differing faces; it appears in divers forms and wears various guises. In a general sense it may mean reformation, or turning from evil to good, without reference to God or Christ or their holy gospel. It might be said, for instance, that if either a Christian or an Islamic or a communistic nation would repent—meaning cease from war, stop crime, turn from immorality, abandon drug addiction, refrain from drunkenness—the people of that nation would be blessed. Any nation—whether Christian, Islamic, or atheistic—that will repent in this sense will have a new birth. The peoples will gain peace; their municipals will be secure in their persons and property; adultery will no longer break up homes and destroy souls; and alcoholics and drug addicts will cease to wear out their lives in degenerate debauchery. Blessings always flow to all people when they conform to those laws upon which their receipt is predicated. But in the full gospel sense, repentance is far more than reformation. The mere fact of maintaining standards of normal decency will not, of itself, qualify men for a celestial inheritance.

In the gospel sense repentance is the system, ordained of God, whereby fallen man may be saved. It is the plan of mercy that enables sinners to be reconciled to God. It is the way whereby all men, being sinners, can escape the grasp of justice and be encircled forever in the arms of mercy. It operates in and through and because of the infinite and eternal atonement; and if there had been no atonement, the doctrine of repentance would serve no purpose and save no souls. Salvation comes because of the atonement and is reserved for those who repent.

Thus repentance follows faith. It is born of faith; it is the child of faith; and it operates only in the lives of those who have faith—faith in the Lord Jesus Christ. Faith comes first and repentance second; one is the first principle of the gospel, the other the second.

Thus repentance is a gift of God conferred upon those who earn the right to receive it. It comes by obedience to law. In order to repent, men must "do works meet for repentance." (Acts 26:20.) It is with repentance as with all the gifts of God: they are bestowed upon worthy recipients and upon none others.

Thus repentance prepares men for that baptism by immersion which is for the remission of sins. It precedes baptism, and to be efficacious it must be followed by baptism. There is no salvation in repentance alone, and in the gospel sense, repentance dies aborning unless the repentant soul is also baptized. Sins are washed away, as it were, in the waters of baptism; they do not simply die and cease because unbaptized persons reform their lives. When unrepentant Pharisees and

Sadducees came to John for baptism, he said: "O generation of vipers, who hath warned you to flee from the wrath to come? Bring forth therefore fruits meet for repentance." (Matthew 3:7-8.)

The relationship between repentance and baptism and the fact that good works precede and are a part of repentance is perfectly set forth in these words of scripture: "All those who humble themselves before God, and desire to be baptized, and come forth with broken hearts and contrite spirits, and witness before the church that they have truly repented of all their sins, and are willing to take upon them the name of Jesus Christ, having a determination to serve him to the end, and truly manifest by their works that they have received of the Spirit of Christ unto the remission of their sins, shall be received by baptism into his church." (D&C 20:37.)

Thus contrition and humility, penitence and godly sorrow, confession and conformity, desires for righteousness and a determination to make amends for past sins and to live better in the future—all these precede and are part of repentance. To gain a remission of sins by repentance, men must not only forsake sin itself, but they must also forgive others their trespasses and affirmatively turn to righteousness in all things.

Those who truly repent forsake the world; they flee unto Christ; they assemble with the saints and worship the Father in spirit and in truth. They die as to carnal and evil things and become alive in Christ, choosing thereby to walk in a newness of life. They repent of their evil deeds and of their false doctrines. A truly repentant person believes the gospel, rejects all heretical views, and goes forward along the course leading to eternal life. Repentance, thus, is not an isolated principle, standing alone by itself; it is part and portion of the plan of salvation, and it is interwoven with the whole gospel scheme of things.

The World and Repentance

The need for repentance is universal. It covers the whole earth, and it presses in upon all men. This need is as all-pervading and as everywhere present as are the effects of the fall; indeed, the fall itself took place so that death and probation and repentance might be the common lot of all men. This mortal life is the time and the day appointed for men to repent and prepare to meet God. Thus, speaking with one voice by way of both doctrine and testimony, the Latter-day Saints affirm: "We know that all men must repent and believe on the name of Jesus Christ, and worship the Father in his name, and endure in faith on his name to the end, or they cannot be saved in the kingdom of God." (D&C 20:29.)

It follows that God, whose right it is, *commands* men to repent. Repentance is an eternal law, the law of the Lord, and he has commanded his children to obey its terms and conditions. Those who do not do so are in rebellion against him and his word. Thus saith the Lord: "I command all men everywhere to repent." (D&C 18:9.) This command goes forth by the mouths of his servants the prophets, whom he sends to represent him in all nations and among all peoples. The Nephite Jacob carried the message by saying: "He commandeth all men that they must repent, and be baptized in his name, having perfect faith in the Holy One of Israel, or they cannot be saved in the kingdom of God." (2 Nephi 9:23.) And Jesus himself, after saying that salvation came to men because of "the repentance of all their sins, and their faithfulness to the end," issued the decree of universal application in these words: "Now this is the commandment," he said: "Repent, all ye ends of the earth, and come unto me and be baptized in my name, that ye may be sanctified by the reception of the Holy Ghost." (3 Nephi 27:19-20.)

Knowing these things, it comes as no surprise to us, as the Lord's servants, to be told by him to cry repentance unto the world, meaning to go forth and preach the gospel to all men. "You are called to cry repentance unto this people," the divine voice directs, "and if it so be that you should labor all your days in crying repentance unto this people, and bring, save it be one soul unto me, how great shall be your joy with him in the kingdom of my Father! And now, if your joy will be great with one soul that you have brought unto me into the kingdom of my Father, how great will be your joy if you should bring many souls unto me! . . . And as many as repent and are baptized in my name, which is Jesus Christ, and endure to the end, the same shall be saved." (D&C 18:14-16, 22.)

The divine commands, "Say nothing but repentance unto this generation" (D&C 6:9) and "Preach naught but repentance" (D&C 19:21), mean that the Lord's ministers are to confine their teachings to the doctrines of the gospel. They are to teach that gospel repentance which is in effect the very plan of salvation itself. Those who conform to the counsel thus given have this promise: "The thing which will be of the most worth unto you will be to declare repentance unto this people, that you may bring souls unto me, that you may rest with them in the kingdom of my Father." (D&C 15:6.)

The perfect pattern for ministerial service was set by the Lord Jesus. Of his ministry among men, the holy word says: "Jesus began to preach, and to say, Repent: for the kingdom of heaven is at hand." (Matthew 4:17.) Also: "The time is fulfilled, and the kingdom of God is at hand: repent ye, and believe the gospel." (Mark 1:15.) Indeed, Christ came to call "sinners to repentance." (Mark 2:17.) His oft-repeated cry was: "Except ye repent, ye shall all likewise perish." (Luke 13:3.) After having thus set the pattern for carrying the gospel to the world, he suffered, died, and rose again the third day, "that repentance and remission of sins should be preached in his name among all nations, beginning at Jerusalem." (Luke 24:47.)

And as it was anciently, so it is today. Christ "sendeth an invitation unto all men, for the arms of mercy are extended towards them, and he saith: Repent, and I will receive you." (Alma 5:33.)

CHAPTER 25

The Church
and Repentance

The Saints and Repentance

To whom does the law of repentance apply, and who among men are in need of repentance? Surely none will dissent from the proposition that evil and carnal men must repent; all will agree that the wicked and ungodly need to forsake their sins. There can be no question that those who live after the manner of the world can be reconciled to God only on conditions of repentance. But as a matter of practical reality, the law of repentance is not limited to those who are outside the fold of Christ.

True though it is that the whole need no physician, only they who are sick; true though it is that repentance is for the wicked, not the righteous; true though it is that the saints have power to sanctify their souls and stand spotless before the Lord—yet, in reality, the generality of them are not as yet prepared to dwell in the divine presence, and all of them are in need of repentance to some degree. Repentance is for the saints; it is for the members of the church and kingdom of God on earth; it is for those who have made covenant in the waters of baptism to serve God and keep his commandments. True it is that the world cannot be saved without repentance, but neither can the saints.

Why must even the saints repent? We answer: Because they are not yet perfect; because they commit sin; because they are only in the process of overcoming the world; because they are yet carnal to some degree. Paul said to the Corinthian saints: "Ye are yet carnal." To prove his point, he asked: "Whereas there is among you envying, and strife, and divisions, are ye not carnal, and walk as men?" (1 Corinthians 3:3.) The attainment of salvation is a long and grueling process; it is the process of renewed, repeated, and continuing repentance, as our needs and circumstances may require. It is the process of overcoming the world, of bridling our passions, of coming to a unity with the Lord, of growing in grace until we become like Him through whose atoning blood we have power to gain eternal life.

The revealed word, given in our day, says: "And surely every man must repent or suffer, for I, God, am endless." Then it explains that judgments, woes, and weeping await the wicked—all of which constitute endless torment and eternal damnation, and all of which they will suffer until they have, in justice, paid the penalty for their sins. Such is the eternal decree for all men: all must forsake the world, repent of their sins, and come unto Christ, or lose the blessings that might have been theirs.

It is in this setting that the Lord says to his saints, to those who believe, to those who have faith and in whose lives the processes of repentance have commenced: "I command you to repent, and keep the commandments which you have received by the hand of my servant Joseph Smith, Jun., in my name." Surely those who hear the message of salvation have a greater responsibility to repent than do those in whose ears the divine voice has never been raised. Surely those whose hearts have been touched and who have come to a knowledge of the truth have a yet greater responsibility to forsake the world and walk in the light than do those whose souls have never felt the power of the Spirit.

"Therefore I command you to repent," the Lord says to his saints, "repent, lest I smite you by the rod of my mouth, and by my wrath, and by my anger, and your sufferings be sore— how sore you know not, how exquisite you know not, yea, how hard to bear you know not." The great Judge, who cannot look upon sin with the least degree of allowance, is no respecter of persons. Carnal persons in the Church will be treated like carnal persons in the world: they will be called upon to pay the penalty for their own sins.

"For behold, I, God, have suffered these things for all, that they might not suffer if they would repent; but if they would not repent they must suffer even as I; which suffering caused myself, even God, the greatest of all, to tremble because of pain, and to bleed at every pore, and to suffer both body and spirit—and would that I might not drink the bitter cup, and shrink—nevertheless, glory be to the Father, and I partook and finished my preparations unto the children of men." It was in Gethsemane and at Golgotha that our Lord bore the sins of all men on conditions of repentance. "Wherefore, I command you again to repent," he continues, "lest I humble you with my almighty power; and that you confess your sins, lest you suffer these punishments of which I have spoken." (D&C 19:4-20.)

How marvelous it is that the saints of God have power to cleanse and perfect their souls if they will repent! Let the same blessings be offered to the world, for the Lord will receive all who come unto him. But let the outpouring of divine goodness and grace come first upon those who believe. The Lord has a greater interest in the welfare of his people, who are struggling upwards along the strait and narrow path, than he has in those who walk in crooked paths. Thus the beloved John says of the saints: "Our fellowship is with the Father, and with his Son Jesus Christ. . . . If we [the saints, those who have aligned themselves in the cause of righteousness] say that we have fellowship with him, and [yet] walk in darkness, we lie, and do not the truth." If we continue in sin after baptism, the darkness of the world enshrouds us. Our profession of fellowship is a lie.

"But if we walk in the light, as he [the Father] is in the light, [then] we have fellowship one with another, and the blood of Jesus Christ his Son cleanseth us from all sin." The Son pays the penalty for our sins if we repent and work righteousness. "If we say that we have no sin, we deceive ourselves, and the truth is not in us." There are sins in us though we are the saints of the Most High; we are not perfect—far from it. Our responsibility is to press forward with a steadfastness in Christ until we overcome the world and rise above all things. "If we confess our sins, he is faithful and just to forgive us our sins, and to cleanse us from all unrighteousness." There is no other way for either saints or sinners. And, "If we [the saints] say that we have not sinned, we make him a liar, and his word is not in us." (1 John 1:3-10.)

In our day the Lord speaks of "the only true and living church upon the face of the whole earth." He says he is "well pleased" with his people, "speaking unto the church collectively and not individually," but that he "cannot look upon sin with the least degree of allowance." The destiny of the Church is assured; church members, however, are not all walking in the light and gaining a forgiveness of their sins. "Nevertheless, he that repents and does the commandments of the Lord shall be forgiven." Repent and obey! "And he that repents not, from him shall be taken even the light which he has received; for my Spirit shall not always strive with man, saith the Lord of Hosts." (D&C 1:30-33.) The saints who do not repent shall lose their standing; the light of testimony that once was theirs shall grow dim; they shall die spiritually and be as other men. The wages of sin is death, in or out of the Church.

The Sins of the Saints

Would it be amiss to ask what sins the saints need to repent of? And would not the answer be, the same sins from which all men must repent? To those outside the Church, the Lord says: "Turn, all ye Gentiles, from your wicked ways; and repent of your evil doings, of your lyings and deceivings, and of your whoredoms, and of your secret abominations, and your idolatries, and of your murders, and your priestcrafts, and your envyings, and your strifes, and from all your wickedness and abominations, and come unto me, and be baptized in my name, that ye may receive a remission of your sins, and be filled with the Holy Ghost, that ye may be numbered with my people who are of the house of Israel." (3 Nephi 30:2.)

Paul says that "the works of the flesh" include "adultery, fornication, uncleanness, lasciviousness, idolatry, witchcraft, hatred, variance, emulations, wrath, strife, seditions, heresies, envyings, murders, drunkenness, revellings, and such like." And, he says, "they which do such things shall not inherit the kingdom of God." (Galatians 5:19-21.) "Be not deceived," our ancient apostolic friend also said, for "neither fornicators, nor idolaters, nor adulterers, nor effeminate, nor abusers of themselves with mankind, nor thieves, nor covetous, nor drunkards, nor revilers, nor extortioners, shall inherit the kingdom of God." Such, he said, were some of the Corinthians before they joined the church, but having forsaken these evils, they were then heirs of salvation. (1 Corinthians 6:9-11.)

Paul also speaks of both men and women who have "vile

affections" for those of their own sex. These are lesbians and homosexuals who change "the natural use" of the body "into that which is against nature." He also heaps divine condemnation upon those who are "filled with all unrighteousness, fornication, wickedness, covetousness, maliciousness; [who are] full of envy, murder, debate, deceit, malignity; [who are] whisperers, backbiters, haters of God, despiteful, proud, boasters, inventors of evil things, disobedient to parents, without natural affection, implacable, unmerciful," saying that all such, without repentance, shall be damned. (Romans 1:26-32.)

Members of the Church are sometimes guilty of the same sins that afflict fallen man generally. When they are, their condemnation is greater than it otherwise would be, because of their greater light and knowledge. In addition, many acts become sinful for the saints that would not be so considered had they not taken upon themselves the obligations of the gospel. Thus the Lord says to his people: "There are those among you who have sinned exceedingly; yea, even all of you have sinned; but verily I say unto you, beware from henceforth, and refrain from sin, lest sore judgments fall upon your heads." All the sins named by Paul and Mormon and others of the prophets sometimes lie at the door of the saints. But there is more of which they must beware. "For of him unto whom much is given much is required; and he who sins against the greater light shall receive the greater condemnation. Ye call upon my name for revelations, and I give them unto you; and inasmuch as ye keep not my sayings, which I give unto you, ye become transgressors; and justice and judgment are the penalty which is affixed unto my law." (D&C 82:2-4.)

Thus, Malachi, having in mind the saints who do not pay their tithes and offerings, asks: "Will a man rob God?" (Malachi 3:8.) The Gentiles who pay no tithes and make no offerings to the Lord are without sin in these respects. But the Lord expects more of those who have taken upon themselves his name and covenanted in the waters of baptism to love and serve him all their days.

Thus Alma, addressing himself to his "brethren of the church," asks: "How will any of you feel, if ye shall stand before the bar of God, having your garments stained with blood and all manner of filthiness? . . . Could ye say, if ye were called to die at this time, . . . that ye have been sufficiently humble? . . . Is there one among you that doth make a mock of his brother? . . . Will ye still persist in the wearing of costly apparel and setting your hearts upon the vain things of the world, [and] upon your riches? . . . Will you persist in turning your backs upon the poor, and the needy, and withholding your substance from them?" (See Alma 5:14-55.)

And thus the Lord says to the saints in our day: "Your minds in times past have been darkened because of unbelief, and because you have treated lightly the things you have received—which vanity and unbelief have brought the whole church under condemnation." Is the Lord telling us we are guilty of sin if we do not believe the doctrines he has given us? If we treat lightly—neither reading, nor pondering, nor obeying—the revelations he has given us, are we guiltless? Is it a sin to believe a false doctrine? To believe, for instance, the evolutionary theories that deny the need for an atoning sacrifice? "And this condemnation"—for unbelief and for treating lightly what we have received—"resteth upon the children of Zion, even all. And they shall remain under this condemnation until they repent and remember the new covenant, even the Book of Mormon and the former commandments which I have given them, not only to say, but to do according to that which I have written—that they may bring forth fruit meet for their Father's kingdom; otherwise there remaineth a scourge and judgment to be poured out upon the children of Zion. For shall the children of the kingdom pollute my holy land? Verily, I say unto you, Nay." (D&C 84:54-59.) Is it a sin to have the Book of Mormon and do nothing about it? to use it neither for our own guidance nor as a means of presenting the message of the restoration to the world?

Is it not a sin to walk in darkness when we have light? Is it not a sin to hold the holy priesthood and do nothing about it? "There are many who have been ordained among you," the Lord says to his saints, "whom I have called but few of them are chosen. They who are not chosen have sinned a very grievous sin, in that they are walking in darkness at noon-day. . . . If you keep not my commandments, the love of the Father shall not continue with you, therefore you shall walk in darkness." (D&C 95:5-6, 12.)

Oh, what a grievous thing it is to receive the light of heaven and yet walk in darkness! As Jesus said to certain people in his day: "If ye were blind, ye should have no sin: but now ye say, We see; therefore your sin remaineth." (John 9:41.)

Return unto the Lord

To the saints and to the world the Lord's voice calls: 'Repent ye, repent ye; why will ye perish?' All men, in and out of the Church, are commanded to repent; otherwise they will be damned. Every faithful saint, no matter how firmly his feet are planted on the strait and narrow path, knows within himself that he yet has sins to forsake and appetites and desires to control. Hence the prophetic calls to repent that are addressed to those who are already within the fold of the Good Shepherd.

"O ye workers of iniquity," Alma said to wayward and straying sheep in his day, "ye that are puffed up in the vain things of the world, ye that have professed to have known the ways of righteousness nevertheless have gone astray, as sheep having no shepherd, notwithstanding a shepherd hath called after you and is still calling after you, but ye will not hearken unto his voice! Behold, I say unto you, that the good shepherd doth call you; yea, and in his own name he doth call you, which is the name of Christ." (Alma 5:37-38.)

Isaiah issued the call to backsliding Israel in this way: "Seek ye the Lord while he may be found, call ye upon him while he is near: Let the wicked forsake his way, and the unrighteous man his thoughts: and let him *return* unto the Lord, and he will have mercy upon him; and to our God, for he will abundantly pardon." (Isaiah 55:6-7. Italics added.) Repent of your wicked ways; repent of your evil thoughts. *Return.* Be as you once were, and the Lord will have mercy upon you.

The Lord, by the mouth of Ezekiel, set forth the law of personal accountability for sins: "The soul that sinneth, it shall die. But if a man be just, and do that which is lawful and right, . . . he shall surely live, saith the Lord God." And again: "The soul that sinneth, it shall die. The son shall not bear the iniquity of the father, neither shall the father bear the iniquity of the son: the righteousness of the righteous shall be upon him, and the wickedness of the wicked shall be upon him. But if the wicked will turn from all his sins that he hath committed, and keep all my statutes, and do that which is lawful and right, he shall surely live, he shall not die. All his transgressions that he hath committed, they shall not be mentioned unto him: in his righteousness that he hath done he shall live." Repent and live, O Israel.

"When a righteous man turneth away from his righteousness, and committeth iniquity, and dieth in them; for his iniquity that he hath done shall he die. Again, when the wicked man turneth away from his wickedness that he hath committed, and doeth that which is lawful and right, he shall save his soul alive. . . . Therefore I will judge you, O house of Israel, every one according to his ways, saith the Lord God. Repent, and turn yourselves from all your transgressions; so iniquity shall not be your ruin. Cast away from you all your transgressions, whereby ye have transgressed; and make you a new heart and a new spirit: for why will ye die, O house of Israel? For I have no pleasure in the death of him that dieth, saith the Lord God: wherefore turn yourselves, and live ye." (Ezekiel 18:4-32.) And what the Lord said to ancient Israel applies in full measure to modern Israel.

Alma the younger—the Nephite Paul, as it were—was the son of the presiding high priest over the church among the American Hebrews. He was himself a member of the church; he had been taught by his father, and he had received baptism, probably when he was eight years of age. But in the wisdom of his own conceits, he was going about with the sons of Mosiah to destroy the faith of the saints. Then it was that the earth trembled and the angel appeared and said: "If thou wilt . . . be destroyed, [so be it; but] seek no more to destroy the church of God." There followed three days and three nights during which Alma could neither speak nor move.

"I was racked with eternal torment," he says, "for my soul was harrowed up to the greatest degree and racked with all my sins. Yea, I did remember all my sins and iniquities, for which I was tormented with the pains of hell; yea, I saw that I had rebelled against my God, and that I had not kept his holy commandments. Yea, I had murdered many of his children, or rather led them away unto destruction; yea, and in fine so great had been my iniquities, that the very thought of coming into the presence of my God did rack my soul with inexpressible horror. Oh, thought I, that I could be banished and become extinct both soul and body, that I might not be brought to stand in the presence of my God, to be judged of my deeds." Alma serves as a pattern. The horror for sin that engulfed him should be felt by every wayward member of the kingdom; then repentance would be forthcoming, as it was with our Nephite friend.

"And now, for three days and for three nights was I racked, even with the pains of a damned soul," he says. "And it came to pass that as I was thus racked with torment, while I was harrowed up by the memory of my many sins, behold, I remembered also to have heard my father prophesy unto the people concerning the coming of one Jesus Christ, a Son of God, to atone for the sins of the world. Now, as my mind caught hold upon this thought, I cried within my heart: O Jesus, thou Son of God, have mercy on me, who am in the gall of bitterness, and am encircled about by the everlasting chains of death." Then he remembered his pains no more; then his soul was no longer harrowed up with the memory of his sins; rather, his soul was lighted with the light of everlasting life. "And oh, what joy, and what marvelous light I did behold; yea, my soul was filled with joy as exceeding as was my pain! . . . There could be nothing so exquisite and so bitter as were my pains. . . . There can be nothing so exquisite and sweet as was my joy." (Alma 36:1-21.) And thus it is with the true saints when the laws of repentance and of forgiveness operate in their lives in full measure.

The Day of Our Repentance

All men may well ask themselves: When must we believe and repent and obey in order to be saved? When must we turn from evil and seek the Lord in order to enter into his rest? When must we lay claim on the cleansing blood of Him who knew no sin, but who died for sinners that we might become clean as he is clean? All this must take place when opportunity affords, be that in this mortal life or in the spirit world where all the dead await the day of resurrection and judgment. All who have opportunity to hear the gospel taught in this life must believe and obey in this life, or they cannot be saved in the kingdom of God. Salvation for the dead is reserved for those, and those only, who would have received the gospel with all their hearts had it been preached to them during this mortal probation.

Addressing himself to those who are privileged to hear the word of eternal truth in the here and now, Amulek says: "Now is the time and the day of your salvation." Mortality is the appointed period of probation. "Therefore, if ye will repent and harden not your hearts, immediately shall the great plan of redemption be brought about unto you." Adam's fall brought death and sin and sorrow for the living present; Christ's atonement swallows up death, triumphs over sin, and brings peace and joy for those in the living present. "For behold, this life is the time for men to prepare to meet God; yea, behold the day of this life is the day for men to perform their labors."

So-called deathbed repentance is not part of the divine plan. It is an attempt to live after the manner of the world during the years of vigor and virility, and then to gain the rewards of the blessed without ever overcoming the lusts of the flesh, lusts that, with old age and death, cease to burn in the mortal soul. Thus Amulek continues: "Do not procrastinate the day of your repentance until the end; for after this day of life, which is given us to prepare for eternity, behold, if we do not improve our time while in this life, then cometh the night of darkness wherein there can be no labor performed." There are no redeeming doctrines, no saving ordinances, no promised kingdoms of glory for such. Those who reject the gospel in this life—having heard the word from the lips of a legal administrator and having been made aware of its glories and truths—and who then accept it in the spirit world shall go to the terrestrial kingdom.

The fact is that those who reject and fight the truth in this life will continue to do so in the life to come. "That same spirit [of evil, wickedness, and rebellion] which doth possess your bodies at the time that ye go out of this life, that same spirit [of evil, wickedness, and rebellion] will have power to possess your body in that eternal world." How could a just God let it be otherwise? If death erased the sins and feelings of mortality, this present life would cease to be a probationary estate, and the purposes of God would come to naught. Accordingly, as Amulek says, "If ye have procrastinated the day of your repentance even until death, behold, ye have become subjected to the spirit of the devil, and he doth seal you his; therefore, the

Spirit of the Lord hath withdrawn from you, and hath no place in you, and the devil hath all power over you; and this is the final state of the wicked." (Alma 34:31-35.)

Sins unto Death

There are sins unto death, meaning spiritual death. There are sins for which there is no forgiveness, neither in this world nor in the world to come. There are sins which utterly and completely preclude the sinner from gaining eternal life. Hence there are sins for which repentance does not operate, sins that the atoning blood of Christ will not wash away, sins for which the sinner must suffer and pay the full penalty personally.

We do not know all of the judgments of God, nor could we understand them even if they were revealed. Our knowledge about sins unto death is limited, but providentially there are relatively few who cannot be redeemed from spiritual death through repentance. "If any man see his brother sin a sin which is not unto death," John tells us, "he shall ask, and he shall give him life for them that sin not unto death." That is, for all sins which are not unto death, repentance and mercy are available. "There is a sin unto death; I do not say that he shall pray for it," John continues. "All unrighteousness is sin: and there is a sin not unto death." (1 John 5:16-17.) There is no way to reclaim a person who has sinned unto death, not through faith and prayer, not through repentance, not through struggles to perform good works, not in any way. "I, the Lord, forgive sins unto those who confess their sins before me and ask forgiveness, who have not sinned unto death." (D&C 64:7.)

What are sins unto death? We can answer this only in part. "Thou shalt not kill; and he that kills shall not have forgiveness in this world, nor in the world to come." (D&C 42:18.) Murder is thus a sin unto death, at least concerning members of the Church, to whom this revelation, which is entitled "the law of the Church," was addressed. We do know that there are murders committed by Gentiles for which they at least can repent, be baptized, and receive a remission of their sins. (See 3 Nephi 30:1-2.)

Adultery, in certain limited cases, is also a sin unto death. "If a man commit adultery, he cannot receive the celestial kingdom of God. Even if he is saved in any kingdom, it cannot be the celestial kingdom." (*History of the Church* 6:81.) The Prophet Joseph Smith in these words is addressing himself to those, and those only, whose calling and election has been made sure. The words do not refer to any others, either in or out of the Church. Having received the added light and knowledge that come in being sealed up unto eternal life, those whose calling and election has been made sure are subject to greater penalties if they transgress. Adulterers, as many scriptures attest and as the practice of the Church confirms, can repent and gain full salvation.

In the "Revelation on Priesthood," given to the Prophet in September 1832, the Lord speaks of the oath and covenant of the Melchizedek Priesthood, which is binding upon all those who receive this higher priesthood. "Whoso breaketh this covenant after he hath received it, and altogether turneth therefrom, shall not have forgiveness of sins in this world nor in the world to come," the revelation states. (D&C 84:41.) This has never been interpreted by the Brethren to mean that those who forsake their priesthood duties, altogether turning therefrom, shall be sons of perdition; rather, the meaning seems to be that they shall be denied the exaltation that otherwise might have been theirs. But, we repeat, we do not know all things relative to sins unto death, only enough to stand as a warning to us to walk in paths of light and truth.

There are some things, however, about the unpardonable sin that we can speak of with some degree of finality. The destiny of those who commit this sin is to be sons of perdition, of whom the Lord has said, "There is no forgiveness in this world nor in the world to come." (D&C 76:34.) These are the ones of whom Jesus spoke when he said: "All manner of sin and blasphemy shall be forgiven unto men: but the blasphemy against the Holy Ghost shall not be forgiven unto men. And whosoever speaketh a word against the Son of man, it shall be forgiven him: but whosoever speaketh against the Holy Ghost, it shall not be forgiven him, neither in this world, neither in the world to come." (Matthew 12:31-32.)

What is the blasphemy against the Holy Ghost of which Jesus speaks? In our day the Lord has said: "The blasphemy against the Holy Ghost, which shall not be forgiven in the world nor out of the world, is in that ye commit murder wherein ye shed innocent blood, and assent unto my death, after ye have received my new and everlasting covenant." (D&C 132:27.) That is to say, the unpardonable sin consists in denying Christ, in fighting the truth, in joining hands with those who crucified him, knowing full well, and with a perfect knowledge, that he is the Son of God; it means pursuing this course after gaining a perfect knowledge, given of the Holy Ghost, that he is Lord of all. The innocent blood thus shed is his blood; those who so sin become murderers by assenting unto his death, an assent that is given with a full and perfect knowledge of his divinity.

Paul tells us that these rebellious ones who choose to become sons of perdition (or angels of the devil) cannot repent. "It is impossible for those who were once enlightened," he says, "and [who] have tasted of the heavenly gift, and were made partakers of the Holy Ghost, and have tasted the good word of God, and the powers of the world to come, if they shall fall away, to renew them again unto repentance; seeing they crucify to themselves the Son of God afresh, and put him to an open shame." (Hebrews 6:4-6.) And also: "If we sin wilfully after that we have received the knowledge of the truth, there remaineth no more sacrifice for sins, but a certain fearful looking for of judgment and fiery indignation, which shall devour the adversaries. He that despised Moses' law died without mercy under two or three witnesses: of how much sorer punishment, suppose ye, shall he be thought worthy, who hath trodden under foot the Son of God, and hath counted the blood of the covenant, wherewith he was sanctified, an unholy thing, and hath done despite unto the Spirit of grace?" (Hebrews 10:26-29.)

CHAPTER 26

The Doctrine of Forgiveness

Gaining Forgiveness After Baptism

Before baptism, the seeker of salvation believes in Christ and gains a knowledge of the plan of redemption, of mercy, and of repentance. He feels in his heart that through our Lord's atoning sacrifice man can be reconciled to God, and he desires, through repentance, to rid himself from the grasp of justice and find mercy in the arms of the Lord. Accordingly, he forsakes his sins, confesses them to the Lord in prayer, and enters the gate of repentance and baptism. His sins are washed away in the waters of baptism; sin and evil are burned out of his soul as though by fire. He finds himself on the strait and narrow path leading to eternal life. If he then presses forward, "with a steadfastness in Christ, having a perfect brightness of hope, and a love of God and of all men"; if he then feasts "upon the word of Christ" and lives by every word that proceedeth forth from the mouth of God; and if he then endures to the end—he shall inherit eternal life. (2 Nephi 31:20.)

But all men sin after baptism; all fall short of the high standard set by the Lord Jesus in his life; all are ensnared again, to one degree or another, in the sins of the world. Some build a barrier of sin across the strait and narrow path and cease to press forward to eternal life. Others turn off the path and wander into bye and forbidden paths of grievous sin. What of all these? How can we gain a remission of the sins committed after baptism? Thanks be to God, there is a way, and it consists in taking seven known steps, as follows.

1. Godly Sorrow for Sin

Addressing baptized members of the church, Paul says: "Let us cleanse ourselves from all filthiness of the flesh and spirit, perfecting holiness in the fear of God." We must, he says, have sorrow, "to repentance"; we must be "made sorry after a godly manner." He is not speaking of sorrow as such, but of a particular kind of sorrow. "For godly sorrow worketh repentance to salvation," he says, "but the sorrow of the world worketh death." And as to those saints who had "sorrowed after a godly sort," Paul cried out in words of praise and exultation: "What carefulness it wrought in you" (now they were watchful and conforming); "yea, what clearing of yourselves" (now the burdens of sin had been lifted); "yea, what indignation" (now they had a horror of sin); "yea, what fear" (now they feared the consequences of sin); "yea, what vehement desire, yea, what zeal" (now they were consumed with desires for righteousness and a zeal for Christ); "yea, what revenge" (now they had slain their sins and taken revenge upon the adversary). (2 Corinthians 7:1-11.)

Godly sorrow is born of the Spirit; it is a gift of God that comes to those who have a broken heart and a contrite spirit. It includes an honest, heartfelt contrition, a frank recognition of sins committed, and a firm determination to go and sin no more. The sorrow of the world, in which there is no salvation, is the sorrow of the thief who is caught and the robber who is imprisoned. It is sorrow for lost status, lost wealth, and lost freedom. In it there is no element of repentance, and it neither reforms nor cleanses a sinning soul.

2.   Abandonment of Sin

That sinners must forsake their sins to gain forgiveness is self-evident. As long as we continue in sin, are we not bound by the chains of sin? As long as we walk in carnal paths, are we not partakers of carnality? "By this ye may know if a man repenteth of his sins," saith the Lord, "behold, he will confess them and forsake them." (D&C 58:43.) And also: "Put away the evil of your doings from before mine eyes; cease to do evil; learn to do well; seek judgment, relieve the oppressed, judge the fatherless, plead for the widow." The Lord is here speaking to his people. "Come now, and let us reason together," he continues, "though your sins be as scarlet, they shall be as white as snow; though they be red like crimson, they shall be as wool." (Isaiah 1:16-18.) There is nothing more important in connection with the whole law of forgiveness than to forsake —utterly, totally, completely—every form of iniquity. Thus saith the Lord unto his penitent people: "Go your ways and sin no more; but unto that soul who sinneth shall the former sins return." (D&C 82:7.)

3. Confession of Sin

Wayward church members are required to confess their sins as one of the prerequisites for gaining forgiveness. In the days of Mosiah and Alma, circumstances arose in which "it became expedient that those who committed sin, that were in the church, should be admonished by the church." Being concerned as to what action he should take relative to them, Alma inquired of the Lord, who told him: "Whosoever transgresseth against me, him shall ye judge according to the sins which he has committed." When church and state each have their own jurisdiction, the church does not pass judgment upon the sinners of the world. But those in the church must be handled by the church for their transgressions. They must, as circumstances require, be brought before the courts of the church and have a just decision rendered.

Continuing to speak of any person in the church who transgresses, the Lord said to Alma: "If he confess his sins before thee and me, and repenteth in the sincerity of his heart, him shall ye forgive, and I will forgive him also." There are thus two confessions and two sources of forgiveness. A sinner must always confess all sins, great and small, to the Lord; in addition, any sins involving moral turpitude and any serious sins for which a person might be disfellowshipped or excommunicated must also be confessed to the Lord's agent, who in most instances is the bishop. The bishop is empowered to forgive sins as far as the church is concerned, meaning that he can choose to retain the repentant person in full fellowship and not impose court penalties upon him. Ultimate forgiveness in all instances and for all sins comes from the Lord and from the Lord only.

It is always hoped that erring church members will repent and retain their standing in the kingdom. When they do not, in the case of serious sins, justice requires that the prescribed penalties be imposed. But because the Lord wants his people to repent and gain the blessings of the gospel, he told Alma: "As often as my people repent will I forgive them their trespasses against me." (Mosiah 26:6-30.) "And him that repenteth not of his sins, and confesseth them not," the Lord said to the church in this day, "ye shall bring before the church, and do with him as the scripture saith unto you, either by commandment or by revelation. And this ye shall do that God may be glorified—not because ye forgive not, having not compassion, but that ye may be justified in the eyes of the law, that ye may not offend him who is your lawgiver." (D&C 64:12-13.)

4. Restitution for Sin

Every repentant person desires by instinct to make amends for the wrongs he has done. The desire to make reparation is an outgrowth of Godly sorrow. Has property or money been taken—it must be returned. Has character been defamed or the truth maligned—now the truth must be spoken. Saul the persecutor must become Paul the defender. Restitution is not always possible, but it must always be made insofar as it can be; the repentant sinner must give whatever equivalent he can to compensate for the loss he has caused. When he has done all he can, the Lord will accept his offering.

5. Obedience to All Law

Forgiveness comes to those who forsake their sins and who also keep the commandments. To cease from sin is a requirement of forgiveness, as when the adulterer stops his immoral acts, thus *commencing* the processes of repentance. But to turn to righteousness and keep the commandments is a greater and more ennobling course, as when the immoral sinner not only forsakes his unchaste ways, but keeps the commandments in general, thus *assuring* himself of forgiveness. "He that repents and does the commandments of the Lord shall be forgiven." (D&C 1:32.) Thus, to gain forgiveness for acts of sex immorality, a man must not only forsake his unclean ways, but he must, for instance, pay his tithes and offerings and spread the word of truth to his fellowmen. As to gaining a forgiveness of certain sins through missionary service, the Lord says: "I will forgive you of your sins with this commandment"—that is, with this proviso, or on this condition—"that you remain steadfast in your minds in solemnity and the spirit of prayer, in bearing testimony to all the world of those things which are communicated unto you." (D&C 84:61.)

6. Forgive One Another

Can we gain forgiveness from the Lord without granting it to our fellowmen? The answer is a thunderous, No! Jesus condensed the divine law into these six words: "Forgive, and ye shall be forgiven." (Luke 6:37.) On one occasion Jesus taught his disciples to pray by saying: "Forgive us our sins; for we also forgive every one that is indebted to us." (Luke 11:4.) On another occasion his saints were counseled to pray: "Forgive us our debts, as we forgive our debtors." Why? Because, he said, "if ye forgive men their trespasses, your heavenly Father will also forgive you: But if ye forgive not men their trespasses, neither will your Father forgive your trespasses." (Matthew 6:12-15.) Forgiveness of others is a condition precedent to the receipt of forgiveness for ourselves.

Can we be reconciled to the Lord and remain at variance with our brethren? Jesus says we cannot. "If ye shall come unto me, or shall desire to come unto me," he says, "and rememberest that thy brother hath aught against thee—go thy way unto thy brother, and first be reconciled to thy brother, and then come unto me with full purpose of heart, and I will receive you." (3 Nephi 12:23-24.) The whole system of salvation under which we operate is one of being reconciled to God through the cleansing blood of Christ. "God was in Christ, reconciling the world unto himself," Paul says, "not imputing their trespasses unto them." (2 Corinthians 5:19.) And we cannot be so reconciled and made free from our sins unless and until we first reconcile ourselves with our brethren.

As we seek reconciliation with the Lord, how often must we forgive one another? That there is no limit to the number of times is implicit in Jesus' words: "If thy brother trespass against thee, rebuke him; and if he repent, forgive him. And if he trespass against thee seven times in a day, and seven times in a day turn again to thee, saying, I repent; thou shalt forgive him." (Luke 17:3-4.) When Peter asked, "Lord, how oft shall my brother sin against me, and I forgive him? till seven times?"

Jesus replied: "I say not unto thee, Until seven times: but, Until seventy times seven," meaning times without number. (Matthew 18:21-22.)

It was through Alma that the Lord gave this command to his saints: "Ye shall also forgive one another your trespasses; for verily I say unto you, he that forgiveth not his neighbor's trespasses when he says that he repents, the same hath brought himself under condemnation." (Mosiah 26:31.) In our day we have received this word from the Lord. "My disciples, in days of old, sought occasion against one another and forgave not one another in their hearts; and for this evil they were afflicted and sorely chastened." It is a grievous sin in itself not to forgive those who claim that they have repented. "Wherefore, I say unto you, that ye ought to forgive one another; for he that forgiveth not his brother his trespasses standeth condemned before the Lord; for there remaineth in him the greater sin." How often even good and true people condemn themselves by refusing to forgive their brethren!

"I, the Lord, will forgive whom I will forgive"—judgment and vengeance are his and he will repay—"but of you it is required to forgive all men." Forgiveness on our part is mandatory. "And ye ought to say in your hearts—let God judge between me and thee, and reward thee according to thy deeds." (D&C 64:8-11.)

7. Partake Worthily of the Sacrament

Baptism is for the remission of sins; it is the ordinance, ordained of God, to cleanse a human soul. Baptism is in water and of the Spirit and is preceded by repentance. The actual cleansing of the soul comes when the Holy Ghost is received. The Holy Ghost is a sanctifier whose divine commission is to burn dross and evil out of a human soul as though by fire, thus giving rise to the expression *baptism of fire,* which is the baptism of the Spirit. Forgiveness is assured when the contrite soul receives the Holy Spirit, because the Spirit will not dwell in an unclean tabernacle.

The sacrament of the Lord's Supper is the ordinance, ordained of God, in which baptized saints are privileged, repeatedly and often, to renew the covenant of baptism. Those who partake worthily of the sacramental emblems, by so doing, covenant on their part to remember the body of the Son of God who was crucified for them; to take upon them his name, as they did in the waters of baptism; and to "always remember him and keep his commandments which he has given them; that they may always have his Spirit to be with them." (D&C 20:77.) Thus those who partake worthily of the sacrament—and the same repentance and contrition and desires for righteousness should precede the partaking of the sacrament as precede baptism—all such receive the companionship of the Holy Spirit. Because the Spirit will not dwell in an unclean tabernacle, they thus receive a remission of their sins through the sacramental ordinance. Through this ordinance the Lord puts a seal of approval upon them; they are renewed in spirit and become new creatures of the Holy Ghost, even as they did at baptism; they put off the old man of sin and put on Christ, whose children they then are.

There are also numerous other sacred occasions when the saints may get in tune with and receive the sanctifying power of the Holy Spirit in their lives. The receipt of this heaven-sent boon always attests that the recipient has forsaken the world and is no longer encumbered by its wicked ways. One of these occasions may attend a proper anointing and blessing of the sick. "Is any sick among you?" James asks. "Let him call for the elders of the church; and let them pray over him, anointing him with oil in the name of the Lord: and the prayer of faith shall save the sick, and the Lord shall raise him up; and if he have committed sins, they shall be forgiven him. Confess your faults one to another, and pray one for another, that ye may be healed." (James 5:14-16.) If the Spirit of the Lord rests upon one who is being blessed by the elders, in connection with this or any other ordinance, it automatically follows that the one blessed receives a remission of his sins; otherwise the Spirit would not be present. We do not want for occasions upon which sins may be remitted. Our problem is one of so living that we are worthy to have the companionship of the Spirit in our lives.

CHAPTER 27

The Doctrine
of Baptism

Baptism—God's Eternal Law

What think ye of baptism? What part does this holy ordinance play in the salvation of men? Is it merely an outward sign of an inward grace, or is it a mandatory requirement without which men will be damned? Is it as eternal, as everlasting, as infinite in nature as God himself, or is it an inconsequential rite that satisfies the feelings of those who choose to attach some importance to it?

Baptism, in all its aspects, has been analyzed and debated in religious conclaves from antiquity. Can we now, in these last days, set forth what the Lord thinks about this ordinance and show how it fits into the eternal scheme of things? We can—at least the answers are found in the revealed word. Let us consider the essential elements of the subject under twelve headings.

1. Baptism—Its Nature and Purpose

Baptism is a holy ordinance ordained of God for the salvation of men. It consists of two parts. The first is immersion in water as a visible, public, and outward sign that a penitent person has come unto Christ, accepted his gospel, and taken our Lord's yoke upon him. The second is immersion in the Spirit through the receipt of the Holy Ghost, which is the invisible, private, and inward witness that lets the penitent person know he has been accepted by the Lord as an heir of salvation. Baptism is thus dual in nature; it is in water and of the Spirit. It is a manifestation before the world and the receipt of an inner and personal peace.

Baptism must—absolutely, invariably, and always—be performed by a legal administrator, or it will have no efficacy, virtue, or force in and after the resurrection from the dead. And it must always, without exception and in every case, be sealed by the Holy Spirit of Promise or it will not admit the repentant penitent to the celestial kingdom of God. It is the first ordinance of salvation, and it sets the pattern for all others, meaning that "all covenants, contracts, bonds, obligations, oaths, vows, performances, connections, associations, or expectations" (D&C 132:7) must also be sealed and ratified by the power of the Spirit or they will not be binding on earth and in heaven.

Baptism is the rite and procedure, given of God, whereby men may be reconciled to him through the atonement of his Only Begotten Son. The gospel itself is the new and everlasting covenant, the covenant Deity makes with men to save them with an eternal salvation. Those who believe and obey gain salvation through the atonement. Baptism as a new and an everlasting covenant is the means whereby each individual signifies his acceptance of the gospel covenant. In baptism each person signs, as it were, the contractual agreement; he promises to live by gospel standards, and the Lord promises to pour out upon him all of the blessings of the gospel, the chief of which is eternal life. Baptism and the resultant conformity to the Lord's laws thus comprise "the doctrine of Christ, and the only and true doctrine of the Father, and of the Son, and of the Holy Ghost." (2 Nephi 31:21.)

2.   Baptism—Part of the Eternal Plan

From the eternal standpoint, the plan of salvation includes the creation, the fall, and the atonement. It is the atonement that puts into full operation all of the terms and conditions of the Father's plan. And the atonement was the work of the Son; it has now been wrought by him, and its blessings are available to all.

From the standpoint of mortal men, the plan of salvation includes the things they must do to receive the blessings offered through the atonement. These revealed things that men must do to work out their salvation with fear and trembling before the Lord are five in number: (a) believe in God and have faith in Christ; (b) forsake the world and repent of all ungodliness; (c) make the covenant of baptism in water; (d) receive the gift of the Holy Ghost; and (e) keep the commandments after baptism, thus living after a Godly manner, thus enduring in righteousness unto the end.

In the beginning, by his own voice, God revealed the plan of salvation to Adam in these perfectly phrased words: "If thou wilt turn unto me, and hearken unto my voice, and believe, and repent of all thy transgressions, and be baptized, even in water, in the name of mine Only Begotten Son, who is full of grace and truth, which is Jesus Christ, the only name which shall be given under heaven, whereby salvation shall come unto the children of men, ye shall receive the gift of the Holy Ghost, asking all things in his name, and whatsoever ye shall ask, it shall be given you." (Moses 6:52.)

3. Why the Lord Requires Baptism

Every law, every truth, and every ordinance in the holy gospel of Him by whom salvation comes has been given to us for a reason. All of the laws, truths, and ordinances of the gospel play their part in the redemption of fallen man. In each instance, the reason they were ordained and established is so eternally important that men are damned if they break the law, reject the truth, or ignore the ordinance. Baptism serves four basic purposes in the eternal scheme of things. These are:

(a)   Baptism is for the remission of sins. No unclean thing can enter the kingdom of God or dwell in his holy presence. Figuratively speaking, sins are washed away in the waters of baptism; in the literal sense, they are burned out of a human soul as though by fire upon the receipt of the Holy Ghost. "Why is it that men must repent and be baptized in water?" Adam asked the Lord. "Behold I have forgiven thee thy transgression in the Garden of Eden," came the reply. (Moses 6:53.) Hence baptism is essential to salvation.

(b)   Baptism admits contrite and repentant souls into the church and kingdom of God on earth. The church administers the gospel, and the gospel brings salvation. Salvation comes by obedience to all of the laws and ordinances of the gospel. Thus, without baptism, without the church, and without the gospel, there would be no salvation. Hence baptism is essential to salvation.

(c) Baptism and repentance are the gate to the strait and narrow path that leads to eternal life. "The gate by which ye should enter is repentance and baptism by water," Nephi says, "and then cometh a remission of your sins by fire and by the Holy Ghost. And then are ye in this strait and narrow path which leads to eternal life." (2 Nephi 31:17-18.) Hence baptism is essential to salvation.

(d) Baptism in water and of the Spirit includes the receipt of the gift of the Holy Ghost. The Holy Ghost is a sanctifier; he alone, by divine appointment, has power to sanctify a human soul; and the sanctified are those "of the celestial world." (D&C 88:2.) No person enters that glorious kingdom unless and until he is clean and spotless and sanctified. Hence baptism is essential to salvation.

4. Baptism and Salvation

Baptism leads to salvation; for accountable persons, the absence of baptism guarantees damnation. Those who are baptized and who thereafter keep the commandments will be saved; with those who are not baptized, it will be otherwise. Salvation is for the clean, the spotless, and the sanctified, and for them only. To us in this day the Lord has said: "He that believeth and is baptized shall be saved, and he that believeth not, and is not baptized, shall be damned." (D&C 112:29.) And also: "Every soul who believeth on your words, and is baptized by water for the remission of sins, shall receive the Holy Ghost. . . . [And] they who believe not on your words, and are not baptized in water in my name, for the remission of their sins, that they may receive the Holy Ghost, shall be damned, and shall not come into my Father's kingdom where my Father and I am." (D&C 84:64, 74.)

Jacob told his Nephite brethren that Christ "commandeth all men that they must repent, and be baptized in his name, having perfect faith in the Holy One of Israel, or they cannot be saved in the kingdom of God. And if they will not repent and believe in his name, and be baptized in his name, and endure to the end, they must be damned." (2 Nephi 9:23-24.)

Our friend Mormon placed baptism and salvation in their proper place in the eternal scheme of things in these inspired words: "The first fruits of repentance is baptism; and baptism cometh by faith unto the fulfilling the commandments; and the fulfilling the commandments bringeth remission of sins; and the remission of sins bringeth meekness, and lowliness of heart; and because of meekness and lowliness of heart cometh the visitation of the Holy Ghost, which Comforter filleth with hope and perfect love, which love endureth by diligence unto prayer, until the end shall come, when all the saints shall dwell with God." (Moroni 8:25-26.)

5. Baptism Is a Commandment

Baptism is not an optional ordinance; it is not something for those only who are especially devout and pious. It is for all men, and it comes from God by way of commandment. Those who are not baptized thereby turn from the order of heaven, defy the will of the Lord, and break one of his great and eternal commandments. "Now this is the commandment," the Risen Lord said to the Nephites: "Repent, all ye ends of the earth, and come unto me and be baptized in my name." (3 Nephi 27:20.) In his ministry among the Jews, speaking of John the Baptist, Jesus said: "All the people that heard him, and the publicans, justified God, being baptized with the baptism of John. But the Pharisees and lawyers rejected the counsel of God against themselves, being not baptized of him." (Luke 7:29-30.)

What answer will the unbaptized give in the day of judgment when the great Judge asks: "Why did you reject the counsel of God, being not baptized? Why did you break my commandment to be baptized in my name?" If we are not baptized, we are not his.

6. The Covenant of Baptism

A covenant is a contract in which two or more parties promise and agree to do certain things. Gospel covenants are made between God and men. Baptism is the covenant in which men promise to keep the commandments of God and he promises to give them eternal life. There are many ways in which men's promises might be recounted. Alma, at the waters of Mormon, summarized them by having each repentant soul swear in substance and thought content:

(a)   to forsake the world, to repent of all his or her sins, to join the true church, "to come into the fold of God."

(b)   to become a saint, to be numbered with the true believers, to take upon me the name of Christ and become one of his family, "and to be called [one of] his people."

(c)   to love and serve his fellowmen, to esteem others as himself, and to bear the burdens of his brethren in the church, "that they may be light."

(d)   to visit the fatherless and the widows in their afflictions, to care for the sick, the helpless, and the bereaved, and "to mourn with those that mourn."

(e)   to proclaim peace, to spread solace, and to "comfort those that stand in need of comfort."

(f)   to preach the gospel, to raise the warning voice, to call sinners to repentance, and to stand as a witness of Christ "at all times and in all things, and in all places . . . even until death."

(g)   to serve the Lord "and keep his commandments"—a promise that is itself infinite and endless, and is so worded as to embrace conformity to every word that proceedeth forth from the mouth of God.

On his part, as Alma expresses it, the Lord promises that those who love and serve him shall receive such great blessings as these:

(a)   He covenants to baptize them with fire and with the Holy Ghost, to give them the companionship of his Holy Spirit, to "pour out his Spirit more abundantly upon" them.

(b)   He covenants that his saints shall be redeemed—redeemed from death, hell, the devil, and endless torment; redeemed temporally and spiritually; redeemed from their spiritual fall so that, having been raised in immortality, they will return to his presence and be inheritors of eternal glory.

(c)   He covenants that they shall "be numbered with those of the first resurrection," that they shall come forth in the resurrection of the just, that they shall rise from death with a celestial body, which can stand the glory of the celestial kingdom.

(d)   He covenants that they shall have eternal life, which is to inherit, receive, and possess the fulness of the glory of the celestial world. It is to be like God. (Mosiah 18:8-10.)

Surely the upright and the honest, the good and the pure,

the decent and the noble, among all sects, parties, and denominations—regardless of their present religious profession—ought to desire with all their hearts both to make and to keep the grand covenant of baptism by which salvation comes!

7. The Baptism of Jesus

Why was Jesus baptized? John was baptizing repentant persons in the murky waters of a now hallowed Jordan River, baptizing them for the remission of sins and promising that one who came after, who was mightier than he, would baptize them with the Holy Ghost and with fire. In the midst of this great religious crusade, the Sinless One came and asked for baptism at John's hand. John knew that Jesus, who knew no sin, had no sins to be washed away in Jordan; John knew that the Son, to whom God had given the Spirit during every moment of his mortal life, had no need to receive the Holy Ghost, which was already his constant companion. To our Lord the Baptist said: "I have need to be baptized of thee, and comest thou to me?" Jesus said simply: "Suffer it to be so now: for thus it becometh us to fulfil all righteousness." Thereupon the Baptist immersed the Son of God in the water, the Spirit of God descended in sweet serenity upon the Mortal Messiah, and the Father said: "This is my beloved Son, in whom I am well pleased." (Matthew 3:7-17.)

The Son of God baptized by mortal man! Why? In what way did he fulfill all righteousness by submitting to the baptism of John? He, being holy, had no need for the remission of sins, no need to come forth in a newness of life, no need to become clean so as to be sanctified by the power of the Spirit.

"But notwithstanding he being holy," Nephi says, "he showeth unto the children of men that, according to the flesh he humbleth himself before the Father, and witnesseth unto the Father that he would be obedient unto him in keeping his commandments." Jesus was baptized as a token of humility, and in his baptism he made a covenant with his Father to love and serve him everlastingly.

But there were other reasons also. His baptism "showeth unto the children of men the straitness of the path, and the narrowness of the gate, by which they should enter, he having set the example before them." Though Jesus was God; though he reigned in the heavenly kingdom; though he was alive spiritually and fit in all respects to return to the presence of the Father —yet he was baptized. He was baptized in order to gain salvation in the celestial kingdom of God, thereby setting the perfect example for all men.

"And he said unto the children of men: Follow thou me. Wherefore, my beloved brethren, can we follow Jesus save we shall be willing to keep the commandments of the Father?" asks Nephi. "The Father said: Repent ye, repent ye, and be baptized in the name of my Beloved Son. And also, the voice of the Son came unto me, saying: He that is baptized in my name, to him will the Father give the Holy Ghost, like unto me; wherefore, follow me, and do the things which ye have seen me do." (2 Nephi 31:5-12.)

8. Preparation for Baptism

Knowing that baptism is of infinite worth unto us, knowing that it is a holy ordinance to which even Jesus was subject, and knowing that no unbaptized person can go where God and Christ are, it follows that no price is too great to pay for the privilege of receiving this holy ordinance. We must prepare ourselves for baptism; we must be worthy to make a covenant with the Holy One; we must have a fixed and unalterable determination to conform to his will. Otherwise baptism profiteth nothing. No ordinance is binding on earth and in heaven unless it is ratified and sealed by the Holy Spirit of Promise, and this Spirit is given only to those who are just and true. Just as those who partake unworthily of the sacrament eat and drink damnation to their souls, so those who are baptized unworthily receive cursings instead of blessings.

"See that ye are not baptized unworthily," Moroni taught. (Mormon 9:29.) To be worthy of baptism, men must have faith in Christ; they must confess their sins and forsake them; they must "manifest by their works that they have received of the Spirit of Christ unto the remission of their sins." (D&C 20:37.) In describing how the church operated in his day, Moroni says that converts "were not baptized save they brought forth fruit meet that they were worthy of it." He says that the elders did not "receive any unto baptism save they came forth with a broken heart and a contrite spirit, and witnessed unto the church that they truly repented of all their sins. And none were received unto baptism save they took upon them the name of Christ, having a determination to serve him to the end." (Moroni 6:1-3.) And thus has it been in all dispensations.

9. After Baptism, What?

Baptism is not an end in itself; rather, it is the beginning of a new way of life. It puts the contrite soul on the path leading to eternal life. The trials and tests of life do not cease at baptism; new converts may expect to be tried and tested after baptism. The Lord has promised to "prove [the saints] in all things," to see if they will "abide in [his] covenant, even unto death." (D&C 98:14.)

Jesus commanded his apostles: "Go ye therefore, and teach all nations, baptizing them in the name of the Father, and of the Son, and of the Holy Ghost: teaching them to observe all things whatsoever I have commanded you." (Matthew 28:19-20.) After baptism, the saints must work out their own salvation with fear and trembling before the Lord.

Nephi asks the members of the church—those who through baptism have their feet planted on the strait and narrow path—"if all is done." Will they be saved by baptism alone, or is more required? Can we believe in Christ, repent of our sins, accept baptism, find fellowship with the saints, and then rest secure in the hope of gaining eternal life? In answer we say: Baptism is a beginning; baptism opens a door; baptism charts a course. After baptism comes obedience—obedience to all of the promises made in the covenant of baptism, obedience to all of the laws and ordinances of the gospel. There is no salvation without baptism, but baptism alone does not save. And Nephi, in answer to his own question, said: "Ye must press forward with a steadfastness in Christ, having a perfect brightness of hope, and a love of God and of all men. Wherefore, if ye shall press forward, feasting upon the word of Christ, and endure to the end, behold, thus saith the Father: Ye shall have eternal life. And now, behold, my beloved brethren, this is the way; and there is none other way nor name given under heaven whereby man can be saved in the kingdom of God." (2 Nephi 31:19-21.)

10. The Antiquity of Baptism

Baptism is an eternal and everlasting ordinance. Men on all the worlds of the Lord's creating are saved by the same gospel, the same plan of salvation, the same laws and ordinances, baptism included. As pertaining to this earth and its inhabitants, baptism began with Adam our father, the first man. "He was caught away by the Spirit of the Lord, and was carried down into the water, and was . . . brought forth out of the water. And thus he was baptized." (Moses 6:64-65.)

And thus the pattern was set: baptism was for Adam and for all the sons of Adam. All of the apostles and prophets had the gospel; all were baptized and all performed baptisms. We have scriptures that speak of baptism in connection with Enoch, Noah, Abraham, and Moses. (Moses 6:47-68; 8:19-24; JST, Genesis 17:3-7; 1 Corinthians 10:1-4.) Isaiah's statement that the "house of Jacob, which are called by the name of Israel and [had] come forth out of the waters of Judah," refers to "the waters of baptism." (Isaiah 48:1; 1 Nephi 20:1.) The very law of Moses itself is "the gospel of repentance and of baptism, and the remission of sins." (D&C 84:27.) The molten sea, standing on twelve brazen oxen in Solomon's Temple, was a baptismal font. The Nephite portion of Israel was baptizing for more than six hundred years before the Lord Jesus ministered among them in resurrected glory. When John the Baptist cried repentance and invited all Jewry to report at Bethabara and have their sins washed away in the Jordan, he was following a familiar pattern. The Jews of that day understood and practiced the law of baptism. It was a normal and natural thing for penitent persons to flock to John and desire immersion at his hands.

The antiquity and efficacy of baptism were confirmed to the Prophet Joseph Smith in the revelation directing the organization of the church in this dispensation. The revealed word says that Christ was crucified, died, rose again, and ascended into heaven "that as many as would believe and be baptized in his holy name, and endure in faith to the end, should be saved—not only those who believed after he came in the meridian of time, in the flesh, but all those from the beginning, even as many as were before he came, who believed in the words of the holy prophets." (D&C 20:25-26.)

Truly baptism is for the believers of all ages—past, present, and future.

11. Baptism and Damnation

Baptism of the type and kind given of God, when performed for penitent persons by a legal administrator, opens the door to celestial salvation. Those who do not believe and are not baptized are damned. There is, as Paul says, "one Lord, one faith, one baptism." (Ephesians 4:5.)

All this is as well known to Satan as it is to us. What is more natural, then, than for him to persuade men to ignore baptism entirely or, if not that, to accept a perverted form that is administered by ministers who have no divine appointment? Such, it is sad to report, is what has transpired from the earliest days where all but a few faithful souls are concerned. Among most of Adam's seed, even at this late date, baptism is unknown and unperformed. And among Christians it is almost universally perverted and is always performed without authority.

As far back as Abraham's day, as the scriptures attest, the Lord said to the Father of the Faithful: "My people have gone astray from my precepts, and have not kept mine ordinances, which I gave unto their fathers; and they have not observed mine anointing, and the burial, or baptism wherewith I commanded them; but have turned from the commandment, and taken unto themselves the washing of children, and the blood of sprinkling: and have said that the blood of the righteous Abel was shed for sins; and have not known wherein they are accountable before me. But as for thee, behold, I will make my covenant with thee, . . . that thou mayest know for ever that children are not accountable before me until they are eight years old." (JST, Genesis 17:4-8, 11.)

There is no change in the law of baptism that strays farther from the divine standard than "the washing of children," or in other words the baptism of children who have not arrived at the age of accountability. It appears from what the Lord told Abraham that infant baptism was practiced in the very earliest days of man's mortal life on planet earth. We know it was had among the Nephites around 400 A.D. About the same time in the Old World it became the established system of the Christian world, and it prevails in many places at the present time.

The practice of infant baptism bears witness that those who espouse it have forsaken the true Christ and no longer rely on his redeeming power. Little children are alive in Christ because of the atonement. They "are redeemed from the foundation of the world through mine Only Begotten," saith the Lord; "wherefore, they cannot sin, for power is not given unto Satan to tempt little children, until they begin to become accountable before me." (D&C 29:46-47.) They cannot sin; they cannot repent; they need no baptism.

12. Baptism for the Dead

If God is a just and holy being who is no respecter of persons and who loves all his children, he will provide a way for all to be saved. If he is a being in whom there is no variableness, neither shadow of turning, he will provide the same plan of salvation for all men in all ages. If those who lived in the meridian of time could be saved through faith, repentance, and baptism, such also must be the case for all who went before and all who came after. If salvation comes by believing in Christ and living the laws of his gospel, then all men must have an equal opportunity to believe and obey. If such an opportunity does not come to them in this mortal life, it must be theirs in the spirit world, before the day of final judgment.

If the living are saved by baptism, the dead must be saved in the same manner; otherwise God would be partial, unjust, a respecter of persons, and would, in fact, be sending many of his children to an eternal hell without even giving them a chance to obtain heaven. It follows that the gospel is preached in the spirit world and that there is an ordinance of baptism for the dead. Thus we find Paul asking: "Else what shall they do which are baptized for the dead, if the dead rise not at all? why are they then baptized for the dead?" (1 Corinthians 15:29.)

Baptisms for the dead and all of the other ordinances of salvation and exaltation are performed vicariously for the dead in holy temples built for that purpose. The performance of these ordinances is one of the evidences of the divinity of the great latter-day work. Where they are performed by legal administrators empowered so to act, there is the true church; and where these performances are not found, there the church and kingdom of God on earth is not.

CHAPTER 28

The Holy Ghost

The Holy Ghost and the Light of Christ

Men ought—above all things in this world—to seek for the guidance of the Holy Spirit. There is nothing as important as having the companionship of the Holy Ghost. Those who first receive this endowment and who then remain in tune with this member of the Eternal Godhead will receive a peace and a comfort that passeth all understanding; they will be guided and preserved in ways that are miraculous; they will be instructed until they receive all truth; they will sanctify their souls so as to dwell spotless before the Sinless One in his everlasting kingdom.

There is no price too high, no labor too onerous, no struggle too severe, no sacrifice too great, if out of it all we receive and enjoy the gift of the Holy Ghost. It follows that faithful people desire to know who or what the Spirit is; to know the part he plays in the plan of salvation; to know the blessings that flow from his hands; to know his relationship to the Father and the Son; to know what mortals must do to be filled with his goodness and grace. It is to these and related matters that we shall now give attention. To guide us in our search, we shall set forth the doctrines involved. They should generate the motivating power that will enable us to gain the blessings so devoutly desired.

The Spirit Personage in the Godhead

There are in the Eternal Godhead three persons or personages each of whom is a holy man having his own body, which body in each instance is a separate eternal soul. The Father and the Son are personages of tabernacle who have bodies "of flesh and bones as tangible as man's." They have each passed through a mortal probation; they have resurrected and immortal bodies in which body and spirit are inseparably connected. "The Holy Ghost has not a body of flesh and bones," however, "but is a personage of Spirit." (D&C 130:22.) He is thus a spirit man, a spirit person, a spirit entity. He lives and moves and has his being separate and apart from his fellow Gods. His spirit body is in all respects comparable to the kind of a body that the Lord Jehovah possessed before that beloved and chosen one made flesh his tabernacle by the process of mortal birth. These three persons —the Father, the Son, and the Holy Ghost—are one God, or in other words, one Godhead, because of the perfect unity that prevails among them in all things.

The Father is the Creator by whom all things are; the Son is the Redeemer by whom all of the terms and conditions of the Father's plan are put into full operation; and the Holy Ghost is their minister and their messenger, the one who does, at their bidding, what must be done for men to make them fit candidates to go where God and Christ are. Each member of the Godhead individually and all of them collectively possess the same character, perfections, and attributes. These we have set forth in our consideration of the Godhead. Each of these holy beings is a God in his own right and, where character, perfections, and attributes are concerned, is one with the others. With reference to the Holy Ghost, for instance, this is illustrated by such scriptural statements as that "the Spirit knoweth all things." (Alma 7:13.)

Who Has Seen the Personage of the Holy Ghost?

Prophets and saints in all dispensations have seen the Lord Jesus Christ, in both the dreams of the night and the visions of the day, and also face to face as a man looketh upon and speaketh with his friends. Some have even been privileged to see the Father also. But with the Holy Ghost it is otherwise. His voice is heard; his influence is felt; his presence is manifest— but his person is kept hidden from view in all but rare instances.

The Father created salvation and offered it to his children; the Son wrought the infinite and eternal atonement that makes the salvation of the Father available to all who will believe and obey. Man's attention is and should be centered in the Father and the Son as far as persons are concerned. The Holy Ghost is their minister and messenger. He brings the word from them; he delivers their message; he bears record of them and their divine goodness. And he seeks to center our attention and affection in those whom he represents. Nonetheless, there have been occasions when the person of the Holy Ghost has been seen. These have been manifest to and can be comprehended by the spiritually enlightened and by none others. Allusions to them are found in holy writ so that those who seek to know the mysteries of godliness may be enlightened and reassured.

Although the account is meager and the record fragmentary, we can point to John the Baptist as one who saw the person of the Holy Ghost. After Jesus was baptized of John in Jordan, as Luke expresses it, "the Holy Ghost descended in a bodily shape . . . upon him." Because the Holy Ghost is a spirit man, the only "bodily shape" John could have seen was that of a spirit personage. Inserted in Luke's account is the phrase "like a dove," clearly meaning that the Spirit came with the calmness, serenity, and peace of which the dove is a symbol. (Luke 3:22.) Mark's account says that John "saw the heavens opened, and the Spirit like a dove descending upon him." (Mark 1:10.) Matthew bears a similar witness. (Matthew 3:16.)

By way of interpretation, the Prophet Joseph Smith said that "the *sign* of the dove" was given as a witness that the baptism had divine approval. "The sign of the dove was instituted before the creation of the world, a witness for the Holy Ghost, and the devil cannot come in the sign of a dove," he said. "The Holy Ghost is a personage, and is in the form of a personage. . . . The Holy Ghost cannot be transformed into a dove; but the sign of a dove was given to John to signify the truth of the deed, as the dove is an emblem or token of truth and innocence." (*History of the Church* 5:261.)

Names of the Holy Ghost

Both the Father and the Son are known by many names. Each name centers our attention on something about their persons, or about their characters, perfections, or attributes, thus enlarging our knowledge of these two supreme beings. So also is it with reference to the Holy Ghost. In the scriptures he is called the Spirit, the Spirit of God, the Spirit of the Lord, the Holy Spirit, the Spirit of Truth, and the Comforter. He can also with propriety be called the Testator, Testifier, Witness, Revelator, and Sanctifier.

Christ is also called the Spirit of Truth and the Second Comforter. Often the scriptures use the same names to identify the gift of the Holy Ghost as they do to single out the person of that member of the Godhead. Some of the names of the Holy Ghost are also used in the revelations to refer to the light of Christ, which the Holy Ghost uses in performing his labors. In some passages the same name may mean both the Holy Ghost and the light of Christ, depending upon the application being made.

Oftentimes in speaking and writing, even some of our most insightful theologians confuse and intermingle passages having reference to different things. In gaining a knowledge of all things, it is incumbent upon us to learn the true and diverse meanings of the same names as they are found and used in different contexts.

The Gift of the Holy Ghost

On the day of Pentecost, Peter said to those who believed his teachings and testimony about the Lord Jesus: "Repent, and be baptized every one of you in the name of Jesus Christ for the remission of sins, and ye shall receive the gift of the Holy Ghost." (Acts 2:38.) This gift is a special endowment of divine grace and goodness that is received after baptism and is conferred upon believing souls by the laying on of hands. It is the right to the constant companionship of the Holy Ghost based on faithfulness. It is the right to receive revelation, to see visions, and to be guided from on high. It opens the door so that spiritual gifts and all that the Lord has in store for the faithful may flow to them in abundant measure.

"There is a difference between the Holy Ghost and the gift of the Holy Ghost," the Prophet taught. (*History of the Church* 4:555.) The Holy Ghost is a personage of Spirit; the gift of the Holy Ghost is the right to receive the companionship and association of the Spirit, together with all the spiritual graces and blessings reserved for the faithful. The Holy Ghost is properly referred to as "he," the gift of the Holy Ghost as "it."

There is also a difference between the gift of the Holy Ghost and the enjoyment of the gift. All saints after baptism receive the gift or right to the sanctifying power of the Spirit; only those who are worthy and who keep the commandments actually enjoy the promised reward. In practice, members of the Church enjoy the companionship of the Spirit from time to time as they manage, by obedience, to get in tune with the Infinite.

The actual enjoyment of the gift of the Holy Ghost is a supernal gift that a man can receive in mortality. The fact of its receipt is a witness that the saints so blessed are reconciled to God and are doing the things that will assure them of eternal life in the realms ahead. Is it any wonder, then, that the Nephite Twelve "did pray for that which they most desired; and they desired that the Holy Ghost should be given unto them." (3 Nephi 19:9.)

The Light of Christ

There is a spirit—the Spirit of the Lord, the Spirit of Christ, the light of truth, the light of Christ—that defies description and is beyond mortal comprehension. It is in us and in all things; it is around us and around all things; it fills the earth and the heavens and the universe. It is everywhere, in all immensity, without exception; it is an indwelling, immanent, ever-present, never-absent spirit. It has neither shape nor form nor personality. It is not an entity nor a person nor a personage. It has no agency, does not act independently, and exists not to act but to be acted upon. As far as we know, it has no substance and is not material, at least as we measure these things. It is variously described as light and life and law and truth and power. It is the light of Christ; it is the life that is in all things; it is the law by which all things are governed; it is truth shining forth in darkness; it is the power of God who sitteth upon his throne. It may be that it is also priesthood and faith and omnipotence, for these too are the power of God.

This light of truth or light of Christ is seen in the light of the luminaries of heaven; it is the power by which the sun, moon, and stars, and the earth itself are made. It is the light that "proceedeth forth from the presence of God to fill the immensity of space." It is "the light which is in all things, which giveth life to all things, which is the law by which all things are governed, even the power of God who sitteth upon his throne, who is in the bosom of eternity, who is in the midst of all things." It is the agency of God's power; it is the means and way whereby "he comprehendeth all things," so that "all things are before him, and all things are round about him." It is the way whereby "he is above all things, and in all things, and is through all things, and is round about all things." Because of it, "all things are by him, and of him, even God, forever and ever." (D&C 88:6-13, 41.)

Thus, when the Mosaic account of the creation says that "the Spirit of God moved upon the face of the waters" (Genesis 1:2), and when Abraham records of those same events that "the Spirit of the Gods was brooding upon the face of the waters" (Abraham 4:2), the revealed word is speaking of the light of Christ. And when Job says that "by his spirit [the Lord] hath garnished the heavens" (Job 26:13), and the Psalmist explains that all things were created because the Lord sent forth his spirit, by which also he "renewest the face of the earth" (Psalm 104:30), both are teaching the same truth. Creation itself came by the light of Christ.

The light of Christ is neither the Holy Ghost nor the gift of the Holy Ghost; but that member of the Godhead, because he along with the Father and the Son is God, uses the light of Christ for his purposes. Thus spiritual gifts, the gifts of God— meaning faith, miracles, prophecy, and all the rest—come from God by the power of the Holy Ghost. Men prophesy, for instance, when moved upon by the Holy Ghost. And yet Moroni says: "All these gifts come by the Spirit of Christ" (Moroni 10:17), meaning that the Holy Ghost uses the light of Christ to transmit his gifts. But the Spirit of Christ, by which the Holy Ghost operates, is no more the Holy Ghost himself than the light and heat of the sun are the sun itself.

The Light of Christ—for All Men

The light of Christ, conforming to the will of that God whose influence and spirit it is, dwells in the hearts of all men. If it were not present, life would cease, for it is the light of life as that life comes from God. It is the instrumentality and agency by which Deity keeps in touch and communes with all his children, both the righteous and the wicked. It has an edifying, enlightening, and uplifting influence on men. One of its manifestations is called conscience, through which all men know right from wrong.

It is the means by which the Lord invites and entices all men to improve their lot and to come unto him and receive his gospel. It is the agency through which the Lord strives with men, through which he encourages them to forsake the world and come unto Christ, through which good desires and feelings are planted in the hearts of decent people. It is the medium of intelligence that guides inventors, scientists, artists, composers, poets, authors, statesmen, philosophers, generals, leaders, and influential men in general, when they set their hands to do that which is for the benefit and blessing of their fellowmen. By it the Lord guides in the affairs of men and directs the courses of nations and kingdoms. By it the Lord gives ennobling art, the discoveries of science, and music like that sung in the courts above. By it he dispenses truth in a host of ways to all who will heed the promptings.

It is the Spirit, promised of old, that is being poured out "upon all flesh" in the last days, thus preparing them for the receipt of the Holy Ghost and that high state of spirituality of which Joel, speaking in the name of the Lord, said: "Your sons and your daughters shall prophesy, your old men shall dream dreams, your young men shall see visions: and also upon the servants and upon the handmaids in those days will I pour out my spirit." (Joel 2:28-29.) It is "the Spirit of God that . . . came down and wrought upon" Columbus, leading him to the Lamanites "who were in the promised land." (1 Nephi 13:12.)

Truly, man does not stand alone. God governs in all the affairs of men, and he does it by the power of his Spirit, the Spirit of Jesus Christ, the light of Christ, which is in all things. In reciting all these things, the scriptures speak as though this light or power or influence or spirit strives and entices and enlightens, although it is in reality the agency through which the Lord himself does all these things.

All men are enlightened by the light of Christ. "I am the true light that lighteth every man that cometh into the world," he says. (D&C 93:2; John 1:9.) The light of Christ is the light of truth. Thus all men have the obligation to seek the truth, to believe the truth, and to live the truth. "The word of the Lord is truth, and whatsoever is truth is light, and whatsoever is light is Spirit, even the Spirit of Jesus Christ." This is the Spirit that God gives to all men. "And the Spirit giveth light to every man that cometh into the world; and the Spirit enlighteneth every man through the world, that hearkeneth to the voice of the Spirit." (D&C 84:45-46.)

All men receive this Spirit, but not all hearken to its voice. Many choose to walk in carnal paths and go contrary to the enticings of the Spirit. It is possible to sear one's conscience to the point that the Spirit will withdraw its influence and men will no longer know or care about anything that is decent and edifying. "For my Spirit shall not always strive with man, saith the Lord of Hosts." (D&C 1:33.) Such was the case among the Jaredites (Ether 2:15) and the Nephites (Mormon 5:16) in the day the Lord withdrew his power and left them to be destroyed by the sword. It was true among the Jews in Jerusalem when they were led away captive by Nebuchadnezzar. (1 Nephi 7:14.) It is true among any people who reject, totally and completely, the words of the apostles and prophets who are sent to them. Of our modern civilization, with all its evils and carnality, the holy word says: "I, the Lord, am angry with the wicked; I am holding my Spirit from the inhabitants of the earth." (D&C 63:32.) When the day comes that modern man is ripened in iniquity, the Spirit will cease to strive with them, and they will be destroyed by the brightness of the Lord's return.

Those who follow the promptings of the Spirit accept the gospel and receive the gift of the Holy Ghost. "And every one that hearkeneth to the voice of the Spirit cometh unto God, even the Father. And the Father teacheth him of the covenant which he has renewed and confirmed upon you, which is confirmed upon you for your sakes, and not for your sakes only, but for the sake of the whole world." (D&C 84:47-48.) By following the light of Christ, men are led to the gospel covenant, to the baptismal covenant, to the church and kingdom. There they receive the Holy Ghost.

Truly, "the natural man is an enemy to God, and has been from the fall of Adam, and will be, forever and ever, unless he yields to the enticings of the Holy Spirit, and putteth off the natural man and becometh a saint through the atonement of Christ the Lord." (Mosiah 3:19.) The Holy Ghost does not strive or entice; his mission is to teach and testify. But those who heed the enticements and submit to the strivings of the Holy Spirit (which is the light of Christ) are enabled to receive the Holy Spirit (which is the Holy Ghost).

We have no better illustration of the full operation of the light of Christ upon an investigator of the gospel than what happened to King Lamoni. After the king had fallen to the earth as though he were dead, the scripture says that Ammon "knew that king Lamoni was under the power of God; he knew that the dark veil of unbelief was being cast away from his mind." He knew that "the light which did light up his mind . . . was the light of the glory of God," and that it "was a marvelous light of his goodness." Ammon knew that "this light had infused such joy into [Lamoni's] soul, [that] the cloud of darkness [had] been dispelled." As to Lamoni: "The light of everlasting life was lit up in his soul." (Alma 19:6.) Thereafter, Lamoni was baptized and received the gift of the Holy Ghost.

There is really no excuse for men to reject the gospel message. When they do so, it is because of spiritual blindness or because their deeds are evil and they love darkness rather than light. If they would but hearken to the voice of conscience, to the voice of the light within them, to the voice of the Spirit, they would come unto Christ and receive the Holy Ghost. If they would but heed the whisperings and respond to the enticings planted in their hearts, all would be well with them. "All things which are good cometh of God," Mormon tells us, "and that which is evil cometh of the devil." God entices to do good; the devil entices to do evil. "That which is of God inviteth and enticeth to do good continu- ally; wherefore, every thing which inviteth and enticeth to do good, and to love God, and to serve him, is inspired of God."

How shall man know good from evil? "The Spirit of Christ is given to every man, that he may know good from evil; wherefore, I show unto you the way to judge," Mormon con- tinues, "for every thing which inviteth to do good, and to per- suade to believe in Christ, is sent forth by the power and gift of Christ; wherefore ye may know with a perfect knowledge it is of God." And "the light by which ye may judge," he says, "is the light of Christ." (Moroni 7:12-18.)

The Holy Ghost—a Gift for the Saints

Before and after baptism, all men are endowed to one degree or another with that Spirit which is the light of Christ. Before baptism they may receive revelation from the Holy Ghost for the purpose of giving them a testimony of the truth and divinity of the Lord's work on earth. After baptism they receive the gift of the Holy Ghost, and it is then their right to have the constant companionship of that member of the Godhead if they keep the commandments. The testimony before baptism, speaking by way of analogy, comes as a flash of lightning blazing forth in a dark and stormy night; it comes to light the path on which earth's pilgrims, far from their heavenly home and lost in the deserts and swamps of the world, must walk if they are to return to the Divine Presence. The companionship of the Holy Ghost after baptism is as the continuing blaze of the sun at noonday, shedding its rays on the path of life and on all that surrounds it.

If a devout truth seeker receives a testimony before baptism and does not step forward and receive the gospel, the light is soon gone; the testimony fades away, for one flash of lightning does not show the path ahead for any great distance. An enduring continuance of light and guidance comes only from the sun after the truth seeker leaves the darkness and storms of the night and chooses to walk in the light and calm of the gospel day.

Moroni invites all men to read, ponder, and pray about the Book of Mormon. He promises each sincere person—each person who asks the Father, in the name of Christ, for a witness that the work is true; each person who asks "with a sincere heart, with real intent, having faith in Christ"—that the Lord "will manifest the truth" of the Book of Mormon unto him "by the power of the Holy Ghost." (Moroni 10:4.) This testimony may come before baptism. Similarly, before baptism sincere truth seekers can come to know, by the power of the Holy Ghost, that Jesus is the Lord and that Joseph Smith is a prophet. They are then invited to keep all the truth they already have and to come and receive the added light and knowledge that has come by revelation in our day.

Peter's witness, a witness borne at Caesarea Philippi by the power of the Holy Ghost that Jesus was "the Christ, the Son of the living God" (Matthew 16:16), was given before the chief apostle had received the gift of the Holy Ghost. That holy endowment did not come until the day of Pentecost. Then, for the first time, he and his fellow apostles received the gift that would teach them all things and bring all things to their remembrance. Similarly, Moroni's promise that "by the power of the Holy Ghost ye may know the truth of all things" (Moroni 10:5) is a promise that will find fulfillment after baptism.

The world cannot receive the Holy Ghost because the world is evil; the Spirit will not dwell in unclean and unholy places. There is no way for carnal men to gain the companionship of the Spirit unless they forsake the world and live by godly standards. In words properly applied to the Holy Ghost, Jesus said: "I will pray the Father, and he shall give you another Comforter, that he may abide with you for ever; even the Spirit of truth; whom the world cannot receive, because it seeth him not, neither knoweth him: but ye know him; for he dwelleth with you, and shall be in you." (John 14:16-17.)

In our day and in all dispensations, the Lord's word to his servants is: "Every soul who believeth on your words, and is baptized by water for the remission of sins, shall receive the Holy Ghost." (D&C 84:64.) The gift of the Holy Ghost comes after baptism. As one illustration among many, let us refer to the taking of the gospel to Samaria in the meridian dispensation. Philip taught and baptized among the Samaritans in the power and authority of the Aaronic Priesthood. Then, when the apostles heard of the success of his labors, "they sent unto them Peter and John," who held the Melchizedek Priesthood. These brethren prayed for the Samaritan converts "that they might receive the Holy Ghost: (For as yet he was fallen upon none of them: only they were baptized in the name of the Lord Jesus.) Then laid they their hands on them, and they received the Holy Ghost." (Acts 8:14-17.) Thus it ever has been and thus it ever shall be. Though all men are guided by the light of Christ, only the faithful return to the presence of God and gain the companionship of the Holy Spirit.

CHAPTER 29

The Mission of the Holy Ghost

The Holy Ghost—Minister for the Father and the Son

God's work and his glory—meaning that of either the Father, or the Son, or the Holy Ghost—is to bring to pass the immortality and eternal life of man. There neither is nor can be any greater labor than this. Such is the business of the Father; it is his full-time, all-occupying, unending, everlasting work. All that the Father does in begetting spirit children, in creating endless worlds, in providing a system of salvation for his children, and in sending his Only Begotten into the world has this end in view; all is designed to enable his children to rise in glorious immortality and to enjoy the same type of existence that now is his.

Such also is the business of the Son; it is his employment, his occupation, his office and calling. He so loved the world that he bowed in agony in Gethsemane, as blood oozed from every pore; and his pure and perfect love was crowned when, during the last three hours on the cross of Calvary, he suffered again an infinite burden, as he took upon himself the sins of all men on conditions of repentance. He is the one by whom immortality comes and through whom eternal life is made available.

And such also is the business of the Holy Ghost; it is his assignment, his mission and commission, his labor and work as one of the Eternal Godhead. He is appointed to reveal the plan of salvation to man, to teach the gospel to all who will attune themselves to his voice, to testify of his fellow Gods, and to cleanse fallen man from sin, so that, being clean, man can dwell with the righteous forever. As Christ our Lord took up his body in immortality by the power of the Spirit, so shall all rise in the resurrection of the dead. The work of the Holy

Ghost, as the minister and messenger of the Gods, is to labor to bring to pass the immortality and eternal life of man. We shall now consider the ways in which he performs his mission.

"Receive the Holy Ghost"

After one is baptized, the hands of a legal administrator are placed on his head and he hears the divine decree: "Receive the Holy Ghost." What happens on this sacred occasion? It depends upon the one to whom the promise is made and the command is given. It is an eternal law that the Spirit will not dwell in an unclean tabernacle. "The Lord hath said he dwelleth not in unholy temples, but in the hearts of the righteous doth he dwell." (Alma 34:36.) It follows that we must be worthy in order to receive the Spirit. We must prepare by faith and repentance and righteous living. We must forsake our sins and have a firm determination to serve God and keep his commandments. Then and then only will we be fit recipients of the Holy Spirit.

Those who are worthy for such a sacred association receive the Holy Ghost either immediately after baptism or at such subsequent time as they become a fit companion for that holy being. Should they thereafter cease to be clean and righteous, they lose the Spirit and are left to wallow in the mire of carnality and to be as other men. Hence Paul's counsel to the saints: "Know ye not that ye are the temple of God, and that the Spirit of God dwelleth in you? If any man defile the temple of God, him shall God destroy; for the temple of God is holy, which temple ye are." (1 Corinthians 3:16-17.)

The Holy Ghost—a Sanctifier

To be sanctified is to be saved; to fall short of sanctification is to fail to gain full salvation. Only the sanctified gain eternal life. To be sanctified is to be clean; it is a state of purity and spotlessness in which no taint of sin is found. Only those who die as to sin and are born again to righteousness, becoming thus new creatures of the Holy Ghost, are numbered with the sanctified.

It is the work and mission and ministry of the Holy Spirit of God to sanctify the souls of men. This is his assigned labor in the Eternal Godhead. How he does it we do not know, except

265

that it is a work that can only be performed by a spirit being, and hence the need for one of his personality, status, and standing in the Supreme Presidency of the universe.

Baptism of the Spirit is the way and the means whereby sanctification is made available. Thus, Jesus commands all the "ends of the earth" to be baptized in water "that ye may be sanctified by the reception of the Holy Ghost, that ye may stand spotless before me at the last day." (3 Nephi 27:20.) Truly, the Holy Ghost is a sanctifier, and the extent to which men receive and enjoy the gift of the Holy Ghost is the extent to which they are sanctified. In the lives of most of us, sanctification is an ongoing process, and we obtain that glorious status by degrees as we overcome the world and become saints in deed as well as in name.

The Holy Ghost—a Revelator

Light and truth and knowledge may be gained in many ways. They come through the senses, from experience, and by reason. When so received, man, of course, may be deceived. In their pure and perfect form they are manifest by revelation, through a process of Spirit speaking to spirit, of the Holy Spirit whispering to the properly attuned spirit within us. This also is his work, mission, and assigned ministry. He is a revelator. According to the eternal laws that govern all things, he has power to convey and reveal truth to a human soul with absolute finality. There is never any deception or uncertainty when the Spirit speaks. And where the truths about God and faith and salvation are concerned, there is no way to gain them except by revelation from the Spirit.

Those who have received the gift of the Holy Ghost have this glorious promise: "God shall give unto you knowledge by his Holy Spirit, yea, by the unspeakable gift of the Holy Ghost, [knowledge] that has not been revealed since the world was until now." (D&C 121:26.) As Paul said: "The Spirit searcheth all things, yea, the deep things of God." (1 Corinthians 2:10.) How do these hidden and unknown things come from the Holy Ghost to us? As to this we know only that it is by obedience to those laws upon which the receipt of such heavenly truths is predicated. These are the laws of righteousness. "I will tell you in your mind and in your heart," the Lord says, "by the [power of the] Holy Ghost, which shall . . . dwell in your heart. Now, behold, this is the spirit of revelation." (D&C 8:2-3.) And the presence of the spirit of revelation identifies the true church and kingdom of God on earth; where this is, there is the true church; and where there is no spirit of revelation, there the true church is not.

The Holy Ghost—a Witness

Every man must know for himself of the truth and divinity of the Lord's work, or he cannot be saved. Every man must know the Father and the Son, or he cannot gain eternal life. Every man must have a testimony, receive revelation, and feel the sanctifying power of the Spirit in his life, or he will not stand pure and spotless before the judgment bar. And the Holy Ghost is the witness, sent of God, to testify to every believing soul of the truth of all things. Every member of the Church receives the gift of the Holy Ghost, which includes the right to receive revelation and to understand all of the doctrines of salvation. Thus, all stand on an equal footing before the Lord. As it is with apostles and prophets, so it is with all the saints—all must gain personal revelation, all must receive the witness of the Holy Ghost in their own hearts, all must be apostles and prophets unto themselves.

The Holy Ghost "witnesses of the Father and the Son" (2 Nephi 2:18); he "beareth record of the Father and the Son" (Moses 1:24); he, and he only, makes known those holy beings whom it is life eternal to know. Jesus said: "He shall testify of me" (John 15:26); and, he "beareth record of the Father and me" (3 Nephi 11:32). And Paul said: "No man can say [meaning know] that Jesus is the Lord, but by the Holy Ghost." (1 Corinthians 12:3.) Thus the Holy Ghost is the source of saving knowledge; his mission, assigned by the Father, is to bear witness to the truth of those things which enable men to gain eternal life. His witness is sure; it cannot be controverted; it will stand forever.

The Holy Ghost—a Teacher

Spiritual things, without which there is no salvation, can be known only by the power of the Spirit. Paul lays it down as an eternal principle that "the things of God knoweth no man, except he has the Spirit of God." (JST, 1 Corinthians 2:11.) It could not be otherwise, for salvation is found in a spiritual realm—in a different dimension of existence, a realm that is separate and apart and removed from this mortal sphere. Hence, the Spirit of God has the divine commission to teach spiritual truths by conformity to which the saints can qualify to gain the promised spiritual heights.

Jesus himself set the pattern for gaining light and truth from the Spirit. "He spake not as other men, neither could he be taught; for he needed not that any man should teach him." (JST, Matthew 3:25.) It was he who comforted his apostles with these words: "The Holy Ghost, whom the Father will send in my name, he shall teach you all things, and bring all things to your remembrance, whatsoever I have said unto you." (John 14:26.) And also: "When he, the Spirit of truth, is come, he will guide you into all truth: for he shall not speak of himself; but whatsoever he shall hear, that shall he speak: and he will shew you things to come. He shall glorify me: for he shall receive of mine, and shall shew it unto you." (John 16:13-14.) Moroni's equivalent promise, given to all the saints, is that "by the power of the Holy Ghost ye may know the truth of all things." (Moroni 10:5.) The promise given in this dispensation to all who are baptized is that they shall receive "the Holy Ghost, even the Comforter, which showeth all things, and teacheth the peaceable things of the kingdom." (D&C 39:6.) Truly the Holy Ghost is a teacher; from him the saints learn all that is required to gain their eternal inheritance with the eternal saints in their eternal home.

The Comforter

Because the Holy Spirit speaks peace to the hearts of weary and disconsolate mortals, he is called the Comforter. He brings peace and solace, love and quiet enjoyment, the joy of redemption and the hope of eternal life. These words of promise are given to all who receive the gift of the Holy Ghost: "Therefore it is given to abide in you; the record of heaven; the Comforter; the peaceable things of immortal glory; the truth of all things; that which quickeneth all things, which maketh alive all things; that which knoweth all things, and hath all power, according to wisdom, mercy, truth, justice, and judgment." (Moses 6:61.) How glorious is the word we have received! How wondrous is the Spirit that dwells in faithful hearts!

The Holy Ghost and the Prophetic Word

Prophecy, scriptures, inspired preaching and writing, divine utterances of every sort and kind, all these come by the power of the Holy Ghost. "The Comforter knoweth all things." (D&C 42:17.) Thus, if there is occasion in the providences of the Lord to send any word to men—any word about that which has been, that which is, or that which yet shall be—the message is delivered by the power of the Holy Ghost. All preaching, all teaching, all gospel presentations, in order to have divine approval and carry converting power, must be by the power of the Spirit. So important is this requirement that the holy word prohibits the Lord's ministers from giving utterance to gospel truths unless they do so by divine power. "If ye receive not the Spirit ye shall not teach," the Lord commands. (D&C 42:14.) And those who go forth carrying the word of salvation have this direction: "Take ye no thought how or what thing ye shall answer, or what ye shall say: for the Holy Ghost shall teach you in the same hour what ye ought to say." (Luke 12:11-12.)

Jesus said: The Holy Ghost "will shew you things to come." (John 16:13.) Peter said of those of old who foretold what they foresaw: "The prophecy came not in old time by the will of man: but holy men of God spake as they were moved by the Holy Ghost." (2 Peter 1:21.) And to the Lord's ministers in this day the counsel is: "They shall speak as they are moved upon by the Holy Ghost. And whatsoever they shall speak when moved upon by the Holy Ghost shall be scripture, shall be the will of the Lord, shall be the mind of the Lord, shall be the word of the Lord, shall be the voice of the Lord, and the power of God unto salvation." (D&C 68:3-4.)

The Spirit Speaks the Word of Christ

Salvation is in Christ, not in the Holy Ghost; our Blessed Lord redeemed us, and the Holy Ghost is his messenger to carry the message of redeeming grace into the hearts of men. Thus, the joyous words spoken by the Holy Ghost are in reality the words of Christ. The Spirit is simply the one who delivers the word.

Jesus said: "He shall not speak of himself. . . . He shall glorify me: for he shall receive of mine, and shall shew it unto you." (John 16:13-14.) To Joseph Smith the Lord said: "I speak unto you with my voice, even the voice of my Spirit." (D&C 97:1.) As is well known, many are called to the Lord's work, but few are chosen for eternal life. So that those who are chosen may be sealed up unto eternal life, the scripture says: "It shall be manifest unto my servant, by the voice of the Spirit, those that are chosen; and they shall be sanctified." (D&C 105:36.) They are chosen by the Lord, but the announcement of their calling and election is delivered by the Spirit.

Many scriptures speak of the Holy Ghost doing or saying something when the words and deeds are in reality those of the Lord. When Agabus bound his own hands and feet with Paul's girdle and said, "Thus saith the Holy Ghost, So shall the Jews at Jerusalem bind the man that owneth this girdle" (Acts 21:11), the words did not originate with the Holy Ghost. The Spirit was simply delivering the word of the Lord. When the Holy Ghost fell upon Adam, saying: "I am the Only Begotten of the Father from the beginning, henceforth and forever, that as thou hast fallen thou mayest be redeemed, and all mankind, even as many as will" (Moses 5:9), the Holy Ghost was not making himself the Only Begotten; he was simply speaking in the first person as though he were the Son.

Spiritual Gifts

Spiritual gifts come from God. They are the gifts of God; they originate with him and are special blessings that he bestows upon those who love him and keep his commandments. Because they come by the power of the Holy Ghost, they are also called the gifts of the Spirit. Hence, they are received only by those who are in tune with the Spirit.

These gifts are infinite in number and endless in their manifestations because God himself is infinite and endless, and because the needs of those who receive them are as numerous, varied, and different as there are people in the kingdom. All saints are commanded to seek earnestly the best gifts. Chief among them are the testimony of Jesus, a believing spirit, divine wisdom, heavenly knowledge, faith in the Lord, the working of miracles, prophecy, the beholding of angels and ministering spirits, the discerning of spirits, tongues and their interpretations, the gift of preaching, administrative ability, and the insight to discern and recognize all of the gifts of God, lest there be confusion or deception in the Church. (D&C 46; Moroni 10; 1 Corinthians 12.)

The Holy Ghost Dwells in Us

Passages too numerous to need citation speak of men being full of the Holy Ghost and of that member of the Godhead dwelling in them. John the Baptist was "filled with the Holy Ghost, even from his mother's womb." (Luke 1:15.) Jesus was "full of the Holy Ghost" at all times. (Luke 4:1.) At some time or other during their ministries, such has been the case with all of the prophets.

What does it mean for the Holy Ghost to dwell in us? First, be it noted, the scriptures say that God, meaning the Father, "dwelleth in us," and that "he that dwelleth in love dwelleth in God, and God in him." (1 John 4:12-16.) Be it remembered also that the same applies to the Son. "Christ liveth in me," Paul said. (Galatians 2:20.) And also: "Christ may dwell in your hearts by faith." (Ephesians 3:17.) And yet again: "Jesus Christ is in you, except ye be reprobates." (2 Corinthians 13:5.) Then the scriptures say that "the Holy Ghost has not a body of flesh and bones," as do the Father and the Son, "but is a personage of Spirit." To this is added the somewhat enigmatic statement: "Were it not so, the Holy Ghost could not dwell in us." (D&C 130:22.)

Knowing as we do that the Holy Ghost is the Minister of the Father and the Son—appointed by them, because he is a spirit, to perform a specialized service for men—the meaning of these passages becomes clear. No member of the Godhead dwells in us in the literal sense of the word, but all of them dwell in us figuratively to the extent that we are like them. If we have "the mind of Christ" (1 Corinthians 2:16), which we receive by the power of the Holy Ghost, then Christ dwells in us. If the love of God abides in our souls, which love is a gift of God that comes by the power of the Holy Ghost, then God dwells in us. In some way beyond our comprehension, all of this is possible by the power of the Holy Ghost.

The Power of the Holy Ghost

We have spoken repeatedly of the power of the Holy Ghost. In the broad and general sense, this is the same thing as the power of God. In the same sense that the Father and the Son are omnipotent, omniscient, and omnipresent, so is it with the Holy Spirit, for he is one with them in all things. But in a special and more particular sense, the power of the Holy Ghost is the power he has, because he is a spirit being, to reveal truth to our spirits, to sanctify our souls, to baptize us with fire, and to do and perform all of the labors of his assigned ministry. He is the one who edifies, enlightens, and teaches the saints. He has a refining, uplifting, ennobling influence upon all who will accept his ministrations. "The gift of the Holy Ghost," in the language of Elder Parley P. Pratt, "quickens all the intellectual faculties, increases, enlarges, expands, and purifies all the natural passions and affections, and adapts them, by the gift of wisdom, to their lawful use. It inspires, develops, cultivates, and matures all the fine-toned sympathies, joys, tastes, kindred feelings, and affections of our nature. It inspires virtue, kindness, goodness, tenderness, gentleness, and charity. It develops beauty of person, form and features. It tends to health, vigor, animation, and social feeling. It invigorates all the faculties of the physical and intellectual man. It strengthens and gives tone to the nerves. In short, it is, as it were, marrow to the bone, joy to the heart, light to the eyes, music to the ears, and life to the whole being." (Parley P. Pratt, *Key to the Science of Theology*, Deseret Book, 1978, p. 61.)

The Holy Spirit of Promise

It is the assigned mission of the Holy Ghost to seal men up unto eternal life so they will rise in the resurrection and pass by the angels and the gods and receive their exaltation in the highest heaven of the celestial world. This mission is performed by putting a ratifying seal of approval upon all the righteous acts and all the authoritatively performed ordinances that are found in the life of each saint. That is, the Holy Spirit of Promise gives a promise of blessing and honor to all who are worthy to receive it. He places the divine seal on everything that has the approval of heaven.

To seal, in the scriptural sense, is to ratify, to justify, and to approve. Any act that is approved by the Lord, any act that is ratified by the Holy Ghost, any act that is justified by the Spirit, is one upon which the Holy Spirit of Promise places a divine seal. "All covenants, contracts, bonds, obligations, oaths, vows, performances, connections, associations, or expectations"—in short, all things—must be sealed by the Holy Spirit of Promise, if they are to have "efficacy, virtue, or force in and after the resurrection from the dead." (D&C 132:7.) All that falls short of this divine approval passes away and has no eternal virtue. Among other things, this provision prevents anyone from gaining an unearned blessing.

The Holy Ghost Reproves the World

All men must receive the Holy Ghost in order to be saved. All have power to gain this holy gift, but few there be that find it. Those who fail to take the Holy Spirit for their guide stand reproved and rejected of the Lord. The Lord Jesus promised to send the Comforter to his saints. "When he is come," Jesus promised, "he will reprove the world of sin, and of righteousness, and of judgment: of sin, because they believe not on me; of righteousness, because I go to my Father, and ye see me no more; of judgment, because the prince of this world is judged." (John 16:8-11.)

Men are convicted of sin when they reject the Spirit-borne witness that Jesus is the Christ. They are convicted for rejecting the witness that he is righteous and that righteousness comes by him. They are convicted of false judgment in rejecting the Lord of life and living instead after the manner of the world. Thus saith the Lord: "Behold, I send you out to reprove the world of all their unrighteous deeds, and to teach them of a judgment which is to come." (D&C 84:87.) Truly, the Holy Ghost, by the mouths of the Lord's agents, reproves the world for sin!

CHAPTER 30

The Holy Ghost—
The Lord's Minister

The Holy Ghost Administers the Gospel and the Church

We have set forth the mission of the Holy Ghost with particular reference to his dealings with men as individuals. We have shown, for instance, that he is the Lord's minister who gives revelation, sanctifies souls, dispenses spiritual gifts, and leads men to all truth. Let us now show that none of the blessings of the Spirit are sent forth in a haphazard manner. The Lord's house is a house of order. "The spirits of the prophets are subject to the prophets," as Paul expresses it, "for God is not the author of confusion, but of peace, as in all the churches of the saints." (1 Corinthians 14:32-33.) Accordingly, the Lord gives his Spirit to the leaders of his church so that they may direct that holy organization in harmony with his mind and will. Let us show how the Spirit administers the gospel and guides the church.

1. *True ministers speak by the power of the Spirit.*

We have no doctrines of our own to preach. There is no way any of us can create a plan of salvation that will save and exalt. Salvation and the doctrines of the gospel come from God; they are his; he reveals them to us by the power of the Holy Ghost. Then when we present them to the world, "we speak, not in the words which man's wisdom teacheth, but which the Holy Ghost teacheth." (1 Corinthians 2:13.)

True ministers always speak by the spirit of inspiration. Because they have the gift of the Holy Ghost, they can "speak with the tongue of angels" (2 Nephi 31:13); and angels, who are but true ministers on the other side of the veil, "speak by the power of the Holy Ghost; wherefore, they speak the word of Christ." (2 Nephi 32:3.) Jesus counsels his ministers: "Take no thought how or what ye shall speak: for it shall be given you in that same hour what ye shall speak. For it is not ye that speak, but the Spirit of your Father which speaketh in you." (Matthew 10:19-20.) And also: "Neither take ye thought beforehand what ye shall say; but treasure up in your minds continually the words of life, and it shall be given you in the very hour that portion that shall be meted unto every man." (D&C 84:85.)

False ministers, on the other hand—those ministering in "churches which are built up, and not unto the Lord," those who teach the doctrines of men and not of the Lord—"they shall contend one with another; and their priests shall contend one with another, and they shall teach with their learning, and deny the Holy Ghost, which giveth utterance." (2 Nephi 28:3-4.)

2. *True ministers conform to revealed procedures.*

We have no procedures, no ordinances, no practices of our own. It is not in our power to create a baptism, or provide a sacramental ordinance, or set up an office or an order of priesthood. How could anyone know how, when, and where to perform endowments, baptisms, and sealings, for the living and the dead, unless God revealed it? Knowledge relative to these and all things in the church must come from beyond the veil, if our performances are to have any efficacy, virtue, or force where eternal salvation is concerned.

After his ascension, Jesus, "through the Holy Ghost [gave] commandments unto the apostles whom he had chosen," directing them to govern all things in his church according to the divine pattern. (Acts 1:2.) Other ministers were soon called by the power of the Spirit and were sent forth to labor in Spirit-chosen fields. For instance: "There were in the church that was at Antioch certain prophets and teachers. . . . As they ministered to the Lord, and fasted, the Holy Ghost said, Separate me Barnabas and Saul for the work whereunto I have called them. And when they had fasted and prayed, and laid their hands on them, they sent them away. So they, being sent forth by the Holy Ghost, departed," on the Lord's errand, unto their designated fields of labor, there to perform, by the promptings of the Spirit, those things which were pleasing to that Lord whom they served. (Acts 13:1-4.)

In our day we follow the same pattern. "Every elder, priest, teacher, or deacon," or other church officer, "is to be ordained according to the gifts and callings of God unto him; and he is to be ordained by the power of the Holy Ghost, which is in the one who ordains him." (D&C 20:60.) Thus, "it shall not be given to any one to go forth to preach my gospel, or to build up my church," saith the Lord, "except he be ordained by some one who has authority, and it is known to the church that he has authority and has been regularly ordained by the heads of the church." (D&C 42:11.) Thereafter the teachings and acts of all such must conform to the dictates of the Spirit; otherwise their words and deeds will not be approved, ratified, and sealed on high.

Man can neither create true religion nor administer the true gospel by his own power. These matters rest with the Lord and are given by him, through his Spirit, to those whom he chooses and to none others. If it were not so, the Lord's house would be a house of confusion—the same confusion, be it noted, that prevails among the churches of men and of devils.

3. *The gifts of administration and discernment come from the Spirit.*

Spiritual gifts, in all their wondrous glory, cannot be received by carnal and wicked men; they are reserved for the faithful saints and for them only. These gifts cannot be understood by the power of the intellect alone; they do not rest on the wisdom of men, but are manifest by the power of God. "The natural man receiveth not the things of the Spirit of God: for they are foolishness unto him: neither can he know them, because they are spiritually discerned." (1 Corinthians 2:14.)

But spiritual gifts can be imitated. There are false prophets, false ministers, and false miracles. Satan can speak in unknown tongues, and all but the very elect can be led astray. There are false gifts, false churches, and false gospels. "I fear, lest by any means, as the serpent beguiled Eve through his subtilty," Paul said to the saints in his day, "so your minds should be corrupted from the simplicity that is in Christ." Almost everything found in all the churches of Christendom bears witness that "the simplicity that is in Christ" died when the apostasy was born. "For if he that cometh preacheth another Jesus, whom we have not preached," the ancient apostle continues, "or if ye receive another spirit, which ye have not received, or another gospel, which ye have not accepted," then beware;

flee from falsehood and cleave unto the truth. (2 Corinthians 11:3-4.)

There are two spiritual gifts in particular—the gifts of administration and of discernment—that the Lord has placed in his church to keep his people from being led astray. The saints need not fall heir to false doctrine; they have no need to accept false ordinances; they need not be led astray by false gifts; and their worship can be kept pure and perfect—as long as these two gifts are in active operation.

Paul says that "there are diversities of gifts, but the same Spirit. And there are differences of administrations, but the same Lord. And there are diversities of operations, but it is the same God which worketh all in all." Then he names some of the spiritual gifts that are administered or dispensed to the individual saints. He compares these gifts to the members or parts of the body, each gift being a separate member, but all of them together forming one body. The church, he says, is "the body of Christ," and each of the saints is a part or member of that body. Apostles, prophets, teachers, miracles, healings, governments—all of these, he says, are found in the true church. And through the officers named, the church is governed and the gospel is administered. (1 Corinthians 12.)

Paul then gives a comparison between charity and the gifts of the Spirit (1 Corinthians 13), followed by a long discussion on the relative importance of prophecy and tongues. Following this, certain conclusions are reached, such as: All things are to be done unto edifying. Only two or three should speak in tongues in one meeting. An interpreter must always be present. Two or three prophets may speak while the other prophets sit in judgment upon their words. All prophetic utterances are subject to and governed by other prophets. Presiding prophets are always in control. There is to be no confusion, no disorder. All things are to be done decently and in order. (1 Corinthians 14.) That is to say, there is order and system in the church. Someone is always in charge. Members do not act independently as their whims dictate. The Lord's house is a house of order. Someone with discernment sits in judgment on what is said and done, rejecting the bad and approving the good.

Moroni says that "there are different ways that these gifts [of God] are administered." (Moroni 10:8.) In the revelation on spiritual gifts that has come in our day, the Lord approaches the problem directly. He says: "Ye are commanded in all things to ask of God, who giveth liberally." It is the Lord's work; he will determine what ought to be done and said in his church. "And that which the Spirit testifies unto you even so I would that ye should do in all holiness of heart, walking uprightly before me, considering the end of your salvation, doing all things with prayer and thanksgiving." Manifestly, anyone who walks in such a godly course will be in tune with the Spirit and will know the mind and will of the Lord. As to why the saints must so seek and so live, the divine word says: "That ye may not be seduced by evil spirits, or doctrines of devils, or the commandments of men; for some are of men, and others of devils. Wherefore, beware lest ye are deceived; and that ye may not be deceived seek ye earnestly the best gifts."

The gifts used in administering and regulating the church are then named: "To some it is given by the Holy Ghost to know the differences of administration, as it will be pleasing unto the same Lord, according as the Lord will, suiting his mercies according to the conditions of the children of men." All of the gifts of the Spirit must be dispensed in an orderly way, according to the needs and conditions of the moment. All of the affairs of the earthly kingdom must be administered as changing needs and circumstances require.

Also: "It is given by the Holy Ghost to some to know the diversities of operations, whether they be of God, that the manifestations of the Spirit may be given to every man to profit withal." It is to the gift of discernment that reference is here made. Appointed leaders must be able to divide true doctrine from false, to single out true prophets from the false, to discern between true spirits and false ones.

"And unto the bishop of the church, and unto such as God shall appoint and ordain to watch over the church and to be elders unto the church, are to have it given unto them to discern all those gifts lest there shall be any among you professing and yet be not of God. And it shall come to pass that he that asketh in Spirit shall receive in Spirit; that unto some it may be given to have all those gifts, that there may be a head, in order that every member may be profited thereby." (D&C 46:7-29.)

As long as the Lord's people enjoy the gifts of the Spirit, including the gifts of administration and discernment, they will

278

never go astray. And "all these gifts, . . . which are spiritual," Moroni says, "never will be done away, even as long as the world shall stand, only according to the unbelief of the children of men." (Moroni 10:19.)

Blasphemy Against the Holy Ghost

Because the Holy Ghost is a personage of spirit, he has power to convey truth to the spirit within us with absolute certainty. From him we can come to know, nothing doubting, that Jesus is Lord of all. When this revealed knowledge is received without limit or bounds, when the heavens are opened and a mortal knows his Maker, when a man gains this perfect knowledge, then, should he fall away, he commits the unpardonable sin. He denies that the sun shines while he sees it. He becomes an enemy of God, and though he had a perfect knowledge of the divine Sonship, he classifies himself as one who would have crucified Christ. This sin is the blasphemy against the Holy Ghost, because the sure and perfect knowledge of God and Christ and their laws can come only by revelation from the Holy Ghost. The principle involved is stated in these words of revelation: "Of him unto whom much is given much is required; and he who sins against the greater light shall receive the greater condemnation." (D&C 82:3.)

"All manner of sin and blasphemy shall be forgiven unto men," Jesus says, "but the blasphemy against the Holy Ghost shall not be forgiven unto men. And whosoever speaketh a word against the Son of man"—not then having the perfect knowledge of which we speak—"it shall be forgiven him: but whosoever speaketh against the Holy Ghost, it shall not be forgiven him, neither in this world, neither in the world to come." (Matthew 12:31-32.) By way of definition and explanation, our latter-day revelation says: "The blasphemy against the Holy Ghost, which shall not be forgiven in the world nor out of the world, is in that ye commit murder wherein ye shed innocent blood"—the innocent blood here involved is Christ's—"and assent unto my death, after ye have received my new and everlasting covenant, saith the Lord God." (D&C 132:27.)

The blasphemy against the Holy Ghost is to deny Christ by denying the sure witness received from the Holy Ghost. "After ye have repented of your sins," the Lord Jesus said to Nephi, "and witnessed unto the Father that ye are willing to keep my commandments, by the baptism of water, and have received the baptism of fire and of the Holy Ghost, and can speak with a new tongue, yea, even with the tongue of angels, and after this should deny me, it would have been better for you that ye had not known me." (2 Nephi 31:14.)

The Eternal Holy Ghost

As a member of the Eternal Godhead, the Holy Ghost is an eternal being. As a gift from Deity to man, the gift of the Holy Ghost has been available everlastingly. It is an essential part of the plan of salvation on this and on all worlds. Unless and until men enjoy the gift of the Holy Ghost, they do not receive the fulness of the everlasting gospel and hence are not heirs of the fulness of salvation. As pertaining to this earth and its inhabitants, Adam received the Holy Ghost and was born again, thus setting the pattern for his seed forever. After his spiritual rebirth "he heard a voice out of heaven, saying: Thou art baptized with fire, and with the Holy Ghost. This is the record of the Father, and the Son, from henceforth and forever; and thou art after the order of him who was without beginning of days or end of years, from all eternity to all eternity. Behold, thou art one in me, a son of God; and thus may all become my sons." (Moses 6:66-68.)

From Adam to Noah, and from Noah to Abraham, and from Abraham to Moses, and from Moses to Jesus and his apostles — all the prophets, and all the saints, and all true believers had the Holy Ghost. As far as we know, there were always prophets and legal administrators in ancient Israel who held the Melchizedek Priesthood, by which power the gift is given. Some of our best doctrinal teachings relative to this superlative gift were given by our Nephite brethren in the so-called pre-Christian era. While Jesus ministered among men, the gift itself was temporarily withheld; one member of the Godhead dwelling with mortals sufficed. During that period, however, the Holy Ghost frequently spoke to righteous persons, as he did to Peter in the coasts of Caesarea Philippi. Just a few hours before Jesus went to Gethsemane and from there to the cross, he told his disciples: "It is expedient for you that I go away: for if I go not away, the Comforter will not come unto you; but if I depart, I will send him unto you." (John 16:7.) This promise— that the constant companionship of the Holy Spirit would be available—was fulfilled on the day of Pentecost.

It is to the writings of Nephi that we turn for what is probably the best recitation in holy writ relative to the eternal nature of this eternal gift. "The Holy Ghost . . . is the gift of God unto all those who diligently seek him," our prophetic friend says, "as well in times of old as in the time that he [Christ] should manifest himself unto the children of men. For he"—our blessed Lord of whom the Holy Ghost testifies—"is the same yesterday, to-day, and forever; and the way is prepared for all men from the foundation of the world, if it so be that they repent and come unto him." And the way is to receive the Holy Ghost and work the works of righteousness. "For he that diligently seeketh shall find; and the mysteries of God shall be unfolded unto them, by the power of the Holy Ghost, as well in these times as in times of old, and as well in times of old as in times to come; wherefore, the course of the Lord is one eternal round." (1 Nephi 10:17-19.)

CHAPTER 31

The Spiritual Birth

Born of the Spirit

There is a natural birth, and there is a spiritual birth. The natural birth is to die as pertaining to premortal life, to leave the heavenly realms where all spirits dwell in the Divine Presence, and to begin a new life, a mortal life, a life here on earth. The natural birth creates a natural man, and the natural man is an enemy to God. In his fallen state he is carnal, sensual, and devilish by nature. Appetites and passions govern his life, and he is alive—acutely so—to all that is evil and wicked in the world.

The spiritual birth comes after the natural birth. It is to die as pertaining to worldliness and carnality and to become a new creature by the power of the Spirit. It is to begin a new life, a life in which we bridle our passions and control our appetites, a life of righteousness, a spiritual life. Whereas we were in a deep abyss of darkness, now we are alive in Christ and bask in the shining rays of his everlasting light. Such is the new birth, the second birth, the birth into the household of Christ.

A wise and good man, one Nicodemus by name, sought counsel in secret from Jesus following the first Passover of our Lord's ministry. Jesus said to him: "Except a man be born again, he cannot see the kingdom of God." Born again! Except a man becomes alive to the things of the Spirit, how can he recognize the truth? Unless the light of heaven rests upon him, how can he ever see within the veil and gain even a glimpse of the celestial world?

Nicodemus was troubled. Being himself as yet dead to the things of the Spirit, he asked: "How can a man be born when he is old? can he enter the second time into his mother's womb, and be born?" The questions were unworthy of one who was a master in Israel. He should have known, and all men should now know, the system that has prevailed among men from Adam to the present. Jesus said: "Verily, verily, I say unto thee, Except a man be born of water and of the Spirit, he cannot enter into the kingdom of God." The reference is to immersion in water, which even then was being performed by the Baptist at Bethabara, and also to immersion in the Spirit, a baptism soon to be performed by the One whose shoe's latchet the Baptist felt unworthy to loose.

There followed, however, a doctrinal explanation. "That which is born of the flesh is flesh; and that which is born of the Spirit is spirit," Jesus said. These are the two births, the natural and the spiritual. "Marvel not that I said unto thee, Ye must be born again," Jesus continued. "The wind bloweth where it listeth, and thou hearest the sound thereof, but canst not tell whence it cometh, and whither it goeth: so is every one that is born of the Spirit." (John 3:3-8.)

Birth from the waters of the Jordan was a visible sign for all to see; witnesses can testify of the occasion when men are born of water. But birth from a state of worldliness is as the spring breeze that blew through Jerusalem that night. None can tell its source or see its destiny. Only the newborn babe in Christ knows if he has been born of the Spirit; he alone can testify of the workings of the Holy Spirit in his heart. But both baptisms, both births, that of water and that of the Spirit, are essential to salvation.

Alma the son of Alma, baptized in his youth but as yet spiritually dead, went about with the sons of Mosiah seeking to destroy the church of God. Rebuked, smitten, condemned by an angelic ministrant, he lay in a trance for three days and three nights. When he gained consciousness again, he said: "I have repented of my sins, and have been redeemed of the Lord; behold I am born of the Spirit." The spiritual regeneration that follows baptism at long last was his. Whereas for long years he had stumbled along in spiritual darkness, now the light of heaven rested upon him, and the course he should now pursue was plainly lighted.

While he lay in a trance, the Lord said to him: "Marvel not that all mankind, yea, men and women, all nations, kindreds, tongues and people, must be born again; yea, born of God, changed from their carnal and fallen state, to a state of righteousness, being redeemed of God, becoming his sons and daughters. And thus they become new creatures; and unless they do this, they can in nowise inherit the kingdom of God." (Mosiah 27:24-26.) Such is the doctrine relative to being born again. And for aught we know, the same Lord who spoke these words to Alma may have recited them over again to Nicodemus more than a century later in John's home in Jerusalem. Truly, all men must be born again!

Sons and Daughters of Jesus Christ

Those who are born again not only live a new life, but they also have a new father. Their new life is one of righteousness, and their new father is God. They become the sons of God; or, more particularly, they become the sons and daughters of Jesus Christ. They bear, ever thereafter, the name of their new parent; that is, they take upon themselves the name of Christ and become Christians, not only in word but in very deed. They become by adoption the seed or offspring of Christ, the children in his family, the members of his household, which is the perfect household of perfect faith. And further: Having become the sons of God (Christ), they also become joint-heirs with him of the fulness of the glory of the Father, thus becoming by adoption the sons of God the Father.

John tells us that the Lord Jesus, who came in time's meridian unto his own, was rejected by them. "But as many as received him," as their Messiah and Savior, "to them gave he power to become the sons of God, even to them that believe on his name." (John 1:12.) Speaking of that same meridian day, the same Lord said in our day: "To as many as received me, gave I power to become my sons." Be it noted that true believers are not automatically born to a newness of life by the mere fact of belief alone. That belief and that acceptance of the Savior gives them power to become the sons of God. And in our day the divine word continues: "Even so will I give unto as many as will receive me, power to become my sons." And how are those who receive the Lord identified? By way of answer, he tells us: "Verily, verily, I say unto you, he that receiveth my gospel receiveth me; and he that receiveth not my gospel receiveth not me." (D&C 39:4-5.) Those who have accepted the fulness of the everlasting gospel as it has come again in our day through the instrumentality of Joseph Smith have power to become the sons of God; those who reject this heaven-sent message of salvation reject that Lord whose message it is and remain outside the Lord's family.

In addressing a congregation of contrite and penitent Nephites, King Benjamin, using that simplicity of speech and clarity of expression in which Book of Mormon prophets so excel, said to his fellow saints: "Because of the covenant which ye have made ye shall be called the children of Christ, his sons, and his daughters." They thus gain a new father, and he gains new children. "For behold, this day he hath spiritually begotten you." Their new birth is not a natural but a spiritual birth. "For ye say that your hearts are changed through faith on his name; therefore, ye are born of him and have become his sons and his daughters."

Thus it is that the saints are born of Christ because they have been born of the Spirit; they are alive in Christ because they enjoy the companionship of the Spirit, and they are members of his family because they are clean as he is clean. "And under this head ye are made free"—being in Christ, they are free from the bondage of sin—"and there is no other head [other than Christ our Head] whereby ye can be made free." Only those who accept Christ and receive the Spirit can free themselves from the sins of the world. "There is no other name given whereby salvation cometh; therefore, I would that ye should take upon you the name of Christ, all you that have entered into the covenant with God that ye should be obedient unto the end of your lives." (Mosiah 5:7-8.)

Those who receive the Lord Jesus and believe in their hearts that he is the Son of God by whom salvation comes; those who then covenant in the waters of baptism to serve him and keep his commandments; those who believe the gospel and are members of the earthly kingdom—these are the ones who have power to become his sons and daughters. Thus they are the ones who take upon themselves his name.

In our day the divine word from the Lord Jesus commands: "Take upon you the name of Christ, and speak the truth in soberness. . . . Behold, Jesus Christ is the name which is given of the Father, and there is none other name given whereby man can be saved; wherefore, all men must take upon them the name which is given of the Father, for in that name shall they be called at the last day; wherefore, if they know not the name by which they are called, they cannot have place in the kingdom of my Father." (D&C 18:21-25.)

It was ever thus. Isaiah prophesied of the "seed" of Christ. (Isaiah 53:10.) Abinadi says "his seed" consists of the prophets and saints who hearken to his word, who believe he will "redeem his people," who gain "a remission of their sins," and who are thus "heirs of the kingdom of God." (Mosiah 15:11.)

Our theologically gifted friend Paul teaches the doctrine of spiritual rebirth and of becoming sons and daughters of both the Father and the Son, explaining that true believers, converted souls, righteous saints, those who are born again, "walk not after the flesh, but after the Spirit." To walk after the manner of the flesh is to live after the manner of the world; to walk after the manner of the Spirit is to overcome the world and live by the standards of the gospel. "For they that are after the flesh do mind the things of the flesh"—they live carnal and evil lives—"but they that are after the Spirit the things of the Spirit." Theirs is a godly course of conduct. "For to be carnally minded is death; but to be spiritually minded is life and peace. Because the carnal mind is enmity against God: . . . so then they that are in the flesh cannot please God." The Lord cannot look upon sin with the least degree of allowance. Those who live after the manner of the flesh are damned; those who bridle their passions and overcome the world are saved.

As to the saints of God, Paul says: "But ye are not in the flesh, but in the Spirit, if so be that the Spirit of God dwell in you. Now if any man have not the Spirit of Christ, he is none of his." In the full and eternal sense, even in the true church, only those saints who enjoy the companionship of the Spirit belong to the Lord; they are the only ones who are the Lord's people in the sense of gaining salvation. "And if Christ be in you, the body is dead because of sin; but the Spirit is life because of righteousness. But if the Spirit of him that raised up Jesus from the dead dwell in you"—if you have the companionship of the Holy Ghost—"he that raised up Christ from the dead shall also quicken your mortal bodies by his Spirit that dwelleth in you." Ye shall be born again; ye shall become new creatures of the Holy Ghost; your bodies shall be quickened, shall be made new, shall become fit tabernacles in which the Spirit may dwell.

"Therefore, brethren, we are debtors, not to the flesh, to live after the flesh." The saints must not live in sin. "For if ye live after the flesh, ye shall die: but if ye through the Spirit do mortify the deeds of the body, ye shall live." Those who live after the manner of the world are spiritually dead; those who control the appetites of the flesh and pursue a godly course are alive spiritually. "For as many as are led by the Spirit of God, they are the sons of God. For ye have not received the spirit of bondage again to fear." Ye are made free from the bondage of sin through Christ. "But ye have received the Spirit of adoption [of sonship], whereby we cry, Abba, Father." *Abba* is an Aramaic word that means father; the meaning here is that we sense and feel our newly found relationship with God the Father and hence feel free to address him in a friendly and familiar way.

"The Spirit itself beareth witness with our spirit, that we are the children of God: And if children, then heirs; heirs of God, and joint-heirs with Christ; if so be that we suffer with him, that we may be also glorified together." That is, because we have been adopted into the family of Christ, because we have taken his name upon us, and because he has accepted us in full, we are also accepted by his Father. We become joint-heirs with the Son. We are adopted into a state of sonship by the Father. Christ is his natural heir, and as adopted sons, we become joint-heirs, receiving, inheriting, and possessing as does the Natural Heir. Because we conform "to the image of his Son," we are also "glorified" with him. (Romans 8:4-30.) And thus, in like manner, the inhabitants of all worlds "are begotten sons and daughters unto God" the Father through the atonement of Christ the Son. (D&C 76:24.)

Born of Water, Blood, and Spirit

Three elements are involved in every valid baptism. Unless they are present, unless they are inseparably connected, unless they act in perfect harmony, there is no legal and lawful baptism. These three are the water, the blood, and the Spirit.

Baptism itself is dual in nature; it consists of two parts, an immersion in water and an immersion in the Spirit. But baptism operates and has efficacy, virtue, and force because of blood, the blood of Christ. Baptism is a birth, a new birth, a birth in water and of the Spirit; but these two births would be mere formalities, useless performances, needless man-made rites without saving power, if it were not for the atoning blood of the Lamb. That is to say: If there had been no atonement of Christ, no agony of blood and sorrow in Gethsemane, no suffering with blood and pain on Calvary, baptism would be a worthless waste of time and effort. The blessings that flow from baptism come because of the shedding of the blood of Christ. Baptism and all else by which salvation comes have power and efficacy because of the atonement.

Two births are essential to salvation. Man cannot be saved without birth into mortality, nor can he return to his heavenly home without a birth into the realm of the Spirit. By obedience and conformity in preexistence, we earned the right to a mortal birth, and by a like course while here, we become fit candidates for the promised Spirit-birth. The elements present in a mortal birth and in a spiritual birth are the same. They are water, blood, and spirit. Thus every mortal birth is a heaven-given reminder to prepare for the second birth.

The Lord commanded Adam to teach his children: "By reason of transgression cometh the fall, which fall bringeth death." That is, death and procreation entered the world with the fall. Both of them appertain to mortality, and Adam lived in a deathless state of immortality before the fall. "And inasmuch as ye were born into the world by water, and blood, and the spirit, which I have made, and so became of dust a living soul," the Lord continued, "even so ye must be born again into the kingdom of heaven, of water, and of the Spirit, and be cleansed by blood, even the blood of mine Only Begotten."

In every mortal birth the child is immersed in water in the mother's womb. At the appointed time the spirit enters the body, and blood always flows in the veins of the new person. Otherwise, without each of these, there is no life, no birth, no mortality.

In every birth into the kingdom of heaven, the newborn babe in Christ is immersed in water, he receives the Holy Ghost by the laying on of hands, and the blood of Christ cleanses him from all sin. Otherwise, without each of these, there is no Spirit-birth, no newness of life, no hope of eternal life.

Why must we be born of the Spirit? The Divine Voice continues: "That ye might be sanctified from all sin, and enjoy the words of eternal life in this world, and eternal life in the world to come, even immortal glory; for by the water ye keep the commandment; by the Spirit ye are justified, and by the blood ye are sanctified." (Moses 6:59-60.)

Those who are born of the Spirit thereby—that is, by virtue of their spiritual rebirth—overcome the world. They die as to carnality and evil; they live as to spirituality and godliness. And it all comes to pass because they have faith in Christ. "Whosoever believeth that Jesus is the Christ is born of God," John says. Those who are born anew love the Lord and keep his commandments. "For this is the love of God, that we keep his commandments. . . . For whatsoever is born of God overcometh the world: and this is the victory that overcometh the world, even our faith." There is no way to overcome the world except by turning to Christ and his gospel. It is by living the gospel that men forsake the world and are born again. "Who is he that overcometh the world, but he that believeth that Jesus is the Son of God?"

Having so taught, John says of our Lord: "This is he that came by water and blood, even Jesus Christ; not by water only, but by water and blood." That is to say: Christ our prototype was born as we are. He came into the world as a mortal by water and blood and spirit. In his birth, as in the birth of each of us, the requisite elements were present. But in his life, these elements were again present in his death. He sweat great drops of blood in Gethsemane as he took upon himself the sins of all men on conditions of repentance. This same agony and suffering recurred on the cross. It was then that he permitted his spirit to leave his body, and it was then that blood and water gushed from his riven side.

Thus it was that his mortal life ended; thus it was that his atoning death fulfilled the Father's plan; and thus it was that the elements of water, blood, and spirit came not only to signify the spiritual rebirth into the kingdom of God, but also were made symbols of the atonement itself. And, be it remembered, it is because of the atonement that an entrance into the kingdom of heaven is possible. "It is the Spirit that beareth witness" of all these things, "because the Spirit is truth."

Then John says: "There are three that bear record in heaven, the Father, the Word, and the Holy Ghost: and these three are one." The three members of the one Godhead bear everlasting witness of eternal truth. "And there are three that bear witness in earth, the spirit, and the water, and the blood: and these three agree in one." Every birth of water, blood, and spirit is a witness that the infant mortal must in due course be born of water, blood, and Spirit into the kingdom of heaven. And every baptism—in water, of the Spirit, and binding because of Christ's shed blood—is a witness that our Lord's atonement, wherein also the water and blood and spirit were present, is the rock foundation upon which all blessings rest. "This is the witness of God which he hath testified of his Son." This the true saints understand. "He that believeth on the Son of God hath the witness in himself." (1 John 5:1-10.)

Baptism of the Spirit

Questions: When do we receive the actual remission of our sins? When are we changed from our carnal and fallen state to a state of righteousness? When do we become clean and pure and spotless so as to be able to dwell with Gods and angels? What is the baptism of fire and of the Holy Ghost?

Answers: Sins are remitted not in the waters of baptism, as we say in speaking figuratively, but when we receive the Holy Ghost. It is the Holy Spirit of God that erases carnality and brings us into a state of righteousness. We become clean when we actually receive the fellowship and companionship of the Holy Ghost. It is then that sin and dross and evil are burned out of our souls as though by fire. The baptism of the Holy Ghost is the baptism of fire. There have been miraculous occasions when visible flames enveloped penitent persons, but ordinarily the cleansing power of the Spirit simply dwells, unseen and unheralded, in the hearts of those who have made the Lord their friend. And the Spirit will not dwell in an unclean tabernacle.

John, who baptized the Lord Jesus, preached the baptism of repentance. He called upon all men to repent and be baptized in water for the remission of their sins, meaning that if they submitted to his Aaronic authority, they would be blessed in due course with the manifestation of Melchizedek authority of Another who would give them a second baptism. "I indeed baptize you with water unto repentance," he said, "but he that cometh after me is mightier than I, whose shoes I am not worthy to bear: he shall baptize you with the Holy Ghost, and with fire." (Matthew 3:11.)

After his resurrection, Jesus told the apostles: "John truly baptized with water; but ye shall be baptized with the Holy Ghost not many days hence." (Acts 1:5.) The blessed fulfillment came on the day of Pentecost, when "suddenly there came a sound from heaven as of a rushing mighty wind, and it filled all the house where they were sitting. And there appeared unto them cloven tongues like as of fire, and it sat upon each of them. And they were all filled with the Holy Ghost." (Acts 2:1-4.)

To his Nephite apostles Jesus said: "Blessed are they who shall believe in your words, and come down into the depths of humility and be baptized, for they shall be visited with fire and with the Holy Ghost, and shall receive a remission of their sins." (3 Nephi 12:2.) Thus has it been in all ages, and thus is it in our day. After baptism in water, legal administrators lay their hands upon a repentant person and say: "Receive the Holy Ghost." This gives him the gift of the Holy Ghost, which is the right to the constant companionship of that member of the Godhead based on faithfulness. Either then or later, depending upon the individual's personal worthiness, the Holy Ghost comes. The baptized person becomes a new creature. He is baptized with fire, sin and evil are burned out of his soul, and he is born again.

Truly baptism is a death, burial, and resurrection! "We are buried" with Christ "by baptism into death." We die as to sin. Then, "like as Christ was raised up from the dead by the glory of the Father, even so we also should walk in newness of life." We live as to righteousness. "Our old man is crucified with him [Christ], that the body of sin might be destroyed, that henceforth we should not serve sin."

Truly baptism prepares us for a glorious resurrection! "For if we have been planted together in the likeness of his [Christ's] death, we shall be also in the likeness of his resurrection." (Romans 6:3-6.) As he came forth in the resurrection with a celestial body, a body free from sin, a body prepared to dwell everlastingly in a celestial kingdom, so shall it be with us.

All those who have been baptized in water for the remission of their sins; all those who have received the gift of the Holy Ghost; all those who are saints in very deed and who seek salvation—all these desire, above all else, to gain the companionship of the Spirit, the baptism of the Spirit, so they can stand spotless before the Holy One in the day of judgment.

CHAPTER 32

The Sacrament of the Lord's Supper

Three Ordinances, One Covenant

There neither is nor can be any covenant greater than the covenant of salvation. "[To] be saved in the kingdom of God," the Lord says, "is the greatest of all the gifts of God." Truly "there is no gift greater than the gift of salvation." (D&C 6:13.) It follows that there neither are nor can be any ordinances of greater import than those by which we first make and then renew this greatest of all covenants.

The gospel in its everlasting fulness is the covenant of salvation; it is the everlasting covenant or, more particularly, the new and everlasting covenant. It is the covenant wherein God promises to save and exalt his children provided they believe his word and keep his law. This gospel covenant is accepted by men in the waters of baptism. In baptism we covenant to love and serve the Lord, to keep his commandments, and to live as becometh saints. He in turn promises us the companionship of the Holy Spirit beginning here and now and the wondrous gift of eternal life in the kingdom of his Father in the realms ahead. Baptism is thus the formal and divinely approved occasion when each penitent person makes for himself the covenant of salvation.

Baptism is a once-in-a-lifetime ordinance. We are baptized on one occasion only—for the remission of our sins, for entrance into the earthly church, and for future admission into the kingdom of heaven. After baptism, all men sin. None obey the Lord's law in perfection; none remain clean and spotless and fit for the association of Gods and angels. But in the goodness of God, provision is made to renew and give continuing efficacy to our baptismal covenant. From Adam to the death of the Lord Jesus, baptized persons were privileged to renew all of the terms and conditions of their own personal covenant of baptism through the performance of sacrificial offerings. And from the night before the crucifixion until the Lord comes again, and thereafter as long at least as the earth shall stand, baptized persons are privileged to renew their own personal covenant of salvation by partaking worthily of the sacramental emblems.

Each of these ordinances—baptism, sacrifice, and sacrament—is performed in similitude of the atoning sacrifice by which salvation comes. Baptism is in similitude of the death, burial, and resurrection of our Lord. Sacrifices were performed in similitude of the coming sacrifice of the Lamb of God. The sacramental emblems are eaten in remembrance of the broken flesh and spilt blood of Him who died on Calvary. Each of these ordinances, when performed by legal administrators for worthy persons, opens or reopens the door to the companionship of the Holy Spirit while in mortality and to an inheritance of eternal life when men are raised in immortality.

Baptism, sacrifice, and sacrament are thus members of the same family. They are offspring of the same parents, are endowed with similar powers, and exert a like influence upon the lives of men. They were conceived by the same father, and they came forth from the same mother. They were then reared in the same household of faith, and they received the same divine commission—to prepare repentant souls for salvation.

Each is a separate ordinance with its own distinctive types and shadows; each has its own personality and does its own work in its own way. But no one of them acts alone. In ancient days, those who were subject to the covenant of baptism were then privileged to gain the blessings of sacrificial offerings. In the so-called Christian era, the blessings of the sacrament are offered to baptized persons. All three are ordinances of salvation, meaning they are essential to salvation. Thus, those in ancient days who were baptized and who then offered sacrifices were candidates for salvation and, in fact, could not be saved without these two ordinances. And thus also those of us in the Christian era who are baptized and who partake worthily of the sacramental emblems become heirs of salvation and, in fact, cannot be saved without each of these ordinances.

Sacrificial ordinances, designed as they were to point the attention of true believers forward to the coming sacrifice of the Son of God, had an end when our Lord was lifted up upon the cross. His atoning sacrifice, wrought by the shedding of his own blood, ended the shedding of the blood of animals. The types and shadows of a future sacrifice were no longer needed when the supreme sacrifice toward which they pointed had been accomplished. Then it was that the sacramental emblems, taken in token of the broken flesh and spilt blood of the Eternal Sacrificial Lamb, became the typifying symbols of the atoning sacrifice.

As animal sacrifice was done away the sacrament was introduced. The ordinance of sacrifice bore its last witness of the Lord when Jesus and the Twelve ate the Paschal Supper in an Upper Room in old Jerusalem. That same night the ordinance of the sacrament bore its first witness of the same Lord. And, indeed, so united was their joint witness that the very rituals and performances of the *last* Paschal Supper were used to form the rituals and performances of the *first* sacrament of the Lord's Supper. The Paschal meal in Jesus' day called for the devout worshippers to bless both bread and wine and to eat and drink. Jesus simply took the symbols of the past and gave them a new meaning for the future. He broke the unleavened bread of the Passover feast and blessed it and said: "Take, eat; this is in remembrance of my body which I give a ransom for you." He blessed the cup of wine and said: "Drink ye all of it. For this is in remembrance of my blood of the new testament, which is shed for as many as shall believe on my name, for the remission of their sins." (JST, Matthew 26:22-24.)

The Doctrine of the Sacrament

What is the doctrine of the sacrament of the Lord's Supper? What part does this holy ordinance play in enabling the Lord's people to work out their salvation with fear and trembling before him? What must we do to gain the glorious blessings promised the faithful when they partake of the emblems of our Lord's death? Can we be saved in the kingdom of God without partaking worthily of the sacrament? Answers to these and all related questions are found in an understanding of the true doctrine of the sacrament. That doctrine may be summarized in the following way:

1. *The covenant of the sacrament.*

When we partake of the sacrament, we enter into a covenant with the Lord. The promises on our part are: (1) to "always remember him"—we eat the broken bread in remembrance of the body of Christ who was crucified for us, and we drink the wine or water in remembrance of the blood of our Lord which was shed for us in Gethsemane and on Calvary; (2) to witness unto the Father that we are willing to take upon us the name of Christ and be numbered with his people; (3) to witness unto the Father that we are willing to keep the commandments of Christ that he has given us.

The promises on the part of Deity are: (1) that we "may always have his Spirit to be with" us (D&C 20:77-79); (2) that we shall have eternal life. "Whoso eateth my flesh, and drinketh my blood, hath eternal life," Jesus said, "and I will raise him up at the last day." (John 6:54.)

2. *The renewal of the covenant of baptism.*

When we are baptized, we covenant to come into the fold of Christ and be members of his church; to be called his people and take upon ourselves his name; to bear the burdens, both temporal and spiritual, of our fellow saints; to mourn with those who mourn; to comfort those who stand in need of comfort; to offer the message of salvation to our Father's other children; and to keep the commandments of God. The Lord on his part promises us that he will "pour out his Spirit more abundantly upon" us; that we will be numbered with those of the first resurrection; and that we shall have eternal life. (Mosiah 18:8-10.) This is the identical covenant made in the sacramental ordinance. That is to say, it becomes our privilege every time we partake of the sacrament to receive anew the promises and blessings first offered to us in baptism.

3. *The sacrament—for church members.*

Because the sacrament is the ordinance in which we renew the covenant made in the waters of baptism, it follows that it is an ordinance reserved for members of the church. Little children who belong to the church partake of the sacrament in anticipation of the covenant they will make when eight years of age. Thus Jesus instructed his Nephite disciples: "Break bread and bless it and give it unto the people of my church, unto all those who shall believe and be baptized in my name." With reference to administering the sacramental wine, he said: "This shall ye always do to those who repent and are baptized in my name."

A nonmember of the church might properly attend a sacrament meeting without partaking of the sacrament. The saints were commanded to pray for such a person, "and if it so be that he repenteth and is baptized in my name," Jesus said, "then shall ye receive him, and shall minister unto him of my flesh and blood." (3 Nephi 18:5, 11, 30.) In our day the scriptural word attests: "The elders or priests are to have a sufficient time to expound all things" unto new converts "previous to their partaking of the sacrament . . . so that all things may be done in order." (D&C 20:68.)

4. *The law of sacramental worthiness.*

Blessings come as a result of obedience. "When we obtain any blessing from God, it is by obedience to that law upon which it is predicated." (D&C 130:21.) It is personal worthiness that qualifies us to receive the blessings and ordinances of the gospel. Every ordinance must be ratified and sealed by the Holy Spirit of Promise, or it will have no efficacy, virtue, or force in the eternal worlds, for the Holy Spirit of Promise is shed forth upon those only who are just and true. Thus we find Moroni counseling: "Do all things in worthiness." The particular objects of his concern are baptism and the sacrament. "See that ye are not baptized unworthily; see that ye partake not of the sacrament of Christ unworthily," he commands. (Mormon 9:29.)

The worthiness to be baptized and the worthiness to partake of the sacrament are one and the same. Recipients of each of these ordinances must meet the same identical standards. In each instance, penitent persons must "come forth with broken hearts and contrite spirits, and witness before the church that they have truly repented of all their sins, and are willing to take upon them the name of Jesus Christ, having a determination to serve him to the end, and [they must] truly manifest by their works that they have received of the Spirit of Christ unto the remission of their sins." (D&C 20:37.) The preparation is the same for each ordinance; the covenant is the same; and the rewards are the same.

Those who make a mockery of sacred things not only fail to receive the promised blessings, but also heap condemnation upon themselves for seeking in unworthiness that which is reserved for those who are true and faithful. Thus we find Jesus commanding the Nephites: "Ye shall not suffer any one knowingly to partake of my flesh and blood unworthily, when ye shall minister it; for whoso eateth and drinketh my flesh and blood unworthily eateth and drinketh damnation to his soul; therefore if ye know that a man is unworthy to eat and drink of my flesh and blood ye shall forbid him." Such a person, Jesus said, should be labored with in the hope that he would repent and be baptized and become worthy. (3 Nephi 18:28-30.) If a nonmember with no ill intent partakes of the sacrament, it is in his case as though he had simply eaten bread and drunk wine or water. He will be judged according to the intent of his heart.

Paul spoke similarly, but with particular reference to unworthy members of the church. Of the sacramental emblems he said: "As often as ye eat this bread, and drink this cup, ye do shew the Lord's death till he come. Wherefore whosoever shall eat this bread, and drink this cup of the Lord, unworthily, shall be guilty of the body and blood of the Lord. But let a man examine himself, and so let him eat of that bread, and drink of that cup. For he that eateth and drinketh unworthily, eateth and drinketh damnation to himself, not discerning the Lord's body. For this cause many are weak and sickly among you, and many sleep." (1 Corinthians 11:26-30.)

5. *The sacrament and the Spirit of the Lord.*

Desire righteousness, love the Lord, seek the Spirit—these are the Christian's goals. Paul calls upon us to partake of "the fruit of the Spirit," to "live in the Spirit," to "walk in the Spirit." (Galatians 5:22-25.) There is no better counsel; there is no better way. Man can have no higher aim, no greater goal; he can pursue no grander course than that of seeking the Spirit. A Christian's whole purpose in life is to enjoy the companionship of the Holy Spirit, for he knows that through such a course he will find peace in this world and gain eternal life in the world to come.

What better provision could the Lord have made in his eternal plan of salvation than to provide, first, a baptism so that man might "be sanctified by the reception of the Holy Ghost" (3 Nephi 27:20), and then, second, a sacrament so that all who partake worthily might have the Spirit to be with them always? Is it any wonder that all men are commanded to repent and be baptized, and that the saints are commanded to meet together often to partake of the sacramental emblems and to remember the Lord's death till he comes? Baptism and the sacrament, these two holy ordinances above all others, are designed to enable and encourage men to seek that Spirit without whose companionship they cannot be saved in the kingdom of God.

When men eat the sanctified bread and drink the sanctified water, they are entitled to be filled with the Holy Spirit. Thus Jesus, speaking of eating the emblem of his broken flesh, said to the Nephites: "This shall ye do in remembrance of my body, which I have shown unto you. And it shall be a testimony unto the Father that ye do always remember me. *And if ye do always remember me ye shall have my Spirit to be with you.*" And thus Jesus, speaking of drinking the emblem of his spilt blood, said to that same ancient people: "Ye shall do it in remembrance of my blood, which I have shed for you, that ye may witness unto the Father that ye do always remember me. *And if ye do always remember me ye shall have my Spirit to be with you.*" (3 Nephi 18:7-11. Italics added.)

And thus it is that we receive a remission of our sins through baptism and through the sacrament. The Spirit will not dwell in an unclean tabernacle, and when men receive the Spirit, they become clean and pure and spotless.

6. *False sacraments.*

Just as there are false churches whose gospels cannot save, just as there are false baptisms that do not open the door to heaven, so there are false sacraments, sacraments that are not of God, sacraments that do not assure men of the companionship of the Spirit in this life nor of eternal life in the world to come. So important is the sacrament to our salvation that it must be performed in the Lord's own way and by his legal administrators, and in no other way and by no other professing priests. After giving the true order of the sacrament to the Nephites, Jesus said: "I give unto you a commandment that ye shall do these things. And if ye shall always do these things blessed are ye, for ye are built upon my rock. But whoso among you shall do more or less than these are not built upon my rock, but are built upon a sandy foundation; and when the rain descends, and the floods come, and the winds blow, and beat upon them, they shall fall, and the gates of hell are ready open to receive them." (3 Nephi 18:12-13.)

Paul, in even stronger language, counseled the Corinthians to "flee from idolatry," a sin that was creeping in among them because of their perversion of the ordinance of the sacrament. "The cup of blessing which we bless, is it not the communion of the blood of Christ?" he asked. "The bread which we break, is it not the communion of the body of Christ?" He called upon the saints in his day to be united in partaking of the true sacrament. "For we being many are one bread, and one body," he said, "for we are all partakers of that one bread." There cannot be two differing and true systems of sacramental administration any more than there can be two approved systems of sacrifice.

Paul continued by comparing their sacramental aberrations with false sacrifices. "The things which the Gentiles sacrifice, they sacrifice to devils, and not to God," he said, "and I would not that ye should have fellowship with devils." His conclusion: "Ye cannot drink the cup of the Lord, and the cup of the devils: ye cannot be partakers of the Lord's table, and of the table of devils." (1 Corinthians 10:14-21.)

False sacrifices, false sacraments—all false ordinances, for that matter—are not of God. True saints do not want to drink from "the cup of the devils" nor to eat the supposed emblems of our Lord's death at "the table of devils."

The Law of the Sabbath

The Sabbath is a day of worship. It is the Lord's day, a day on which we renew our allegiance to that Lord on whose errand we serve. On the Sabbath day we feed our spirits, we feast upon the word of Christ, and we renew our covenants to serve him with all our might, mind, and strength. The Sabbath is a day of rest from our temporal pursuits, a day in which we do no servile work.

Man does not live by bread alone. He must also take into his soul the word of God. Temporal bread feeds the body, and the word of the Lord feeds the spirit. Body and spirit together, when nourished and strengthened by the fruit of the earth and the fruit from heaven, become the kind of eternal soul that attains salvation. Thus the law of the Sabbath decrees: "Six days shalt thou labour, and do all thy work: But the seventh day is the sabbath of the Lord thy God: in it thou shalt not do any work." (Exodus 20:9-10.) The law of the Sabbath requires that man labor in the fields of the earth, in the spirit of the gospel, for six days so that his body may be fed, and that he then labor in the spirit on the seventh day so that his spirit may be fed.

The Sabbath is the leaven of life. Our conduct on all days is influenced by what we do on the Lord's day. Ancient Israel received this command: "Bear no burden on the sabbath day. . . . Hallow ye the sabbath day." That is: 'Rest from your labors, and worship the Lord.' Had they done so, the Lord would have preserved their kingdom forever. (Jeremiah 17:20-27.) Similarly, if we would keep the Sabbath, the Lord would bless and prosper us beyond anything we have ever known.

The Sabbath is the day appointed on which we should chart a course to eternal life. On it we partake of the sacrament and make the covenant that enables us to have the Lord's Spirit with us on all days and at all times. The course we must pursue to keep this day holy is set forth for us in latter-day revelation. These words of revelation set the tone for the day: "Thou shalt thank the Lord thy God in all things." It is a day to praise God from whom all blessings flow. The Lord's people are a thankful people, and he is pleased with those who recognize his hand in all things.

"Thou shalt offer a sacrifice unto the Lord thy God in righteousness," the divine word continues, "even that of a broken heart and a contrite spirit." Those whose hearts are broken and whose spirits are contrite are candidates for salvation. It is with them as it was with their forebears in Israel who renewed their covenant of salvation by performing sacrificial ordinances. They are offering sacrifices in their hearts and are blessed as were the ancients who shed the blood of animals in similitude of the sacrifice of the Lamb of God.

"And that thou mayest more fully keep thyself unspotted from the world," the Lord continues, "thou shalt go to the house of prayer and offer up thy sacraments upon my holy day." Offer up thy sacraments! A sacrament is a spiritual covenant between God and man. It is a personal covenant between each man and his Maker, a pledge and promise on man's part to forsake personal sins, knowing that if he does so he will be blessed by the Lord. When the saints partake of the ordinance of the sacrament, they promise not simply to keep the commandments in general, but also to serve and conform and obey where they as individuals have fallen short in the past. Every man's sacraments are thus his own; he alone knows his failures and sins, and he alone must overcome the world and the flesh so that he can have fellowship with the saints.

"For verily this [my holy day] is a day appointed unto you to rest from your labors, and to pay thy devotions unto the Most High." Cease from servile work on the Sabbath; rest as pertaining to temporal pursuits; do the Lord's work on the Lord's day. Worship the Lord. "Nevertheless thy vows shall be offered up in righteousness on all days and at all times." True worship goes on seven days a week. Sacraments and vows and covenants of renewal ascend to heaven daily in personal prayer. "But remember that on this, the Lord's day, thou shalt offer thine oblations and thy sacraments unto the Most High, confessing thy sins unto thy brethren, and before the Lord." Our oblations are our offerings to the Lord; they are both temporal and spiritual. We pay our fast offerings and make our means available for the furtherance of the Lord's work on earth. Such offerings are temporal. But we also offer to the Lord a broken heart and a contrite spirit. These offerings are spiritual, and when we make them, it is accounted unto us as though we had put all things on the altar.

"On this day thou shalt do none other thing, only let thy food be prepared with singleness of heart that thy fasting may be perfect, or, in other words, that thy joy may be full. Verily, this is fasting and prayer, or in other words, rejoicing and prayer." Rejoice in the Lord on his holy day! Fast; pray; worship. Pay thy devotions! It is the Lord's day; do thereon the things he wants done. He has given us six days to do our own work. On the Lord's day we do the Lord's work. Can we not labor one day for him, knowing that if we do we shall reap great blessings in the fields of mortality? As it was anciently, so it is today: temporal as well as spiritual blessings come to those who keep the Sabbath. "And inasmuch as ye do these things with thanksgiving . . . the fulness of the earth is yours." (D&C 59:7-16.) Such is the law of the Sabbath.

ARTICLE 5

*We believe
that a man must be called of God,
by prophecy,
and by the laying on of hands
by those who are in authority,
to preach the Gospel
and administer in the ordinances thereof.*

CHAPTER 33

Priesthood—Its Nature and Power

The Doctrine of Authority in the Ministry

Some truths are self-evident. They shed forth the evidence of their own verity, and to state them is to prove them. No proof is needed to show that man exists, that he dwells on an earth, and that he will die in due course.

Some truths are so obvious and their proof so universally evident that every rational being accepts them the moment they come to his attention. No biblical scriptures need be quoted, no textbooks need be studied, and no sermons need be preached to convince men that the sun rises in the eastern sky, that birds fly in the aerial heavens, and that fish swim in the waters of the world. Anyone who opens his eyes and lets a glimmer of reason enter his mind automatically knows and believes these things.

Such also is the case with reference to authority in the ministry. There is no doctrine of the gospel, no truth revealed from heaven, no eternal verity given of God to man that is more self-evident than the fact that a man must be called and empowered by the Lord in order to preach the gospel and administer in its ordinances.

It is self-evident and axiomatic that man cannot create God, or salvation, or the gospel. Man cannot resurrect himself, and he cannot raise himself unto eternal life. And man cannot presume to be a true minister of salvation unless he is called of God, unless he receives revelation so as to learn what he is to do and say, and unless he holds the Holy Priesthood. "No man taketh this honour unto himself," Paul said with reference to the power to perform in a priestly capacity, "but he that is called of God, as was Aaron." Even the Lord Jesus Christ, the very Son of God, "glorified not himself to be made an high priest" (Hebrews 5:4-5), but was called of God to perform the ministry to which he was appointed.

If there is a plan of salvation, it can be known only by revelation. If the gospel is revealed to men, it must come from God to prophets of God's own choosing. If Deity reveals the ordinances of salvation, he must choose and authorize ministers to perform them. If there are no prophets to whom the Lord speaks, then his gospel, his mind and will, and his saving truths cannot be known. And if there are no legal administrators to preach the true gospel, to regulate the earthly kingdom, and to perform the saving ordinances, there will be no salvation. Thus Paul taught: "Whosoever shall call upon the name of the Lord shall be saved." Salvation comes from God and from him only. But: "How then shall they call on him in whom they have not believed? and how shall they believe in him of whom they have not heard? and how shall they hear without a preacher? And how shall they preach, except they be sent?" True ministers must be called and empowered from on high. "So then faith cometh by hearing" the word of truth as it is taught by the power of the Spirit, "and hearing [comes] by the word of God." (Romans 10:13-17.) The word goes forth by those who are called of God and to whom he gives the revelations of his mind and will.

Thus, to understand the doctrine of authority in the ministry, men must accept and believe the following verities:

1. There is a God in heaven whose powers and authority are infinite. He is the author and creator of salvation, and he has offered salvation to men on his own terms and on no others.

2. The Lord's house is a house of order. He has given a law unto all things, and all blessings come by obedience to those laws upon which their receipt is predicated.

3. Salvation is available to men through the gospel. The gospel is, in fact, the plan of salvation, and in it are set forth the terms and conditions upon which God offers salvation to men.

4. Deity calls his own prophets, his own ministers, and his own legal administrators to preach his gospel and to administer the affairs of his earthly kingdom, all so that salvation may be made available to his earthly children.

What then is the doctrine of authority in the ministry? And how does it apply to men? Nowhere in all the scriptures is the doctrine set forth in such perfection as in these words of the Lord to his latter-day prophet: "All covenants, contracts, bonds, obligations, oaths, vows, performances, connections, associations, or expectations, that are not made and entered into and sealed by the Holy Spirit of promise, of him who is anointed, both as well for time and for all eternity, and that too most holy, by revelation and commandment through the medium of mine anointed, whom I have appointed on the earth to hold this power, . . . are of no efficacy, virtue, or force in and after the resurrection from the dead; for all contracts that are not made unto this end have an end when men are dead."

Men can do what they please and make any assumptions they like as to the validity of any of their acts in this life. But as the Lord lives, nothing they do will endure in heaven unless it meets the divine standard here set forth. It must be done in righteousness; it must be approved by the Spirit; and it must be performed and sealed by a legal administrator.

"Behold, mine house is a house of order, saith the Lord God, and not a house of confusion." (D&C 132:7-8.) Is it rational to suppose that doctrines of every varying sort and ordinances of every conflicting kind, and that churches which are at war with each other, are all part of the Lord's house of order? "Is Christ divided?" (1 Corinthians 1:13.) "Will I accept of an offering, saith the Lord, that is not made in my name?" Has he appointed the worship of those who do not even approach the Father in his name? "Or will I receive at your hands that which I have not appointed?" Has he appointed infant baptism, or the ritualistic maze of the mass, or marriages that couple divorce at death with wedlock for life? "And will I appoint unto you, saith the Lord, except it be by law, even as I and my Father ordained unto you, before the world was?" Can man create his own religion, his own power to preach, his own salvation?

To those into whose souls the light of heaven, rising as the sun in the firmament, has begun to gleam, the answers are self-evident and axiomatic. "I am the Lord thy God," cries the Divine Voice, "and I give unto you this commandment—that no man shall come unto the Father but by me or by my word, which is my law." There is no other way. "And everything that is in the world"—there are no exceptions—"whether it be

307

ordained of men, by thrones, or principalities, or powers, or things of name, whatsoever they may be, that are not by me or by my word, saith the Lord, shall be thrown down, and shall not remain after men are dead, neither in nor after the resurrection, saith the Lord your God."

By me or by my word! Either the Lord must do it personally or he must appoint a legal administrator to stand in his place and stead; otherwise the deed will be as the nothingness of dust in the day of judgment. "For whatsoever things remain are by me; and whatsoever things are not by me shall be shaken and destroyed." (D&C 132:9-14.)

All men are bound to find true ministers who preach the true gospel and who have power to perform the true ordinances of salvation so they will be binding on earth and in heaven. Such is the Lord's way, and he has no other.

Priesthood and Keys—Their Nature and Eternity

Authority in the ministry! The right and power to speak for the Lord, to state what he wants stated, to say what he would say if he personally were here! Divine power, the power to perform the ordinances of salvation, the power to bind on earth and have it sealed everlastingly in the heavens! Without all these things, there is no true gospel, no divine church, no salvation for fallen man.

Authority in the ministry means men must hold the priesthood, for that is the name of the authority of God himself. If men hold the holy priesthood, they are the Lord's agents. As agents, they are authorized to represent the Eternal Principal, saying and doing, with delegated authority, what he would say and do in his own person under the same circumstances. If men do not hold the priesthood, and yet assume to preach the gospel and administer its ordinances, they are false agents, false teachers, false ministers. Their acts are not binding upon the Eternal Principal, for he neither employed them in his business nor sent them forth on his errand.

Of his truly appointed ministers, the Lord says: "As ye are agents, ye are on the Lord's errand; and whatever ye do according to the will of the Lord is the Lord's business." (D&C 64:29.) But those whom he has not called are not engaged in "the Lord's business." Any promises they make are not binding upon him, and the ordinances they perform have no efficacy, virtue, or force in and after the resurrection from the dead.

Priesthood—without which no man can represent the Lord; without which no man can be a true minister; without which no man can bind on earth and seal in heaven—priesthood is the very power of God himself. In the broadest sense, priesthood and faith, the two welded together as one, constitute the power by which the worlds were and are and everlastingly shall be made. Through the priesthood, the sidereal heavens were framed. By this power, worlds without number have been created, peopled, and redeemed. By it, all the eternal purposes of the Almighty are accomplished. "The Priesthood is an everlasting principle," the Prophet Joseph Smith said, and has "existed with God from eternity, and will to eternity, without beginning of days or end of years." (*Teachings of the Prophet Joseph Smith*, p. 157.)

As pertaining to this mortal sphere, priesthood is the power and authority of God, delegated to men on earth, to act in all things for the salvation of men. It is the same power held by the noble and great spirits before the foundations of this world were laid. It is the same power carried into the spirit world by the faithful elders when they depart this life. It is the same power the redeemed of the Lord will possess when they rise in glorious immortality and enter into their exaltation, when, reigning from eternal thrones, they will exercise this supreme power forever.

The keys of the priesthood are the right and power of presidency. They are the directing, controlling, and governing power. Those who hold them are empowered to direct the manner in which others use their priesthood. Every ministerial act performed by a priesthood holder must be done at the proper time and place and in the proper way. The power of directing these labors constitutes the keys of the priesthood. Every elder, for instance, has the power to baptize, but no elder can use this power unless he is authorized to do so by someone holding the keys.

The keys of the kingdom are the power, right, and authority to preside over the kingdom of God on earth, which is the Church, and to direct all of its affairs. The keys of any particular ministerial service authorize the use of the priesthood for that purpose. Thus, the restoration by Moses of the keys of the gathering of Israel and the leading of the Ten Tribes from the land of the north opened the door so the priesthood could be used to gather Israel, the Ten Tribes included, into the true fold of their ancient Shepherd.

There were priesthood holders in preexistence; there are many who have held and do hold priestly powers in this probationary estate; and exalted beings will rule with this divine power to all eternity. "The Priesthood was first given to Adam; he obtained the First Presidency, and held the keys of it from generation to generation," the Prophet said. "He obtained it in the Creation, before the world was formed." (*Teachings,* p. 157.) Certainly this was also true of the other noble and great ones. Those who sided with Christ and Adam and who joined with them in taking of the materials that existed and in making an earth—certainly they all acted in the power and authority of the same priesthood held by Jehovah and Michael.

Then, as a mortal and after his baptism, Adam again received the priesthood. Upon its receipt he was told by the Lord: "Thou art after the order of him who was without beginning of days or end of years, from all eternity to all eternity. Behold, thou art one in me, a son of God; and thus may all become my sons." (Moses 6:67-68.)

"Christ is the Great High Priest; Adam next." (*Teachings,* p. 158.) These two set the pattern; they are the great prototypes. They held the priesthood before the world was, again in mortality, and now in immortal glory. Each of them, as a mortal, performed his foreordained labors. And so should it be with all of the Lord's ministers, with reference to whose foreordination in preexistence and reordination in mortality the Prophet said: "Every man who has a calling to minister to the inhabitants of the world was ordained to that very purpose in the Grand Council of heaven before this world was." (*Teachings,* p. 365.) And, be it noted, every holder of the priesthood has a calling to minister, in one way or another, to the inhabitants of the earth.

As to the priesthood received by Adam, the scripture says: "Now this same Priesthood, which was in the beginning, shall be in the end of the world also." (Moses 6:7.) From Adam it went to Seth, Enos, Cainan, Mahalaleel, Jared, Enoch, Methuselah, Lamech, and Noah, the great patriarchs who lived before the flood, and to all of the brethren in their days who were righteous. (D&C 107:41-52.) After the flood, the spiritual giants who bore with honor the holy priesthood included Shem and his descendants; Melchizedek, who conferred it upon Abraham; and Esaias, Gad, Jeremy, Elihu, Caleb, and Jethro, under whose hands it was given to Moses. (D&C 84:6-16.)

Abraham received a promise that his seed, the literal seed of his body, should have a right to the priesthood through all their generations. (Abraham 2:8-11.) There were at many times, and may have been at all times, prophets in Israel who held the higher priesthood, although much of the time the government of the people was in the hands of the lesser priesthood. Elijah, who restored the keys of the sealing power, is an illustration of a prophet in Israel who held the higher priesthood. The Nephite branch of the house of Israel was subject to the higher priesthood during all its history. The Lord's intent and purpose in ancient Israel was to raise up a holy nation who would be a kingdom of priests after the order of Melchizedek, of whom Jesus in due course would be one. (Exodus 19:5-6.)

Jesus and his apostles and hosts of believers in their day were all priests after this higher order, which Peter called "a royal priesthood." (1 Peter 2:5-9.) But with the martyrdom of the apostles, save John only, the keys of the kingdom were taken from mortals. The priesthood could no longer be conferred upon men, and the long night of apostate darkness fell upon the earth. During that day, only translated beings held the priesthood, and it so continued until those arose whose right it was by lineage to claim the holy order again in the day of restoration. (D&C 86:8-11.)

CHAPTER 34

The Priesthood
and Exaltation

The Oath and Covenant of the Priesthood

Salvation, eternal life, exaltation—these three are all one. In the true sense they are identically the same thing and consist of an inheritance in the highest heaven of the celestial world, where alone the family unit continues. Those who so obtain gain the fulness of the glory of the Father and become like him in all things. The whole purpose and end of the Melchizedek Priesthood is to enable men to gain this exalted state in which they will be as their God is.

Celestial marriage is an "order of the priesthood." It is the patriarchal order that opens the door to a continuation of the family unit in eternity. Those who enter this order of matrimony, "meaning the new and everlasting covenant of marriage" (D&C 131:2), and who are true and faithful, will have "a continuation of the seeds forever and ever." They will have a "continuation of the lives" in the realms ahead. Their reward will be "eternal lives," meaning endless lives or eternal increase. (D&C 132:19-24.) Thus Joseph Smith said: "Except a man and his wife enter into an everlasting covenant and be married for eternity, while in this probation, by the power and authority of the Holy Priesthood, they will cease to increase when they die; that is, they will not have any children after the resurrection. But those who are married by the power and authority of the priesthood in this life," and who are true and faithful in all things, "and continue without committing the sin against the Holy Ghost, will continue to increase and have children in the celestial glory." (*Teachings,* pp. 300-301.)

When we receive the Melchizedek Priesthood, we enter into a covenant with the Lord. It is the covenant of exaltation. In it, we promise to magnify our callings in the priesthood, to keep the commandments, "to give diligent heed to the words of eternal life," to "live by every word that proceedeth forth from the mouth of God," and to enter the patriarchal order, which leads to a continuation of the family unit in the realms ahead. In return, the Lord covenants and promises that we shall inherit eternal life. Of those who keep their part of the covenant, he says: "[They] are sanctified by the Spirit unto the renewing of their bodies." That is, they are born again; they become alive in Christ; they are new creatures of the Holy Ghost; they become the sons of God and thus joint-heirs with Christ. "They become the sons of Moses and of Aaron and the seed of Abraham, and the church and kingdom, and the elect of God." They become heirs of the promises made to the fathers, the promises made to Abraham, Isaac, and Jacob that their seed after them would have the right to the gospel and the priesthood and eternal life.

"And also all they who receive this priesthood receive me, saith the Lord; for he that receiveth my servants receiveth me; and he that receiveth me receiveth my Father; and he that receiveth my Father receiveth my Father's kingdom; therefore all that my Father hath shall be given unto him." What more does the Father have than eternal life, than exaltation and Godhood? Is not eternal life the very name of the kind of life Deity lives?

"And this is according to the oath and covenant which belongeth to the priesthood. Therefore, all those who receive the priesthood, receive this oath and covenant of my Father, which he cannot break, neither can it be moved." (D&C 84:33-44.) That there neither is nor can be a covenant more wondrous and great is self-evident. This covenant, made when the priesthood is received, is renewed when the recipient enters the order of eternal marriage.

It takes two parties to make a covenant, but any person alone can swear an oath. Man and Deity enter into the covenant of the priesthood, but only the Lord, meaning the Father, swears the oath. As to this oath, the scriptures, which both acclaim the greatness of the man Melchizedek and set forth the power of the priesthood which bears his name, say this: "Now Melchizedek was a man of faith, who wrought righteousness; and when a child he feared God, and stopped the mouths of lions, and quenched the violence of fire. And thus, having been approved of God, he was ordained an high priest after the order of the covenant which God made with Enoch, it being after the order of the Son of God; which order came, not by man, nor the will of man; neither by father nor mother; neither by beginning of days nor end of years; but of God; and it was delivered unto men by the calling of his own voice, according to his own will, unto as many as believed on his name." How great, how wondrous, how holy is that divine order which has borne successively the names of Enoch and Melchizedek!

"For God having sworn unto Enoch and unto his seed with an oath by himself; that every one being ordained after this order and calling should have power, by faith, to break mountains, to divide the seas, to dry up waters, to turn them out of their course; to put at defiance the armies of nations, to divide the earth, to break every band, to stand in the presence of God; to do all things according to his will, according to his command, subdue principalities and powers; and this by the will of the Son of God which was from before the foundation of the world. And men having this faith, coming up unto this order of God, were translated and taken up into heaven." (JST, Genesis 14:26-32.)

God's decrees are immutable; his promises never fail; he always and everlastingly fulfills that which he says. Thus, those who abide by the conditions of the holy covenant of the priesthood shall have power, by faith, to govern and control all things upon the earth, and they shall "stand in the presence of God," being as he is and living the kind of life he lives. And to show the immutability of his word, he swears with an oath, by himself and in his own name, that all these things shall surely come to pass.

"The power of the Melchizedek Priesthood is to have the power of 'endless lives'; for the everlasting covenant cannot be broken," the Prophet Joseph Smith said. "Those holding the fulness of the Melchizedek Priesthood are kings and priests of the Most High God, holding the keys of power and blessings. In fact, that Priesthood is a perfect law of theocracy, and stands as God to give laws to the people, administering endless lives to the sons and daughters of Adam." (*Teachings,* p. 322.) Endless lives are eternal lives; they are a continuation of the lives or a continuation of the seeds; they are spirit children in the resurrection. The blessing of so obtaining comes to those who receive the fulness of the priesthood; they become, thus, inheritors of eternal life through the continuation of the family unit in eternity.

Christ: The Prototype of Exaltation

The Blessed Jesus, who is the Christ, is our prototype, pattern, and model. As he gained glory and exaltation, so shall we if we do as he did. In all things—in word, in deed, in belief, in doctrine, in faith, in ordinances, in personal righteousness— in all things he says: "Follow thou me." (2 Nephi 31:10.) As he obtained the fulness of the Melchizedek Priesthood in order to gain exaltation, so must we. As Joseph Smith said: "If a man gets a fullness of the priesthood of God he has to get it in the same way that Jesus Christ obtained it, and that was by keeping all the commandments and obeying all the ordinances of the house of the Lord." (*Teachings,* p. 308.)

In setting forth as much as can, with propriety, be spoken outside of the temple, the Lord says that "the fulness of the priesthood" is received only in the temple itself. This fulness is received through washings, anointings, solemn assemblies, oracles in holy places, conversations, ordinances, endowments, and sealings. (D&C 124:40.) It is in the temple that we enter into the patriarchal order, the order of priesthood that bears the name "the new and everlasting covenant of marriage."

As to Christ and his priesthood, David uttered this great Messianic prophecy: "The Lord hath sworn, and will not repent, Thou art a priest for ever after the order of Melchizedek." (Psalm 110:4.) That is to say: The Father swore with an oath that his Son would be an everlasting priest of the holy order. He would minister in the holy Melchizedek Priesthood in time and in eternity, and, reigning as a king and a priest forever, he would thus have eternal life and be as the Father. True, it was his priesthood and he had used it as a spirit being, as did others associated with him, but he was to receive it again in mortality and carry it with him into immortality.

Thus Paul tells us that "Christ glorified not himself to be made an high priest," while in this life, but that he was "called of God, as was Aaron," all in harmony with David's promise.

"In the days of his flesh," Paul tells us, Christ "offered up prayers and supplications," even as Melchizedek had done, "with strong crying and tears unto him that was able to save him from death, and [he] was heard." Then the ancient apostle records this wondrous word: "Though he were a Son, yet learned he obedience by the things which he suffered; and being made perfect, he became the author [or, rather, the cause] of eternal salvation unto all them that obey him; called of God an high priest after the order of Melchisedec." (Hebrews 5:4-10.)

Then Paul applies his teaching that Christ would be a high priest forever in exaltation to all of the faithful saints. To them he says: "God is not unrighteous to forget your work and labour of love, which ye have shewed toward his name, in that ye have ministered to the saints, and do minister. And we desire that every one of you do shew the same diligence to the full assurance of hope unto the end: that ye be not slothful, but followers of them who through faith and patience inherit the promises." (Hebrews 6:10-12.) That is, the Lord remembers and blesses his ministers. Those who minister to the saints and are true and faithful in all things shall be rewarded along with Him whose very name is "Faithful and True," who is also "called The Word of God," and the "KING OF KINGS, AND LORD OF LORDS." (Revelation 19:11, 13, 16.) These faithful ministers are followers of them of old who ministered with like zeal; and, as we have seen, they thus become "the sons of Moses and of Aaron and the seed of Abraham." (D&C 84:34.)

"For when God made promise to Abraham," Paul continues, "because he could swear by no greater, he sware by himself, saying, Surely blessing I will bless thee, and multiplying I will multiply thee. And so, after he had patiently endured, he obtained the promise." (Hebrews 6:13-15.) The promises of God to Abraham, which were renewed by Deity with Isaac and again with Jacob, thus making them "the promises made to the fathers" (D&C 2:2), were the promises that in them and in their seed all generations should be blessed, or, rather, that they and their seed would be a blessing to all nations (D&C 110:12). "Thou shalt be a blessing unto thy seed after thee, that in their hands they shall bear this ministry and Priesthood unto all nations," the Lord said to Abraham. And further: "I give unto thee a promise that this right shall continue in thee, and in thy seed after thee (that is to say, the literal seed, or the seed of the body) shall all the families of the earth be blessed, even with the blessings of the Gospel, which are the blessings of salvation, even of life eternal." (Abraham 2:9-11.) Thus, Abraham and his seed have a *right* to the priesthood, to the gospel, and to eternal life.

Abraham and his seed, of whom Christ was one, have a right to the most glorious blessings ever offered to man. Christ, who was destined to stand as the prototype for all others, was the Chief Seed of Abraham, as we learn from Paul. "Now to Abraham and his seed were the promises made," the ancient apostle says, adding, with reference to our Lord, "and to thy seed, which is Christ." (Galatians 3:16.)

Because the blessings of Abraham exceed anything else on earth or in heaven, Deity uses the most solemn language known to man to confirm their verity. That is, he swears with an oath in his own name that these blessings shall rest upon the faithful forever. "For men verily swear by the greater," Paul continues in his exposition to the Hebrews, "and an oath for confirmation is to them an end of all strife." When men anciently swore with an oath in the Lord's name to perform an act, they thereby made God their partner; and because God does not fail, they were then bound to perform the act or lay down their lives in the attempt. When God himself swears with an oath, he puts his own Godhood on the line: either what he promises shall come to pass or he ceases to be God. And thus the holy word continues: "Wherein God, willing more abundantly to shew unto the heirs of promise the immutability of his counsel, confirmed it by an oath: that by two immutable things, in which it was impossible for God to lie, we might have a strong consolation, who have fled for refuge to lay hold upon the hope set before us." God swore not one oath but two that the promises made to Abraham— that he and his seed had a right to the priesthood, to the gospel, and to eternal life—would surely come to pass.

These are the promises that give us the hope of eternal life. Of this hope the scripture says: "Which hope we have as an anchor of the soul, both sure and stedfast, and which entereth into that within the veil." And this hope of eternal life is the same one had by the Lord Jesus, of whom the record says: "Whither [that is, within the veil] the forerunner is for us entered, even Jesus, made an high priest for ever after the order of Melchisedec." (Hebrews 6:16-20.)

Having thus shown that God swears with an oath that his Son shall stand as a priest of the Melchizedek order in time and in eternity, thus receiving eternal exaltation, our ancient apostolic friend sets forth that this same oath is sworn with reference to every person who receives the Melchizedek Priesthood. "For this Melchizedek, king of Salem, priest of the most high God, who met Abraham returning from the slaughter of the kings, and blessed him," he says, "to whom also Abraham gave a tenth part of all; first being by interpretation King of righteousness, and after that also King of Salem, which is, King of peace; for this Melchizedek was ordained a priest after the order of the Son of God, which order was without father, without mother, without descent, having neither beginning of days, nor end of life. And all those who are ordained unto this priesthood are made like unto the Son of God, abiding a priest continually." (JST, Hebrews 7:1-3.)

Jesus was "made" a high priest "after the similitude of Melchisedec," thus gaining "the power of an endless life" (Hebrews 7:15-16), or in other words, the promise of eternal life and exaltation. He is our prototype, and all who receive the Melchizedek Priesthood become heirs of the same promise; sworn with the same oath; the promise of glory and honor everlasting as joint-heirs with him in the kingdom of his Father.

CHAPTER 35

Modern-day Legal Administrators

Priesthood and Keys—Their Restoration

Because there neither has been nor is nor ever can be any hope of salvation for fallen man unless God intervenes in the affairs of men, revealing himself and his plan of salvation, we ask: *To whom, if anyone, has that revelation come in our day?*

Because this revelation always has and always will come to legal administrators, called and empowered by the Lord himself, we ask: *Where, if anywhere, are the modern legal administrators who have power to represent the Lord on earth?*

Because no man can assume, unilaterally and by one or many acts on his part alone, the prerogative to be the mouthpiece or agent of Deity, we ask: *If there are legal administrators now on earth, how and in what way were they called of God?*

Because God is the same yesterday, today, and forever, because he esteems a soul to be just as precious today as it was in ancient times, because he has always dealt through apostles and prophets, we ask: *Where, if anywhere, are the apostles and prophets today?*

Because there has been a universal apostasy and the faith once delivered to the saints has *not* come down from the fathers unto us, we ask: *What of men today? How can they be saved? What hope is there for the decent and the good and the upright of the earth who are willing to believe and obey all that the Lord will reveal to them?*

To all these questions, and others that are kin to them, there is only one answer. It is: There has been a glorious restoration of the truths and powers of salvation in our day. The Lord has given again every power, right, prerogative, priesthood, and key ever held by any mortal in days gone by. We live in the dispensation of the fulness of times, which means the dispensation of the fulness of dispensations. This is the promised day that bears the name "the times of restitution of all things." In it, all things "which God hath spoken by the mouth of all his holy prophets since the world began" either have been or will be restored. So far this restoration has included the basic doctrines of salvation and all of the powers and keys needed to seal men up unto eternal life. In due course, "when the times of refreshing shall come from the presence of the Lord" (Acts 3:19-21), when the Lord Jesus comes in power and glory to reign personally upon the earth, then all of the truths and doctrines ever known, together with others that have been kept hidden from the foundations of the world, will be revealed by a gracious God to his children on earth.

Prophets and apostles of old held such powers and keys as were needed in their respective days to do the work assigned them. None of them assumed the prerogative to go forth in the Lord's name; all of them were called of God in the same way he always chooses those whom he sends forth on his errand. All of them had divine power. For instance, Jesus "called unto him his twelve disciples [and] gave them power against unclean spirits, to cast them out, and to heal all manner of sickness and all manner of disease." (Matthew 10:1.) Of these apostles Jesus said: "Ye have not chosen me, but I have chosen you, and or-dained you." (John 15:16.) The ancient apostles were ordained; they received the holy priesthood; they were en-dowed with power from on high. After they had received the priesthood, all of them were given the keys of the kingdom.

"I will give unto thee the keys of the kingdom of heaven," Jesus promised Peter. Holding these keys, Peter would have power to preside over and regulate all of the affairs of that church which is the kingdom of God on earth and which pre-pares men for an inheritance in the kingdom of God in heaven. Hence, Jesus promised: "Whatsoever thou [Peter] shalt bind on earth shall be bound in heaven: and whatsoever thou shalt loose on earth shall be loosed in heaven." (Matthew 16:19.) Thus Peter would have power to do all that was necessary to assure men of an inheritance of eternal life in the kingdom of heaven.

320

Jesus and Moses and Elijah gave the keys of the kingdom to Peter, James, and John on the Mount of Transfiguration. (*Teachings*, p. 158.) Thereafter the keys were given to all of the Twelve. (Matthew 18:18.) "As my Father hath sent me, even so send I you," Jesus told them. And then, referring to the keys vested in them all, he said: "Whose soever sins ye remit, they are remitted unto them; and whose soever sins ye retain, they are retained." (John 20:21-23.) By obedience to the laws and ordinances of the gospel, as administered by those holding the keys, men can free themselves from sin and become fit candidates for a celestial inheritance; otherwise their sins are retained and they pay the penalty for the deeds done in the flesh.

As it was anciently, so it is today. Priesthoods and keys and heavenly powers are just as important as they ever were. Where they are present, there is a hope of salvation; if they are absent, there is no true gospel, no power of God unto salvation, no redeeming power, no hope of eternal life.

But thanks be to God, all that mortals possessed anciently in the way of priesthoods and keys has been restored. John the Baptist, ministering as a resurrected and glorified being, on the 15th day of May in 1829, conferred upon Joseph Smith and Oliver Cowdery the Aaronic Priesthood and all of the keys and powers that unto it do appertain. It "holds the keys of the ministering of angels, and of the gospel of repentance, and of baptism by immersion for the remission of sins." (D&C 13.) It is the power by which Aaron and his sons and the Levites in general administered the temporal and spiritual affairs of the Lord in ancient Israel. What those ancient worthies did in their day, legal administrators can do now, because the same ancient power is vested in modern hands. (JS–H 1:68-72.)

Soon thereafter Peter and James, in resurrected glory, and John their fellow minister, serving as a translated being, came also to Joseph Smith and Oliver Cowdery. These heavenly ministrants conferred upon their mortal fellows the Melchizedek Priesthood, the keys of the kingdom of God, and the keys of the dispensation of the fulness of times. (D&C 27:12-13.) This higher priesthood embraces within it the holy apostleship and is the power by which the gospel and the Church are administered, and by which the gift of the Holy Ghost and salvation in its eternal fulness are made available to men. Being thus empowered from on high, the recipients of so great a boon were able to organize the church and kingdom of God on earth, which they did on the 6th of April in 1830.

Thereafter, to fulfill the ancient promise—"I will reveal unto you the Priesthood, by the hand of Elijah the prophet, before the coming of the great and dreadful day of the Lord" (D&C 2:1)—that ancient Israelitish seer came to modern Israelitish souls. On April 3, 1836, in the Kirtland Temple, he conferred upon the first and second elders of the latter-day kingdom the keys of the sealing power, even as he and the Lord Jesus had given these same powers and keys to Peter, James, and John on the Mount of Transfiguration.

That same day "Elias appeared, and committed the dispensation of the gospel of Abraham," meaning the great commission given to Abraham that he and his seed had a right to the priesthood, the gospel, and eternal life. Accordingly, Elias promised those upon whom these ancient promises were then renewed that in them and in their seed all generations should be blessed. (D&C 110:12-16.) Thus, through the joint ministry of Elijah, who brought the sealing power, and Elias, who restored the marriage discipline of Abraham, the way was prepared for the planting in the hearts of the children of the promises made to the fathers. (D&C 2:2.) These are the promises of eternal life through the priesthood and the gospel and celestial marriage.

Also on that glorious April day, Moses appeared and conferred the keys of the gathering of Israel, including the Ten Tribes, from all the lands into which they have been scattered. (D&C 110:11.) These keys authorize priesthood holders to gather the lost sheep of Israel into the same church and fold where their ancestors were so bounteously watered and fed.

We do not know all of the places and times when angelic ministrants brought back their ancient powers. We do know that all of the rivers of the past flow into the ocean of the present. We do know that "it is necessary in the ushering in of the dispensation of the fulness of times . . . that a whole and complete and perfect union, and welding together of dispensations, and keys, and powers, and glories should take place, and be revealed from the days of Adam even to the present time." We do know that Michael, Gabriel, Raphael, and "divers angels, from Michael or Adam down to the present time," have appeared to mortals—"all declaring their dispensation, their rights, their keys, their honors, their majesty and glory, and the power of their priesthood." (D&C 128:18, 21.)

As to the restoration of all these keys and powers and authorities, suffice it to say: They are now held by the First Presidency and the Twelve who preside over The Church of Jesus Christ of Latter-day Saints. And they will continue so to be held, by these brethren and their successors in interest, until the Lord Jesus Christ descends in the clouds of glory to reign personally upon the earth for a thousand years. Truly, "the keys of the kingdom of God are committed unto man on the earth, and from thence shall the gospel roll forth unto the ends of the earth, as the stone which is cut out of the mountain without hands shall roll forth, until it has filled the whole earth." (D&C 65:2.)

How Men Are Called of God

Our Article of Faith sets forth that a man must be called of God in two ways in order to do two things. He must be called of God by prophecy, and by the laying on of hands of those who are in authority. Having been thus called, he has power to preach the gospel and to administer in the ordinances thereof.

These terms and expressions must be clearly understood if we are to envision how and in what manner the Lord's true ministers perform the divine service to which they are called. It is because they are misunderstood or completely disregarded that we find the loose and tangled web of assumed authority that prevails in the sectarian world. According to the revealed word, their true meaning is as follows:

1. *To be called of God by prophecy* means to be called by the spirit of inspiration. It means that the one making the call has the gift of prophecy, which is the testimony of Jesus. It means that he has the spirit of revelation; that he is in tune with the Holy Spirit of God; that he makes the call by the power of the Holy Ghost. In other words, the call comes from the Lord, by the mouth of his servant, as that servant is moved upon by the Spirit. One man does not call another to the ministry. It is the Lord's call, and a servant of the Lord simply conveys to the called person the glad tidings that the Lord has chosen him and is granting him the requisite divine power to accomplish the work. Men are called of God in the literal and true sense, and if

God does not call them by prophecy, they are not his ministers. The Lord's house is a house of order.

2. *To be called by the laying on of hands of those who are in authority* means that more than one person approves the call and that the Lord's servants—formally, officially, and by the performance of an ordinance—convey the power and authority needed to do the ministerial work involved. Men who desire to serve God are not left free to assume, because of some inner feeling, that the Lord wants them to labor in his vineyard. They must receive a formal call from a legal administrator, and they must feel the hands of the Lord's servants on their heads as the words of ordination or conferral or authorization are spoken. The Lord's house is a house of order.

3. *To preach the gospel with divine approval* means just that. It means that the preacher has been called of God and that he preaches the gospel of God. It means that the doctrine taught is the Lord's doctrine. It is what the Lord would say if he personally were present. It is what he wants said under whatever circumstances prevail. It is his mind, his will, and his voice; the words spoken are his words. Hence, the gospel is and can be preached by the power of the Holy Ghost and in no other way. The Holy Ghost, as a revelator, must tell the preacher what to say; otherwise the minister cannot truly represent the Lord and do the Lord's will. It is because men deny the Holy Ghost who giveth utterance, and preach instead their own ideas of what the scriptures mean, that there are so many false and vain and foolish notions in so-called Christendom, making of the Lord's house so-called a house of confusion rather than of order.

4. *To administer the ordinances of the gospel with divine approval* means that legal administrators must perform the right ordinances, for the approved individuals, by the power of the Holy Ghost. They must baptize those whom the Lord would baptize if he were doing it; they must ordain those whom the Lord wants ordained. It is his work and not man's. No man can create a baptism or make any ordinance that will have efficacy, virtue, and force in eternity. The Lord alone can do that. True ordinances are his ordinances, and he must authorize and approve all that are performed by his servants; otherwise they will be of no avail. The various ordinances performed in divers ways by those devoid of priestly authority

stand as a witness that the Lord's hand is not manifest in the churches of men. Truly, the Lord's house is a house of order and not of confusion.

The whole body of revealed writ attests to the verity of the concepts here summarized. For instance, as a pattern for what others also are called to do, the Lord said to the Twelve in this dispensation: "Behold, you are they who are ordained of me to ordain priests and teachers; to declare my gospel, according to the power of the Holy Ghost which is in you, and according to the callings and gifts of God unto men." (D&C 18:32.)

To all the elders of his kingdom the Lord commands: "Ye shall go forth in the power of my Spirit, preaching my gospel, two by two, in my name, lifting up your voices as with the sound of a trump, declaring my word like unto angels of God. And ye shall go forth baptizing with water, saying: Repent ye, repent ye, for the kingdom of heaven is at hand." And then, so that all men may know how and in what manner and by whom the word is to be preached and the ordinances performed, the divine word continues: "It shall not be given to any one to go forth to preach my gospel, or to build up my church, except he be ordained by some one who has authority, and it is known to the church that he has authority and has been regularly ordained by the heads of the church." The Lord's house is a house of order.

"And again, the elders, priests and teachers of this church [and all the other officers placed in the church since the day of this revelation] shall teach the principles of my gospel, which are in the Bible and the Book of Mormon, in the which is the fulness of the gospel. And they shall observe the covenants and church articles to do them, and these shall be their teachings, as they shall be directed by the Spirit. And the Spirit shall be given unto you by the prayer of faith; and if ye receive not the Spirit ye shall not teach." (D&C 42:6-14.) On another occasion this divine word was forthcoming: "Go ye into all the world, preach the gospel to every creature, acting in the authority which I have given you, baptizing in the name of the Father, and of the Son, and of the Holy Ghost." (D&C 68:8.)

Let us, then, reason together along this wise:

If the Lord himself—the great God who governs and controls his affairs on earth—personally called a man to be a minister or a prophet or an apostle, who would doubt the legality and efficacy of the call? This, of course, is what he did when he ministered among men.

If an angel, sent from heaven, came down and called one of his mortal fellowservants, one who had the testimony of Jesus, to serve as a minister of Christ, surely the one called would be a true legal administrator. Angels speak and act by the power of the Holy Ghost; they represent the Lord, and their acts are his acts.

Similarly, if mortal men who themselves are the servants of the Lord, acting by the spirit of prophecy and revelation, call others to the ministry, those so chosen are the very persons the Lord himself, if ministering personally, would have called. What difference does it make whether the Lord acts personally, or sends angelic ministrants to deliver the call, or directs his mortal servants, by the Spirit, to make the appointment? Whether it is done by his own voice or by the voice of his servants, it is the same. And there is no other way.

Let us, then, conclude that calls to service in the ministry of the Master must—

1. come from an authorized minister, one who himself holds the holy priesthood and who has been directed from on high to call others to serve on the Lord's errand;

2. be made by prophecy, meaning by the spirit of inspiration and revelation as directed by the Holy Spirit;

3. be confirmed and finalized by the laying on of hands, as the means of conferring the authority involved and of testifying, visibly and without question, that the powers or keys of prerogatives are vested in the recipient; and

4. be known and announced to the Church and have the approval of the heads of the Church.

"Behold, mine house is a house of order, saith the Lord God, and not a house of confusion." (D&C 132:8.)

ARTICLE 6

We believe
in the same organization
that existed in the Primitive Church,
namely,
apostles, prophets, pastors,
teachers, evangelists,
and so forth.

CHAPTER 36

The Church—Its Nature and Purpose

The Eternal Church

Even as the Lord God is known by many names and identified in numerous ways, all to the end that men may know more about him and his laws, so it is with his church. Through the ages the prophetic word has described, identified, and named the Lord's people in various ways, all of which, viewed and analyzed in their proper settings, throw a wondrous flood of light on the nature and purpose of the Church. And yet, be it remembered, there is but one true and living God and one true and saving church. The one Lord is the author of salvation, and the one church offers salvation to men. To bring the true church and its message and purpose into a proper perspective, we shall organize our subject under ten headings, as follows.

1. The Church Is the Organized Body of True Believers

Our Lord's church, the one true church, the sole center of true and perfect worship, is an organized body of true believers. It is a formal and official organization with prescribed officers, defined units, approved doctrines, and authorized ordinances. Its ministers are endowed with power from on high; they hold the holy priesthood, and they are empowered to act in the place and stead of the Lord Jesus. Miracles and gifts of the Spirit always abound within its folds; its way of worship is always pure and perfect Christianity. And it always bears the name of that Lord whose church it is.

Above all else, the church is the Lord's. He establishes it; he directs its affairs; he gives it to whomsoever he will; and he takes it from unworthy hands. Man can accept a divine invitation to join the Lord's organization. He can by full obedience gain all the blessings that flow therefrom. But he cannot alter, amend, change, add to, diminish from, or improve upon that which the Lord, whose church it is, has himself arranged. If at any time man assumes any of these prerogatives, he thereby runs counter to the divine will, the Spirit of the Lord withdraws, and the realigned and rearranged church becomes the church of a man. It is no longer the Lord's church.

2. The Church Administers the Gospel

In the eternal scheme of things, there are three divine realities that always go together. They cannot be separated. Where any one of them is found, there the other two always are. These three divine things are: the gospel, the priesthood, and the church.

Priesthood is the power of God; where we are concerned, it is the power and authority of God delegated to man on earth to act in all things for the salvation of men. With reference to the Melchizedek Priesthood, the revealed word attests: "This greater priesthood administereth the gospel." (D&C 84:19.) The gospel, so administered, is the plan of salvation; it includes all that is needed to save and exalt men in the highest heaven. And the church is the organization that houses, regulates, controls, and administers the gospel and makes its blessings available to men. Gospel truths, doctrines, ordinances, gifts, and powers are offered to the world through the church. They are available to those who repent and are baptized and receive the enlightening power of the Holy Spirit; they are available, in their saving fulness, to the members of the church. Thus the church is the organization through which salvation is made available to man.

And thus the priesthood, the gospel, and the church go hand in hand. Indeed, that Lord whose church it is defines his church in these words: "Behold, this is my doctrine—whosoever repenteth and cometh unto me, the same is my church." The church consists of those who believe the gospel, repent of their sins, and accept baptism under the hands of the legal administrators who represent the Lord. "Whosoever declareth more or less than this," the divine word continues, "the same is not of me, . . . therefore he is not of my church." Church members are limited to those who believe the gospel and accept its ordinances as these are performed by those who hold the holy priesthood. "And now, behold, whosoever is of my church," saith the Lord, "and endureth of my church to the end, him will I establish upon my rock, and the gates of hell shall not prevail against them." (D&C 10:67-69.) And thus it is that faithful members of the church are saved.

The Aaronic Priesthood administers the preparatory gospel; the Melchizedek Priesthood administers the fulness of the everlasting gospel. In reasoning with the Hebrews, who had the law of Moses, which is the preparatory gospel, and who were administering that lesser law by the power of the Aaronic Priesthood, Paul said: "If therefore perfection were by the Levitical priesthood, (for under it the people received the law), what further need was there that another priest should rise after the order of Melchisedec, and not be called after the order of Aaron?" That is, why do the scriptures say Christ will come as a priest of the Melchizedek order if men can gain a fulness of salvation through the lesser law?

Then our ancient apostolic friend made the great pronouncement: "For the priesthood being changed, there is made of necessity a change also of the law." (Hebrews 7:11-12.) That is, the very fact that the higher priesthood came, to supersede a lesser though a divine order, proves that salvation comes through the fulness of the gospel and not through the Mosaic law alone. Truly, the gospel, the priesthood, and the church are all one.

3.   The Church Is Eternal and Everlasting

The gospel, the priesthood, and the church are everlasting, eternal, unending. They have and do and will exist in all worlds, in all ages, everlastingly. Like God himself, they are without beginning and without end. As to the gospel, it is the gospel of the galaxies; it is the everlasting gospel; it is the eternal plan of salvation. As to the priesthood, it has existed with God from all eternity; it is the very power of God; by it the worlds were made and souls are saved. As to the church, it is the Lord's organized system of administration; it has existed in all dispensations; it is organized in heaven above and on the earth beneath. What we have here is patterned after what gods and angels have there.

331

With reference to the church on earth, and the priesthood by which it is governed, the revelations say: "The Holy Priesthood" was handed down from Adam to his seed, "which priesthood continueth in the church of God in all generations, and is without beginning of days or end of years." (D&C 84:6, 17.) Whenever the Melchizedek Priesthood has been on earth, the church of God has also been present; and, conversely, when and where there is no Melchizedek Priesthood, there is no true church.

Adam was the president of the church in his day, Melchizedek in his; both were high priests in that holy order called "the Holy Priesthood, after the Order of the Son of God." And in the day of Melchizedek—because he "was such a great high priest," and also "out of respect or reverence to the name of the Supreme Being, to avoid the too frequent repetition of his name"—it was "the church, in ancient days, [that] called that priesthood after Melchizedek, or the Melchizedek Priesthood." (D&C 107:2-4.) Thus the pattern was set for all ages; the church was, and is, and everlastingly shall be the agency set up by the Lord to save his children.

4.   Zion Is the Church

Anciently "the Lord called his people ZION, because they were of one heart and one mind, and dwelt in righteousness." Enoch was their presiding officer, and he and his people "built a city that was called the City of Holiness, even ZION." This is that Zion which "in process of time, was taken up into heaven." (Moses 7:18-21.) To us the divine word acclaims: "Let Zion rejoice, for this is Zion—THE PURE IN HEART." (D&C 97:21.)

In the meridian of time and in our day, the Lord calls his people *saints* because they are of one heart and one mind, and dwelling in righteousness, they are one with the saints beyond the veil. The latter-day saints as well as former-day saints forsake the world and gather to Zion, or in other words they join the church, for Zion is the church. Those who are thus gathered into the fold of Christ are the pure in heart, becoming thus when their sins are washed away in the waters of baptism.

As the saints in Enoch's day built the City of Zion—a City of Holiness, a place of refuge from the carnality of the world—

so the saints in our day are organized into stakes of Zion. These stakes are part of the church structure, and all who forsake the world and who seek to be one with those of Enoch's day gather into the stakes of Zion, where they find refuge from the carnality and evils of the world.

5. Israel Is the Church

Ancient Israel was a nation, a kingdom, and a church all wrapped in one. Moses in his day was the prophet, seer, and revelator; Aaron was the presiding bishop; the twelve princes of Israel, one heading each of the tribes, held an equivalent status to that of the Twelve whom Jesus chose; and the seventy elders, who with Moses and Aaron saw the Lord, were what we would call the First Quorum of the Seventy. There were elders and judges (bishops) and other officers, presiding, as circumstances warranted, over tens and fifties and hundreds and thousands. Israel operated as a theocracy, as a congregation of the Lord's people, as a church.

When we speak thus of Israel, we are not speaking of all of the literal seed of Jacob who are Israel, but of those who were true and faithful. We are speaking of those "Israelites," as Paul identified them, "to whom pertaineth the adoption, and the glory, and the covenants, and the giving of the law, and the service of God, and the promises." Rebellious descendants of Jacob were excommunicated anciently as they are today. Hence, in Paul's language, "they are not all Israel, which are of Israel. . . . That is, They which are the children of the flesh, these are not the children of God." (Romans 9:4-8.)

Israelitish history abounds in periods of apostasy and rebellion in which the people forsook the Lord, rejected his gospel, and fell away from his church. They were scattered for their sins and rebellion. And when they are gathered again in the last days, it is and will be because they return to the Lord, accept his everlasting gospel, and join his church. Thus it is that Jacob speaks of "the covenants of the Lord that he has covenanted with all the house of Israel," covenants that tell the destiny of that chosen people, "even from the beginning down, from generation to generation, until the time comes that they shall be restored to the true church and fold of God." (2 Nephi 9:1-2.) Israel once belonged to "the true church," and this blessed privilege is once again available for those who hearken to the voice of the same Lord who spoke to their fathers.

It is worthy of note that the Old Testament, as we now have it, speaks not of the church of Israel but of the congregation of Israel. For that matter, Matthew is the only one of the Gospel authors in whose writings the term *church* has been preserved. There are about two hundred and thirty references to the church in the Book of Mormon, nearly all of which refer to the church between 600 B.C. and A.D. 34. Nephi speaks "of the brethren of the church" who dwelt in Jerusalem before Lehi's family left that city of sin and iniquity. (1 Nephi 4:26.) It is clear that if we had the full Old Testament accounts, they would speak plainly and profusely about the church and all that appertains to it.

6. Jehovah's Fold Is His Church

No better imagery could have been devised for pastoral Israel than to refer to the Lord's church among them as the sheepfold of Jehovah. Those in the sheepfold were safe from the wolves of sin and preserved from the deserts of thirst. Within the fold they fed in green pastures and drank from the still waters because Jehovah was their Shepherd. Jesus said he was the Good Shepherd who gave his life for the sheep. Peter called Christ the Chief Shepherd.

To the lost sheep among the Nephites, Alma issued this call: "O ye workers of iniquity; ye that are puffed up in the vain things of the world, ye that have professed to have known the ways of righteousness nevertheless have gone astray, as sheep having no shepherd, notwithstanding a shepherd hath called after you and is still calling after you, but ye will not hearken unto his voice! Behold, I say unto you, that the good shepherd doth call you; yea, and in his own name he doth call you, which is the name of Christ; and if ye will not hearken unto the voice of the good shepherd, to the name by which ye are called, behold, ye are not the sheep of the good shepherd." (Alma 5:37-38.) Akin to this is Mormon's statement: "If ye have not faith in him then ye are not fit to be numbered among the people of his church." (Moroni 7:39.) Truly, in his church, we find the sheep of the Lord's pasture being fed true doctrine and being watered at the wells of righteousness.

7.   The Church Is the Kingdom of God on Earth

The church of the living God is not a democracy; its laws are not made by men; its doctrines are not devised in conferences and conclaves. The church is a kingdom; it is God's kingdom, the kingdom of God on earth, and as such is designed to prepare men for an inheritance in the kingdom of God in heaven, which is the celestial kingdom. Our Lord Jesus Christ is the Eternal King; his representative on earth is the President of the church.

Laws and doctrines and officers and forms of administration and standards of judgment and all else come to the church from the Eternal King by the voice of the one who heads his work on earth.

Speaking in the name of the Lord, the Prophet Joseph Smith said that "the kingdom of God" has been "set up on the earth from the days of Adam to the present time [w]henever there has been a righteous man on earth unto whom God [has] revealed His word and [given] power and authority to administer in His name." The church and kingdom are eternal. "Where there is a priest of God," the Prophet said, "a minister who has power and authority from God to administer in the ordinances of the gospel and officiate in the priesthood of God, there is the kingdom of God." The gospel, the priesthood, and the church always go together.

"Where there is no kingdom of God there is no salvation." Without the church, man cannot be saved. "What constitutes the kingdom of God?" What constitutes the church of Christ? "Where there is a prophet, a priest, or a righteous man unto whom God gives His oracles, there is the kingdom of God; and where the oracles of God are not, there the kingdom of God is not."

Thus: "Whenever men can find out the will of God and find an administrator legally authorized from God, there is the kingdom of God; but where these are not, the kingdom of God is not. All the ordinances, systems, and administrations on earth are of no use to the children of men, unless they are ordained and authorized of God; for nothing will save a man but a legal administrator; for none others will be acknowledged either by God or angels." (*Teachings of the Prophet Joseph Smith,* pp. 271-72, 274.)

8.   The Church Bears the Name of Christ

Before the church was organized again among men in these last days, the Lord said to the Prophet: "If you shall build up my church, upon the foundation of my gospel and my rock, the gates of hell shall not prevail against you." The true church has the true gospel; any church that relies upon false doctrines is not the Lord's church.

That Joseph Smith and his associates might proceed properly in the great work of establishing the latter-day kingdom, the divine word continued: "Take upon you the name of Christ, and speak the truth in soberness." No one can belong to the church unless and until he takes upon him the name of the One whose church it is. "And as many as repent and are baptized in my name, which is Jesus Christ, and endure to the end, the same shall be saved." Repentance and baptism are the gate to that strait and narrow path which leads to eternal life. "Behold, Jesus Christ is the name which is given of the Father, and there is none other name given whereby man can be saved; wherefore, all men must take upon them the name which is given of the Father, for in that name shall they be called at the last day; wherefore, if they know not the name by which they are called, they cannot have place in the kingdom of my Father." (D&C 18:5, 21-25.)

This same direction was given by the same Lord to his Nephite disciples. "Ye must take upon you the name of Christ, which is my name," he confirmed. This is done in the waters of baptism and in partaking of the sacramental emblems. "And whoso taketh upon him my name, and endureth to the end, the same shall be saved at the last day. Therefore, whatsoever ye shall do, ye shall do it in my name; therefore ye shall call the church in my name; and . . . if it be called in my name then it is my church, if it so be that they are built upon my gospel." (3 Nephi 27:5-8.)

9.   The Church of Jesus Christ of Latter-day Saints

We have taken upon ourselves the name of Christ; it is in his name we are called in these last days, and we know that his is the only name given under heaven whereby salvation comes. We have joined his church, The Church of Jesus Christ of Latter-day Saints. This church is the kingdom of God on earth. It administers the gospel and is in turn administered by the Holy Priesthood. It is "the only true and living church upon the face of the whole earth." (D&C 1:30.) It is the one place where salvation is found, where the fulness of the everlasting gospel is taught in plainness and perfection, and where there are legal administrators who have power to seal men up unto eternal life.

This kingdom—because it is the Lord's and because it is true—shall roll forward and increase in size and influence until it fills the whole earth, until every living soul on earth is embraced within its fold. This consummation, devoutly to be desired and zealously sought for by the faithful, shall come to pass when that Lord whose church it is comes to reign personally upon the earth with his saints for a thousand years. Until that day, we shall go forward as best we can, living the gospel, gathering the elect, and saving the righteous.

10. The Church of the Firstborn

The Church of the Firstborn is the church among exalted beings in the highest heaven of the celestial world. It is the church among those for whom the family unit continues in eternity. In a sense it is the inner circle within the Lord's church on earth. It is composed of those who have entered into that patriarchal order which is called the new and everlasting covenant of marriage. As baptism admits repentant souls to membership in the earthly church, so celestial marriage opens the door to membership in the heavenly church.

The purpose of the church on earth is to prepare us for an inheritance in the church in heaven. Those who so obtain, having overcome all things, shall pass by the angels and the gods and enter into their exaltation. "They are they who are the church of the Firstborn. They are they into whose hands the Father has given all things—they are they who are priests and kings, who have received of his fulness, and of his glory; and are priests of the Most High, after the order of Melchizedek, which was after the order of Enoch, which was after the order of the Only Begotten Son. Wherefore, as it is written, they are gods, even the sons of God—wherefore, all things are theirs, whether life or death, or things present, or things to come, all are theirs and they are Christ's, and Christ is God's." (D&C 76:54-59.)

CHAPTER 37

False Churches

Apostasy Creates False Churches

One of the great and eternal verities that all men are required by their Creator to accept without reservation is that there is only one true church. How can churches that teach conflicting doctrines and perform differing ordinances all be true? Are we wrong in saying that truth is truth, and one truth is always in perfect harmony with every other truth?

There is only one true and living God; he is what he is and not something else, and he cannot be two opposite or disagreeing things. There is only one gospel, one faith, one plan of salvation, one eternal heaven.

Everyone knows, of course, that there are in this sad and sorry world of ours churches of every sort, kind, and nature. There is a place somewhere for every wind of doctrine, every creedal vagary, every conceivable rite and performance, every nonsensical notion that the minds of men or the devisings of devils can imagine. The mere fact that there are churches that believe and teach different ways whereby salvation comes proves that there has been an apostasy. Adam started out with the true church, and anything differing from what he had is in the very nature of things false.

One of the most emphatic things Paul ever wrote was in condemnation of those who perverted, even in his day, the pure and perfect gospel he had preached. "Though we, or an angel from heaven, preach any other gospel unto you than that which we have preached unto you," he said, "let him be accursed." How could language be stronger? Simply by repetition. "As we said before, so say I now again," he continued, "if any man preach any other gospel unto you than that ye have received, let him be accursed." (Galatians 1:8-9.)

338

That Paul's priesthood, Paul's gospel, and Paul's church came from God is not open to question. All of them had been restored in the meridian of time, and Paul as an apostle gloried in them. The issue facing modern Christendom is whether pure and perfect Christianity continued on down through the ages. In gaining an answer to this problem, Elder James E. Talmage suggests a consideration of the following facts:

"Since the period immediately succeeding that of the ministrations of the apostles of old, and until the nineteenth century, no organization had maintained a claim to direct revelation from God; in fact, the teachings of professed ministers of the Gospel for centuries have been to the effect that such gifts of God have ceased, that the days of miracles have gone, and that the present depends for its guiding code wholly upon the past. A self-suggesting interpretation of history indicates that there has been a great departure from the way of salvation as laid down by the Savior, a universal apostasy from the Church of Christ. Scarcely had the Church been organized by the Savior, whose name it bears, before the powers of darkness arrayed themselves for conflict with the organized body. Even in the days of our Lord's personal ministry in the flesh, persecution was waged against Him and the disciples. Commencing with the Jews, and directed first against the Master and His few immediate associates, this tide of opposition soon enveloped every known follower of the Savior, so that the very name Christian was used as an epithet of derision.

"In the first quarter of the fourth century, however, a change in the attitude of paganism toward Christianity was marked by the so-called conversion of Constantine the Great, under whose patronage the Christian profession grew in favor and became in fact the religion of State. But what a profession, what a religion was it by this time! Its simplicity had departed; earnest devotion and self-sacrificing sincerity were no longer characteristic of the ministers of the Church. These professed followers of the humble Prophet of Nazareth, those self-styled representatives of the Lord whose kingdom was not of earth earthy, those loudly proclaimed lovers of the Man of Sorrows acquainted with grief, lived amidst conditions strangely inconsistent with the life of their divine Exemplar. Church offices were sought after for the distinction of honor and wealth accompanying them; ministers of the Gospel affected the state of secular dignitaries; bishops exhibited the pomp of princes, arch-bishops lived as kings and popes like emperors. With these innovations came many changes in the ordinances of the so-called church—the rites of baptism were perverted; the sacrament was altered; public worship became an exhibition of art; men were canonized; martyrs were made subjects of adoration; blasphemy grew apace, in that men without authority essayed to exercise the prerogatives of God. Ages of darkness came upon the earth; the power of Satan seemed almost supreme." (James E. Talmage, *The Articles of Faith*, pp. 200-201.)

The Church of the Devil

"In relation to the kingdom of God," Joseph Smith said, "the devil always sets up his kingdom at the very same time in opposition to God." (*Teachings of the Prophet Joseph Smith*, p. 365.) And since the kingdom of God or true church has been on earth from age to age, so also has the kingdom of the devil or the church of the devil. Adam and Abel had true worship and offered sacrifices in the way the Lord ordained. On the other hand, "Cain loved Satan more than God." That is, he chose to live after the manner of the world, and it was Satan, not the Lord, who told Cain, "Make an offering unto the Lord." (Moses 5:18.) Thus the pattern was set for all ages. Satan tells men to worship the Lord, but the proposed worship that he gives them is false and without saving power.

Thus, Alma, addressing himself to those who "are not the sheep of the good shepherd," that is, to those who do not belong to the true church, asked: "And now if ye are not the sheep of the good shepherd, of what fold are ye?" His answer: "Behold, I say unto you, that the devil is your shepherd, and ye are of his fold; and now, who can deny this? Behold, I say unto you, whosoever denieth this is a liar and a child of the devil."

Then Alma states this obvious truism: "For I say unto you that whatsoever is good cometh from God, and whatsoever is evil cometh from the devil." And then, by way of application, he says: "Therefore, if a man bringeth forth good works he hearkeneth unto the voice of the good shepherd, and he doth follow him. But whosoever bringeth forth evil works," the account continues, "the same becometh a child of the devil, for he hearkeneth unto his voice, and doth follow him." (Alma 5:38-41.)

Those who have hearkened unto Satan and become his children, in all ages, are more numerous than those who have become, by faith, the sons and daughters of Christ. In the so-called pre-Christian era they included all the peoples of the earth except the chosen seed and races. Since the coming of Christ, they include all except those who have the pure and perfect worship of Jesus and the apostles and saints of that day.

Our especial concern is in the falling away from the ancient faith that took place after New Testament times. This day of dire and dark apostasy was abundantly foretold by biblical authors, as reference to their writings and to numerous commentaries shows. Let us, however, note briefly some of the plain and powerful language of the Book of Mormon prophets relative to the spiritual darkness that was destined to cover the minds of men after Jesus ascended into heaven.

Nephi saw in vision the church that would arise after the death of the ancient apostles and that would have dominion over nations and kingdoms down to the time of the discovery of America by Columbus. "I saw among the nations of the Gentiles the formation of a great church," he said. With reference to this church an angel told Nephi: "Behold the formation of a church which is most abominable above all other churches, which slayeth the saints of God, yea, and tortureth them and bindeth them down, and yoketh them with a yoke of iron, and bringeth them down into captivity."

All of the churches of men and of devils are not immersed in iniquity to the same degree. What Nephi here saw is a church that exceeds all others in abominations. "I beheld this great and abominable church," he said, "and I saw the devil that he was the founder of it." Then he saw "the desires of this great and abominable church"—gold and silver, silks and scarlets, fine twined linen and precious clothing, and many harlots. (1 Nephi 13:4-8.) All of this is descriptive of that which prevailed in the dark ages.

Then, seeing what would be in the latter days, after the restoration of the gospel, Nephi was told by his angelic friend: "Look, and behold that great and abominable church, which is the mother of abominations, whose founder is the devil." Then, in this setting, one in which there were many churches

341

in addition to the true church, the angel said: "Behold there are save two churches only; the one is the church of the Lamb of God, and the other is the church of the devil; wherefore, whoso belongeth not to the church of the Lamb of God belongeth to that great church, which is the mother of abominations; and she is the whore of all the earth." (1 Nephi 14:9-10.) Thus we come back to Alma's teaching that unless men are in the sheepfold of Christ, their shepherd is the devil and they will be rewarded by him whom they list to obey. (Alma 5:41.)

Churches in the Last Days

There now are thousands of churches on earth. The trend is for churches to increase in number and diverge in doctrine. True, some professing ministers perform as many good works as their light and knowledge allow, and they will be blessed accordingly. Others, however, are engaged in priestcrafts, pure and simple. And according to the prophetic word: "Priestcrafts are that men preach and set themselves up for a light unto the world, that they may get gain and praise of the world; but they seek not the welfare of Zion." These ministers also will be rewarded according to the deeds done in the flesh.

Nephi saw that in our day "the Gentiles," being lifted up in pride and stumbling because of false doctrines, "built up many churches." He saw their ministers "put down the power and miracles of God, and preach up unto themselves their own wisdom and their own learning, that they may get gain and grind upon the face of the poor." He saw a day of division and contention and debate in which men gave little heed to the voice of the Lord. "There are many churches built up which cause envyings, and strifes, and malice," he said. "And there are also secret combinations, even as in times of old, according to the combinations of the devil, for he is the founder of all these things; yea, the founder of murder, and works of darkness; yea, and he leadeth them by the neck with a flaxen cord, until he bindeth them with his strong cords forever." (2 Nephi 26:20-22.)

In the midst of false churches of every sort, the Lord promised to build up his true kingdom again among men. "If this generation harden not their hearts, I will establish my church among them," he said. And "whosoever belongeth to my church need not fear, for such shall inherit the kingdom of heaven." As to all others, the divine word is: "It is they who do not fear me, neither keep my commandments but build up churches unto themselves to get gain, yea, and all those that do wickedly and build up the kingdom of the devil—yea, verily, verily, I say unto you, that it is they that I will disturb, and cause to tremble and shake to the center." (D&C 10:53-56.)

Moroni described and identified the day in which the Lord would bring forth the Book of Mormon, restore the gospel, and set up anew the true church among men. It would be a day of apostasy—a day when men would deny miracles; when there would be wars and pollutions and abominations; when there would be lyings and whoredoms and robbing and murder; when iniquity would abound and the love of men wax cold. "Yea, it shall come in a day when the power of God shall be denied," he said, "and churches become defiled and be lifted up in the pride of their hearts; yea, even in a day when leaders of churches and teachers shall rise in the pride of their hearts, even to the envying of them who belong to their churches. . . . Yea, it shall come in a day when there shall be churches built up that shall say: Come unto me, and for your money you shall be forgiven of your sins."

Moroni saw in vision the people who would live in the day of restoration. Speaking to them he said: "I know your doing. And I know that ye do walk in the pride of your hearts; and there are none save a few only who do not lift themselves up in the pride of their hearts, unto the wearing of very fine apparel, unto envying, and strifes, and malice, and persecutions, and all manner of iniquities; and your churches, yea, even every one, have become polluted because of the pride of your hearts. For behold, ye do love money, and your substance, and your fine apparel, and the adorning of your churches, more than ye love the poor and the needy, the sick and the afflicted." (Mormon 8:26-37.)

How long, O Lord, can these conditions continue? When, oh when, will truth triumph and false churches cease to control the minds of men? Hear the prophetic answer: "The time speedily shall come that all churches which are built up to get gain, and all those who are built up to get power over the flesh, and those who are built up to become popular in the eyes of the world, and those who seek the lusts of the flesh and the things of the world, and to do all manner of iniquity; yea, in fine, all those who belong to the kingdom of the devil are they who need fear, and tremble, and quake; they are those who must be brought low in the dust; they are those who must be consumed as stubble; and this is according to the words of the prophet." (1 Nephi 22:23.)

CHAPTER 38

Organization of the Kingdom

Orders of the Priesthood

There is one God, one gospel, one church, and one priesthood. There are, of course, false gods, perverted gospels, apostate churches, and imitation priesthoods. As to the one true priesthood, which in reality and in truth is the very power of God as found both on earth and in heaven, Joseph Smith said: "All priesthood is Melchizedek, but there are different portions or degrees of it." (*Teachings of the Prophet Joseph Smith,* p. 180.) This, in the very nature of things, is and must be true because there is only one God, and the power he has is his power, and that power is priesthood.

However, there are two orders of the priesthood. One is the order of Melchizedek, the other the order of Aaron; that is, each of these orders is a portion or degree of the power of God and is named after either Melchizedek or Aaron because these ancient brethren served so valiantly in the fields of their assignment. We have come to consider these orders or systems of priesthood as two different priesthoods, each functioning in its own field and sphere. Hence the revealed word says: "There are, in the church, two priesthoods, namely, the Melchizedek and Aaronic, including the Levitical Priesthood."

As to the Melchizedek Priesthood, it is written: "All other authorities or offices in the church are appendages to this priesthood." That is, all authorities and powers, all offices and officers, all organizations and programs, all members of the Church—there are no exceptions—all are subject to the Melchizedek Priesthood. All exist and operate under the direction of this priesthood; all gain their power and authority from it. All things in the Church are but appendages to the priesthood; they grow out of it, and such efficacy, virtue, and force as they possess come because of it. The priesthood is supreme; it administers the gospel in all its parts and portions and is the very power by which eternal life is gained.

"But there are two divisions or grand heads—one is the Melchizedek Priesthood, and the other is the Aaronic or Levitical Priesthood." (In the true sense of the word, the names Aaronic and Levitical are synonymous; they are one and the same priesthood, although all of the sons of Levi did not perform all of the ordinances of the Aaronic Priesthood anciently, even as deacons today do not use the fulness of Aaronic authority that bishops do.)

"The Melchizedek Priesthood holds the right of presidency, and has power and authority over all the offices in the church in all ages of the world, to administer in spiritual things." This is the greater priesthood, the higher priesthood, the highest and holiest order ever conferred upon men; it is the very priesthood used by the Lord Jesus in his ministry, by means of which, through faith, he performed his mighty miracles.

"The second priesthood is called the Priesthood of Aaron, because it was conferred upon Aaron and his seed, throughout all their generations. Why it is called the lesser priesthood is because it is an appendage to the greater, or the Melchizedek Priesthood, and has power in administering outward ordinances. . . .

"The power and authority of the higher, or Melchizedek Priesthood, is to hold the keys of all the spiritual blessings of the church—to have the privilege of receiving the mysteries of the kingdom of heaven, to have the heavens opened unto them, to commune with the general assembly and church of the Firstborn, and to enjoy the communion and presence of God the Father, and Jesus the mediator of the new covenant." (D&C 107:1-19.) It is on this basis that the Lord says to all his ministers, to all who hold the Melchizedek Priesthood, to every elder in his kingdom: "It is your privilege, and a promise I give unto you that have been ordained unto this ministry, that inasmuch as you strip yourselves from jealousies and fears, and humble yourselves before me, . . . the veil shall be rent and you shall see me and know that I am." (D&C 67:10.)

In contrast with and preparatory to receiving such an infinitely great spiritual experience, we have this pronouncement relative to the order of Aaron: "The power and authority of the lesser, or Aaronic Priesthood, is to hold the keys of the ministering of angels, and to administer in outward ordinances, the letter of the gospel, and baptism of repentance for the remission of sins, agreeable to the covenants and commandments." (D&C 107:20.)

The ministries of two of the ancient prophets dramatize the difference between Aaronic and Melchizedek authority. John the Baptist was the last legal administrator under the Mosaic law who held both the Aaronic Priesthood and "the keys of the ministering of angels, and of the gospel of repentance, and of baptism by immersion for the remission of sins." (D&C 13.) This priesthood and these keys are what he conferred upon Joseph Smith and Oliver Cowdery in the early days of this dispensation. The Lord Jesus was the first legal administrator of the new meridian dispensation. He was ordained a high priest forever after the order of Melchizedek, and, of course, he held the keys of the kingdom of heaven. This priesthood and these keys he conferred upon Peter, James, and John and then upon all of the ancient Twelve. In modern times he sent angelic ministrants to confer these same authorities and keys upon Joseph Smith and Oliver Cowdery. The difference between the ministry of Jesus and that of John is summarized by the Baptist in these words: "I indeed baptize you with water unto repentance: but he that cometh after me is mightier than I, whose shoes I am not worthy to bear: he shall baptize you with the Holy Ghost, and with fire." (Matthew 3:11.) Thus the Aaronic Priesthood performs the outward ordinance of baptism, but it takes the Melchizedek Priesthood to bring the inward and spiritual change by which sin and evil are burned out of a human soul as though by fire.

Officers of the Kingdom

The Lord our God always organizes his earthly kingdom in the same basic and general way. He is a God of order and system; constancy and consistency attend his doings, and he always walks in the same path, doing the same things under the same circumstances. His house is a house of order. This means that the church, his earthly kingdom, is always governed by apostles and prophets who hold the keys of the kingdom; it is always administered by those holding the Melchizedek Priesthood; and there are always such office holders as the needs of the day require.

Each dispensation has its own special needs, and the church organization in it is suited to the spiritual, social, cultural, economic, and other circumstances then prevailing. Auxiliary organizations change as times change. It is the higher priesthood and the keys of the kingdom that are always present. There was no need for Aaronic Priesthood officers before the flood; they had their beginning under the Mosaic order. Even during the Mosaic dispensation there were no Aaronic Priesthood holders among the Nephites, for there were no Levites among them, and the Aaronic Priesthood in that day was confined to the sons of Levi. The priests and teachers among the Nephites held the Melchizedek Priesthood.

Our avowed belief in "the same organization that existed in the Primitive Church" means that we have the same keys, the same priesthood, and the same priesthood offices as were had in the meridian of time, though this has not always been the way the earthly kingdom has been organized. Paul promised that apostles, prophets, evangelists, pastors, and teachers would remain in the true church until that Millennial day when there was a "unity of the faith." (Ephesians 4:11-13.) In setting forth some of the essential identifying characteristics of that true church, the ancient apostle wrote: "God hath set some in the church, first apostles, secondarily prophets, thirdly teachers, after that miracles, then gifts of healings, helps, governments, diversities of tongues." (1 Corinthians 12:28.) And the "Revelation on Priesthood" given in our day says of the two orders of priesthood now found in the earthly kingdom: "Of necessity there are presidents, or presiding officers growing out of, or appointed of or from among those who are ordained to the several offices in these two priesthoods." (D&C 107:21.)

We shall now consider the priesthood offices, the positions of presidency, and the helps and governments, given of God for the administration of his kingdom in this our day.

1. *Apostles*

This is the supreme office in the church in all dispensations because those so ordained hold both the fulness of the priesthood and all of the keys of the kingdom of God on earth. The

President of the Church serves in that high and exalted position because he is the senior apostle of God on earth and thus can direct the manner in which all other apostles and priesthood holders use their priesthood. An apostle is an ordained office in the Melchizedek Priesthood, and those so ordained (with an occasional exception that does not rank the person so involved along with those of whom Paul writes and of whom the other revelations speak) are set apart as members of the Quorum of the Twelve and are given the keys and power to preside over the church and kingdom and regulate all of the affairs of God on earth.

Apostles are "special witnesses of the name of Christ in all the world." They are also "a Traveling Presiding High Council, to officiate in the name of the Lord, under the direction of the Presidency of the Church, agreeable to the institution of heaven; to build up the church, and regulate all the affairs of the same in all nations, first unto the Gentiles and secondly unto the Jews." (D&C 107:23, 33.)

2. *Prophets*

Next to apostles come prophets. They are persons who have "the testimony of Jesus," which "is the spirit of prophecy." (Revelation 19:10.) That is, those having prophetic status are people who know by personal revelation that Jesus Christ is the Son of the living God who was crucified for the sins of the world. Having thus gained revelation from the Holy Spirit, they are in a position to gain added revelations that foretell the future or set forth the mind and will and purposes of the Lord in whatever respect is pleasing to Him whose servants they are.

The prophetic position is not an ordained office in the priesthood, although every person who holds the priesthood is or should be a prophet. "Would God that all the Lord's people were prophets, and that the Lord would put his spirit upon them!" was the great cry of Moses. (Numbers 11:29.) All faithful brethren should be prophets in their own right, gaining thus the inspiration of the Lord in their personal affairs and for their families. Those called to preside over quorums, wards, stakes, or other organizations in the church should be prophets to those over whom they preside. The First Presidency and the Twelve are sustained as prophets, seers, and revelators to the church. The President is the presiding prophet on earth and as such is the one through whom revelation is sent forth to the world and for the guidance of the whole body of believing saints.

3. *The First Presidency*

"Of the Melchizedek Priesthood, three Presiding High Priests, chosen by the body [of the Twelve], appointed and ordained to that office, and upheld by the confidence, faith, and prayer of the church, form a quorum of the Presidency of the Church." (D&C 107:22.) They constitute the First Presidency because they preside over all other presidencies, take precedence in all things, and speak the final word on all issues. The President of the Church is the first elder, the presiding high priest, the senior apostle, the president of the high priesthood, the presiding officer of the Church, the prophet of God on earth, the mouthpiece of the Almighty, and the only one who can exercise, at any one time, the keys of the kingdom in their eternal and unlimited fulness.

4. *The Seventy*

Three great councils preside over and govern the kingdom of God on earth. Number one is the First Presidency, the second is the Quorum of the Twelve Apostles, and the third is the Seventy, meaning the First Quorum of the Seventy. "The Seventy are also called to preach the gospel, and to be especial witnesses unto the Gentiles and in all the world." They "are to act in the name of the Lord, under the direction of the Twelve or the traveling high council, in building up the church and regulating all the affairs of the same in all nations, first unto the Gentiles and then to the Jews. . . . It is the duty of the traveling high council to call upon the Seventy, when they need assistance, to fill the several calls for preaching and administering the gospel, instead of any others." (D&C 107:25, 34, 38.) The calling of a seventy is an ordained office in the Melchizedek Priesthood. In addition to the Seventy who have administrative responsibility in all the Church and in all the world, there are other seventies in the stakes of Zion whose especial responsibilities lie in the missionary field.

5. *High Priests*

The calling of a high priest is an ordained office in the higher priesthood. "High priests after the order of Melchizedek"—as distinguished from high priests after the order of Aaron, who served in ancient Israel—"have a right to officiate in their own standing, under the direction of the presidency [meaning the First Presidency], in administering spiritual things, and also in the office of an elder, priest (of the Levitical order), teacher, deacon, and member." (D&C 107:10.) Their work is to perfect the saints and to serve as standing presidents in church organizations. They may also serve as missionaries and do anything that an elder or seventy may do.

There is no separate or ordained office of Presiding High Priest, although all high priests serving in presiding capacities are presiding high priests to the organization involved. Thus, the President of the Church is the "President of the High Priesthood of the Church; or, in other words, the Presiding High Priest over the High Priesthood of the Church." The First Presidency itself consists of "three Presiding High Priests." (D&C 107:22, 65-66.) The stake president is the presiding high priest in the stake, and the bishop is the presiding high priest in the ward. These brethren all serve in those capacities for a time and a season only; those who hold the ordained office of high priest continue as such in time and in eternity because it is an ordained office.

6. *Elders*

In the Church, the designation elder has two meanings. It is an ordained office in the Melchizedek Priesthood, and it refers to all holders of that priesthood irrespective of their office. Thus apostles, patriarchs, high priests, and seventies are also elders. "The high priest and elder are to administer in spiritual things, agreeable to the covenants and commandments of the church." (D&C 107:12.) Elders are to perfect the saints, preach the gospel, and serve as standing ministers. They are "to teach, expound, exhort, baptize, and watch over the church; and to confirm the church by the laying on of the hands, and the giving of the Holy Ghost. . . . The elders are to conduct the meetings as they are led by the Holy Ghost, according to the commandments and revelations of God." (D&C 20:42-45.) From an eternal perspective, there is no greater office than that of an elder. All elders hold all of the priesthood and have it in their power to gain eternal life through celestial marriage and keeping the commandments.

7. *Patriarchs or Evangelists*

The patriarchal or evangelical office is one of blessing and not of administration, although all who are so ordained also serve as high priests and as elders. Holders of this ordained office in the Melchizedek Priesthood are appointed to give patriarchal blessings to the saints. These blessings include an inspired declaration of lineage and such prophetic utterances as the Spirit dictates with reference to each person blessed.

8. *Bishops*

Bishops are the overseers, shepherds, pastors, and judges of their flocks. Their office is one of the ordained offices in the Aaronic Priesthood. Anciently the bishops (judges) were "literal descendants of Aaron." Their office had its beginning with Aaron, who was the presiding bishop of the church. Even in our dispensation, "the firstborn among the sons of Aaron" has "a legal right to the bishopric, . . . for the firstborn holds the right of the presidency over this priesthood, and the keys or authority of the same." That is, it is his right to be the Presiding Bishop of the Church, if he is selected and approved by the First Presidency. So far in our day the lineage through which the office of Presiding Bishop will descend "from father to son" has not been revealed. Until then, high priests of the Melchizedek Priesthood are chosen to officiate in this office and also as ward bishops. (D&C 68:16-21.)

9. *Priests*

For our day and time, those who serve as priests hold an ordained office in the Aaronic Priesthood. They are legal administrators empowered "to preach, teach, expound, exhort, and baptize, and administer the sacrament, and visit the house of each member, and exhort them to pray vocally and in secret and attend to all family duties." (D&C 20:46-47.)

10. *Teachers*

There are in the Church many teachers, by which is meant persons, both male and female, who act as instructors and preachers. But there are also those brethren who are ordained to the office of a teacher in the Aaronic Priesthood. Both of these kinds of teachers are essential identifying characteristics of the true church. Ordained teachers are appointed "to watch over the church always, and be with and strengthen them; and see that there is no iniquity in the church, neither hardness with each other, neither lying, backbiting, nor evil speaking: and see that the church meet together often, and also see that all the members do their duty. . . . They are . . . to warn, expound, exhort, and teach, and invite all to come unto Christ." (D&C 20:53-59.)

11. *Deacons*

These brethren hold ordained offices in the Aaronic Priesthood and are "appointed to watch over the church, [and] to be standing ministers unto the church." (D&C 84:111.) They assist the teachers in all their duties and are "to warn, expound, exhort, and teach, and invite all to come unto Christ." (D&C 20:59.)

12. *Helps and Governments*

There are in the Melchizedek Priesthood five ordained offices: elder, seventy, high priest, patriarch, and apostle. In the Aaronic Priesthood there are four ordained offices: deacon, teacher, priest, and bishop. Holders of each of these offices (except patriarchs) are organized into quorums, which are self-governing organizations having their own presiding officers who are appointed to counsel, teach, and guide the destinies of those over whom they preside.

Those upon whom the Melchizedek Priesthood is conferred receive that priesthood in its entirety. They are then ordained to offices in the priesthood and assume thus the responsibility to perform the particular ministerial service inherent in their designated office. No office adds any power, dignity, or authority to the priesthood; all offices derive their rights, powers, and prerogatives from the priesthood. All offices are appendages to the priesthood. Thus, it is greater to hold the Melchizedek Priesthood than to be an apostle, patriarch, high priest, seventy, or elder, although no one could hold any of these offices without first having the priesthood conferred upon him.

Congregations of believers are organized into wards or branches. Groups of these local units form stakes of Zion. There are also missions, districts, and such auxiliary organizations as the needs of the moment require. These auxiliary organizations aid priesthood quorums in caring for the spiritual, social, cultural, and other needs of women, the youth of Zion, and the children of the Church. Both secular and religious education is provided as the needs of the people require and the strength and means of the Church allow.

A church and kingdom guided by the inspiration of heaven will always have whatever helps and governments are needed to save men temporally and spiritually. A religion that does not have power to save a man temporally and to care for all of his needs in this life certainly does not have power to save him spiritually and provide for all of his needs in the life to come.

ARTICLE 7

*We believe
in the gift of tongues, prophecy,
revelation, visions, healing,
interpretation of tongues,
and so forth.*

CHAPTER 39

A God of Gifts
and Miracles

Gifts for All Mankind

All good things are given of God as gifts for the benefit and blessing of men. He organized the sidereal heavens, the universe, the unending worlds and spheres that roll through a boundless immensity. He made this earth and all that on it is. He created Adam and his seed, all from the dust of the earth, and he breathes the breath of life into countless beings and creatures, all as his eternal providences dictate. And all of these gifts are free.

This same gracious God, in his goodness and mercy, provides for his earthly children all that their needs require. This earth whereon we dwell is full and there is enough and to spare of all those things needed to fill the belly and clothe the body and gladden the soul. It is a good earth, well appointed, well prepared, well endowed, containing all that heaven's pilgrims need in their journey far from home. On it, the Father of us all sends seedtime and harvest, showers his bounties upon all men, and cares for the fowls and the flowers. "He maketh his sun to rise on the evil and on the good, and sendeth rain on the just and on the unjust." (Matthew 5:45.)

All these things and ten thousand times ten thousand more, of every kind and sort, are gifts from God. We did not create them, nor devise them, nor make them available. We do not pay for them, give aught in exchange for them, nor go in debt because of their receipt. They are free gifts, freely given, generously bestowed. They are the natural inheritance of all mankind.

And further: All men are enlightened from on high, all are endowed with the gift of conscience, all—inherently, innately, through no act or power of their own—know right from wrong. "There is a spirit in man: and the inspiration of the Almighty giveth them understanding." (Job 32:8.) There is a light, a spirit, a power—the light of Christ—which proceedeth forth from the presence of God to fill the immensity of space. This "Spirit of Christ is given to every man, that he may know good from evil." (Moroni 7:16.) This "Spirit giveth light to every man that cometh into the world." (D&C 84:46.) This heaven-sent, universally present, all-pervading Spirit is a free gift, given of God to all his children without reference to good works, or personal righteousness, or any deeds done in the flesh.

But none of these things, however great and marvelous, however miraculous and beyond mortal understanding, none of them classify as the gifts of the Spirit, as the spiritual gifts, as the signs that follow those who believe. The Eternal Giver of Gifts has special endowments of divine grace, special gifts and blessings for those who love and serve him with all their hearts. These gifts are freely offered to all men but are given to those only who meet the divine standard upon which their receipt is predicated.

The greatest gift ever given of God to man on earth was the gift of his Son. "For God so loved the world, that he gave his only begotten Son, that whosoever believeth in him should not perish, but have everlasting life." (John 3:16.) The Father gave the Son so that through his atoning sacrifice all of the terms and conditions of the great and eternal plan of salvation might be made operative. Our Blessed Lord himself came to bring to pass the immortality and eternal life of man. Immortality comes as a free gift to all men. Eternal life, which from an eternal perspective is "the greatest of all the gifts of God" (D&C 14:7), is reserved for those who believe and obey.

The Holy Ghost is Christ's gift to men because the companionship of that member of the Godhead is made available through the atonement. This Comforter is sent by the Father in the name of the Son. (John 14:26.) He comes to minister in the place and stead of the Lord Jesus, giving the message and bearing the testimony that would come from the Son of God if he were ministering personally to men. "When the Comforter is come, whom I will send unto you from the Father," Jesus said, "he shall testify of me." (John 15:26.) "It is expedient for you that I go away," our Lord continued, "for if I go not away, the Comforter will not come unto you; but if I depart, I will send him unto you." (John 16:7.)

And further: As the Father gave his Son, a gift to the world, as he gave him to proclaim the gospel and atone for the sins of the world, so the Son gives gifts of a like nature to his fellow-men. As Paul expressed it, "Christ . . . ascended up on high," that is, he rose in glorious immortality and ascended to his Father, and "gave gifts unto men." Those whom he gives as his gifts are his ministers and representatives. They are to proclaim the gospel, to perfect the saints, to work in the ministry, to bring the blessings of the atonement into the lives of men. Who are they? The scripture says of Christ: "He gave some, apostles; and some, prophets; and some, evangelists; and some, pastors and teachers." (Ephesians 4:7-14.) That is to say, all legal administrators who labor as the Lord did for the salvation of men are gifts, given of Christ, for the blessing and benefit of all who will heed their words. It is with them, though in a lesser degree, as it was with their Lord and Master. They are among the greatest of the gifts of God to men.

The Gifts and Callings of God

And yet again: Those ministers and preachers of righteousness who are given of God to proclaim his word to the world, and to perform their assigned labors in his earthly kingdom, are themselves endowed with special spiritual talents or gifts that enable them to perform their appointed work. These personal gifts are not earned, as far as this life is concerned. They do not result either from faith, repentance, and baptism, or from any special training in this life. Rather they are talents earned and acquired in preexistence, and at birth into mortality, they are given of God to those whom he foreordained to be his ministers. Hence, as Paul says, "as concerning the gospel, . . . the gifts and calling of God are without repentance." (Romans 11:28-29.) They are given to whomsoever the Lord wills.

In our dispensation, Joseph Smith stands supreme as the most highly gifted of all the prophets. While yet in his fifteenth year, and before he had been schooled or trained to any degree in the things of the Spirit, he saw the Father and the Son.

All those whose priesthood and power stem back to Joseph Smith have a like but lesser divine call: they were all foreordained and are all endowed, at birth, with gifts and talents that will enable them to succeed in their ministries if they choose to follow Him who has called them and from whom their gifts come. Thus the Lord says to those called to the holy apostleship in this dispensation: "You are they who are ordained of me . . . to declare my gospel, according to the power of the Holy Ghost which is in you, and according to the callings and gifts of God unto men." (D&C 18:32.) That all who are called of God to his ministry are the very ones to whom he has given the gifts and upon whom he has showered the talents that will enable them to do their assigned labors is implicit in these words of scripture: "Every elder, priest, teacher, or deacon is to be ordained according to the gifts and callings of God unto him; and he is to be ordained by the power of the Holy Ghost, which is in the one who ordains him." (D&C 20:60.)

All of those called to the ministry, all who receive callings in the priesthood, all who are called of God by prophecy are given the gifts needed to perform the work whereunto they are called. These gifts are always the ones needed for the particular work at hand. In the revealed word, we have illustrations of how these gifts are given, increased, and on occasion withdrawn from men, all as the divine purposes require.

Joseph Smith was given the gift to translate the Book of Mormon (D&C 5:30-31), a gift that he lost temporarily when the 116 pages of manuscript went out of the possession of Martin Harris (D&C 10:1-3, 18). To Joseph Smith and Oliver Cowdery, the Lord gave these words, words applicable to each of them, and in one degree or another to an endless host of his other latter-day ministers: "Behold thou hast a gift, and blessed art thou because of thy gift." All who have gifts earned in the preexistence are blessed in mortality as a direct result of that premortal obedience. "Remember it [thy gift, whatsoever it may be] is sacred and cometh from above." Let God be praised by gifted men for the endowments that are theirs; let not the mortal vessels boast in earthly achievements, for it is the Eternal Potter who shapeth all vessels as they are. "And if thou wilt inquire, thou shalt know mysteries which are great and marvelous"—this is an invitation, given of God to all his ministers—"therefore thou shalt exercise thy gift, that thou mayest find out mysteries, that thou mayest bring many to the knowledge of the truth, yea, convince them of the error of their ways." (D&C 6:10-11.) The sons of Mosiah are a perfect illustration of ministers of Christ who used and increased their divine gifts in bringing souls into the kingdom. "They had waxed strong in the knowledge of the truth; for they were men of a sound understanding and they had searched the scriptures diligently, that they might know the word of God. . . . They had given themselves to much prayer, and fasting; therefore they had the spirit of prophecy, and the spirit of revelation, and when they taught, they taught with power and authority of God." (Alma 17:2-3.)

Continuing the counsel, applicable to all of his ministers, the Lord said through Joseph Smith: "Make not thy gift known unto any save it be those who are of thy faith." Boast not before the world of divine endowments. "Trifle not with sacred things." And then, having worked the works of righteousness and having used the gifts of God to the full, prepare to receive the greatest of all gifts: "If thou wilt do good, yea, and hold out faithful to the end, thou shalt be saved in the kingdom of God, which is the greatest of all the gifts of God; for there is no gift greater than the gift of salvation."

Then to Oliver Cowdery in particular the Lord said: "I grant unto you a gift, if you desire of me"—all men ought to desire and seek the gifts of God—"to translate, even as my servant Joseph." The historical fact is that Oliver Cowdery neither desired nor sought this gift with that divine fervor which should attend the labors of the Lord's ministers, and he therefore failed to gain the promised gift and to translate the ancient records that the Lord had in store for his people. "Verily, verily, I say unto you," Oliver was promised, "there are records which contain much of my gospel, which have been kept back because of the wickedness of the people; and now I command you, that if you have good desires—a desire to lay up treasures for yourself in heaven—then shall you assist in bringing to light, with your gift, those parts of my scriptures which have been hidden because of iniquity. And now, behold, I give unto you, and also unto my servant Joseph, the keys of this gift, which shall bring to light this ministry." (D&C 6:12-13, 25-28.)

With particular reference to translating the Book of Mormon, Oliver was told by the Lord: "Assuredly as the Lord liveth, who is your God and your Redeemer, even so surely shall you receive a knowledge of whatsoever things you shall ask in faith, with an honest heart, believing that you shall receive a knowledge concerning the engravings of old records, which are ancient, which contain those parts of my scripture of which has been spoken by the manifestation of my Spirit." That is to say: The Lord offered Oliver Cowdery the gift and power to translate the Book of Mormon on the same basis that this gift was enjoyed by the Prophet Joseph Smith. "Yea, behold, I will tell you in your mind and in your heart, by the [power of the] Holy Ghost, which shall come upon you and which shall dwell in your heart," the Lord said. The Book of Mormon could be translated by the power of the Holy Ghost and in no other way. "Now, behold, this is the spirit of revelation. . . . Therefore this is thy gift; apply unto it, and blessed art thou, for it shall deliver you out of the hands of your enemies, when, if it were not so, they would slay you and bring your soul to destruction. Oh, remember these words, and keep my commandments. Remember, this is your gift." At this point the Lord told Oliver of another gift, "the gift of Aaron," that also was his. (D&C 8:1-6.) The reasons for Oliver's failure to use his gift and translate the Book of Mormon are set forth in a subsequent revelation. (D&C 9:1-14.)

The Lord's servants have it in their power, through faith, to gain the gifts and powers needed to succeed in their work and to do the things appointed unto them by Him in whose name they minister. Thus, as an ensample, the Lord said to Hyrum Smith: "Thou hast a gift, or thou shalt have a gift if thou wilt desire of me in faith, with an honest heart, believing in the power of Jesus Christ, or in my power which speaketh unto thee." (D&C 11:10.) Indeed, salvation itself comes to those, and those only, who "believe in the gifts and callings of God by the Holy Ghost." (D&C 20:27.) All such have the Lord's promise: "If you keep my commandments, and endure to the end you shall have eternal life, which gift is the greatest of all the gifts of God." (D&C 14:7.)

The Gifts and Miracles of God

Miracles and spiritual gifts always attend the faithful. Signs always follow those who believe the true gospel. The fruits of faith always grow on the tree of faith. Whenever the Lord has a people on earth, he endows them with power from on high. The presence of miracles, signs, wonders, and gifts of the Spirit stands as conclusive proof of the divine commission of those whom the Lord has called to minister in his place and stead among the children of men. All this we have heretofore set forth in our analysis of faith and in discussing the powers and ministry of the Holy Spirit. We shall now speak more particularly of the miraculous nature of those spiritual gifts reserved for and abundantly showered upon the saints.

In the ultimate sense, all that God does is a miracle; this includes every word that he speaks, every creative act, every control exercised over matter or men or angels. It includes all that he does in the sidereal heavens, all that appertains to this earth, all that is involved where every form of life is concerned. That is, all these things are miracles from man's standpoint. To the Lord they are the normal way of life of an exalted being who has all power, with whom all things originate, and in whom all things center. But because they are beyond our power to perform, because they can be done only by those who are granted the requisite divine power, they are miracles to us mortals. Similarly, a radio or television broadcast would have been classified as miraculous by Abraham or Moses, but to us, having learned to use the laws of nature involved, such broadcasts are a way of life.

To us, all spiritual gifts are miracles and all miracles come by the power of the Spirit. That these gifts and miracles have always been poured out upon the Lord's people in past ages is common knowledge. The Bible tells of one miracle after another. The miracle-filled ministries of Jesus, of the ancient apostles, and of the faithful saints in the meridian of time are as well known as anything connected with Christianity. And that gifts and miracles, as then known, ceased in the early days of the Christian era is also known and taught and wondered about by the whole of modern Christendom.

Quite aptly and manifesting a penetrating spiritual insight,

John Wesley, one of the great Protestant reformers, speaks of the departure of spiritual gifts from the apostate:

"It does not appear that these extraordinary gifts of the Holy Spirit were common in the church for more than two or three centuries. We seldom hear of them after that fatal period when the emperor Constantine called himself a Christian, and from a vain imagination of promoting the Christian cause thereby, heaped riches and power and honor upon Christians in general, but in particular upon the Christian clergy. From this time they almost totally ceased; very few instances of the kind were found. The cause of this was not as has been supposed because there was no more occasion for them—because all the world was become Christians. This is a miserable mistake; not a twentieth part of it was then nominally Christian. The real cause of it was the love of many, almost all Christians, so called, was waxed cold. The Christians had no more of the Spirit of Christ than the other heathens. The Son of Man, when he came to examine His Church, could hardly find faith upon the earth. This was the real cause why the extraordinary gifts of the Holy Ghost were no longer to be found in the Christian Church—because the Christians were turned heathens again, and only had a dead form left." (Wesley's Works, vol. 7, 89:26, 27, cited in James E. Talmage, *The Articles of Faith*, p. 495.)

Though spiritual gifts are unknown in the world, they are commonplace among those who have forsaken the world and have come unto Christ with full purpose of heart. And they are, thus, one of the signs of the true church. "I speak unto you who deny the revelations of God," Moroni writes, "and say that they are done away, that there are no revelations, nor prophecies, nor gifts, nor healing, nor speaking with tongues, and the interpretation of tongues." Those so addressed are the generality of mankind; they include all of the non-Christian world and with minor exceptions all of those who profess to follow the lowly Nazarene. It is the general contention of these professing Christians that gifts and miracles, in the full and true sense, were needed only in the formative days of the church. Since then, they say that men in their wisdom, unshackled by the creeds and mysticism of the past, no longer need the kind of spiritual guidance that was necessary to save the apostles and prophets of old. That such a contention is not worthy of refutation is self-evident.

But what is Moroni's message to those who no longer believe in spiritual gifts? "Behold I say unto you," he continues, "he that denieth these things knoweth not the gospel of Christ; yea, he has not read the scriptures; if so, he does not understand them." To deny the continuing and everlasting need for spiritual gifts in this present probationary sphere is to reject the gospel and deny the scriptures. "For do we not read that God is the same yesterday, today, and forever, and in him there is no variableness neither shadow of changing?" If such words describe the true God, every faithful man from Adam to the end of time, every man who obeys the law upon which their receipt is predicated, will receive, possess, and enjoy the gifts of the Spirit.

"And now, if ye have imagined up unto yourselves a god who doth vary, and in whom there is shadow of changing, then have ye imagined up unto yourselves a god who is not a God of miracles." Such are the imaginings of those who worship the god of the creeds. "But behold, I will show unto you a God of miracles, even the God of Abraham, and the God of Isaac, and the God of Jacob; and it is that same God who created the heavens and the earth, and all things that in them are." This God is identified as the one who created Adam, the man by whom the fall came, and because of which fall came Jesus Christ and the redemption of man. This God is named as the one through whom immortality and eternal life come; as the one who brings to pass the resurrection of the dead; as the Holy One before whose bar all men will be judged. Then, with an insight born of the Spirit, Moroni asks and answers these questions:

"And now, O all ye that have imagined up unto yourselves a god who can do no miracles [and who no longer, therefore, gives spiritual gifts to the children of men], I would ask of you, have all these things passed, of which I have spoken? Has the end come yet?" Will not great miracles attend the Second Coming of the Son of Man? Have all things transpired that the Lord has in store for this earth and its inhabitants? "Behold I say unto you, Nay; and God has not ceased to be a God of miracles."

How wondrous are things past, things present, and things to come. "Behold, are not the things that God hath wrought marvelous in our eyes? Yea, and who can comprehend the marvelous works of God?" Who can even imagine the gifts and miracles and wonders yet to be? How foolish to say that there are no gifts for the faithful because we, being faithful, have received none!

"Who shall say that it was not a miracle that by his word the heaven and the earth should be; and by the power of his word man was created of the dust of the earth; and by the power of his word have miracles been wrought? And who shall say that Jesus Christ did not do many mighty miracles? And there were many mighty miracles wrought by the hands of the apostles." None can deny these things; they are the great truths of eternity and are among the basic verities of revealed religion. "And if there were miracles wrought then, why has God ceased to be a God of miracles and yet be an unchangeable Being?" All those with spiritual insight of their own know the answer to this question and to all of Moroni's questions.

Hence, as though the thunders of heaven rolled forth the proclamation for all men to hear, Moroni concludes: "And behold, I say unto you he changeth not; if so he would cease to be God; and he ceaseth not to be God, and is a God of miracles." (Mormon 9:7-19.)

What then of spiritual gifts? They come from God by the power of his Spirit. They are miracles; they are the fruits of faith; they are the signs that follow true believers. Where they are, there is the church and kingdom of God on earth; and where they are not, the true church, the true gospel, and the power of God unto salvation are not found among mortals.

CHAPTER 40

Spiritual Gifts

Spiritual Gifts Come by Faith

Those gifts of God that come to faithful people by the power of the Holy Ghost are called spiritual gifts or gifts of the Spirit. They come from God, they are administered by the Holy Ghost, and they are transmitted to men by the Spirit of Christ, which is the light of Christ, which is the agency of God's power. Their receipt is predicated upon faith, obedience, and personal righteousness; hence they are reserved for the saints of God, for those who believe in his name and live his laws. They are the signs and miracles that follow those who believe, and their receipt, in one degree or another, is essential to salvation. No one can be saved in the celestial kingdom unless he receives some or many of the gifts of the Spirit.

Why do signs and miracles cease in certain ages? Why are they not found at all times and among all peoples? Were those of old entitled to greater blessings than those of us who now dwell on the same earth that once was theirs? Moroni answers: "The reason why" a God of gifts and miracles "ceaseth to do miracles among the children of men," and to pour out his gifts upon them, "is because that they dwindle in unbelief, and depart from the right way, and know not the God in whom they should trust." They worship false gods whom they define in their creeds, and they no longer walk in the same paths pursued by the saints of former days.

It is men who have changed, not God; he is the same everlastingly. All men who have the same faith and live the same law will reap the same blessings. "Whoso believeth in Christ, doubting nothing," saith Moroni, "whatsoever he shall ask the Father in the name of Christ it shall be granted him; and this promise is unto all, even unto the ends of the earth." Moroni

then quotes the promise of the Lord Jesus about signs following those who believe, which promise concludes with these
wondrous words: "And whosoever shall believe in my name,
doubting nothing, unto him will I confirm all my words, even
unto the ends of the earth." (Mormon 9:20-25.)

Then, after setting forth many of the spiritual gifts by name,
Moroni exhorts us to remember that God "is the same yesterday, today, and forever, and that all these gifts, . . . which are
spiritual, never will be done away, even as long as the world
shall stand, only according to the unbelief of the children of
men." And as his custom was, he again anchored his words to
those of his Master. "And Christ truly said unto our fathers: If
ye have faith ye can do all things which are expedient unto
me." Knowing this and being guided by the Spirit, Moroni proclaimed: "And now I speak unto all the ends of the earth—that
if the day cometh that the power and gifts of God shall be done
away among you, it shall be because of unbelief."

Sad to say, the gifts of God were done away in the Americas
with the death of Moroni, and in the Old World shortly after
the death of the apostles. "And wo be unto the children of
men if this be the case," Moroni said of that dire and fateful era;
"for there shall be none that doeth good among you, no not
one. For if there be one among you that doeth good, he shall
work by the power and gifts of God. And wo unto them who
shall do these things away and die, for they die in their sins,
and they cannot be saved in the kingdom of God; and I speak
it according to the words of Christ; and I lie not." (Moroni
10:19-26.)

Seek Spiritual Gifts

Is it proper to seek for spiritual gifts? Should we plead with
the Lord for the gift of prophecy, or of revelation, or of
tongues? Is it fitting and right to pray for the soul-sanctifying
privilege of seeing the face of the Lord Jesus while we yet dwell
as mortals in a sin-filled world? Does the Lord expect us to
desire and seek for spiritual experiences, or do the divine
proprieties call for us simply to love the Lord and keep his
commandments, knowing that if and when he deems it proper
he will grant special gifts and privileges to us?

By way of answer, it almost suffices to ask such questions

as these: Are we not expected to seek salvation, the greatest of all the gifts of God? Why, then, should we not prepare ourselves for this greatest of all boons by seeking the enjoyment of the lesser ones? If we are to see his face in that eternal realm, where the same sociality that exists among us here, then coupled with eternal glory, shall endure everlastingly, can we go amiss by seeking to establish that sociality here and now? Are we not commanded: Ask and ye shall receive; seek and ye shall find; knock and it shall be opened? Why, then, should we smother a desire to heal the sick or raise the dead or commune with friends beyond the veil?

Also by way of answer to the queries at hand, we might with propriety reason along this line: If spiritual gifts are interwoven with and form part of the very gospel of salvation itself, can we enjoy the fulness of that gospel without possessing the gifts that are part of it? If gifts and miracles shall—inevitably, always, and everlastingly—follow those who believe, how can we be true believers without them? And if we are to seek the gospel, if we are to hunger and thirst after righteousness, if our whole souls must cry out for the goodness of God and his everlasting association, how can we exempt ourselves from seeking the gifts of the Spirit that come from and prepare us for his presence?

If such be our thoughts, we are in harmony with the counsel given in the divine word. Paul says: "Covet earnestly the best gifts" (1 Corinthians 12:31), "desire spiritual gifts," and be "zealous of spiritual gifts," seeking "that ye may excel to the edifying of the church" (1 Corinthians 14:1, 12). Moroni says: "Lay hold upon every good gift." (Moroni 10:30.) But the great exhortation to seek for spiritual gifts is found in latter-day revelation.

"Ye are commanded in all things to ask of God, who giveth liberally," the holy word acclaims. Note the Lord's language: We are commanded to seek the gifts of the Spirit; if we do not do so, we are not walking in that course which is pleasing to Him whose gifts they are. "And that which the Spirit testifies unto you even so I would that ye should do in all holiness of heart, walking uprightly before me, considering the end of your salvation, doing all things with prayer and thanksgiving." These are the words of the Lord; they summarize the course he desires us to pursue. Why should we ask, and seek, and obey?

He answers: "That ye may not be seduced by evil spirits, or doctrines of devils, or the commandments of men; for some are of men, and others of devils." If we do not receive gifts and guidance and doctrine and commandments from on high, we shall of necessity receive them from some other source. Others have guidance to offer, doctrine to teach, and commandments to give. We must choose what to believe and elect how we shall live. "Wherefore, beware lest ye are deceived; and that ye may not be deceived seek ye earnestly the best gifts, always remembering for what they are given."

Why, for what purpose, and to whom are the gifts given? "Verily I say unto you, they are given for the benefit of those who love me and keep all my commandments, and him that seeketh so to do; that all may be benefited that seek or that ask of me, that ask and not for a sign that they may consume it upon their lusts." It is inherent in the whole plan of righteousness that those who seek the gifts of the Spirit do so for their own salvation and for the glory of God, and not for lustful and selfish and worldly reasons.

"And again, verily I say unto you, I would that ye should always remember, and always retain in your minds what those gifts are, that are given unto the church." (D&C 46:7-10.) Truly all of the Lord's saints should seek him, should seek his Spirit, should seek his gifts. Where these gifts are, there is the true and saving gospel, and where they are not, there is no hope of salvation.

Gifts Given the Saints

There are three scriptural accounts which name a limited few of the gifts of the Spirit that are reserved for the saints. They come from the pens of Paul and Moroni and from the lips of the Lord Jesus as he spoke to Joseph Smith. Interweaving the three accounts together, we gain the following overview of the matter:

1. *Faith Precedes the Miracle*
The gifts of the Spirit come to those who receive the Spirit. Men must receive the gift of the Holy Ghost before that member of the Godhead will take up his abode with them and begin the supernal process of distributing his gifts to them. The gift of the Holy Ghost is the right to the constant companion-

ship of that member of the Godhead, based on faithfulness. It is given at baptism. Those saints who keep the commandments and walk in paths of truth and righteousness after baptism actually receive the promised companionship—not at all times, but from time to time, for no man is perfect; none in mortality walk eternally and unceasingly in the blazing light of heaven. Thus the gifts of the Spirit are for believing, faithful, righteous people; they are reserved for the saints of God. They come from God in heaven to man on earth in a miraculous manner. Their receipt is a miracle, and faith precedes the miracle.

2. *Gifts Without Number*

Spiritual gifts are endless in number and infinite in variety. Those listed in the revealed word are simply illustrations of the boundless outpouring of divine grace that a gracious God gives those who love and serve him. "All have not every gift given unto them; for there are many gifts, and to every man [who is true and faithful] is given a gift by the Spirit of God. To some is given one, and to some is given another, that all may be profited thereby." (D&C 46:11-12.) "And there are different ways that these gifts are administered; but it is the same God who worketh all in all; and they are given by the manifestations of the Spirit of God unto men, to profit them." (Moroni 10:8. See also 1 Corinthians 12:4-7.)

3. *The Gift of Testimony*

Testimony is the first and greatest of all the gifts given of God to mortals. It is the rock foundation upon which men build their houses of faith and righteousness and salvation. It is the beginning of all righteousness, and because of it, faithful men endure all things as though they constantly saw the face of "the invisible God" in whose image Christ came. (Colossians 1:14-15.) A testimony is to know the doctrine of the divine Sonship by personal revelation from the Holy Ghost. It comes when Spirit speaks to spirit, when the Holy Spirit of God speaks to the spirit within us, giving knowledge with absolute certainty. "To some it is given by the Holy Ghost to know that Jesus Christ is the Son of God, and that he was crucified for the sins of the world." (D&C 46:13.) "And ye may know that he is, by the power of the Holy Ghost." (Moroni 10:7.) Indeed, "No man can say [or rather, know] that Jesus is the Lord, but by the Holy Ghost." (1 Corinthians 12:3.)

4. Believing the Lord's Witnesses

Prophets and apostles and the elders of Israel preach the gospel and testify of Christ and his divine Sonship, having first received the divine message by personal revelation. Some believe their words and know in their hearts that they have heard the truth. The truths taught may be new and strange to the hearers, but their acceptance is instinctive, automatic, without restraint; they need hear no further arguments. The Spirit-guided words find firm lodgment in their souls by the power of the Spirit. This ability to believe is a gift of God.

Individuals who have not yet advanced in spiritual things to the point of gaining for themselves personal and direct revelation from the Holy Ghost may yet have power to believe what others, speaking by the power of the Spirit, both teach and testify. They have power to recognize the truth of the words of others who do speak by the power of the Spirit, even though they cannot attune themselves to the Infinite so as to receive the divine word direct from heaven and without the helps of others to teach them. Thus it is written: "To others [the hearers of whom we speak] it is given to believe on their words [that is, on the words of those who have the message direct from God in heaven], that they also might have eternal life if they continue faithful." (D&C 46:14.) Thus, men can obey and be saved even though they do not see the Lord, or entertain angels, or receive, independent of any other persons, the heaven-sent word of salvation.

5. The Gifts of Administration and Discernment

These gifts, given to those who administer the church and who are appointed to discern between true and false spirits, are considered in Chapter 31, "The Holy Ghost—The Lord's Minister."

6. Wisdom and Knowledge

Worldly wisdom and knowledge gained by intellectual talents are available to all men. But the knowledge of God and his eternal laws—gospel knowledge, saving knowledge, the hidden wisdom that comes from on high, the wisdom of those to whom the wonders of eternity are an open book, divine wisdom—all these are gifts of the Spirit. "The things of God knoweth no man, but the Spirit of God." (1 Corinthians 2:11.)

Among the true saints are those endowed with divine knowledge and heavenly wisdom "that all may be taught to be wise and to have knowledge." (D&C 46:17-18. See also Moroni 10:9-10; 1 Corinthians 12:8.) Of those so endowed, Paul says: "We have received, not the spirit of the world, but the spirit which is of God; that we might know the things that are freely given to us of God. Which things also we speak, not in the words which man's wisdom teacheth, but which the Holy Ghost teacheth." (1 Corinthians 2:12-13.)

7. *The Gift of Faith*

Faith itself—faith in all its glory, wonder, and power—is a gift of God. Some have it; some do not. Among those so endowed are those who have faith to heal, or to be healed, or to work miracles, or to do all things according to the will of Him in whom they trust. (D&C 46:19-20; Moroni 10:11; 1 Corinthians 12:9.) Faith, and all that appertains to it, we have heretofore considered at some length.

8. *The Working of Miracles*

Healing and being healed and raising the dead are only the beginning of miracles. Properly gifted persons control the elements, move mountains, turn rivers out of their course, walk on water, quench the violence of fire, are carried by the power of the Spirit from one congregation to another, are translated and taken up into heaven, or—and this above all—gain for themselves an eternal inheritance in the presence of Him who is Eternal. Miracles are now, have always been, and always will be part and portion of the true gospel of that God who is a God of miracles. They are gifts of the Spirit. (D&C 46:21; Moroni 10:12; 1 Corinthians 12:10.)

9. *The Gift of Prophecy*

The gift of prophecy is an extension and an enlargement of the gift of testimony. "The testimony of Jesus is the spirit of prophecy." (Revelation 19:10.) A person who gains personal revelation from the Holy Spirit that Jesus is Lord of all, being thus attuned to the Infinite, "may prophesy concerning all things." (Moroni 10:13. See also D&C 46:22; 1 Corinthians 12:10.) There is no difference between receiving revelation that Jesus was crucified for the sins of the world and receiving revelation that he shall soon come again in all the glory of his Father's kingdom. Thus it is that Peter said of the holy word given anciently by the mouths of the prophets: "Prophecy came not in old time by the will of man: but holy men of God spake as they were moved by the Holy Ghost." (2 Peter 1:21.)

And even as men seek for a testimony so should they desire the gift of prophecy. Thus it is that Paul says: "Let the prophets speak. . . . For ye may all prophesy one by one. . . . Wherefore, brethren, covet to prophesy." (1 Corinthians 14:29, 31, 39.)

10. *Beholding Angels and Discerning Spirits*

If a man has power to part the veil and converse with angels and with the ministering spirits who dwell in the realms of light, surely this is a gift of the Spirit. Also, how can anyone discern between the spirits sent of God and the evil spirits that do the devil's bidding except by revelation? Among us, there are those so endowed.

11. *The Gift of Tongues and Their Interpretation*

These are of two kinds: (1) learning to speak foreign tongues, to understand the words spoken by aliens, and to translate what is written in other languages; and (2) speaking or understanding alien and unknown languages without premeditation. The first kind is by far the more important and more commonly conferred; the second type is more dramatic and may involve languages spoken by others now living or dead languages long unknown among men. Some have spoken, for instance, in the pure Adamic language.

Both the gift of tongues and the gift of interpretation of tongues are given primarily for the preaching of the gospel. Missionaries learn the languages of those among whom they labor, and sometimes they are given power, for a short time, to preach and understand without the labor of study and the struggle for understanding. Moroni speaks both of "tongues" and of "the interpretation of languages and of divers kinds of tongues." (Moroni 10:15-16. See also D&C 46:24; 1 Corinthians 12:10.) Joseph Smith's translation of the Book of Mormon from Reformed Egyptian into English falls within this broad scope.

Tongues and their interpretation are the most dangerous and most easily imitated of all the gifts of God. Men can speak and interpret by intellectual power and thus use their abilities to teach lies and foster heresies. Lucifer can cause his disciples to give forth nonsensical gibberish in tongues known to devils. In a long discourse about tongues and their proper usage, Paul counsels the saints to restrict them in their dramatic form. Interpreters, he says, must always be present. And, having in mind their proper purpose, he says of himself: "I had rather speak five words with my understanding, that by my voice I might teach others also, than ten thousand words in an unknown tongue." (1 Corinthians 14:19.)

12. *Revelation and Visions*

Revelation and prophecy and testimony and visions—these are the foundation upon which the Lord builds his earthly church. As gifts of the Spirit, they are poured out upon the saints. Revelation is the making known of divine truths by communication from heaven; it is God speaking to man in numerous available ways; it is the giving of saving truths to unsaved mortals. One means is by rending the heavens and permitting fallen man to entertain angels and see within the veil; in vision the faithful are thus permitted to see the wonders of eternity and to come to know their Maker. When revelation dips into the future beyond what mortal eyes can see, it becomes prophecy. The earthly kingdom is governed and guided and sustained by the spirit of prophecy and the spirit of revelation. Testimony is the beginning of personal revelation in the life of a believing soul. And "upon this rock"—the rock of testimony and personal revelation—"I will build my church," saith the Lord, "and the gates of hell shall not prevail against it." (Matthew 16:18.)

Visions and revelation are always found in the true church. They always abound among the saints of God, and without them there would be no divine kingdom on earth. Without them there is no true religion, no salvation, no hope of eternal glory, no way in which man can be as his Maker. They are as much a part of true religion as sunshine and rain are part of mortal existence. Unless the sun shines and the rains fall, men could not live on earth; and when visions and revelations cease, men die spiritually. Is it any wonder, then, that the divine word intones, "Deny not the spirit of revelation, nor the spirit of prophecy, for wo unto him that denieth these things"? (D&C 11:25.)

Good and Evil Gifts

"It must needs be," Lehi taught, "that there is an opposition in all things." (2 Nephi 2:11.) In the very nature of things this must be so. It is inherent in the whole scheme of life and being. Life itself depends upon the existence of opposites. Without evil, there could be no good; without misery, no happiness; without death, no life. (2 Nephi 2.) Thus, if there are good gifts that come from God, there are also evil gifts that spring forth from Satan. Heaven is the source of all that is good; hell, of all that is evil.

Satan and his fallen angels abide on earth. They seek to destroy men and doom them to an everlasting perdition. If they alone had influence and there were no help from above, men would slide everlastingly downward until, bound by the chains of hell, they would be in bondage to that evil spirit who fell from the presence of the Eternal God. As we have seen, God gives gifts to men to lift them up, to light their way back to heaven, to let them gain glimpses, while yet on their mortal pilgrimages, of that eternal home whence they came. These good gifts are shown forth in the midst of a world filled with evil gifts. And as we have also seen, these good gifts are given so that men need "not be seduced by evil spirits, or doctrines of devils, or the commandments of men." The Lord's people are to "beware lest [they] are deceived; and that [they] may not be deceived," they are to "seek . . . earnestly the best gifts." (D&C 46:7-8.)

After discoursing upon "the gifts of God," Moroni says: "And I would exhort you, my beloved brethren, that ye remember that every good gift cometh of Christ." (Moroni 10:18.) The biblical word, as phrased by James, teaches: "Every good gift and every perfect gift is from above, and cometh down from the Father of lights, with whom is no variableness, neither shadow of turning." (James 1:17.) The Father and the Son are the source of all that is good; conversely, Lucifer originates all that is evil.

Is there a gift of preaching by the power of the Holy Ghost that enlightens spiritual souls and leads them to eternal life? So also there is a gift of intellectual persuasion, a gift of sophistry and delusion, that pleases carnal men and lets them feel that they can believe what they will and live after the manner of the world, and yet be saved.

Is there a gift of charity, of enjoying and possessing the pure love of Christ, that leads men to peace in this present world and assures them of eternal life in that world which is to be? So also there is a gift of selfishness, of putting one's own interests first in all things, of spewing forth hatred and animosity upon others, all of which leads to war and desolation here and now and to everlasting destruction hereafter.

Are there gifts of purity, of chastity, of clean thoughts, of upright living, all of which cleanse and perfect the souls of men and prepare them to be at ease in the fellowship of angels and holy beings hereafter? So also there are gifts of lust, of lewdness, of profane and evil speaking, of filling one's mind with carnal and evil thoughts, all of which lead to vulgar and immoral acts that prepare men for the continuing association of evil spirits in the realms ahead.

It was Mormon who addressed these words to the true believers of his day: "All things which are good cometh of God; and that which is evil cometh of the devil; for the devil is an enemy unto God, and fighteth against him continually, and inviteth and enticeth to sin, and to do that which is evil continually. But behold, that which is of God inviteth and enticeth to do good continually; wherefore, every thing which inviteth and enticeth to do good, and to love God, and to serve him, is inspired of God."

This mortal probation is so designed that it requires each person to choose for himself what he will believe and how he will live. And "the Spirit of Christ is given to every man," Mormon says, "that he may know good from evil." The great and eternal standard of judgment is given in these words: "Every thing which inviteth to do good, and to persuade to believe in Christ, is sent forth by the power and gift of Christ; wherefore ye may know with a perfect knowledge it is of God. But whatsoever thing persuadeth men to do evil, and believe not in Christ, and deny him, and serve not God, then ye may know with a perfect knowledge it is of the devil." (Moroni 7:12-17.)

The grand conclusion of the whole matter is couched by Moroni in this exhortation: "Lay hold upon every good gift, and touch not the evil gift, nor the unclean thing." (Moroni 10:30.) To this, it seems appropriate to add only these words of the Lord. Question: "What doth it profit a man if a gift is bestowed upon him, and he receive not the gift?" Answer: "Behold, he rejoices not in that which is given unto him, neither rejoices in him who is the giver of the gift." (D&C 88:33.)

CHAPTER 41

The Divine Gift of Prayer

Prayer: A Gift of God

Prayer—blessed, blessed prayer—is a gift of God offered by a loving and gracious Father to all his children. It is the means provided for earth's pilgrims, far from their heavenly home and shut out from the personal presence of Him who sent them on their journey, to report their labors and receive further direction. The Father of us all spoke to each of us personally in the realms of glory whence we came. Now, in this sphere of toil and trial and testing, he offers to continue his speech if we will abide the law that makes such possible. That law is prayer.

Prayer is the way ordained of God whereby mortal men can converse, by the power of the Spirit, with their Immortal Father. As a heaven-sent boon, it is offered to all without money and without price. It is a free gift. Those who receive the gift, who learn thereby how to communicate with their Maker, and who conform in full to the true law of prayer are on the path leading to the celestial kingdom of heaven. "For whosoever shall call upon the name of the Lord shall be saved." (Romans 10:13.) They are the ones for whom prayer becomes in the full and true sense a gift of the Spirit because they learn to pray by the power of the Spirit.

In prayer, man asks and Deity answers. Those who do not ask receive no answer. "Ask, and it shall be given you," Jesus said; "seek, and ye shall find; knock, and it shall be opened unto you." Why? Because the promise is: "Every one that asketh receiveth; and he that seeketh findeth; and to him that knocketh it shall be opened." Such is the divine law. Having so stated, the Lord Jesus reasoned thus: "What man is there of you, whom if his son ask bread, will he give him a stone? Or if he ask a fish, will he give him a serpent?" Even the wicked and ungodly are kind to their children. "If ye then, being evil," Jesus continued, "know how to give good gifts unto your children, how much more shall your Father which is in heaven"—who is perfect in all his attributes—"give good things to them that ask him?" (Matthew 7:7-11.)

James, our Lord's brother after the manner of the flesh, in writing "to the twelve tribes which are scattered abroad," gave this counsel: "If any of you lack wisdom, let him ask of God, that giveth to all men liberally, and upbraideth not; and it shall be given him." These are the very words that led Joseph Smith, himself one of the lost sheep of Israel, to ask which of all the sects was true so that he might know which to join. And then came the First Vision with all that it portends. "But let him ask in faith," James continued, "nothing wavering. For he that wavereth is like a wave of the sea driven with the wind and tossed." Ask in faith, that pure and perfect assurance which pulls down the blessings of heaven! No answer shall be forthcoming for an unbeliever. "For let not that man"—the man without faith—"think that he shall receive any thing of the Lord." (James 1:5-7.) It is by faith that men attune themselves to the Infinite and hear the answers sent from heaven. Truly, "all things, whatsoever ye shall ask in prayer, believing, ye shall receive." (Matthew 21:22.)

There is scarcely a better illustration of the blessings of prayer in the lives of the saints than to point to healings that attend the prayers of the faithful. "Is any sick among you?" James asks the Lord's people. If so, he counsels, "let him call for the elders of the church," those brethren who, like Peter and the ancient apostles, hold the holy Melchizedek Priesthood. "And let them pray over him, anointing him with oil in the name of the Lord." As the Lord's agents, they pray and minister in the place and stead of their Master. "And the prayer of faith shall save the sick"—save him physically and save him spiritually—"and the Lord shall raise him up." He shall be healed unless he is appointed unto death. "And if he have committed sins, they shall be forgiven him." Of course they will be, if he is in tune with and receives the Spirit, for that sanctifying member of the Godhead will not dwell in an unclean tabernacle. "Confess your faults one to another," James continues, "and pray one for another, that ye may be healed. The effectual fervent prayer of a righteous man availeth much." (James 5:14-16.)

How aptly Nephi said: "Pray always, and [do] not faint." And also: "Ye must not perform any thing unto the Lord save in the first place ye shall pray unto the Father in the name of Christ, that he will consecrate thy performance unto thee, that thy performance may be for the welfare of thy soul." (2 Nephi 32:9.)

The True Doctrine of Prayer

All three members of the Godhead are involved in and concerned with our prayers. Each of them stands in his specific and appointed position and performs his designated service for men. Their labors in this respect are identifiable and distinct and must not be confused or misunderstood. The true doctrine of prayer is this: We worship and pray to the Father, in the name of the Son, by the power of the Holy Ghost. This is the one and only approved order; there is no other. It is this true order of prayer that we shall now set forth.

1. *We worship and pray to the Father.*

This is the most basic verity in the whole plan of salvation. The Father, in the ultimate sense, is the Creator. He ordained and established the gospel for the salvation of all his spirit children, Christ included. Thus, the revealed summary of the eternal verities on which salvation rests proclaims: "There is a God in heaven, who is infinite and eternal, from everlasting to everlasting the same unchangeable God, the framer of heaven and earth, and all things which are in them." The Father is God above all. He is our God, and he is Christ's God. He is the ultimate source of all life and being; all good gifts come from him, and no one takes his place.

Speaking of the Father, the divine word continues: "He created man, male and female, after his own image and in his own likeness, created he them." Mortal man is fashioned and patterned after the Father of us all. We were his children first in the premortal life, and we are his children here again in this mortal sphere. And it was the Father who directed how and in what manner mortal men should worship. He "gave unto them commandments that they should love and serve him, the only living and true God, and that he should be the only being whom they should worship." Having thus set forth the true and only order of true worship, the scripture tells how this "Almighty God gave his Only Begotten Son" to work out the infinite and eternal atonement and to put all of the terms and conditions of his plan of salvation into operation. (D&C 20:17-21.)

Thus—because the Father is the Creator, Originator, and Source of all that is; and because the Son is the Redeemer of all things, and (as we shall shortly set forth) the Prototype of salvation for all men—thus the divine word that came to Adam, for himself and his posterity, decreed: "Thou shalt do all that thou doest in the name of the Son, and thou shalt repent and call upon God in the name of the Son forevermore." (Moses 5:8.) The pattern of worship and prayer being thus set, the Nephite Jacob said of his people and of those who preceded them: "We knew of Christ, and we had a hope of his glory many hundred years before his coming; and not only we ourselves had a hope of his glory, but also all the holy prophets which were before us. Behold, they believed in Christ and worshiped the Father in his name, and also we worship the Father in his name." (Jacob 4:4-5.)

2. *We pray and worship in the name of the Son.*

Christ is not only the Savior and Redeemer, the one by whom salvation comes, the one whose atoning sacrifice puts into operation all of the terms and conditions of his Father's plan. He is also the Prototype, the Pattern, the Type, and the Model of salvation. He is the great Exemplar. He came to earth and worked out his own salvation by worshipping the Father so that all men—as his brethren in the spirit and as his fellow mortals in mortality—could pattern their lives after his and become themselves joint-heirs of God and inheritors with the Son of the fulness of the glory of the Father.

All this is set forth in a wondrous manner in the revealed word, first recorded by John the Baptist, then by John the Revelator, and now revealed to us, in which John saw that Christ "received not of the fulness at the first, but received grace for grace," and that he "continued from grace to grace, until he received a fulness." That "fulness of the glory of the Father" finally came after the resurrection, when "he received all power, both in heaven and on earth." That is, the Lord Jesus, born of Mary, came to earth as a mortal man. In this state he progressed from one degree of intelligence to another until, having overcome the world and having been obedient in all things, he attained a state of resurrected glory. Then he gained a fulness of joy and that full and unlimited glory which can come only to those for whom body and spirit are inseparably connected. This sets the pattern for all men. If we do what he did, praying, worshipping, and obeying as he did, we shall gain eternal life as he did. He is our Prototype.

This recitation of how Christ worshipped the Father, thus gaining exaltation for himself, has been revealed to us in this day for a specific reason. "I give unto you these sayings," he says—those sayings that set forth how he was saved by worshipping the Father—"that you may understand and know how to worship, and know what you worship, that you may come unto the Father in my name, and in due time receive of his fulness. For if you keep my commandments you shall receive of his fulness, and be glorified in me as I am in the Father; therefore, I say unto you, you shall receive grace for grace." (D&C 93:12-20.)

"Come unto the Father in my name." Worship in the name of Christ. Act in his name; speak in his name; pray in his name. Indeed, in the waters of baptism we have taken upon ourselves his name so that it becomes our name. We take his name upon us anew each time we partake worthily of the sacrament of the Lord's Supper. It is a holy and sacred name, the only "name under heaven given among men, whereby we must be saved." (Acts 4:12.)

When we act in the name of another, we place ourselves in his position; we act in his place and stead; our words become his words, our deeds his deeds, our prayers his prayers. Thus, if we pray to the Father, or worship the Father, in the name of Christ, it is as though Christ himself did what we are doing. Our way of worship becomes his way of worship because we have done it in his name; we have done it in his place and stead, as though we were the Lord Jesus, for we are acting in his name. We are doing what he would do; he is our Prototype.

Thus, with particular reference to prayer, which is itself

one of the most important parts of true worship, the Lord Jesus commands: "Ye must watch and pray always, lest ye be tempted by the devil, and ye be led away captive by him." But how shall we pray? What pattern shall we follow? He answers: "As I have prayed among you even so shall ye pray in my church, among my people who do repent and are baptized in my name. Behold I am the light; I have set an example for you." Both the New Testament and the Book of Mormon tell us how Christ prayed; they record the example of which he speaks.

"Therefore," he continues, "ye must always pray unto the Father in my name." If we follow his example and pray as he would pray in any given situation, we are praying in his place and stead, as it were, or in other words, in his name. "And whatsoever ye shall ask the Father in my name, which is right, believing that ye shall receive, behold it shall be given unto you." And further: "Pray in your families unto the Father, always in my name, that your wives and your children may be blessed." And yet further, with reference to those outside the Church who are seeking the truth, he says: "Ye shall pray for them," in the proper way, that is, "ye shall pray for them unto the Father, in my name."

Our prayers, as the saints of the Most High, should conform to the divine standard because they are patterned after the prayers of Him in whose name we pray. "Hold up your light that it may shine unto the world," he says. "Behold I am the light which ye shall hold up—that which ye have seen me do. Behold ye see that I have prayed unto the Father," and ye shall do likewise. (3 Nephi 18:15-24.)

3. *We pray and worship by the power of the Holy Ghost.*

In the pure and perfect and proper sense, no one can speak or pray in the name of Christ unless he speaks or prays by the power of the Holy Ghost. It is within our capability, as the Lord's people, to do this because "we have the mind of Christ." (1 Corinthians 2:16.) That is, we have the gift of the Holy Ghost, which is the right to the constant companionship of that member of the Godhead, based on faithfulness. Indeed, one of the chief reasons for the restoration of the gospel in our day was to enable "every man [to] speak in the name of God the Lord, even the Savior of the world." (D&C 1:20.) This includes the power whereby every man who is true and faithful can pray in that same holy name, saying the words and seeking the blessings that would be said and sought by Him in whose name the prayer is uttered.

Thus, in the revelation on spiritual gifts, the Lord gives this promise: "He that asketh in Spirit shall receive in Spirit." Why? Because "he that asketh in the Spirit asketh according to the will of God; wherefore it is done even as he asketh." God grants the petition because, having been offered in the name of the Son, it is, in fact, the petition of the Son. Hence this added word of revealed truth: "All things must be done in the name of Christ, whatsoever you do in the Spirit; And ye must give thanks unto God in the Spirit for whatsoever blessing ye are blessed with." (D&C 46:28-32.)

Perfect prayers are always answered; proper petitions are always granted. The Lord never rejects a prayer uttered by the power of the Spirit, or denies a petition sought in the name of Christ, that accords with the divine will. "If ye are purified and cleansed from all sin," he says, "ye shall ask whatsoever you will in the name of Jesus and it shall be done. But know this, it shall be given you what you shall ask." (D&C 50:29-30.) Thus perfect prayers are spoken by the power of revelation.

The Law of Prayer

As with everything else that God has ordained—everything that is part and portion of his everlasting gospel; everything, both temporal and spiritual, that exists and is and shall be—as with all things, prayer is governed by law. "There is a law, irrevocably decreed in heaven before the foundations of this world, upon which all blessings are predicated"—prayer included. "And when we obtain any blessing from God, it is by obedience to that law upon which it is predicated." (D&C 130:20-21.)

The law of prayer operates by faith; it is perfected by obedience; it has greater power when there is conformity and uprightness in the lives of those who petition their God. When we have faith, when we keep the commandments, when we live righteously, the Lord is more inclined to answer our prayers. "I, the Lord, am bound when ye do what I say," he says, "but when ye do not what I say, ye have no promise." (D&C 82:10.)

It is written: "The Lord . . . heareth the prayer of the righteous." (Proverbs 15:29.) It is also written: "And whatsoever we ask, we receive of him, because we keep his commandments, and do those things that are pleasing in his sight." (1 John 3:22. See also 5:14-15.) And it was Jesus himself who said: "If ye abide in me, and my words abide in you, ye shall ask what ye will, and it shall be done unto you." (John 15:7.) Thus, prayers are heard and prayers are answered when those who seek their God do so in righteousness. Only the true and living God hears prayers. He alone grants the petitions of the penitent, and as with all else that he does, he is bound by the laws of obedience and faith and personal righteousness that he himself has ordained.

In a stirring plea, Amulek calls upon the saints to pray always for all their needs, both temporal and spiritual. Above all, we are to call upon the Lord for mercy lest, being sinners, we remain subject to the demands of justice and be required with a relentless certainty to pay the penalty for all our evil deeds. Prayer confers upon us the merciful goodness of a gracious Lord who bore our sins and who seeks to wash us clean in his blood. "Cry unto him for mercy," Amulek exhorts, "for he is mighty to save." All of the great and eternal spiritual blessings that prepare mortals for eternal life are available through prayer.

We are also to call upon the Lord against the power of our enemies; "against the devil, who is an enemy to all righteousness"; "over the crops of [our] fields, that [we] may prosper in them"; and "over the flocks of [our] fields, that they may increase." Our hearts are to "be full, drawn out in prayer unto him continually for [our] welfare, and also for the welfare of those who are around [us]." And it is in this setting that this grand counsel is forthcoming: "My beloved brethren, . . . do not suppose that this is all; for after ye have done all these things, if ye turn away the needy, and the naked, and visit not the sick and afflicted, and impart of your substance, if ye have, to those who stand in need—I say unto you, if ye do not any of these things, behold, your prayer is vain, and availeth you nothing, and ye are as hypocrites who do deny the faith. Therefore, if ye do not remember to be charitable, ye are as dross, which the refiners do cast out." (Alma 34:17-29.)

Truly, prayer is as broad and expansive as life itself. Its

power may be felt in temporal and spiritual fields; it transcends the bounds of mortality and affects the living and the dead. Those who offer perfect prayers—to the Father, in the name of Christ, by the power of the Holy Ghost—gain peace in this world and eternal life in the world to come. Such is the law where faithful saints are concerned; such is the power of prayer in the lives of believing souls.

But, sadly, there are evil prayers as well as righteous. Of those who do not walk in paths of truth and righteousness, the scripture saith: "Ye ask, and receive not, because ye ask amiss, that ye may consume it upon your lusts." (James 4:3.) And also: "God hath said a man being evil cannot do that which is good; for if he offereth a gift, or prayeth unto God, except he shall do it with real intent it profiteth him nothing. For behold, it is not counted unto him for righteousness. . . . And likewise also is it counted evil unto a man, if he shall pray and not with real intent of heart; yea, and it profiteth him nothing, for God receiveth none such." (Moroni 7:6-9.)

"O then despise not, and wonder not, but hearken unto the words of the Lord, and ask the Father in the name of Jesus for what things soever ye shall stand in need. Doubt not, but be believing, and begin as in times of old, and come unto the Lord with all your heart, and work out your own salvation with fear and trembling before him. Be wise in the days of your probation; strip yourselves of all uncleanness; ask not, that ye may consume it on your lusts, but ask with a firmness unshaken, that ye will yield to no temptation, but that ye will serve the true and living God." (Mormon 9:27-28.)

ARTICLE 8

We believe
the Bible to be the word of God
as far as it is translated correctly;
we also believe
the Book of Mormon
to be the word of God.

CHAPTER 42

The Holy Bible

Scripture—the Word of the Gospel

Salvation in its everlasting fulness; life in that realm where God and Christ are; life, eternal life, life of the kind and sort that God lives; peace in this realm, and exaltation and glory and honor everlasting in the realms ahead—all these come through the glorious gospel of God. The gospel is the power of God unto salvation. And the means, the conduit, the way, whereby salvation is revealed from heaven is called *scripture.*

God alone can save; he only can create a celestial glory, and his plan—and his plan only—will lead fallen men to heights beyond the skies. He must speak; he must reveal; he must make known his laws. And what he speaks, the things he reveals, the laws he makes known—these are scripture. When Deity speaks, his words are scripture; when men or angels speak by the power of the Holy Ghost, the words are the Lord's, and hence are scripture. When Christ speaks, his doctrine is not his, but the Father's whose fellow-God he is. Angels speak by the power of the Holy Ghost, and their words are the words of Christ. Prophets and inspired men, endowed and enlightened with power from on high, speak words of heavenly origin. Their words are scripture.

Scripture is the word of the gospel. It is the spoken word that points the way to peace in this life and eternal life in the world to come; it is the recorded word that preserves the heaven-sent message for others to read and heed. The Lord's ministers, those who have been called by him and who are in line of their duty, "speak as they are moved upon by the Holy Ghost." The words are not their own; they are the Lord's, and they are spoken in his name, meaning for and on his behalf. "And whatsoever they shall speak when moved upon by the

Holy Ghost shall be scripture, shall be the will of the Lord, shall be the mind of the Lord, shall be the word of the Lord, shall be the voice of the Lord, and the power of God [leading] unto salvation." (D&C 68:3-4.)

There is no salvation in scripture as such, standing alone; it is simply the message telling those in darkness what they must do to walk in the light that leads to salvation. Salvation-seekers must believe the message and conform to the directions it contains. "Our gospel came not unto you in word only," as the scripture itself asserts, "but also in power, and in the Holy Ghost, and in much assurance." (1 Thessalonians 1:5.) To be saved requires power, the power that comes to those who heed the divine word, to those who conform to the word contained in the scripture.

Thus we are commanded "to give diligent heed to the words of eternal life" and to "live by every word that proceedeth forth from the mouth of God." (D&C 84:43-44.) Jesus told the Jews, "Search the scriptures," meaning the Old Testament, because those ancient records bore testimony of him. (John 5:39.) Paul told Timothy, "The holy scriptures," meaning those found in the Old Testament, "are able to make thee wise unto salvation through faith which is in Christ Jesus." It was not the scriptures that would save, but they would prepare the way for that faith in Christ without which there neither is nor can be any salvation. "All scripture is given by inspiration of God," the ancient apostle continued, "and is profitable for doctrine, for reproof, for correction, for instruction in righteousness: that the man of God may be perfect, throughly furnished unto all good works." (2 Timothy 3:15-17.)

To the Old Testament, of which Jesus and Paul spoke in such glowing terms, has now been added the New Testament, the two together comprising the Holy Bible. This volume of holy writ is the foremost of the standard works of the church; that is, it is the first of the accepted, approved, canonized volumes of scripture used by the saints as the standards by which all doctrines and procedures are judged. The other standard works are the Book of Mormon, the Doctrine and Covenants, and the Pearl of Great Price. Of all of these we may well say, as did the Psalmist of old of the holy writ of his day: "The law of the Lord is perfect, converting the soul: the testimony of the Lord is sure, making wise the simple. The statutes of the Lord are right, rejoicing the heart: the commandment of the Lord is pure, enlightening the eyes. The fear of the Lord is clean, enduring for ever: the judgments of the Lord are true and righteous altogether. More to be desired are they than gold, yea, than much fine gold: sweeter also than honey and the honeycomb. Moreover by them is thy servant warned: and in keeping of them there is great reward." (Psalm 19:7-11.)

As the translators of the King James Version of the Bible so aptly said of the scriptures: "If we be ignorant, they will instruct us; if out of the way, they will bring us home; if out of order, they will reform us; if in heaviness, comfort us; if dull, quicken us; if cold, inflame us. . . . The Scriptures then being acknowledged to be so full and so perfect, how can we excuse ourselves of negligence, if we do not study them?" (Cited in J. Reuben Clark, Jr., *Why The King James Version,* pp. xxxi, xxxii.)

The Bible—What It Is

The holy Bible—as of now—is the most influential book ever written in the entire history of the world. As presently constituted, it contains those portions of the sacred writings of Judaism and of Christianity which have come down to us in relative purity. In its pure and primeval state it was composed of divine revelations and inspired writings. In substance and thought content, the word of the Lord, thus written by the apostles and prophets and inspired men of old, has been preserved for us by the transcribers and translators through whose hands it has passed. It is thus a divine library, a heaven-sent volume of holy scripture, a voice from the past that contains the mind and will and law of the Lord. It is a partial and fragmentary record of God's dealings with his ancient covenant people, a people who had either the fulness of the everlasting gospel or were being schooled by the preparatory gospel as time and circumstances dictated.

The Old Testament contains a revealed and abbreviated account of the creation of this earth, of man, and of all forms of life. It tells of the fall of man and of the Lord's dealings with Adam and the ancient patriarchs before the flood. It speaks of the Abrahamic and Israelitish covenants. A major portion tells how Israel became a nation, possessed their promised land, and, as the sheep of the Lord's pasture, were fed the prophetic word down through the ages. Included are poetical, prophetic, legalistic, doctrinal, didactical, and historical books. And, above all, interwoven through the whole account, from Adam to Malachi, is the promise of a Savior, a Redeemer, a Deliverer, a Messiah, a Suffering Servant, a Son of God, who would be born of woman, atone for the sins of the world, die and rise again in glorious immortality, and then return to that God whose Son and witness he was. The Old Testament is designed and prepared to teach the truths of salvation and to bear witness of the one who should come to redeem mankind and put into full operation all of the terms and conditions of the Father's great and eternal plan of salvation.

As to the New Testament, it recounts the fulfillment of the ancient promises; tells of the birth and ministry and atoning sacrifice of the Promised One; expounds the saving doctrines of his everlasting gospel; records the growth and expansion of the gospel cause in the meridian day; predicts the universal falling away from the faith once delivered to the saints; promises a glorious restoration of the gospel in the last days; and foretells, in graphic and dramatic imagery, the events preceding, attending, and succeeding the Second Coming of the Son of Man. Its chief purpose is to bear witness of Christ and to teach those doctrines, ordinances, and ways of life and worship which lead penitent souls to an eternal oneness with those Gods who themselves are one.

The Bible—Viewed in True Perspective

The Bible is a Judeo-Christian book. Our Jewish brethren accept the Old Testament; Christians in general are wedded to the concept that both testaments are holy scripture. It is the book of books, accepted by believers of every hue and tone and in every sect and church as the source of their doctrine, their ethical standards, and their very way of life. Salvation itself, so they suppose, is dependent upon belief in and an understanding of the sacred sayings found in this canonized volume.

We need not define, collate, or summarize the wealth of organized data that analyzes, explains, and interprets the biblical books. There are countless texts and biblical dictionaries that cover every known aspect of the origin, preservation, translation, and publishing of the ancient holy word. For our purposes it suffices to say that the King James Version of the Bible, as published in the English tongue, is probably the best Bible ever prepared and preserved by the scholars among men. It is the version brought into being for use in the restoration processes that brought forth the fulness of the gospel again among men. The Joseph Smith Translation—an inspired version—both corrects errors and reintroduces lost passages, all by the spirit of revelation, thus making this version the best source of biblical knowledge. Joseph Smith did not complete this revision in the sense of making all the corrections and additions that some day will be made, although he did approve for publication the work as it now stands.

For our purposes, we shall simply set forth a few concepts and perspectives that will guide the sincere student in his study and use of Bible scripture. It is far more important to know what the Bible teaches and its true place in the eternal scheme of things than to know anything else about it. Accordingly, be it noted that:

1. *The Bible is the book of books.*

It has done more, with greater numbers of people, to preserve Christian culture, uphold gospel ethics, and teach true doctrine than any other book ever written, many times over. Nations have been born and have died, continents have been conquered, and hemispheres settled because of biblical influence. There is no way to overstate the worth and blessing of the Bible for mankind.

2. *The Bible and the Book of Mormon are companion volumes.*

That Lord who is no respecter of persons, who loves all his children, and in whose sight all souls are precious has also spoken to nonbiblical nations, and they have preserved his sayings in volumes of holy scripture. The Book of Mormon account is one of these. And to keep all things in perspective, we hasten to testify that the Nephite record—we say it reverently and discreetly—will one day, ere long if it please God, rival even the Bible in power and influence over the minds of men. It is the Book of Mormon, not the Bible, that prepares men, in the full and true sense, for the Second Coming of the Son of Man. And when the eternal ledgers are finally balanced, more souls will have been saved in the celestial kingdom—ten thousand times over—because of the Book of Mormon than have so obtained because of the Bible. It is the Book of Mormon that proves the restoration of the gospel; that converts penitent souls to its saving doctrines; that gathers Israel from all the nations of the earth; that guides and inspires those sainted souls who are preparing themselves to abide the day of the coming of the Lord; and that will continue to guide and inspire gathered Israel in the great Millennial day that lies ahead.

3. *There is no salvation in the Bible as such.*

Neither the Bible nor the Book of Mormon, nor any volume of scripture, is or can be more than a guide, a help, a means to an end. Every volume of revealed writ stands as a teacher of truths and a preserver of principles. But the word of the gospel as found in any of them is a heavenly seed that has power to bring forth faith and righteousness and salvation. The Bible itself is only an account of what other people have believed, known, and felt. All of us who gain salvation with the ancients must believe and know and feel and be as they were. The Bible charts the course; we must walk in the way there set forth.

4. *Belief in the Bible presupposes belief in the Book of Mormon.*

All scripture comes from God; all scripture is true; and every divine word accords with every other word from the same heavenly source. The Bible bears witness of the Book of Mormon, and the Book of Mormon testifies of the Bible. They are both true; they both came from God; neither is false, and both are accepted by true believers. Those who believe one believe the other, and those who reject one reject, in a very real sense, the other. Mormon put it just this bluntly: If ye believe the Bible, ye will believe the Book of Mormon also. (Mormon 7:9.) Nephi said, "No man will be angry at the words which I have written" in the Book of Mormon, "save he shall be of the spirit of the devil." And: "If ye shall believe in Christ ye will believe in these words, for they are the words of Christ, and he hath given them unto me; and they teach all men that they should do good." (2 Nephi 33:5, 10.)

5. *The Bible is true.*

The Bible, as far as it is translated correctly, is scripture and thus is true, with the possible exception of the Song of Solomon, which probably is not inspired writing. We accept the Bible as the mind and will of the Lord and as binding upon the saints, with the reservation pertaining to the accuracy of transcription and the verity of translation. Whatever the scholars of the world may think, and however much liberal scriptural exegetes may attempt to explain away the verity of the ancient word, we proclaim boldly that we believe the Bible. Indeed, the Book of Mormon itself came forth for the express purpose of "proving to the world that the holy scriptures are true." (D&C 20:11.) By "holy scriptures" is here meant the holy Bible.

6. *Not all scripture is in the Bible.*

Scripture—the heaven-sent guide to a heavenly inheritance—is one thing; the Bible is quite another. Scripture is as broad as eternity, as comprehensive as the limitless bounds of truth, as all-pervading as the immanent spirit that goes forth from the presence of God to fill the immensity of space. Scripture includes all that is spoken or written by the power of the Holy Ghost. (D&C 68:1-4.) It is, thus, spoken on earth and in heaven; it is written by men and angels and Gods; and it gives direction to the spirits yet unborn, to us mortals in our low and fallen state, to the dead who await the day of the resurrection, and to those who have come forth in immortal glory to dwell everlastingly in the kingdoms that are prepared. But the Bible is something else. It contains a small part of the divine word, a part of what was given of God to the ancient patriarchs, prophets, and apostles in the Old World. It is only an acorn growing on a mighty oak; but it is an acorn that, if planted, watered, cultivated, and impelled by the living rays of the sun, can grow into a majestic tree in its own right.

7. *The Bible does not contain "all things necessary to salvation."*

Contrary to that which is written in the formal declarations of sectarianism, more truths are needed to save souls than are recorded in the Bible as it now exists. "Holy Scripture containeth all things necessary to salvation," it is commonly said, "so that whatsoever is not read therein, nor may be proved thereby, is not to be required of any man, that it should be believed as an article of the Faith, or be thought requisite or necessary to salvation." (*Book of Common Prayer,* p. 686.) It is then common to name the canonical books that contain the aforesaid word, and they are usually the same as contained in the King James Version of the Bible.

In truth and in fact, however, the Bible does not contain all that is needed to guide men to salvation, except in the sense that if men believed what it contains and lived as it directs, they would receive the added light and knowledge needed to perfect their souls. It does contain many allusions to gospel doctrines and references to divine practices, but it does not set forth these doctrines or define these practices in full. There are references to the doctrine of salvation for the dead and the practice of baptism for the dead, but the whole doctrine and the prescribed mode of vicarious baptism are not set forth. There are references to the Aaronic and Melchizedek priesthoods, but nowhere is the doctrine of the priesthood summarized in a definitive way. It is clear in principle that the biblical saints understood and practiced marriage for time and all eternity, but the records coming down to us do not set forth this doctrine in a whole and complete and perfect way.

8. *The Bible contains only a portion of the Lord's word.* Though the holy Bible is a book beyond compare; though it shines as the sun upon a world in spiritual darkness; though it is the very voice of the Almighty to his fallen children—yet it contains only a portion, a small portion, a fragmentary portion, of eternal truth. And it was never intended nor designed by the Great Designer himself that it should be otherwise. He gives unto men that portion of his word, and no more, that they are able to bear. Milk must precede meat. Before they can receive the Vision of the Degrees of Glory, given in latter days, they must first ponder what is meant in the biblical accounts with reference to coming forth in the resurrection of life or of damnation. When men are rebellious and have low levels of spiritual enlightenment, they receive little of the Lord's word; when they are obedient and receptive, their cups overrun. We

have only the basic portion of the Book of Mormon, not the sealed portion. Others more faithful than we are, however, were not so limited in their day.

As to the Bible, it contains simply that portion of the Lord's word which he granted unto the children of men who lived from about the end of the first century down to A.D. 1830, a period of over seventeen hundred years. It does not contain, and was never intended to contain, all of the scriptural word that faithful saints have enjoyed in generations past. And as we look at the iniquity and rebellion in the world today; as we see men tread under foot even the biblical portion of the eternal word; as we shudder at the way self-appointed biblical exegetes wrest the holy word from its true and real intent—we are made aware that, even now, it contains more divine truth than many men are prepared to receive.

9. *Many biblical books have been lost.*

Even that portion of the divine word that we are qualified to receive has not been preserved for us within the covers of the Bible. The holy book itself makes repeated references to other prophetic books, other inspired historical accounts, and other apostolic epistles, none of which are now extant. And even within the accounts we now have, there are references and allusions, by the thousands, to sermons preached, prophecies made, visions seen, and miracles performed that are not there recorded and of which we know nothing. The Bible is what it is, for which we praise the Lord, but someday in his eternal providences it will become, by the addition of the lost and withheld portions and books, what it might have been had men in general been prepared to receive more of heaven's light.

10. *The Bible prepares men for latter-day revelation.*

As the law was a schoolmaster to prepare backsliding Israel to receive Christ and his gospel; as John prepared the way before that Messianic Lord whom all devout men sought; as the dawning rays of a rising sun herald the coming brilliance of its noonday rays—so the Bible prepares men for the endless outpouring of eternal truth that is to be showered upon the faithful in the last days.

As the Lord reveals his mind and will line upon line and precept upon precept; as growing mortals must drink the milk of the word before they feast at tables heaped high with the delicacies of eternity; as men must taste the good word of God before they can feast upon the mysteries of the kingdom —so they must drink at the biblical fountain before they quench their thirst for righteousness at the great fountains from which the words of eternal life flow in our day.

Our present Bible is an initial, preparatory book of scripture. It has been given to test mankind. How much more they receive of the mind and will of the Lord depends upon the heed and diligence they give to that which has come down to them from the prophets and apostles of old. By accepting the Bible in the true and full sense of the word, men qualify for that added light and knowledge which is available to those who love and serve the Eternal Theologian with full purpose of heart.

11. *The Bible proves the great apostasy.*

In its present form, the Bible bears a powerful and persuasive witness of the falling away from the faith once delivered to the saints. Its prophetic pages describe in detail the apostasy that now is. It records the doctrines, ordinances, and way of life of the ancient saints, none of which have any material similarity to their equivalents found in the Christian world today. But, even above these verities, the very fact that the Bible ceased to grow through the ages is itself proof positive of the great apostasy. True, there was a dusky twilight as the gospel sun sank in the western skies, during which a few saintly souls communed with their Maker and enjoyed the light of heaven in their lives. But the prophetic word that guided the church ceased with the end of the apostolic era. The darkness that followed left the Bible without the added words that might have been appended.

12. *The Bible invites men to seek revelation.*

The very existence of the Bible is itself an invitation to all men to seek for more revelation. From Genesis to Revelation, every word that is recorded is a witness that God hears the petitions of his children and answers them from heaven by sending his revealed word, a word that always fits the needs of the very hour. Be it Noah, Abraham, or Moses; be it Isaiah, Ezekiel, or Malachi; be it Jesus, Peter, or Paul—always and without fail the Lord gives the revelation needed to solve the problems of the day. If there is anything the world needs today, it is divine guidance in solving its problems, and if there is anything the Bible teaches, it is that guidance and power from on high are available to those who have faith like that of the ancients.

13. *The Bible contains the fulness of the gospel.*

According to the revealed word, the Book of Mormon contains the fulness of the everlasting gospel; so also does the Bible, and so do both the Doctrine and Covenants and the Pearl of Great Price. Each of them contains the word of the gospel; each of them is a record of God's dealings with a people who had the fulness of the gospel; each of them is a scriptural record that summarizes the plan of salvation and sets forth what men must do to gain the fulness of reward in the mansions that are prepared. The gospel itself is the power of God by which salvation comes; it is the power that saves a human soul; and the fulness of the gospel is all of the truths and powers needed to enable men to gain a fulness of reward in the highest heaven of the celestial world. Thus, properly speaking, the fulness of the gospel consists in having the Melchizedek Priesthood and the gift of the Holy Ghost, without either of which salvation is not available to men. The Bible—glorious and wondrous book that it is—contains the word of the gospel, the word to which men must conform in order to get the power of the gospel into their lives. No book can ever do more than chart a course leading to eternal life.

14. *To whom was the Bible written?*

To understand the Bible, we must realize that it was written to people who already had the gospel, the priesthood, and the gift of the Holy Ghost. It was written to true believers, not to worldly skeptics. Paul's epistles were written to congregations of saints; the prophets of Israel spoke to the house of Israel; the Gospels were written to strengthen the faith of the meridian saints. All of the holy word is beneficial to all men, in and out of the kingdom, but its full meaning and power are manifest only to the saints to whom it is addressed.

15. *There is only one way to understand the Bible.*

Granted that a knowledge of the language, customs, traditions, and life of those to whom any scripture is addressed will aid in determining the intent and meaning of the message, yet, in the true and full sense of the word, there is only one way to understand the scriptures. That way is by the power of the Holy Ghost. There is in reality no way, absolutely no way, either on earth or in heaven, to understand the Bible except by the power of the Spirit. All prophecies, all inspired writing, everything that constitutes the mind and will of the Lord, is given by the power of the Holy Ghost. And the things of God can only be understood by the power of the Spirit of God. Hence, the scriptures are of no private interpretation; they mean only what the original author intended them to mean.

CHAPTER 43

The Biblical Word

The Bible—Its Origin and Canonization

What think ye of the words of life as they are found in the Holy Bible? They are wondrous words of light and truth. As they fell from seeric lips and flowed from prophetic pens, they were perfect, manifesting the mind and will of the Lord to mortals. Since then there have been additions and deletions, editorial and other changes, and translations into tongues that oftentimes have no equivalent words or phrases to convey the original and precise meaning of the once perfect divine word. And the holy word is now in the hands of peoples whose social, economic, cultural, and other circumstances bear little resemblance to like conditions among those of old to whom it was first directed. As a result, many allusions, illustrations, parables, and comments are misunderstood or misapplied.

The Bible—*ta biblia,* the books—originally meant the books accepted as scripture by the Lord's people (those living in the second century A.D.) and accepted by them as the deposit of the then available divine revelation. It is now rendered in the singular and has reference to the thirty-nine books of the Old Testament and the twenty-seven books of the New Testament, to which compilation the various apocryphal books are added in Catholic versions.

Revelations are always given to men "after the manner of their language, that they might come to understanding." (D&C 1:24.) Prophets preach to be heard and seers speak to be understood; a revelation given in a foreign and unknown tongue would be as sounding brass and tinkling cymbals. The Old Testament was written in Hebrew and Aramaic, the New Testament in Greek.

Adam, Enoch, Noah, Abraham, and Moses, and the patriarchs and apostles in general, wrote the various books of scripture. Fragments of these have come down to us in a condensed and abbreviated way or have been revealed anew to subsequent prophets. The Lord revealed to Joseph Smith many of the words originally written by Enoch and Abraham and Moses. And it was common for prophets of one age to copy or paraphrase the words of their predecessors. It seems obvious that Paul and Moroni both had before them the words of some previous prophet relative to faith, hope, and charity, which they in turn adopted and used as their own. Nephi, nearly 600 B.C., and Malachi, two hundred years later, both say the same things about the Second Coming, and Nephi attributes them to an unnamed prophet who preceded him, leaving us to suppose that Malachi also had this common source before him when the Spirit guided his prophetic pen. Paul wrote many things, as, for instance, those about Melchizedek, which are not in our Bible, but which were restored to the Old Testament by the Prophet Joseph Smith, making it clear that the apostle had before him a more extended and better Old Testament account than is found in our modern versions. The only biblical account of the creation was revealed directly to Moses, but we are left to suppose that he copied or condensed the historical portions of Genesis from the writings of Noah, Melchizedek, Abraham, and the patriarchs. The fourteenth and fiftieth chapters of Genesis, both as restored by Joseph Smith, must have been written respectively by Melchizedek and Joseph (the son of Jacob) in the first instance. Exodus, Leviticus, Numbers, and Deuteronomy were written by or under the direction of Moses. Prophets and inspired poets and historians wrote the balance of the Old Testament.

Hebrew became a dead language in the second century before Christ, and the scriptures of the chosen people were then translated into various languages. The most renowned translation, made in the second and third centuries B.C., is the Septuagint. This rendition into Greek is supposed to have been made by about seventy scholars, the number reminiscent of the seventy elders called by Moses and of the total membership of the Great Sanhedrin. The Septuagint, commonly cited as LXX, is the first known translation of a major work into a foreign language. It was done by the wisdom of men and not by the spirit of inspiration. Portions are well translated; others are not. Scholars say the Pentateuch (the five books of Moses) is a serviceable translation; that the Psalms and Isaiah show signs of obvious incompetence; that part of Jeremiah is unintelligibly literal; and that Daniel is a mere Midrashic paraphrase, meaning that it is more an exposition than a translation. The LXX is, however, the most authentic of the ancient versions and is used at the present time by the Greek Catholics and other eastern churches.

The translation of the Septuagint from Hebrew to Greek illustrates the problems that have attended translations ever since. Aside from the sorry state of the text due to scholastic incompetence, there was a far more serious problem, namely, the theological bias of the translators. This caused them to change the meaning or paraphrase texts that were either unclear or embarrassing to them. Concrete terms in Hebrew came out as abstract terms in Greek. Expressions about God—deemed by the Greek translators to be crude or offensive because they described Deity as the Holy Man that he is, rather than the immanent spirit they supposed him to be—were changed or toned down or deleted entirely. Passages setting forth the so-called anthropomorphic nature of Deity were simply assumed by the translators to be false and were translated, paraphrased, and changed accordingly.

Jesus and the apostles quoted from the Septuagint and from the Hebrew accounts. In their day in the synagogues in Palestine, the Jews read and quoted from the Hebrew. The people spoke Aramaic and understood little Hebrew, and so it was the practice for one person to read from the Hebrew scriptures and then for another to targum (translate or paraphrase) it into Aramaic. Our present Old Testament was translated from the Hebrew and not the Greek. Hence the frequent differences between the Old and New Testaments in rendering the same passage.

As long as inspired men are the keepers of holy writ; as long as prophets and apostles are present to identify and perfect the scriptures by revelation; as long as scriptural translations (as in the instance of the Book of Mormon) are made by the gift and power of God—all will be well with the written word. But when the gospel sun sets and apostate darkness shrouds the minds of men, the scriptural word is in jeopardy.

From Adam to Malachi, the ancient biblical word was in prophetic hands. For the next three or four centuries, uninspired men kept the records, adding and deleting as they chose and for their own purposes. During these dark days, apocryphal and pseudepigraphic writings—intermingling as they do the truths of heaven with the heresies from beneath—arose in great numbers. And there were no prophetic voices either to condemn or to canonize them.

History repeated itself in New Testament times. The inspired word flowed from Spirit-guided pens; inspired men kept the records; and true believers rejoiced in the truths that thus were theirs. True, there were apostates and traitors even while the apostles lived, but at least there was divine guidance that identified the true word and kept the faithful from following every false and evil wind of doctrine. But after the passing of those who held the keys by which the mind and will of the Lord can be gained; after the holy apostles mingled their blood with that of the prophets who were before them; after the age of inspiration ceased—all was no longer well with the written word. Wolves scattered the flock and tore the flesh of the saints; false teachers led the church into apostate darkness; the post-apostolic fathers wrote their own views—and there was no way to distinguish with divine certainty the light from above the darkness that soon covered the earth.

Let us illustrate what happened. Paul wrote to the saints in Corinth. His words, now unknown to us, set forth a divine solution to some unspecified problem about marriage that existed among them. Highly prized, his words were read in sacrament meetings; copies were made by many faithful elders; other copies were sent to distant congregations; and soon there were copies of copies unto the tenth or hundredth generation. Some errors crept in through inadvertence; it could not have been otherwise. Then toward the end of the second century and during the third century, as false doctrines relative to God and marriage and miracles and many things crept into the church and became common among the so-called Christians, uninspired men changed Paul's words to conform to their views. His words no longer breathed the spirit of celestial marriage and the eternal blessings reserved for worthy members of an eternal family unit. Instead, they were made to appear as though even Paul himself was unmarried and was counseling ministers in general to live a celibate life. These perverted manuscripts were also copied, and they begat children to the tenth and hundredth generation. And being in the hands of the church, in its low and fallen state, they were the manuscripts that were preserved.

This same thing happened with reference to many of the other doctrines taught by Paul and his fellows. On the same basis, deletions and changes were made in the Old Testament so that passages about baptism, the priesthood, the coming of the Messiah, the universal apostasy after New Testament times, the restoration of the gospel in the last days, the Second Coming of the Son of Man, and the final triumph of truth were all deleted. Many of these have now been restored and are found in the Book of Moses in the Pearl of Great Price.

There are also differences—so numerous that no one has ever counted them—among the various copies of the ancient manuscripts. These differences are not numbered in the tens, or hundreds, or even the thousands; scholars have found them by the scores of thousands, and the end is by no means in sight. It follows that to arrive at an approved text relative to any questionable passage involves a process of continuing research, of comparison, of analysis, and, finally, of making an educated guess.

We speak of the Bible as being a canon of scripture, meaning it consists of books that are recognized as authoritative guides in matters of faith, doctrine, and conduct. A canon is a standard, or principle, or rule of doctrine and faith by which all else is measured. It is common among Latter-day Saints to speak of their four volumes of scripture as the standard works. Thus the Book of Mormon, the Doctrine and Covenants, and the Pearl of Great Price, as well as the Bible, are canonical books.

These volumes of added latter-day scripture were selected by prophetic insight and then approved by the voice of the people in conference assembled, to stand as canonical measuring rods. As to them, the issue is clear, but with the Bible it is otherwise. How came the ancient biblical word to have the sanctity and stamp of divine approval that is now universally attributed to it? This is not an easy question to answer, and—

aside from the statements in our revelations and in our Article of Faith that we believe the Bible as far as it is translated correctly—there is no heaven-approved way of knowing that the Bible as now constituted is true.

It was as hard to determine by worldly wisdom which books should be included in the Bible as it is to gain, from that same uninspired source, a sure knowledge of the verity with which any given passage is translated. Those who compiled the books of the Bible were neither prophets nor seers nor revelators. They were simply men who made their choices, not by the power of the Spirit, but by the power of the intellect. Those books in the Bible that now is ours were chosen by a process of disagreement and debate, of contention, compromise, and confusion. Various councils approved different sets of books. Every prominent bishop and theologian of renown, down through the dark and dreary apostate centuries, had his own self-selected and self-approved books. To this day the scholars of sectarianism contend about the authorship, content, and inspiration of the various books. Few among them, for instance, so much as believe that Paul wrote the book of Hebrews. Neither in the dark ages nor in modern Christendom is there any unity of feeling, coming from the Holy Spirit of God, as to the truth and divinity of the Bible.

As now constituted, the Bible simply contains those portions of the divine word that survived the confusion of the centuries. Other books of equal worth are not there. Providentially, that which is now published, at least in the Protestant world, does have a general stamp of divine approval; in the main, and in substance and thought content, as far as it goes, it is true. Indeed, in the light of all that has transpired historically, it is a marvelous and wondrous thing to find the Bible as accurate and sound as it is. Truly, to the degree consistent with His providence, a divine hand has been over the preservation and translation of his holy word.

Perverting the Biblical Word

Every good thing is opposed by an evil power. Every true principle is condemned by those who believe false doctrines. The gospel is rejected by carnal men; the blood of the righteous is spilt by those whose deeds are evil, and the revelations from above are denied, desecrated, and perverted by those whose inspiration comes from beneath. In like manner, the true Bible is opposed by false teachers, by false ministers, and by those whose deeds it condemns. During the dark ages the Bible itself was withheld from the people, and many is the martyr who was burned at the stake or slain by the sword for the crime of reading its pages and preaching its doctrines. In our age of enlightenment, the worldly wise deny its divinity and spiritualize away its plain teachings.

We are now at that point in time when there is no way to know whether the Bible is true except by revelation. And further: There is no way to know how much of the original divine word is preserved on its pages unless the Lord lifts the curtain and lets us see, in true perspective, what happened to the holy scriptures through the ages. As it happens, we have a revelation that tells us that the Book of Mormon came forth for the express purpose of "proving to the world that the holy scriptures [meaning the Bible] are true." (D&C 20:8-11.) And we also have an inspired account in the Book of Mormon that defines and sets forth both the wonder and the shortcomings of the Bible.

Nephi saw in vision the crucifixion of Christ, the subsequent warfare of the world against the apostles and saints of the primitive church, the great apostasy that followed the apostolic day, the formation by the devil of a great and abominable church, the rise of Gentile nations in Europe, the discovery of America by Columbus, the peopling of America by the Gentiles, and the revolutionary war that freed them from European domination. Then he saw a book—the Bible!—go forth among the people, for at last it had been prepared, translated, and printed.

Thereupon an angelic ministrant said to Nephi: "The book that thou beholdest is a record of the Jews, which contains the covenants of the Lord, which he hath made unto the house of Israel." The Bible recounts the Lord's dealings with the Jews and with all the house of Israel. To Nephi, the Jews were those of the kingdom of Judah whence the Lehites came. Also, the Jews were those who returned from Babylon, who built up the waste places of Palestine again, and to whom Jewish Jesus and the Jewish apostles ministered. "And it also containeth many," but by no means all, "of the prophecies of the holy prophets," the angel continued, "and it is a record like unto the engravings which are upon the plates of brass, save there are not so many." The clear inference is that the brass plates contained much that was not preserved for inclusion in the Bible. We know that somewhere along the line the writings of Zenos, Zenock, Neum, and Ezias, and no doubt many other prophets —all found on the brass plates—were lost in their entirety. "Nevertheless, they [the biblical writings] contain the covenants of the Lord, which he hath made unto the house of Israel; wherefore, they are of great worth unto the Gentiles." Notwithstanding the losses, changes, and deletions, the Bible yet contains a general summary of the covenants made with the chosen people; there is enough there to point the attention of all men to the fuller and plainer accounts that have come by latter-day revelation.

"Thou hast beheld," Nephi's angelic friend continued, "that the book"—the Bible: both the Old and the New Testaments—"proceeded forth from the mouth of a Jew." Jewish writers composed, compiled, and preserved both the ancient records and those that came forth in the meridian of time. "And when it proceeded forth from the mouth of a Jew it contained the fulness of the gospel of the Lord, of whom the twelve apostles bear record; and they bear record according to the truth which is in the Lamb of God." As with the Book of Mormon, so with the Bible; both contain the fulness of the gospel, meaning that the word of the gospel is recorded in them, the word by which men may chart a course leading to the fulness of reward hereafter.

"Wherefore, these things go forth from the Jews in purity unto the Gentiles, according to the truth which is in God." They were not complete, but they were true; the accounts did contain the mind and will and voice of the Lord to all men. But then they suffered an awful fate; they fell into evil hands; they became the tools of those who rose up to fight against God in the name of religion. Hence, thus saith the angel: "And after they go forth by the hand of the twelve apostles of the Lamb, from the Jews unto the Gentiles"—after the primitive saints began to send them, and the fulness of the gospel which they contained, to all the world as they had been commanded— "thou seest the formation of that great and abominable church, which is most abominable above all other churches." The church here described is the church of the devil, the church of which he was the founder, the church that arose after the day of the apostles, the church into whose hands the scriptures had fallen.

And what then happened to the Bible? "Behold, they have taken away from the gospel of the Lamb many parts which are plain and most precious," saith the angel, "and also many covenants of the Lord have they taken away." (1 Nephi 13:20-26.) What effect did this have upon true worship? The answer to this question becomes apparent by asking such other questions as these: What happened to celestial marriage, to baptism for the dead, and to those holy ordinances by which mortals are endowed with power from on high? Where do we find churches that lay on hands for the present conferral of the gift of the Holy Ghost? How is it that the churches of Christendom do not have apostles, prophets, high priests, seventies, and all of the New Testament offices and callings? Has baptism by immersion for the remission of sins been replaced by infant baptism or discarded entirely, as the case may be? Indeed, how did infant baptism find its way into the churches of the day? Is the sacrament of the Lord's Supper the same simple ceremony that it once was? Whence came the numerous ordinances and performances, so common in Christendom, that have no biblical precedent? How does modern Christianity compare with that of the primitive saints? Have we lost the simplicity that was in Christ?

As to the changes in the biblical word, the angel continued: "All this have they done that they might pervert the right ways of the Lord, that they might blind the eyes and harden the hearts of the children of men." Is modern Christianity the same as primitive Christianity?

And in large measure it all came to pass because of the perversion of a book. "Wherefore, thou seest that after the book hath gone forth through the hands of the great and abominable church, that there are many plain and precious things taken away from the book, which is the book of the Lamb of God. And after these plain and precious things were taken away it goeth forth unto all the nations of the Gentiles." First came the perversions. They arose beginning in the second century after Christ and continuing until the invention of printing and the promulgation of the word among the people, and then, for the first time, the Bible became available to men generally.

409

"And after it goeth forth unto all the nations of the Gentiles, yea, even across the many waters which thou hast seen with the Gentiles which have gone forth out of captivity, thou seest—because of the many plain and precious things which have been taken out of the book, which were plain unto the understanding of the children of men, according to the plainness which is in the Lamb of God—because of these things which are taken away out of the gospel of the Lamb, an exceedingly great many do stumble, yea, insomuch that Satan hath great power over them."

Why are the churches of modern Christendom in such an "awful state of blindness" with reference to the doctrines of salvation? Why do they worship a spirit essence rather than the Holy Man of whom the original Bible spoke? Why do they say there is no marrying or giving in marriage in heaven when, in fact, celestial marriage is the gate to eternal life? Why all the mystery and darkness that keeps ordinary minds from turning to the Lord and his church? This is the answer the angel gave Nephi: It is "because of the plain and most precious parts of the gospel of the Lamb which have been kept back by that abominable church, whose formation thou hast seen."

It is in this setting that the great promise is made of a restoration of the fulness of the everlasting gospel; it is in view of all these things that the Lord promises to open the heavens and reveal anew that which has been taken by evil men from his holy word; it is because of his infinite mercy and his desire to save souls that he will start anew in the last days and make salvation available as it was in days of old. Therefore, thus saith the Lord: "After the Gentiles do stumble exceedingly, because of the most plain and precious parts of the gospel of the Lamb which have been kept back by that abominable church, which is the mother of harlots, saith the Lamb—I will be merciful unto the Gentiles in that day, insomuch that I will bring forth unto them, in mine own power, much of my gospel, which shall be plain and precious, saith the Lamb."

Then the Lord said that these "plain and precious things" should be written by the Nephites, and that in the last days they should "come forth unto the Gentiles, by the gift and power of the Lamb. And in them shall be written my gospel, saith the Lamb, and my rock and my salvation." The account of which he here speaks is the Book of Mormon.

"And after it [the Book of Mormon] had come forth unto them," Nephi said, "I beheld other books, which came forth by the power of the Lamb, from the Gentiles unto them, unto the convincing of the Gentiles and the remnant of the seed of my brethren, and also the Jews who were scattered upon all the face of the earth, that the records of the prophets and of the twelve apostles of the Lamb are true." These other books include the Doctrine and Covenants, and Pearl of Great Price, and others that shall yet come forth by the power of God and the inspiration of heaven.

Then from the angelic lips Nephi heard these words of wisdom: "These last records [those that have come forth by latter-day revelation], which thou hast seen among the Gentiles, shall establish the truth of the first [the Bible], which are of the twelve apostles of the Lamb, and shall make known the plain and precious things which have been taken away from them; and shall make known to all kindreds, tongues, and people, that the Lamb of God is the Son of the Eternal Father, and the Savior of the world; and that all men must come unto him, or they cannot be saved." (1 Nephi 13:27-40.)

To learn some of the things that have been restored to the Bible itself, we need but compare the King James Version with the Joseph Smith Translation. For instance, the book of Genesis, down to Genesis 6:13, contains 151 verses. This identical account in the book of Moses in the Pearl of Great Price contains 356 verses, with most of the new and added verses being twice as long as the normal biblical verses. The content of the added material is such that it completely changes our whole concept of how and why and in what manner the Lord has dealt with his people in dispensations past.

To envision the extent to which plain and precious things have been made known through the Book of Mormon and latter-day revelation, we need but compare the doctrines of salvation as set forth in the Bible with those same doctrines revealed anew in our dispensation. The Bible shines with a dim and reflected light, showing forth portions of what holy men of old believed and taught; the modern word blazes forth in all the brilliance of the noonday sun, chasing darkness away and testifying in plain words what all men must believe and do to gain peace in this life and eternal life in the world to come.

Having so spoken and so analyzed with reference to the

wondrous word of scripture—*ta biblia,* the books—we are now ready to turn our attention to the Book of Mormon and the same holy word as it has come anew in plainness and perfection in our day.

CHAPTER 44

The Book of Mormon: Its Nature and Divinity

What Is the Book of Mormon?

We await the day when someone with heaven-sent talent will define and describe and introduce the Book of Mormon in such a way as to touch the hearts of men. We long to read the living words that someday will set forth the wonder and glory of this ancient Nephite record with its appendage of Jaredite origin. No one as yet has even come close to writing the introductory and fire-filled language that this volume of holy writ deserves. Nor will anyone, we suppose, until that Millennial day when the sealed portion of the ancient record is translated and read from the housetops. And surely, even then, it will take someone with the seeric insight of Isaiah, the literary craftsmanship of Paul, and the linguistic simplicity of Peter. To frame words that will reveal the full feelings and true meaning of what the Lord and his prophets proclaim is beyond human capacity. Such words, like some written in days of old and now withheld from us, would cause men who read them to be overpowered by the Spirit.

True it is that the Book of Mormon ignites the fires of one intense passion or another in the hearts of men. Among devout people whose souls are filled with fervor for one cause or another, it is rated as either a good or an evil book. There is no middle ground. True it is also that there are indifferent and unconcerned souls who could not care less whether it is a divine or a devilish book. But they are the ones who have the same thoughtless feelings about the Bible and the things of the Spirit in general. Among those who are aware of the Book of Mormon and its claims, and who are concerned about religion and salvation, who are active in this or that religious circle, who have a proselyting zeal for their chosen cause—all such have strong feelings about this book of modern scripture. They either accept or reject it with feelings of emotion, even of passion.

Here is a man who gains a copy of this blessed book, begins to read it, and continues without eating or sleeping, day and night, until, having read it all, his famished soul is filled with the bread of life. He cannot lay it aside or ignore its teachings. It is as though the waters of life are flowing into the barren deserts of his soul, quenching the arid, empty feeling that theretofore separated him from his God.

Here is another man who reads the book and before he has finished the first chapter he cries out: "It is true! I believe! Thank God for his holy word!" And from that hour he is born again so as to see the kingdom of God, which he so much desires to enter.

Here is yet another, reading on into the night, marveling at the plain and precious truths he is learning, and saying: "Either God or the devil wrote this book; no man could have done it. I have never read anything that so clearly unfolds the meaning of so many hidden biblical doctrines."

And here is still another who drinks in its living truths, as an arid and sandy wasteland absorbs the gentle rain from heaven, and who, believing what he reads, leaves lands and houses and wealth and position and family and all that the world has to offer, to join with the saints of God in their humble and lowly state.

But sadly there are others—and they are many—who, reading the same words but having a different spirit, wear out their lives counting the misspelled words, the commas that are out of place, the textual changes that bring the account into full conformity with the original manuscript and the intent of the inspired authors, and such like—all with a view to crying: "Delusion! Falsehood! Flee this imposture!" These are the ones who reject the ancient doctrine, revealed anew, for the salvation of all who, as with the ancients, will believe the word of truth sent in their day.

What, then, shall we, in our weak way, say of the Book of Mormon? Let us speak hesitantly, temperately, wisely, for it is beyond our power to fashion phrases and create sentences that will portray what God hath wrought in this perfect rendition of a portion of his word. But let us speak also with boldness, wishing that we had the voice of ten legions of angels, thundering forth with all the might of omnipotence; for we know, at least in small measure, of the wonder and worth of the holy word as arranged and edited by our friend Mormon.

What is the Book of Mormon? It is a voice from the dust, the voice of an ancient and once faithful people, the voice of a fallen people. It is the voice of Jaredites and Nephites and Lamanites speaking from their graves, of whole nations that fell from grace and now burn in the fires of Gehenna, of kindreds and races who acclaim, as the flames of sorrow sear their souls, "Be not as we were. Flee from carnal things. Care not for the passing pleasures and the worthless baubles of earth, lest ye also come to this pit of sorrow and gloom."

It is a voice from the dust, the voice of prophets and apostles, of holy men of old, of preachers of righteousness, of mortals who spake as the Holy Ghost gave them utterance— all testifying of Christ, all teaching his doctrine, all telling us what we must do to be saved, all testifying: "This is the way, the only way to God. Come, walk ye in it, and as the Lord lives, you shall at death find rest and peace in paradise, and then shall rise from death and find joy and rejoicing in immortal glory."

It is the voice of the holy gospel, the voice of peace in this world and of eternal life in the realms ahead. It contains the words of eternal life to be cherished and pondered above all, and points the way to immortal glory for all who believe and obey. It contains the mind and will of the Lord; it is holy scripture; it testifies of Christ; it speaks of the salvation that is in him; it is, in fine, the voice of God to every living soul in this final day of grace.

What is the Book of Mormon? It is "Another Testament of Jesus Christ," a new and living witness for Christ, and a holy book that proclaims the divine Sonship of our Lord. It is a volume of holy writ that contains the fulness of the everlasting gospel, meaning that it contains a record of God's dealings with a people who had the fulness of the gospel, and that their prophets summarized on its pages the things all men must do to gain the fulness of salvation. Those who believe the witness it bears and obey the doctrines it teaches will be led to that further light and knowledge revealed in this day, and to the mysteries of the kingdom that the saints alone can receive. It was "written by way of commandment, and also by the spirit of prophecy and revelation." And it came forth "to show unto the remnant of the House of Israel what great things the Lord hath done for their fathers; and that they may know the covenants of the Lord, that they are not cast off forever." And it came forth, above all, "to the convincing of the Jew and Gentile that JESUS is the CHRIST, the ETERNAL GOD, manifesting himself unto all nations." (Title page.)

What is the Book of Mormon? It is the Lord Jesus administering in resurrected glory to his Nephite kinsmen: giving them his gospel; inviting thousands to feel the prints of the nails in his hands and feet and to thrust their hands into his riven side; calling twelve apostles; preaching anew the Sermon on the Mount; healing their sick; administering the emblems of his broken flesh and spilt blood; expounding the scriptures; foretelling the restoration of the gospel, the triumph of Israel in the last days, and his return in that day to the New Jerusalem; and much, much more.

It is Nephi summarizing the plan of salvation, as no biblical prophet of whom we know ever did, and promising the saints that if they press forward with a steadfastness in Christ, having a perfect brightness of hope and a love of God and of all men, feasting upon the words of Christ and enduring to the end, they shall have eternal life.

It is an angel coming down from God in heaven to preach a sermon on the Messiah and the infinite and eternal atoning sacrifice he will make for the sins of the world. It is the angelic proclamation "that there shall be no other name given nor any other way nor means whereby salvation can come unto the children of men, only in and through the name of Christ, the Lord Omnipotent," and that "salvation was, and is, and is to come," in and through his atoning blood. (Mosiah 3:17-18.)

It is King Benjamin telling his people that they must take upon them the name of Christ and be born again, that they must become "the children of Christ, his sons, and his daughters," if they are to find place with him in the kingdom of his Father. (Mosiah 5:7-8.) It is Alma telling how all men, including those in the church who hold the holy priesthood, must be born again, changed from a carnal and fallen state, if they are to be heirs with Him who has redeemed them with his blood. It is Alma foretelling the coming of the Son of God, reciting the state of the soul between death and the resurrection, setting forth the eternal plan of redemption, and testifying that all shall come forth from the grave in their proper and perfect form.

It is Lehi's teachings about the fall of Adam; Moroni's explanations about faith, hope, and charity; Jacob's discourse on the atonement and the eternal judgment awaiting all men; Amulek's teachings about justice and mercy and prayer, and his proclamation as to what the saints must do in the here and now to save themselves; Alma's discourses on priesthood and on faith—all of which are superior, far superior, to any discourses on the same subjects in the Bible.

But the Book of Mormon is more than a recitation of pure doctrine, more than a witness of spiritual things, more than sermons and exhortations and prophecies. It is also a book about people. It tells of their wars and dissensions, of the calamities that befell them, of their foibles and sorrows and sins—and of the destruction of whole civilizations when they forsook the Lord and walked after the manner of the world.

It tells of Nephi, confronted with the awful decision involving life or death, as he was constrained by the Spirit to slay Laban. It tells of Korihor, to whom the devil appeared as an angel of light, being struck dumb at the word of Alma. It recounts how Helaman's two thousand sons were miraculously preserved in battle; how General Moroni raised the banner of liberty and saved his people; how Abinadi was burned at the stake by King Noah and his wicked priests; how Kishkumen murdered Pahoran as he sat on the judgment seat; how two hundred and thirty thousand Nephite soldiers were slain in a battle at Cumorah; how Nephi and Lehi, the sons of Helaman, being imprisoned for their teachings, were encircled about with fire from heaven; and so on and so on.

Truly, there is no book like the Book of Mormon. As of now only about one-third of it has been translated. The sealed portion, which contains the deep and hidden doctrines of the kingdom, is yet to come forth, probably not, however, until the Millennial era. The portion we have received is to try our faith and prepare us for that which is to come. When we exercise faith in Christ like unto those who once rejoiced in the mysteries of the kingdom now withheld from us, then we shall receive that which they enjoyed. In the meantime, "He that will contend against the word of the Lord, let him be accursed;

417

and he that shall deny these things [those in the portion of the Book of Mormon that we have received], let him be accursed; for unto them will I show no greater things, saith Jesus Christ." (Ether 4:8.)

"Truth Shall Spring Out of the Earth"

Every book of scripture is a witness of the truth and divinity of every other volume of holy writ. No compilation of the divine word stands alone; all join in bearing the same witness and in teaching the same truths. Their settings vary; their miracles fit their own needs; their prophets have different names and speak the local languages. But the message of salvation is the same. Always the scriptures bear witness of Christ; always they teach the truths of salvation; always they call upon fallen man to forsake the world and be reconciled to God through the atonement of his Son; always they speak peace to sorrowing souls in this world and hold out to them the hope of eternal life in the world to come.

Scripture is scripture no matter who receives it or in what volume it is compiled. When there are prophets, there will be scripture. And every people, having prophets and scripture of their own, know that the same Lord gives the same word to his servants in all ages. Such people wait upon the Lord continually, pleading with him for more revelation, for more of his mind and will, for more scripture. And they expect to find one volume speaking of another volume that either has been or yet will be. Why should the Lord withhold from people in one age knowledge that other peoples in past and future ages have been and yet will be his people?

Thus we find living prophets praising dead prophets and also speaking of prophets yet unborn. Thus we find one book of scripture quoting former books and speaking of yet other volumes to be written by future prophets. There will always be new prophets and new scripture among the Lord's people; and should they cease, it will be because the sheep of the Lord's fold have strayed from the green pastures and are lost in the deserts of despair and darkness.

Thus we find the Old Testament setting the stage for the New, and the New Testament testifying of the truth of the Old. Thus we find the biblical prophets speaking of the Book of

Mormon and the Nephite prophets bearing witness of the truth and verity of the biblical word. The Old Testament itself is simply a compilation of the inspired writings of one prophet after another. Implicit in this coming of new scripture, age after age, is the fact that there will be a New Testament to record the sayings and doings of the Chief Prophet of whom all the ancient prophets bore witness. And both the Chief Prophet and his New Testament colleagues unite in testifying of the eternal verity of the word of the ancient prophets.

In the case of the Bible and the Book of Mormon, these two volumes of scripture, arising from different peoples who dwelt a continent apart, speak of and describe each other. As we have seen, the Book of Mormon testifies that the Bible is true and also tells of the loss of many plain and precious doctrines from its pages. It also announces, in general terms, what the Revelator John will write in his day in the book of Revelation. And as we shall soon show, the Bible speaks of the Book of Mormon in a rather detailed and extended way. By way of perspective, for instance, there is more in the Bible about the Book of Mormon, as a book of scripture, than there is in the Old Testament about the New Testament.

Before there was either a Bible or a Book of Mormon, the Lord revealed to Enoch his plans and purposes and what he had in mind, in part at least, in the realm of scripture. Enoch was told of the dire and evil day of apostasy and tribulation that would cover the earth before the Second Coming and of the restoration of the gospel in that day of wickedness and vengeance. As to the piercing of the gloom of sullen darkness, the Lord said: "Righteousness will I send down out of heaven; and truth will I send forth out of the earth, to bear testimony of mine Only Begotten; his resurrection from the dead; yea, and also the resurrection of all men."

How will the gospel be restored? Heaven and earth will unite in one grand act of grace and goodness. Revelation will commence anew; angelic ministrants will come down from the courts of glory to give keys and powers; righteousness in all its forms will come down from the Son of Righteousness. And the very earth itself will speak forth anthems of eternal praise to the King Immanuel. Righteousness from a living heaven and truth from the dead earth shall unite to proclaim the glad tidings. Men shall hear a voice from the dust, a voice of truth springing out of the earth, an account of God's dealings with the Lehites and Jaredites, both of whom had the fulness of his everlasting gospel. The Book of Mormon—long lost to the knowledge of men; indeed, buried in the earth for more than fourteen hundred years—shall come forth proving the resurrection of that Lord who was slain on Calvary, and proving also, because he rose from the dead, that he is the Son of God whose gospel is binding upon us all.

"And righteousness and truth"—these two, coming from heaven above and from the earth beneath—"will I cause to sweep the earth as with a flood," saith the Lord, "to gather out mine elect from the four quarters of the earth, unto a place which I shall prepare, an Holy City, that my people may gird up their loins, and be looking forth for the time of my coming; for there shall be my tabernacle, and it shall be called Zion, a New Jerusalem." (Moses 7:60-62.) The restored gospel and the knowledge of the true God as set forth therein shall sweep the earth; this gospel and this knowledge shall cover the earth as the waters cover the mighty deep. Israel shall gather to Zion. What power will bring the Israelites from the ends of the earth to their New Jerusalem? It will be the gospel from heaven and the gospel from the dust. Note it and note it well: It is the power of the Book of Mormon that gathers Israel in the last days.

Both Isaiah and David, as guided by the Spirit, and perhaps having Enoch's record before them, bore a like witness. Isaiah, using the poetic and prophetic language in which he surpasses all others, records these words from the same Lord who spoke to Enoch: "Drop down, ye heavens, from above, and let the skies pour down righteousness: let the earth open, and let them bring forth salvation, and let righteousness spring up together; I the Lord have created it." (Isaiah 45:8.) Salvation comes because God speaks from heaven, and a voice from the dust echoes his divine words. Echoes? Nay, the voice from the dust recites anew what the heavenly voice said to holy men of old as they were moved upon by the Holy Ghost.

David, whose inspired psalms were composed by the power of the Spirit, gave forth this heaven-sent word: "I will hear what God the Lord will speak," he said. Oh, that all men might feel to lend a listening ear to the words of the Almighty! Let the Lord speak, and let all the earth keep silence. "For he will speak peace unto his people, and to his saints." The gospel message is always a message of peace, of a peace that passeth understanding in this life and of an eternal peace in the life that is to be. And always the message is received by those who are saints indeed. "Surely his salvation is nigh them that fear him; that glory may dwell in our land. Mercy and truth are met together; righteousness and peace have kissed each other." Salvation comes because God speaks from heaven; mercy is reserved for those who accept his truths; peace comes to the righteous. And then the climax of the whole matter: "Truth shall spring out of the earth; and righteousness shall look down from heaven." (Psalm 85:8-11.) How glorious it is when the heavens rain righteousness and the earth brings forth truth! Truly, such a day is a day of salvation for all who "will hear what God the Lord will speak."

CHAPTER 45

The Record of Joseph

Joseph and the Book of Mormon

Except for a few brief chapters about the Jaredites, the entire Book of Mormon is a record of God's dealings with a branch of the house of Israel. Lehi was of Manasseh, Ishmael of Ephraim, thus making their united descendants an ideal representation of the house of Joseph. Such other tribes—Judah, for one, in the case of Mulek—were swallowed up in the dominant Lehite and Ishmaelite lineages.

Jacob, who is Israel, gave patriarchal blessings to each of his twelve sons. These blessings were in reality tribal blessings and set forth the destiny of the tribe over which the respective son held patriarchal presidency. Such fragments of these blessings as have come down to us are found in chapter 49 of Genesis. Only in the case of Joseph is there any extended recitation about the posterity that will yet be his. Of Joseph, who was sold into Egyptian slavery by his jealous brothers, father Jacob, speaking prophetically, said: "Joseph is a fruitful bough, even a fruitful bough by a well; whose branches run over the wall." 'Joseph's posterity shall be great; millions shall claim him as their father; though they are well situated in Canaan, branches from his house shall even extend over the wall of water that separates the continents.' How expertly the prophetic mind devises figures and illustrations that remain in our minds forever, bearing repeated and continuous witness of the great realities to which they allude. The reference here is, of course, to the Lehite migration from Jerusalem, across the Indian Ocean, and then over the wide Pacific to the western coast of America.

Jacob continues his blessing: "The mighty God of Jacob,"

the Good Shepherd to his people, the Stone of Israel, "the God of thy father, . . . shall help thee," and "the Almighty . . . shall bless thee with blessings of heaven above, blessings of the deep that lieth under, blessings of the breasts, and of the womb." The Great God—the God of Abraham, Isaac, and Jacob, who is the Lord Jehovah—shall bless Joseph in three respects: (1) with the blessings of heaven, meaning wisdom and understanding and revelation—the blessings of the gospel, the priesthood, eternal marriage, all that comes from the Lord in heaven to those on earth who love and serve him; (2) with the blessings of the deep, meaning the oceans shall separate his seed from the Gentile nations, thus freeing them from the religious bondage and political slavery of the nations of the earth; and (3) with the blessings of the breasts and of the womb, meaning a posterity in this world to whom the gospel will come, a posterity not unlike that of faithful Abraham, his great-grandfather.

"The blessings of thy father have prevailed above the blessings of my progenitors unto the utmost bound of the everlasting hills." Joseph's father, Jacob himself—the very father of the Lord's people Israel—shall be blessed because of the posterity of Joseph. That posterity shall, in the last days, be established in the tops of the mountains, in the far distant everlasting hills, in the mountain where the house of God shall be built unto which all nations shall flow. Truly America, and the United States in particular, is the land of Joseph, to which many of scattered Israel have come in our day to learn of the God of Jacob and to walk in his ways.

And "they"—all of the eternal blessings of which his patriarchal blessing speaks—"shall be on the head of Joseph, and on the crown of the head of him that was separate from his brethren." (Genesis 49:22-26.) Again the figure and allusion is expertly woven into the great tapestry. Even as Joseph was separated from his brothers, for their ultimate temporal salvation in the day of famine and want of bread, so Joseph's seed, the branches of Ephraim and Manasseh known as the Nephites and Lamanites, were separated from their Old World brethren. Then, dwelling alone in the Americas for a thousand years, they brought salvation to a greater number of souls than were saved in all Israel in all their long history in the Old World. And yet again, in the last days the house of Joseph is separated from their fellows in Israel, as they build anew the Zion of God to which all Israel shall yet look for eternal salvation.

Joseph of old sought the Lord—this we cannot doubt—to gain the blessings promised him by Jacob. As his years ebbed to a close, "Joseph said unto his brethren, I die, and go unto my father; and I go down to my grave with joy. . . . For the Lord hath visited me, and I have obtained a promise of the Lord, that out of the fruit of my loins, the Lord God will raise up a righteous branch out of my loins." He then told them of their coming Egyptian bondage and of their deliverance by Moses as he gathered them back to the land of their promised inheritance. "And it shall come to pass that [Israel] shall be scattered again," he continued, "and a branch shall be broken off, and shall be carried into a far country." Those of whom he thus speaks are, of course, the Lehite peoples. His continuing words tell of this branch and also speak of the Prophet Joseph Smith and the restoration of the gospel in the last days. All of this was written on the Brass Plates and has been restored in chapter 50 of Genesis in the Joseph Smith Translation. Lehi, finding these things about his people on the Brass Plates, quoted relevant portions that are preserved for us in the Book of Mormon. It is to this source we now turn for a full explanation of what is involved.

"Joseph truly saw our day," Lehi said. "And he obtained a promise of the Lord, that out of the fruit of his loins the Lord God would raise up a righteous branch unto the house of Israel; not the Messiah, but a branch which was to be broken off, nevertheless, to be remembered in the covenants of the Lord that the Messiah should be made manifest unto them in the latter days, in the spirit of power, unto the bringing of them out of darkness unto light—yea, out of hidden darkness and out of captivity unto freedom." The Messiah, after his resurrection, is to visit the Nephites, for they are to be remembered in the covenants of the Lord and are to rejoice in that fulness of gospel light which prepares men for the fulness of glory in the Lord's eternal kingdom.

Lehi quotes these words of the Lord, given to Joseph of old: "A seer will I raise up out of the fruit of thy loins; and unto him will I give power to bring forth my word unto the seed of thy loins." This has reference to Joseph Smith, the coming forth of the Book of Mormon, and its proclamation to all of the seed of Joseph of old, including his Lamanite seed and his other seed mingled with and among scattered Israel. "And not to the bringing forth my word only, saith the Lord, but to the convincing them of my word, which shall have already gone forth among them." The Book of Mormon will establish the truth and divinity of the Bible. "Wherefore, the fruit of thy loins [the Nephites] shall write; and the fruit of the loins of Judah [the prophets in ancient Israel] shall write; and that which shall be written by the fruit of thy loins [the Book of Mormon], and also that which shall be written by the fruit of the loins of Judah [the Bible], shall grow together unto the confounding of false doctrines and laying down of contentions, and establishing peace among the fruit of thy loins, and bringing them to the knowledge of their fathers in the latter days, and also to the knowledge of my covenants, saith the Lord." If ever there was a book of prophecy and revelation that needs divine interpretation, it is the Bible, as is shown by the mere existence of the numerous diverse doctrines and varied views espoused by the conflicting sects of Christendom. And that the Book of Mormon is and shall ever be the interpreter and expounder of the Bible, who can doubt?

The missions and labors and names of Moses, Aaron, and Joseph Smith were all revealed to our ancient father Joseph. Moses was named as the one who would deliver Israel from Egyptian bondage and unto whom the Lord would give his law. However, his tongue would not be loosed so as to make him mighty in speaking. Joseph Smith is described as the seer who would be like unto Joseph of old and who would bring salvation unto the Lord's people. "And out of weakness he shall be made strong, in that day when my work shall commence among all my people, unto the restoring thee, O house of Israel, saith the Lord." Aaron is identified as the spokesman for Moses in that he would proclaim the law, given to his younger brother, Moses, by revelation.

Then, in this setting of one person writing the Lord's law and another proclaiming it, the Lord said to Joseph of old: "I will raise up unto the fruit of thy loins; and I will make for him a spokesman." As Moses wrote and Aaron proclaimed the law given in the Old World, so someone in the New World, some-one of the seed of Joseph, would write the Lord's law, and yet another, a spokesman, would declare it. In this case the writer and the spokesman are not identified by name; rather, we are left, based on our knowledge of what has transpired in this and previous dispensations, to identify those whose missions were of such import as to have them revealed thousands of years before the events transpired. Mormon wrote the Book of Mormon, quoting, condensing, and summarizing from many ancient records as the Spirit directed. And Joseph Smith trans-lated the ancient word by the gift and power of God and pro-claimed it to all men, and to the seed of Joseph in particular, as the mind and will and voice of Him by whom salvation comes.

With this in mind, note these words of the Lord: "And I, behold, I will give unto him [Mormon] that he shall write the writing of the fruit of thy loins [the Nephites], unto the fruit of thy loins [the Lamanites]; and the spokesman of thy loins [Joseph Smith] shall declare it." That is, Mormon wrote the Book of Mormon, but what he wrote was taken from the writ-ings of the Nephite prophets; and these writings, compiled into one book, were translated by Joseph Smith and sent forth by him unto the Lamanites unto whom, as the title page of the Book of Mormon attests, they were originally written. And further, they are sent forth to all the seed of Joseph, whether in the Lamanite branch of Israel or not.

"And the words which he [Mormon] shall write shall be the words which are expedient in my wisdom should go forth unto the fruit of thy loins." They were selected by inspiration, and they contain that portion of the word that is designed to bring fallen Israel again into the true sheepfold, where they will be taught the deeper doctrines, including the mysteries of the kingdom. "And it shall be as if the fruit of thy loins [the Nephites] had cried unto them [their Lamanite brethren, in particular] from the dust; for I know their faith." Many were the ancient Book of Mormon prophets who pled with the Lord that the gospel might go in due course and in his providences to the remnant of Lehi's seed.

"And they [the Nephites] shall cry from the dust [for as a nation they have been destroyed and have no living voice with which to speak]; yea, even repentance unto their brethren, even after many generations have gone by them. And it shall come to pass that their cry [in the Book of Mormon] shall go, even according to the simpleness of their words. Because of their faith their words [in the Book of Mormon] shall proceed forth out of my mouth"—the Book of Mormon is the word of the Lord; it is as though the words fell from his own lips— "unto their brethren [the Lamanites] who are the fruit of thy [Joseph's] loins; and the weakness of their words will I make strong in their faith, unto the remembering of my covenant which I made unto thy fathers." (2 Nephi 3:4-21.) With Joseph's fathers—Abraham, Isaac, and Jacob—the Lord covenanted that in them and in their seed all generations shall be blessed. These blessings are now available to the seed of Joseph because of the coming forth of the Book of Mormon and the restoration of the gospel.

Other Sheep of the Same Shepherd

All the world knows of the house of Judah and of the Bible that came through them, but what of the house of Joseph and of the scriptures destined to come forth through them? All the world knows that in the days of his flesh, the Messiah ministered to the house of Judah. But what of the house of Joseph to whom such great promises were made—should not the Messiah also minister to them? Is it not true that there is one God and one Shepherd over all the earth, and that if he calls his Jewish sheep, his voice should also be heard by his other sheep? Is not the God of Israel the Lord both of gathered and scattered Israel? And for that matter, is he not the God of the whole earth, to whom all men must come if they are to be saved in his Father's kingdom?

Jesus gave us the key to these matters in his great sermon on the Good Shepherd. In this sermon he acclaimed his own divine Sonship and spoke of his other Israelitish sheep. First, to gain a congregation that would, at the peril of their salvation, be bound to heed his words, Jesus healed, on his own motion, a man blind from birth. Then a great contention arose among the people as to the power by which the healing came. Thereupon, speaking to a people who accepted Jehovah as their Shepherd, Jesus announced himself as the Good Shepherd who would give his life voluntarily for the sheep because his Father had so commanded. As charges of blasphemy formed in the hearts of the sheep of his Jewish fold, because Jesus thus equated himself with Jehovah and thus made himself God, and as though to let them know that they alone did not comprise the chosen people, he said: "Other sheep I have, which are not of this fold: them also I must bring, and they shall hear my voice; and there shall be one fold, and one shepherd." (John 10:16.)

Jehovah is their Shepherd. He maketh his sheep to lie down in green pastures; he leadeth them beside the still waters. Those who follow the Good Shepherd shall not want. Israel is his people, his chosen ones, those with whom he covenanted in days of old. They are the sheep of his pasture. It was to Israel that he said: "Ye my flock, the flock of my pasture, are men, and I am your God, saith the Lord God." (Ezekiel 34:31.) What then of the house of Joseph and of the lost tribes—shall they not all hear his voice and learn his word and be gathered into his sheepcote?

After his resurrection, the Lord Jesus appeared to his Nephite saints. He taught them the gospel, organized his church and kingdom, and called twelve disciples to govern and regulate all the affairs of his kingdom in the Western Hemisphere. To these twelve he said: "Ye are my disciples; and ye are a light unto this people, who are a remnant of the house of Joseph." Was not Joseph of old promised that the Lord would minister to those of his seed who were separated from their brethren? "And behold, this is the land of your inheritance; and the Father hath given it unto you." The Americas are the land of Joseph; they were in Nephite times and they are now. The kingdom as now established on earth, with headquarters in Salt Lake City, will so continue until they build the New Jerusalem to which the other tribes will come to receive their blessings, under the hands of Ephraim, according to the promises.

"And not at any time hath the Father given me commandment that I should tell it unto your brethren at Jerusalem. Neither at any time hath the Father given me commandment that I should tell unto them concerning the other tribes of the house of Israel, whom the Father hath led away out of the land. This much did the Father command me, that I should tell unto them: That other sheep I have which are not of this fold; them also I must bring, and they shall hear my voice; and there

shall be one fold, and one shepherd." How could it be otherwise? Are not these the sheep of the house of that Joseph who
was favored above all the tribes of Israel? Only in one thing
was he excelled: that Shilo came through Judah.

"And now, because of stiffneckedness and unbelief they
understood not my word." He is speaking not alone of the
rebellious Jews who opposed him, but of the saints in
Jerusalem and of the apostles and prophets who led them.
"Therefore I was commanded to say no more of the Father
concerning this thing unto them." In this connection we are
left to wonder how much there is in this day that is withheld
from us because of our stiffneckedness and unbelief.

"But, verily, I say unto you that the Father hath commanded me, and I tell it unto you, that ye were separated from
among them because of their iniquity; therefore it is because of
their iniquity that they know not of you. And verily, I say unto
you again that the other tribes hath the Father separated from
them; and it is because of their iniquity that they know not of
them." And in like manner is it with us: we know only that the
lost tribes are scattered in all the nations of the earth, and that
when they are gathered, it will be on the same basis and in the
same way that any converts are made. As yet, because we are
not prepared to receive it, we do not know of the Lord's resurrected ministry among them, though we are safe in assuming
that it was patterned after his Nephite ministry.

"And verily I say unto you, that ye are they of whom I said:
Other sheep I have which are not of this fold; them also I must
bring, and they shall hear my voice; and there shall be one
fold, and one shepherd. And they understood me not, for they
supposed it had been the Gentiles; for they understood not
that the Gentiles should be converted through their preaching.
And they understood me not that I said they shall hear my
voice; and they understood me not that the Gentiles should
not at any time hear my voice—that I should not manifest
myself unto them save it were by the Holy Ghost. But behold,
ye have both heard my voice, and seen me; and ye are my
sheep, and ye are numbered among those whom the Father
hath given me." (3 Nephi 15:12-24.) Thereafter Jesus told the
Nephites that he had yet other sheep, the lost tribes, to whom
he would then minister, that they too might see his face and
hear his voice and be numbered among his sheep.

CHAPTER 46

A Voice
from the Dust

Woe to Ariel and to the Nephites

How wondrous it is to read and ponder and interpret the prophetic word; to discover its deep and hidden meanings; to know that the conclusions reached, and the truths learned, are the very ones that had their origin in the prophetic mind. In the full sense this can only be done by the power of the Spirit; only those enlightened by the same Spirit that gave the ancient word can discover its true meaning and discern its true intent.

There are few chapters in all the prophetic word that can compare in content and import with Isaiah 29. It is, as with all words of scripture, variously understood and interpreted by the uninspired commentators of the world. But in the providences of the Lord, Nephi, a prophet like unto Isaiah, has given us an interpreting paraphrase of this marvelous chapter, doing so because it deals with his own people and with the scriptural records preserved by them. Nephi's words, coupled with some other revealed truths that have come forth in this dispensation, enable us to catch the vision of what Israel's ancient seer foretold pertaining to the Lehite civilization and to the great day of restoration in which we live.

On the eve of the Assyrian assault against Jerusalem by Sennacherib, which brought much sorrow and suffering upon Judah; more than a hundred years before the Chaldeans led by Nebuchadnezzar destroyed Jerusalem, which resulted in the Babylonian captivity; about eight hundred years before the Romans under Titus overran the Holy City, tore the temple apart stone by stone, slaughtered more than a million Jews, and made slaves of the others—the Lord, by the mouth of Isaiah, proclaimed: "Woe to Ariel, to Ariel, the city where David dwelt!"

Why this symbolic name, *Ariel,* to describe Jerusalem—
Jerusalem, the Holy City; the city in which all Israel assembled
three times a year to worship the King; the site of the ancient
Zion and of the temple of Jehovah? The choice of this name
was pure inspiration, for the message to be delivered included
these words: "I will distress Ariel, and there shall be heaviness
and sorrow." (Isaiah 29:1-2.) *Ariel* is a Hebrew word of several
meanings. Literally it denotes the "Hearth of God (El)" and was
used to describe the altar-hearth whereon sacrifices were
offered. It is also rendered "Lion of God" and "Mount of
God." Thus Isaiah's utterance means 'Woe to Jerusalem, the
principal place where God is worshipped; woe to Mount Zion
and the Temple of the Lord; woe to the city that considers
herself as invincible as a lion—for heaviness and sorrow and
bondage and captivity and death shall fall upon her inhabitants.'

Be it remembered that the Lord Jesus also wept over
doomed Jerusalem; described it as the city "that killest the
prophets, and stonest them which are sent unto thee"; and
then said to the Jewish people: "Behold, your house is left
unto you desolate." (Matthew 23:37-38.) And be it remembered also that Jesus foretold the desolations yet to be wrought
by Titus and his legions in these words: "For then, in those
days, shall be great tribulation on the Jews, and upon the
inhabitants of Jerusalem, such as was not before sent upon
Israel, of God, since the beginning of their kingdom until this
time; no, nor ever shall be sent again upon Israel." (JS–M 1:18.)

This proclamation of woes that shall befall Ariel—woes in
which they will be slain and slaughtered as animals upon the
Lord's altar; woes that will bring burnings and fires and
devastation upon them—this proclamation is the setting for
like woes that shall come upon another people, a people who
went out from Jerusalem to become a great nation, but who, in
turn, through sin fell from grace and became "as Ariel." Those
who are to be "as Ariel" are the Nephites, as we learn from
chapter 3 of Second Nephi, Nephi's paraphrase of Isaiah 29.

Of those who shall be "as Ariel," the Lord says: "I will
camp against thee round about, and will lay siege against thee
with a mount, and I will raise forts against thee." (Isaiah 29:3.)
In the days of her warfare, Jerusalem was besieged and smitten
and made desolate. In the days of Titus, women hungering for

bread ate their children, blood flowed in rivers through the streets, and dead bodies, unburied, were heaped in stacks. But so likewise was it among the Lehites. Through the centuries the Nephites and Lamanites slaughtered each other, sometimes in such great numbers that they did not even count the dead. Then came the final great war of extermination. It lasted for more than forty years: and on the final day of battle alone, the Lamanites slew two hundred and thirty thousand Nephite warriors. During the whole period blood and carnage covered the land, and it was one complete revolution everywhere. Dead bodies were heaped up as dung; the wicked slew the wicked; captive Nephite women and children were sacrificed to Lamanite idols. As Mormon viewed these scenes, he cried out in anguish of spirit: "It is impossible for the tongue to describe, or for man to write a perfect description of the horrible scene of the blood and carnage which was among the people, both of the Nephites and of the Lamanites; and every heart was hardened, so that they delighted in the shedding of blood continually. And there never had been so great wickedness among all the children of Lehi, nor even among all the house of Israel." (Mormon 4:11-12.)

However great were the destructions upon Ariel—as the sword of Sennacherib, the battering rams of Nebuchadnezzar, and the arrows and fire of Titus shed Israelitish blood—yet who shall say that these Nephites were not as Ariel? And how better could Isaiah have foretold their downfall than to compare their destruction with that of the city whence they fled in the days of Zedekiah?

"And thou"—ye Nephites, saith the Lord—"shalt be brought down, and shalt speak out of the ground, and thy speech shall be low out of the dust, and thy voice shall be, as of one that hath a familiar spirit, out of the ground, and thy speech shall whisper out of the dust." Where else in all history are there two better examples of peoples who were brought down and utterly destroyed than the Jaredites and Nephites? And whose voices, being stilled in death, yet speak from their graves for all to hear? Does not their united voice have a familiar spirit? Is it not whispering out of the ground the same prophetic message that is now and always has been the burden of the living prophets? Does not the Book of Mormon proclaim a familiar message, one already written in the Bible?

"Moreover"—that is, in addition—"the multitude of thy strangers shall be like small dust, and the multitude of the terrible ones shall be as chaff that passeth away: yea, it shall be at an instant suddenly. Thou shalt be visited of the Lord of hosts with thunder, and with earthquake, and great noise, with storm and tempest, and the flame of devouring fire." (Isaiah 29:4-6.) In Abraham's day, before there was a house of Israel, the Lord rained fire and brimstone upon Sodom and Gomorrah, Adamah and Zeboim, destroying the people and all that grew from the ground. In his anger and in his wrath, he sent brimstone and salt and burning so that seeds could not sprout nor any grass grow. But what was the destruction of four Gentile cities as compared to the utter extinction of sixteen Nephite cities, plus horrendous destruction in a host of others, at the time of our Lord's crucifixion? For the space of three hours—in "an instant suddenly," as it were—the earth shook, the rocks were rent, and the whole face of the land was changed. At that time, "there arose a great storm, such an one as never had been known in all the land. And there was also a great and terrible tempest; and there was terrible thunder, insomuch that it did shake the whole earth as if it was about to divide asunder. And there were exceedingly sharp lightnings, such as never had been known in all the land." (3 Nephi 8:5-7.) Cities were burned with fire; others sank into the sea; yet others were buried in the depths of the earth; and among those that remained, their buildings were shaken and destroyed and many of their inhabitants killed.

After describing the destructions of that day, the holy word says: "He that hath the scriptures, let him search them, and see and behold if all these deaths and destructions by fire, and by smoke, and by tempests, and by whirlwinds, and by the opening of the earth to receive them, and all these things are not unto the fulfilling of the prophecies of many of the holy prophets." (3 Nephi 10:14.) And not the least of these prophets was Isaiah.

The Voice—Heard in the Day of Darkness

The scene of Isaiah's seeric sayings now changes. Leaving the Nephite days and all the devastation that attended the crucifixion and the warfare at Cumorah, his prophetic pen dips into that future which now is and which yet shall be. He must reassure Israel of her eventual triumph; Ariel must finally become the Holy City in which the soles of Jehovah's feet will again tread. After scattered Israel has suffered the sorrows of Sennacherib, borne the devastations of Nebuchadnezzar, and been trodden under the feet of Titus, she must rise again and receive her promised inheritance.

In the day when all nations are gathered at Jerusalem to fight against the chosen people; in the day when the house of Judah accepts Him in whose hands and feet are the nail marks of Calvary; when they look upon him whom they have pierced and ask, "What are these wounds in thine hands?" (Zechariah 13:6); and when he identifies himself as their God—in that day, the Lord of Hosts, the ancient God of battles, shall again fight their battles. Israel shall triumph. Their enemies shall be destroyed. All who fight against Ariel shall fade away and be forgotten, as are the nightmarish dreams of the night. With reference to that day, Isaiah says: "The multitude of all the nations that fight against Ariel, even all that fight against her and her munition, and that distress her, shall be as a dream of a night vision. It shall be as when an hungry man dreameth, and, behold, he eateth; but he awaketh, and his soul is empty: or as when a thirsty man dreameth, and, behold, he drinketh; but he awaketh, and, behold, he is faint, and his soul hath appetite: so shall the multitude of all the nations be, that fight against mount Zion."

This day of triumph and glory for the Lord's redeemed, and of sorrow and vengeance for their enemies, shall not come to pass until the cup of iniquity of the ungodly is full. It will take place in an evil day, a day of sin and wickedness, a day when the nations of the earth are without prophetic guidance. Thus Isaiah says: "Stay yourselves, and wonder; cry ye out, and cry: they are drunken, but not with wine; they stagger, but not with strong drink. For the Lord hath poured out upon you the spirit of deep sleep, and hath closed your eyes: the prophets and your rulers, the seers hath he covered." (Isaiah 29:7-10.) How dire and awful the apostasy is in the last days! Men are drunken spiritually; they stagger spiritually; they are sick spiritually; they are dead spiritually—dead to the things of righteousness and of the Spirit. They are without seers and without prophets; they have none of the saving powers of the holy gospel. Their rulers walk in darkness. As far as the things of God are concerned, they are in a deep sleep.

Knowing all this, Nephi gives us this interpreting explanation of Isaiah: "Behold, in the last days, or in the days of the Gentiles—yea, behold all the nations of the Gentiles and also the Jews, both those who shall come upon this land [the Western Hemisphere] and those who shall be upon other lands, yea, even upon all the lands of the earth, behold, they will be drunken with iniquity and all manner of abominations." He is speaking of the day of universal apostasy; of the day in which the gospel is to be restored; of the day preceding the Second Coming, in which evil and iniquity and sorrow will increase.

"And when that day shall come they [those who then dwell in all lands] shall be visited of the Lord of Hosts, with thunder and with earthquake, and with a great noise, and with storm, and with tempest, and with the flame of devouring fire." We have seen these things as they were manifest among the Nephites at the time of the crucifixion of Christ. We have seen them in the wars and butchery of modern times, particularly where atomic weapons are involved. And we shall yet see them, in a measure never before manifest on earth, when all nations gather against Jerusalem in the days of the coming Armageddon. This Nephi knew, and this we know.

Continuing to use Isaiah's language, and viewing, as it were, these final calamities of earth, Nephi says: "All the nations that fight against Zion, and that distress her, shall be as a dream of a night vision; yea, it shall be unto them, even as unto a hungry man which dreameth, and behold he eateth but he awaketh and his soul is empty; or like unto a thirsty man which dreameth, and behold he drinketh but he awaketh and behold he is faint, and his soul hath appetite; yea, even so shall the multitude of all the nations be that fight against Mount Zion." Let us be reminded that most of the wars fought from the fall of man to this hour have been religious wars. It was so before the flood; it was so in ancient Israel; it was so with the Jaredites and Nephites. It was so in England and in Europe and among those of Islam; it is so when the powers of communism invade and enslave; and it will be so—a thousand times over—in the coming Armageddon. The nations that distress Jerusalem in that day will be in opposition to the Lord Jehovah. They will be fighting against Mount Zion.

At this point Nephi addresses himself to the apostate and fallen peoples of the earth—those to whom the Book of Mormon is destined to go—and in doing so clarifies and improves the words of Isaiah: "For behold, all ye that doeth iniquity, stay yourselves and wonder, for ye shall cry out, and cry; yea, ye shall be drunken but not with wine, ye shall stagger but not with strong drink. For behold, the Lord hath poured out upon you the spirit of deep sleep. For behold, ye have closed your eyes, and ye have rejected the prophets; and your rulers, and the seers hath he covered because of your iniquity." (2 Nephi 27:1-5.)

Nephi and Moroni Speak from the Dust

The Book of Mormon prophets knew that their words would whisper forth as a voice from the dust and would stand as a witness of Christ and his gospel for all generations. They knew and understood and rejoiced in Isaiah's words. Let us— also knowing and understanding and rejoicing in the words of Israel's ancient seer—sample the words of Nephi, the first prophetic Book of Mormon writer, and of Moroni, the last, so that we too, if properly guided by the Spirit, may also believe as they believed and eventually be saved with them.

"Behold, I prophesy unto you concerning the last days," Nephi said, "concerning the days when the Lord God shall bring these things forth unto the children of men." He is speaking of the coming forth of his words and of the words of all his fellow prophets; and such of them as the world is now worthy to receive bear the title Book of Mormon, which is "Another Testament of Jesus Christ."

These are the words of his prophecy: "After my seed [the Nephites] and the seed of my brethren [the Lamanites] shall have dwindled in unbelief, and shall have been smitten by the Gentiles [the European nations that overran the Americas]; yea, after the Lord God shall have camped against them round about, and shall have laid siege against them with a mount, and raised forts against them [as he did at Cumorah and elsewhere]; and after they shall have been brought down low in the dust, even that they are not, yet the words of the righteous shall be written, and the prayers of the faithful shall be heard, and all those who have dwindled in unbelief shall not be forgotten." The once mighty Nephites have perished; they are dead; but their words live on!

"For those who shall be destroyed [the Nephites] shall speak unto them [who have dwindled in unbelief] out of the ground, and their speech shall be low out of the dust, and their voice shall be as one that hath a familiar spirit; for the Lord God will give unto him power, that he may whisper concerning them, even as it were out of the ground; and their speech shall whisper out of the dust. For thus saith the Lord God: They [the Nephites] shall write the things which shall be done among them, and they shall be written and sealed up in a book [in the Book of Mormon], and those who have dwindled in unbelief [the Lamanites] shall not have them, for they seek to destroy the things of God. Wherefore, as those who have been destroyed [the Nephites] have been destroyed speedily; and the multitude of their terrible ones shall be as chaff that passeth away—yea, thus saith the Lord God: It shall be at an instant, suddenly—And it shall come to pass, that those who have dwindled in unbelief [the Lamanites] shall be smitten by the hand of the Gentiles," after the discovery of the Americas. (2 Nephi 26:14-19.)

Nephi next prophesies of the false churches, of priestcrafts, and of evils that shall be among the Gentiles, and of many things that shall transpire in the last days. Then he comes back to the records of his people, which shall come out of the earth, be given to the Gentiles, and then be taken by them to the remnant of the Lehite peoples. "And now, I would prophesy somewhat more concerning the Jews and the Gentiles," he said. "For after the book of which I have spoken [the Book of Mormon] shall come forth, and be written unto the Gentiles [the Book of Mormon is for the Gentiles as well as the Lamanites], and sealed up again unto the Lord, there shall be many which shall believe the words which are written; and they shall carry them forth unto the remnant of our seed." The Gentiles shall take the Nephite record to the Lamanites, a thing that we are now doing.

"And then shall the remnant of our seed know concerning us, how that we came out from Jerusalem, and that they are descendants of the Jews." All the theories of men as to the origin of the ancient inhabitants of the Americas are as nothing compared with the divine declaration that these peoples are descendants of the Jews and are of the house of Israel. "And the gospel of Jesus Christ shall be declared among them; wherefore, they shall be restored unto the knowledge of their fathers, and also to the knowledge of Jesus Christ, which was had among their fathers." (2 Nephi 30:3-5.)

And then, finally, from the depths of a thankful and testifying heart, this father of the Nephite branch of Joseph, the branch that ran over the ocean wall, said: "I, Nephi, have written what I have written, and I esteem it as of great worth, and especially unto my people. . . . And the words which I have written in weakness will be made strong unto them; for it persuadeth them to do good; it maketh known unto them of their fathers; and it speaketh of Jesus, and persuadeth them to believe in him, and to endure to the end, which is life eternal." What better purpose could any writings have?

"And it speaketh harshly against sin, according to the plainness of the truth; wherefore, no man will be angry at the words which I have written save he shall be of the spirit of the devil. . . . And now, my beloved brethren, and also Jew, and all ye ends of the earth"—how well Nephi knew to whom his words would go—"hearken unto these words and believe in Christ; and if ye believe not in these words believe in Christ. And if ye shall believe in Christ ye will believe in these words, for they are the words of Christ, and he hath given them unto me; and they teach all men that they should do good.

"And if they are not the words of Christ, judge ye—for Christ will show unto you, with power and great glory, that they are his words, at the last day; and you and I shall stand face to face before his bar; and ye shall know that I have been commanded of him to write these things, notwithstanding my weakness. . . .

"And now, my beloved brethren, all those who are of the house of Israel, and all ye ends of the earth, I speak unto you as the voice of one crying from the dust: Farewell until that great day shall come." (2 Nephi 33:3-13.)

And now the words and testimony of Moroni: "And whoso receiveth this record [the Book of Mormon], and shall not condemn it because of the imperfections which are in it, the same shall know of greater things than these. Behold, I am Moroni. . . . I am the same who hideth up this record unto the Lord. . . . And if there be faults they be the faults of a man. But behold, we know no fault; nevertheless God knoweth all things; therefore, he that condemneth, let him be aware lest he shall be in danger of hell fire. . . .

"Search the prophecies of Isaiah. Behold, I cannot write them. Yea, behold I say unto you, that those saints who have gone before me, who have possessed this land, shall cry, yea, even from the dust will they cry unto the Lord; and as the Lord liveth he will remember the covenant which he hath made with them."

And now, having in mind the words of Isaiah and of Nephi about the low and fallen and evil state of men in the day when the blessed book shall come forth, let us hear these words of Moroni: "And no one need say they shall not come, for they surely shall, for the Lord hath spoken it; for out of the earth shall they come, by the hand of the Lord, and none can stay it; and it shall come in a day when it shall be said that miracles are done away; and it shall come even as if one should speak from the dead.

"And it shall come in a day when the blood of saints shall cry unto the Lord, because of secret combinations and the works of darkness. Yea, it shall come in a day when the power of God shall be denied, and churches become defiled and be lifted up in the pride of their hearts; yea, even in a day when leaders of churches and teachers shall rise in the pride of their hearts, even to the envying of them who belong to their churches.

"Yea, it shall come in a day when there shall be heard of fires, and tempests, and vapors of smoke in foreign lands; and there shall also be heard of wars, rumors of wars, and earthquakes in divers places.

"Yea, it shall come in a day when there shall be great pollutions upon the face of the earth; there shall be murders, and robbing, and lying, and deceivings, and whoredoms, and all manner of abominations; when there shall be many who will say, Do this, or do that, and it mattereth not, for the Lord will uphold such at the last day. But wo unto such, for they are in the gall of bitterness and in the bonds of iniquity.

"Yea, it shall come in a day when there shall be churches built up that shall say: Come unto me, and for your money you shall be forgiven of your sins." (Mormon 8:12-32.)

How pointed and plain is the holy word! Surely none can fail to see the evidence, on every hand, of all those things of which Moroni spoke.

CHAPTER 47

The Sealed Book

Why Is the Book Sealed?

How shall the triumph of Israel be brought to pass in the last days? It shall come through the restoration of the same gospel possessed by their ancient forebears; it shall be when they worship again the God of their fathers; it shall come when they forsake the world, flee from fallen and apostate churches, and come unto Christ with full purpose of heart.

And where will this new knowledge, this new way of life be found? It will be written in a book, a sealed book, a book that has been hidden and sealed for more than fourteen hundred years. It will be found in a book that even now is sealed, except for the introductory part, which part has been translated by the gift and power of God and is known as the Book of Mormon.

When a voice whispers from the dust, what message will it deliver? If the righteous dead of ages past could cry out from their graves, what would they say to their descendants on earth? The voice from the dust, the words of the prophets of old, would be the same voice and the same words they used in mortality. Their message would be the most important ever given to men; it would be the message of salvation, the message of the gospel. How will the message come? It will be written in a book—a book that contains the fulness of the everlasting gospel, a book that tells men what they must do to gain peace in this life and eternal life in the realms ahead.

When truth springs out of the earth, as righteousness looks down from heaven, what truths will be involved? They will be the truths about Christ and his divine Sonship; about his atoning sacrifice and the ransom he paid to redeem men temporally and spiritually; about his resurrection and the resurrection of all men. And all these things shall be written in a book for men to read.

How shall the night of awful darkness that covers the earth come to an end? What light will pierce the enshrouding gloom? How shall those who are drunken but not with wine, and who stagger but not with strong drink, be reclaimed? What will bring spiritual sobriety into their souls? Again the answer is a book—a book that contains the mind and will and voice of the Lord, a book that whispers from the dust.

And so Isaiah speaks of the glorious restoration of the everlasting gospel, which is to take place in the last days, and he introduces that restoration by speaking of the book so long sealed and even now only partially opened. He says: "The vision of all is become unto you as the words of a book that is sealed, which men deliver to one that is learned, saying, Read this, I pray thee: and he saith, I cannot; for it is sealed: And the book is delivered to him that is not learned, saying, Read this, I pray thee: and he saith, I am not learned." (Isaiah 29:11-12.)

How much more Isaiah may have taught about the sealed book we do not know. As we have seen, he did speak prophetically about the Nephites and of their destruction. And he is the prophet who said that "the remnant that is escaped of the house of Judah"—meaning the Lehites—"shall yet again take root downward, and bear fruit upward. For out of Jerusalem shall go forth a remnant, and they that escape out of mount Zion: the zeal of the Lord of hosts shall do this." (2 Kings 19:30-31.) But in any event, Nephi, who was closer to the divine scene than even Isaiah, took up Isaiah's words, expounding, amplifying, explaining, testifying—all while the spirit of prophecy and of revelation rested upon him.

These are Nephi's words: "And it shall come to pass that the Lord God shall bring forth unto you"—that is, unto those who are in darkness because they have rejected the prophets, and who are drunken but not with wine, and who stagger but not with strong drink—"the words of a book, and they shall be the words of them which have slumbered. And behold the book shall be sealed; and in the book shall be a revelation from God, from the beginning of the world to the ending thereof. Wherefore, because of the things which are sealed up, the things which are sealed shall not be delivered in the day of the wickedness and abominations of the people. Wherefore the book shall be kept from them." (2 Nephi 27:6-8.)

What a marvelous thing this is! There is actually a book in which prophets of old have written about preexistence, the creation, the fall, the histories of all nations, the gospel through the ages, the great and abominable church, life in paradise and hell, the Second Coming of the Son of Man, the Millennial era, the resurrection and final judgment, and a host of other things that have not so much as entered our minds. We have little slivers of knowledge about all these things. How wondrous it would be to know it all. What would men give to read such a book, to know the mysteries of the kingdom recorded therein, and to know in full the answer to the Whence, Why, and Whither of life?

But sadly, the book is sealed; its contents are being kept from men in this day. Indeed, it is not even now in the possession of mortals; it was returned by Joseph Smith to Moroni, its divinely appointed custodian. Nor did even Joseph Smith either read or translate it. We know of no one among mortals since Mormon and Moroni who have known its contents. It was known among the Nephites during the nearly two hundred years of their Golden Era. But for the present, the book is kept from us; only the portion upon which no seal was placed has been translated.

Why are these plates of Mormon sealed? The answer is obvious. They contain spiritual truths beyond our present ability to receive. Milk must precede meat, and whenever men are offered more of the mysteries of the kingdom than they are prepared to receive, it affects them adversely. In instructing his Jewish disciples, for instance, Jesus said: "Go ye into the world, saying unto all, Repent, for the kingdom of heaven has come nigh unto you. And the mysteries of the kingdom ye shall keep within yourselves; for it is not meet to give that which is holy unto the dogs; neither cast ye your pearls unto swine, lest they trample them under their feet. For the world cannot receive that which ye, yourselves, are not able to bear; wherefore ye shall not give your pearls unto them, lest they turn again and rend you." (JST, Matthew 7:9-11.) Thus also Alma said: "It is given unto many to know the mysteries of God; nevertheless they are laid under a strict commandment that they shall not impart only according to the portion of his word which he doth grant unto the children of men, according to the heed and diligence which they give unto him." (Alma 12:9.)

The sealed portion of the Book of Mormon contains an account of what the brother of Jared saw. Of this account Moroni said: "I have written upon these plates the very things which the brother of Jared saw; and there never were greater things made manifest than those which were made manifest unto the brother of Jared. Wherefore the Lord hath commanded me to write them; and I have written them. And he commanded me that I should seal them up; and he also hath commanded that I should seal up the interpretation thereof; wherefore I have sealed up the interpreters, according to the commandment of the Lord. For the Lord said unto me: They shall not go forth unto the Gentiles until the day that they shall repent of their iniquity, and become clean before the Lord.

"And in that day that they shall exercise faith in me, saith the Lord, even as the brother of Jared did, that they may become sanctified in me, then will I manifest unto them the things which the brother of Jared saw, even to the unfolding unto them all my revelations, saith Jesus Christ, the Son of God, the Father of the heavens and of the earth, and all things that in them are. And he that will contend against the word of the Lord, let him be accursed; and he that shall deny these things, let him be accursed; for unto them will I show no greater things, saith Jesus Christ." (Ether 4:4-8.)

Opening the Sealed Book

John the Revelator saw the Lord sitting upon his heavenly throne, holding in his right hand a book sealed with seven seals. This book "contains the revealed will, mysteries, and works of God; the hidden things of his economy concerning this earth during the seven thousand years of its continuance, or its temporal existence. . . . The first seal contains the things of the first thousand years, and the second also of the second thousand years, and so on until the seventh." (D&C 77:6-7.) John heard an angelic voice ask: "Who is worthy to open the book, and to loose the seals thereof?" No man on earth was able to do so, but "the Lion of the tribe of Juda, the Root of

David" (Revelation 5:2-5), who is Christ, prevailed and opened the book, and a few slivers of that which has occurred and will occur in each thousand years was revealed.

We wonder if this sealed book is the same one that was sealed by the hands of Mormon and of Moroni, that its teachings would remain hidden until Christ the Lord opened it to those who had faith in him like unto the brother of Jared. If it is not, it certainly is a companion volume that—as is the case with the Bible and Book of Mormon—bears the same witness and speaks of the same hidden mysteries.

In any event, Nephi, speaking of the sealed book on the plates of Mormon, says: "But the book shall be delivered unto a man." That is, Joseph Smith shall receive the actual book, the plates, the very record upon which the ancient American prophets had inscribed their teachings and testimonies. "And he shall deliver the words of the book, which are the words of those who have slumbered in the dust, and he shall deliver these words unto another." Joseph Smith shall copy some of the very words, in their original tongue; he will attach to these words a literal translation, and he will then give the words and their translation to Martin Harris.

"But the words which are sealed he shall not deliver, neither shall he deliver the book." The words copied by Joseph Smith and his translation shall come from the unsealed portion of the book; they will not be taken from the sealed portion; and the book itself—the actual plates of Mormon— shall remain in prophetic hands to be seen by those only who are called of God to receive so great a privilege. "For the book shall be sealed by the power of God, and the revelation which was sealed shall be kept in the book until the own due time of the Lord, that they may come forth; for behold, they reveal all things from the foundation of the world unto the end thereof." It is perfectly clear that, at least in substance and thought content, if not in actual words, this book contains the same information that is in the sealed book seen by John.

"And the day cometh that the words of the book which were sealed shall be read upon the house tops." The sealed portion of the Book of Mormon shall yet be translated by the gift and power of God; the words so translated shall be published to the world; all men everywhere will be entitled to hear them. This means that all men will have the faith of the brother of Jared, a state that will not prevail until that Millennial day, after the destruction of the wicked, when the Lord Jesus reigns personally upon the earth. "And they shall be read by the power of Christ." The Lion of the tribe of Judah shall open the sealed book. "And all things shall be revealed unto the children of men which ever have been among the children of men, and which ever will be even unto the end of the earth." (2 Nephi 27:9-11.)

Witnesses of the Book of Mormon

How can we prove that any words purporting to come from the Lord are true? How can it be known that the Bible is true? Or the Book of Mormon? Or any writings that claim to be from an inspired source?

In answer let us say: (1) It takes a revelation to prove the verity of a revelation. The Holy Spirit of God must bear witness of the truth of any other revealed verity. (2) All scripture carries within itself the evidence of its own divinity. If, for instance, no man could have written the Book of Mormon—setting forth therein in such clarity and perfection the doctrines of salvation, and conforming so perfectly with the Bible—then that book must be of God. (3) Others of respected integrity, knowing of the truth of whatever scripture is involved, may bear witness of its divine origin. Those who saw and handled and hefted and examined the plates of Mormon, for instance, may bear witness in words of soberness that they actually exist. Indeed, such witnesses are sent to bear testimony so that others shall be left without excuse when they stand before the bar of the Judge of all the earth. (4) Reason, logic, internal consistencies, archeological discoveries, ethnological considerations, and a thousand other things may bear a supplemental witness of the truth and divinity of any compilation of the divine word.

Witnesses, testifying of the truth and divinity of any given gospel verity, prepare the way for others to gain the same sure knowledge possessed by the one who bears the original testimony. Thus Nephi tells us: "By the words of three, God hath said, I will establish my word. Nevertheless, God sendeth more witnesses, and he proveth all his words." (2 Nephi 11:3.) Such is the law of witnesses.

And so, continuing his prophecies about the sealed book, Nephi says: "Wherefore, at that day when the book shall be delivered unto the man of whom I have spoken, the book shall be hid from the eyes of the world, that the eyes of none shall behold it save it be that three witnesses shall behold it, by the power of God, besides him to whom the book shall be delivered; and they shall testify to the truth of the book and the things therein." (2 Nephi 27:12.) The book is the plates of Mormon; the man who has the book is Joseph Smith; and the three witnesses to whom the book is shown are Oliver Cowdery, David Whitmer, and Martin Harris.

These three brethren were shown the plates by a holy angel, and they heard the voice of God bear record that the Book of Mormon is true and was translated correctly. They were commanded to bear record of what they had seen and heard, and their testimony is published to the world in every copy of the Book of Mormon.

Moroni, knowing what Nephi knew, wrote of the plates that he was about to bury in Cumorah: "Unto three shall they be shown by the power of God; wherefore they shall know of a surety that these things are true. And in the mouth of three witnesses shall these things be established; and the testimony of three, and this work, in the which shall be shown forth the power of God and also his word, of which the Father, and the Son, and the Holy Ghost bear record—and all this shall stand as a testimony against the world at the last day." (Ether 5:3-4.) The witnesses and the word: together they bear a testimony that will condemn all who do not believe.

Nephi continues his prophetic word: "And there is none other which shall view it, save it be a few according to the will of God, to bear testimony of his word unto the children of men; for the Lord God hath said that the words of the faithful should speak as if it were from the dead." Those few here mentioned are the Eight Witnesses. They did not stand in the angelic presence nor hear the voice of God, but they examined and hefted the plates, and their testimony also is published in the Book of Mormon.

"Wherefore, the Lord God will proceed to bring forth the words of the book," Nephi continues, "and in the mouth of as many witnesses as seemeth him good will he establish his word; and wo be unto him that rejecteth the word of God!" (2

Nephi 27:13-14.) Today there are millions of witnesses, all of whom know by the power of the Holy Ghost that the Book of Mormon is true; all of whom thank God from the depths of their souls that he has restored the plain and precious things long lost from the world; all of whom will stand alongside Nephi and Moroni and the prophets of old, before the bar of God, as witnesses that this holy book is the mind and will and voice of the Lord to all men in these last days.

The Sealed Book Dialogue

"But behold, it shall come to pass," Nephi continues, "that the Lord God shall say unto him [Joseph Smith] to whom he shall deliver the book: Take these words which are not sealed and deliver them to another [Martin Harris], that he may show them unto the learned [a certain Professor Charles Anthon], saying: Read this, I pray thee. And the learned shall say: Bring hither the book, and I will read them. And now, because of the glory of the world and to get gain will they say this, and not for the glory of God. And the man [Martin Harris] shall say: I cannot bring the book, for it is sealed. Then shall the learned say: I cannot read it." (2 Nephi 27:15-18.)

These ancient words, according as they do with those of Isaiah, were fulfilled in a rather dramatic experience of Martin Harris. "I went to the city of New York," he recounts, "and presented the characters which had been translated, with the translation thereof, to Professor Charles Anthon, a gentleman celebrated for his literary attainments." He was truly a learned man. "Professor Anthon stated that the translation was correct, more so than any he had before seen translated from the Egyptian." The record on the plates was written in reformed Egyptian, meaning in the Hebrew tongue by means of Egyptian characters that had been altered to meet the Nephite needs. "I then showed him those which were not yet translated, and he said that they were Egyptian, Chaldaic, Assyriac, and Arabic; and he said they were true characters. He gave me a certificate, certifying to the people of Palmyra that they were true characters, and that the translation of such of them as had been translated was also correct. I took the certificate and put it into my pocket, and was just leaving the house, when Mr. Anthon called me back, and asked me how the young man found out that there were gold plates in the place where he found them. I answered that an angel of God had revealed it unto him.

"He then said to me, 'Let me see that certificate.' I accordingly took it out of my pocket and gave it to him, when he took it and tore it to pieces, saying that there was no such thing now as ministering of angels, and that if I would bring the plates to him he would translate them. I informed him that part of the plates were sealed, and that I was forbidden to bring them. He replied, 'I cannot read a sealed book.' I left him and went to Dr. Mitchell, who sanctioned what Professor Anthon had said respecting both the characters and the translation." (JS–H 1:64-65.)

Truly, the Lord's ways are not man's ways, and the Lord will bring the Book of Mormon forth by his own power. "Wherefore it shall come to pass," Nephi prophesies, "that the Lord God will deliver again the book and the words thereof to him that is not learned; and the man that is not learned shall say: I am not learned.

"Then shall the Lord God say unto him [the words that follow are directed to Joseph Smith]: The learned shall not read them, for they have rejected them, and I am able to do mine own work; wherefore thou shalt read the words which I shall give unto thee. Touch not the things which are sealed, for I will bring them forth in mine own due time; for I will show unto the children of men that I am able to do mine own work. Wherefore, when thou hast read the words which I have commanded thee, and obtained the witnesses which I have promised unto thee, then shalt thou seal up the book again, and hide it up unto me, that I may preserve the words which thou hast not read, until I shall see fit in mine own wisdom to reveal all things unto the children of men. For behold, I am God; and I am a God of miracles; and I will show unto the world that I am the same yesterday, today, and forever; and I work not among the children of men save it be according to their faith." (2 Nephi 27:19-23.)

CHAPTER 48

The Book of Mormon and the Restoration

Isaiah, the Book, and the Restoration

After foretelling the sorrows and wars and utter destruction of the Nephites; after announcing that they would speak with a familiar spirit out of the dust; after telling of the sealed book wherein their words would be found; after calling attention to the dire and dark apostasy that would enshroud the earth—then Isaiah (and, of course, Nephi) announces the restoration of the gospel in the last days. That is to say, the Book of Mormon is the foundation upon which the house of the restoration is built. Take it away and there is no restoration, no true church and kingdom of God on earth, no plan of salvation, no power and authority whereby man may be saved and exalted.

We shall quote Isaiah's words (Isaiah 29:13-24) as they have been amplified and improved by Nephi. The first major improvement is the announcement that they are addressed specifically to the Prophet Joseph Smith. Nephi says: "It shall come to pass that the Lord shall say unto him [Joseph Smith] that shall read the words [on the plates of Mormon] that shall be delivered to him: Forasmuch as this people draw near unto me with their mouth, and with their lips do honor me, but have removed their hearts far from me, and their fear towards me is taught by the precepts of men—Therefore, I will proceed to do a marvelous work among this people, yea, a marvelous work and a wonder, for the wisdom of their wise and learned shall perish, and the understanding of their prudent shall be hid." (2 Nephi 27:24-26.)

These words announce the restoration. Universal apostasy shall cease, darkness shall flee, and righteousness shall rain down from heaven. And, indeed, on that glorious spring day in 1820, when the two Personages, glorious beyond description, stood before the young prophet-to-be, the appointed time of restoration had arrived. Young Joseph asked which of all the churches was right and which he should join. "I was answered that I must join none of them," he said, "for they were all wrong; and the Personage who addressed me said that all their creeds were an abomination in his sight; that those professors were all corrupt; that: 'they draw near to me with their lips, but their hearts are far from me, they teach for doctrines the commandments of men, having a form of godliness, but they deny the power thereof.' " (JS–H 1:19.) How well Isaiah knew the very words the Great God would speak in the day of restoration!

And as to the "marvelous work and a wonder," it is the restored gospel. Many were the revelations in the early days of this dispensation that spoke of it, such as: "By your hands I will work a marvelous work among the children of men," saith the Lord, "unto the convincing of many of their sins, that they may come unto repentance, and that they may come unto the kingdom of my Father." (D&C 18:44.)

The Lord's words—given by Isaiah, interpreted by Nephi, and addressed to Joseph Smith—continue: "Wo unto them that seek deep to hide their counsel from the Lord!" Woe unto them that oppose the Lord's work and follow evil counsel in the day of restoration! "And their works are in the dark"—because their deeds are evil—"and they say: Who seeth us, and who knoweth us? And they also say: Surely, your turning of things upside down shall be esteemed as the potter's clay." Some think their opposition to the truth is unknown; others, that the complete revolution in religion, which is born of the restoration, is of no more worth than discarded clay from the potter's wheel.

"But behold, I will show unto them, saith the Lord of Hosts, that I know all their works." Their deeds are recorded in heaven; they are known to Him who notes even the sparrow's fall. How, then, can they escape the condemnation that attends rejecting the new revelations? "For shall the work say of him that made it, he made me not? Or shall the thing framed say of him that framed it, he had no understanding?" God, who made all things, shall in his infinite wisdom properly judge all men according to the deeds done in the flesh.

"But behold, saith the Lord of Hosts: I will show unto the

children of men that it is yet a very little while and Lebanon shall be turned into a fruitful field; and the fruitful field shall be esteemed as a forest." Lebanon, both the mountain and the valley, and adjoining Galilee, and all of Palestine—however desolate they may have been over the years—shall begin to blossom almost as soon as the gospel is restored. It is well known that for many years, Jewish Israel has been engaged in turning its desert homelands into gardens throughout all the land of Palestine.

"And in that day"—that is, in this present hour, when the ancient Israelitish lands, for long intervening generations a desert, are becoming again a fruitful field, as it was in the days of ancient Israel—"shall the deaf hear the words of the book, and the eyes of the blind shall see out of obscurity and out of darkness." The book—the sealed book, the Book of Mormon —shall come forth in that day. And many who have been spiritually deaf and spiritually blind shall hear and see the things of the Spirit, as it was among those anciently who had the pure gospel. "And the meek also shall increase"—the meek are the God-fearing and the righteous—"and their joy shall be in the Lord, and the poor among men shall rejoice in the Holy One of Israel." As it was in the day of Jesus, the poor shall have the gospel preached unto them, and they shall glory in Him who is revealed in the book.

"For assuredly as the Lord liveth they shall see that the terrible one is brought to naught, and the scorner is consumed, and all that watch for iniquity are cut off; and they that make a man an offender for a word, and lay a snare for him that reproveth in the gate, and turn aside the just for a thing of naught." The saints shall see their enemies confounded and destroyed in each category here named. This has its beginning now, but the complete fulfillment shall await the day of vengeance when all the proud and they who do wickedly shall be consumed at His coming.

"Therefore, thus saith the Lord, who redeemed Abraham, concerning the house of Jacob: Jacob shall not now be ashamed, neither shall his face now wax pale." Gathered Israel, as it was with Paul of old, shall not be ashamed of the gospel of Christ, neither shall they fear the face of men. "But when he [Israel] seeth his children, the work of my hands, in the midst of him, they shall sanctify my name, and sanctify the Holy One of Jacob, and shall fear the God of Israel." Israel shall return to the Lord God of their fathers.

Finally—and this brings us back to the book that is so much a part of the restoration—"They also that erred in spirit shall come to understanding, and they that murmured shall learn doctrine." (2 Nephi 27:27-35.) Such is one of the great purposes of the Book of Mormon.

Ezekiel, the Book, and the Restoration

Israel's long and tempestuous history has been one of unity and disunity, of great righteousness and dire iniquity, of serving Jehovah and following Baal; and her divine destiny is to stand supreme as the Lord's chosen people during the coming Millennium. Why has she risen to the heights in one age and sunk to the depths in another? And how will she be reclaimed from her present lost and fallen state so as to inherit the promised blessings?

From the time of the covenant God made with Abraham to the Exodus from Egypt was four hundred and thirty years. On that day, as Israel passed through the Red Sea, with a wall of water on the right hand and on the left, she was born as a free nation; she became a people set apart from the kingdoms of the world; and she reaffirmed the choice of the Lord Jehovah as her King. Then, for more than five hundred years—for more than half a millennium—she remained one people, led by prophets, judged by judges, and reigned over by three kings: Saul, David, and Solomon.

After Solomon came the two kingdoms, the Kingdom of Israel and the Kingdom of Judah. These two nations of kinsmen—divided, unruly, rebellious, sometimes united together against Gentile powers, sometimes fighting each other—never again became the one nation that they once were. After some two and a half centuries, the Kingdom of Israel was carried into Assyrian captivity, whence they—the so-called Ten Tribes—have been lost to the knowledge of men. After nearly four hundred years of their separate kingdom, the Kingdom of Judah—the Jews—were carried into Babylonian captivity, whence a remnant returned in due course to establish the nation and people who dwelt in Palestine in the day of the Lord Jesus.

Ezekiel was one of those carried into Babylon. Knowing that both of the nations of Israel had lost their inheritance in that land which God had promised to Abraham and his seed for an everlasting inheritance, and knowing also that scattered Israel one day must be gathered home to the land of their inheritance and once again be one people, he wondered how it all could come to pass. How shall Israel be gathered? How will they become not just two divided nations, but one kingdom as they were in the days when the Lord was their King and his judges ruled over them?

The answer: it will be brought to pass, in the destined day, by a book and by the restoration of the gospel. Let us hear the word of the Lord on these issues as that word came to Ezekiel the prophet, as he lived in an anguished bondage in a worldly Babylon.

"Moreover, thou son of man, take thee one stick," saith the Lord, "and write upon it, For Judah, and for the children of Israel his companions: then take another stick, and write upon it, For Joseph, the stick of Ephraim, and for all the house of Israel his companions: and join them one to another into one stick; and they shall become one in thine hand." (Ezekiel 37:16-17.) Whether these sticks were boards on which something was written or sticks around which rolls of papyrus were wrapped matters little. The symbolism is the same, and the reference in each instance is to a book, a divine record, a volume of holy scripture kept by the respective peoples. One record is to flow from the Kingdom of Judah, composed in that day of Judah, Benjamin, and those of such other tribal lineages as dwelt in that kingdom. The stick of Judah is the Bible. The other stick, the stick of Joseph in the hands of Ephraim, is symbolical of the Book of Mormon. This record was kept by the house of Joseph, of whom the Nephites were a branch; and because the Church today is composed chiefly of the seed of Ephraim, that record is now in the hands of Ephraim. Moroni, the last of the Nephite prophets, who holds "the keys of the record of the stick of Ephraim" (D&C 27:5), brought that ancient record to light in modern times. Both records, the one from Judah and the one from Joseph, are for the benefit and blessing of all the house of Israel. And these records shall be one in the Lord's hands because they testify of the same Christ, teach the same gospel, breathe the same spirit, and come from the same source.

That God should write his word to more nations than one is not only a glorious truth, but a verity that is so obvious that it ought to be assumed. Are not the remnants of scattered Israel in the Americas as precious in his sight as their kinsmen in the Old World? Is he not the God of the whole earth and not just of the seed of Abraham? And surely he will send prophets to proclaim his word to all those who are prepared and worthy to receive it. And thus it is that he said to Nephi: "I command all men, both in the east and in the west, and in the north, and in the south, and in the islands of the sea, that they shall write the words which I speak unto them; for out of the books which shall be written I will judge the world, every man according to their works, according to that which is written."

Then the Lord particularizes even more than he did to Ezekiel: "For behold, I shall speak unto the Jews and they shall write it; and I shall also speak unto the Nephites and they shall write it; and I shall also speak unto the other tribes of the house of Israel, which I have led away, and they shall write it; and I shall also speak unto all nations of the earth and they shall write it." Can the Lord speak to too many people? Are there nations outside the pale of saving grace who should be denied his word? If such is the case, for a time or a season, it is because they do not hearken unto the light of Christ that leads them to the covenant the Father offers to all men.

"It shall come to pass," saith the Lord, "that the Jews shall have the words of the Nephites, and the Nephites shall have the words of the Jews; and the Nephites and the Jews shall have the words of the lost tribes of Israel; and the lost tribes of Israel shall have the words of the Nephites and the Jews." How many records there are yet to come forth! The world has the Bible, not as it once was but as it now is, and it is the record of the Jews. We have also the Book of Mormon, which is a part of the record of Joseph; and we have received some of the writings of Abraham and Enoch and Moses—some but by no means all. Could it be that if we had more faith and believed and lived in harmony with what we have already received, the Lord would give us more, even now, without waiting for that Millennial day when he will reveal all things?

"And it shall come to pass that my people, which are of the house of Israel, shall be gathered home unto the lands of their possessions; and my word also shall be gathered in one. And I will show unto them that fight against my word and against my people, who are of the house of Israel, that I am God, and that I covenanted with Abraham that I would remember his seed forever." (2 Nephi 29:11-14.) These words of divine origin, given to Nephi in the Western Hemisphere, are akin to and teach the same truths we find in the continuing recitation of the Lord's word by Ezekiel.

"And when the children of thy people shall speak unto thee, saying, Wilt thou not shew us what thou meanest by these? say unto them, Thus saith the Lord God; Behold, I will take the stick of Joseph, which is in the hand of Ephraim, and the tribes of Israel his fellows, and will put them with him, even with the stick of Judah, and make them one stick, and they shall be one in mine hand. And the sticks whereon thou writest shall be in thine hand before their eyes." (Ezekiel 37:18-20.) The Book of Mormon—now in the hands of Ephraim and such of his fellows as have gathered with him, and having a familiar spirit and being like unto the Bible—is now put with that ancient Jewish record, and the two are one in the Lord's hand. We wonder, in this connection, if Ezekiel did not say more to the people than is here recorded. There is no reason why he should not have told them of the remnant of Joseph that escaped from Jerusalem and whose appointment it was to take root downward and bear fruit upward, as Isaiah had prophesied.

But Ezekiel's two sticks that became one are intended to do more than announce the writing of two volumes of scripture that became one. They are a symbol of the gathering of the two kingdoms of Israel into one kingdom in the last days. "And say unto them [thy people], Thus saith the Lord God; Behold, I will take the children of Israel from among the heathen, whither they be gone, and will gather them on every side, and bring them into their own land: and I will make them one nation in the land upon the mountains of Israel; and one king shall be king to them all: and they shall be no more two nations, neither shall they be divided into two kingdoms any more at all." (Ezekiel 37:21-22.)

Israel—all Israel, including those of the Kingdom of Judah

and those of the Kingdom of Israel, who are the Ten Tribes—shall gather, be one, and have one King. There is nothing mysterious or hidden or unknown as to how and why and in what manner Israel—all Israel—shall gather. "Turn, O backsliding children, saith the Lord," by the mouth of Jeremiah, "for I am married unto you: and I will take you one of a city, and two of a family, and I will bring you to Zion. . . . In those days the house of Judah shall walk with the house of Israel, and they shall come together out of the land of the north to the land that I have given for an inheritance unto your fathers." (Jeremiah 3:14, 18.) The process of gathering is now and always will be one in which the scattered remnants of Jacob—those of all tribes—believe the Book of Mormon, accept the restored gospel, and come to the latter-day Zion, there to receive the same blessings that once were showered upon their fathers. This gathering will be one person here, and two there, and a few somewhere else—all by the power of a book, the stick of Joseph joined with the stick of Judah.

When they gather and become one people, they will be a new and a changed people. "Neither shall they defile themselves any more with their idols, nor with their detestable things, nor with any of their transgressions: but I will save them out of all their dwellingplaces, wherein they have sinned, and will cleanse them: so shall they be my people, and I will be their God." They will believe in Christ, repent of their sins, be baptized for the remission of sins, and receive the gift of the Holy Ghost, thereby being cleansed and having their sins burned away as though by fire.

"And David my servant shall be king over them; and they all shall have one shepherd: they shall also walk in my judgments, and observe my statutes, and do them. And they shall dwell in the land that I have given unto Jacob my servant, wherein your fathers have dwelt; and they shall dwell therein, even they, and their children, and their children's children for ever: and my servant David shall be their prince for ever." In that day there shall be one God and one Shepherd over all the earth, and he shall reign forever and ever, for he is Christ, the Second David. And all Israel, gathered securely into his fold, shall keep his commandments and obey his laws.

"Moreover I will make a covenant of peace with them; it shall be an everlasting covenant with them: and I will place

457

them, and multiply them, and will set my sanctuary in the midst of them for evermore. My tabernacle also shall be with them: yea, I will be their God, and they shall be my people. And the heathen shall know that I the Lord do sanctify Israel, when my sanctuary shall be in the midst of them for evermore." (Ezekiel 37:23-28.) In that day all Israel, gathered in from their long dispersion, shall receive the everlasting covenant, which is the everlasting gospel. The Lord's temple shall be in their midst, wherein the other tribes shall come to Ephraim to receive their blessings, according to the promises. There also will be tabernacles of assembly wherein the people will worship. And all men will know that the Lord has fulfilled his promises to Israel, that they are his people and he is their God.

And it will all be brought to pass by a book—the Book of Mormon—and by the restoration to them of the same gospel in which their forebears rejoiced.

CHAPTER 49

Is the
Book of Mormon True?

Opposition to the Book of Mormon

Millions of sincere and devout people now living believe, in the depths of their souls and with all the fire and fervor of a Peter or a Paul, that the Book of Mormon is true, that it is the mind and will and voice of God, that it is holy scripture, and that no person on earth can please the Lord and be saved in his kingdom unless he has such a testimony. This of itself presents no special problem. Believing souls in all ages have been prepared to die for their professions of faith.

The issue centers in nonbelievers. Why should they become exercised in mind and disturbed in spirit because their neighbors and friends and relations choose to believe in any religious system, as long as such does not destroy the rights of others? Religion is a personal matter, and all men are entitled to worship any God of their own choosing, in any way that suits them, as long as their course is decent and does not destroy the rights and freedoms of others.

But, almost strangely, there are other millions of sincere and devout persons who disbelieve, oppose, and openly fight the Book of Mormon. We suppose that the book has more enemies than friends. Why is this so? What is it about some words on a printed page—all of which are clean and uplifting and pertain to historical and doctrinal matters—that arouses such violent antagonisms?

Men ordinarily do not rise up to fight the Bible; they do not organize mobs and incite them to shed the blood of others because such persons believe in the scripture of the Old World. Why should they do so with reference to a companion volume of holy writ based on New World peoples and prophets?

There are those who disbelieve the Bible, of course, but this does not cause them to put to death others who do believe. Neither the atheists nor the communists have any use for the Bible, but they wage no open warfare against the book per se; they do not wear out their lives trying to show that it is false. Even those in Islam, whose whole religion is Koran-based, find no especial fault with the Bible. It is true that they pointedly deny the divinity of Christ and rank him as a prophet like Moses or Abraham, but they do not devote their lives to belittling the book that speaks of Jesus and his ministry. Liberal theologians manage to spiritualize away the plain meaning of many biblical passages, but their assaults are intellectual, and they simply view with contempt and disdain those who are so unlearned as to believe the biblical fables, as they assume the scriptural recitations to be. Many Christians are prone to view the Bible as one-sided history or great literature, but not as inspired writing. Again there is no open warfare on their part against the people who think otherwise.

There is, however, one great difference between the Bible and the Book of Mormon that shows why some people can disbelieve the Bible and let the matter drop, but disbelieving the Book of Mormon, they find themselves compelled to arise in wrath and defame the Nephite record. It is that people who believe the Bible, as they suppose, can also believe any creed of their choice and belong to any church that suits them. But belief in the Book of Mormon presupposes the acceptance of Joseph Smith as a prophet as well as membership in the church organized by him. Such believers accept no creed except the creed of the scriptures and are bound by no code except the code of righteousness.

Further, the Bible is difficult to interpret and understand, and reasonable men, approaching it wholly from an intellectual standpoint, can reach divergent conclusions on almost all doctrines—hence, the many contending sects in Christendom. The Bible is indeed the perfect tool to support every conceivable doctrinal view. But the Book of Mormon is otherwise; this American scripture sets forth the doctrines of salvation in simplicity and plainness so that reasonable men, even from an intellectual standpoint, can scarcely disagree. This leaves religionists in the position where they must freely accept or openly oppose the Nephite scripture. There is no middle ground, no readily available gray area, no room for compromise.

Either the Book of Mormon is true or it is false; either it was translated by the gift and power of God or it was not; either Moroni delivered the ancient record to Joseph Smith or he did not. This brings us to the heart and core of the matter, which is: either Joseph Smith was a prophet or he was not. He and the Book of Mormon go together. Why do men oppose the Book of Mormon? For precisely the same reason they oppose Joseph Smith. The issue is not limited to a book; it embraces the great latter-day work of the Lord in all its parts. If the Book of Mormon is true, Joseph Smith was a prophet; if he was sent of God, The Church of Jesus Christ of Latter-day Saints, which he organized, is the only true and living church upon the face of the whole earth; if this church, and this church only, is the Lord's earthly kingdom, then all other churches are false. Hence, all who contend for some other way of life and salvation must, of necessity, oppose that which would destroy their system.

This, as it happens, was the identical reasoning of those who opposed and crucified Christ. Either the man Jesus, the carpenter's son as they contended, was the Promised Messiah or he was not. And if he was the Son of God, then his words were true, and the whole Mosaic system of worship, with its sacrifices and formalities, was fulfilled in him; and if the day of the law was over and the day of Christ was at hand, then men must accept the new order or be damned. There was no middle ground. If they chose to stand by the traditions of their fathers, they rejected Jesus and his apostles.

Thus, those who oppose Joseph Smith and the Book of Mormon are in the same position as were those who fought and imprisoned and sought to slay the ancient apostles. They must contend against all that has been revealed in our day or admit their system of religion is false. Oh, that they would take the wise advice of Gamaliel, given when those in the Great Sanhedrin "took counsel to slay" the apostles. Said he: "Refrain from these men, and let them alone: for if this counsel or this work be of men, it will come to nought: but if it be of God, ye cannot overthrow it; lest haply ye be found even to fight against God." (Acts 5:33, 38-39.) But such fairmindedness is not to be. Satan lives; the devil is not dead; and he has and does and everlastingly shall oppose the Lord's work. And as we have heretofore shown: "No man will be angry" at the Book of Mormon "save he shall be of the spirit of the devil." (2 Nephi 33:5.)

In truth and in fact, the violent opposition to the Book of Mormon is one of the great evidences of its divinity. If it were not of God, Lucifer would not overly concern himself with it. What is one other book about religion to him, unless it teaches the truth and leads men to love and serve Christ and to prepare for an eternal inheritance with him in the kingdom of his Father?

Let us, then, hear what the Lord has to say about those who reject and oppose the Book of Mormon. "My words"—as set forth in the Nephite record—"shall hiss forth unto the ends of the earth," saith the Lord, "for a standard unto my people, which are of the house of Israel." Scattered Israel in all the nations of the earth shall be guided and governed and gathered by the Book of Mormon. It is the standard around which they shall rally in the last days.

"And because my words shall hiss forth—many of the Gentiles shall say: A Bible! A Bible! We have got a Bible, and there cannot be any more Bible." They refer to the Book of Mormon as the Mormon Bible, and they write in their creeds and stipulate in their articles of religion that the Bible is all sufficient, that it contains all things necessary to salvation, that no doctrine is to be believed unless it is found therein, and— this almost above all—that there will be no new and added revelations to append to those given of old.

"But thus saith the Lord God: O fools, they shall have a Bible; and it shall proceed forth from the Jews, mine ancient covenant people. And what thank they the Jews for the Bible which they receive from them? Yea, what do the Gentiles mean? Do they remember the travails, and the labors, and the pains of the Jews, and their diligence unto me, in bringing forth salvation unto the Gentiles?" (2 Nephi 29:2-4.) If the hearts of the Christians of the world were truly centered on the Bible, as they profess, would they not have an entirely different feeling toward the Jews? Did not Jesus say that "salvation is of the Jews"? (John 4:22.) Was not Jesus a Jew, and did not the Bible come to us through Jewish hands? Can anyone truly believe and reverence the Bible without honoring and thanking the Jews?

"O ye Gentiles, have ye remembered the Jews, mine ancient covenant people? Nay; but ye have cursed them, and have hated them, and have not sought to recover them. But behold, I will return all these things upon your own heads; for I the Lord have not forgotten my people." The true gospel is for all men, Jew and Gentile alike. Those who obey the true gospel love all men, Jew and Gentile alike. That love impels true believers to offer the gospel and all of its blessings, without money and without price, to all of our Father's children. Has this been done through the ages by those who profess to glory in the Jewish Bible and who say that it, and it alone, suffices to bring salvation? Rather, as we view Jewish history during the Christian era, we see little but ill will and hate and bloodshed heaped by Christians upon Jews.

"Thou fool, that shall say: A Bible, we have got a Bible, and we need no more Bible. Have ye obtained a Bible save it were by the Jews?" When the Lord God calls a man a fool, we rather suppose he is a fool; let us remember that what the Lord has spoken, he has spoken, and neither he nor we need make any excuse for it.

"Know ye not that there are more nations than one? Know ye not that I, the Lord your God, have created all men, and that I remember those who are upon the isles of the sea; and that I rule in the heavens above and in the earth beneath; and I bring forth my word unto the children of men, yea, even upon all the nations of the earth?" This is one of those grand occasions in which the Lord reasons with men after the manner of their understanding. And to the questions he asks, there are no sensible answers except those that support and sustain the giving of scripture to receptive people everywhere.

At this point the Lord asks a question that should be an end to all controversy: "Wherefore murmur ye, because that ye shall receive more of my word?" (2 Nephi 29:5-8.) What a plaque these words would make to hang on the door of every cathedral in Christendom! Would any but a fool close the mouth of God and say his words should cease? Speaking of receiving the word of God, Jesus said: "For whosoever receiveth, to him shall be given, and he shall have more abundance;

but whosoever continueth not to receive, from him shall be taken away even that he hath." (JST, Matthew 13:10-11.)

"Know ye not that the testimony of two nations is a witness unto you that I am God, that I remember one nation like unto another? Wherefore, I speak the same words unto one nation like unto another. And when the two nations shall run together the testimony of the two nations shall run together also. And I do this that I may prove unto many that I am the same yesterday, today, and forever; and that I speak forth my words according to mine own pleasure." It is God, not man, who determines when and what the Almighty shall say. Man can no more close the mouth of the Lord than he can stop the sun from rising.

"And because that I have spoken one word ye need not suppose that I cannot speak another; for my work is not yet finished; neither shall it be until the end of man, neither from that time henceforth and forever. Wherefore, because that ye have a Bible ye need not suppose that it contains all my words; neither need ye suppose that I have not caused more to be written." (2 Nephi 29:8-10.) This, then, is the Lord's answer to those who suppose that all of his word is in the Bible and that there is no need for the Book of Mormon. And who can refute the divine logic?

The Blessed Book Is True

Is the Book of Mormon true? So much hinges on the answer to this simple question that there is no way to overstate its importance. It is akin to asking, Was Joseph Smith called of God? Or has the fulness of the everlasting gospel been restored in these last days? Or has the church and kingdom of God been set up again on earth, and is it the one place where men in our day may find salvation? It is not amiss to state that salvation itself depends upon learning the true answers to these and all like questions.

Volumes have been and yet will be written analyzing the Book of Mormon from every aspect. Always the basic issue has been and will continue to be whether the Nephite record is what it purports to be or whether it is a cunningly devised fable and fraud. For our present purposes, we can best serve the cause of truth and righteousness by setting forth the way and means whereby all men may learn whether this American volume of scripture is true or false. Manifestly, our analysis will deal with spiritual things, for we are in the realm of religion, and we are making inquiry about revelations that have come from God in heaven to man on earth. And providentially, the Lord has provided a way whereby these things can be tested and proved so that honest men may know for a surety what the true facts are.

As Moroni came to the close of his own appendages to the monumental work of his father Mormon, this last Nephite prophet recorded "a few words by way of exhortation." They are addressed to us. "When ye shall read these things," he said of the Book of Mormon, "remember how merciful the Lord hath been unto the children of men, from the creation of Adam even down until the time ye shall receive these things, and ponder it in your hearts." He is not, be it noted, asking us to draw a curtain around the Book of Mormon as though it were the only book of scripture ever to flow from prophetic pens. All things must be kept in perspective. He is asking us to ponder what is in the biblical record and to put the writings of Mormon in their proper relationship to all else that has come from the Lord. All these things are to be pondered.

"And when ye shall receive these things," Moroni continues, "I would exhort you that ye would ask God, the Eternal Father, in the name of Christ, if these things are not true; and if ye shall ask with a sincere heart, with real intent, having faith in Christ, he will manifest the truth of it unto you, by the power of the Holy Ghost. And by the power of the Holy Ghost ye may know the truth of all things." (Moroni 10:2-5.) In these plain words of scripture, the way is set forth for the man of God to know by revelation of the truth and divinity not only of the Book of Mormon, but of all things. The truth seeker must read, ponder, and pray—pray sincerely, in faith, with real intent, desiring to receive a witness by the power of the Holy Ghost. Let us consider these three requirements.

1. *Read the Book of Mormon.*

Read it carefully, thoughtfully, in the spirit of prayer and thanksgiving. Read it with an open mind; a mind unshackled by the prejudices of men; a mind open to truth and anxious to learn. Read it as you read the Bible, knowing beforehand that it will overflow with profound truths and that many passages will have deep and hidden meanings. Read it in the spirit of faith, with a believing heart and a contrite spirit. Read it as one who hungers and thirsts after righteousness, who desires to feast upon the words of Christ, who yearns to drink the living water that flows from the Eternal Fountain. Ponder as you read, and pray as you ponder.

2. *Ponder the Book of Mormon doctrines and teachings.*

Casual reading of the Book of Mormon, alone and without more, does not lead to the desired testimony. Words and sentences remain a dead letter until they begin to live in the heart and mind of a reader. Before anyone can sit in judgment on the truth or falsity of the Book of Mormon, he must know what the words say and what they mean. Hence the need to ponder upon the holy word; to give deep consideration to it; to weigh each concept carefully; to meditate, reason, and wonder— indeed, to brood over the whole matter.

There is no promise that the Lord will pour a testimony into a vacuum. Man on his part must do all he can, by himself and alone, before he qualifies for divine guidance. After Oliver Cowdery tried and failed to translate from the plates of Mormon, the Lord told him: "You took no thought save it was to ask me. But, behold, I say unto you, that you must study it out in your mind; then you must ask me if it be right, and if it is right I will cause that your bosom shall burn within you; therefore, you shall feel that it is right." (D&C 9:7-8.) So it is, in like manner, with all who seek a testimony of that which Joseph Smith by faith did, in fact, translate. They must study the matter out in their own minds, reach a conclusion in their own minds, and then ask the Lord for a spiritual confirmation of the conclusion they, by their agency, have already reached.

In this connection, a sincere, searching student may well ask himself, over and over and over again, as he reads and ponders the Book of Mormon: "Could any man have written this book?" Is it too much to ask that this question be asked— in the spirit of faith and with an open heart—one thousand times in the course of reading and pondering the Nephite record? If such a course is followed, there is an absolute guarantee that somewhere between the first and the thousandth time the question is asked, the genuine truth seeker will come to know, by the power of the Spirit, that the book is true.

Here, also, is a suggested personal study program that will

open the eyes of the spiritually blind and unstop the ears of the spiritually deaf. Choose the one hundred most basic doctrines of the gospel, and under each doctrine make two parallel columns, one headed *Bible* and the other *Book of Mormon.* Then place in these columns what each book of scripture says about each doctrine. The end result will show, without question, that in ninety-five of the one hundred cases, the Book of Mormon teaching is clearer, plainer, more expansive, and better than the biblical word. If there is any question in anyone's mind about this, let him take the test—a personal test. The scriptures are before you. Search them; find out for yourself; and in the process, gain a sure and absolute knowledge of the truth and divinity of that which came forth in our day by the hand of Joseph Smith.

3. *Pray for a testimony of the Book of Mormon.*

Ask the Lord if the conclusions you have reached in your study are correct. Ask, and ye shall receive; knock, and it shall be opened unto you. If any of you lack wisdom, let him ask of God—in faith—and it shall be given. Pray in the approved manner—to the Father, in the name of Christ. The answer will come by the power of the Holy Ghost. "I will tell you in your mind and in your heart," saith the Lord, "by the Holy Ghost, which shall come upon you and which shall dwell in your heart. Now, behold, this is the spirit of revelation." (D&C 8:2-3.)

As to the truth and divinity of the Book of Mormon, let us record but one testimony. It is a testimony couched in the most solemn language known to the human tongue; it is a witness that is sworn with an oath; it is the testimony of the Lord God himself. To the Three Witnesses he said of Joseph Smith: "He [the great seer of latter days] has translated the book, even that part which I have commanded him, and as your Lord and your God liveth it is true." (D&C 17:6.)

"The Keystone of Our Religion"

It is written: God "gave him [Joseph Smith] power from on high, by the means which were before prepared [the Urim and Thummim and the power of faith], to translate the Book of Mormon; which contains a record of a fallen people,"—it is an inspired history—"and the fulness of the gospel of Jesus Christ to the Gentiles and to the Jews also." It is also holy scripture. "Which"—meaning the Book of Mormon—"was given by inspiration [to the ancient prophets], and is confirmed to others by the ministering of angels [confirmed to Joseph Smith and the witnesses by angelic ministrations], and is declared unto the world by them." Such is the scriptural setting for the inspired proclamation that the Book of Mormon came forth; "proving to the world that the holy scriptures are true, and that God does inspire men and call them to his holy work in this age and generation, as well as in generations of old; thereby showing that he is the same God yesterday, today, and forever." (D&C 20:8-12.)

In this same connection, Joseph Smith said: "I told the brethren that the Book of Mormon was the most correct of any book on earth, and the keystone of our religion, and a man would get nearer to God by abiding by its precepts, than by any other book." (*Teachings of the Prophet Joseph Smith,* p. 194.) The keystone is the crown of an arch, the stone that holds the whole structure in place; it is thus the force on which all associated things depend.

Thus it is that the Book of Mormon proves, sustains, and upholds all things connected with our whole system of revealed religion. It proves that the Bible is true, that Joseph Smith was a prophet, that the gospel has been restored, that The Church of Jesus Christ of Latter-day Saints is true, and so on and so on. Let us illustrate the reasoning involved.

If the Book of Mormon is true, then Jesus Christ is the Son of the living God and he was crucified for the sins of the world, salvation comes in and through his atoning blood and in no other way, and men may be saved if they obey the laws and ordinances of his gospel. Why? Because this is the teaching of the Book of Mormon.

If the Book of Mormon is true, then Joseph Smith was the prophet called of God to restore the fulness of the gospel and to set up anew among men the church and kingdom of God on earth. How so? Because Joseph Smith received the plates from an angel—a resurrected being—and translated them by the gift and power of God, and received the divine assurance that the translation was correct.

If the Book of Mormon is true, there was a falling away

from the faith once delivered to the primitive saints; a great and abominable church then gained power over nations and kingdoms; there was to be a restoration of eternal truth in the last days; the eventual gathering of all Israel into the true church and fold and to the lands of their inheritance was assured; the American continent would be a land of Zion; gifts and powers and miracles would be restored; and so on and so on and so on—all because the Book of Mormon says so.

The Church and the priesthood and our hope of salvation all stand or fall on the truth or the falsity of the Book of Mormon. It is the keystone of our whole system of revealed religion. There is no impropriety—indeed, there is great wisdom—in such statements as these:

I know that the Father and the Son appeared to Joseph Smith—because the Book of Mormon is true.

I know that Moses and Elias and Elijah and divers angels from dispensations past restored their keys, powers, and authorities, and the majesty of their priesthood—because the Book of Mormon is true.

I know that our chief purpose in life is to create for ourselves eternal family units patterned after the family of God our Heavenly Father; that through celestial marriage and obedience to the eternal laws involved, the family unit continues in eternity; that the glorious gospel of God has provision for the salvation of both the living and the dead; that there will be a literal resurrection, a day of judgment, and a final inheritance for all men in either a celestial, a terrestrial, or a telestial kingdom—because the Book of Mormon is true.

It is implicit in all we have said that the Book of Mormon is the way and means provided by the Lord for presenting to the world the message of the restoration. In all dispensations, ours included, the conclusive and binding witness of the truth is borne by legal administrators who are sent of God to teach his doctrine and testify of his word. But as pertaining to anything that has been or will be written, the Book of Mormon is the greatest of all missionary tools. It contains that portion of the Lord's word which opens the door to salvation for all men in all nations.

One of the sins of the Church is our failure to accept it for what it is and to use it in the divinely appointed way. As to this, the Lord says: "Your minds in times past have been darkened because of unbelief, and because you have treated lightly the things you have received—which vanity and unbelief have brought the whole church under condemnation." Question: What are the things we have received? Answer: The Book of Mormon and the revelations of heaven, which set us apart from the world. It is not our province to rest our case solely on the Bible or upon the word of the Lord as given to ancient peoples. We are to use and rejoice in that which has come to us.

"And this condemnation resteth upon the children of Zion, even all," the revealed word continues. "And they shall remain under this condemnation until they repent and remember the new covenant, even the Book of Mormon and the former commandments which I have given them, not only to say, but to do according to that which I have written—that they may bring forth fruit meet for their Father's kingdom; otherwise there remaineth a scourge and judgment to be poured out upon the children of Zion." To free ourselves of the folly of going along with the world in their teachings—using in the process the ancient word to an almost exclusive degree—we must instead center our attention anew upon the Book of Mormon and upon latter-day revelation.

"For I will forgive you of your sins"—sins of omission; of treating lightly the things that have come to us in this dispensation; of not centering our attention upon the First Vision, upon the restoration of the priesthood, upon the revelations in the Doctrine and Covenants, upon the new covenant that is the Book of Mormon—yes, "I will forgive you of your sins with this commandment—that you remain steadfast in your minds in solemnity and the spirit of prayer, in bearing testimony to all the world of those things which are communicated unto you." (D&C 84:54-61.)

Let us, then, hear the conclusion of the whole matter where the Book of Mormon is concerned. It is holy scripture; it is true; it is another testament of Jesus Christ. It charts the course leading to eternal life. It came forth to testify of Christ; to teach the doctrines of salvation; to stand as an irrefutable witness of the truth and divinity of the Lord's work in the last days. It ties all dispensations together because it proves that the

Bible is true; that Adam and the ancients walked in paths of righteousness; that the gospel has been restored to prepare a people for the Second Coming of the Son of Man; that Israel shall gain her promised Millennial glory; that all mankind may be saved by obedience to the laws and ordinances of the gospel. Indeed, no man in our day can be saved unless he believes the Book of Mormon.

ARTICLE 9

*We believe
all that God has revealed,
all that He does now reveal,
and we believe
that He will yet reveal many great
and important things
pertaining to the Kingdom of God.*

CHAPTER 50

Revelation—the Voice of God

Revelation and Salvation

In ages past we dwelt as spirits in the Divine Presence on some distant sphere; we saw God, heard his voice, and knew he was our Father; we then walked by sight. In this present age we dwell as mortals, cast out of our heavenly home, abiding on the earth of our assignment. We no longer see the face of the Lord, or hear his voice, or remember that he was our Father; a curtain has been lowered between us and the Divine Presence, and we are now walking by faith.

In ages past he ordained and established the plan of salvation, which would enable us to advance and progress and become like him. 'Walk in my ways; do as I say; keep my commandments—and ye shall become as I am,' he said. In that day we knew his law: knew that it came from him, and that he was the author of the plan of salvation; knew that if we obeyed his will, we would be blessed, and that if we walked contrary thereto, we would be cursed.

Now, as fallen men, far from those heavenly heights where light and truth flow ever forth, we are left to ourselves. We have changed, but the eternal plan of the Eternal God goes on everlastingly the same. He is God, and neither he nor his word ever varies. If we are to continue our progress on the road to immortality and eternal life, we must find the way and do whatever is necessary to walk in that blessed course.

This brings us to the great and eternal principle of revelation. Either God speaks and we hear his voice, or the damning curtain of ignorance, unbelief, and disobedience will forever shut us out from his presence. In this sense revelation is the beginning and the end; it is the first great requisite leading to salvation, the one principle upon which all others rest, the rock foundation upon which the whole house of salvation is built. Without revelation there is no witness; with it there is light and truth and knowledge and a hope of eternal life. Revelation is essential to salvation.

If it is life eternal to know the only true God and the Mediator whom he sent to reconcile fallen man to himself; if that God and that Mediator must be revealed or remain forever unknown; if there is such a thing as salvation in the kingdom of God; if there are laws and requirements by obedience to which salvation comes; if, for mortal men, there is a divine way of life leading to a divine reward—all this must be revealed. If there are laws and ordinances and covenants and promises, they must be made manifest. If baptism is essential to salvation; if men must be endowed in holy places with power from on high; if celestial marriage is the gate to exaltation; if there are ways to make one's calling and election sure; if there are certain things we must know to qualify us to stand, free from trembling, before the bar of the Great Jehovah; if, in fine, there is a gospel of the Lord Jesus Christ that is, in fact, the power of God unto salvation—all such must be revealed.

Either there is revelation or we receive nothing from the spiritual realm; either there is revelation or there is no purpose in life, no hope in the future, no glory in Christ or in his atonement. Revelation is truly the beginning and the end, the reality that makes all things possible, the great and grand principle that separates the saints from those in the world who are without God and without hope.

This entire work is a witness testifying that God and his laws must be revealed or he and they will remain forever unknown. Such is implicit in the teachings of each chapter. We have shown that all men receive revelation in the sense of being guided by the light of Christ; that those who follow the promptings and enticings of this good Spirit are led to the covenant of baptism and that the faithful saints then receive revelations in dreams and visions; that angelic ministrants attend them from time to time; that some hear the voice of God and even see his face; and that all are enlightened by the power of the Holy Ghost. In the case of seers, whose office entitles them to use the Urim and Thummim, as Joseph Smith did, revelations are oftentimes given for the benefit and blessing of the Church. It now behooves us to consider a few added concepts relative to this heaven-sent blessing of receiving the mind and will of Him whose we are.

Revelation for the Church

Whenever the Lord has had a people on earth, they have received revelation from appointed prophets, apostles, and seers. If at any time they ceased to receive revelation, they ceased to be the Lord's people. This has been the unvarying course from Adam to the present moment. The receipt of revelation is one of the chief identifying characteristics of the true saints; where there are saints there is revelation, and where there is no revelation the saints of the Most High cease to exist among men. In the same sense, where there is revelation, there is the true church and kingdom of God on earth, and where there is no revelation—coming from apostles, prophets, and seers—there the true church is not. The true church receives revelation from those who are called of God to receive his mind; false churches are not guided by prophets, do not have living apostles and seers, and do not receive the mind and will of the Lord for their day and time.

From Adam to Jesus and his apostles, there was an almost unbroken period of some four thousand years during which appointed leaders received the word of the Lord and announced it to the people. From Adam to Noah, there was no break whatever, nor was there after the flood until those periods in Israelitish history when there was utter and complete rebellion and when the people worshipped Baal or other false gods. It was this rebellion that led, ultimately, to the dispersion of that once-favored people. Prophetic guidance was slight from the days of Malachi to the coming of John the son of Zacharias, although the Aaronic Priesthood itself continued without a break, and many who held it must have been zealous and true to their covenants and ministry. In the Old World the great apostasy was complete sometime during the second century A.D., and in the New World it gained the ascendancy in the fifth century with the destruction of the Nephites.

During the age of universal apostasy, when darkness covered the earth and gross darkness the minds of the people, there was no revelation in the true and full and saving sense. The light of Christ did strive with all men, except those who utterly rebelled and defied every principle of decency and uprightness. Such Satan-led souls, like the Nephites and the Jaredites in the days of their degeneracy and destruction, were evil and wicked persons with whom the Spirit ceased to strive. Many good and noble souls lived during the dark ages, however; and they received guidance from that Spirit which enlighteneth every person born into the world, and in turn gave guidance and direction to nations and peoples. But until the rending of the heavens in 1820, there were no open visions, no angelic ministrations, no prophetic utterances, no seeric sayings, no heavenly guidance of the sort that qualifies men for salvation. From our day forward, on through the Millennial era, and for the short season thereafter, including the day of the great winding-up scene, there will always be revelation from on high for the benefit and blessing of believing souls.

Revelation for the Church and for the world generally, no matter what age is involved, always falls into two categories. First, the Lord reveals the truths of salvation; he tells fallen men of the salvation that is in Christ; and he charts for them the course leading to eternal life. This revelation is the revelation of the gospel, which gospel is the plan of salvation. Second, he gives the special, limited, and single-instance revelations that are needed for the temporal and spiritual salvation of those to whom they are addressed. Thus, Enoch was commanded to build a City of Holiness and to prepare his people to be taken up into heaven without tasting death. Noah was directed to build an ark and save seed through the flood; Moses received the divine commission to lead Israel out of Egypt, through the Red Sea, to the borders of their promised land; and Lehi was called to lead a remnant of Joseph to the New World, where they might take root downward and bear fruit upward according to the prophetic word. By revelation, the meridian saints were led out of Jerusalem before the iron hand of Rome turned the city into rubble and its people into corpses and slaves. Thus it is in every age: the Lord gives his people the direction they need at the moment of their peril and danger. And surely in the days ahead there will be times when nothing but the wisdom of God, descending from heaven and flowing forth from prophetic lips, will be able to save his people.

We do not know the detailed church organization that has existed in all ages. We do know that there have always been keys and priesthood and offices and callings therein; that prophets and apostles have never gone their own independent ways free from the divine discipline of presiding officers. Above all we know that the Lord's house is a house of order and not a house of confusion.

In the dispensation of the fulness of times, which began in the spring of 1820 with the appearance of the Father and the Son to Joseph Smith, revelation has always come through the presiding elder of the kingdom, who is also the President of the Church. During the initial tempering, schooling, preparatory period—from the spring of 1820 to the 6th of April, 1830, when the Church as a formal organization came into being— Joseph Smith, as a prophet, received and delivered such of the mind and will of the Lord as was needed to lay the foundation for what lay ahead. This included the coming forth of the Book of Mormon and the receipt of keys and priesthoods from John the Baptist and from Peter, James, and John. The revealed word contained in sections 2 through 21 of the Doctrine and Covenants came during this period.

Between April 6, 1830, and February 14, 1835, when the first apostles were ordained, the Prophet Joseph Smith led the Church, receiving at least eighty-seven of the sections in the Doctrine and Covenants, and made monumental revisions in the Bible, including the newly revealed material in the Book of Moses. During this early period the as yet untried and spiritually unschooled saints had much to learn about the receipt of revelation, and in some instances some of them were deceived by evil powers. Satan gave some revelations to Hiram Page that deceived even Oliver Cowdery, the second elder and the one who held the keys of the kingdom jointly with the Prophet. As a consequence, in a revelation given through the Prophet in September 1830, the Lord told Oliver Cowdery: "No one shall be appointed to receive commandments and revelations in this church excepting my servant Joseph Smith, Jun., for he receiveth them even as Moses." Oliver might speak, teach, and command as the Comforter directed. "But thou shalt not write by way of commandment, but by wisdom; and thou shalt not command him who is at thy head, and at the head of the church." No one ever receives a true revelation for anyone in a position higher than his. "For I have given him [Joseph Smith] the keys of the mysteries, and the revelations which are sealed, until I shall appoint unto them another in his stead. . . . And thou shalt have revelations, but write them not by way of commandment." (D&C 28:2-8.)

Later, in February 1831, when some members of the Church were disturbed by people making false claims as revelators, the Lord referred to the revelations and commandments given through Joseph Smith and then said: "This ye shall know assuredly—that there is none other appointed unto you to receive commandments and revelations until he be taken, if he abide in me." The Lord always honors his prophets, and he never sends others to do what they suppose the prophets have left undone. "And this shall be a law unto you, that ye receive not the teachings of any that shall come before you as revelations or commandments; and this I give unto you that you may not be deceived, that you may know they are not of me." (D&C 43:2-6.)

After the organization of the Church was perfected, with the President of the Church appointed "to be a presiding elder over all my church, to be a translator, a revelator, a seer, and prophet"; after "the First Presidency" was appointed "to receive the oracles for the whole church" (D&C 124:125-126); after the Twelve were called "to officiate in the name of the Lord, under the direction of the Presidency of the Church, agreeable to the institution of heaven; to build up the church, and regulate all the affairs of the same in all nations" (D&C 107:33); and after the Twelve were given, in 1844 in Nauvoo, all of the keys and powers held by the Prophet himself—then fifteen men were called and sustained as prophets, seers, and revelators in the full and complete sense of the word. As any one of these magnifies his calling, he may speak in the name of the Lord, acting for and on behalf of Him whose witness he is, teaching, counseling, exhorting, pleading. But in the full and unrestricted sense his prophetic calling, so far as leading and commanding the Church to walk in a particular course is concerned, lies dormant unless and until he becomes the senior apostle of God on earth. Then he, as the President of the Church, exercises the keys of the kingdom and all of the prophetic, seeric, and revelatory endowments, in their fulness. Then, and then only, can he direct the Church to pursue whatever course the Lord intends.

Truly, the Lord's house is a house of order, and no one need be deceived as to where to look for revelation or whose voice to follow.

Revelations of the Future

Revelation is as eternal as God himself; he is the Eternal Revelator. When he speaks, his words are revelation; they set forth what is in his heart and mind, and he cannot exist without speaking. Should revelation cease, God would cease to be God, the purposes of creation would come to naught, and all things would vanish away—all of which is beyond the realm of possibility. The receipt of revelation by mortals is quite another thing. Such is gained by obedience to law. The Eternal Broadcaster may send forth his word throughout all immensity, but only those whose souls are attuned to the same wave band on which he is speaking are able to hear and receive the divine word.

Revelations came in days past; revelations come now; and revelations will continue as long as the earth shall stand. Those saints whose souls are attuned to the Infinite believe all that God has revealed; they need only be taught that any particular truth came by revelation, and they automatically believe it. These same contrite souls believe all that God does now reveal. Those of Gentile blood or leanings may say within themselves: "I must test this newly announced revelation; I must compare it with all else I know, whether from spiritual or secular sources. Surely the Lord expects me to use my agency and make an intelligent decision. I, therefore, am the one who must determine whether the prophetic voice is speaking for the Lord or only as an uninspired man." But those who are enlightened by the power of the Spirit know by spiritual instinct, without argument, without persuasion, without debate, that any authoritatively announced revelation came from the Divine Source.

In like manner, true saints not only believe (and know!) that God will yet reveal many great and important things pertaining to his kingdom both on earth and in heaven, but they also, in a very real sense, believe in advance the divine word that is yet to come. It was Alma who said: "It has thus"—

through mighty fasting and prayer—"been revealed unto me, that the words which have been spoken by our fathers are true." Alma believed the revelations of the past; his knowledge came by the spirit of prophecy as poured out by the Spirit of God. And further: "I say unto you, that I know of myself that whatsoever I shall say unto you, concerning that which is to come, is true." (Alma 5:47-48.) Alma believed the revelations that were yet to come. His spiritual maturity permitted him to know that whatever he—or anyone—should thereafter say by the power of the Holy Ghost would in the very nature of things be true. Spiritually enlightened minds always know that the word of the Lord is truth; God did not lie in the past, nor does he now, nor will he do so to all eternity. Thus the true saints say in their hearts: "Speak, Lord. Let thy servants hear, and we will believe thy word. If it runs counter to our previous views or to the wisdom of the worldly wise, no matter. Thou knowest all things, and we believe thy word, let it be whatsoever it may be."

False churches rely on the revelations of the past and somehow assume that because men of old had the faith to pull down the revelations of heaven, men today, without that faith, are yet heirs of the same blessings. In the true church the emphasis is not on the past or even on the present alone, but on the future. The testimony of the Latter-day Saints, borne by the spirit of prophecy and revelation at the time of the organization of the Church, is that we shall neither add to nor diminish from the revelations of John, nor the prophecy of his book, nor the holy scriptures (meaning the Bible), nor "the revelations of God which shall come hereafter by the gift and power of the Holy Ghost, the voice of God, or the ministering of angels." (D&C 20:35.) Members of the true church always rejoice in the revelations of the present but look forward with joyful anticipation to those of the future. "For I deign to reveal unto my church," saith the Lord, "things which have been kept hid from before the foundation of the world, things that pertain to the dispensation of the fulness of times." (D&C 124:41.)

There is an awful woe pronounced upon those who "deny . . . the spirit of revelation" and "the spirit of prophecy." (D&C 11:25.) "Wo be unto him that shall say: We have received the word of God, and we need no more of the word of God, for we have enough! For behold, thus saith the Lord God: I will give unto the children of men line upon line, precept upon precept, here a little and there a little; and blessed are those who hearken unto my precepts, and lend an ear unto my counsel, for they shall learn wisdom; for unto him that receiveth I will give more; and from them that shall say, We have enough, from them shall be taken away even that which they have." (2 Nephi 28:29-30.)

We know only droplets of truth taken from an immense ocean; we have drunk only a few swallows from the streams of living water; there is so much more to learn. Why, then, should we take offense if the God of Truth chooses to make more of his eternal word available to us?

There is so much that we do not know—more, in fact, than all the understanding that now is ours. We know but little about God and his glory and the laws by which he created worlds without number. What do we know about the sidereal heavens and the endless galaxies spinning through boundless space? Our knowledge of the creation of even this little dot of dust known as planet earth is so slight that we can scarcely envision its place in the eternal orbits and its relationship to the endless worlds that roll everlastingly forth from the Creator's hand. What of life in all its forms and varieties, on this and other worlds, and in the realm of the spirit and of mortality?

We have only a bare outline of our birth as spirits; of the life we then lived, its length, and the nature of our premortal tests; and of our associations there and the affinities we had one for another. What do we know of life in the Edenic paradise, of the fall of man and all forms of life, and even of the earth itself? And what of the nations of men both before the flood and since the day those earth-covering waters swept over the highest peaks and immersed the earth according to the baptismal similitude? How did the various nations come into being, and why the differences in physical characteristics?

What also of the sheep of the Lord's pastures in days gone by? When they come to light, what will we find in the writings of Joseph the son of Jacob, of Gad the seer in Israel, of Zenos, Zenock, Neum, and Ezias, all of whom were Israelitish prophets? Do the Brass Plates contain the writings of other prophets than these, writings that are yet to come forth? Did Adam and Seth, Enos and Cainan, Mahalaleel and Jared, Lamech and Noah—all of whom had patriarchal stature before the flood—write the mind and will of the Lord in their days? We assume they did, and if so, such will surely be revealed in due course. And what of Jethro, Caleb, Elihu, Jeremy, Gad, and Esaias of Abraham's day, through all of whom the holy priesthood descended—who are they, what peoples did they minister among, and what records have they left? And Enoch, the seventh from Adam, than whom there has scarcely been a more righteous man on earth, what of him and his writings and the people whom he guided to translation so that they were taken up into heaven without tasting death—what of Enoch and all his people? And, for that matter, there is John the Revelator and also the Three Nephites, all living on earth until the Second Coming—where are they, with whom do they labor, and why are they so appointed?

Do we know so much as a thousandth part of the doings and sayings of our Lord among the Jews? Or among the Nephites? We know nothing as yet of his ministry to the lost tribes of the house of Israel. Ought not all these things to come forth for our edification and enlightenment? And what else is there in the way of lost scripture, the existence of which has not even crossed our minds? We can think also of the Second Coming, life during the Millennial era, what is going on in paradise and hell, the nature and manner of the resurrection, life in the kingdoms of glory, and ten thousand times ten thousand other things, all of which are so little known by us mortals. Would it violate some great and eternal purpose for us to learn all things as rapidly as we are able to receive added light and knowledge from the Source of Truth?

We rejoice in the revelations that have come since March 1, 1842, when the Prophet sent forth the word in the Articles of Faith, including the pronouncement that more things were yet to be revealed. Since that day the wondrous concepts in sections 130 and 131 of the Doctrine and Covenants have come to us; also the great truths relative to salvation for the dead in sections 127, 128, and 138; and more recently, as announced on June 8, 1978, the heaven-sent word that the holy priesthood, celestial marriage, and all of the blessings of the gospel are now to go to all men, without reference to race or culture. That the receipt of this revelation on priesthood is one of the signs of the times is now apparent to all. And what has been revealed—in all fields—is but prelude to what yet shall come forth, for the voice of God shall never cease to speak, and the words that fall from his lips are endless.

How soul-satisfying it is to know that we stand on the threshold of the house of revelation and that that which is yet to come will know no bounds. It will include the restoration of all that has ever been revealed in any dispensation of the past and also "knowledge . . . that has not been revealed since the world was until now; which our forefathers have awaited with anxious expectation to be revealed in the last times, which their minds were pointed to by the angels, as held in reserve for the fulness of their glory." All of the hopes and yearnings and desires of all the holy prophets will find fruition in the coming day; all of their prophecies will be fulfilled, and they will join with mortals in the great winding-up scenes yet to be enacted.

We look forward to the future with joy; it will be "a time to come in the which nothing shall be withheld, whether there be one God or many gods, they shall be manifest. All thrones and dominions, principalities and powers, shall be revealed and set forth upon all who have endured valiantly for the gospel of Jesus Christ. And also, if there be bounds set to the heavens or to the seas, or to the dry land, or to the sun, moon, or stars— all the times of their revolutions, all the appointed days, months, and years, and all the days of their days, months, and years, and all their glories, laws, and set times, shall be revealed in the days of the dispensation of the fulness of times—according to that which was ordained in the midst of the Council of the Eternal God of all other gods before this world was, that should be reserved unto the finishing and the end thereof, when every man shall enter into his eternal presence and into his immortal rest." (D&C 121:26-32.)

How wondrous it is to know that "when the Lord shall come, he shall reveal all things—things which have passed, and hidden things which no man knew, things of the earth, by which it was made, and the purpose and the end thereof— things most precious, things that are above, and things that are beneath, things that are in the earth, and upon the earth, and in heaven." (D&C 101:32-34.)

Fools say, "Revelation has ceased, and the canon of scripture is full." The saints of God testify, "Revelation has scarcely begun; and if we are true and faithful, we shall receive revelation upon revelation until we know all things and therefore become like Him from whom revelation comes."

CHAPTER 51

Personal Revelation

Personal Revelation—Essential to Salvation

Revelation is essential to salvation; without it, no one can be saved in the kingdom of heaven. The Lord God is the author of salvation. He created a heavenly kingdom as a home for saved beings, and he ordained and established the laws by obedience to which an inheritance may be won in that eternal realm. But unless and until he speaks, those laws remain unknown; man remains in his lost and fallen state; and the heavenly kingdom is a house unoccupied. Hence, the Lord calls prophets and seers to whom he reveals the plan of salvation so that they in turn can teach its truths to the residue of men. Without revelation—the general revelation to the Church and to the world of the plan of salvation—there could be no salvation for anyone on earth.

But there is more to the doctrine of revelation than the calling of apostles and prophets and the sending of them forth to proclaim the gospel to the world. The very gospel plan itself requires that every believing soul attune himself to the Infinite and get personal revelation in order to be saved. Personal revelation to the weak and the simple and the lowly is as essential to salvation as is the general revelation that comes to the spiritual giants who proclaim light to the world.

Almost always the first revelation received by an investigator is called a testimony. By definition and in its nature, a testimony is to know, by revelation from the Holy Ghost, that Jesus Christ is the Son of the Living God; that he was crucified for the sins of the world; that Joseph Smith is the prophet called of God to restore the fulness of the everlasting gospel and to stand as a legal administrator in this day and time; and that The Church of Jesus Christ of Latter-day Saints is the kingdom of God on earth, the sole place where salvation may be found for all persons now living. Again, almost always, this testimony comes by the power of the Holy Ghost to those who read, ponder, and pray about—in faith and with a sincere heart—that holy book, the Book of Mormon.

There is no such thing as gaining a testimony without receiving revelation, because a testimony consists of learning from a divine source of the truth and verity of the Lord's latter-day work. It comes by the power of the Holy Ghost, and as Joseph Smith so aptly expresses it, "No man can receive the Holy Ghost without receiving revelations. The Holy Ghost is a revelator." (*Teachings of the Prophet Joseph Smith,* p. 328.)

After baptism, believing souls receive the gift of the Holy Ghost by the laying on of hands. This gift is the right to the constant companionship of that member of the Godhead, based on faithfulness. Those who actually enjoy the gift are thus in a position to gain continuing revelations from the Revelator, all in harmony with Moroni's promise: "And by the power of the Holy Ghost ye may know the truth of all things." (Moroni 10:5.) This gift of the Holy Ghost is offered to everyone. Peter, on the day of Pentecost, said to a great congregation assembled out of many nations: "Repent, and be baptized every one of you in the name of Jesus Christ for the remission of sins, and ye shall receive the gift of the Holy Ghost. For the promise is unto you, and to your children, and to all that are afar off, even as many as the Lord our God shall call." (Acts 2:38-39.) The receipt of this gift, which cannot come without revelation, thus makes revelation itself available to all. The receipt of this heaven-sent boon is not limited to prophets, seers, and revelators; it is for every member of the Church.

The Holy Ghost, as Nephi expresses it in a passage of superlative meaning and beauty, "is the gift of God unto all those who diligently seek him, as well in times of old as in the time that he should manifest himself unto the children of men. For he is the same yesterday, to-day, and forever; and the way is prepared for all men from the foundation of the world, if it so be that they repent and come unto him. For he that diligently seeketh shall find; and the mysteries of God shall be unfolded unto them, by the power of the Holy Ghost, as well in these times as in times of old, and as well in times of old as in times to come; wherefore, the course of the Lord is one eternal round."

(1 Nephi 10:17-19.) In harmony with these words of transcendent beauty are those of latter-day revelation that say simply to every member of the Church: "God shall give unto you knowledge by his Holy Spirit, yea, by the unspeakable gift of the Holy Ghost." (D&C 121:26.) Such is the promise, and the promise is sure. The sole need on the part of any individual is to comply with the law that entitles him to receive the promised revelation.

Thus revelation—personal revelation—is the rock foundation upon which the church and kingdom of God is built. After Peter had borne witness that our blessed Lord was "the son of the living God," Jesus commended and blessed the Chief Apostle and said: "Flesh and blood hath not revealed it unto thee, but my Father which is in heaven," by the power of the Holy Ghost. Peter at that very moment had received personal revelation. "And upon this rock"—the rock of revelation—"I will build my church; and the gates of hell shall not prevail against it," Jesus said. (Matthew 16:16-18.) Every member of the Church must stand where Peter stood and receive the same personal revelation that came to him; and as long as such is the case in the church and kingdom on earth, the gates of hell shall not prevail against the Lord's people. It is only when they lose their testimonies and no longer are in tune with the promptings of the Holy Spirit that Satan takes over and apostasy and evil prevail.

Paul bore a comparable witness about himself. In exhorting the Galatians to believe only that gospel which he had preached to them, he testified: "I certify you, brethren, that the gospel which was preached of me is not after man." Man did not originate it; it came from God. "For I neither received it of man, neither was I taught it, but by the revelation of Jesus Christ." (Galatians 1:11-12.) It was with Paul as it is with us—of course we are taught the gospel by others; of course we study it out of the revealed word; but in the final analysis, it comes to us by revelation, the Holy Spirit of God bearing witness to the spirit within us that the holy word is true. In the ultimate and true sense, it does not come to us by the power of man, but by the power of God. And thus we build our house of salvation upon the rock of revelation.

Personal revelation is not limited to gaining a testimony and knowing thereby that Jesus, through whom the gospel came, is Lord of all, nor is it limited to receiving guidance in our personal and family affairs—although these are the most common examples of revelation among the Lord's people. In truth and in verity, there is no limit to the revelations each member of the Church may receive. It is within the power of every person who has received the gift of the Holy Ghost to see visions, entertain angels, learn the deep and hidden mysteries of the kingdom, and even see the face of God.

If all things operate by law, and they do; if God is no respecter of persons, and certainly he is perfectly impartial; if his course is one eternal round, never varying from age to age, and such truly is the case—then all of the gifts and graces and revelations ever given to any prophet, seer, or revelator in any age will be given again to any soul who obeys the law entitling him so to receive. While discoursing about the Second Comforter, and in setting forth that those whose callings and elections have been made sure have the privilege of seeing the face of the Lord while they yet dwell in the flesh, the Prophet Joseph Smith said: "God hath not revealed anything to Joseph, but what He will make known unto the Twelve, and even the least Saint may know all things as fast as he is able to bear them." (*Teachings of the Prophet Joseph Smith,* p. 149.)

Paul quoted Isaiah's inspired teachings about the mysteries of the kingdom in this way: "Eye hath not seen, nor ear heard, neither have entered into the heart of man, the things which God hath prepared for them that love him." Then the ancient apostle made this pronouncement, which only one guided by the same Spirit that possessed Isaiah could make: "But God hath revealed them unto us by his Spirit: for the Spirit searcheth all things, yea, the deep things of God." (1 Corinthians 2:9-10.) Truly, as Jesus said: "The Spirit of truth . . . will guide you into all truth." (John 16:13.) By his power men may know the truth of all things, see all visions, learn all the mysteries.

One of the grandest visions ever given to men on earth came to Joseph Smith and Sidney Rigdon on the 16th day of February in 1832. As an introduction to this unfolding of the degrees of glory in the resurrection, we have these divine words: "For thus saith the Lord—I, the Lord, am merciful and gracious unto those who fear me, and delight to honor those who serve me in righteousness and in truth unto the end." Be it noted that the Lord desires and seeks to give revelations and visions to his servants; nothing pleases him more than to have them attain that state of spiritual perfection in which they can be enlightened from on high. Of those so attaining, he continues: "Great shall be their reward and eternal shall be their glory. And to them will I reveal all mysteries, yea, all the hidden mysteries of my kingdom from days of old, and for ages to come, will I make known unto them the good pleasure of my will concerning all things pertaining to my kingdom. Yea, even the wonders of eternity shall they know, and things to come will I show them, even the things of many generations. And their wisdom shall be great, and their understanding reach to heaven; and before them the wisdom of the wise shall perish, and the understanding of the prudent shall come to naught. For by my Spirit will I enlighten them, and by my power will I make known unto them the secrets of my will— yea, even those things which eye has not seen, nor ear heard, nor yet entered into the heart of man." (D&C 76:5-10.)

Father Lehi's family gives us one of the best illustrations in all the scriptures of how personal revelation comes to men. First, Lehi searched the scriptures (the Brass Plates), pondered their truths in his heart, sought the Lord in prayer, and then received visions and revelations. These, along with many prophetic words, he expounded to his family. Then Nephi sought for the same blessings. "It came to pass," he said, "after I had desired to know the things that my father had seen, and believing that the Lord was able to make them known unto me, as I sat pondering in mine heart I was caught away in the Spirit of the Lord." (1 Nephi 11:1.) Nephi then saw what his father had seen and more.

Later, Nephi's brethren were disputing among themselves about Lehi's teachings. They said: "Behold, we cannot understand the words which our father hath spoken." Nephi responded: "Have ye inquired of the Lord?" Their reply: "We have not; for the Lord maketh no such thing known unto us." To this Nephi exclaimed: "How is it that ye do not keep the commandments of the Lord? How is it that ye will perish, because of the hardness of your hearts? Do ye not remember the things which the Lord hath said?—If ye will not harden your hearts, and ask me in faith, believing that ye shall receive, with diligence in keeping my commandments, surely these things shall be made known unto you." (1 Nephi 15:7-11.)

The Crowning Revelation of Life

What greater personal revelation could anyone receive than to see the face of his Maker? Is not this the crowning blessing of life? Can all the wealth of the earth, all of the powers of the world, and all of the honors of men compare with it? And is it an unseemly or unrighteous desire on man's part to hope and live and pray, all in such a way as to qualify for so great a manifestation?

There is a true doctrine on these points, a doctrine unknown to many and unbelieved by more, a doctrine that is spelled out as specifically and extensively in the revealed word as are any of the other great revealed truths. There is no need for uncertainty or misunderstanding; and surely, if the Lord reveals a doctrine, we should seek to learn its principles and strive to apply them in our lives. This doctrine is that mortal man, while in the flesh, has it in his power to see the Lord, to stand in his presence, to feel the nail marks in his hands and feet, and to receive from him such blessings as are reserved for those only who keep all his commandments and who are qualified for that eternal life which includes being in his presence forever. Let us at least sample the holy word and see what the Lord has promised as to seeing his face and being in his presence while we are yet pilgrims far removed from our heavenly home.

1. *The pure in heart shall see God.*

Our text for the whole presentation relative to seeing the Lord comes from the very Sermon on the Mount itself; the matter is just that basic. "Blessed are all the pure in heart, for they shall see God." (3 Nephi 12:8; Matthew 5:8.) And who are those to whom such a glorious promise is made? They are those among the saints who in full measure are free from sin. Purity of heart is a figure for purity of soul. They are the ones who received a remission of their sins in the waters of baptism; who, after baptism, have so lived as to retain a remission of sins; who have had their sins burned out of their souls as though by fire by the power of the Holy Ghost. They are God-fearing and righteous souls; and being pure, they qualify to see and associate with other pure beings, the chief of whom is the Lord of Purity who dwells in the heavens, but on occasion visits his pure saints here on earth.

2. *The saints shall see the Lord.*

How sweet, how tender, how loving and gracious are these kind words spoken by the Lord of Heaven to his saints on earth: "Behold, ye are little children and ye cannot bear all things now." You have just begun to grow in gospel grace and wondrous wisdom. "Ye must grow in grace and in the knowledge of the truth." You must learn my word and believe my doctrine. "Fear not, little children, for you are mine, and I have overcome the world, and you are of them that my Father hath given me; and none of them that my Father hath given me shall be lost." Such is the ancient promise; such is the promise to those who believe in this day. "The Father and I are one. I am in the Father and the Father in me; and inasmuch as ye have received me, ye are in me and I in you." The Lord and his saints are one because the saints have the mind of Christ. "Wherefore, I am in your midst, and I am the good shepherd, and the stone of Israel. He that buildeth upon this rock shall never fall. And the day cometh that you shall hear my voice and see me, and know that I am." (D&C 50:40-45.) Can it be otherwise with the pure in heart? Our sole need is to keep the commandments and grow in grace until we qualify to receive the promised blessing.

3. *We should seek his face.*

Does it seem unseemly to seek such a spiritual reward as seeing the face of the Lord? Is it presumptuous, improper, beyond the bounds of propriety? Hear this divine counsel to the saints: "Care for the soul, and for the life of the soul. And seek the face of the Lord always, that in patience ye may possess your souls, and ye shall have eternal life." (D&C 101:37-38.) We seek eternal life, which is life in the Divine Presence. To receive this greatest of all the gifts of God, we must be worthy to dwell in that Celestial Presence. Ought we not—nay, must we not—then become worthy, here and now, and thus qualify for the divine association that we hope to enjoy forever in the realms ahead?

4. *Those who believe and obey shall see him.*

There is scarcely a more profound and glorious promise in all holy writ than is contained in these words of the Lord to his great latter-day prophet: "It shall come to pass that every soul who forsaketh his sins and cometh unto me, and calleth on my name, and obeyeth my voice, and keepeth my commandments, shall see my face and know that I am." (D&C 93:1.) Come unto Christ; forsake your sins; pray mightily; keep the commandments; live as becometh a true saint—all this in full measure—and the Lord will unveil his face to you as he has done in days past to others who pursued the same course in their day.

5. *Those who are sanctified shall see the Father.*

Without "the power of godliness," meaning without righteousness, "no man can see the face of God, even the Father, and live." The unrighteous would be consumed in his presence. "Now this Moses plainly taught to the children of Israel in the wilderness, and sought diligently to sanctify his people that they might behold the face of God." To be sanctified is to be clean, pure, spotless, free from sin. In the ultimate and final day, the sanctified will be those of the celestial kingdom, the kingdom where God and Christ dwell. "But they [the children of Israel] hardened their hearts and could not endure his presence"—because they would not become pure in heart—"therefore, the Lord in his wrath, for his anger was kindled against them, swore that they should not enter into his rest while in the wilderness, which rest is the fulness of his glory." (D&C 84:21-24.) All Israel might have seen the Lord had they taken the counsel of Moses, but only a few did. On one occasion, for instance, Moses and Aaron, Nadab and Abihu who were Aaron's sons, and "seventy of the elders of Israel . . . saw the God of Israel," while the hosts with whom Moses had labored remained in their dark and benighted state. (Exodus 24:9-10.)

6. *Those who see God are quickened and transfigured.*

Moses "saw God face to face, and he talked with him, and the glory of God was upon Moses; therefore Moses could endure his presence." Speaking of this personal visitation of the Almighty, Moses said: "Mine own eyes have beheld God; but not my natural, but my spiritual eyes, for my natural eyes could not have beheld; for I should have withered and died in his presence; but his glory was upon me; and I beheld his face, for I was transfigured before him." (Moses 1:2, 11.) Again the message is one of personal righteousness, for which there is no substitute.

7. *No sinful man can see the Lord.*

On one occasion "the Lord spake unto Moses face to face,

as a man speaketh unto his friend." On another the Lord said to the great lawgiver of Israel: "Thou canst not see my face at this time, lest mine anger be kindled against thee also, and I destroy thee, and thy people; for there shall no man among them see me at this time, and live, for they are exceeding sinful. And no sinful man hath at any time, neither shall there be any sinful man at any time, that shall see my face and live." (JST, Exodus 33:11, 20.) And again the message is one of personal righteousness.

8. *The righteous see him while in the flesh.*

We must not wrest the scriptures and suppose that the promises of seeing the Lord refer to some future day, either a Millennial or a celestial day, days in which, as we all know, the Lord will be present. The promises apply to this mortal sphere in which we now live. This is clearly set forth in the Vision of the Degrees of Glory. After Joseph Smith and Sidney Rigdon had seen the Father and the Son, concourses of angels, and the wonders of each kingdom of glory, and after they had written the account thereof, their continuing language says: "Great and marvelous are the works of the Lord, and the mysteries of his kingdom which he showed unto us, which surpass all understanding in glory, and in might, and in dominion; which he commanded us we should not write while we were yet in the Spirit, and are not lawful for man to utter; neither is man capable to make them known, for they are only to be seen and understood by the power of the Holy Spirit, which God bestows on those who love him, and purify themselves before him; to whom he grants this privilege of seeing and knowing for themselves; that through the power and manifestation of the Spirit, while in the flesh, they may be able to bear his presence in the world of glory." (D&C 76:114-118.) While in the flesh! For those who "purify themselves before him," this is the time and the day and the hour when they have power to see their God!

9. *The Melchizedek Priesthood prepares men to see the Lord.*

Everything connected with the Melchizedek Priesthood is designed to prepare men for eternal life in the presence of God. That preparation goes on in this life. Hence, as the revealed word attests, those who hold this holy order "have the privilege of receiving the mysteries of the kingdom of heaven, to have the heavens opened unto them, to commune with the general assembly and church of the Firstborn, and to enjoy the communion and presence of God the Father, and Jesus the mediator of the new covenant." (D&C 107:19.) This priesthood prepares men to see both the Father and the Son. "This greater priesthood administereth the gospel and holdeth the key of the mysteries of the kingdom, even the key of the knowledge of God." And it was because ancient Israel refused to use this holy priesthood to prepare themselves to see God that the Lord "took Moses out of their midst, and the Holy Priesthood also." (D&C 84:19, 25.)

10. *The elders of Israel may see the Lord.*

To all who hold the Melchizedek Priesthood, the Lord gives this promise: "It is your privilege, and a promise I give unto you that have been ordained unto this ministry, that inasmuch as you strip yourselves from jealousies and fears, and humble yourselves before me, for ye are not sufficiently humble, the veil shall be rent and you shall see me and know that I am—not with the carnal neither natural mind, but with the spiritual. For no man has seen God at any time in the flesh, except quickened by the Spirit of God. Neither can any natural man abide the presence of God, neither after the carnal mind. Ye are not able to abide the presence of God now, neither the ministering of angels; wherefore, continue in patience until ye are perfected. Let not your minds turn back; and when ye are worthy, in mine own due time, ye shall see and know that which was conferred upon you by the hands of my servant Joseph Smith, Jun." (D&C 67:10-14.) If seventy of the elders of Israel saw the Lord in Moses' day, should not seventy thousand see him today? Or, better, should not all the elders of the kingdom receive the privilege that is theirs? The answer is that they have fears, jealousies, and lack humility; they are yet carnal and have not overcome the world. When they become worthy, they shall see the Lord, for such is their privilege. Ordination to any office in the Melchizedek Priesthood is an open invitation to see the face of Him whose priesthood it is.

11. *Temple ordinances prepare us to see the Lord.*

Thus saith the Lord: "Sanctify yourselves that your minds become single to God, and the days will come that you shall see him; for he will unveil his face unto you, and it shall be in his own time, and in his own way, and according to his own will. Remember the great and last promise which I have made unto you; cast away your idle thoughts and your excess of laughter far from you. . . . Sanctify yourselves; yea, purify your hearts, and cleanse your hands and your feet before me, that I may make you clean." Whoso hath ears to hear, let him hear; those with understanding will envision what the Lord is here saying. And all of it has this end in mind: "That I may testify unto your Father, and your God, and my God, that you are clean from the blood of this wicked generation; that I may fulfil this promise, this great and last promise [this promise of seeing my face], which I have made unto you, when I will." (D&C 88:68-75.)

12. *The Lord may be seen in the temple.*

A temple is a house of the Lord; it has been given to him as a place where he may lay his head, as it were; it is his earthly abode. What is more natural, when he visits an area of the earth, than to come to his house in that area? This is his practice; so he said with reference to one of his temples, and it applies in principle to them all: "Inasmuch as my people build a house unto me in the name of the Lord, and do not suffer any unclean thing to come into it, that it be not defiled, my glory shall rest upon it; yea, and my presence shall be there, for I will come into it, and all the pure in heart that shall come into it shall see God. But if it be defiled I will not come into it, and my glory shall not be there; for I will not come into unholy temples." (D&C 97:15-17.)

13. *Faith and knowledge prepare us to see the Lord.*

Scriptural accounts of the appearances of the Lord to prophets and righteous men of old are patterns for us. They let us know that if we obey the same laws obeyed by those of old, we shall receive and inherit in our day as they did in theirs. Thus, in commenting upon the appearance of the Lord Jesus to Jared's brother (Moriancumer), Moroni says: "Because of the knowledge of this man he could not be kept from beholding within the veil; and he saw the finger of Jesus, which, when he saw, he fell with fear; for he knew that it was the finger of the Lord; and he had faith no longer, for he knew, nothing doubting. Wherefore, having this perfect knowledge of God, he could not be kept from within the veil; therefore he saw Jesus;

and he did minister unto him." (Ether 3:19-20.) If there is a message to us, perhaps it may be couched in these words: "Go, and do thou likewise."

14. *The Son will reveal the Father to men.*

Jesus said: "All things are delivered unto me of my Father: and no man knoweth the Son, but the Father; neither knoweth any man the Father, save the Son, and he to whomsoever the Son will reveal him." (Matthew 11:27.) The Son reveals the Father to men! And in like manner the Father testifies to men of the Son. "And no man hath seen God at any time, except he hath borne record of the Son; for except it is through him no man can be saved." (JST, John 1:19.)

15. *Both the Father and the Son may be seen by men.*

In his great discourse on the Second Comforter—perhaps as deep and wondrous a sermon as he ever delivered—the Lord Jesus promised: "I will not leave you comfortless: I will come to you. . . . He that hath my commandments, and keepeth them, he it is that loveth me: and he that loveth me shall be loved of my Father, and I will love him, and will manifest myself to him. . . . If a man love me, he will keep my words: and my Father will love him, and we will come unto him, and make our abode with him." (John 14:18-23.) The concluding sentence in this quotation is John 14:23, of which the revealed word, given in our day, says: "The appearing of the Father and the Son, in that verse, is a personal appearance; and the idea that the Father and the Son dwell in a man's heart is an old sectarian notion, and is false." (D&C 130:3.)

16. *Those whose calling and election has been made sure may see the Lord.*

When a man has "his calling and election made sure, then it will be his privilege to receive the other Comforter," the Second Comforter, the Prophet Joseph Smith tells us. Then he asks: "Now what is this other Comforter?" His answer: "It is no more nor less than the Lord Jesus Christ Himself; and this is the sum and substance of the whole matter; that when any man obtains this last Comforter, he will have the personage of Jesus Christ to attend him, or appear unto him from time to time, and even He will manifest the Father unto him, and they will take up their abode with him, and the visions of the heavens will be opened unto him, and the Lord will teach him face to face, and he may have a perfect knowledge of the mysteries of the Kingdom of God; and this is the state and place the ancient Saints arrived at when they had such glorious visions—Isaiah, Ezekiel, John upon the Isle of Patmos, St. Paul in the three heavens, and all the Saints who held communion with the general assembly and Church of the Firstborn." (*Teachings of the Prophet Joseph Smith*, pp. 150-51.)

17. *The sons of God shall see the Lord at the Second Coming.*

Those who believe and obey the gospel in its eternal fulness become, by adoption, the sons of God; they are sons and daughters of Jesus Christ, as King Benjamin taught. Those among them who are living at the Second Coming shall see their Lord. As John said: "Now are we the sons of God," and "we know that, when he shall appear, we shall be like him; for we shall see him as he is. And every man that hath this hope in him purifieth himself, even as he is pure." (1 John 3:2-3.)

18. *Our eternal association is with the Lord.*

We saw him in the premortal life; we were the children of the Father, and the Lord Jesus was our Elder Brother; our association then was with them. He has sent us forth, for the moment, as pilgrims in a fallen world, and he has given all of us the power and privilege to return to his celestial presence and there take up our eternal abode. In the not distant future the Lord Jesus, who dwelt once as a mortal among men, will return in glorious immortality to live and reign on earth for the space of a thousand years, during which time all of earth's inhabitants shall see him. Why should it be thought a thing unseemly, or beyond reasonable probability, for us to seek his face during our travels here on earth?

19. *Who has seen the Lord?*

There is no way of knowing this. In all of the scriptures, ancient and modern, there are accounts of his visits to prophets, seers, apostles, and others. He dwelt with his people in the city of Enoch. He appeared to a great congregation at Adam-ondi-ahman. He ministered to tens of thousands among the Nephites after his resurrection, and also visited those in the lost tribes of Israel. Could there have been other than a host of appearances to righteous Nephites during the near two centuries of their Golden Era? Those who see his face ordinarily do not cast this "pearl before swine" lest men trample it under their feet and rend the recipient of so great a blessing.

ARTICLE 10

We believe
in the literal gathering of Israel
and in the restoration
of the Ten Tribes;
that Zion (the New Jerusalem)
will be built upon
the American continent;
that Christ will reign personally
upon the earth;
and, that the earth will be renewed
and receive its paradisiacal glory.

CHAPTER 52

The Abrahamic–Israelitish Covenant

The Abrahamic Covenant

Israelite history begins not with father Jacob, who is Israel, nor with his tribal descendants who adopted his name as theirs, but with Abraham, their father. In the true and spiritual sense of the terms, Abraham was the first Hebrew, the first Israelite, and the first Jew, although none of these names originated with or had their first application to him. But Abraham was the father of the faithful, the progenitor of the chosen people, the one through whose loins the Lord promised to raise up a righteous nation and people, the one with whom God made an eternal covenant that would save him and his seed after him, the one of whom Jehovah said: "I know him, that he will command his children and his household after him, and they shall keep the way of the Lord, to do justice and judgment." (Genesis 18:19.)

There are many great patriarchal fathers to whom all the faithful look. Chief among them are Adam, Noah, and Abraham. Adam is the first man, the first mortal flesh upon the earth, the Presiding High Priest over all the earth, the head of the mortal and immortal patriarchal chains. He stands next to Christ in the eternal hierarchy. All men on earth are Adam's seed as mortals. Those who gain exaltation and live in the family unit in celestial glory shall live and reign as his immortal children, being thus subject to him forever. Noah is in the same position. He stands next to Adam in priestly power and authority; he is the father of all mortals and will stand preeminent above all who have lived since his day and who gain exaltation. His position in the patriarchal chain of exalted beings will be above that of all who have lived since the flood.

Abraham stands in the same position as Noah for all who

have lived since his day, as far as eternal blessings are concerned. Even those who are not his literal seed shall receive their eternal blessings through him and the covenant God made with him. The Lord made repeated promises to Abraham that he would become a great nation and also that in him should "all families of the earth be blessed." (Genesis 12:2-3.) He was promised the land of Canaan as an everlasting inheritance for him and for his seed. "And I will make thy seed as the dust of the earth: so that if a man can number the dust of the earth, then shall thy seed also be numbered." (Genesis 13:16.) This has reference to eternal increase, for no man's seed could exceed in number the dust particles of the earth. "Look now toward heaven," the Lord said, "and tell the stars, if thou be able to number them: and he said unto him, So shall thy seed be." And Abraham "believed in the Lord; and he counted it to him for righteousness." (Genesis 15:5-6.) All these things are part of the Abrahamic covenant.

And yet again the Lord said to Abraham: "As for me, behold, my covenant is with thee, and thou shalt be a father of many nations. . . . And I will make thee exceeding fruitful, and I will make nations of thee, and kings shall come out of thee. And I will establish my covenant between me and thee and thy seed after thee in their generations for an everlasting covenant, to be a God unto thee, and to thy seed after thee. And I will give unto thee, and to thy seed after thee, the land wherein thou art a stranger, all the land of Canaan, for an everlasting possession; and I will be their God." (Genesis 17:4-8.) Abraham thus covenants for himself and for his seed that he and they will serve the Lord Jehovah, who in turn promises them eternal increase.

In its purest and best form, as far as the ancient word is concerned, the Abrahamic covenant is thus set forth: "I will make of thee a great nation," saith Jehovah, "and I will bless thee above measure, and make thy name great among all nations, and thou shalt be a blessing unto thy seed after thee, that in their hands they shall bear this ministry and Priesthood unto all nations." We, as the seed of Abraham today, are doing this very thing; we are offering to the faithful in all nations all of the blessings of the covenant that God made with Abraham of old.

"And I will bless them [those in all nations and of every

lineage] through thy name; for as many as receive this Gospel shall be called after thy name, and shall be accounted thy seed, and shall rise up and bless thee, as their father." Those of alien or Gentile lineage who believe the gospel and live its laws are adopted into Abraham's family and shall inherit the blessings of the covenant as fully and completely as though they had been born in the chosen lineage. "And I will bless them that bless thee, and curse them that curse thee; and in thee (that is, in thy Priesthood) and in thy seed (that is, thy Priesthood), for I give unto thee a promise that this right shall continue in thee, and in thy seed after thee (that is to say, the literal seed, or the seed of the body) shall all the families of the earth be blessed, even with the blessings of the Gospel, which are the blessings of salvation, even of life eternal." (Abraham 2:9-11.)

What, then, is the Abrahamic covenant? It is that Abraham and his seed (including those adopted into his family) shall have all of the blessings of the gospel, of the priesthood, and of eternal life. The gate to eternal life is celestial marriage, which holy order of matrimony enables the family unit to continue in eternity, so that the participating parties may have posterity as numerous as the sands upon the seashore or the stars in heaven. The Abrahamic covenant enables men to create for themselves eternal family units that are patterned after the family of God our Heavenly Father. A lesser part of the covenant is that the seed of Abraham have the Millennial destiny of inheriting as an everlasting possession the very land of Canaan whereon the feet of the righteous have trod in days gone by.

The Descent of the Abrahamic Covenant

The Lord did not covenant with Abraham for himself alone; it is not the divine intent that only one man and his immediate family should be saved. Salvation is for all, and all may be saved on the same terms and conditions. The Abrahamic covenant was for him and for his seed, with the express understanding that any and all of his seed who were worthy to reap its blessings must live the same law that Abraham their father lived.

This brings us to the descent of the Abrahamic covenant from his day to ours. Isaac, a child of divine promise, was the first to inherit the blessings of the covenant, all pursuant to the word of Jehovah to Abraham: "In Isaac shall thy seed be called." (Genesis 21:12.) That is, the blessings of the covenant were to go to Isaac and to his seed after him. But first, on Mount Moriah, because Abraham had not withheld his only son—in similitude of the Eternal Father, who did not withhold his Only Begotten Son on Calvary—the Lord renewed the covenant with Abraham, saying: "I will multiply thy seed as the stars of the heaven, and as the sand which is upon the sea shore. . . . And in thy seed shall all the nations of the earth be blessed." (Genesis 22:17-18.) Then, after Isaac's marriage to Rebekah and the birth of Jacob and Esau, the Lord appeared to Abraham's son and said: "I will perform the oath which I sware unto Abraham thy father; and I will make thy seed to multiply as the stars of heaven, . . . and in thy seed shall all the nations of the earth be blessed." (Genesis 26:2-4.)

After Isaac comes Jacob. To him the Lord said: "I am the Lord God of Abraham thy father, and the God of Isaac: the land whereon thou liest, to thee will I give it, and to thy seed; and thy seed shall be as the dust of the earth, and thou shalt spread abroad to the west, and to the east, and to the north, and to the south: and in thee and in thy seed shall all the families of the earth be blessed." (Genesis 28:13-14.)

And after Jacob came his twelve sons, the tribal heads, and their sons, and their sons' sons, to all generations. The Lord did not appear to each of them, as he had to their fathers, but whenever they were worthy, they possessed the holy priesthood, the glorious gospel, and that never-ending order of eternal marriage with its consequent hope of eternal life. After the day of Moses, the ruling, governing, theocratic power in Israel was the Aaronic Priesthood. But most of the time, if not at all times, there were prophets and seers and congregations of brethren who held the Melchizedek Priesthood, which enabled them to perform celestial marriages.

During all their long history, the Nephite peoples had the gospel and the priesthood and the blessings of the Abrahamic covenant. When the Risen Lord appeared to them toward the end of that memorable thirty-fourth year, during which he had been crucified and then rose from the dead, he said: "Behold, ye are the children of the prophets; and ye are of the house of Israel; and ye are of the covenant which the Father made with your fathers, saying unto Abraham: And in thy seed shall all the kindreds of the earth be blessed. The Father . . . raised me up unto you first, and sent me to bless you in turning away every one of you from his iniquities; and this because ye are the children of the covenant." (3 Nephi 20:25-26.) As yet, the record of the Lord's resurrected ministry among the lost tribes of Israel has not come forth, but there can be no question that they, being also of the house of Jacob, were children of the covenant and inheritors of the same blessings with their Israelite kinsmen.

And as with Nephite Israel, so with modern Israel. We also are the children of the covenant; we have received, as did they of old, the holy priesthood and the fulness of the everlasting gospel; and we rejoice in that crowning gospel ordinance, which is celestial marriage. And perhaps there is no scriptural word that ties the whole doctrine of the Abrahamic covenant together as well as do these words of the Lord to Joseph Smith: "Abraham received promises concerning his seed, and of the fruit of his loins—from whose loins ye are, namely, my servant Joseph—which were to continue so long as they were in the world; and as touching Abraham and his seed, out of the world they should continue; both in the world and out of the world should they continue as innumerable as the stars; or, if ye were to count the sand upon the seashore ye could not number them." These words interpret and give meaning to those spoken anciently to Abraham, Isaac, and Jacob.

And then come the words that show that the promises are not restricted to the ancients. "This promise is yours also." Why? "Because ye are of Abraham, and the promise was made unto Abraham"—that is, it was given to Abraham for himself and for his righteous seed. "And by this law is the continuation of the works of my Father, wherein he glorifieth himself." It is the Lord's glory as well as his work to bring to pass the immortality and eternal life of man. And whenever any man gains eternal life, which is exaltation, which is the continuation of the family unit in eternity, this adds to the kingdoms and therefore to the glory of the Father. And then comes the exhortation: "Go ye, therefore, and do the works of Abraham; enter ye into my law and ye shall be saved. But if ye enter not into my law ye cannot receive the promise of my Father, which he made unto Abraham." (D&C 132:30-33.)

When he is married in the temple for time and for all eternity, each worthy member of the Church enters personally into the same covenant the Lord made with Abraham. This is the occasion when the promises of eternal increase are made, and it is then specified that those who keep the covenants made there shall be inheritors of all the blessings of Abraham, Isaac, and Jacob. All of this is made possible because of the ministry of two holy beings from dispensations past—Elijah and Elias.

Elijah brought back the sealing power so that marriages and other ordinances that are bound on earth shall be eternally sealed in the heavens. Those married by this authority are husband and wife in this life, and they so remain in the life to come, if they are true and faithful in all things. When Elias appeared to Joseph Smith and Oliver Cowdery on that third day of April in 1836 in the Kirtland Temple, he "committed the dispensation of the gospel of Abraham, saying that in us and our seed all generations after us should be blessed." (D&C 110:12.) That is, Elias restored the great commission, given of God to Abraham our father, whereby the seed of Abraham has power to gain eternal blessings forever through eternal marriage; that is, Elias restored the marriage discipline that had eternal efficacy, virtue, and force in the days of Abraham, Isaac, and Jacob.

One of the grandest concepts in the whole plan of salvation is that these same blessings, given to worthy mortals whenever the fulness of the gospel is on earth, are also available to all those who have died without a knowledge of the gospel but who would have received it with all their hearts had it been offered to them while they dwelt in the flesh. This is what is involved in the promise that the Lord would reveal unto us "the Priesthood, by the hand of Elijah the prophet, before the coming of the great and dreadful day of the Lord." By restoring the sealing keys, Elijah revealed the greatest use to which the priesthood may be put by mortals on earth. "And he [Elijah] shall plant in the hearts of the children the promises made to the fathers, and the hearts of the children shall turn to their fathers." (D&C 2:1-2.)

The fathers are Abraham, Isaac, and Jacob. The promises are the provisions of the Abrahamic covenant whereby the seed of the ancient patriarchs are entitled to receive the priesthood, the gospel, and eternal life (including celestial marriage). We are the children, and after we receive these blessings for ourselves, our attention turns almost by instinct to the well-being of our ancestors who died without a knowledge of the gospel. We are Abraham's seed, and they were Abraham's seed —through Isaac, through Jacob, and through the house of Israel. It thus becomes our privilege, on the basis of salvation for the dead, to search out our ancestors—to whom the same blessings have been promised as have come to us—and to make these blessings available to them through the vicarious ordinances of the house of the Lord.

And as we shall now see, backsliding Israel was scattered because she rejected the Abrahamic covenant. Her scattered remnants will be gathered, one of a city and two of a family, as they receive again that same glorious covenant that so blessed their fathers.

CHAPTER 53

Israel—The Chosen People

Israel—From Eternity to Eternity

Israel—blessed, blessed Israel; a people favored above all the inhabitants of the earth; a people after the Lord's own heart—Israel is the people of the Lord in and by and through whom he brings to pass his eternal purposes. Israel comes first, and all other nations and peoples and kingdoms stand aside and are subject to her. Israel is the people of peoples, the nation of nations, and the kingdom of kingdoms.

It is the work and glory of the Almighty to bring to pass the immortality and eternal life of man. This work is accomplished in and by and through the house of Israel. Out of her come the prophets and seers and apostles; she is the source of the revealed word; all of the holy scriptures have been and are in her care and custody. Jehovah himself is the Holy One of Israel; the Lord Jesus Christ is the God of Israel; and the Only Begotten of the Father was born into mortality as the Son of David. Israel's King is the King of kings.

Jesus said: "Salvation is of the Jews." (John 4:22.) And so it is, for he himself by whom salvation comes was a Jew, and they were the only known portion of the house of Israel in his day. Our present Bible has come to us by way of the Jews, and the apostles of old were members of that chosen race. But in a larger and more comprehensive sense, "salvation is of the house of Israel," for Christ is the God of all Israel. The Israelites are the ones who accept his gospel, and through them the word of truth and salvation is taken to all the nations of the earth.

Israel is an eternal people. She came into being as a chosen and separate congregation before the foundations of the earth were laid; she was a distinct and a peculiar people in preexistence, even as she is in this sphere. Her numbers were known before their mortal birth, and the very land surface of the earth was "divided to the nations [for] their inheritance . . . according to the number of the children of Israel." (Deuteronomy 32:8.)

Certain lands were given to Israel for an inheritance in time and in eternity. America is the land of Joseph; it was the home of Nephite Israel, who were of Joseph, for a thousand years, and it is the headquarters of the Church in this final dispensation in which the church and kingdom of God are in the hands of Ephraim. Palestine was given to the seed of Jacob anciently, and they shall receive it again in the resurrection. "Behold, O my people," saith the Lord, "I will open your graves, and cause you to come up out of your graves, and bring you into the land of Israel. . . . And shall put my spirit in you, and ye shall live, and I shall place you in your own land." (Ezekiel 37:12-14.) And there are no doubt other places, now unknown to us, which are reserved as an eternal inheritance for designated portions of the house of Israel.

Israel was a separate and distinct and identifiable nation for a millennium and a half, from the day she went out of Egypt until her people were scattered in all nations. Remnants of Israel are known today. Members of the Church are of Israel, and portions of Jewish Israel hold forth in various nations or have gathered in a political sense to the land of their fathers. This gathering, however, is simply one that puts persons of the proper lineage in the same geographic locale where their ancestors dwelt; it is not the true gathering of Israel of which the prophets speak, as we shall set forth shortly.

Israel's Millennial destiny is to be gathered again under circumstances where she will be one nation and one people and have one King—the Lord Jesus Christ. In that day her kingdom will be composed of the righteous dead who have come forth to live and reign on earth with Christ for a thousand years, and also of the billions of mortals who will be undergoing their mortal probation during the Millennial era. And the final destiny of all the righteous who have lived from the day of Abraham to the last man on earth is to find place in the house of Israel in the celestial kingdom, there to live and reign in exaltation and glory forever.

The Election of Israel

All men are the spirit children of the Eternal Father; all dwelt in his presence, awaiting the day of their mortal probation; all have come or will come to earth at an appointed time, in a specified place, to live among a designated people. In all of this there is no chance. A divine providence rules over the nations and governs in the affairs of men. Birth and death and mortal kinship are the Lord's doings. He alone determines where and when and among what people his spirit children shall undergo their mortal probation.

Is it inappropriate to ask: Why are there different races of men? Why is there a white, a yellow, and a black race? In the days of Israel's first bondage, why did the Lord send some spirits in the lineage of enslaved Jacob and others to their Egyptian overlords? Why were some spirits sent to earth among the Amalekites, the Assyrians, and the Babylonians, while others at the same moments found birth in the house of Israel? Why was Antipas sent as the son of a debauched and evil Herod, while John the Baptist came into the home of a priestly Zacharias and a saintly Elisabeth?

All of these things operate by law; they are the outgrowth of long years of personal preparation in preexistence on the part of each individual; they come to pass according to the laws that the Lord has ordained. This second estate is a continuation of our first estate; we are born here with the talents and capacities acquired there. Abraham was one of the noble and great spirits in the premortal life. He was chosen for his mortal ministry and position before he was born, and as with the father of the faithful, so with all of the spirits destined to be born as his seed.

The greatest and most important talent or capacity that any of the spirit children of the Father could gain is the talent of spirituality. Most of those who gained this talent were chosen, before they were born, to come to earth as members of the house of Israel. They were foreordained to receive the blessings that the Lord promised to Abraham and to his seed in all their generations. This foreordination is an election, Paul tells us, and truly it is so, for those so chosen, selected, or elected become, in this life, the favored people. Though all mankind may be saved by obedience, some find it easier to believe and obey than others. Hence the concept, taught by Jesus, that his sheep know his voice and will not follow the dissident voices of the world.

It is of the house of Israel that Paul is speaking when he says: "All things work together for good to them that love God, to them who are called according to his purpose." Those in Israel are called to receive certain blessings because they earned the right in their first estate so to inherit in this life. "For whom he did foreknow [that is, in preexistence], he also did predestinate [foreordain] to be conformed to the image of his Son, that he might be the firstborn among many brethren." They were foreordained to be joint-heirs with Christ, to gain his image, to be like him, to be exalted with him. "Moreover whom he did predestinate [foreordain], them he also called: and whom he called, them he also justified: and whom he justified, them he also glorified." (Romans 8:28-30.)

Those of whom Paul here speaks are the house of Israel. It is the privilege of all of them to gain all of the blessings of Abraham, Isaac, and Jacob, though some rebel and forfeit the high reward that otherwise would have been theirs. They are "Israelites," Paul continues, "to whom pertaineth the adoption, and the glory, and the covenants, and the giving of the law, and the service of God, and the promises; whose are the fathers, and of whom as concerning the flesh Christ came, who is over all, God blessed for ever." He then explains how Jacob, "that the purpose of God according to election might stand," was chosen to have precedence over Esau, even before they were born. All this is done so that the Lord "might make known the riches of his glory on the vessels of mercy, which he had afore prepared unto glory." (Romans 9:4-11, 23.) That is to say: All Israel, according to the doctrine of foreordination, have it in their power to gain exaltation; to be like the Son of God, having gained his image; to be joint-heirs with him; to be justified and glorified; to be adopted into the family of God by faith; to be participators with their fathers in the covenant that God made with them; and to be inheritors, to the full, of the ancient promises. Implicit in all this is the fact that they are foreordained to be baptized, to join the Church, to receive the priesthood, to enter the ordinance of celestial marriage, and to be sealed up unto eternal life.

In another place Paul says that God the Father "hath

chosen us in him before the foundation of the world [that is, he foreordained us while we dwelt in his presence], that we should be holy and without blame before him in love: having predestinated [foreordained] us unto the adoption of children by Jesus Christ to himself, according to the good pleasure of his will." He says that "we have obtained an inheritance, being predestinated [foreordained] according to the purpose of him who worketh all things after the counsel of his own will." (Ephesians 1:3-5, 11.) That is, we, the house of Israel, have been foreordained to become pure, spotless, and holy through baptism and obedience until we are adopted into the family of Christ and become joint-heirs with him of all that the Father hath.

Having before us, then, the nature of the covenant God made with Abraham, and also an understanding of Israel's eternal status, and also the doctrine of election, as it applies to the whole house of Israel, we are in a position to consider: (1) what the Lord offered to ancient Israel; (2) why they were scattered and dispersed among the nations; and (3) what really is involved in the gathering of Israel.

It was the Lord's design and purpose to save Israel along with saved Abraham. They were to be his people, and he was to be their God. He invited them to sanctify themselves so they could see his face and stand in his presence. Moses sought diligently to guide them in this course and failed. The Lord offered them all of the blessings of Abraham, Isaac, and Jacob—all of the blessings of the eternal Abrahamic covenant. "If ye will obey my voice indeed, and keep my covenant," he said, "then ye shall be a peculiar treasure unto me above all people: for all the earth is mine: and ye shall be unto me a kingdom of priests, and an holy nation." (Exodus 19:5-6.)

What did the Lord give to ancient Israel? He gave them the everlasting gospel, the holy priesthood, and his own church and kingdom—the church then being his congregation, and the kingdom being a theocracy. He gave them baptism and the gift of the Holy Ghost, temple endowments, and celestial marriage. He gave them his statutes, his laws, and the revelations of heaven. He renewed with them the covenant made with Abraham, Isaac, and Jacob, that they should have eternal increase and that in them and in their seed all generations would be blessed. He poured out upon them his gifts and graces, gave them the spirit of prophecy and revelation, and sent prophets and seers to guide them. He gave them judges and kings to rule over them, and he put to flight the armies of the aliens that fought against them. All these things overflowed in the days of their righteousness. Always his call to them was: "Ye shall be holy: for I the Lord your God am holy." (Leviticus 19:2.) Always he commanded: "Thou shalt love the Lord thy God, and keep his charge, and his statutes, and his judgments, and his commandments, alway." (Deuteronomy 11:1.)

Why was Israel scattered? The answer is clear; it is plain; of it there is no doubt. Our Israelite forebears were scattered because they rejected the gospel, defiled the priesthood, forsook the church, and departed from the kingdom. They were scattered because they turned from the Lord, worshipped false gods, and walked in all the ways of the heathen nations. They were scattered because they forsook the Abrahamic covenant, trampled under their feet the holy ordinances, and rejected the Lord Jehovah, who is the Lord Jesus, of whom all their prophets testified. Israel was scattered for apostasy. The Lord in his wrath, because of their wickedness and rebellion, scattered them among the heathen in all the nations of the earth.

What, then, is involved in the gathering of Israel? The gathering of Israel consists in believing and accepting and living in harmony with all that the Lord once offered his ancient chosen people. It consists of having faith in the Lord Jesus Christ, of repenting, of being baptized and receiving the gift of the Holy Ghost, and of keeping the commandments of God. It consists of believing the gospel, joining the Church, and coming into the kingdom. It consists of receiving the holy priesthood, being endowed in holy places with power from on high, and receiving all the blessings of Abraham, Isaac, and Jacob, through the ordinance of celestial marriage. And it may also consist of assembling to an appointed place or land of worship.

Having this concept of the scattering and gathering of the chosen seed, we are able to understand the prophetic word relative thereto. That word we shall examine in due course.

Modern Israelite Myths

There is an aura of mystery surrounding the house of Israel. Born as a separate nation among the plagues of Egypt, she preserved her identity until the Assyrian captivity of Israel in about 721 B.C. and the Babylonian bondage of Judah after 600 B.C. After seventy years in Babylon, a Jewish remnant returned to Palestine, there to labor amid blood and tears, in suffering and agony, for another six hundred years as they sought to establish and perfect their national status. In A.D. 71, they were scattered and slain and enslaved by their Roman overlords. Since then Jewish enclaves have managed to survive in nearly all nations of the earth; and today portions of these, seemingly impelled by a power greater than man's, are assembling again in the land of their fathers, where they have established a political nation called Israel.

Because most of the Old Testament is a record of God's dealings with ancient Israel; because it speaks in great plainness of the scattering and gathering of this chosen people; because Jesus himself confined his ministry to the lost sheep of the house of Israel; because he initially sent his apostles and seventies to their Israelite kinsmen and to none others; because Paul and the other New Testament writers expound so elaborately about Israel and her destiny—because of all these things, the whole Christian world knows that the Lord has some plans and purposes, now seemingly hidden, concerning his ancient covenant people.

Because the Book of Mormon is a history of God's dealings with a portion of the house of Israel; because the Nephite prophets expound, interpret, and add to the Old Testament word about the scattering and gathering of Israel; because our latter-day revelations speak *in extenso* about the gathering of the saints in the last days; because Moses restored the keys of the gathering of Israel and of the leading of the Ten Tribes from the land of the north; because the Ten Tribes have not as yet been restored to the lands of their ancient inheritance, according to the promises; because our patriarchs, as guided by the spirit of inspiration, announce the tribal status of church members—because of all these things, the Latter-day Saints have a knowledge beyond that of the world relative to the house of Jacob, both anciently and modernly. Indeed, inspired and wise Latter-day Saint authors have reached the very proper conclusion that for almost four thousand years, from the time Jehovah first made covenant with Abraham and his seed, the history of Israel has been the history of the world. And, of course, we look forward to the Millennial day when a triumphant Israel, serving their King, will stand supreme above all peoples.

Our knowledge about Israel's past, her present, and her future comes from many scriptures. The settings vary; different ages and peoples are involved; and the terminology often has different definitions. There are also some legends that have come down from those long dead that postulate this or that about those who are assumed to have descended from Father Jacob. It is no surprise, therefore, to discover, both in the world and in the Church, various illusions and myths that are without substance and are not based on the bedrock of revelation. Some of these are total fabrications, having no more verity than the fitful dreams of a disturbed sleep; others have shreds of truth interwoven with them; and yet others come so near to the eternal verity that they even deceive some of the very elect. These are the most prominent among the false Israelite myths:

1. *The British Israel myth.*

This illusion postulates that the British people are identical with the Ten Tribes of Israel; that Jeremiah, the prophet, brought Tephi, a daughter of Zedekiah, to the north of Ireland; that she married into the royal line and her descendants now sit upon the throne of England, thereby providing divine continuity for the throne of David; and that—and this is the most important part—all of the ancient prophecies relative to the restoration of Israel have been or will be fulfilled in and through Great Britain as a nation. There is not one chance in a million, or in ten thousand million, that any of the historical assumptions are true; and if they were, it would not make one particle of difference—the doctrinal view would still be false. The ancient word concerning the gathering is to find fulfillment in and through the restoration of the gospel, the coming forth of the Book of Mormon, and the setting up again on earth of the same kingdom once possessed by Israel of old. Providentially, this British Israel concept, once so prevalent in the British Isles and elsewhere, has gone pretty much out of vogue and is not taken as seriously as it once was.

2. *The Spiritual Israel myth.*

Being aware of the prophetic word about Israel, but not understanding that this word can be fulfilled only by a restoration of the gospel, the sectarian world has devised the doctrine of a spiritual Israel. Under this view, all who become Christians are part of a new spiritual Israel, and they inherit the blessings of ancient Israel. This view enables them to spiritualize away the plain meaning of the prophetic word and yet to have the secure feeling that the Christendom of the sects is indeed that which Jesus and the apostles professed. This doctrine of a spiritual Israel is, of course, on a par with the whole sectarian system; it is as false as their concept of God, or of salvation by grace, or of any of the other great basics of revealed religion.

3. *The Davidic myth.*

This wresting of the written word assumes that someone of prophetic stature will arise in the Church in the last days, to preside as a Second David, and to prepare the way before the Second Coming of the Son of Man. That there may be one or many brethren called David who preside over the Church in this dispensation is of no moment. The scriptures that speak of King David reigning in the last days are Messianic; they have reference to the Millennial reign of the Lord Jesus Christ.

4. *False ideas about the Gentile fulness.*

Israelites are called Gentiles in those scriptures which speak of the gospel going first to the Gentiles and then to the Jews in the last days. Thus the Book of Mormon came forth by way of the Gentile; Joseph Smith was the Gentile who brought it forth; and the United States is a Gentile nation. This is an instance of all men being divided into two categories—Jews and Gentiles, with the Jews being those who are descendants of the Kingdom of Judah. This categorizes the Lost Tribes of Israel as Gentiles, though, in fact, they are of the literal blood of Israel. Joseph Smith was of Ephraim, and the so-called Gentiles who are receiving the gospel in this day, before it goes to the Jews in full measure, are of the house of Israel.

5. *False ideas about a nation being born in a day.*

This phrase is often used to describe a future day when the Lamanites or Jews or some other part of Israel will be converted almost overnight by the tens and hundreds of thousands. It has a true application; such conversions will occur after the Second Coming among those who have abided the day. In the meantime, the whole house of Israel will be converted one by one and two by two. And any comments about a nation being born in a day are simply figurative and apply to comparatively rapid buildups of the Church in one area or another.

6. *The Lamanite-temple myth.*

An occasional whiff of nonsense goes around the Church acclaiming that the Lamanites will build the temple in the New Jerusalem and that Ephraim and others will come to their assistance. This illusion is born of an inordinate love for Father Lehi's children and of a desire to see them all become now as Samuel the Lamanite once was. The Book of Mormon passages upon which it is thought to rest have reference not to the Lamanites but to the whole house of Israel. The temple in Jackson County will be built by Ephraim, meaning the Church as it is now constituted; this is where the keys of temple building are vested, and it will be to this Ephraim that all the other tribes will come in due course to receive their temple blessings.

7. *The myth that the gathering of Israel is to the United States only.*

The idea that the United States is the sole gathering place for Israel in the last days is false. As Israel was scattered by stages, so she will be gathered by stages. There was a day when all Israel was called to the mountains of Israel in the United States. Now the new converts are called into the stakes of Zion in their own lands and are expected to build up the kingdom there. In due course, representatives at least of all the tribes will assemble in Palestine, and representatives may be gathered at the New Jerusalem when it is built. But the gathering of Israel, in its fulness, will be worldwide and in every nation and among every people, and church members in these nations will not be invited to forsake their own nations and come to an American Zion.

8. *The myth of the Jewish gathering.*

Judah will gather to old Jerusalem in due course; of this, there is no doubt. But this gathering will consist of accepting Christ, joining the Church, and receiving anew the Abrahamic covenant as it is administered in holy places. The present assembling of people of Jewish ancestry into the Palestinian nation of Israel is not the scriptural gathering of Israel or of Judah. It may be prelude thereto, and some of the people so assembled may in due course be gathered into the true church and kingdom of God on earth, and they may then assist in building the temple that is destined to grace Jerusalem's soil.

But a political gathering is not a spiritual gathering, and the Lord's kingdom is not of this world.

9. *The notion that the scattering of Israel is all past.*

It is assumed, in an unthinking sort of way, that Israel was scattered in ancient days and is being gathered in modern times. In reality, the scattering of Israel is still going on. Those already scattered continue to be shifted hither and yon, as witness the travails and sorrows of the Jews as they flee from one nation to another. But also, some of gathered Israel is being scattered yet again. It is no different in our day than in ancient Palestine: when any of the house of Israel forsake the Lord, worship false gods, and join apostate churches, have they not withdrawn from the true sheepfold and joined themselves again with the lost sheep of Israel? And those so going back to Babylon, as it were, often find it in their interest to move physically to cities and nations where they can be swallowed up by the world and not have everlastingly before them the sight of Israel worshipping in her latter-day congregations.

10. *The myth of the location of the lost tribes of Israel.*

There is something mysterious and fascinating about believing the Ten Tribes are behind an iceberg somewhere in the land of the north, or that they are on some distant planet that will one day join itself with the earth, or that the tribe of Dan is in Denmark, the tribe of Reuben in Russia, and so forth. A common cliché asserts: "If we knew where the Lost Tribes were, they would not be lost." True it is that they are lost from the knowledge of the world; they are not seen and recognized as the kingdom they once were; but in general terms, their whereabouts is known. They are scattered in all the nations of the earth, primarily in the nations north of the lands of their first inheritance.

11. *The myth of the Ten Tribes returning as guided by their prophets.*

This simply is not true; there will be no prophets among them except the elders of Israel who belong to The Church of Jesus Christ of Latter-day Saints. The Ten Tribes are to come back like anyone else: by accepting the Book of Mormon and believing the restored gospel. There cannot be two separate and independent church organizations on earth at one and the same time; at least it cannot be in a day when it is possible to govern the Church from one place. The President of the Church holds the keys whereby the Ten Tribes will be led from the lands of the north to their Palestinian homeland. He, not they, will direct their return. But will they not bring their scriptures with them? Probably not; at least there is no such promise. Yes, we and they will have their scriptures; and those scriptures will tell of the visit of the Risen Lord among their forebears. How they shall be brought to light is not known. It may be in much the same way the Book of Mormon was revealed to the world. And once again it will be by or under the direction of the President of the Church, for he holds the keys of the mysteries of the kingdom and of the things that are sealed and hidden up.

12. *Notions about the triumphal return of the Ten Tribes.*

Many of these ideas, though true when properly interpreted, give a wholly false view of what is to be when they are simply paraphrased from the scriptures. In the literal sense of the word, the Ten Tribes will not return with armies and trumpets and banners; with the ice flowing down at their presence; on a highway spanning oceans and continents over which their legions shall march in regal majesty. Their return will be marvelous, with miracles attending. They will tread the highway of righteousness, and it will be as though a nation had been born in a day, because the wicked will have been destroyed and the Lord himself will be reigning on earth. The return of the Ten Tribes is, of course, a Millennial event.

CHAPTER 54

Moses and the Destiny of Israel

Moses Teaches the Scattering and Gathering of Israel

Moses, the man of God, continued the work of Abraham, Isaac, and Jacob in standing as a father and friend and founder of the family of Israel. In the providences of the Lord, Moses led the chosen people out of Egypt, through the Red Sea, and into the wilderness of their wanderings and sorrows. There for forty years he was their leader, their lawgiver, and the legal administrator under whose hands they received the ordinances of salvation and exaltation. As the mediator of the old covenant, he stood between the people and their God, pleading their cause and entreating the Lord, in his mercy and goodness, to pour out upon them the fulness of his glory and to make them a nation of kings and priests who could see the face of God, even the Father, and live.

To Moses—"whom the Lord knew face to face" (Deuteronomy 34:10), and with whom he spoke plainly and not in dark similitudes—the destiny and future of Israel was revealed. The Lord set this destiny before them in the form of blessings or cursings—blessings for obedience and curses for disobedience. The accounts are detailed, extensive, and specific. Included in the blessings are these provisions: "If ye walk in my statutes, and keep my commandments, and do them, . . . I will have respect unto you, and make you fruitful, and multiply you, and establish my covenant with you. . . . And I will walk among you, and will be your God, and ye shall be my people." Above all else, obedience would bring them all of the blessings of the Abrahamic covenant, so that it would be with them as it was with faithful Abraham, meaning that they would be exalted and that their seed after them to all generations would inherit like blessings.

"But if ye will not hearken unto me, and will not do all these commandments; and if ye shall despise my statutes, or if your soul abhor my judgments, so that ye will not do all my commandments, but that ye break my covenant"—then, as the holy word sets forth, almost unbelievable curses and pestilence and plagues and war and desolations would befall them. "And I will scatter you"—the whole house of Israel—"among the heathen, and will draw out a sword after you: and your land shall be desolate, and your cities waste. . . . And upon them that are left alive of you I will send a faintness into their hearts in the lands of their enemies; and the sound of a shaken leaf shall chase them; and they shall flee, as fleeing from a sword; and they shall fall when none pursueth." When the power of the Lord departs from his people, they are left weaker and more filled with fear than the heathen who never rested on the arm of the Lord.

"And they shall fall one upon another, as it were before a sword, when none pursueth." Israel shall fight Israel as the nations in which they are scattered wage war against each other. "And ye shall have no power to stand before your enemies. And ye shall perish among the heathen, and the land of your enemies shall eat you up." How awful is the fate of a people who once walked in the light and love of the Lord, when they sink into the mire and sin of heathendom!

"And they that are left of you shall pine away in their iniquity in your enemies' lands; and also in the iniquities of their fathers shall they pine away with them." During the age upon age in which there are no prophets, no apostles, no angelic ministrants, no true gifts and miracles; during the long night of apostate darkness, in which men draw near to the Lord with their lips, but their hearts are far from him; during all those days in which Israel and her heathen overlords, both together as one people, worship false gods—during all this period, Israel pines away in sorrow, without hope.

Then comes the day of restoration; then the heavens are rent; then the everlasting covenant is made again with men on earth. Then the Lord says of his scattered people: "If they shall confess their iniquity, and the iniquity of their fathers, with their trespass which they trespassed against me, and that also they have walked contrary unto me; and that I also have walked contrary unto them, and have brought them into the land of their enemies; if then their uncircumcised hearts be humbled, and they then accept of the punishment of their iniquity: Then will I remember my covenant with Jacob, and also my covenant with Isaac, and also my covenant with Abraham will I remember." The covenant made with the fathers was that their seed after them should receive the same gospel, the same priesthood, the same promise of salvation, that blessed the lives of those with whom the covenant was first made.

As to the seed of Jacob in the day of restoration: "They shall accept of the punishment of their iniquity: because, even because they despised my judgments, and because their soul abhorred my statutes. And yet for all that, when they be in the land of their enemies, I will not cast them away, neither will I abhor them, to destroy them utterly, and to break my covenant with them: for I am the Lord their God. But I will for their sakes remember the covenant of their ancestors, whom I brought forth out of the land of Egypt in the sight of the heathen, that I might be their God." (Leviticus 26:3-45.) When Israel worships again the same God who led their fathers out of Egypt, they will become again inheritors of the same blessings so abundantly showered upon those fathers.

Moses also gave this inspired word to his Israelitish fellows: "When thou shalt beget children, and children's children, and ye shall have remained long in the land"—he is looking seven, eight, and nine centuries into the future—"and shall corrupt yourselves, and make a graven image, or the likeness of any thing, and shall do evil in the sight of the Lord thy God, to provoke him to anger: I call heaven and earth to witness against you this day, that ye shall soon utterly perish from off the land whereunto ye go over Jordan to possess it; ye shall not prolong your days upon it, but shall utterly be destroyed." Destruction would come upon them, and no power could stay it, when they approached that fulness of iniquity that prevailed among the Nephites before that branch of Israel was utterly destroyed as a nation. Wickedness always does and always will beget destruction in every nation and particularly among those who have been enlightened from on high and who then turn to evil.

"And the Lord shall scatter you among the nations"—all nations—"and ye shall be left few in number among the heathen, whither the Lord shall lead you. And there ye shall serve gods, the work of men's hands, wood and stone, which neither see, nor hear, nor eat, nor smell." What better language could there be to describe the gods of modern Christendom? How can a three-in-one spirit essence that is everywhere and nowhere in particular present, and that was created by men in their councils and defined in their creeds, either see or hear or eat or smell, all of which things the true God does?

"But if from thence thou shalt seek the Lord thy God"— the God who sees and hears and eats and smells, who is a personal being in whose image man is made, and who is indeed the literal Father of the spirits of all flesh—"thou shalt find him, if thou seek him with all thy heart and with all thy soul." This search must come in the day of restoration when once again the heavens have been rent, when the voice of God is heard again, when the Lord Jehovah and the Almighty Elohim both unveil their faces, as in ancient times.

"When thou art in tribulation, and all these things are come upon thee, even in the latter days, if thou turn to the Lord thy God, and shalt be obedient unto his voice"—a voice that once again is heard among men—"(For the Lord thy God is a merciful God;) he will not forsake thee, neither destroy thee, nor forget the covenant of thy fathers which he sware unto them." (Deuteronomy 4:25-31.) Israel is thus gathered when they worship the God of their fathers and receive for themselves the same covenant that an unchanging Lord always makes with those who love and serve him, which is the Abrahamic covenant. As it happens, we now live in the latter days, and that covenant has once again been given to men so that all who will may come and enter therein and be saved with the same eternal fulness that blessed the lives of the ancients.

Moses Announces Blessings and Cursings for Israel

In some of the most pointed and piercing language ever written with a mortal pen, Moses blesses Israel on condition of obedience and curses her if she rejects God and walks in the ways of the world. Included in the cursings are these prophetic words: Thou "shalt be removed into all the kingdoms of the earth." Scattered Israel, all of it, all of the twelve tribes, is everywhere, in all nations. "The Lord shall bring thee, and thy king which thou shalt set over thee, unto a nation which neither thou nor thy fathers have known; and there shalt thou serve other gods, wood and stone." In the days of their initial scattering, the rebels of the house of Jacob worshipped gods of wood and stone in the literal sense; in this present age of supposed enlightenment, their seed, in whose veins the blood of Israel yet flows, worship the equally false gods of an apostate Christendom or a heathen Mohammedanism.

"And thou shalt become an astonishment, a proverb, and a byword, among all nations whither the Lord shall lead thee." This is particularly true of the Jews whose identity is known. "Thou shalt beget sons and daughters, but thou shalt not enjoy them; for they shall go into captivity." Interwoven with the divine announcement of the scattering of Israel is the repeated explanation as to why it occurs. It is: "Because thou servedst not the Lord thy God with joyfulness, and with gladness of heart, for the abundance of all things; therefore shalt thou serve thine enemies which the Lord shall send against thee, in hunger, and in thirst, and in nakedness, and in want of all things: and he shall put a yoke of iron upon thy neck, until he have destroyed thee" as a nation.

Even before Israel gained her inheritance in Canaan, Moses told them: "Ye shall be plucked from off the land whither thou goest to possess it. And the Lord shall scatter thee among all people, from the one end of the earth even unto the other; and there thou shalt serve other gods, which neither thou nor thy fathers have known, even wood and stone." This was said after Israel left Egypt, while she was in the wilderness, and before she entered the Promised Land. And part of the destined dispersion of the chosen people included this prophecy: "And the Lord shall bring thee into Egypt again, . . . and there ye shall be sold unto your enemies for bondmen and bondwomen, and no man shall buy you." (Deuteronomy 28:1-68.) Israel—scattered Israel—returns to Egypt! Moses led them out of Egypt once—out of bondage, away from Pharaoh and his gods, into a land where, as a separate people, they were free to worship the Lord and walk in his ways. But forsaking the Lord, and beginning again to worship false gods, they thereby returned to the Egypt of the world. Their deliverance a second time from Egyptian bondage occurs as they forsake the Egyptian gods, as it were, and turn again to the Lord their God.

After Israel is scattered and Palestine made desolate, men in all nations shall ask: "Wherefore hath the Lord done thus unto this land? what meaneth the heat of this great anger?" Why has he scattered his own chosen people to the ends of the earth? "Then men shall say, Because they have forsaken the covenant of the Lord God of their fathers, which he made with them [again] when he brought them forth out of the land of Egypt: for they went and served other gods, and worshipped them, gods whom they knew not, and whom he had not given unto them: . . . the Lord rooted them out of their land in anger, and in wrath, and in great indignation, and cast them into another land." (Deuteronomy 29:24-28.)

But there is to be a day of restoration—a day when the gospel, the priesthood, the eternal covenant, and the knowledge of God and Christ and their laws shall all be revealed anew. As it is written: "It shall come to pass, when all these things are come upon thee, the blessing and the curse, which I have set before thee, and thou shalt call them to mind among all the nations, whither the Lord thy God hath driven thee, and shalt return unto the Lord thy God, and shalt obey his voice according to all that I command thee this day, thou and thy children, with all thine heart, and with all thy soul; that then the Lord thy God will turn thy captivity, and have compassion upon thee, and will return and gather thee from all the nations, whither the Lord thy God hath scattered thee." The gathering will be as extensive and all-embracing as was the scattering.

"If any of thine be driven out unto the outmost parts of heaven, from thence will the Lord thy God gather thee, and from thence will he fetch thee: and the Lord thy God will bring thee into the land which thy fathers possessed, and thou shalt possess it; and he will do thee good, and multiply thee above thy fathers." Israel shall be more glorious in the day of her deliverance from the second Egypt than she was when she went out from the first Egypt. In that day she shall be established in Palestine, her ancient homeland.

The day of gathering will be a day of conversion. "The Lord thy God will circumcise thine heart, and the heart of thy seed, to love the Lord thy God with all thine heart, and with all thy soul, that thou mayest live. . . . And thou shalt return and obey the voice of the Lord, and do all his commandments which I command thee this day. And the Lord thy God will make thee plenteous in every work of thine hand, in the fruit of thy body, and in the fruit of thy cattle, and in the fruit of thy land, for good: for the Lord will again rejoice over thee for good, as he rejoiced over thy fathers, if thou shalt hearken unto the voice of the Lord thy God, to keep his commandments and his statutes which are written in this book of the law, and if thou turn unto the Lord thy God with all thine heart, and with all thy soul." (Deuteronomy 30:1-10.)

Is it amiss to point out that the lost sheep of Israel, as they return to the ancient sheepcote, are blessed and prospered because they keep the commandments, obey the ordinances, and walk in all the ways of the God of Israel—and not simply because they confess the Lord Jesus with their lips and assume that his atoning sacrifice has done all that is necessary to save the elect? It is obedience and personal righteousness that saves all men, Israel included.

Moses Empowers Men to Gather Israel

Why was Israel scattered? Again the divine word attests: because "he forsook God which made him, and lightly esteemed the Rock of his salvation," who is Christ. "They provoked him to jealousy with strange gods, with abominations provoked they him to anger. They sacrificed unto devils, not to God; to gods whom they knew not, to new gods that came newly up, whom your fathers feared not." These new gods are the gods of the creeds of Christendom. "Of the Rock that begat thee thou art unmindful, and hast forgotten God that formed thee. And when the Lord saw it, he abhorred them, because of the provoking of his sons, and of his daughters. And he said, I will hide my face from them, I will see what their end shall be: for they are a very froward generation, children in whom is no faith."

Hence: "I said, I would scatter them into corners, I would make the remembrance of them to cease from among men." How aptly this describes the situation with reference to the Ten Tribes who are now lost to the knowledge of men. "For they are a nation void of counsel, neither is there any understanding in them. O that they were wise, that they understood this, that they would consider their latter end!" (Deuteronomy 32:15-29.)

How shall Israel be gathered? First will come the conversion and gathering of the tribe of Joseph. Then Joseph shall gather the other tribes. "His horns are like the horns of the unicorns [wild oxen]: with them he shall push the people together to the ends of the earth." It will not be an easy work. Every lost sheep must be taught the gospel; every new convert must believe the Book of Mormon; all must repent and forsake the world and come voluntarily, often in the face of great opposition, into the latter-day kingdom of the God of their fathers. Missionaries must labor with zeal and in the face of great odds. They must "push the people together." And who shall do this work? Moses says: "They are the ten thousands of Ephraim, and they are the thousands of Manasseh." (Deuteronomy 33:17.) And such is an apt and accurate definition of the missionary force of the great latter-day kingdom.

Moses—mighty, mighty Moses—acting in the power and authority of the holy order, gathered Israel once. What is more fitting than for him to confer upon mortals in this final dispensation the power and authority to lead latter-day Israel out of Egyptian darkness, through a baptismal Red Sea, into their promised Zion?

Moses, who mediated the cause of his erring brethren in ancient times, and to whom the Lord revealed the doctrine of the scattering and the doctrine of the gathering, is the very one who came in resurrected glory to give the needed authorization and keys to Joseph Smith and Oliver Cowdery. As the holy word attests: "Moses appeared before us, and committed unto us the keys of the gathering of Israel from the four parts of the earth, and the leading of the ten tribes from the land of the north." (D&C 110:11.)

Two things are involved in this commission. First, Israel—all Israel, the Ten Tribes included—is to be gathered "from the four parts of the earth," out of every nation and from among every people. They are to be gathered into the true church and fold of the God of Israel. This gathering is primarily spiritual, but it is also temporal in that the gathered sheep are assembled into the stakes of Zion where the living waters flow. But, next, this commission directs the one who holds the keys of the gathering, meaning the President of the Church, to lead the Ten Tribes from the land of the north to their destined Palestinian homeland. They will be led to their promised inheritances after they join the Church, after they return unto the

Lord, after they believe in Christ and accept his gospel, after they receive, individually and collectively, the Abrahamic covenant again. This part of the gathering of Israel is Millennial, for that is the assigned period in which the Ten Tribes are to come forth; that is the day in which the kingdom will be restored to Israel in the political as well as the ecclesiastical sense.

Just before our Lord's ascension into heaven to sit down on the right hand of the Father and reign forever in eternal glory, the ancient apostles asked: "Lord, wilt thou at this time restore again the kingdom to Israel?" (Acts 1:6.) Jesus left the question unanswered, directing his ancient apostolic witnesses to do the work assigned to them and to leave the future in divine hands. And so it is with us; the restoration of the kingdom to Israel, in the full and literal sense of the word, will not take place in our day unless some of us live to see the Second Coming of the Son of Man. It is in that day that Israel will triumph in the full sense and the Ten Tribes will be led to their destined inheritance.

CHAPTER 55

Israel and the Prophetic Word

Why Israel Was Scattered

What think ye of the scattering and gathering of Israel? Surely it is all part of a great and divine purpose. Can there be any doubt that the Lord gathers his people for their salvation, scatters them when they turn to apostate ways of worship, and then gathers them again when they turn again to him with all their heart? All this is set forth in the Mosaic word.

Moses, who labored to save the elect of God in his day; Moses, who wore out his days in service to that congregation which the Lord put in his charge; Moses, who, as a dispensation head, stands supreme above all the prophets of Israel— Moses is the one, as we have seen, to whom the Lord revealed the scattering and the gathering of his people. He is the one who gathered them out of the first Egypt, and it is by his authorization and in the power and authority and majesty of the same priesthood he held that they are now being gathered out of the second Egypt. But the prophets who came after echoed the words of the great lawgiver. They also spoke by the spirit of revelation and of prophecy, and they amplified, expounded, and wove added details into the grand tapestry begun by Moses. We shall now sample the inspired utterances of those who came after the one who parted the Red Sea and who led Israel to that Jordan which, crossing over, placed them in their Promised Land.

When Solomon departed this life, Israel, who had been one people, divided into two kingdoms—Judah under Rehoboam and Israel under Jeroboam. And it was Jeroboam who led a whole nation into dire and evil apostasy. He made molten images, created his own priests, and caused his people to become as the aliens who dwelt in the land before them. In this setting Ahijah the prophet sent this word unto Jeroboam: "The Lord shall smite Israel, as a reed is shaken in the water, and he shall root up Israel out of this good land, which he gave to their fathers, and shall scatter them beyond the river, because they have made their groves, provoking the Lord to anger. And he shall give Israel up because of the sins of Jeroboam, who did sin, and who made Israel to sin." (1 Kings 14:15-16.)

Centuries later these prophetic words were fulfilled to the very letter. The kingdom of Israel was conquered and carried captive into Assyria, whence they later departed by miraculous means and have since been lost to the knowledge of men. With this Assyrian siege and captivity—with all its blood and horror—vividly impressed upon the mind of the inspired chronicler, he recited the reasons for the fall of Israel in these sad and simple words: "For so it was, that the children of Israel had sinned against the Lord their God, which had brought them up out of the land of Egypt, from under the hand of Pharaoh king of Egypt, and had feared other gods, and walked in the statutes of the heathen, whom the Lord cast out from before the children of Israel, and of the kings of Israel, which they had made." The Lord gave Israel her liberty and her land. He freed his people from bondage and gave them a choice land in which to dwell. He drove out the nations that preceded them and established his people as a great nation and a mighty people. And yet they forsook their God and observed the statutes and laws and practices of the heathen nations that were before them.

"And the children of Israel did secretly those things that were not right against the Lord their God, and they built them high places in all their cities, from the tower of the watchmen to the fenced city." False worship was everywhere. Every city and village had its own high place whereon a heathen altar stood. And even the unwalled country towns, and the lodging places for shepherds, and the country areas where only towers stood to shelter the watch in time of danger—they all had their high places and their altars.

"And they set them up images [pillars] and groves [or, probably, idols as of Ashtoreth] in every high hill, and under every green tree: and there they burnt incense in all the high places, as did the heathen whom the Lord carried away before them; and wrought wicked things to provoke the Lord to anger: for they served idols, whereof the Lord had said unto them, Ye shall not do this thing." The heathen worship to which Israel reverted was unspeakably lewd and licentious. Ashtoreth, for instance, was the Canaanite goddess of sensual love, and the worship conducted in her honor was licentious, evil, and immoral. When the cup of iniquity of the early Canaanite inhabitants of the land was full, the Lord destroyed them and gave their land to Israel; when Israel's wickedness approached that of the Amorite, a not dissimilar fate befell her.

"Yet the Lord testified against Israel, and against Judah, by all the prophets, and by all the seers, saying, Turn ye from your evil ways, and keep my commandments and my statutes, according to all the law which I commanded your fathers, and which I sent to you by my servants the prophets." Neither the kingdom of Israel nor the kingdom of Judah went unwarned. They were told in plainness and in power what would befall them if they did not worship the Father, in the name of the Son, by the power of the Spirit.

"Notwithstanding they would not hear, but hardened their necks, like to the neck of their fathers, that did not believe in the Lord their God. And they rejected his statutes, and his covenant that he made with their fathers, and his testimonies which he testified against them; and they followed vanity, and became vain, and went after the heathen that were round about them, concerning whom the Lord had charged them, that they should not do like them. And they left all the commandments of the Lord their God, and made them molten images, even two calves, and made a grove, and worshipped all the host of heaven, and served Baal." That is to say: Israel forsook the gospel, left the church, rejected the Abrahamic covenant, robbed God by retaining their tithing, kept not the passover, dishonored the sabbath, and in place of all this, chose to believe and worship as the heathens did.

They became true sectarians, splitting off in diverse directions—some worshipping this idol, others bowing before a different one. Some worshipped the sun, moon, and stars, and yet others bowed before Baal. Baal, a Canaanite deity, was the son of El, the father of the gods; he is also identified as the son of Dagon. As the farm god, he was thought to give increase to family and field and to flocks and herds, and he was worshipped in temples and at "high places" by sacrifices, ritualistic meals, and licentious dances. Male prostitutes and sacred harlots were provided at these high places, and the whole system of worship was lewd and licentious in nature. But there was even a greater depth of depravity than this to which Israel fell.

"And they caused their sons and their daughters to pass through the fire, and used divination and enchantments, and sold themselves to do evil in the sight of the Lord, to provoke him to anger." The divination and enchantment spoken of are those that involve communion with evil spirits. This is spiritualism in its most degrading form. Men seek devils for guidance, and they get what it pleases Lucifer to give them. And also they sacrificed their children to Molech. This was the most abhorrent and detestable of all the ancient evils. It is difficult to conceive how fanatical and wicked a people must become in order to offer, freely, their children in sacrifice, as burnt offerings, to an image made with men's hands. But so it was with those whom the Lord in his wrath scattered among all nations.

"Therefore the Lord was very angry with Israel, and removed them out of his sight: there was none left but the tribe of Judah only." Israel was carried away by the Assyrians; Judah, later by the Babylonians. "Also Judah kept not the commandments of the Lord their God, but walked in the statutes of Israel which they made. And the Lord rejected all the seed of Israel, and afflicted them, and delivered them into the hand of spoilers, until he had cast them out of his sight." (2 Kings 17:1-20.) Is there a sadder story in all history than this?

By way of addendum, we now refer to that holy word written after the fate of Israel became the fate of Judah. Zedekiah, king of Judah, rebelled against Nebuchadnezzar and broke his oath to the Babylonian ruler. "Moreover all the chief of the priests, and the people, transgressed very much after all the abominations of the heathen; and polluted the house of the Lord which he had hallowed in Jerusalem." As it had been in Israel, so now it was in Judah; the cup of their iniquity was full. "And the Lord God of their fathers sent to them by his messengers, rising up betimes, and sending; because he had compassion on his people, and on his dwelling place: but they mocked the messengers of God, and despised his words, and misused his prophets, until the wrath of the Lord arose against his people, till there was no remedy. Therefore, he brought upon them the king of the Chaldees, who slew their young men with the sword in the house of their sanctuary, and had no compassion upon young man or maiden, old man, or him that stooped for age: he gave them all into his hand." (2 Chronicles 36:14-17.) And all this came to pass according to the word of Moses, the man of God, who was a father to Israel and who sought to save them, but they would not.

Isaiah and the Gathering of Israel

Between Moses, the man of God, and the one like unto Moses, who is Christ, the prophet in Israel who had the greatest spiritual stature, fame, renown, and enduring influence was Isaiah. His prophetic language, filled with poetry and imagery, was written to his fellow Israelites, to the Nephites, to the Jews of Jesus' day, and, above all, to latter-day Israel—to Israel in the day of her gathering and Millennial triumph.

Among those Christians who concern themselves with anything more than the social gospel, Isaiah is esteemed as the Messianic prophet, because of the powerful witness he bears of the Promised Messiah. In a greater sense, as the Latter-day Saints know, he is the prophet of the restoration, for the great burden of his message deals with the Lord's work in the last days.

With reference to the house of Israel, Isaiah simply built on the Mosaic foundation. He renewed the scriptural truisms that the Lord's people were scattered for their iniquity and would be gathered for their righteousness. That righteousness, he proclaimed, would result from obedience to the laws and ordinances of the restored gospel. We have already considered his prophetic words relative to the coming forth of the Book of Mormon; those about the sealed book, yet to be revealed; those that prefigured the First Vision; and those that foretold the restoration of the gospel, which gospel was called by Israel's seer a marvelous work and a wonder. In all of this, Isaiah's mind was on Israel's future, not her past. He chose to issue a call of hope and triumph and glory for the chosen seed in the day they returned to the Lord.

"My people are gone into captivity, because they have no knowledge," saith the Lord, "and their honourable men are famished, and their multitude dried up with thirst." Isaiah, be it remembered, lived after the kingdom of Israel had been carried, as a nation, into Assyria. Why were they called upon so to suffer and so to be scattered? "Because they have cast away the law of the Lord of hosts, and despised the word of the Holy One of Israel. Therefore is the anger of the Lord kindled against his people, and he hath stretched forth his hand against them, and hath smitten them: and the hills did tremble, and their carcases were torn in the midst of the streets." Such is what had happened to the kingdom of Israel, and such is what lay in store for the kingdom of Judah.

But what of the future? "For all this his anger is not turned away, but his hand is stretched out still," saith Isaiah. "And he will lift an ensign to the nations from far, and will hiss unto them from the end of the earth: and, behold, they shall come with speed swiftly." (Isaiah 5:13-26.) In all the history of the world, has there ever been an ensign like the gospel ensign—an ensign raised to all Israel in all nations and to all men everywhere, inviting them to rally around the standard of salvation?

And who shall carry the message to the world? Those to whom it is first revealed and those who first believe its doctrines and obey its ordinances. To them Isaiah's word is: "Go, ye swift messengers," go ye elders of Israel, go ye messengers of the kingdom, "to a nation scattered and peeled, to a people terrible from their beginning hitherto; a nation meted out and trodden down, whose land the rivers have spoiled!" Let the word go forth! And what counsel hath Isaiah for those who hear the word? "All ye inhabitants of the world, and dwellers on the earth, see ye, when he [Israel's God] lifteth an ensign on the mountains; and when he bloweth a trumpet, hear ye." (Isaiah 18:2-3.) That ensign, the fulness of the everlasting gospel, has now been raised; and that trumpet, the gospel trumpet, is now sounding its clarion call. This is the day when the root of Jesse is standing "for an ensign of the people"; when "the Lord shall set his hand again the second time to recover the remnant of his people," from all the lands and islands of their dispersion; when "he shall set up an ensign for the nations, and shall assemble the outcasts of Israel, and gather together the dispersed of Judah from the four corners of the earth." (Isaiah 11:10-12.)

When the lost and scattered sheep of Israel find place again in the fold of their Ancient Shepherd, they do so by forsaking the world and joining the true church. They leave the deserts of sin and lie down in the green pastures. They leave Babylon and return to Zion. Hence the call: "Go ye forth of Babylon, flee ye from the Chaldeans, with a voice of singing declare ye, tell this, utter it even to the end of the earth; say ye, The Lord hath redeemed his servant Jacob." (Isaiah 48:20.)

When Israel gathers, she returns to the Lord and worships again him that made heaven and earth and the sea and the fountains of waters. In the world "every man walketh in his own way, and after the image of his own god, whose image is in the likeness of the world, and whose substance is that of an idol, which waxeth old and shall perish in Babylon." (D&C 1:16.) In the true church men worship again the true God. Hence the call: "Assemble yourselves and come; draw near together, ye that are escaped of the nations." As to those yet in Babylon, the holy word says: "They have no knowledge, . . . and pray unto a god that cannot save." Let them heed the call: "Look unto me," saith the Lord Jehovah, who is Christ, "and be ye saved, all the ends of the earth: for I am God, and there is none else. I have sworn by myself, the word is gone out of my mouth in righteousness, and shall not return, that unto me every knee shall bow, every tongue shall swear. . . . In the Lord shall all the seed of Israel be justified, and shall glory." (Isaiah 45:20-25.)

One prophet after another proclaims that those of Israel will be gathered when they turn again to the God of their fathers and worship him as their forebears did. Isaiah does more. He tells how the true God will be known to the seed of Israel. "I am the Lord thy God, the Holy One of Israel, thy Saviour." Thus spoke the Lord Jesus Christ to his ancient chosen people. "Since thou wast precious in my sight, thou hast been honourable, and I have loved thee." Blessed, blessed Israel—how loved they were of the Lord in the days of their faith and righteousness! But they are not, in their scattered and desolate state, to be forsaken forever. "Fear not: for I am with thee," saith the Lord. "I will bring thy seed from the east, and gather thee from the west; I will say to the north, Give up; and to the south, Keep not back: bring my sons from far, and my daughters from the ends of the earth; even every one that is called by my name."

Israel—all Israel—shall assemble from the four corners of the earth; they shall be gathered from the four winds and the seven seas, from every kingdom and out of every nation, and from the isles of the seas. Who shall come? Those who have exercised the gospel power given them to become the sons of God; those who are the sons and daughters of Jesus Christ; those who know the name by which they are called; those who have taken upon them the name of Christ, by covenant, and who are striving to be worthy of membership in his family —these are the ones who shall gather with the saints. "Bring forth the blind people that have eyes, and the deaf that have ears." Those who once were blind to the truth shall have their eyes opened; those who once were deaf and unable to hear the promptings of the Holy Spirit shall have their ears opened. "Let all the nations be gathered together, and let the people be assembled." Let all the witnesses be heard; let it be determined which of all the gods men shall worship.

Then, in that day, the God of Israel shall say to the seed of his ancient people: "Ye are my witnesses, saith the Lord, . . . that ye may know and believe me, and understand that I am he: before me there was no God formed, neither shall there be after me." Christ and Christ alone is the Savior; there was none before him, and there will be none after. "I, even I, am the Lord; and beside me there is no saviour. . . . . Therefore, ye are my witnesses, saith the Lord, that I am God. . . . I am the Lord, your Holy One, the creator of Israel, your King." Let others say, Lo, here is Christ, or, Lo, there; let the exponents of the creeds proclaim that a three-in-one, all-pervading, everywhere present, spirit essence is God; let men talk of salvation by grace alone, or of salvation through ordinances and penance and indulgences; let the witnesses be heard. And above all, know this: The elders of Israel are the Lord's witnesses. They know the Lord, and they testify of him. And he is and can be known and found and accepted by testimony and in no other way.

In that day—and it has arrived—shall men look to a dead past or to a living present? "Remember ye not the former things, neither consider the things of old," saith the Lord. Look not back to dead prophets and to saints who are now in another sphere. "Behold, I will do a new thing; now it shall spring forth; shall ye not know it?" The gospel is new as well as everlasting, and it has sprung forth in our day. "This people have I formed for myself; they shall shew forth my praise. . . . I, even I, am he that blotteth out thy transgressions for mine own sake, and will not remember thy sins." (Isaiah 43:3-25.)

How glorious is the day when the Lord gathers Israel! Of that day he said to our ancient fathers: "I will pour my spirit upon thy seed, and my blessing upon thine offspring." By this scattered seed his voice is heard, saying: "I have formed thee; thou art my servant: O Israel, thou shalt not be forgotten of me. I have blotted out, as a thick cloud, thy transgressions, and, as a cloud, thy sins: return unto me; for I have redeemed thee. Sing, O ye heavens; for the Lord hath done it: shout, ye lower parts of the earth: break forth into singing, ye mountains, O forest, and every tree therein: for the Lord hath redeemed Jacob, and glorified himself in Israel." (Isaiah 44:3, 21-23.)

The crowning blessings of the gospel are received in temples, in holy sanctuaries apart from the world, in the places where only the faithful assemble. It is in temples—whether they be the portable tabernacle of testimony used by Moses, or the magnificent wonder of the world built by Solomon, or the temples of the latter days—that the saints receive the mysteries of godliness. It is in these holy houses that faithful couples enter into the ordinance of celestial marriage through which they become parties to the Abrahamic covenant, the covenant of eternal increase, the covenant that in them and in their seed all generations shall be blessed.

Thus Israel gathers for the purpose of building temples in which the ordinances of salvation and exaltation are performed for the living and the dead. And thus it comes as no surprise to find the ancient prophets speaking of the temples of the Most High and doing it in the setting of the gathering of Israel. "And it shall come to pass in the last days," saith Isaiah, "that the mountain of the Lord's house shall be established in the top of the mountains, and shall be exalted above the hills; and all nations shall flow unto it." This has specific reference to the Salt Lake Temple and to the other temples built in the top of the Rocky Mountains, and it has a general reference to the temple yet to be built in the New Jerusalem in Jackson County, Missouri. Those in all nations, be it noted, shall flow to the houses of the Lord in the tops of the mountains, there to make the covenants out of which eternal life comes.

"And many people shall go and say, Come ye, and let us go up to the mountain of the Lord, to the house of the God of Jacob; and he will teach us of his ways, and we will walk in his paths: for out of Zion shall go forth the law, and the word of the Lord from Jerusalem." (Isaiah 2:2-3.) Following this prophecy, the divine word speaks of the Second Coming of the Son of Man. And so it is that the elders of Israel have gone forth to the nations for a hundred years, inviting believing souls to gather with Israel where the temples of the Lord now stand, there to be endowed with power from on high. And so it shall yet be in a future day when, during the Millennial era, there are two great world capitals—one in the Zion of America, the New Jerusalem, whence the law shall proceed, and the other in the Zion of old, the Old Jerusalem, whence the word of the Lord shall go forth. Truly the great marvels of the gathering of Israel lie ahead, marvels that shall come to pass during the Millennium.

CHAPTER 56

Israel Shall Be Gathered

Jeremiah and the Gathering of Israel

"Hath God cast away his people?" (Romans 11:1.) Hath he scattered Israel forever? When will he look again with tender mercies upon the seed of Jacob? Should not our chief interest today be not in the scattering of Israel, but in the gathering of that once-favored nation?

As we have seen, the Lord's people were scattered because they forsook the Lord, worshipped false gods, joined false churches, and adopted the lewd and evil ways of the world. "My people have committed two evils," saith the Lord; "they have forsaken me the fountain of living waters, and hewed them out cisterns, broken cisterns, that can hold no water." (Jeremiah 2:13.) And as we are aware, they will be gathered again when they return to the Lord and quench their thirst from that Eternal Fountain whence streams of living water flow.

Without repeating the dire and evil deeds that caused the dispersion, let us turn to some of the comforting prophecies that tell of the gathering of Israel and the glory that shall attend it. For, "I will yet plead with you, saith the Lord, and with your children's children will I plead." (Jeremiah 2:9.)

We live in the day when the Lord is pleading with his children. The elders of Israel have received a commission from him to go forth and plead with their scattered brethren. Their instructions are: "Go and proclaim these words toward the north, and say, Return, thou backsliding Israel, saith the Lord; and I will not cause mine anger to fall upon you: for I am merciful, saith the Lord, and I will not keep anger for ever. Only acknowledge thine iniquity, that thou hast transgressed against the Lord thy God, and hast scattered thy ways to the strangers under every green tree, and ye have not obeyed my voice, saith the Lord." The lost sheep of Israel have worshipped idols "under every green tree," as it were, and have bowed before false gods everywhere. Now they are invited to come unto Christ, and through him to the Father, that they may receive the Holy Ghost and be cleansed from all their sins.

"Turn, O backsliding children, saith the Lord; for I am married unto you: and I will take you one of a city, and two of a family, and I will bring you to Zion: and I will give you pastors according to mine heart, which shall feed you with knowledge and understanding." The whole house of Israel, the Ten Tribes included, will be gathered one by one as their hearts are touched by the Spirit of Christ. After they join the Church and receive the gift of the Holy Ghost, they will be taught the doctrines of salvation and will learn the mysteries of the kingdom.

"And it shall come to pass, when ye be multiplied and increased in the land"—that is, when great multitudes have gathered and the true church is once again well established in the nations—then, "in those days, saith the Lord, they shall say no more, The ark of the covenant of the Lord: neither shall it come to mind: neither shall they remember it; neither shall they visit [miss] it; neither shall that be done any more." The old rituals of Israel shall be forgotten. No longer will they look to the mercy seat that rests on the ark; rather, it will be the day of the new covenant—and all Israel will have direct access to the Lord. "At that time they shall call Jerusalem the throne of the Lord"—this is yet future; it is Millennial—"and all the nations shall be gathered unto it, to the name of the Lord, to Jerusalem: neither shall they walk any more after the imagination of their evil heart. In those days the house of Judah shall walk with the house of Israel, and they shall come together out of the land of the north to the land that I have given for an inheritance unto your fathers." In that glorious day the Lord will say to his gathered saints: "Thou shalt call me, My Father; and shalt not turn away from me."

The plea to scattered Israel is: "Return, ye backsliding children, and I will heal your backslidings." It is: Repent and come unto Christ and accept him as did your fathers; forsake your sins; and the Lord, through the waters of baptism, will heal you.

And the response of believing souls is: "Behold, we come unto thee; for thou art the Lord our God. Truly in vain is salvation hoped for from the hills, and from the multitude of mountains: truly in the Lord our God is the salvation of Israel." (Jeremiah 3:12-23.) Salvation is not found through worshipping false gods in the hills and mountains, nor at the shrines or in the churches of the world. Israel gathers because salvation is in Christ as he is revealed in the Book of Mormon and the revelations of latter days.

In one of the greatest prophecies about the scattering and gathering of Israel, the Lord says by the mouth of Jeremiah: "Your fathers have forsaken me, saith the Lord, and have walked after other gods, and have served them, and have worshipped them, and have forsaken me, and have not kept my laws"—this is being said after the Assyrian captivity of Israel and before the Babylonian captivity of Judah—"and ye have done worse than your fathers; for, behold, ye walk every one after the imagination of his evil heart, that they may not hearken unto me: Therefore will I cast you out of this land into a land that ye know not, neither ye nor your fathers; and there shall ye serve other gods day and night; where I will not shew you favour." All Israel, in their dire and scattered state, will serve false gods; all Israel will belong to false churches and walk in evil ways, becoming carnal, sensual, and devilish. And be it remembered that the gods of the creeds, which are the gods of Christendom, are just as false as are the gods of the Assyrians, Babylonians, Muslims, Amorites, Hittites, or any other peoples, excepting only the members of the true church. There is but one living and true God—a thing that many, even in the Church, find it difficult to envision.

"Therefore, behold, the days come, saith the Lord, that it shall no more be said, The Lord liveth, that brought up the children of Israel out of the land of Egypt; but, The Lord liveth, that brought up the children of Israel from the land of the north, and from all the lands whither he had driven them: and I will bring them again into their land that I gave unto their fathers." The magnitude, glory, wonder, and greatness of the latter-day gathering of Israel is beyond mortal comprehension. We see little trickles and streams that will one day unite to become such a flood that it will sweep everything on earth before it. A wall of water on the right hand and a wall of water on the left, with more than two million people marching between them on dry ground, as the Red Sea parted, will be nothing by way of comparison, when the full and yet future glory of the gathering of Israel is manifest before men.

"Behold, I will send for many fishers, saith the Lord, and they shall fish them; and after will I send for many hunters, and they shall hunt them from every mountain, and from every hill, and out of the holes of the rocks." It is not in the divine program to gather Israel amid worldly splendor. A trumpet will not call legions forth, arrayed in battle splendor, with weapons at the ready, to march to a Promised Land. Moroni's trumpet is symbolical. An angel's voice will not be raised in every ear. Israel will be gathered as one fish is caught on a line cast into a river, and a few more are seined in by a net cast into the sea. A hunter will find one hart on a high mountain, a few hares in a plainal area, a wild boar in a forest thicket, a slumbering bear in a secluded cave. The elect of God will come in one by one and family by family.

"For mine eyes are upon all their ways: they are not hid from my face, neither is their iniquity hid from mine eyes," saith the Lord. "And first I will recompense their iniquity and their sin double; because they have defiled my land, they have filled mine inheritance with the carcases of their detestable and abominable things." Scattered Israel lives in sin; they are evil; their deeds are an abomination in the Lord's sight. They are no different than the heathen whose servants and companions they are. Along with all sinners, they have suffered and do and will suffer for their evil deeds; they will be beaten with many stripes; and they will not be free from sin and suffering until they repent and accept the cleansing power of the blood of Him who died that they might live.

"O Lord, my strength, and my fortress, and my refuge in the day of affliction, the Gentiles shall come unto thee from the ends of the earth, and shall say, Surely our fathers have inherited lies, vanity, and things wherein there is no profit. Shall a man make gods unto himself, and they are no gods?" In Jeremiah's day, everyone was a Gentile except the Jews, who were nationals of the kingdom of Judah. Thus, in effect, all men, Jew and Gentile alike, when they gain a knowledge of the true God, will know in their hearts that they and their fathers have been deceived. It is no grave sin to inherit false teachings from the traditions of one's ancestors; the sin is for men to hear the truth and then choose to walk in the darkness of those whose doctrines were formulated in the dark ages. The gods of Christendom, for instance, are gods who were created by men in the creeds of an apostate people. There is little profit or peace in serving them, and certainly there is no salvation available through them.

"Therefore, behold, I will this once cause them to know, I will cause them to know mine hand and my might; and they shall know that my name is The Lord." (Jeremiah 16:11-21.) For one final time, just once only, the Lord will reveal himself anew to men. In this final dispensation, the dispensation of the fulness of times, he, as Christ, will announce himself as the Jehovah of old. This he has done. The gospel has been restored for the last time. The revelation as to the nature and kind of being God is began in the spring of 1820 with the appearance of the Father and the Son to Joseph Smith. It has progressed through the flesh and bones statement in the Doctrine and Covenants, through the grand concepts presented in the King Follett Sermon—than which Joseph Smith never preached a greater—and it is now at the place where every elder has power, by faith, through righteousness, to see the face of God for himself and to gain a perfect knowledge of Him whom it is eternal life to know.

Israel—Gathered by Stages

Prophecies about the gathering of Israel by the same prophet might seem to be repetitive. In part they are, for repetition is sound pedagogy, but they also tell of gatherings that will occur by stages and in different locations. Israel was not scattered at one time; indeed, the main phases of the scattering went forward for a thousand years. And Israel will not be gathered all at one time. The gathering commenced with the organization of The Church of Jesus Christ of Latter-day Saints in 1830; it was formalized and took on a divine impetus with the restoration of the keys by Moses in 1836; and it has grown in scope and intensity ever since. Once it was centered in Kirtland, Ohio, then in Missouri, and then in Illinois. For nearly a hundred years the new converts flowed to the tops of the Rocky Mountains, and now they are counseled to remain in the stakes of Zion in the nations of their inheritance. It will thus continue on a worldwide basis until the Second Coming and then go on into the Millennium for as long as is necessary to perfect the work and convert the world. We see no reason why this Millennial phase should take longer than a single generation.

Thus the Lord tells Jeremiah: "I will gather the remnant of my flock out of all countries whither I have driven them, and will bring them again to their folds, and they shall be fruitful and increase." After they are gathered, they will not be left without guidance. "And I will set up shepherds over them which shall feed them"—the Church will be organized and perfected among them, and the Lord's pastors will preserve and care for his flocks—"and they shall fear no more, nor be dismayed, neither shall they be lacking, saith the Lord." (Jeremiah 23:3-4.) "And I will give them an heart to know me, that I am the Lord: and they shall be my people, and I will be their God: for they shall return unto me with their whole heart." (Jeremiah 24:7.)

One of the great phases of the gathering is set forth by Jeremiah in these wondrous words: "There shall be a day, that the watchmen upon the mount Ephraim shall cry, Arise ye, and let us go up to Zion unto the Lord our God." Ephraim having first been gathered sends forth the call to the fellows of his tribe and to all Israel to come to him, to come to the house of the God of Jacob in the tops of the mountains, there to receive their blessings.

"For thus saith the Lord; Sing with gladness for Jacob, and shout among the chief of the nations: publish ye, praise ye, and say, O Lord, save thy people, the remnant of Israel." This is the day and the time of our salvation; as the Lord appointed a day in David and a day in the meridian of time, so has he appointed a day today. The word is here; salvation is free; and all who will, may come and drink of the waters of life, without money and without price.

"Behold, I will bring them from the north country, and gather them from the coasts of the earth, and with them the blind and the lame, the woman with child and her that travaileth with child together: a great company shall return thither. They shall come with weeping, and with supplications, will I lead them: I will cause them to walk by the rivers of waters in a straight way, wherein they shall not stumble: for I am a father to Israel, and Ephraim is my firstborn." The poor, to whom the Master's word is preached; the halt and lame and blind, who find refuge with the saints; mothers caring for children and women in sorrow and travail; companies slogging their way behind oxen-drawn wagons or pushing handcarts containing all their worldly possessions; the weak and the humble and the outcasts—in the eyes of the world they are the offscourings of the earth, and yet these, rich in faith, loving the Lord, worshipping again the true God, wear out their bodies and lay down their lives to travel as an organized body from Nauvoo, along the rivers of waters, to the Great Salt Lake. Who is to say that Jeremiah did not see these remnants, singing, "All is well," as they went forth to establish their latter-day Zion?

"Hear the word of the Lord, O ye nations, and declare it in the isles afar off, and say, He that scattered Israel will gather him, and keep him, as a shepherd doth his flock. For the Lord hath redeemed Jacob, and ransomed him from the hand of him that was stronger than he. Therefore they shall come and sing in the height of Zion, and shall flow together to the goodness of the Lord. . . . And my people shall be satisfied with my goodness, saith the Lord." (Jeremiah 31:6-14.)

"Behold, I will gather them out of all countries, whither I have driven them in mine anger, and in my fury, and in great wrath; and I will bring them again unto this place, and I will cause them to dwell safely." Not only will Israel assemble in the tops of the mountains in western America; they will also flow together, one by one, and company by company, to the very land and soil where the feet of their ancestors once trod. The gathering of Israel is to many places, under divers circumstances and in differing periods. "And they shall be my people, and I will be their God: and I will give them one heart, and one way, that they may fear me for ever, for the good of them, and of their children after them: and I will make an everlasting covenant with them, that I will not turn away from them, to do them good; but I will put my fear in their hearts, that they shall not depart from me." (Jeremiah 32:37-40.) In the full sense, the fulfillment of these words is Millennial. But, be it noted, always and under all circumstances, whenever Israel gathers, the Lord makes an everlasting covenant with them—the gospel covenant, the new and everlasting covenant, the same covenant he made with Abraham their father.

Nearly all of the prophecies about the gathering of Israel are fulfilled a little at a time, line upon line and precept upon precept, as it were. Most of them have a partial pre-Millennial fulfillment in our day, but in all their grandeur and beauty and fulness they will not come to pass until the wicked are destroyed and the God of Israel has come to reign over his own who are Israel. Thus, in a Millennial setting, in a day when "the Lord cometh" (Isaiah 26:21), "he shall cause them that come of Jacob to take root: Israel shall blossom and bud, and fill the face of the world with fruit." Then, in that day, "ye shall be gathered [gleaned] one by one, O ye children of Israel." (Isaiah 27:6, 12.) In that day the whole earth, having become Zion in all its parts, will be a gathering place; those of Israel in all nations will gather in their own areas. Indeed, in that day the nations of the earth as separate political divisions will cease. "I will make a full end of all the nations whither I have driven thee," saith the Lord, "and Jacob shall return, and be in rest and at ease, and none shall make him afraid." (Jeremiah 46:27-28.)

One of the greatest prophecies for which there has been a partial fulfillment up to this time, and which awaits a far grander and greater fulfillment in the days ahead, is given in these words: "Behold, the days come, saith the Lord, that I will make a new covenant with the house of Israel, and with the house of Judah: not according to the covenant that I made with their fathers in the day that I took them by the hand to bring them out of the land of Egypt; which my covenant they brake, although I was an husband unto them, saith the Lord." The Mosaic covenant, the law of carnal commandments, the lesser law, the preparatory gospel—all these shall have an end. They will be replaced with the gospel, the higher law, the eternal fulness that includes the covenant God made with Abraham.

"But this shall be the covenant that I will make with the house of Israel; After those days, saith the Lord, I will put my law in their inward parts, and write it in their hearts; and will be their God, and they shall be my people." This is the gospel covenant. With whom shall it be made? Those who receive it will be the lost sheep of Israel, those who are a scattered remnant of the ancient Israelite people. The Lord's sheep shall hear his voice and be gathered into his fold. To a small extent and for a limited period, this covenant was made in the meridian of time; then came the day of universal apostasy. To a like extent it has been made again with us through the restoration of eternal truth in our day.

Why do we say it has been made so far only to a limited degree? Because, as the holy word affirms, it involves more than the mere receipt of the gospel. A covenant, to have full force and validity, must be accepted in full both by God in heaven and by man on earth. The grand part of the covenant is this: "They shall teach no more every man his neighbour, and every man his brother, saying, Know the Lord: for they shall all know me, from the least of them unto the greatest of them, saith the Lord: for I will forgive their iniquity, and I will remember their sin no more." (Jeremiah 31:31-34.) As Joseph Smith taught in his great sermon on the Second Comforter, this promise has reference to the receipt of that added Comforter, which means that they have the personage of Jesus Christ to attend them and to appear unto them from time to time. Those so blessed are the ones who remain after the destruction of the wicked at the ushering in of the Millennium. (*Teachings of the Prophet Joseph Smith,* p. 149.) That is to say, the complete fulfillment is Millennial.

The prophetic word speaks of Israel, of the remnants of that once-favored people who are now scattered in all the nations of the earth, of the literal seed of the bodies of the prophets of old; it says that these—the descendants of the ancients—shall be gathered. Of this there is no question. But what of the Gentiles in the last days? Is not the gospel for them also? In answer we ask: What of the Gentiles in the days of ancient Israel? Were they not the children of the Father of us all? And did not the Lord offer salvation to them as he did to his chosen seed? The answer is that the eternal blessings were offered preferentially to the seed of Jacob, but that the strangers within Israel's gates were invited to come also and partake of the blessings promised the faithful. In dedicating the temple in his day, Solomon prayed that the blessings of Israel might also rest upon the strangers among them, provided those who were alien to Israel sought the Lord and kept his commandments. And so it is today, and so it is with reference to the gathering of Israel. There is to be also a gathering of the Gentiles, and all the Gentiles who gather with Israel by accepting and living the gospel shall be adopted into the house of Israel and shall rise up and bless Abraham as their father.

In most pointed and precise language, Isaiah says, concerning the gathering of the Gentiles in the last days, that it shall be with them as it was with the righteous Gentiles in ancient days. "Neither let the son of the stranger, that hath joined himself to the Lord, speak, saying, The Lord hath utterly separated me from his people: neither let the eunuch say, Behold, I am a dry tree." Are the Gentiles denied gospel blessings? Shall the eunuchs have no hope of eternal families in the realms ahead?

"For thus saith the Lord unto the eunuchs that keep my sabbaths, and choose the things that please me, and take hold of my covenant; even unto them will I give in mine house and within my walls a place and a name better than of sons and of daughters: I will give them an everlasting name, that shall not be cut off." Gentiles and eunuchs and strangers may all be saved if they will join with Israel and keep the commandments. Indeed, rich blessings are reserved for them because they rise above their environment.

And as to the day of gathering, the holy word continues: "Also the sons of the stranger, that join themselves to the Lord, to serve him, and to love the name of the Lord, to be his servants, every one that keepeth the sabbath from polluting it, and taketh hold of my covenant; even them will I bring to my holy mountain, and make them joyful in my house of prayer: . . . for mine house shall be called an house of prayer for all people." The God of Israel is also the God of the whole earth; he seeks to save Israel and he seeks to save all men. The gospel goes first to Israel and then to all others.

Hence: "The Lord God which gathereth the outcasts of Israel saith, Yet will I gather others to him, beside those that are gathered unto him." (Isaiah 56:3-8.) All mankind may be saved by obedience to the laws and ordinances of the gospel. The gospel goes first to the chosen seed and from them to all others. In our day it is expanding out to include the seed of Cain from whom the curse has now been lifted. Even they, long denied these blessings, may now join with Israel in receiving the gospel, the priesthood, celestial marriage, and the fulness of the blessings and glories that come by faith and righteousness.

Jeremiah has a like prophecy about the gathering of the Gentiles. "Behold, I will pluck them out of their land," out of their ancient lands. That is, the Gentile nations shall be scattered. "And it shall come to pass, after that I have plucked them out I will return, and have compassion on them, and will bring them again, every man to his heritage, and every man to his land." They are promised not an inheritance in the lands of Israel, but in their own lands. "And it shall come to pass, if they will diligently learn the ways of my people, to swear by my name, . . . then shall they be built in the midst of my people. But if they will not obey, I will utterly pluck up and destroy that nation, saith the Lord." (Jeremiah 12:14-17.)

Ezekiel and the Gathering of Israel

Ezekiel himself was taken captive into Babylon, leaving us to suppose that the word of the Lord to him about the gathering of Israel must have had a deep and personal impact. Let us note some of his prophetic utterances about Israel. "Although I have cast them far off among the heathen, and although I have scattered them among the countries," saith the Lord, "yet will I be to them as a little sanctuary in the countries where they shall come." The Lord will not entirely forsake his people, even in their scattered state; his Spirit—the light of Christ—will strive with them and be as "a little sanctuary," as a temple in their hearts, preparing them for the day of gathering.

For "thus saith the Lord God; I will even gather you from the people, and assemble you out of the countries where ye have been scattered, and I will give you the land of Israel." They shall come again, literally, into their ancient homeland, which is Palestine—a gathering yet future. "And they shall come thither, and they shall take away all the detestable things thereof and all the abominations thereof from thence." They will repent; they will forsake the ways of their fathers; they will no longer walk in the abominations of the past.

"And I will give them one heart, and I will put a new spirit within you; and I will take the stony heart out of their flesh, and will give them an heart of flesh: that they may walk in my statutes, and keep mine ordinances, and do them: and they shall be my people, and I will be their God." They will forsake the world, receive the gospel, enjoy the gift of the Holy Ghost, become new creatures by the power of the Spirit.

"But as for them whose heart walketh after the heart of their detestable things and their abominations, I will recompense their way upon their own heads, saith the Lord God." (Ezekiel 11:16-21.) Those who do not repent and gather spiritually into the Church will not be privileged to gather temporally. "For they are not all Israel, which are of Israel," as Paul so well expressed it. (Romans 9:6.)

Among all the prophecies of the gathering of Israel, these words of Ezekiel are unique; there is no other prophetic word comparable to them. They are: "As I live, saith the Lord God, surely with a mighty hand, and with a stretched out arm, and with fury poured out, will I rule over you: and I will bring you out from the people, and will gather you out of the countries wherein ye are scattered, with a mighty hand, and with a stretched out arm, and with fury poured out." These words are reminiscent of the day of plagues and power and miracles that attended the deliverance of Israel from Egypt. The Lord in his wrath and in his fury cursed the Egyptians, even to the point of slaying the eldest son in every Egyptian home from Pharaoh on his throne to the least and weakest among them. As the Millennium is ushered in and wars and desolations sweep the earth, we can suppose there will be some like things in connection with the coming triumph of the Lord's people.

The comparison with the gathering out of Egypt is continued in these words: "I will bring you into the wilderness of the people, and there will I plead with you face to face. Like as I pleaded with your fathers in the wilderness of the land of Egypt, so will I plead with you, saith the Lord God." Between the parting of the Red Sea to the crossing of the Jordan, Israel spent forty years of preparation in the wilderness; the rebels were purged out; a new generation arose; and the people were prepared to enter their Promised Land. It would appear that after Israel gathers out of the latter-day Egypt, there will also be a period of preparation and training in "the wilderness of the people" before they are worthy and prepared to cross over Jordan again.

"And I will cause you to pass under the rod, and I will bring you into the bond of the covenant." The saints will bow beneath the gospel rod; they will make the everlasting gospel covenant the controlling power in their lives. "And I will purge out from among you the rebels, and them that transgress against me"—the Church will be cleansed; the inactive and rebellious will be sloughed off; only the faithful will inherit the promises—"I will bring them forth out of the country where they sojourn, and they shall not enter into the land of Israel: and ye shall know that I am the Lord." (Ezekiel 20:33-38.) Though some gather with the saints, they shall not be found worthy, following the preparatory tests in the wilderness, to receive their inheritance in the land of promise.

If there is one recurring theme in all the prophecies relative to the gathering of Israel, it is that the new Israel will have a new heart and a new spirit and will keep the commandments; it is that they will receive the everlasting covenant, becoming thus the Lord's people, he being also their God; it is that they will be saved with an everlasting salvation because they become again as their ancient fathers once were. "I will take you from among the heathen, and gather you out of all countries, and will bring you into your own land," saith the Lord. After gathered Israel has come where the temple of God is, "Then will I sprinkle clean water upon you, and ye shall be clean: from all your filthiness, and from all your idols, will I cleanse you." Those with understanding will know the meaning of this. "A new heart also will I give you, and a new spirit will I put within you: and I will take away the stony heart out of your flesh, and I will give you an heart of flesh. And I will put my spirit within you, and cause you to walk in my statutes, and ye shall keep my judgments, and do them. And ye shall dwell in the land that I gave to your fathers; and ye shall be my people, and I will be your God. I will also save you from all your uncleanness." (Ezekiel 36:24-29.)

What greater blessings could there be than these? In the true sense they embrace all things. The Lord be praised for the gathering of his people!

CHAPTER 57

The Book of Mormon and the Gathering of Israel

The Doctrine of the Gathering of Israel

As far as the gathering of Israel is concerned, the Book of Mormon is the most important book that ever has been or ever will be written. It is the book that gathers Israel and that reveals, in plainness and perfection, the doctrine of the gathering of the chosen seed. It is the book, given of God, to prove the truth and divinity of his great latter-day work. It contains the fulness of the everlasting gospel and carries with it the evidence of its own divinity. Every person who is truly converted knows by the revelations of the Holy Ghost to the spirit within him that the Book of Mormon is the mind and will and voice of the Lord to the world today. It is the Book of Mormon that causes people to believe the gospel and join the Church, and, as we have heretofore seen, it is the power that brings to pass the gathering of Israel. If there were no Book of Mormon, from a practical standpoint, the gathering of the Lord's people in the last days would come to a standstill. The lost sheep of Israel hear the voice of their Shepherd as it is found in that book and, heeding that voice, come into the true sheepfold. There is no way of overstating the importance of this book of Nephite scripture in the salvation of men in the last days.

We shall now see what the Book of Mormon has to say about the doctrine of the gathering of Israel. The biblical prophets, in profuse abundance, tell of the scattering and gathering of the house of Israel. They set forth the sins and evils that caused the scattering and prescribe the righteousness and good works that underlie the gathering. But they do not use the words *gospel* and *church* and *Messiah* and *Zion* and *covenant* as clearly and plainly and with the same full meaning that these words have in the Nephite account. As with almost all the doctrines of the gospel, the Book of Mormon adds a perspective and gives a view of eternal truth that can be received in no other way.

The Book of Mormon people knew of the Assyrian captivity of the kingdom of Israel, and they fled Jerusalem in 600 B.C. to escape the coming Babylonian captivity of the kingdom of Judah, a desolation of which they later learned by revelation. As a people they were Jews, coming as they did from the kingdom of Judah. In the very nature of things they were more interested in the scattering and gathering of the Jews than of the other tribes of Israel. But as Israel is one people, and Jacob is one house, and Abraham is one father, so they, of necessity, spoke also of the whole house of Israel. What then is the word they gave, and what is the doctrine they taught?

Lehi taught his little group of Jewish emigrants from Jerusalem that after the Jews had been "carried away captive into Babylon, . . . they should return again" and "possess again the land of their inheritance"; that the Messiah, who is the "Savior of the world," should come among them and be rejected and slain; and that after the gospel was preached among the Jews they would dwindle in unbelief. Lehi also compared "the house of Israel," all twelve of the tribes, to "an olive-tree, whose branches should be broken off and should be scattered upon all the face of the earth." Thus Israel—all of the tribes— had been or would be scattered everywhere, in all nations, among every people, and become part of those kindreds speaking every tongue.

Then Lehi added a dimension to the scattering of Israel that is not found in the biblical word. He said that his people, the Lehites and Nephites and all who would become part of them, would be led "into the land of promise [the Americas], unto the fulfilling of the word of the Lord, that we [all Israel] should be scattered upon all the face of the earth." Thus, portions of Israel were scattered physically and geographically, not for their wickedness but for their righteousness, so that the Lord might preserve remnants of the Lord's covenant people in those lands and under such circumstances that they might serve him and continue to inherit the blessings of their fathers.

"And after the house of Israel should be scattered they should be gathered together again," Lehi taught. "Or, in fine, after the Gentiles [those not of the kingdom of Judah] had received the fulness of the Gospel, the natural branches of the olive-tree, or the remnants of the house of Israel, should be grafted in, or come to the knowledge of the true Messiah, their Lord and their Redeemer." (1 Nephi 10:1-14.) Thus Israel, be they of the kingdom that served Rehoboam or the kingdom that chose Jeroboam and his evil ways, all Israel shall gather if, as, and when they receive the fulness of the gospel and accept the Lord Jesus Christ as their Messiah, Lord (Jehovah), Savior, and Redeemer. There is no biblical prophecy that sets forth what is to occur as well and as plainly as do these teachings of Father Lehi.

Nephi picked up the theme of his father and expounded about Israel, the Jews and Gentiles, and the seed of Lehi, to this effect: "The house of Israel was compared unto an olive-tree, by the Spirit of the Lord which was in our father; and behold are we not broken off from the house of Israel, and are we not a branch of the house of Israel?" He is speaking to his brethren who neither believed nor understood what their father Lehi had taught.

"And now, the thing which our father meaneth concerning the grafting in of the natural branches through the fulness of the Gentiles, is, that in the latter days, when our seed shall have dwindled in unbelief, yea, for the space of many years, and many generations after the Messiah shall be manifested in body unto the children of men, then shall the fulness of the gospel of the Messiah come unto the Gentiles, and from the Gentiles unto the remnant of our seed." Both Lehi and Nephi divide all men into two camps, Jews and Gentiles. The Jews were either the nationals of the kingdom of Judah or their descendants; all others were considered to be Gentiles. Thus, we are the Gentiles of whom this scripture speaks; we are the ones who have received the fulness of the gospel; and we shall take it to the Lamanites, who are Jews, because their fathers came from Jerusalem and from the kingdom of Judah.

"And at that day," when the gospel goes from us to the Lamanites, "shall the remnant of our seed know that they are of the house of Israel, and that they are the covenant people of the Lord; and then shall they know and come to the knowledge of their forefathers, and also to the knowledge of the gospel of their Redeemer, which was ministered unto their fathers by him; wherefore, they shall come to the knowledge of their Redeemer and the very points of his doctrine, that they may know how to come unto him and be saved." This is a perfect description of the gathering of Israel. The lost sheep of Israel return when they believe in Christ, their Savior and Redeemer; when they accept his gospel; when they learn the doctrines of salvation and walk in the course leading to salvation.

"And then at that day will they not rejoice and give praise unto their everlasting God, their rock and their salvation? Yea, at that day, will they not receive the strength and nourishment from the true vine? Yea, will they not come unto the true fold of God?" Will they not join the true church, receive the gift of the Holy Ghost, perform miracles, and work out their salvation with fear and trembling before the Lord? "Behold, I say unto you, Yea; they shall be remembered again among the house of Israel; they shall be grafted in, being a natural branch of the olive-tree, into the true olive-tree." The allegory of Zenos, as recorded in Jacob 5, is a marvelous hidden-yet-plain exposition of the scattering and gathering of Israel with particular reference to the Lehite civilization.

"This is what our father meaneth," Nephi continues, "and he meaneth that it will not come to pass until after they [our seed] are scattered by the Gentiles; and he meaneth that it shall come by way of the Gentiles, that the Lord may show his power unto the Gentiles, for the very cause that he shall be rejected of the Jews, or of the house of Israel." The Lamanites will not be grafted in and receive their proper place on the Israelite olive-tree until after the restoration of the gospel through Joseph Smith. Then, as they believe the Book of Mormon and learn of the covenants of the Lord with their fathers, they will again find grace in the sight of Him who is full of grace and truth.

Lehi's chief concern was with his own seed, as all of ours should be with our posterity. But everything that applies to the Lamanites applies also in principle to the whole house of Israel; unless this is understood, it is sometimes difficult to put some Book of Mormon passages in their proper perspective. "Wherefore, our father hath not spoken of our seed alone," Nephi explains, "but also of all the house of Israel, pointing to the covenant which should be fulfilled in the latter days; which covenant the Lord made to our father Abraham, saying: In thy seed shall the kindreds of the earth be blessed." Nephi also taught his brethren of "the restoration of the Jews in the latter days," and of the restoration of the whole house of Israel, and made the promise that "after they were restored they should no more be confounded, neither should they be scattered again." (1 Nephi 15:12-20.) One of the chief and distinctive characteristics of the setting up of the kingdom of God on earth in the last days is that the kingdom will prevail; the gospel never again will be lost or given to another people; and the cause of Christ will triumph over all else.

Numerous Book of Mormon references lead us to believe that Zenos was one of the greatest prophets in Israel. None of his inspired utterances are found in our present Bible, but they were on the Brass Plates, and they were known to Nephi. Zenos spoke at length about the crucifixion of Christ and the part the Jews would play in it. Nephi expounds some of these teachings in this way: "As for those [the Jews] who are at Jerusalem, saith the prophet [Zenos], they shall be scourged by all people, because they crucify the God of Israel, and turn their hearts aside, rejecting signs and wonders, and the power and glory of the God of Israel." This is the one thing in the realm of religion that all men seem to know: that the Jews have been driven and smitten and cursed and scourged and slain and enslaved, all because they crucified their King. They are now in every nation, where they have suffered as perhaps no other people on earth have. The Jews constitute the one portion of Israel that is known by all to be scattered and cursed. And the end for them is not yet.

"And because they turn their hearts aside, saith the prophet [Zenos], and have despised the Holy One of Israel, they shall wander in the flesh, and perish, and become a hiss and a byword, and be hated among all nations." This is both a truism and an understatement. No man can tell the sufferings of this people—under Titus, under Hitler, in Russia, and in many nations and under divers rulers. Christians, to their sorrow, having little of the milk of human kindness, little of the compassion of those who are Christ's, during the long ages from Golgotha to the present have damned themselves by scourging and slaying the Jews.

"Nevertheless, when that day cometh, saith the prophet [Zenos], that they [the Jews] no more turn aside their hearts against the Holy One of Israel, then will he remember the covenants which he made to their fathers." He will remember the covenants made with Abraham, Isaac, and Israel concerning their seed; he will remember the promises of all the holy prophets that he would gather in from their long dispersion all of his chosen people, including the scattered remnants of the kingdom of Judah.

"Yea, then will he remember the isles of the sea; yea, and all the people who are of the house of Israel, will I gather in, saith the Lord, according to the words of the Prophet Zenos, from the four quarters of the earth. Yea, and all the earth shall see the salvation of the Lord, saith the prophet; every nation, kindred, tongue and people shall be blessed." (1 Nephi 19:13-17.)

Nephite Light on a Biblical Doctrine

In expounding Isaiah, chapters 48 and 49, which tell of Israel being gathered with power in the last days, Nephi says: "It appears that the house of Israel, sooner or later, will be scattered upon all the face of the earth, and also among all nations." This is a biblical thesis that we have already set forth somewhat *in extenso*. "Behold, there are many who are already lost from the knowledge of those who are at Jerusalem." Hence the expression "the Lost Tribes of Israel"—they are lost from the knowledge of those who do not understand the scriptures and who are not enlightened by the power of the Spirit; to others, in general terms, their whereabouts is known. "Yea, the more part of all the tribes have been led away; and they are scattered to and fro upon the isles of the sea; and whither they are none of us knoweth, save that we know that they have been led away." The Ten Tribes—"the more part of all the tribes"—were already scattered in all nations and among all peoples in the days of Nephi. In this sense they are not lost and their locale is known, though being thus intermixed with the Gentiles, it takes the spirit of inspiration, in a patriarchal blessing or otherwise, to identify one or many of them.

"And since they have been led away, these things [the words of Isaiah] have been prophesied concerning them, and also concerning all those who shall hereafter be scattered and be confounded, because of the Holy One of Israel; for against him will they harden their hearts; wherefore, they shall be scattered among all nations and shall be hated of all men." This last, referring to a scattering subsequent to the time of Nephi, speaks of the Jews in particular and the hatred all nations will have for them.

"Nevertheless, after they [all Israel] shall be nursed by the Gentiles [in the day of gathering], and the Lord has lifted up his hand upon the Gentiles and set them up for a standard"—the Gentiles here mentioned are those who are not Jews in the sense of being descendants of the kingdom of Judah; we are part of them though, in fact, in the literal blood sense of the word, we are of Israel, and in this sense it is to the Gentiles that the Book of Mormon came; it is to the Gentiles (the non-Jews) that the restored gospel was given—"and [after] their children [Israel's children] have been carried in their [the Gentile's] arms, and their daughters have been carried upon their shoulders, behold these things of which are spoken are temporal." The gathering of Israel is a literal and temporal thing as well as a spiritual gathering into the church and kingdom. "For thus are the covenants of the Lord with our fathers; and it [the account in Isaiah] meaneth us in the days to come, and also all our brethren who are of the house of Israel." That is, because the Nephites are a part of Israel, the prophecies relative to all Israel apply to them as well as to their kindred in other tribes.

"And it [the holy word] meaneth that the time cometh that after all the house of Israel have been scattered and confounded, that the Lord God will raise up a mighty nation among the Gentiles, yea, even upon the face of this land; and by them shall our seed be scattered." There is no way in which Nephi could have gained this understanding of Isaiah's words except by the spirit of inspiration, which, however, is the only perfect and sure way of interpreting anything the prophets have said.

"And after our seed [the seed of Lehi] is scattered the Lord God will proceed to do a marvelous work among the Gentiles, which shall be of great worth unto our seed; wherefore, it is likened unto their being nourished by the Gentiles and being carried in their arms and upon their shoulders." The marvelous work spoken of is the restoration of the gospel, including the coming forth of the Book of Mormon. When these things are offered to the Lamanites, it is with great effort and at great cost. The new converts are coddled and helped and encouraged and led along, easily and quietly, until they attain a secure spiritual stature; they are helped both temporally and spiritually by the Gentiles; and it is as though the Gentiles carried them in their arms and on their shoulders.

"And it"—the marvelous work, the gospel—"shall also be of worth unto the Gentiles." Of course it will! Jew and Gentile alike are all saved by the same belief and the same obedience and the same righteousness. A gospel that will save a Lamanite is also a gospel that will save a Gentile. Not only will it be of worth "unto the Gentiles but unto all the house of Israel, unto the making known of the covenants of the Father of heaven unto Abraham, saying: In thy seed shall all the kindreds of the earth be blessed." The gospel and the Book of Mormon have come forth for the salvation of all the tribes of Israel, the Ten Tribes included, and those of the whole house of Israel will be saved on the same terms and conditions that apply to Lehi's seed.

"And I would, my brethren, that ye should know," Nephi continues, "that all the kindreds of the earth cannot be blessed unless he [the Lord] shall make bare his arm in the eyes of the nations." If those in all nations are to be blessed, then the whole earth must hear the message; they must see the hand of the Lord in the glorious work of restoration and gathering that transpires in the last days.

"Wherefore, the Lord God will proceed to make bare his arm in the eyes of all the nations, in bringing about his covenants and his gospel unto those who are of the house of Israel." There is to be a day, as all the faithful know, when the ends of the earth shall inquire after the name of Joseph Smith and shall seek after the glorious gospel that has been restored through his instrumentality.

"Wherefore, he [the Holy One of Israel] will bring them [his ancient covenant people] again out of captivity, and they shall be gathered together to the lands of their inheritance; and they shall be brought out of obscurity and out of darkness; and they shall know that the Lord is their Savior and their Redeemer, the Mighty One of Israel." Israel will not all come to one land or to one nation; there are many lands and many nations where the righteous will assemble. America is the land of Joseph. The Jews will flee to Jerusalem. At least a representative portion of the Ten Tribes will establish themselves in ancient Canaan. But what is equally important, Israel in all nations will be established in the lands of their inheritance, in the nations of their birth, in the places where stakes of Zion are now being and yet shall be established.

At this point Nephi says some things that enable us to understand a host of Old Testament prophecies about the triumph of Israel over her enemies. He begins to talk of what will happen to gathered Israel in the final winding-up scenes incident to the Second Coming. We thus learn that the day of Israel's ultimate triumph and glory will be Millennial. The pre-Millennial day of gathering will take place in a day of darkness and apostasy, of war and commotion. "And the blood of that great and abominable church, which is the whore of all the earth, shall turn upon their own heads," Nephi says of the happenings of that day. "For they shall war among themselves, and the sword of their own hands shall fall upon their own heads, and they shall be drunken with their own blood." This refers to the day in which we live. The evil church, founded by the devil, is in all nations, and as these nations wage war with each other, the abominable church is thus bathed in its own blood.

It is in this setting, a setting describing the apostasy and evils and wars of the last days, that the prophetic word acclaims: "And every nation which shall war against thee, O house of Israel, shall be turned one against another, and they shall fall into the pit which they digged to ensnare the people of the Lord. And all that fight against Zion shall be destroyed." By Nephi's ending the quotation at this point, as in substance and thought content the equivalent Old Testament passages do, we are left to wonder how Israel shall come off victorious over her enemies in the last days. The inference is that the Gentile powers will array themselves in battle against Israel, as was the case in ancient Palestine, and that the Lord will preserve and defend his people as he did in days of old.

But Nephi comes forth with a clarifying pronouncement that gives an entirely new perspective to the scriptures that speak of the latter-day triumphs of Israel over the Gentile nations. "All that fight against Zion shall be destroyed," he declares. That is to say, Israel's triumph over her enemies will occur not because her marching armies defeat their foes in battle, but because her enemies will be destroyed, simply because every corruptible thing will be consumed at the Second Coming. In that day the Lord will truly fight the battles of his saints, for as he descends from heaven, amid fire and burning, all the proud and they that do wickedly shall be burned as stubble.

"For behold, saith the prophet"—perhaps Nephi is still quoting Zenos—"the time cometh speedily that Satan shall have no more power over the hearts of the children of men; for the day soon cometh that all the proud and they who do wickedly shall be as stubble; and the day cometh that they must be burned." This language has reference to the burning of the vineyard at the beginning of the Millennium. (Interestingly, if Nephi is quoting Zenos, as seems reasonably certain, then that Israelite prophet may well be the original source from whom Malachi gained the similar expressions he made about the great and dreadful day of the Lord.)

"For the time soon cometh that the fulness of the wrath of God shall be poured out upon all the children of men; for he will not suffer that the wicked shall destroy the righteous." Israel are the righteous among mankind; they are the ones who worship the true God; they believe the true gospel, belong to the true church, and seek to walk in paths of truth and righteousness. The wicked are those whose whole hearts are not centered on their Creator, upon the God who made heaven and earth and the seas and the fountains of waters. "Wherefore, he will preserve the righteous by his power"—Israel shall come off triumphant—"even if it so be that the fulness of his wrath must come, and the righteous be preserved, even unto the destruction of their enemies by fire. Wherefore, the righteous [Israel!] need not fear; for thus saith the prophet, they shall be saved, even if it so be as by fire. . . . For behold, the righteous shall not perish; for the time surely must come that all they who fight against Zion shall be cut off." Worldly people always have been and always will be the ones who oppose the church, who persecute the saints, who fight against Zion.

Nephi then spells out the Millennial nature of Israel's day of triumph in these words: "And the time cometh speedily that the righteous must be led up as calves of the stall"—this also is an expression later used by Malachi—"and the Holy One of Israel must reign in dominion, and might, and power, and great glory." Christ will reign personally upon the earth, and Israel will be his people. "And he gathereth his children from the four quarters of the earth"—in that Millennial day—"and he numbereth his sheep, and they know him; and there shall be one fold and one shepherd; and he shall feed his sheep, and in him they shall find pasture." One fold! One people upon the mountains of Israel! No longer two kingdoms, but one kingdom! Judah and Israel united as one nation with David their King, the Second David, ruling over them forever! How glorious Israel will be in the day of her final gathering and triumph!

"And because of the righteousness of his people [Israel], Satan has no power; wherefore, he cannot be loosed for the space of many years; for he hath no power over the hearts of the people, for they dwell in righteousness, and the Holy One of Israel reigneth. And now behold, I, Nephi, say unto you that all these things must come according to the flesh. But, behold, all nations, kindreds, tongues, and people shall dwell safely in the Holy One of Israel if it so be that they will repent." (1 Nephi 22:3-28.) Yea, even the Gentiles shall be blessed with Israel when they become as Israel.

There are many other Book of Mormon prophecies about the gathering of Israel from which added insights may be gained. For instance:

No one is ever gathered with Israel until they accept the Crucified One. Jacob says of the Jews: "When they shall come to the knowledge of their Redeemer," whom he identifies as the one they crucified, "they shall be gathered together again to the lands of their inheritance." (2 Nephi 6:11.) And the Lord himself says: "When the day cometh that they shall believe in me, that I am Christ, then have I covenanted with their fathers that they shall be restored in the flesh, upon the earth, unto the lands of their inheritance. And it shall come to pass that they shall be gathered in from their long dispersion, from the isles of the sea, and from the four parts of the earth." (2 Nephi 10:7-8.)

Israel's enemies shall be destroyed after Israel accepts Christ, not before. "He [their Redeemer] will manifest himself unto them in power and great glory, unto the destruction of their enemies, when that day cometh when they shall believe in him; and none will he destroy that believe in him." (2 Nephi 6:14.) The present gathering of the Jews to Palestine is political, not spiritual, and it is not the gathering of Israel of which the prophecies speak.

The gathering of Israel consists of joining The Church of Jesus Christ of Latter-day Saints, which church is the only true and living church upon the face of the whole earth. "All the house of Israel" shall remain in a lost and fallen and scattered state "until the time comes that they shall be restored to the true church and fold of God."

There are many lands and many places where Israel shall gather. After they join the true church, "they shall be gathered home to the lands of their inheritance, and shall be established in all their lands of promise." (2 Nephi 9:1-2.)

That God who is no respecter of persons, who curses the rebellious and blesses the obedient, both scatters and gathers all Israel on the same basis. We can, therefore, take what has happened to the Jews as a pattern and an illustration. In principle it applies to the whole house of Jacob. "Because of their iniquities, and the hardness of their hearts, and the stiffness of their necks"; because they rejected and scourged their Messiah; because they crucified the Lord of Glory—they have been scattered among all nations.

What of their gathering? How shall it be brought to pass? Thus saith Nephi: "After they have been scattered, and the Lord God hath scourged them by other nations for the space of many generations, yea, even down from generation to generation until they shall be persuaded to believe in Christ, the Son of God, and the atonement, which is infinite for all mankind—and when that day shall come that they shall believe in Christ, and worship the Father in his name, with pure hearts and clean hands, and look not forward any more for another Messiah, then, at that time, the day will come that it must needs be expedient that they should believe these things.

"And the Lord will set his hand again the second time to restore his people from their lost and fallen state. Wherefore, he will proceed to do a marvelous work and a wonder among the children of men." He will restore again the fulness of his everlasting gospel. "Wherefore, he shall bring forth his words unto them"—in the Book of Mormon and in the revelations to modern prophets—"which words shall judge them at the last day, for they shall be given them for the purpose of convincing them of the true Messiah, who was rejected by them; and unto the convincing of them that they need not look forward any more for a Messiah to come, for there should not any come, save it should be a false Messiah which should deceive the people; for there is save one Messiah spoken of by the prophets, and that Messiah is he who should be rejected of the Jews." (2 Nephi 25:12-18.)

CHAPTER 58

Israel Gathers to Zion

Zion—Its Nature and Site

Few things about Israel seem to give the saints greater concern than to identify the place or places to which the returning remnants shall gather. Will it be in America or in Palestine? Where will the Ten Tribes take up their abode when they are led out of the land of the north? Are the saints to gather to Salt Lake City or to Jerusalem, where once our Lord ministered? What of Jackson County—will there be a day when the saints go there to receive an inheritance that will include lands and houses and room to dwell? What of the statement, true in all respects, that all of North and South America is Zion?

In reality, these and related questions should be matters of lesser concern. It is the spiritual rather than the temporal or literal gathering of Israel that is of the greatest moment. But it must be clearly understood that there is also a literal gathering together of the chosen people; if such did not occur, the prophetic word, given at length and in detail, would fail; and if this concept of a literal gathering is not woven into our religious views, then those views cannot contain the fulness of the gospel. Nevertheless, the spiritual gathering takes precedence over the temporal. The locale or locales, the site or sites, the places where houses will be built and crops sown is of secondary concern. Men can be saved wherever they live, but they cannot be saved, regardless of their abode, unless they accept the gospel and come unto Christ wherever he may be found.

Interwoven with all that we have heretofore said about the gathering of Israel is the fact of a gathering over a long period of time and to many places. Now we shall turn our attention to the concept that Israel is destined to gather to Zion. If we can identify what Zion is and find the place or places of its locale, such may do more than almost anything else to put into a true perspective what is meant by a literal gathering of Israel.

Once there was a day—a day of which carnal men can scarcely conceive—when "the Lord came and dwelt with his people, and they dwelt in righteousness." (Moses 7:16.) This was in the day of that Enoch of whom Paul said: "By faith Enoch was translated that he should not see death; and was not found, because God had translated him: for before his translation he had this testimony, that he pleased God." (Hebrews 11:5.) In that day, "the fear of the Lord was upon all nations, so great was the glory of the Lord, which was upon the people. And the Lord blessed the land, and they were blessed upon the mountains, and upon the high places, and did flourish." Of course, the people prospered temporally, but conceive, if such be possible, of the spiritual blessings that attended them, day in and day out, because of the faith and purity of life that permitted them to see the face of the Lord Jesus Christ, and to partake of his wisdom and goodness and grace.

It is in this setting that the scripture saith: "And the Lord called his people ZION, because they were of one heart and one mind, and dwelt in righteousness; and there was no poor among them." (Moses 7:17-18.) The revealed definition of Zion, given through the Prophet Joseph Smith, is: "This is Zion —THE PURE IN HEART." (D&C 97:21.) "And blessed are all the pure in heart, for they shall see God." (3 Nephi 12:8.)

Thus Zion is people—pure people; people who walk with God; people from whose souls sin and evil have been burned by the sanctifying power of the Holy Ghost. Thus Zion is the saints of God—saints who have been baptized for the remission of sins; saints who keep the commandments and walk in all the ways of the Lord; saints who have put on Christ and are partakers of his Holy Spirit. Zion is what all people must become if they are to inherit the same eternal fulness enjoyed by those of old who attained such supreme spiritual heights.

But Zion is also a place, for "Enoch continued his preaching in righteousness unto the people of God. And it came to pass in his days, that he built a city that was called the City of Holiness, even ZION." What was more natural than to name the city after the people? The pure in heart called their abode by the name City of Holiness. Their every thought was 'Holiness to the Lord, and blessed be he that cometh in the name of the Lord. Hosanna in the highest!'

"And it came to pass that Enoch talked with the Lord; and he said unto the Lord: Surely Zion shall dwell in safety forever," a most natural thought to have, seeing that the Lord always preserves and blesses those of perfect faith and righteousness. "But the Lord said unto Enoch: Zion have I blessed, but the residue of the people have I cursed. And . . . Zion, in process of time, was taken up into heaven. And the Lord said unto Enoch: Behold mine abode forever." Thereafter, others, attaining a like spiritual stature with those already translated, "were caught up by the powers of heaven into Zion." (Moses 7:19-27.)

In all subsequent days, whenever people have forsaken the world and sought, by congregations, to perfect themselves in Christ, they, as a people, have become Zion. And they have chosen to call all or part of the places of their abodes by the same name. Jerusalem, Israel's ancient capital city, is called Zion; a New Jerusalem, yet to be built up in Jackson County, Missouri, carries the same name. The Church (a body of pure worshippers) is called Zion, and whenever large congregations of saints are accessible to each other, they are organized into stakes of Zion. The Zion people in Enoch's day built a holy city called Zion, wherein they worshipped the Lord, and the Zion people today build stakes of Zion for the same reason.

Thus, the gathering of Israel is both spiritual and temporal. The lost sheep gather spiritually when they join the Church, and they gather temporally when they come to a prepared place—that is, to Zion or one of her stakes. There they can strengthen each other in the Lord; there they can receive for themselves, in holy houses built for that very purpose, the covenant made in days of old with Abraham, Isaac, and Israel. There they can redeem their dead through the vicarious ordinances of the temples. Speaking of places and locales, Zion itself (the New Jerusalem) has not as yet been established in our day, but it will be in due course. For the present, the Lord's people, who are Zion, are called to gather in the stakes of Zion as these are established in the lands of their inheritance.

However, Zion is likened by the prophets to a great tent held up by poles and cords and stakes. The tent is a place of refuge, a covert from the storms, a gathering place where, sheltered from the rains and winds of the world, the Lord's people can worship him in spirit and in truth. There is no difference between Zion, as a single city, and other Zions wherever they may be located. The same blessings are available in them all. In the true sense of the word, every part of the tent is a part of Zion; thus, wherever there is a stake of Zion, that area of the earth becomes a part of Zion. And when stakes of Zion cover the earth as they will during the Millennium, then every dot of ground in every site and location will be part of Zion. Zion will cover the whole earth.

"Come to Zion, Come to Zion"

What does the holy word say about the gathering of Israel to Zion?

First, Zion is described as a glorious place—and how could it be otherwise when it is the place where the saints of God reside? Any place is made better when righteous people choose it as their home. "Beautiful for situation, the joy of the whole earth, is mount Zion, . . . the city of the great King. God is known in her palaces for a refuge." (Psalm 48:2-3.) "The Lord loveth the gates of Zion more than all the dwellings of Jacob. Glorious things are spoken of thee, O city of God. . . . And of Zion it shall be said, This and that man was born in her: and the highest himself shall establish her. The Lord shall count, when he writeth up the people, that this man was born there." (Psalm 87:2-6.) How wondrous it would have been to be born in the City of Enoch, or to have lived among the Nephites during their Golden Era! What a blessing it would be to have one's mortal probation during the Millennium, when children will grow up without sin unto salvation. So be it; but how infinitely great it is to be born among the saints in any age, or to accept the gospel, leave the world, and assemble with those who serve the God of Jacob!

Next, the blessings attendant upon gathering to Zion are set forth, and the chief blessing to be gained is salvation. "I will place salvation in Zion for Israel my glory," saith the Lord. (Isaiah 46:13.) That is, Come to Zion and be saved. Salvation is not available to any who do not gather with the lost sheep of Israel into the true fold of the Good Shepherd.

"Sing, O heavens; and be joyful, O earth; and break forth

into singing, O mountains: for the Lord hath comforted his people, and will have mercy upon his afflicted." Let the very rocks and stones cry out for joy at the glories available through the gathering of Israel. "But Zion said, The Lord hath forsaken me, and my Lord hath forgotten me." So it would seem to the spiritually untutored, as the long days of the dispersion are brought to mind. But the Lord has an answer: "Can a woman forget her sucking child, that she should not have compassion on the son of her womb? yea, they may forget, yet will I not forget thee. Behold, I have graven thee upon the palms of my hands; thy walls are continually before me." (Isaiah 49:13-16.) What is there of greater concern to the Lord than to gather his people so they can be saved? For what purpose did he create the earth, man, and all things, except to bring to pass the immortality and eternal life of his spirit children?

"The Redeemer shall come to Zion, and unto them that turn from transgression in Jacob, saith the Lord. As for me, this is my covenant with them, saith the Lord; my spirit that is upon thee [upon gathered Israel], and my words which I have put in thy mouth, shall not depart out of thy mouth, nor out of the mouth of thy seed, nor out of the mouth of thy seed's seed, saith the Lord, from henceforth and for ever." (Isaiah 59:20-21.) There is an eternal decree, issued in heaven above by the Lord himself. It is that in the day of gathering, when for the last time he assembles the outcasts of Israel, he will never again forsake them. They and their seed forever shall remain steadfast to the truth. The gospel will never be given to another people, nor the kingdom placed in other hands. The Lord's work will roll forward until the conversion of the world is completed.

The holy word also says that the way to come to Zion is to accept the Lord Jesus Christ; to believe his word, his doctrine, his gospel; to worship the Father, in his name, by the power of the Holy Ghost. "Come unto Christ" is the plea of Moroni, addressed to the Lamanites and to all the scattered sheep of Israel. "And awake, and arise from the dust, O Jerusalem." Let Jerusalem of old become as she once was; let her be glorious because of the righteousness of those who dwell within her walls. "Yea, and put on thy beautiful garments, O daughter of Zion." Wear again the garments of righteousness. "And strengthen thy stakes and enlarge thy borders forever, that thou mayest no more be confounded, that the covenants of the Eternal Father which he hath made unto thee, O house of Israel, may be fulfilled. Yea, come unto Christ, and be perfected in him, and deny yourselves of all ungodliness." (Moroni 10:30-32.) The covenants of God, made with Israel of old, all promised that he would save their seed in the day when they believed in Christ, accepted his gospel, and lived his laws.

And again, the holy word acclaims that Israel will be gathered and Zion built up by the power and authority of the holy priesthood. Indeed, what other power and authority has the Lord ever used to govern his people? And where is this priesthood but among the saints of the Most High? And so we read in Isaiah one of the passages Moroni had before him in his call to the Lamanites and to all Israel. By Isaiah the Lord calls: "Awake, awake; put on thy strength, O Zion; put on thy beautiful garments, O Jerusalem, the holy city: for henceforth there shall be no more come into thee the uncircumcised and the unclean." (Isaiah 52:1.)

"What is meant by the command . . . which saith: Put on thy strength, O Zion—and what people had Isaiah reference to?" Answer: "He had reference to those whom God should call in the last days, who should hold the power of priesthood to bring again Zion, and the redemption of Israel; and to put on her strength is to put on the authority of the priesthood, which she, Zion, has a right to by lineage; also to return to that power which she had lost." (D&C 113:7-8.) When the work here proclaimed is fully accomplished, the Millennium will be upon us, and no unclean person will be left to go into Jerusalem or Zion or any of the cities of the earth, for the wicked will be burned at His coming.

And, yet again, we read in the holy word that Israel will gather to Zion when she forsakes her sins and looses the bands that bind her; that she, being worthy, will receive revelation and come again to know the Lord; that this will be brought to pass by the preaching of the restored gospel; and that the converts who gather to Zion will be perfectly united in belief, in doctrine, in obedience—all to the extent that they see eye to eye in all things. And so the word in Isaiah says: "Shake thyself from the dust; arise, and sit down, O Jerusalem: loose thyself from the bands of thy neck, O captive daughter of Zion. For thus saith the Lord, Ye have sold yourselves for nought; and ye shall be redeemed without money." (Isaiah 52:2-3.)

Question: "What are we to understand by Zion loosing herself from the bands of her neck?" Answer: "We are to understand that the scattered remnants are exhorted to return to the Lord from whence they have fallen; which if they do, the promise of the Lord is that he will speak to them, or give them revelation. . . . The bands of her neck are the curses of God upon her, or the remnants of Israel in their scattered condition among the Gentiles." (D&C 113:9-10.) Such is the inspired interpretation given in latter days.

As to the revelation that will attend the gathering of Israel and be received by those who gather to Zion, the Lord says through Isaiah: "Therefore my people shall know my name: therefore they shall know in that day that I am he that doth speak: behold, it is I." And how could Israel be gathered without revelation? Who would so much as know who belongs to the house of Israel, unless that knowledge came from on high? Any why would any individual choose to gather with Israel unless he had a personal revelation that God has spoken again, giving to men at long last the fulness of his gospel? And as to the building of Zion, what is Zion, where is the building site, what laws are involved, and who will govern the resultant City of Holiness?

As to the work to be done by preachers, the divine word says: "How beautiful upon the mountains are the feet of him that bringeth good tidings, that publisheth peace; that bringeth good tidings of good, that publisheth salvation; that saith unto Zion, Thy God reigneth!" Let the glad tidings of salvation be carried to all men, and to the lost sheep of Israel in particular, by the legal administrators whom the Lord calls in this the dispensation of the fulness of times. Praise God for the missionary system and for the missionaries!

And as to unity, how better has the proclamation ever been made than in these words: "Thy watchmen"—those on the towers of Zion—"shall lift up the voice; with the voice together shall they sing: for they shall see eye to eye, when the Lord shall bring again Zion." To a modest degree this promise finds fulfillment in the lives of faithful Latter-day Saints who place the things of God's kingdom first in their lives and who are guided and enlightened by the power of the Holy Ghost. Its complete and glorious fulfillment will, of course, be Millennial.

Is it any wonder, then, that Isaiah breaks forth into poetic, prophetic praise? "Break forth into joy, sing together, ye waste places of Jerusalem: for the Lord hath comforted his people, he hath redeemed Jerusalem." This is not yet, but by and by. "The Lord hath made bare his holy arm in the eyes of all the nations; and all the ends of the earth shall see the salvation of our God." So it is now, but so shall it be in particular in that great Millennial day that is soon to dawn. And both for now and for the future the call is: "Depart ye, depart ye"—go ye out from Babylon; forsake the world—"go ye out from thence, touch no unclean thing; go ye out of the midst of her; be ye clean, that bear the vessels of the Lord. For ye shall not go out with haste, nor go by flight: for the Lord will go before you; and the God of Israel will be your rereward." (Isaiah 52:6-12.)

The holy word also affirms that Israel gathers to Zion to escape the abomination of desolation that shall be poured out upon a wicked world in the last days. In Zion there will be safety; in the world, naught but sorrow and tribulation and desolation. To all the members of The Church of Jesus Christ of Latter-day Saints the Lord commands: "Arise and shine forth, that thy light may be a standard for the nations; and that the gathering together upon the land of Zion, and upon her stakes, may be for a defense, and for a refuge from the storm, and from wrath when it shall be poured out without mixture upon the whole earth." (D&C 115:5-6.)

But let us hear the conclusion of the whole matter and recite the crowning reason for gathering to Zion or to her stakes. It is to receive the blessings found in the temples of the Lord. There and there only are the saints endowed with power from on high after the ancient pattern. There and there only can they enter into the same eternal covenants that Jehovah made with Abraham, Isaac, and Jacob, that through celestial marriage they might have a continuation of the seeds forever and ever. There and there only can they perform the ordinances of salvation and exaltation for their ancestors who died without a knowledge of the gospel, but who would have received it with all their hearts had it come to them in their day.

Thus—and this is an illustration only—the Lord commanded: "Let the city, Far West, be a holy and consecrated land unto me; and it shall be called most holy, for the ground upon which thou standest is holy. Therefore, I command you to build a house unto me, for the gathering together of my saints, that they may worship me." (D&C 115:7-8.) Indeed, all of the places appointed for the gathering of the saints are holy places, and the center and crown of each place is that sacred sanctuary, that holy temple, wherein the fulness of the blessings of heaven may be received.

CHAPTER 59

The Building Up of Zion

The Pre-Millennial Zion

Even before the Book of Mormon, which contains the fulness of the gospel, was published to the world; even before the coming of John the Baptist, and of Peter, James, and John, and of other angelic ministrants, each bringing their priesthoods, keys, powers, and authorities; even before the Church, as an organized body of believers, was set up again on earth in this final dispensation of grace—before all this, the Lord by revelation said to one person after another: "Keep my commandments, and seek to bring forth and establish the cause of Zion." (D&C 6:6; 11:6; 12:6; 14:6.) After the coming forth of the Book of Mormon, the restoration of priesthood and keys, and the organization of the Church, the command went forth to every elder in the kingdom: "Thou art called to labor in my vineyard, and to build up my church, and to bring forth Zion, that it may rejoice upon the hills and flourish." (D&C 39:13.)

The building up of Zion—that is our work! All that we do in this life should be judged by this grand standard: does it further the cause of Zion? What does it profit a man if he gain the wealth of the world, the power of kingdoms, the dominion of Caesars, unless what he does furthers the interests of Zion? Those interests are both temporal and spiritual and are concerned, solely and exclusively, with the salvation of the souls of men.

How do we go about building up Zion and strengthening her cause in all the earth? Between now and the Second Coming, our course is one of building up the Church and strengthening its influence among men. As the Mosaic law was a schoolmaster preparing Israel for the higher law of the gospel, so this pre-Millennial period is one in which the saints prepare for that Millennial glory reserved for those who abide the day of His coming.

Our work is to preach the gospel to every nation and kindred and tongue and people, in plainness and perfection, by the power of the Spirit, unto the convincing of those who hear our words. It is to gather believing souls from Babylon and establish their feet in the mountains of Israel, far from the damning evils of the world.

Our work is to perfect the lives of the saints, leading them gently and quietly in the way of righteousness, until, in the full bloom of spiritual perfection, they have received all the ordinances of the house of the Lord, have sanctified their souls, and are fit to dwell in the Glorious Presence for a thousand years. This is the work in which the Church and all its organizations are engaged, early and late, day in and day out, and they will continue so to labor until the perfect day dawns.

Our work is to redeem our dead, to offer them through vicarious ordinances the same blessings—those of Abraham, Isaac, and Jacob—which we have received in our own *propria persona,* that they with us, the family units being thus perfected, may enter into that rest of the Lord which is the fulness of his glory.

Our work is to call more missionaries; to preach in more nations; to organize new stakes; to build more temples; to free ourselves from the blood and sins of this generation; to keep the commandments; to stand in holy places; to remain on the highway the Lord has cast up whereon gathered Israel may march to their Millennial Zion. Our work is to prepare a people for the Second Coming. Temples must be built in Old Jerusalem and in the New Jerusalem. And when all things are accomplished, the Great Jehovah will say the work is done. Until then we have no choice but to use our means, talents, and time in the building up of the Lord's work on earth and the establishment of Zion.

Those who labor in the cause of Zion shall not go unrewarded. "Blessed are they who shall seek to bring forth my Zion," saith the Lord, "for they shall have the gift and the power of the Holy Ghost; and if they endure unto the end they shall be lifted up at the last day, and shall be saved in the everlasting kingdom of the Lamb; and whoso shall publish peace, yea, tidings of great joy, how beautiful upon the mountains shall they be." (1 Nephi 13:37.)

Zion in the limited sense of the word, meaning the New Jerusalem, will be built in Jackson County, Missouri, in due course as the Lord shall direct. Zion in the broad and general sense of the word, meaning the church and kingdom of God on earth, which does or should consist of the pure in heart, is in process of being built up in one part of the earth after another as rapidly as our strength and means permit. Whenever the growth of the Church in any area is sufficient, a stake of Zion is organized, thus making that area, in the general sense of the word, a part of Zion. The gathering of Israel is to Zion and her stakes, and since Zion proper is yet to be built, the gathering of Israel as of now is into the stakes of Zion wherever they may be. "For Zion must increase in beauty, and in holiness; her borders must be enlarged; her stakes must be strengthened; yea, verily I say unto you, Zion must arise and put on her beautiful garments." (D&C 82:14.)

It is self-evident that not all of the saints can dwell in the Zion called the New Jerusalem. Hence, saith the Lord, "I have other places which I will appoint unto them, and they shall be called stakes, for the curtains or the strength of Zion." (D&C 101:21.) Hence the inspired prayer, offered at the dedication of the Kirtland Temple: "Whatsoever city thy servants shall enter, and the people of that city receive their testimony, let thy peace and thy salvation be upon that city; that they may gather out of that city the righteous, that they may come forth to Zion, or to her stakes, the places of thine appointment, with songs of everlasting joy." (D&C 109:39.) And hence the divine promise: "That the gathering together upon the land of Zion, and upon her stakes, may be for a defense, and for a refuge from the storm, and from wrath when it shall be poured out without mixture upon the whole earth." (D&C 115:6.)

This process of gathering the righteous together into the stakes of Zion will continue until stakes are organized in many nations. Then the Lord will come. He will come to the people who have been schooled and prepared in the stakes to receive their King. Nephi saw the Church in our day when we are struggling to bring forth the cause of Zion; he saw the growth and stability it would have when the Lord comes; and he compared the Lord's earthly kingdom with the power and dominion of the forces of evil that would almost cover the earth in that day. "I beheld the church of the Lamb of God," he said, "and its numbers were few, because of the wickedness and abominations of the whore who sat upon many waters." So it is today, and so shall it be until the Second Coming. Though there will be millions of faithful people on earth when the Lord returns, they will be few compared to the armies of evil.

Where and in what nations will the saints be found when their Lord returns? Though they are comparatively few in number, Nephi continues, "nevertheless I beheld that the church of the Lamb, who were the saints of God [and who are gathered Israel], were also upon all the face of the earth." He is seeing stakes of Zion in the nations of the earth. "And their dominions upon the face of the earth were small, because of the wickedness of the great whore whom I saw." We are few; they are many. The righteous are a handful; the wicked are a host. It is their world, a world of carnality and evil; and for the moment they, measured by the standards of the world, are coming off triumphant.

"And it came to pass that I beheld that the great mother of abominations did gather together multitudes upon the face of all the earth, among all the nations of the Gentiles, to fight against the Lamb of God. And it came to pass that I, Nephi, beheld the power of the Lamb of God, that it descended upon the saints of the church of the Lamb, and upon the covenant people of the Lord, who were scattered upon all the face of the earth; and they were armed with righteousness and with the power of God in great glory." (1 Nephi 14:12-14.) After the wars and desolations of the last days, the Lord will come, bringing triumph and glory with him; the wicked will be destroyed, and the Millennial era, with its great and glorious day of gathering, will be ushered in.

Is All Well in Zion?

As we build up Zion and strengthen her stakes in one nation after another; as the lost sheep of Israel come to Zion and find place in her stakes, with a desire to serve God and keep his commandments; as new congregations of true believers break forth on the right hand and on the left—what of the overall progress of the kingdom? Are we going forward in full harmony with the divine will? Is all well in Zion?

Unfortunately, the answer is No. We rejoice in the glorious restoration of eternal truth; in the going forth of the Lord's servants to proclaim the everlasting word; in the rich harvest that attends their labors; in the organizing of stakes and the building of temples at the ends of the earth; in the tithes and offerings and service and good works of the faithful; in the gifts of the Spirit found in the households of faith; and (perhaps inordinately) in the temporal prosperity so bounteously showered upon us. Truly, the contrast between the saints and the world is sharp; between us and them there is a great gulf; but sadly, many of the house of Israel backslide today as did their fathers of old. Some cross the gulf and join the world; others try to compromise and have what they assume is the best of both worlds. Foreseeing this, Nephi prophesied: "Others will he [Lucifer] pacify, and lull them away into carnal security, that they will say: All is well in Zion; yea, Zion prospereth, all is well—and thus the devil cheateth their souls, and leadeth them away carefully down to hell." (2 Nephi 28:21.)

The children of Zion fail in their great mission for two reasons: (1) Oftentimes they set their hearts upon temporal things and are more concerned with amassing the things that moth and rust corrupt, and that thieves break through and steal, than in laying up for themselves treasures in heaven. Hence the divine direction: "But the laborer in Zion shall labor for Zion; for if they labor for money they shall perish." (2 Nephi 26:31.) (2) Others fail to live by the high standards of belief and conduct imposed by the gospel. Of them the divine word says: "Your minds in times past have been darkened because of unbelief, and because you have treated lightly the things you have received—which vanity and unbelief have brought the whole church under condemnation. And this condemnation resteth upon the children of Zion, even all. And they shall remain under this condemnation until they repent and remember the new covenant, even the Book of Mormon and the former commandments which I have given them, not only to say, but to do according to that which I have written— that they may bring forth fruit meet for their Father's kingdom;

otherwise there remaineth a scourge and judgment to be poured out upon the children of Zion." (D&C 84:54-58.)

This scourge was, in part at least, poured out upon them in the early days of this dispensation as they were smitten and persecuted and driven from one place to another. "And, now, behold, if Zion do these things"—keep the commandments!—"she shall prosper," saith the Lord, "and spread herself and become very glorious, very great, and very terrible. And the nations of the earth shall honor her, and shall say: Surely Zion is the city of our God, and surely Zion cannot fall, neither be moved out of her place, for God is there, and the hand of the Lord is there; and he hath sworn by the power of his might to be her salvation and her high tower. . . . Therefore, . . . let Zion rejoice, while all the wicked shall mourn." Such is the Lord's promise to Zion—to the Zion of the latter days.

Why was the promise given? Because "vengeance cometh speedily upon the ungodly as the whirlwind," saith the Lord, "and who shall escape it?" Because "the Lord's scourge shall pass over by night and by day, and the report shall vex all people; yea, it shall not be stayed until the Lord come; for the indignation of the Lord is kindled against their abominations and all their wicked works." Such is the state of things in the world, a state that will surely worsen in the days ahead.

"Nevertheless, Zion shall escape if she observe to do all things whatsoever I have commanded her. But if she observe not to do whatsoever I have commanded her, I will visit her according to all her works, with sore affliction, with pestilence, with plague, with sword, with vengeance, with devouring fire." (D&C 97:18-26.) Our forebears—the first inhabitants, as it were, of the latter-day Zion—failed to gain all of the promised blessings and in part, at least, reaped the resultant curses. Our course today is not much different than theirs was, leaving us to ponder, anxiously, what our fate shall be. The true fulfillment of the promises relative to the greatness and preservation of Zion will be Millennial.

The Millennial Gathering to Zion

We live in the Saturday night of time. Tomorrow the Millennial Sunday will dawn with all its peace and glory; it will be a sabbath of rest in which Israel will no longer be scattered and smitten and scourged. Then, in the true and full sense, she will gather to Zion, build the Old and New Jerusalem, and triumph gloriously over all who oppressed her.

But we are of Israel and have already gathered to a pre-Millennial Zion, a Zion that is a forerunner, an Elias, as it were, of the Zion that is yet to be. Our interest is centered primarily in the prophetic word that speaks of this pre-Millennial gathering, of this pre-Millennial Zion, of the restoration of the gospel, which prepares the way for the restoration of the kingdom to Israel. We are part of and participants in this great preparatory work, a work that is preparing a people for the coming of their King, our Lord, Jesus Christ, to reign over them forever. And we must not suppose that the prophetic word about the gathering of Israel and the building of Zion is to be fulfilled in all its fulness and perfection in our day. The great day of fulfillment is Millennial, though the same prophetic word may be quoted to show what is now taking place and also to open our minds and enlarge our vision of what will be when the Lord comes. Ours is a day of beginnings, a day of slight and partial fulfillment of the divine word. The great day for the Lord's people lies ahead. Let us sample enough of the prophetic word to see how this concept operates.

After the restoration of the gospel; after converts are made in all nations; after the true saints who belong to "the church of the Lamb" become again "the covenant people of the Lord," then, as Nephi prophesied, these Latter-day Saints will be "armed with righteousness and with the power of God in great glory." Then—and this day is yet future, for we are not as yet established in all nations—then "the wrath of God" is to be "poured out upon the great and abominable church"; then there will be "wars and rumors of wars among all the nations and kindreds of the earth." There has been a slight foretaste of this in our day, but the great day in which the wrath of God is to be poured out upon the Babylonish whore will be at the Second Coming. Then and not until then will Babylon, which is the great and abominable church, be destroyed.

"And when the day cometh that the wrath of God is poured out upon the mother of harlots, which is the great and abominable church of all the earth, whose founder is the devil, then, at that day"—the day when the Millennium is ushered in —"the work of the Father shall commence, in preparing the way for the fulfilling of his covenants, which he hath made to his people who are of the house of Israel." (1 Nephi 14:12-17.) The destruction of the wicked when the Lord comes will make possible the triumph of the Lord's people in the full and complete sense of the word.

It is also of the Millennium that the biblical word says: "They shall not hurt nor destroy in all my holy mountain: for the earth shall be full of the knowledge of the Lord, as the waters cover the sea. And in that day . . . the Lord shall set his hand again the second time to recover the remnant of his people." (Isaiah 11:9-11.) In an initial and preparatory way, the Lord is now gathering his people; during the coming sabbath of peace, all the people of the whole earth will be involved, in one way or another, in this gathering.

"For the Lord shall comfort Zion: he will comfort all her waste places; and he will make her wilderness like Eden, and her desert like the garden of the Lord; joy and gladness shall be found therein, thanksgiving, and the voice of melody." These words of holy writ have reference to the renewed earth. And when the Lord comforts Zion, "the redeemed of the Lord shall return, and come with singing unto Zion; and everlasting joy shall be upon their head: they shall obtain gladness and joy; and sorrow and mourning shall flee away." In that day the Lord will say unto Zion, "Thou art my people."

Because of all this, the cry will go forth: "Awake, awake, stand up, O Jerusalem, which hast drunk at the hand of the Lord the cup of his fury; thou hast drunken the dregs of the cup of trembling, and wrung them out." (Isaiah 51:3-16.) O Jerusalem, Jerusalem, the once Holy City, how thou hast been a battleground through the ages; how thou didst sink to the depths as "the great city, which spiritually is called Sodom and Egypt, where also our Lord was crucified" (Revelation 11:8); how thou art even now trodden down of the Gentiles, until the day of thy redeemed shall come; and how thou shalt continue to suffer until thy bands are loosed in the devastation of that Armageddon which is to be.

What city has been like unto Jerusalem? "Therefore hear now this, thou afflicted, and drunken, but not with wine: Thus saith thy Lord the Lord, and thy God that pleadeth the cause of his people, Behold, I have taken out of thine hand the cup of trembling, even the dregs of the cup of my fury; thou shalt no more drink it again: but I will put it into the hand of them that afflict thee; which have said to thy soul, Bow down, that we may go over: and thou hast laid thy body as the ground, and as the street, to them that went over." (Isaiah 51:21-23.)

O Jerusalem, thou shalt yet ascend to the heights; thou shalt yet overcome all things. "Awake, awake; put on thy strength, O Zion;" put on the authority of that priesthood to which thou hast a right by lineage; "put on thy beautiful garments, O Jerusalem, the holy city"; put on the robes of righteousness; "for henceforth there shall no more come into thee the uncircumcised and the unclean." (Isaiah 52:1.) This is reserved for the day when the wicked have been destroyed by the brightness of His coming; this is the day when those who remain, those who have abided the day, will qualify to enter the Holy City.

That these words of Isaiah, and much else that he wrote about Zion and the gathering of Israel, will have Millennial fulfillment is attested to by the Lord Jesus himself. "I will gather my people together as a man gathereth his sheaves into the floor," he told the Nephites. He then spoke of the restoration of the gospel, that it should go to the Lamanites and then, in due course, to the Jews. For, said he, "I will remember the covenant which I have made with my people; and I have covenanted with them that I would gather them together in mine own due time, that I would give unto them again the land of their fathers for their inheritance, which is the land of Jerusalem, which is the promised land unto them forever, saith the Father." The Jews shall gather to Jerusalem. That is their homeland; that will be where their holy city shall stand.

"And it shall come to pass that the time cometh, when the fulness of my gospel shall be preached unto them; And they shall believe in me, that I am Jesus Christ, the Son of God, and shall pray unto the Father in my name." The day of Jewish conversion, except for an isolated few, will be at the Second Coming when they see the nail marks in his hands and feet and the spear wound in his side. "Then shall their watchmen lift up their voice, and with the voice together shall they sing; for they shall see eye to eye. Then will the Father gather them together again, and give unto them Jerusalem for the land of their inheritance. Then shall they break forth into joy—Sing together, ye waste places of Jerusalem; for the Father hath comforted his people, he hath redeemed Jerusalem. The Father hath made bare his holy arm in the eyes of all the nations; and all the ends of the earth shall see the salvation of the Father; and the Father and I are one."

At this point the Lord Jesus quotes Isaiah 52. He calls upon Jerusalem to awake, put on her strength, clothe herself with righteousness, and attain her redemption. It is of this Millennial setting that, using Isaiah's words, he says: "Then shall a cry go forth: Depart ye, depart ye, go ye out from thence, touch not that which is unclean; go ye out of the midst of her; be ye clean that bear the vessels of the Lord. For ye shall not go out with haste nor go by flight; for the Lord will go before you, and the God of Israel shall be your rearward." (3 Nephi 20:18, 29-42.)

Isaiah 54 continues in the same vein; so also do Isaiah 60, 61, and 62. In one divine outpouring of heavenly wisdom after another, Isaiah speaks of the Millennial glory and righteousness of the people who were scattered by Jehovah for their sins in days of old. Other chapters in Isaiah and elsewhere speak prophetically of all phases of the scattering and gathering of the Lord's chosen people. No attempt is made in this brief work to cover all that the scriptures contain.

But in the light of all that the Lord and his prophets have said, we are led to ask: How can any church be true that does not believe in the literal gathering of Israel and in the restoration of the Ten Tribes?

Or even more importantly: How can any person be saved unless he joins with gathered Israel and receives for himself the blessings of the covenant made with Abraham, Isaac, and Israel?

CHAPTER 60

Zion and the New Jerusalem

Israel Builds the New Jerusalem

There is no occasion for uncertainty or anxiety about the building up of Zion—meaning the New Jerusalem—in the last days. The Lord once offered his people the chance to build that Zion from which the law shall go forth to all the world. They failed. Why? Because they were unprepared and unworthy, as is yet the case with those of us who now comprise the kingdom. When we as a people are prepared and worthy, the Lord will again command us and the work will go forward —on schedule, before the Second Coming, and at the direction of the President of the Church. Until then, none of us need take any personal steps toward gathering to Missouri or preparing for a landed-inheritance there. Let us, rather, learn the great concepts involved and make ourselves worthy for any work the Lord may lay upon us in our day and time. Some things must yet precede the building up of Jackson County.

First, Israel shall gather to prepare for the Second Coming of the Son of Man; she shall gather to Zion in all nations; she shall gather into the stakes created everywhere among all peoples. "I will gather my people together as a man gathereth his sheaves into the floor," was the promise of the Risen Lord to his Nephite sheep. "And it shall come to pass that I will establish my people, O house of Israel." This is the gathering that is now going on. And every gathering place, for the scattered remnants who there assemble, becomes to them as a New Jerusalem. It becomes a City of Holiness, a place where they can worship the Father in spirit and in truth, a place where temples are available in which they may receive the fulness of the priesthood, a place where no blessing is denied them.

Then, before the Second Coming, gathered Judah, as

directed by Ephraim, shall build up anew the Old Jerusalem and prepare therein a holy temple; and gathered Ephraim, aided by Manasseh, shall build a New Jerusalem in an American Zion and prepare therein a holy temple. It is to these two temples in particular that the Lord shall come at his glorious return, and it is from these two cities—Zion in America and Jerusalem in Old Canaan—that the governance and worship of the world will be directed. Thus Jesus, continuing his preaching to the Nephites, said: "And behold, this people"— this Lehite remnant of Israel—"will I establish in this land, unto the fulfilling of the covenant which I made with your father Jacob; and it shall be a New Jerusalem." Jacob is Israel, and Israel is the one with whom the Lord made covenant that his seed should inherit the blessings of Abraham, Isaac, and Israel. "And the powers of heaven shall be in the midst of this people; yea, even I will be in the midst of you." (3 Nephi 20:18, 21-22.) After gathered Israel builds the New Jerusalem, the Lord will come and dwell with his people.

The building of these two world capitals will commence before the Second Coming and continue during the Millennium. Classifying scattered Israel as Gentiles, because they are not nationals of the kingdom of Judah (the Jews), the Lord Jesus said: "If they will repent and hearken unto my words, and harden not their hearts, I will establish my church among them, and they shall come in unto the covenant and be numbered among this the remnant of Jacob, unto whom I have given this land for their inheritance." We are the ones here named; the gospel spoken of came through Joseph Smith; we are of the house of Joseph to whom the land of America has been given as an inheritance, even as it was given to the Nephite portion of Joseph's seed. "And they [the Latter-day Saints] shall assist my people, the remnant of Jacob, and also as many of the house of Israel as shall come, that they may build a city, which shall be called the New Jerusalem." Israel—all gathered remnants assisting each other—shall build the New Jerusalem in America.

"And then shall they [that Israel which builds the New Jerusalem] assist my people that they may be gathered in, who are scattered upon all the face of the land, in unto the New Jerusalem. And then shall the power of heaven come down among them; and I also will be in the midst." Israel gathers; the New

Jerusalem is built; Israel continues to gather; and the Lord comes to reign personally in the midst of his people. Then an even greater gathering takes place, which includes the restoration of the Ten Tribes to the lands of their inheritance. Then, when the Lord is in the midst of his people, "shall the work of the Father commence at that day, even when this gospel shall be preached among the remnant of this people. Verily I say unto you, at that day shall the work of the Father commence among all the dispersed of my people, yea, even the tribes which have been lost, which the Father hath led away out of Jerusalem." (3 Nephi 21:22-26.)

John the Revelator saw in vision the holy city come down from God in heaven twice. First he saw the City of Enoch, a Holy City called the New Jerusalem, come down after the Second Coming to remain with men on earth a thousand years. Then with seeric eyes he beheld the celestial Jerusalem, the Holy City where God and angels dwell, come down from heaven to be with men forever in that day when this earth becomes a celestial sphere.

As to the return of the City of Enoch, John said: "And I saw a new heaven and a new earth: for the first heaven and the first earth were passed away; and there was no more sea." This is the Millennial earth that is to be after the Lord returns. "And I John saw the holy city, new Jerusalem, coming down from God out of heaven, prepared as a bride adorned for her husband." Enoch's people, now resurrected and glorified, shall return in all their glory to that earth which once was theirs. "And I heard a great voice out of heaven saying, Behold, the tabernacle of God is with men, and he will dwell with them, and they shall be his people, and God himself shall be with them, and be their God." The Lord Jesus shall dwell on earth with men again.

And what of life during that Millennial day? In answer, John proclaimed: "God shall wipe away all tears from their eyes; and there shall be no more death, neither sorrow, nor crying, neither shall there be any more pain: for the former things are passed away." That these words have reference to the Millennium is set forth in D&C 101:22-32.

In his vision of the Celestial Jerusalem, John saw "the holy Jerusalem, descending out of heaven from God, having the glory of God. . . . The street of the city was pure gold, as it were transparent glass." There was no temple therein, neither the need for the sun nor moon to give light, "for the glory of God did lighten it, and the Lamb is the light thereof." (Revelation 21.)

The New Jerusalem—An American Zion

Ether, whose teachings are summarized for us by Moroni, speaks of the New Jerusalem (Enoch's city) that shall come down out of heaven, of the New Jerusalem to be built upon the American continent, and of the building up anew of the Old Jerusalem in Palestine. His words show the relationship of these three Jerusalems to the Second Coming.

As Moroni records, Ether taught that America "was the place of the New Jerusalem, which should come down out of heaven, and the holy sanctuary of the Lord. Behold, Ether saw the days of Christ, and he spake concerning a New Jerusalem upon this land." One Jerusalem is to be built up in America after the latter-day restoration of the gospel; the other is to come down from heaven after the Lord returns.

"He spake also concerning the house of Israel, and the Jerusalem from whence Lehi should come—after it should be destroyed it should be built up again, a holy city unto the Lord; wherefore, it could not be a new Jerusalem for it had been in a time of old; but it should be built up again, and become a holy city of the Lord; and it should be built unto the house of Israel." The Lord's people will build up Old Jerusalem again; they shall do it in righteousness, including the placing of a holy temple within its walls. Joseph Smith says this temple must be built before the Second Coming.

Ether also taught "that a New Jerusalem should be built up upon this land [America], unto the remnant of the seed of Joseph." We and the Lehite descendants are remnants of Joseph. "Wherefore, the remnant of the house of Joseph shall be built upon this land; and it shall be a land of their inheritance; and they shall build up a holy city unto the Lord, like unto the Jerusalem of old; and they shall no more be confounded, until the end come when the earth shall pass away." This is the New Jerusalem that is to be built in Jackson County, Missouri, in due course.

"There shall be a new heaven and a new earth; and they

shall be like unto the old save the old have passed away, and all things have become new." This is the Millennial or renewed or paradisiacal earth. "And then cometh the New Jerusalem." Enoch's city will come to join with the New Jerusalem built by the saints. "Blessed are they who dwell therein, for it is they whose garments are white through the blood of the Lamb; and they are they who are numbered among the remnant of the seed of Joseph, who were of the house of Israel."

It is in this Millennial setting that Old Jerusalem, built before the Second Coming, will receive its full glory and attain its true divine stature. "Then also cometh the Jerusalem of old; and the inhabitants thereof, blessed are they, for they have been washed in the blood of the Lamb; and they are they who were scattered and gathered in from the four quarters of the earth, and from the north countries, and are partakers of the fulfilling of the covenant which God made with their father, Abraham." (Ether 13:3-12.)

Enoch and his people, being translated, were taken away from the carnal and evil society of the world. But they went with the promise that when the earth was cleansed and made new, they would return again. Speaking of the latter days, after the restoration of the gospel, the Lord said to Enoch: "Righteousness and truth will I cause to sweep the earth as with a flood, to gather out mine elect from the four quarters of the earth, unto a place which I shall prepare, an Holy City, that my people may gird up their loins, and be looking forth for the time of my coming; for there shall be my tabernacle, and it shall be called Zion, a New Jerusalem." The New Jerusalem in Jackson County will be built before the Second Coming.

"Then [after the Second Coming] shalt thou and all thy city meet them there," the Lord said, "and we will receive them into our bosom, and they shall see us; and we will fall upon their necks, and they shall fall upon our necks, and we will kiss each other; and there shall be mine abode, and it shall be Zion, which shall come forth out of all the creations which I have made; and for the space of a thousand years the earth shall rest." (Moses 7:62-64.)

The New Jerusalem—When?

If there is one grand heaven-held secret that the saints would like to learn, it is this: When will the Lord return to dwell and reign among the sons of men? Akin to this question, which has stirred the hearts of men since that day on Olivet when, as he ascended, angelic ministrants acclaimed, "This same Jesus, which is taken up from you into heaven, shall so come in like manner as ye have seen him go into heaven" (Acts 1:11), akin to and associated with the desire to know when he will come again, are these questions: When will Zion be redeemed? When will the saints build the New Jerusalem and crown its holy ground with the very temple to which earth's returning King will come? Are there things we should be doing now to prepare for a return to Jackson County and the building of the temple at the appointed place?

As to the Second Coming, the time is fixed, the hour is set, and, speaking after the manner of the Lord, the day is soon to be. The appointed day can be neither advanced nor delayed. It will come at the decreed moment, chosen before the foundations of the earth were laid, and it can be neither hastened by righteousness nor put off by wickedness. It will be with our Lord's return as it was with his birth to Mary: the time of each coming was fixed by the Father.

True, no man knows or shall know the day or the hour of our Lord's return; that knowledge is retained in the bosom of heaven, for good and sufficient reasons. But all men may read the signs of the times, and those whose souls are attuned to the things of the Spirit know that the great and dreadful day of the Lord is near, even at the door. But they also know there are many things yet to be done before earth's rightful King comes to change the kingdoms of this world into the kingdom of our God and of his Christ. One of these is the building of the New Jerusalem in Jackson County, Missouri.

As to the building of the New Jerusalem, different criteria apply than those pertaining to the Second Coming. Zion could have been redeemed a century and a half ago. If the newly called saints of that day had kept the commandments and seen eye to eye as did the saints of Enoch's day, they too could have built a City of Holiness, called Zion, and the glory of God would have rested upon it. That day of opportunity passed, however, and the Lord's people began the arduous process of establishing stakes of Zion in all nations as part of a schooling process to prepare them for the day when they would build Zion itself.

The stakes of Zion that now are must be strengthened and perfected before they can uphold and sustain that Zion which is destined to be. When Zion is fully established, it will be by obedience to the law of the celestial kingdom, which law is operative in the stakes of Zion only in part. As of now, we are living under a preparatory law, as it were; as the Mosaic law was a schoolmaster to prepare Israel for the fulness of the gospel, so the church and kingdom, as now constituted, is a schoolmaster to prepare the saints for an inheritance in that perfect society of souls of which Zion will be composed. The most obvious illustration of this concept is that we today have the law of tithing, which we do not live perfectly, but when Zion is built we will have the law of consecration in its fulness. It follows that the righteousness of the saints can hasten the redemption of Zion. And, viewing the present state of the Church, good as it is when compared with the world, the day of the building of Zion seems to be some years away.

CHAPTER 61

The Lord's American Zion

The Saints Shall Build Zion

A summary of the revealed word and a recitation of what has happened in our dispensation with reference to the redemption of Zion and the building of the New Jerusalem with its temple of temples will be instructive. The hope and longing for the New Jerusalem was deeply rooted in the hearts of the early saints. As early as February 9, 1831, the Lord said: "The time shall come when it shall be revealed unto you from on high, when the city of the New Jerusalem shall be prepared, that ye may be gathered in one, that ye may be my people and I will be your God." (D&C 42:9.)

This revelation, in an initial sense, was not long delayed, although, as we shall see, the ultimate and actual time for the building of the holy city is yet to be revealed. On March 7, 1831, after speaking of the signs of the times and the wars and desolations to be poured out upon the world, the Lord said: "Gather ye out from the eastern lands, assemble ye yourselves together ye elders of my church: go ye forth into the western countries, call upon the inhabitants to repent, and inasmuch as they do repent, build up churches unto me." Always and everlastingly the call is to go forth to all men, inviting them to come and be one with the saints and to be inheritors of that joy and peace and eternal reward promised the faithful.

But the elders of the kingdom are to do more than spread the gospel. "With one heart and with one mind, gather up your riches that ye may purchase an inheritance which shall hereafter be appointed unto you." Zion is to be purchased, built, and established by gathered Israel. "And it shall be called the New Jerusalem, a land of peace, a city of refuge, a place of safety for the saints of the Most High God." Zion shall be set apart from the world; though war and desolation overshadow all nations, Zion shall be at rest. How could it be otherwise when perfect righteousness prevails?

"The glory of the Lord shall be there, and the terror of the Lord also shall be there, insomuch that the wicked will not come unto it, and it shall be called Zion. And it shall come to pass among the wicked, that every man that will not take his sword against his neighbor must needs flee unto Zion for safety." These are the conditions that prevailed in the day of Enoch; they are descriptive of his Zion; and they are to prevail again in the latter-day Zion that is to be.

"There shall be gathered unto it out of every nation under heaven; and it shall be the only people that shall not be at war one with another." As yet this has never happened. "And it shall be said among the wicked: Let us not go up to battle against Zion, for the inhabitants of Zion are terrible; wherefore we cannot stand. And it shall come to pass that the righteous shall be gathered out from among all nations, and shall come to Zion, singing with songs of everlasting joy."

None of this was fully consummated during the lives of those to whom the divine word came. From our perspective it is perfectly clear that the promises cannot be fulfilled until Millennial conditions prevail on earth. That is to say, all this lies in futurity, a fact that the concluding words of the revelation bear out: "For when the Lord shall appear he shall be terrible unto them [those in the world who are the enemies of the saints], that fear may seize upon them, and they shall stand afar off and tremble. And all nations shall be afraid because of the terror of the Lord, and the power of his might." (D&C 45:64-75.)

Independence, Missouri—Center Place

These promises fed the hopes and made sure the desires of the little flock who alone were the Lord's saints in that day. Some four months later, in July 1831, in Jackson County, Missouri, "the Prophet exclaimed in yearning prayer: 'When will the wilderness blossom as the rose? When will Zion be built up in her glory, and where will thy Temple stand, unto which all nations shall come in the last days?' " (Heading, D&C 57.)

In the true sense, the wilderness shall blossom as the rose when the earth is renewed and receives its paradisiacal glory. In the full sense, Zion shall regain her ancient glory, and attain that grandeur and might promised in the prophetic word, only during the Millennium, though the work of establishing Zion and building the New Jerusalem must precede our Lord's return. And as to the temple unto which all nations shall come in the last days, it shall be built in the New Jerusalem before the Second Coming, all as a part of the preparatory processes that will make ready a people for their Lord's return.

And so the Lord, giving line upon line, as his purposes mandate, revealed to the Prophet a partial answer to his yearning plea. He named the heaven-selected site of the temple and also what the little flock should then do relative to the building of that holy house. "The land of Missouri . . . is the land which I have appointed and consecrated for the gathering of the saints. Wherefore, this is the land of promise, and the place for the city of Zion. And thus saith the Lord your God, if you will receive wisdom here is wisdom. Behold, the place which is now called Independence is the center place; and a spot for the temple is lying westward, upon a lot which is not far from the courthouse." (D&C 57:1-3.)

The center place! Let Israel gather to the stakes of Zion in all nations. Let every land be a Zion to those appointed to dwell there. Let the fulness of the gospel be for all the saints in all nations. Let no blessing be denied them. Let temples arise wherein the fulness of the ordinances of the Lord's house may be administered. But still there is a center place, a place where the chief temple shall stand, a place to which the Lord shall come, a place whence the law shall go forth to govern all the earth in that day when the Second David reigns personally upon the earth. And that center place is what men now call Independence in Jackson County, Missouri, but which in a day to come will be the Zion of our God and the City of Holiness of his people. The site is selected; the place is known; the decree has gone forth; and the promised destiny is assured.

The Purchase of the Land of Zion

What, then, did the Lord, in July 1831, expect of his little flock? "Wherefore, it is wisdom that the land should be purchased by the saints," he said, "and also every tract lying westward, even unto the line running directly between Jew and Gentile; and also every tract bordering by the prairies, inasmuch as my disciples are enabled to buy lands. Behold, this is wisdom, that they may obtain it for an everlasting inheritance." Sidney Gilbert was appointed "an agent unto the church, to buy land in all the regions round about, inasmuch as can be done in righteousness, and as wisdom shall direct." Edward Partridge was appointed to "divide unto the saints their inheritance," and the Lord's people were to be planted in the land. (D&C 57:4-8.) Some lands were acquired, and these planting processes had an initial beginning before the saints were driven by murderous mobs from their Missouri homeland-to-be.

Knowing the end from the beginning and that in reality the New Jerusalem would not be built in that day, the Lord, on August 1, 1831, cautioned his saints in these words: "Give ear to my word, and learn of me what I will concerning you, and also concerning this land unto which I have sent you." Knowing what has, in fact, taken place since the Lord first cautioned and commanded his people, it may be that we are in a better position than they were to envision the full import of the divine word that then came forth. Following an initial decree to them to keep the commandments, the early saints were told: "Ye cannot behold with your natural eyes, for the present time, the design of your God concerning those things which shall come hereafter, and the glory which shall follow after much tribulation. For after much tribulation come the blessings. Wherefore the day cometh that ye shall be crowned with much glory; the hour is not yet, but is nigh at hand."

Is the Lord warning them that all will not go well with their efforts to build the New Jerusalem? Are they being told that tribulation and trials and persecutions and mobbings lie ahead? And are they being reassured that after much tribulation, and though driven from their promised land, they will yet be crowned with eternal glory?

"Remember this, which I tell you before, that you may lay it to heart, and receive that which is to follow." Are they being strengthened for the trials ahead? "Behold, verily I say unto you, for this cause I have sent you—that you might be obedient, and that your hearts might be prepared to bear testimony of the things which are to come; and also that you might be honored in laying the foundation, and in bearing record of the land upon which the Zion of God shall stand." Truly, the doctrine relative to Zion and the New Jerusalem is being revealed to them, and they are laying the foundation, a foundation upon which their successors in interest shall yet build. How glorious it was for them to commence the work, and how filled with wonder and awe is the prospect before us of building upon the foundation they laid.

Then the Lord speaks of the gospel feast and of the supper of the Lord to which all nations are invited. The word relative thereto is to "go forth from Zion, yea, from the mouth of the city of the heritage of God." Edward Partridge is again named as the one "to divide the lands of the heritage of God unto his children," as the Lord's judges in ancient Israel divided the promised land among the ancient chosen people. Counsel is next given about obedience and the proper use of agency, and then come these rather enigmatic words: "Who am I that made man, saith the Lord, that will hold him guiltless that obeys not my commandments? Who am I, saith the Lord, that have promised and have not fulfilled? I command and men obey not; I revoke and they receive not the blessing. Then they say in their hearts: This is not the work of the Lord, for his promises are not fulfilled. But wo unto such, for their reward lurketh beneath, and not from above."

Do these words contain a message about the building up of Zion and the New Jerusalem? Are the shadows of coming events being cast before? Are they being forewarned and prepared for a future commandment that will deny them the privilege of building the City of Holiness and of dwelling within its sacred walls? Whatever the Lord's intent is, his next words are: "And now I give unto you further directions concerning this land." He then directs Martin Harris to stand forth as "an example unto the church, in laying his moneys before the bishop of the church." All others who come "unto this land to receive an inheritance" are commanded to do likewise. Lands are to be "purchased in Independence" for various purposes and for certain named persons.

Then this shadow of coming events is cast before them: "And now, verily, I say concerning the residue of the elders of my church, the time has not yet come, for many years, for them to receive their inheritance in this land, except they desire it through the prayer of faith, only as it shall be appointed unto them of the Lord." They are to preach the gospel and "build up churches" in other places.

Even now, a century and a half later, are we not still subject to the same decree that many years must pass before Zion is redeemed? And yet if we had faith and desired to build on the foundations of our forebears, would not the Lord direct us to go forward? The building up of Zion, be it remembered, depends upon the faith and righteousness of the Lord's people.

The revealed word then speaks of collecting "moneys to purchase lands in Zion." Sidney Rigdon is told to "write a description of the land of Zion, and a statement of the will of God, as it shall be made known by the Spirit unto him." This inspired writing is to be used to collect moneys to purchase lands. The gathering is to continue, and Elder Rigdon is to "consecrate and dedicate this land, and the spot for the temple, unto the Lord." (D&C 58:1-57.)

In August 1831, the Lord renewed the commands to purchase lands in Zion and to gather to that sacred spot. "This is the will of the Lord your God concerning his saints," he said, "that they should assemble themselves together unto the land of Zion, not in haste, lest there should be confusion, which bringeth pestilence."

An everlasting principle underlies this command. The Lord's newly converted saints must flee from Babylon lest they be swallowed up by the world and, walking with the world, partake again of the ways of the world. Always and in all ages the Lord's people must gather—gather to those places where true worship prevails; gather into congregations where they can strengthen and perfect each other; gather to holy temples where the ordinances of salvation and exaltation are performed; and, particularly in our day, gather to the holy houses wherein their dead may be redeemed. The law of the gospel includes the law of gathering. But the Lord's house is a house of order; his saints must be organized; the gathering is not a hasty, unprepared foray to a new locale. It is a wisely planned and prearranged assembling; provision must be made for food, clothing, shelter, travel, and even a future livelihood, if possible.

And, further, lands must be purchased whereon the

assembling hosts may dwell. Hence the decree: "Behold, the land of Zion—I, the Lord, hold it in mine own hands; nevertheless, . . . I the Lord will that you should purchase the lands, that you may have . . . claim on the world, that they may not be stirred up unto anger. For Satan putteth it into their hearts to anger against you, and to the shedding of blood." Satan would slay all of the saints if he could; he managed, rather quickly, to do away with all of them in the meridian of time, and he would do the same again in this dispensation if he could. What a pretext he would have for persecution and slaughter if the saints gained the lands that are to be theirs by any means except those set forth in the laws of the land!

"Wherefore, the land of Zion shall not be obtained but by purchase or by blood, otherwise there is none inheritance for you. And if by purchase, behold you are blessed; And if by blood, as you are forbidden to shed blood, lo, your enemies are upon you, and ye shall be scourged from city to city, and from synagogue to synagogue, and but few shall stand to receive an inheritance." The reasoning is right and the decree is clear: the saints are to render unto Caesar the things that are Caesar's.

Next the Lord speaks of the decreed wars in which the wicked shall slay the wicked until the day of his coming. "Wherefore, seeing that I, the Lord, have decreed all these things upon the face of the earth, I will that my saints should be assembled upon the land of Zion"—the one place where peace and safety might prevail—"and that every man should take righteousness in his hands and faithfulness upon his loins, and lift a warning voice unto the inhabitants of the earth; and declare both by word and by flight that desolation shall come upon the wicked." The gathering of the saints to Zion or to any of her stakes is a sign to the world and a witness to all men that the gospel has been restored and is in process of preparing a people for the coming of the Lord.

And all those who take part in the glorious gathering and who use their influence and means to build up Zion have this divine promise: "He that sendeth up treasures unto the land of Zion shall receive an inheritance in this world, and his works shall follow him, and also a reward in the world to come." (D&C 63:24-48.) Surely where a man's treasure is, there will his heart and his inheritance be also.

Saints in Zion Live the United Order

When Zion is fully established, in a yet future day, the divine promise, given September 11, 1831, shall be fulfilled: "Zion shall flourish, and the glory of the Lord shall be upon her; and she shall be an ensign unto the people, and there shall come unto her out of every nation under heaven. And the day shall come when the nations of the earth shall tremble because of her, and shall fear because of her terrible ones." (D&C 64:41-43.) To a degree the stakes of Zion now flourish and the lost sheep of Israel are gathering to them, but the day when all the earth shall tremble and fear because of the Zion of God is yet to be.

To prepare his people for such a glorious reward and for such a grand state of excellence, in March 1832 the Lord said this about the United Order, the order through which the divine principle of consecration was and is destined to operate: "The time has come, and is now at hand; and behold, and lo, it must needs be that there be an organization of my people, in regulating and establishing the affairs of the storehouse for the poor of my people, both in this place [Ohio] and in the land of Zion [Missouri]." As is well known, the saints attempted to live in the United Order and failed. That it will yet be operated in its fulness among the Latter-day Saints is also well known. What concerns us here is to set forth the principles upon which that order, destined to prevail in Zion, must operate.

This heaven-sent organization came, the Lord said, "for a permanent and everlasting establishment and order unto my church, to advance the cause, which ye have espoused, to the salvation of man, and to the glory of your Father who is in heaven; that you may be equal in the bonds of heavenly things, yea, and earthly things also, for the obtaining of heavenly things. For if ye are not equal in earthly things ye cannot be equal in obtaining heavenly things. For if you will that I give unto you a place in the celestial world, you must prepare yourselves by doing the things which I have commanded you and required of you." (D&C 78:3-7.) These are the principles underlying the establishment of Zion; these are the laws that must be lived in the New Jerusalem; these are the standards set by the Lord for the saints of latter days. Let every man judge for himself how nearly we approach them at this time.

Building the Temple in Jackson County

Now we come to the much misunderstood revelation that gives the direction for building the temple in the New Jerusalem. Given September 22 and 23, 1832, it is: "The word of the Lord concerning his church, established in the last days for the restoration of his people, as he has spoken by the mouth of his prophets, and for the gathering of his saints to stand upon Mount Zion, which shall be the city of New Jerusalem." The Church, which is to build the city and the temple, is set up upon the earth as the organization to which Israel shall gather. Those who gather are the Lord's saints; they shall stand upon Mount Zion which is the New Jerusalem.

"Which city shall be built, beginning at the temple lot, which is appointed by the finger of the Lord, in the western boundaries of the State of Missouri, and dedicated by the hand of Joseph Smith, Jun., and others with whom the Lord was well pleased. Verily this is the word of the Lord, that the city New Jerusalem shall be built by the gathering of the saints, beginning at this place, even the place of the temple, which temple shall be reared in this generation. For verily this generation shall not all pass away until an house shall be built unto the Lord, and a cloud shall rest upon it, which cloud shall be even the glory of the Lord, which shall fill the house. . . . For the sons of Moses and also the sons of Aaron shall offer an acceptable offering and sacrifice in the house of the Lord, which house shall be built unto the Lord in this generation, upon the consecrated spot as I have appointed—and the sons of Moses and of Aaron shall be filled with the glory of the Lord, upon Mount Zion in the Lord's house, whose sons are ye; and also many whom I have called and sent forth to build up my church." (D&C 84:2-5, 31-32.)

It is perfectly clear that the New Jerusalem, crowned by the Holy Temple to which our Lord shall come, was destined to be built within the promised generation. The fact is that neither the city nor the temple yet graces Missouri's soil, and the generation is long since gone by. Why so? This is the foreshadowed case in which the Lord said he commanded and then revoked, and we are left to say naught except, Blessed be the name of the Lord. As to why he revoked, that is quite another thing. Could it be other than because his people did not climb the gospel heights that it was in their power to reach? Their faith was imperfect, as is ours, and their enemies drove them from their inheritance. It could have been otherwise had they, as ancient Israel did on occasions, persuaded the Lord to fight their battles, with two of them putting their tens of thousands to flight.

After the saints were driven from Missouri; after keys and powers had been given in a preparatory house of the Lord built in Kirtland, Ohio; after the refiner's fire had purified the saints to a degree—the Lord deigned to give them a temple in Nauvoo, Illinois, in which the fulness of the ordinances of his kingdom might be administered for the living and the dead.

In the Nauvoo Temple—as will be the case in due course in the temple in Missouri—the saints were to receive "the fulness of the priesthood" through celestial marriage, which is the patriarchal order. In it they were to "be baptized for those who are dead"; in it they were to receive honor and glory, washings, anointings, oracles, conversations, statutes and judgments, and much else—all "for the beginning of the revelations and foundation of Zion, and for the glory, honor, and endowment of all her municipals." In this house the Lord promised to reveal "things which have been kept hid from before the foundation of the world, things that pertain to the dispensation of the fulness of times." That is to say, the revelations, endowments, ordinances, covenants, promises, and eternal truths received in this and all subsequent temples are for the express purpose of preparing and purifying the Lord's people, freeing them from the blood and sins of the world, so they will be ready in due course to build the New Jerusalem and the temple in that center place.

With reference to the saints in the days of Nauvoo and to the temple to be built in that Illinois city, the Lord said: "If ye labor with all your might, I will consecrate that spot [where the Nauvoo Temple is to be built] that it shall be made holy." That temple and all those temples built thereafter stand on holy ground, ground consecrated to the Lord for the salvation of his children. "And if my people will hearken unto my voice, and unto the voice of my servants whom I have appointed to lead my people, behold, verily I say unto you, they shall not be moved out of their place." It is within the power of the Lord's people to gather to Zion, to her stakes, or to whatever place the Lord directs, there to be preserved, protected, and blessed, if they keep the commandments.

"But if they will not hearken to my voice, nor unto the voice of these men whom I have appointed, they shall not be blest, because they pollute mine holy grounds, and mine holy ordinances, and charters, and my holy words which I give unto them." In part, but not in full, the saints conformed to this standard. Hence, for their failures, they were driven from state to state and finally from the confines of the United States itself to the mountains of western America.

"And it shall come to pass that if you build a house unto my name, and do not the things that I say, I will not perform the oath which I make unto you, neither fulfil the promises which ye expect at my hands, saith the Lord. For instead of blessings, ye, by your own works, bring cursings, wrath, indignation, and judgments upon your own heads, by your follies, and by all your abominations, which you practise before me, saith the Lord." Who can doubt that the saints today—sadly—are as the saints were in Nauvoo, as yet unworthy to receive all the blessings that might be theirs.

It is in this setting that the Lord gives the reason why the temple was not built in Jackson County in the designated generation. The general principle is set forth in these words: "Verily, verily, I say unto you, that when I give a commandment to any of the sons of men to do a work unto my name, and those sons of men go with all their might and with all they have to perform that work, and cease not their diligence, and their enemies come upon them and hinder them from performing that work, behold, it behooveth me to require that work no more at the hands of those sons of men, but to accept of their offerings. And the iniquity and transgression of my holy laws and commandments I will visit upon the heads of those who hindered my work, unto the third and fourth generation, so long as they repent not, and hate me, saith the Lord God." Such is the law of the Lord.

As to its application to the Missouri temple situation, the divine word continues: "Therefore, for this cause have I accepted the offerings of those whom I commanded to build up a city and a house unto my name, in Jackson county, Missouri, and were hindered by their enemies, saith the Lord your God." The command to purchase lands, to build the New Jerusalem, to build the chief temple of this dispensation in the appointed generation—all these were revoked by the same power that gave the commands in the first instance. The Lord's people were to retreat, regroup, and prepare themselves for the great battles of the future.

"And I will answer judgment, wrath, and indignation, wailing, and anguish, and gnashing of teeth upon their heads [the heads of the enemies of the saints], unto the third and fourth generation, so long as they repent not, and hate me, saith the Lord your God. And this I make an example unto you, for your consolation concerning all those who have been commanded to do a work and have been hindered by the hands of their enemies, and by oppression, saith the Lord your God. For I am the Lord your God, and will save all those of your brethren who have been pure in heart, and have been slain in the land of Missouri, saith the Lord." (D&C 124:28-54.)

Though the city and the temple were not built within the appointed generation, and though the early saints were excused from that labor, yet the ultimate triumph of the cause of Zion remains unchanged. On March 8, 1833, the Lord promised: "I, the Lord, will contend with Zion, and plead with her strong ones, and chasten her until she overcomes and is clean before me. For she shall not be removed out of her place." (D&C 90:36-37.) Zion remains where she has ever been; the New Jerusalem shall yet be built in the appointed place, and the Latter-day Saints will build the decreed temple in that day which the mouth of the Lord shall name.

In the midst of her struggles, on August 2, 1833, the Lord sent this word to Zion: "If Zion do these things"—build the temple and become pure in heart so as to qualify, as a people, to see the face of the Lord—"she shall prosper, and spread herself and become very glorious, very great, and very terrible." This has not yet happened; neither will it, nor can it, until the inhabitants of Zion attain the spiritual stature specified.

"And the nations of the earth shall honor her, and shall say: Surely Zion is the city of our God, and surely Zion cannot fall, neither be moved out of her place, for God is there, and the hand of the Lord is there; and he hath sworn by the power of his might to be her salvation and her high tower." No matter what might have been, it seems clear to us now that the fulfill- ment of this promise awaits the day when "God is there," when the great Millennium arrives and the Lord dwells with his people.

"Therefore, verily, thus saith the Lord, let Zion rejoice, for this is ZION—THE PURE IN HEART; therefore, let Zion rejoice, while all the wicked shall mourn." As pertaining to his saints, the time of the Lord's return is *The Year of His Redeemed.* As far as the wicked are concerned, it is *The Day of Vengeance.*

"For behold, and lo, vengeance cometh speedily upon the ungodly as the whirlwind; and who shall escape it?" This refers to the great and dreadful day of the Lord when the wicked will be as stubble. But before that day comes, "the Lord's scourge shall pass over by night and by day, and the report thereof shall vex all people; yea, it shall not be stayed until the Lord come: for the indignation of the Lord is kindled against their abominations and all their wicked works." We live in the day of the indignation of the Lord, when the wicked are slaying the wicked and there are abominations on every hand.

"Nevertheless, Zion shall escape if she observe to do all things whatsoever I have commanded her. But if she observe not to do whatsoever I have commanded her, I will visit her according to all her works, with sore affliction, with pestilence, with plague, with sword, with vengeance, with devouring fire." If the saints—those in Zion or in any of her stakes—live after the manner of the world, they will inherit the curses and plagues destined to be poured out without measure upon the ungodly. The saints are no better than any other sinners, if they remain in their carnal and fallen state and do not have the Holy Spirit for their guide.

"Nevertheless, let it be read this once to her ears, that I, the Lord, have accepted of her offering; and if she sin no more none of these things shall come upon her; and I will bless her with blessings, and multiply a multiplicity of blessings upon her, and upon her generations forever and ever, saith the Lord your God." (D&C 97:18-28.) Let every man ponder upon the state of that Zion which might have been in Missouri, and also upon that Zion which now exists in the stakes of Zion that are beginning to dot the earth. Who is there among us who does not desire to escape the Lord's scourge?

On October 12, 1833, the Lord sent this word to his

people: "And now I give unto you a word concerning Zion," he said. "Zion shall be redeemed, although she is chastened for a little season." We are now in process of finding out how long a little season is to the Lord. "Therefore, let your hearts be comforted; for all things shall work together for good to them that walk uprightly, and to the sanctification of the church. For I will raise up unto myself a pure people, that will serve me in righteousness; and all that call upon the name of the Lord and keep his commandments, shall be saved." (D&C 100:13-17.) Obedience, walking uprightly, purity, righteousness, prayer, sanctification, salvation—always these are the things that the Lord associates with Zion and her redemption. The extent to which they exist in the hearts of the saints is the extent to which Zion prospers.

CHAPTER 62

The Future Redemption
of Zion

Why Zion Was Not Redeemed

We now come to section 101 of the Doctrine and
Covenants, a revelation of wondrous worth and infinite
import. It was given December 16, 1833, after the mobs had
driven the saints from their homes in Jackson County, Missouri. Satan seemed to have the upper hand. The Lord's
people had lost their clothing, furniture, livestock, property,
crops, homes, and lands. What of the Zion they so devoutly
sought? Why, oh why, had their God permitted these persecutions and drivings?

To Joseph Smith, then in Kirtland, the Lord revealed his
mind and will about Zion and her future in one of the grandest of all the divine outpourings: "Verily I say unto you, concerning your brethren who have been afflicted, and persecuted, and cast out from the land of their inheritance—I, the
Lord, have suffered the affliction to come upon them,
wherewith they have been afflicted, in consequence of their
transgressions; yet I will own them, and they shall be mine in
that day when I shall come to make up my jewels." They were
not perfect, nor are we—far from it—and though they were
called upon to suffer for their failures and imperfections, yet
they (and we devoutly hope the same applies to us) shall yet
be saved with an everlasting salvation.

"Therefore, they must needs be chastened and tried, even
as Abraham, who was commanded to offer up his only son."
Why should it be any different with the saints in this day than
it has ever been? "For all those who will not endure chasten-
ing, but deny me, cannot be sanctified." Praise God for the
faith of our forebears, and God grant that we shall be at least
as faithful as they were.

"Behold, I say unto you, there were jarrings, and contentions, and envyings, and strifes, and lustful and covetous desires among them; therefore by these things they polluted their inheritances." They were not a pure people, and the inhabitants of Zion must be pure in heart, for the Lord will be there, and only the pure in heart can see God. But "they were slow to hearken unto the voice of the Lord their God; therefore, the Lord their God is slow to hearken unto their prayers, to answer them in the day of their trouble. In the day of their peace they esteemed lightly my counsel; but, in the day of their trouble, of necessity they feel after me." The Latter-day Saints—how similar they are to those of former days. The wheat and tares together grow, and in almost all ages the saints have been and are weak, struggling, striving mortals who love the Lord but who seldom do all that they can and should do in the cause of righteousness. "Verily I say unto you, notwithstanding their sins, my bowels are filled with compassion towards them. I will not utterly cast them off; and in the day of wrath I will remember mercy." Truly the Lord has been and yet will be merciful unto his people.

In contrast, he pours out his wrath upon their persecutors. "I have sworn . . . that I would let fall the sword of mine indignation in behalf of my people; and even as I have said, it shall come to pass." The destructions preceding and attending the Second Coming will be to save the saints from the evils of the world. "Mine indignation is soon to be poured out without measure upon all nations; and this will I do when the cup of their iniquity is full." When men become again as they were in Noah's day, they again will be destroyed, this time by the fires that consume every corruptible thing.

"And in that day"—that day when the Lord returns— "all who are found upon the watch-tower, or in other words, all mine Israel, shall be saved." Then, in that day when the Lord returns, "they that have been scattered shall be gathered," including those scattered from Palestine and those scattered from Missouri. "And all they who have mourned shall be comforted. And all they who have given their lives for my name shall be crowned." When the Lord comes, his people shall triumph.

"Therefore, let your hearts be comforted concerning Zion; for all flesh is in mine hands; be still and know that I am

God. Zion shall not be moved out of her place, notwithstanding her children are scattered." Zion is where Zion is, and there she shall ever remain. Where the soles of the feet of the saints once trod, they shall tread again.

"They that remain," having abided the day of his coming, "and are pure in heart, shall return, and come to their inheritances, they and their children, with songs of everlasting joy, to build up the waste places of Zion—and all these things that the prophets might be fulfilled." How can the saints build up the waste places of Zion (in Missouri) unless those lands are first wasted by the desolations to precede and attend the Second Coming?

"And, behold, there is none other place appointed than that which I have appointed; neither shall there be any other place appointed than that which I have appointed, for the work of the gathering of my saints—until the day cometh when there is found no more room for them; and then I have other places which I will appoint unto them, and they shall be called stakes, for the curtains or the strength of Zion." In our day the gathering of Israel is into the stakes of Zion; it will so remain until the appointed time when selected ones are called from the stakes to go to the center place and build the promised city and temple.

"Behold, it is my will, that all they who call on my name, and worship me according to mine everlasting gospel, should gather together, and stand in holy places; and prepare for the revelation which is to come, when the veil of the covering of my temple, in my tabernacle, which hideth the earth, shall be taken off, and all flesh shall see me together." Let Israel gather to the multitude of holy places so that they may be prepared, as a people, for the return of their rightful King.

At this point the revelation speaks in some detail about the glory that will prevail during the Millennium. "And all they who suffer persecution for my name, and endure in faith, though they are called to lay down their lives for my sake yet shall they partake of all this glory." The slain saints shall rise again and dwell in Zion after their resurrection.

Returning to Zion and her state and fate, the Lord says: "Behold, here is wisdom concerning the children of Zion, even many, but not all; they were found transgressors, therefore they must needs be chastened—he that exalteth himself shall be abased, and he that abaseth himself shall be exalted."

Having said all these things, the Lord continues: "And now, I will show unto you a parable, that you may know my will concerning the redemption of Zion." This parable speaks of a nobleman who plants twelve olive trees in a choice land; of watchmen appointed to build a tower and care for the vineyard; of dissension among them and their failure to stand true to their trust; of the enemy overrunning the vineyard; of the Lord of the vineyard gathering an army to redeem his property and again "possess the land." Then a servant asks: "When shall these things be?" The answer: "When I will; go ye straightway, and do all things whatsoever I have commanded you; and this shall be my seal and blessing upon you —a faithful and wise steward in the midst of mine house, a ruler in my kingdom. And his servant went straightway, and did all things whatsoever his lord commanded him; and after many days all things were fulfilled." Parables are not intended to reveal truths with the same clarity that attends a simple recitation of whatever is involved. It is clear from this recitation, however, that the Lord's servants, for the present, are to be about their Father's other business, becoming thereby rulers in his kingdom, and that the redemption of Zion, as of 1833, was delayed for a long period.

Following this parable, the Lord speaks of a continuation of the gathering of all the saints "unto the places which I have appointed." They are not to gather in haste nor by flight, and all things must be prepared before them. They are to purchase lands adjacent to "the land of Zion," including land in Jackson County "and the counties round about." The children of Zion are to importune to the government for redress of their grievances, and they have the assurance that Zion will one day be established in the appointed place. (D&C 101.)

Righteousness and the Redemption of Zion

Time and time again the early saints in this dispensation were offered the precious privilege of building up Zion, of establishing the New Jerusalem, and of crowning that Holy City with the temple of temples. But always the promises were conditional. Always the divine provisos set forth the need for faith, obedience, righteousness, and complete conformity to the high, holy, and heavenly law. Sad to say, the Lord's people failed to gain the promised blessing. Obeying only in part, they received only a partial reward. Failing to live the fulness of the divine law, they were denied an inheritance in the Holy City in the days of their mortal probation.

It was with the Latter-day Saints as it had been with their ancestors in the days of Moses. The Lord Jehovah offered ancient Israel the fulness of his eternal gospel; by the mouth of Moses and others of the prophets, he pled with his people to sanctify themselves and receive the fulness of his glory while in the wilderness and again after they entered their promised Canaan. A few in Israel gained wondrous gifts and powers, but the generality of the people, obeying only in part, rose no higher in spiritual stature than provided for in the lesser law. And yet in that law, always and everlastingly, there was a call to higher things. The very law itself was a schoolmaster to prepare the people for the fulness of the gospel.

And so it has been among us. Though the newly called saints of the nineteenth century failed to build their promised Zion, yet they retained the glorious gospel, with all its hopes and promises. They were left in that state which now exists among us. What we now have is a schoolmaster to prepare us for that which is yet to be. We are now seeking to build Zion in our hearts by faith and personal righteousness as we prepare for the day when we will have power to build the city whence the law will go forth when He rules whose right it is.

Thus, on February 24, 1834, after the saints had been scattered and driven from their lands in Jackson County, the Lord gave these words of comfort and counsel to his people: "I will give unto you a revelation and commandment . . . concerning the salvation and redemption of your brethren, who have been scattered on the land of Zion; being driven and smitten by the hands of mine enemies, on whom I will pour out my wrath without measure in mine own time." Those who persecute the saints and oppose the cause in which they are engaged are the enemies of God. Whether their opposition is directed against the Lord personally or against his servants, it is the same. And when the great and dreadful day arrives and the

Lord returns to take vengeance upon the ungodly, then his wrath will be poured out upon them without measure.

"For I have suffered them thus far," that is, 'I have permitted mine enemies to persecute my people,' "that they [the enemies of God] might fill up the measure of their iniquities, that their cup might be full; and that those who call themselves after my name"—that is, the saints who have taken upon themselves the name of Christ—"might be chastened for a little season with a sore and grievous chastisement, because they did not hearken altogether unto the precepts and commandments which I gave unto them." Though his people believed the gospel and sought righteousness, yet they had not attained that perfection—a perfection born of full obedience—that would enable them to establish Zion.

"But verily I say unto you, that I have decreed a decree which my people shall realize, inasmuch as they hearken from this very hour unto the counsel which I, the Lord their God, shall give unto them." The door is not yet closed; it is still the hour in which Zion can be redeemed and the New Jerusalem built—all on conditions of obedience and worthiness. "Behold they [my people] shall, for I have decreed it, begin to prevail against mine enemies from this very hour. And by hearkening to observe all the words which I, the Lord their God, shall speak unto them, they shall never cease to prevail until the kingdoms of the world are subdued under my feet, and the earth is given unto the saints, to possess it forever and ever." By obedience, the saints have power to redeem Zion, to prevail in all things against their enemies, and to stand triumphant over earth and hell, even down to the Millennial day when the kingdoms of this world cease and only the kingdom of our God remains.

"But inasmuch as they keep not my commandments, and hearken not to observe all my words, the kingdoms of the world shall prevail against them." That the evil and worldly powers did prevail over them to the extent that they were finally driven from the confines of the United States to a destined inheritance in the mountains of western America is now known to us all. "For they were set to be a light unto the world, and to be the saviors of men; and inasmuch as they are not the saviors of men, they are as salt that has lost its savor, and is thenceforth good for nothing but to be cast out and trodden under foot of men." And even now, to some extent, the saints are trodden underfoot of men and are suffering many things that need not befall them, all of which is permitted because we are no better than our forebears who in their day failed to exercise the power that was theirs to build the Zion that might have then been.

"But verily I say unto you, I have decreed that your brethren which have been scattered shall return to the lands of their inheritances, and shall build up the waste places of Zion." Even then the power was in them to accomplish the work that must yet be performed. "For after much tribulation, as I have said unto you in a former commandment, cometh the blessing. Behold, this is the blessing which I have promised after your tribulations, and the tribulations of your brethren—your redemption, and the redemption of your brethren, even their restoration to the land of Zion, to be established, no more to be thrown down." All of this, as so emphatically and repetitiously stated, was dependent upon their faith and devotion to the gospel cause.

"Nevertheless, if they pollute their inheritances they shall be thrown down; for I will not spare them if they pollute their inheritances." And that they did pollute their inheritances is now one of the unchangeable facts of history.

"Behold, I say unto you, the redemption of Zion must needs come by power." It would have taken power in that day, and it will take power in the day when it is destined to be. "Therefore, I will raise up unto my people a man, who shall lead them like as Moses led the children of Israel." Joseph Smith was such a man for his day, and another like him shall wear his mantle when the future hour of our redemption arrives.

"For ye are the children of Israel, and of the seed of Abraham, and ye must needs be led out of bondage by power, and with a stretched-out arm." Why should it be any different with us than it was with our fathers? They were led out of Egyptian bondage to their promised land; we shall yet be led out of the bondage of the world to that Zion which it is our destined mission to build as soon as we are prepared for the wondrous work. "And as your fathers were led at the first, even so shall the redemption of Zion be." Plagues and desolation shall prepare the way; the pharaoh of worldly opposition shall be destroyed; and miracles, comparable to the parting of the Red Sea, shall attend.

"Therefore, let not your hearts faint, for I say not unto you as I said unto your fathers: Mine angel shall go up before you, but not my presence. But I say unto you: Mine angels shall go up before you, and also my presence, and in time ye shall possess the goodly land." The saints shall possess the lands of their inheritance while they dwell as mortals on earth. The New Jerusalem with its temple shall rise before the Lord comes to reign in Millennial glory.

Having so promised, the Lord commanded Joseph Smith to issue this call to the strength of his house: "Gather yourselves together unto the land of Zion, upon the land which I have bought with money that has been consecrated unto me." The army of valiant souls so involved were to purchase more lands, to curse their enemies if need be, and to be willing to lay down their lives in the Lord's cause. Out of this command came Zion's Camp, which traveled from Kirtland to Missouri to succor their afflicted brethren in that area. Their instructions were: "Organize my kingdom upon the consecrated land, and establish the children of Zion upon the laws and commandments which have been and which shall be given unto you." Even at this time it was still within their power to build up Zion and accomplish all that they were commanded to do. And this was the condition placed upon them: "All victory and glory is brought to pass unto you through your diligence, faithfulness, and prayers of faith." (D&C 103.)

The Lord Delays the Building of Zion

Mob violence increased in Missouri. Organized bodies of the Lord's enemies declared their intent to destroy his people, and Zion's Camp, with the Prophet at its head, came to Missouri, bringing clothing and provisions for the suffering saints. In Missouri, while encamped near Fishing River, the Prophet received the revelation that relieved the saints of the immediate necessity to build up the center place of the Lord's American Zion. It was June 22, 1834, and this was the word: "Verily I say unto you who have assembled yourselves together that you may learn my will concerning the redemption of mine afflicted people—behold, I say unto you, were it not for the transgressions of my people, speaking concerning the church and not individuals, they might have been redeemed even now." As a unit, as the Lord's congregation, as a body of true believers, as the saints of the Most High, as the collective body of souls comprising the Church, they had not measured up to the required divine standard. Many individuals had, but the kingdom of the saints was to be established by the hosts of Israel; it was not a work for a few, but for many; a few individuals standing alone do not build great cities.

"But behold, they [the saints in general] have not learned to be obedient to the things which I required at their hands, but are full of all manner of evil, and do not impart of their substance, as becometh saints, to the poor and afflicted among them." They were not living the revealed law of consecration; the United Order, given of God for the blessing of his people, was not prospering.

"And [they] are not united according to the union required by the law of the celestial kingdom; and Zion cannot be built up unless it is by the principles of the law of the celestial kingdom; otherwise I cannot receive her unto myself." So it was in the Zion of Enoch in former days, and so must it be in the Zion of the saints in the latter days. If those of old, in the coming day, are to descend from heaven and be one with those in the latter-day Zion, both peoples must have the same faith and be living the same laws. In the providences of a just God, how could it be otherwise?

Hence: "My people must needs be chastened until they learn obedience, if it must needs be, by the things which they suffer." Both we and our forebears in this dispensation are now learning obedience in this manner. But, "I speak not concerning those who are appointed to lead my people, who are the first elders of my church, for they are not all under this condemnation; but I speak concerning my churches abroad—there are many who will say: Where is their God? Behold, he will deliver them in time of trouble, otherwise we will not go up unto Zion, and will keep our moneys." Are not those who lack faith the ones who find fault with the Lord and his work? Do those who love the Lord declaim against him or his people or their leaders? How true it is that where your treasure is, there will your heart be also.

"Therefore, in consequence of the transgressions of my

people, it is expedient in me that mine elders should wait for a little season for the redemption of Zion—that they themselves may be prepared, and that my people may be taught more perfectly, and have experience, and know more perfectly concerning their duty, and the things which I require at their hands." A little season—how long will it last? Will it be two hundred years? or three hundred? Though the day of the Second Coming is fixed, the day for the redemption of Zion depends upon us. After we as a people live the law of the celestial kingdom; after we gain the needed experience and learn our duties; after we become by faith and obedience as were our fellow saints in the days of Enoch; after we are worthy to be translated, if the purposes of the Lord should call for such a course in this day—then Zion will be redeemed, and not before.

"This cannot be brought to pass until mine elders are endowed with power from on high. For behold, I have prepared a great endowment and blessing to be poured out upon them, inasmuch as they are faithful and continue in humility before me." As of this time the ordinances of the house of the Lord had not been revealed, and the endowment of power from on high received through them was needed in the heavenly work that lay ahead. "Therefore it is expedient in me that mine elders should wait for a little season, for the redemption of Zion." (D&C 105:1-13.) And so we wait, wondering the while how long the "little season" is destined to last. As to its length, we cannot say. This much only do we know: the "little season" is the appointed period of preparation for the Latter-day Saints. In it we must attain the same spiritual stature enjoyed by those who built the original Zion. Then and then only will we build our latter-day City of Holiness.

Zion Shall Be Redeemed with Power

As we await the day and as we prepare ourselves as a people, we are comforted with these added words of revelation: "Behold, I do not require at their hands"—the hands of mine elders—"to fight the battles of Zion; for, as I said in a former commandment, even so will I fulfil—I will fight your battles." We need not suppose our swords must slay the enemies of God, or that any mortal power must cleanse the land and make it available for the saints. The building of the New Jerusalem is the Lord's work, and he will prepare the way for his people when that people have prepared themselves to perform the heaven-given labors.

"Behold, the destroyer I have sent forth to destroy and lay waste mine enemies." Destructions, wars, calamities, the violence of nature—those things that men call "acts of God" —shall sweep over the land. "And not many years hence"—the "little season" shall last for years—"they shall not be left to pollute mine heritage, and to blaspheme my name upon the lands which I have consecrated for the gathering together of my saints." We are thus left to conclude that the wicked will slay the wicked, and the God of Nature will loose the forces of nature to destroy those who oppose the manifest destiny of his saints. If the Lord cursed old Egypt and overthrew Pharaoh in order to free his ancient covenant people from bondage, will he not curse modern Egypt, as it were, and overthrow the powers of the world, as he prepares the way for his covenant saints to build the capital city of their latter-day promised land?

As to Zion's Camp, which had come to the Fishing River site, their mission had been to redeem Zion, to gather the Lord's people, and to throw down the towers of his enemies. "But the strength of mine house have not hearkened unto my words," the Lord said. Only a few had responded to the call; though they were worthy to do the holy work and inherit the promised rewards, the great body of the saints were not. "But inasmuch as there are those who have hearkened unto my words, I have prepared a blessing and an endowment for them, if they continue faithful. I have heard their prayers, and will accept their offering; and it is expedient in me that they should be brought thus far for a trial of their faith."

The Lord then counsels his people to be wise and discreet and not stir up opposition as they gather together. "Talk not of judgments, neither boast of faith nor of mighty works," they are commanded, "but carefully gather together, as much in one region as can be, consistently with the feelings of the people." They are to seek "favor in the eyes of the people, until the army of Israel becomes very great." Joseph Smith and the appointed elders are told: "Gather up the strength of my house," and send "wise men, to fulfil that which I have commanded concerning the purchasing of all the lands in Jackson county that can be purchased, and in the adjoining counties round about." In spite of their prior failures, the hope is still held out to them that in their lifetimes Zion can be redeemed.

"For it is my will that these lands should be purchased; and after they are purchased that my saints should possess them according to the laws of consecration which I have given." Those who dwell in the perfect Zion must be qualified to live the law of consecration, and obedience to that law is the very way in which the New Jerusalem will be built. As is well known, the early saints attempted to live the law of consecration as it operated through a United Order, but they failed. And up to this point in time we are living only the lesser law of tithing, though some of the principles of consecration are found in the Church Welfare Program.

"And after these lands are purchased, I will hold the armies of Israel guiltless in taking possession of their own lands, which they have previously purchased with their moneys, and of throwing down the towers of mine enemies that may be upon them, and scattering their watchmen, and avenging me of mine enemies unto the third and fourth generation of them that hate me." Even now, a century and a half later, and for many years to come—we do not know how many—there are and will be those of the third and fourth generation who inhabit the lands that are to become holy unto the Lord when his Zion is built upon them.

"But first"—before the redemption of Zion—"let my army become very great," saith the Lord. The building of the capital city of the world, the city whence the law shall go forth for a thousand years, the city of the Great King who shall reign personally upon the earth—the building of such a glorious place is not the work for a few hundred, a few thousand, or even for tens of thousands. The Lord's people—his army—must become very great, greater by far than it is even now. "And let it [the army of the Lord] be sanctified before me, that it may become fair as the sun, and clear as the moon, and that her banners may be terrible unto all nations; that the kingdoms of this world may be constrained to acknowledge that the kingdom of Zion is in very deed the kingdom of our God and his Christ; therefore, let us become subject unto her laws."

Again the word is this: The worthiness of the Lord's

people, their sanctified state, their purity and uprightness before him—these are the things that will enable them to build the New Jerusalem, for Zion is the City of Holiness. When it is built, as it was in Enoch's day, its grandeur and glory and power must be such that those in all nations, from one end of the earth to the other, standing in awe, will feel inclined to be subject to such a mighty city, whence comes such a perfect law. The day in which the latter-day Zion will have such renown and be held in such unlimited awe is clearly Millennial.

Before Zion is built, the elders of the kingdom are to be endowed with power from on high; they are to be endowed in holy temples built for that very purpose. "Let those commandments which I have given concerning Zion and her law be executed and fulfilled, after her redemption." The New Jerusalem is to be built before the Second Coming, but all of the things concerning her glory and her laws shall not come to pass until the Millennium is ushered in. The greatness and the power will come to pass "after her redemption."

"There has been a day of calling," a day in which all the elders of the kingdom were invited to come forward and build the New Jerusalem, "but the time has come for a day of choosing." The response of his early Latter-day Saints having been inadequate, the Lord will now choose, when he will, those who are to accomplish the great work. "And let those be chosen that are worthy." When the day comes, none but those who qualify by obedience and righteousness will participate in the work. "And it shall be manifest unto my servant"— the President of the Church who then governs the kingdom—"by the voice of the Spirit, those that are chosen; and they shall be sanctified; and inasmuch as they follow the counsel which they receive, they shall have power after many days to accomplish all things pertaining to Zion." (D&C 105:14-37.)

After many days, a designated period in which we still live, those who are called, chosen, selected, appointed, and sent forth by the voice of the Spirit, as it speaks to the President of the Church, shall build the New Jerusalem and the holy temple to which the Lord Jesus Christ shall come in power and glory as the great Millennium is ushered in. In the meantime, our work as a people is to keep the commandments and sanctify ourselves so that if the call comes in our day, we shall be worthy to respond.

CHAPTER 63

The Second Coming of the Son of Man

The First and Second Comings of Christ

Our Blessed Lord, Mary's Son, whose father is God, was destined from before the foundations of the earth to stand on two occasions as the Chief Citizen on this lowly orb. He was foreordained to come to earth twice, once in mortal guise as the Atoning One, then in glorious immortality as King and Lord. These two comings, the first past and the second future, are inextricably woven together; neither can be understood by itself alone, and both are essential to complete the salvation of man. One took place in a corner with few men aware of the earthwide and universe-filled effect of the infinite act there performed; the other will be heralded by angelic hosts and will usher in such changes in the whole earth, changes both physical and spiritual, that it will be as though all flesh saw the Lord and viewed his glory at one and the same moment.

The most transcendent event that ever has occurred or ever will occur, from creation's dawn through all the unending ages of eternity, took place in a garden and on a cross in the meridian of time. It was the infinite and eternal atonement. There, in Gethsemane and on Golgotha, because he was the Son of the Immortal Elohim and the mortal Mary, he ransomed men from the temporal and spiritual death that fell upon Adam's seed when the first man of all men chose to become mortal so that man might be. There, in agony beyond compare, suffering both body and spirit in a way incomprehensible to us, he bore the sins of all men on conditions of repentance. There, as he sweat great gouts of blood from every pore, and shrinking because of pain (would—had such been possible—that he might not drink the bitter cup), he paid the penalty for a broken law and poured out his soul unto death. There, as none but a God could do, he fulfilled his Father's will; brought life and immortality to light through the gospel; put all of the terms and conditions of his Father's plan into operation; ransomed this earth and all that on it is from an endless death and a mindless oblivion; made possible the victory over the grave; and sealed the fate of Lucifer and the enemies of God who seek to enthrone themselves above the stars of heaven.

There is no language known to the human tongue; there are no words that mortals can speak or write; there are no feelings that can fill the heart of an earthbound soul; there is no way by the power of the greatest intellect—to even begin to portray the infinite power and eternal wonder of the atoning sacrifice. All this occurred in time's meridian; all this we must know if we are to keep in perspective the glory and grandeur of that which is yet to be in the fulness of times.

Indeed, the soon-to-be coming of the Lord Jesus Christ in the clouds of heaven, attended by angelic legions and in all the glory of his Father's kingdom, is but an outgrowth and a result of the atonement. It is the day when the Son of David, rejected by his own and slain by wicked men, will return as the Second David to rule and reign over the house of Israel forever. It is the day when the hopes and desires and longings of all the prophets and all the saints of all the ages will reach a glorious fulfillment. Then the wicked will be destroyed, Satan will be bound, peace and plenty will abound, righteousness will cover the earth as the waters cover the sea, and all who call upon the name of the Lord will be saved. Though the infinite power that atones was manifest in all its death-defying force in the meridian of time, the eternal glory, the splendor, and the triumph over the world of evil remains to be shown forth in the coming Millennial day.

This earth is destined to be renewed and receive its paradisiacal glory during the Millennium. This renewal and return to earth's Edenic state will be brought to pass by the Second Coming of the Son of Man. To envision the glories and wonders of that Millennial day, we must first understand and believe the doctrine of the Second Coming.

All, in and out of the Christian fold, who are aware of the facts of history know that a man called Jesus lived some two thousand years ago in a place called Palestine. They know that reliable historians attribute to him a life of good works and miracles and that he was crucified by Roman hands at the instigation of his Jewish brethren. True Christians believe he was the Son of God and that he rose from the dead, becoming thus the firstfruits of them that sleep. They believe and know that his resurrection proves his divine Sonship, and that because he was the Son of God, the gospel he preached has power to save men in the kingdom of God. True believers also know that all the prophets from Adam to John the Baptist foretold his mortal coming and testified of the works he would do and the atonement to be wrought by him.

It behooves us now to make but a brief outline of the revealed word relative to the Second Coming as a foundation for our consideration of the personal reign of earth's King on the paradisiacal earth that is soon to be.

The Signs of the Times

Jesus our Lord, though he was the Son of the living God, "made himself of no reputation, and took upon him the form of a servant, and was made in the likeness of men." In this state he dwelt among mortals for some thirty-three years. His active ministry of preaching, healing, and saving was just over three years. Then came Gethsemane and the day of atonement, "and being found in fashion as a man, he humbled himself, and became obedient unto death, even the death of the cross." (Philippians 2:7-8.) After his death, resurrection, and another forty days spent with his apostolic witnesses, he ascended into heaven. Then, on that holy ground called Olivet, "while they beheld, he was taken up; and a cloud received him out of their sight." Angelic ministrants attended. "Ye men of Galilee," they said, "why stand ye gazing up into heaven? this same Jesus, which is taken up from you into heaven, shall so come in like manner as ye have seen him go into heaven." (Acts 1:9-11.) Thus Christ the Lord came; he ministered; he atoned; he was resurrected and ascended into heaven; and he shall come again, being at that appointed day the same loving and compassionate friend who ate and drank with them of old after he rose from the dead.

Knowing that the Lord whom we seek "shall descend from heaven with a shout, with the voice of the archangel, and with the trump of God," we await with great expectancy that glorious day. We "know perfectly that the day of the Lord so cometh as a thief in the night"; that he will not be expected by the world; and that he will take vengeance upon the ungodly in that day. Sudden destruction will come upon them "as travail upon a woman with child; and they shall not escape." But the saints of God, who are "the children of light, and the children of the day," shall not be in darkness. They know the generation of his return, and hence they await and watch and are sober. (1 Thessalonians 5:2-6.) They can read the signs of the times. That is, they know and recognize the things that must occur after the ascension and before the Second Coming and thus are in a position to have an intelligent opinion as to when the great and dreadful day of the Lord will come. We shall now note some of the major signs of the times.

1. *Universal apostasy prevails.*

This is the first great sign of the times; out of it all others grow. It contains the seeds of evil from which the fruits of wickedness, despair, and doom are harvested. There is no hope for the world except through the gospel of the Lord Jesus Christ; without it, all men remain carnal, sensual, and devilish by nature and are never reconciled to their God through the mediation of his Son. And this gospel in its fulness and perfection was lost to the world shortly after the death of the apostles. As Paul said, "The Lord Jesus shall be revealed from heaven with his mighty angels, in flaming fire taking vengeance on them that know not God, and that obey not the gospel of our Lord Jesus Christ," but "that day shall not come, except there come a falling away first, and that man of sin be revealed, the son of perdition." (2 Thessalonians 1:7-8; 2:3.)

From the day the early church was swallowed up by the world until now, the man of sin, who is Lucifer, has held sway, and his works have been revealed on every hand. It has been, "as with the people, so with the priest; as with the servant, so with his master; as with the maid, so with her mistress; as with the buyer, so with the seller; as with the lender, so with the borrower; as with the taker of usury, so with the giver of usury to him." All have gone astray; darkness has covered the earth, and gross darkness the minds of the people. "The earth also is defiled under the inhabitants thereof; because they have transgressed the laws, changed the ordinance, broken the everlasting covenant." (Isaiah 24:2, 5.) If there was ever a sad, sorry, and terrible state—and it is one of which scriptures by the hundreds testify—it is that dire, dark everywhere-present apostasy would envelope the earth shortly after the ascension of the Lord Jesus.

2. *Iniquity abounds.*

Jesus said: "Iniquity shall abound." (JS–M 1:30.) How could it be otherwise? Without the gospel to guide them, men are easily led into Lucifer's sheepcote. It is because men "changed the truth of God into a lie," by forsaking the gospel, apostatizing from the truth, and turning from the light to darkness, that "God also gave them up to uncleanness through the lusts of their own hearts." (Romans 1:24-25.) Since the day of Noah, when all but eight souls were swept off the earth by a flood, there has never been such a day of wickedness and evil as now exists. It is a sign of the times, and it will so continue, in a worsening degree, until every corruptible thing is consumed by the brightness of His coming.

3. *False Christs arise.*

Speaking of our day, the Lord Jesus said: "If any man shall say unto you, Lo, here is Christ, or there, believe him not; for in those days there shall also arise false Christs, and false prophets, and shall show great signs and wonders, insomuch, that, if possible, they shall deceive the very elect, who are the elect according to the covenant. Behold, I speak these things unto you for the elect's sake." (JS–M 1:21-23.) False Christs are false systems of religion, false ways of worship, false claims as to how and in what manner men may be saved, all of which are taught by false ministers who are false prophets. And such is the state of modern Christendom. Voices on every hand call out: "Lo, here is Christ, or, Lo, there."

4. *False churches flourish.*

False ways of worship, based on false doctrines, are found in false churches, "churches which are built up, and not unto the Lord." And "their priests shall contend one with another, and they shall teach with their learning, and deny the Holy Ghost, which giveth utterance." How well it is said of them:

"Because of pride, and because of false teachers, and false doctrine, their churches have become corrupted, and their churches are lifted up; because of pride they are puffed up. . . . Because of pride, and wickedness, and abominations, and whoredoms, they have all gone astray." (2 Nephi 28:3-14.) And how well it was said to Joseph Smith that he should "join none of them, for they were all wrong," that their "professors were all corrupt," and that they drew near to the Lord "with their lips, but their hearts" were far from him, and that they taught "for doctrines the commandments of men, having a form of godliness," but denying "the power thereof." (JS–H 1:19.)

5. *Satan's church reigns.*

John and Nephi, in detail and with a power of expression seldom seen even in the prophetic word, speak of the church founded by the devil, whose adherents desire wealth and power and carnal living; a church whose wickedness is like that of ancient Babylon; a church that sells the souls of men; a church that is a harlot and the mother of harlots and that persecutes and slays the saints of God. (See Revelation 17 and 18; 1 Nephi 13 and 14.) Moroni, writing centuries after John and Nephi, shows how evils of false religion, found in many churches, would be shown forth in the last days. "There shall be churches built up that shall say, Come unto me, and for your money you shall be forgiven of your sins." (Mormon 8:32.) Indeed, the evils and abominations performed in the name of religion are so great that it sickens the soul to read of them, both in the prophetic word and in the annals of history past and history present. But all that now is, in this respect, is provided for in the divine plan and is descriptive of that which is and shall be before the great and dreadful day of the Lord.

6. *Secret combinations destroy freedom.*

From the day of Cain, who slew his brother Abel, to the present, there have always been secret combinations whose members have reveled in carnal deeds and sought power and dominion over others by evil means. Through the ages these have taken many forms and borne many names. There are powers and forces and combinations of nations and kingdoms where freedom is denied today. Some of these are as autocratic and deny freedom of worship as forcefully as any of the ancient empires. Some profess to be godless; others mandate

the worship of a particular God. Some have political philosophies that run counter to gospel principles; others wage wars
against neighboring nations to spread and impose their views
upon the minds of men. There are those who would control,
govern, and enslave the whole world if they could. Moroni
warns us that "whatsoever nation shall uphold [these] secret
combinations," whose goal is "to get power and gain . . . shall
be destroyed." He says these combinations seek "to overthrow the freedom of all lands, nations, and countries," and to
bring "to pass the destruction of all people," for they are "built
up by the devil, who is the father of all lies." (Ether 8:22-25.)
They are part of the church of the devil and will be over-
thrown when the Lord comes to take vengeance upon the
ungodly.

7. *False prophets are everywhere.*

One of the surest and most certain signs of the times is
the near-omnipresence of false prophets. "There shall also
arise . . . false prophets," saith the holy word. (JS – M 1:22.) It
is now almost as though every fool or near-fool, and every
person filled with self-conceit and a desire to be in the spot-
light of adulation, fancies himself a prophet of religion or
politics, or what have you. On every hand there are those who
suppose they know how to save society, to save nations, to
save souls. They preach all sorts of gospels—a social gospel; a
racial gospel; a gospel of freedom or communism, of socialism
or free enterprise, of military preparedness or reliance upon
the wispy promises of foreign foes; a gospel of salvation by
grace alone, or of this or that doctrine. Streets and stadiums
and temples are overrun, as the ancient prophets foretold, with
the false ministers and teachers and politicians of the latter
days. And all this shall continue until the greedy, the power
hungry, and the self-called preachers go the way of all the earth
when He comes to rule whose right it is both to instruct and to
govern.

8. *There shall be an age of restoration.*

As the apostasy is the first great sign of the times, so the restoration is the second. As there are many parts and phases of
the apostasy, so there are many signs and events involved in
the restoration. The greatest of these is that an actual period of
time must commence in which the Lord of heaven will begin

to restore every truth, doctrine, and teaching; every power, priesthood, and key; every ordinance, performance, and rite— all that has ever been had by faithful men in ages past. This restoration began in the spring of 1820 with the appearance of the Father and the Son to Joseph Smith. That was the commencement of "the times of restitution" of which Peter spoke. This ancient apostle said that "a times of refreshing shall come from the presence of the Lord," a time of renewal, a time when the earth would receive again its paradisiacal glory. So shall it be at the Second Coming, when the Millennium is ushered in. In that day, God "shall send Jesus Christ" again, the same Jesus "which before was preached" unto the Jews. But, Peter continued—note it and note it well—this Jesus must remain in heaven until something happens. He is the one "whom the heaven must receive until the times of restitution of all things, which God hath spoken by the mouth of all his holy prophets since the world began." (Acts 3:19-21.) That is, this Jesus came once; he ministered among men; he ascended into heaven; there he must remain; and he will not come again to dwell among men until a certain age in the earth's history commences.

That age is called the times of restitution or, in other words, the age of restoration. In it, all things are to be restored that were had by any of the saints in any past dispensation. The promise is not that all things will be restored before the Second Coming, but that the age of restoration will commence before our Lord returns. The fact is that many things—indeed, most things—will be restored after he comes. But the age itself is here—we live in it—and the hour of his coming is known, thereby, to be nearer than the world supposes.

9.   *Preparation is made for the age of restoration.*

For half a millennium, from the fourteenth century to the nineteenth century, great social, cultural, educational, economic, industrial, and religious movements prepared the way for the age of restoration. The rays of the Renaissance pierced the deep gloom of the dark ages, and men began again to think for themselves. The shackles of the dominant church were loosed; papal absolutism was challenged; and there were even futile and failing attempts to reform Western Catholicism. Printing was discovered and used, universities were established, and a new age of learning was ushered in. In the religious realm, the Protestant reformation grew out of the Renaissance, and because of it the minds and souls of many were prepared for the added light and knowledge soon to come by revelation.

10. *The American nation is established.*

The establishment of the United States of America as a free and powerful nation is one of the political miracles of the ages. Never has such a system of government been devised before; indeed, it was brought into being in our day by the power of the Lord for the accomplishment of his own purposes. Those purposes include the restoration of the gospel, the setting up of the true church, and the sending of the word of truth from this American Zion to all the nations and peoples of the world. Columbus discovered America; Gentile peoples fled from European bondage to find freedom in America; the American colonists received divine help in the Revolutionary War; the Constitution of the United States, with its guarantees of religious freedom, came into being; the people of the United States were established as a free people by the power of the Lord—all as part of the eternal plan, which provided for the restoration of the gospel and the salvation of the children of men.

11. *The glorious gospel is restored.*

What is the gospel? It is the plan of salvation; it is the way and means whereby fallen man may find place again in the heaven of heavens; it is the power of God whereby salvation comes. John saw in vision that this everlasting gospel would be brought from heaven to earth, by angelic ministration, to prepare a people for the hour of the Lord's judgment, which judgment shall take place at his Second Coming. (Revelation 14:6-7.) This promised restoration proves the universal apostasy, for if any nation, kindred, tongue, or people had the gospel, it would not be necessary to reveal it anew so that it might be taught to them. Moroni and other heavenly beings brought back to mortals the Lord's system of salvation, and the fulness of the everlasting gospel is now resident with men on the earth. This restoration includes the doctrines of salvation, the priesthoods and powers by which salvation comes, and the keys of presidency whereby all things in the Lord's earthly kingdom are governed.

12. *Elias shall restore all things.*

Referring to our day, Jesus said: "Elias truly shall first come, and restore all things, as the prophets have written." (JST, Matthew 17:10.) No single ancient prophet, standing alone, returned to restore all things. Angelic ministrants came from all of the great dispensations of the past. This promised Elias is, in effect, all of the angelic ministrants who have come in the latter days to restore truths and powers and keys, all of the things that, taken together, compose "all things." It was in this way that our dispensation became the dispensation of the fulness of times, meaning the dispensation of the fulness of all dispensations past. Someone came from each of these ancient dispensations to bring to us what was had among mortals in his day. Hence these words of Jesus about Elias as they are here explained.

13. *Elijah shall return before the great and dreadful day.*

Thus saith the Lord: "Behold, I will send you Elijah the prophet before the coming of the great and dreadful day of the Lord." (Malachi 4:5.) It is just that simple; the Lord Jesus will not return in power and glory to take vengeance upon the wicked until Elijah returns and does a preparatory work. Elijah came on the third day of April in 1836 to Joseph Smith and Oliver Cowdery, conferring upon them the keys of the sealing power that he held as a mortal. (D&C 110:13-16.) These keys are the power to bind on earth and seal everlastingly in the heavens, and without these keys, no people can possess the fulness of the gospel.

14. *The Lord's messenger prepares the way.*

It is with reference to the Second Coming that the ancient word promises: "Behold, I will send my messenger, and he shall prepare the way before me." (Malachi 3:1.) John the Baptist did this very thing in the meridian of time, but it remained for Joseph Smith to perform the glorious work in our day. He is the latter-day messenger who was sent to restore the gospel, which itself prepares a people for the return of the Lord. This gospel, first revealed in modern times to Joseph Smith, is itself personified in these words of latter-day scripture: "I have sent mine everlasting covenant into the world," saith the Lord, "to be a light to the world, and to be a standard for my people, and for the Gentiles to seek to it, and to be a messenger before my face to prepare the way before me." (D&C 45:9.)

15. *The gospel will be preached in all nations.*

There is but one gospel—the everlasting gospel; the gospel preached by Peter, James, and John, and by Jesus Christ our Lord; the gospel administered by the kingdom of God on earth; the gospel lost from the earth during the long night of universal apostasy; the gospel restored by the opening of the heavens to Joseph Smith. Jesus said: "This Gospel of the Kingdom shall be preached in all the world, for a witness unto all nations, and then shall the end come, or the destruction of the wicked." (JS–M 1:31.) The gospel is to go to every nation and kindred and tongue and people before the Lord returns. All peoples are to hear the warning voice so they can prepare for the coming of Him who will take vengeance upon the wicked and ungodly. This requisite has yet to be fulfilled; indeed, we have done little more than scratch the surface where our worldwide preaching commission is concerned. This labor cannot be accomplished in full until the Church is much bigger and stronger than it now is.

16. *The Church will be established in the nations of the earth.*

A measure and degree of success shall attend the preaching of the restored gospel in all the world in the last days; converts will be made and church organizations established among many peoples before the Lord returns. Though the Latter-day Saints will be few in number compared to the masses of men, yet the Lord's people will be found in every nation, speaking every tongue. "I beheld that the church of the Lamb, who were the saints of God, were also upon all the face of the earth," Nephi said. (1 Nephi 14:12.) These choice souls, who love the Lord and seek his face, will be a leavening and refining influence wherever they are found. They will be members of The Church of Jesus Christ of Latter-day Saints, and they will be organized as their circumstances warrant. The righteous in all nations will seek safety and salvation in the stakes of Zion as the dreadful day approaches. Truly the true church and kingdom will be established to some degree in all nations before the Second Coming.

17. *The Book of Mormon prepares the way.*

Many of Israel's ancient prophets and seers—Jacob who was Israel; Joseph who was sold into Egypt; David the sweet singer of Israel; Isaiah, Ezekiel, Zenos, and others—foretold the coming forth of the Book of Mormon to prepare the way before the Lord in the last days. That holy book was to be the power that gathered Israel (the Ten Tribes included) and made them one nation again upon their ancient mountains; it was to open the ears of the spiritually deaf, give sight to those who were blind spiritually, cause those who erred in spiritual things to come to understanding, and teach true doctrine to those who murmured. It would bear witness of Christ, proclaim the doctrines of salvation, and stand as irrefutable proof of the truth and divinity of the Lord's great latter-day work. To all of these things the holy word attests. (See, for example, JST, Genesis 49 and 50; Psalm 85; Isaiah 29; Ezekiel 37; 2 Nephi 3; and Jacob 5.)

18. *Israel shall be gathered to her ancient Shepherd.*

Israel shall gather both before and after the Second Coming, for her great and glorious day is Millennial; then she shall be exalted as the Lord himself dwells and reigns among his people. That is the day when the kingdom shall be restored to Israel in the full sense of the word; that is the day when the Lord's people will become again as they once were—a nation and a kingdom set apart from all others, a realm in which every man is a king and a priest in his own right. But Israel shall gather by the tens of millions into the true church before the Lord comes; she shall assemble to the stakes of Zion in all nations; she shall enjoy the fulness of the blessings of the ecclesiastical kingdom before the Lord comes; and thereafter the political kingdom also will be hers.

19. *The Lamanites will be gathered into the fold.*

"The Son of Man cometh," saith the Lord. "But before the great day of the Lord shall come, Jacob shall flourish in the wilderness, and the Lamanites shall blossom as the rose." (D&C 49:22, 24.) Throughout the whole Book of Mormon account, the Lehite prophets looked forward to that glorious day when the Lamanites—then a dark and benighted and loathsome people—would again become pure and delightsome. The fulfillment of these promises is pre-Millennial, and it is now beginning to occur, particularly in South America, where Father Lehi's seed are coming into the Church in such great numbers.

20. *The two Jerusalems will be built.*

As we have heretofore set forth in some detail, the building up of Old Jerusalem in Palestine and the establishment of the New Jerusalem in America are both destined to occur before our Lord returns. Both events are yet future. As to the American Zion that is to be, one of our scriptures proclaims: "The Son of Man cometh. . . . But before the great day of the Lord shall come, Jacob shall flourish in the wilderness. . . . Zion shall flourish upon the hills and rejoice upon the mountains, and shall be assembled together unto the place which I have appointed." (D&C 49:22, 24-25.) We, as the seed of Jacob, now flourish in the wilderness of western America, and at the appointed time the saints shall gather to their promised Zion in Missouri.

21. *The Jewish portion of Israel will be gathered.*

As with the Ten Tribes, so with the Jews—the day of their real gathering is Millennial. Scattered representatives of the Kingdom of Judah and the Kingdom of Israel will be gathered into the true fold of Christ before he comes, but the great day of the gathering of these ancient peoples will be after the King of Israel has taken his place as the ruler of the earth. "The Jews which are scattered," Nephi says, "also shall begin to believe in Christ; and they shall begin to gather in upon the face of the land; and as many as shall believe in Christ shall also become a delightsome people." (2 Nephi 30:7.) This is now in process. A few of these ancient covenant people are returning to the sheepfold of their fathers, but most of them are not. When the Lord comes, in the midst of that Armageddon then in process, the Jews, as a body and as a people, will look upon him and inquire about the wounds in his hands and feet. He will then introduce himself as that Jesus whom their fathers crucified. They will then weep for the sins of their ancestors, be converted, and become the valiant souls that the children of the prophets should be.

22.   *The two temples will be built.*

A temple shall be built in the New Jerusalem and another in Old Jerusalem before the Second Coming. It is to these holy houses, among others, that the Lord shall suddenly come. We have already set forth much detail relative to the temple in Independence, Missouri. Relative to the temple in Old Jerusalem, the Prophet Joseph Smith said: "Judah must return, Jerusalem must be rebuilt, and the temple; . . . and all this must be done before the Son of Man will make His appearance." (*Teachings of the Prophet Joseph Smith,* p. 286.)

23.   *The times of the Gentiles will be fulfilled.*

Incident to the Second Coming, in a gradual way and over a period of time, the preferential treatment now offered to the Gentiles (the non-Jews) will come to an end and the gospel will go preferentially to the Jews, as it did in the day of our Lord's personal ministry among them. We live in that generation, or age, when "the times of the Gentiles [shall] be fulfilled," although this will not be complete until the Lord comes. (D&C 45:30.)

24.   *Wars, plagues, pestilence, and desolation will take place.*

Before the Lord comes, the whole earth will be in turmoil. Wars and rumors of wars will spread death and destruction and disease that will dwarf anything ever known among men. Plagues and pestilence and pain will punish the people to a degree never before known. Men will be cursed physically and spiritually; the flesh of many will fall from their bones and their eyes from their sockets. Earthquakes will destroy many cities and bring death to their municipals; fire and hail will destroy the crops of the earth; rivers and seas and deserts and mountains will be contaminated; the waters of the world will be polluted; famines and poisons and dead bodies will be commonplace. No tongue can tell the desolations and sorrows that are yet to be, all of which will be climaxed by the burning of the vineyard, at which time every corruptible thing will be consumed.

Truly, the signs of the times are many. No man can name them all, and all of them come as a warning and to prepare the way before the face of Him who yet shall reign in triumph and glory. The saints of the Most High have power to read the signs of the times; they need not be deceived as to what has been and what yet shall be, all as a prelude to the ushering in of the great Millennium. Accordingly, all those with understanding are watching, seeking to be ready, and striving to prepare themselves to abide the day of his coming.

CHAPTER 64

The Personal Reign

Ushering In the Personal Reign

As to the signs of the times—those ominous and portentous yet wondrous events that shall precede the Second Coming of the Lord Jesus—most of them are passed; some are now being shown forth; and a few others have yet to rear their ugly and hateful heads before the eyes of all men. Our views and understanding of the glorious events immediately preceding and concurrent with the Second Coming will come into sharp focus if we give attention to the signs now blazing forth like mighty comets in the firmament of heaven, and also if we name and identify the decreed desolations, wars, and portents that lie just around the corner. These include the following:

1. *The generation of the Lord's return.*

No man knows the day nor the hour when the Lord Jesus —resplendent in glory, omnipotent in might, amid legions of holy angels—shall come again to rule among the sons of men. Nor do the very angels of God in heaven possess this knowledge, for they too, as part of their decreed destiny, are awaiting the day when their salvation will be perfected. But they and we know the generation, the age, the general period of time when earth's rightful King shall return to rule on the throne of David. They and we are the children of light, and so we know the generation or age of the Second Coming. That generation is now; we live in it, and it is rolling speedily along toward that consummation for which the saints so devoutly pray when they plead, "Thy kingdom come. Thy will be done in earth, as it is in heaven." (Matthew 6:10.)

2. *Will he come in our lifetimes?*

Or will it be while our children, or grandchildren, are still laboring through their probationary estates? This we do not know. We do know that in the Lord's perspective, his coming is near, even at the door. And we do have some rather pointed, though general, designations that indicate the approximate time of his return. Shortly before his martyrdom, the Prophet Joseph Smith said, as given utterance by the Spirit, "There are those of the rising generation who shall not taste death till Christ comes." (*Teachings of the Prophet Joseph Smith,* p. 286.) There will be many of that rising generation who will be living when the twenty-first century is ushered in. Our revelations state categorically that the Lord will come "in the beginning of the seventh thousand years" of this earth's temporal continuance. They speak of events destined to occur "in the beginning of the seventh thousand years," which events will be "the preparing of the way before the time of his coming." (D&C 77:12.) This revealed word can only mean that the Lord will come sometime after the beginning of the named time, but whether that coming will be ten or a hundred years thereafter, we are left to wonder.

3. *Prophets shall again be martyred in Jerusalem.*

Just before the Lord comes, two witnesses—mighty prophets of the restoration—shall be slain in Jerusalem because they testify of Joseph Smith and the restoration and the imminent return of Him whose witnesses they are. "And their dead bodies shall lie in the street of the great city, which spiritually is called Sodom and Egypt, where also our Lord was crucified." (Revelation 11:8.) The enemies of God will rejoice over the death of these prophets, but after three and a half days the spirit of life will enter their bodies, and they will ascend up on high. And at the same hour Jerusalem will be shaken by the great earthquake that ushers in her ancient King.

4. *Pouring out of the seven last plagues.*

In those days, which shall be in the beginning of the seventh thousand years, as explained in *The Millennial Messiah,* the Lord will pour out the seven last plagues. These are: (1) a noisome and grievous sore; (2) the seas become blood and their life dies; (3) all water turns to blood and is diseased; (4) the sun scorches men and the earth; (5) darkness, pain, and sores in the kingdoms of the world; (6) false miracles as the world prepares for Armageddon; and (7) war, upheavals of nature, and the fall of Babylon.

5.   *The promised signs and wonders appear.*

Near to and almost concurrent with the Second Coming, there will be certain promised signs and wonders that exceed and excel any like events of the past. These may appropriately be collated under the following headings: (1) Manifestations of blood, and fire, and vapors of smoke. (2) The sun shall be darkened and the moon turned into blood. (3) The stars shall hurl themselves from heaven. (4) The rainbow shall cease to appear in the mists and rains of heaven. (5) The sign of the Son of Man shall make its appearance. (6) A mighty earthquake, beyond anything of the past, shall shake the very foundations of the earth. As with other matters pertaining to the Second Coming, these are considered at length in *The Millennial Messiah.*

6.   *Armageddon—the greatest battle of the ages.*

When the Lord Jesus comes again, it will be not as the Prince of Peace, not as the Suffering Servant, not as one who descends below all things, but as the Man of War and the God of Battles who will wage war and overthrow kingdoms and spread destruction as he did when Joshua and Gideon and David led his people anciently. The Millennial era will not be ushered in by the righteousness of the people. Christ will come in the midst of war such as has never been known before in the whole history of the world. All the nations of the earth will be engaged. Those who oppose freedom and liberty and Christianity and the Jews will attack Jerusalem. The focal point will be the ancient battlegrounds of Megiddo and Armageddon. In the midst of this war, "this same Jesus" who ascended from Olivet "shall so come in like manner" as he went up into heaven. (Acts 1:11.) His feet shall once again stand upon the Mount of Olives. And in the Valley of Jehoshaphat, which is between Jerusalem and Olivet, he shall sit to judge the heathen nations.

7.   *Armageddon—the abomination of desolation.*

As it was in the days of Titus, so shall it be in the day of the coming of the Son of Man. Titus and his legions destroyed the Holy City, slew more than a million Jews, and enslaved the remainder. Not one stone was left upon another in the temple of Jehovah. But the primitive saints were preserved by divine power; they were led to safety before the abomination that maketh desolate fell upon the doomed city. And once again, in the coming Armageddon, Jerusalem shall be destroyed, and only the coming of the Lord Jesus will save the saints.

8. *The Jewish conversion and cleansing.*

Out of Armageddon will come the conversion and cleansing of those Jews who are not destroyed by the brightness of His coming. They are the ones who will ask: "What are these wounds in thine hands and in thy feet?" They are the ones to whom their returning Lord will say: "These wounds are the wounds with which I was wounded in the house of my friends. I am he who was lifted up. I am Jesus that was crucified. I am the Son of God." (D&C 45:51-52.) Then they and those in all nations who have not accepted Christ, as he has been revealed by his prophets, shall weep and lament for their unbelief and iniquities. "In that day there shall be a fountain opened to the house of David and to the inhabitants of Jerusalem for sin and for uncleanness." (Zechariah 13:1.) That is to say, they will be baptized and will come into the earthly kingdom and be one with the Lord's people.

9. *Armageddon—Gog and Magog.*

Holy writ describes the battle of Armageddon as the war of Gog and Magog. These accounts relative to Gog and Magog add to the Armageddon concept the fact that this final war will be religious in nature. Nations bearing the pseudonyms Gog and Magog will attack the Lord's covenant people. These evil forces will be destroyed by fire; the Lord will rain fire and brimstone upon them. That is, they will be burned at his coming. Their destruction will include the overthrow of the political kingdom on earth of Lucifer and the fall of the great and abominable church. The final triumph in this war of wars will bring to pass the triumph of Israel as a people and as a nation.

10. *The fall of Babylon.*

The destruction of Gog and Magog constitutes the fall of Babylon, the overthrow of the great and abominable church, and the destruction of the wicked. Babylon is the world; it is carnality, sensuality, and devilishness; it is the church of the devil; it is every religious and political kingdom and power that is not of God. Within its folds are found Catholics, Protestants, and Latter-day Saints; communists, worldly peoples, and godless nations; the Islamics, the Buddhists, and all who worship any God but the Lord; atheists, humanists, and evolutionists—yes, within its folds are all those who live after the manner of the world. And they all "shall be cast down by devouring fire" (D&C 29:21), as Ezekiel said with reference to Gog and Magog.

11. *The great and dreadful day of the Lord.*

Our Lord's return is called the great and dreadful day of the Lord, having particular reference to the dread and sorrow to be poured out upon the wicked and ungodly. It will be a day of burning, as we shall note particularly in considering the new heaven and the new earth. As pertaining to the wicked, it will be a day of vengeance; as pertaining to the righteous, it will usher in the year of the Lord's redeemed.

12. *The day of judgment.*

That great day when our Lord returns will be a day of judgment. Christ himself shall be the judge of all the earth. All men shall be judged by his law—the law of the gospel. One of the chief purposes of his coming will be to execute judgment upon all and to render to every man according to his deeds. In that day there will be an entire separation of the righteous and the wicked; only those who are worthy shall abide the day.

13. *He cometh in glory.*

When all things are in readiness; when the conditions precedent are fulfilled; when every jot and tittle of the Messianic word has come to pass; when the day and hour, before prepared and known to the Father from the beginning, has arrived; when all is as it is destined to be—and not before—then the Lord will come. "Our God shall come, and shall not keep silence: a fire shall devour before him, and it shall be very tempestuous round about him." (Psalm 50:3.) Then he shall reign personally upon the earth in great power and glory, which reign we shall now consider.

The Lord Reigns

"We believe . . . that Christ will reign personally upon the earth" (Article of Faith 10), meaning, as the Prophet tells us, that he will "visit it," from time to time, "when it is necessary to govern it." (*Teachings of the Prophet Joseph Smith,* p. 268.) The personal reign of the Lord Jesus Christ! What wonders yet lie in store for this fallen earth!

Mary's son—he who was foretold by the prophets; conceived by the Father; introduced by Gabriel; born in a stable; cradled in a manger; welcomed by angelic choirs; circumcised when eight days old; worshipped by wise men from the east; exiled to Egypt; disciplined in Nazareth; trained in carpentry in Galilee; matured and grown in grace in the Holy Land; baptized at Bethabara; tested in the wilderness; a Holy Man who ministered in Judea and Galilee and Samaria and beyond the borders of Israel; preached and wrought miracles throughout all the land; cast out devils; healed lepers; cured the lame; opened blind eyes; walked on the Sea of Galilee; fed thousands with a few loaves and fishes; raised the dead in Capernaum and Nain and Bethany; proclaimed his own divine Sonship; the Son who was transfigured on the mount; atoned in Gethsemane; tried before Annas and Caiaphas and Herod and Pilate; crucified on Calvary; resurrected in the Garden; and ascended from Olivet—Mary's son, once a mortal, who "made himself of no reputation, and took upon him the form of a servant, and was made in the likeness of men" (Philippians 2:7), shall come again, as the Immortal King, to rule and reign over Israel and all the earth for a thousand years! Let us now speak of the personal reign of our Pattern, Savior, Friend, and King.

1. *He cometh to Adam-ondi-Ahman.*

Before the Son of Man comes to reign personally upon the earth; before he descends in flaming fire with ten thousands of his saints to execute judgment upon the ungodly; before he comes in the clouds of heaven, in all the glory of his Father's kingdom; before he sets his feet once again upon the Mount of Olives, which is before Jerusalem; before he stands with 144,000 high priests on Mount Zion in Missouri; before he suddenly comes to his temple; before he utters his voice from the land of Zion and from Old Jerusalem; before all flesh shall see him together; before all of the appearances that, taken together, comprise the Second Coming—before all these, he will come in private to Adam-ondi-Ahman. Why and for what reason? To receive back from his servants of all ages the keys they have used to govern his earthly kingdom. Then and then only will he deign to reign personally. Now the voice of his servants is his voice, and they act pursuant to the divine commission he has given them. Then the keys will vest again in their rightful owner, and his voice and his power will be manifest to all men.

2. *The Kingdom shall be restored to Israel.*

The kingdom is to be restored to Israel after the Second Coming, not before. Israel is now in process of gathering into the stakes of Zion. These stakes are cities of holiness, as it were, to which the outcasts of that once-favored people may now flee to escape the abomination of desolation that awaits a wicked world. In this way, a people is being prepared for the day of glory and triumph that lies ahead. But the great day of gathering, the gathering into both a political and an ecclesiastical kingdom, is reserved for the Millennium.

Our ancient apostolic colleagues asked the same Master whom we serve, just before his ascension into heaven, "Lord, wilt thou at this time restore again the kingdom to Israel?" They already had the keys of the kingdom; theirs was the power and privilege to preside over the church and kingdom of God on earth, and they had received the divine commission to carry the gospel of salvation to every nation and kindred and tongue and people. But they had not been commissioned to set up again the ancient kingdom of Israel. How, then, could the prophecies of all the prophets of Israel be fulfilled? When would the promised day come, the day in which Israel would rule over the Gentiles and have the worldwide dominion of which the prophets foretold?

Jesus replied: "It is not for you to know the times or the seasons, which the Father hath put in his own power." (Acts 1:6-7.) The setting up of the promised kingdom was Millennial, not meridian. They were counseled, rather, to do the work assigned them and to leave the great work of establishing the kingdom of Israel to those who would be called in the latter days. This is the Millennial kingdom over which the Second David will reign; it is the one whose political capital shall be in Missouri and whose ecclesiastical capital will be in Old Jerusalem.

3. *The Ten Tribes shall return.*

In the coming Millennial day, Israel—which, since the death of Solomon, had been divided into two divisive, warring, rebellious kingdoms: the Kingdom of Israel, with its Ten Tribes, and the Kingdom of Judah, with the residue; two kingdoms long since destroyed and taken captive, with their municipals scattered in all the earth—Israel shall again become one nation, upon the mountains of Israel, in the Palestinian home of their fathers. Ephraim and Manasseh, with occasional scattered remnants of other tribes, are now gathering into stakes of Zion as rapidly as these are established in all nations. After the Lord returns, a highway shall be cast up—Isaiah calls it the way of holiness where none of the unclean can pass, meaning that it is the strait and narrow path leading to eternal life—and upon this highway the Ten Tribes shall return. They shall once again believe the gospel and receive the blessings of baptism, even as these were theirs in the day when the Risen Lord ministered among them. These blessings and the blessings of the temple will be administered to them by the hands of Ephraim. And then, at the appointed time and at the direction of the President of the Church, who holds the keys of the gathering of Israel and the leading of the Ten Tribes from the land of the north, at least representative and appointed portions of the Kingdom of Israel shall go from the lands north of Palestine, back to their ancient inheritance, to the very soil promised Abraham, Isaac, and Jacob as an everlasting inheritance.

4. *The Son of David reigneth.*

Prophecies by the hundreds—there is scarcely anything about which the ancient prophets were more prolific—tell of the personal reign of the Lord on the earth in the last days. As the Son of David, he shall have dominion over all Israel forever. As the King of the whole earth, he shall make a full end of all nations, and they, combining under one head, shall become the kingdom of our God and of his Christ, and he shall reign forever and ever. There will be no law but his law when he comes, and he shall restore his judges and rulers as at the first.

5. *Mortal man after the Second Coming.*

Life during the Millennium—how wondrous and great, how marvelous it will be when contrasted with that benighted state of affairs that now is! As the coming day of life and righteousness dawns, our present day of death and wickedness shall cease. All of the proud and they who do wickedly; all who are carnal, sensual, and devilish; all who are evil and corrupt; all who live after the manner of the world—all these shall be burned at His coming. Every corruptible thing—man and beast, fowl and fish—shall be consumed. Death as we know it shall cease; life as we know it shall change. Man shall live to be a hundred years old, when he will be changed from Millennial mortality to eternal immortality. Procreation will continue among mortals and all forms of life, and children will grow up without sin unto salvation. The comparatively few who survive the Millennial fires will multiply without measure, and it is not unreasonable to suppose that more people will live on earth during the Millennium than in all prior ages combined many times over. It will be a day of peace and plenty and pure worship, and the Lord alone shall be exalted.

6. *Millennial worship.*

How and in what manner will men worship their God during the Millennium? In answer, we can only call attention to the pure and perfect worship ordained to be in that blessed age. We cannot find language—nor does such exist—that will define and describe the spiritual feelings or make known the holy peace that will then fill the hearts of worshipping saints. This we know: the Millennium is designed to save souls; Satan will be bound, and sin as we know it will cease; all false religions and every rite and practice that is not of God will go the way of all the earth; and true worship, untainted, unalloyed, unabridged, will fill the hearts of all men. The gospel in its fulness and perfection will fill every heart; all people will be baptized; all shall glory in the gift of the Holy Ghost; all men will hold the priesthood and magnify their callings; and there will be no marriage but eternal marriage. It will be a day of personal revelation, a day when the knowledge of God will cover the earth as the waters cover the sea, a day when no man need say to his neighbor, "Know the Lord," for all shall know him from the greatest to the least. In that day the blessings of the Second Comforter will be poured out upon the saints, and every man will be his own king and his own priest, and the will of God shall be done on earth as it is in heaven. What more need we say?

CHAPTER 65

The Paradisiacal Earth

The Day of Burning

"We believe . . . that the earth will be renewed and receive its paradisiacal glory." (Article of Faith 10.) This is a basic and fundamental doctrine of the gospel; it is one of the first principles of revealed religion. True, it is outside the realm of our experience; nothing of this sort has happened from the time when life was first planted on this planet to the present moment. But for that matter, the three greatest verities of the whole gospel system—the temporal creation, the fall of man, and the atonement of the Lord Jesus Christ—are also outside the realm of any experience of mortal men. Nevertheless, these verities are realities; they did occur; and so also, at its appointed time, will this fallen earth rise again and receive that paradisiacal glory which once was found upon its face.

Unless we, as the saints of the Most High, understand the doctrine of the renewal of the earth, we cannot envision the true nature of the temporal creation, nor of the fall that grew out of it, nor of the atonement that came to ransom us from the effects of the fall. Without a knowledge of the transfigured earth that is to be, we are denied the hope of Millennial glory for us or our seed, and we so narrow our gospel perspective that the Lord cannot be pleased with our ignorance of his laws and purposes. As to this day of burning and renewal, ushered in as it will be by the Second Coming of the Son of Man, let us note the following:

1. *He comes—in flaming fire.*

Echoing the sentiments of David, Isaiah, Micah, Nahum, Habakkuk, Malachi, and almost all of the prophets who prophesied of the Second Coming, Paul recorded these heaven-sent words: "The Lord Jesus shall be revealed from heaven with his mighty angels, in flaming fire taking vengeance on them that know not God, and that obey not the gospel of our Lord Jesus Christ." (2 Thessalonians 1:7-8.) Fire, flaming fire, literal fire, fire that burns trees, melts ore, and consumes corruption—such shall accompany the Lord Jesus and cover the earth when he returns in all the glory of his Father's kingdom.

2. *He comes—and the elements melt.*

Not only will the Lord come in flaming fire, but that fire will produce fervent, glowing, intense heat, heat that has not been known in the entire history of the earth, heat that will cause the very elements to melt, the mountains to flow down at his presence, and the very earth itself, as now constituted, to dissolve. Nowhere is this better expounded than by Peter. "The day of the Lord will come as a thief in the night," he says, "in the which the heavens shall pass away with a great noise, and the elements shall melt with fervent heat, the earth also and the works that are therein shall be burned up." In this dread day when "the heavens being on fire shall be dissolved, and the elements shall melt with fervent heat," there will come into being "new heavens and a new earth, wherein dwelleth righteousness." (2 Peter 3:10-13.)

3. *He comes—to cleanse his vineyard.*

What of men in the coming day of burning? How can they survive the flaming fire and fervent heat? What of life in all its forms when fire from the Lord melts the mountains and causes the oceans of water to boil? In the coming day when the vineyard of the Lord is burned, some few will abide the day, but the masses of men will be destroyed. Only those who are quickened, as were Shadrach, Meshach, and Abednego in the furnace of Nebuchadnezzar, shall be able to abide the day of burning. In that day, as Isaiah says, the flame from the Holy One shall "burn and devour his thorns and his briers in one day." Then shall it "consume the glory of his forest, and of his fruitful field, both soul and body. . . . And the rest of the trees of his forest shall be few, that a child may write them." (Isaiah 10:17-19.) And also: "The inhabitants of the earth are burned, and few men left." (Isaiah 24:6.) And in our day the Lord has said: "Every corruptible thing, both of man, or of the beasts of the field, or of the fowls of the heavens, or of the fish of the sea, that dwells on all the face of the earth, shall be consumed;

and also that of element shall melt with fervent heat; and all things shall become new, that my knowledge and glory may dwell upon all the earth." (D&C 101:24-25.)

4. *He comes—for it is the end of the world.*

When the Lord comes, it will be the end of the world, the end of an age that has lasted for six thousand years, the end of the carnal and corrupt way of life that has prevailed among the generality of mankind since the fall. The world is the evil, sensual, devilish way of life that prevails among ungodly men. It includes those who lie and steal and cheat; who take advantage of their neighbor for a word; who set their hearts on money and power and worldly applause; who are lewd, lascivious, and immoral; who rob and plunder and murder; who are adulterers, homosexuals, and pornographically oriented; who are vulgar and whose minds dwell on unclean and indecent things. And the end of the world is their destruction, the destruction of the wicked. Our old world of wickedness shall soon die, and a new heaven and a new earth, whereon righteousness dwells, shall be born. An age shall end, a new era begin. A worldly way of life shall cease and a righteous way of living take its place. In our present probationary estate we are in the world, but we should not be of the world. If we overcome the world and walk thereby in paths of righteousness, we shall abide the day of His coming and be numbered among those who inherit Millennial glory.

5. *"Who may abide the day of his coming?"*

This question, posed by Malachi and others of the ancient prophets, is intended to bring the reality of the Second Coming close to home. "Who shall stand when he appeareth? for he is like a refiner's fire." (Malachi 3:2.) The prophetic answer, given in varying settings and differing language, always attests to the same eternal verity: the righteous shall abide the day, the wicked shall be consumed. When "the day cometh, that shall burn as an oven," then "all the proud, yea, and all that do wickedly, shall be stubble: and the day that cometh shall burn them up." (Malachi 4:1.) But the righteous, the God-fearing, the meek—indeed, as we shall see, all those who are living at least a terrestrial law—these are the ones who shall continue to live on the new earth and breathe the air of the new heavens. They will include faithful members of The Church of Jesus Christ of Latter-day Saints and other upright and decent people who, following the light of Christ, have managed to rise above the world and walk in paths of decency and uprightness. These latter, without much question, will soon join the Church and become inheritors of all the blessings of Israel.

6. *The day of separation.*

In this present evil and dark day, iniquity abounds. Never since the day of Noah, when the Lord destroyed all save eight souls, has there been so great wickedness among men. There are now social enclaves of homosexuals, sodomists, adulterers, murderers, Gadianton robbers, as it were, and those of every like evil ilk. Interspersed among the masses of devilish people are a few who love the Lord and let their light shine in the dark dens of sin. Our society is polarized. Though saints and sinners intermingle, they are poles apart in belief and conduct. The saints stand by themselves at one pole; evil forces without number assemble at the other pole; and in between are some who know not which way to go, and for whose souls the Lord and Lucifer are at war. Even in the Church, the tares and wheat together grow.

All of this is preparing for the day when the wicked shall be cut off from among the people; when the tares, bound in bundles, shall be burned; when two shall be grinding at the mill and one shall be taken and the other left; when there shall be "an entire separation of the righteous and the wicked." (D&C 63:54.)

The New Heaven and New Earth

Man—marvelous, marvelous man—is the center of all our interests and concerns. Man is the offspring of God; he it is that was created in the image of his Maker; he is the one for whom the whole plan of salvation was established. Man may become as his Maker, attain exaltation, inherit eternal life, and be a god in his own right. It is man for whom the earth and all forms of life were created; all else, this earth and every form of life on the face thereof, is to serve man, the crowning creature of God's creating.

What interest have we, then, in the earth and life on its face? Simply this: If man is to understand himself and the processes by which he is saved, he must know his relationship to Deity, to the earth, and to other forms of life. He must understand the overall purposes of the Great Creator and know why the earth and all life came into being as they first were, as they now are, and as they yet shall be. He must know how to use created things to work out his salvation. Hence the revealed word relative to an Edenic earth, a fallen earth, a renewed earth, and finally a celestial earth.

This earth, as with man and all forms of life, was first created spiritually. Thereafter came the temporal creation—the paradisiacal or Edenic creation, the creation of the earth and man and all forms of life as they were before the fall. In that day there was no death, not for man nor for any form of life. In that day there was no mortality and no procreation, not for man nor for any form of life. All things were created in a state of paradisiacal immortality. Adam and Eve were on earth in bodies of flesh and bones; their spirits had entered the tabernacles of clay created for them from the dust of the earth; they were living souls. But without the fall, "they would have remained in a state of innocence, having no joy, for they knew no misery; doing no good, for they knew no sin." And without the fall, "all things which were created must have remained in the same state in which they were after they were created; and they must have remained forever, and had no end." (2 Nephi 2:22-23.)

In that Edenic day, the earth and all life were pronounced very good by the Creator. There was no disease or evil or death. Life was destined to go on forever. The lion ate straw like the ox, and the wolf and the lamb were friends. Light and life and peace and immortality reigned in every department of creation. Such was life on the Edenic earth, on the temporal earth that had been created in a paradisiacal state. The earth was in a terrestrial state; it was temporal and earthy, and neither spiritual nor celestial.

Then came the fall. Mortality was born; procreation began; disease and death and sorrow covered the earth. The probationary estate had its beginning. Having sinned, man was no longer innocent; he could now feel joy, for he knew misery, and he could do good, for he knew sin. The earth and man and all forms of life fell to a telestial state—the state that now is; the state in which there are high mountains and pleasant valleys; in which there are arid deserts and salty wastelands; in which there are thorns and thistles and briars and noxious weeds to overrun the crops of the earth.

If man is to be saved, he must be reclaimed from his lost and fallen state. He must gain full immortality and, by obedience, obtain eternal life. And so with the earth and all forms of life; they too must become immortal, if they are to endure forever. Thus there is a plan of salvation that involves the earth and all life. The earth's final destiny is one of celestial glory. As it is written: "The earth abideth the law of a celestial kingdom, for it filleth the measure of its creation, and transgresseth not the law—wherefore, it shall be sanctified; yea, notwithstanding it shall die, it shall be quickened again, and shall abide the power by which it is quickened, and the righteous shall inherit it." (D&C 88:25-26.)

In the course of abiding the law given of God to govern it, the earth is to be renewed and receive again its paradisiacal glory. It is to rise from its fallen telestial state to the terrestrial state it once enjoyed. It cannot be renewed—becoming again paradisiacal and terrestrial—unless it once possessed those very states. When the change comes, it will be so dramatic and the earth will be altered in so many respects that it will have a new aerial heaven and become, in fact, a new earth. In that day, the former things will not be remembered nor come to mind, and men will rejoice in the Lord and glory in the good things that are theirs.

We have already spoken of the day of burning in which the very rocks and soil will be dissolved, in which the elements melt with fervent heat, and the mountains, as wax, flow down at the presence of the Lord. The prophetic word also speaks of every valley being exalted, of the mountains being made low, and the rough places smoothed as a plain. It tells of an earthquake beyond anything the earth has ever known; of the earth reeling to and fro as a drunken man; of the mighty deep returning to the land of the north where it once was; of the continents becoming one land as they were in the day before they were divided; of the ice flowing down from the polar regions; of the burning deserts blossoming as the rose; of springs of water springing up in the arid wastelands; of the whole earth becoming as the Garden of Eden. Who knows but what the very axis of the earth will shift so that the seasons cease and the whole earth enjoys both seedtime and harvest at all times.

It is also written that the wolf shall dwell with the lamb and the leopard shall lie down with the kid. The enmity of men and beasts and all flesh shall cease. The cow and the bear shall feed together, and the lion shall eat straw like the ox. How could it be otherwise when there is no death, and when at the appointed time life is blessed with everlasting immortality?

Above all else there will be perfect peace and heaven-guided worship. Children will grow up without sin unto salvation. Wars will cease. Disease will no longer afflict man, and there will be no graves. Neither will there be any sorrow, for there will be no death. The earth will bring forth abundantly, and every man will sit under his own vine and his own tree enjoying the fruits of his garden.

During the Millennium there will be both mortal and immortal people on earth. Those who are receiving their temporal bodies for the first time, and who are marrying and begetting children, will be living lives comparable to ours, except they will not be subject to disease and death. Our Lord, who shall reign as King and Lord, is immortal, as also are all who have been redeemed "out of every kindred, and tongue, and people, and nation," and of whom it is written: "Thou [the Lamb, who] wast slain . . . hast made us unto our God kings and priests: and we shall reign on the earth." (Revelation 5:9-10.) Thus, they, under Christ, each man in his own place and sphere, will also reign on earth. Those who are mortals—who have the paradisiacal type of mortality that will then exist—shall be changed to immortality in the twinkling of an eye when they become a hundred years old.

The Post-Millennial Earth

After the Millennium, what? Can there be any social order greater than the one over which the Son of God himself, aided by the righteous from all ages, shall rule and reign? What more could man desire than to associate with the Lord Jesus and serve under his just and loving guidance for a thousand years? And yet in the providences of Almighty God, of that Elohim who made men that they might become as he is, there is more.

Man may gain his own kingdom, serve as his own king and ruler, and have everlasting dominion—always under the Father!—over his own spirit children forever. Such shall be the reward of those who gain celestial exaltation.

In Eden's Garden—call it a primeval paradise, if you will—man dwelt in paradisiacal glory. The temporal creation of all things was terrestrial in nature. Then came the fall, a fall from a terrestrial to a telestial state. Men became carnal, sensual, and devilish by nature; the earth became the kind of orb on which lewd, lascivious, and wicked persons can live. Anyone who lives a telestial law—the law of worldliness—can live on an earth that is in a telestial state. Soon the new earth, an earth of Millennial mien, will come into being. Renewed and changed, it will return to its paradisiacal or terrestrial state. Then none can abide on its face save those who live at least a terrestrial law. Such is the law of uprightness and decency found among those who have avoided the depravity and degeneracy of the world. Indeed, the dawning of this new day is the end of the world that now is, the end of that evil and carnality and wickedness which prevails among the masses of men; and it will be brought to pass by the destruction of the wicked.

After the thousand years of peace, wickedness will again be found on earth. We suppose it will come in gradually, by degrees, as it did among the Nephites after their Golden Era. And as the Nephites turned totally to sin until, ripened in iniquity, they were destroyed, so shall it be with the post-Millennial inhabitants of the earth. The earth will be spared for a little season, perhaps a thousand years, and then cometh the end. The battle of Gog and Magog, another Armageddon, as it were, will be fought again. And then, following the triumph of Michael, who also led the armies of the Lord in the war in heaven, Lucifer will again be cast out and the vineyard will again be burned. Again there will be a new heaven and a new earth, but this time it will be a celestial rather than a terrestrial sphere, and when it becomes a celestial sphere, no one can live on it who does not conform to a celestial law. Hence, in that day it will be reserved for those who are saved and exalted.

When the Lord comes, those who died in him and who were true and faithful in the gospel cause, who took the Holy Spirit for their guide, and who were sanctified by obedience to celestial law—all these shall rise from the grave with celestial bodies. These bodies qualify for celestial glory found only in a celestial kingdom. They are Christ's, the firstfruits. Theirs is an inheritance of glory everlasting. After the Second Coming, those who lived a terrestrial law shall be called forth; their glory and kingdom shall be terrestrial. Then after the Millennium the residue of men, including those who lived a telestial law, will come forth. Those who have lived a telestial law shall gain telestial bodies and shall merit and gain a telestial glory found in a telestial kingdom. The sons of perdition, after their resurrection, will be cast out eternally with the devil and his angels.

As to those who are born after the Millennium and who turn to unrighteousness, their state will be awful. We suppose they will continue to live on an earth where there is no death and that they will be numbered among those of whom Isaiah said: "The child shall die an hundred years old; but the sinner being an hundred years old shall be accursed." (Isaiah 65:20.) Surely there shall be many sons of perdition in that day, for many shall come out in open rebellion against God, knowing perfectly that he is supreme and that they are fighting him and his plan of salvation.

How glorious it is to have the truth and to know the truth and to live the truth. How awful it is to fight against God and go down to perdition.

ARTICLE 11

We claim
the privilege of worshiping
Almighty God
according to the dictates of our own conscience,
and allow all men
the same privilege,
let them worship how, where, or what they may.

CHAPTER 66

Freedom of Worship

The Doctrine of Freedom of Worship

Freedom of worship is one of the basic doctrines of the gospel. Indeed, in one manner of speaking it is the most basic of all doctrines, even taking precedence over the nature and kind of being that God is, or the atoning sacrifice of the Son of God, or the vesting of priesthood and keys and saving power in the one true church. By this we mean that if there were no freedom of worship, there would be no God, no redemption, and no salvation in the kingdom of God. Let us now reason, as the prophets have done, on this matter.

In chapter 11, "The Agency of Man," we discussed the philosophy of agency, showing that it is an eternal principle, that there can be no salvation without agency, and that both rewards and punishments depend on its free exercise. Let us now apply these principles to the doctrine of freedom of worship. Agency is the law of opposites. "It must needs be, that there is an opposition in all things," the scripture saith. Without opposites, without opposition, "all things must needs be a compound in one," having no independent existence of their own. Without darkness, there can be no light; without cold, nothing could be hot; without a down, there could be no up. And without damnation, there could be no salvation. Lehi carries this reasoning to the point of proving that without opposites, there "is no God. And if there is no God we are not, neither the earth; for there could have been no creation of things, neither to act nor to be acted upon; wherefore, all things must have vanished away." (2 Nephi 2:11-13.)

Lucifer, in the Grand Council when the Great God presented the plan of agency and salvation, proposed instead to save all men. "I will redeem all mankind, that one soul shall not be lost, and surely I will do it," he said. (Moses 4:1.) That is, none would be damned; damnation would not be a viable alternative to salvation; there would be no agency—no freedom of choice, no election to serve God or to flee from evil and turn to righteousness. But if there is no freedom of choice between damnation and salvation, how can either exist? They are opposites; without one you cannot have the other. Lucifer's proposal to amend the Father's plan could not be; it was philosophically impossible to accomplish. He could not save all mankind, because unless some were damned, there would be no salvation, for nothing can so much as exist unless it has an opposite. Agency and freedom of worship are just that basic and important in the eternal plan of salvation.

Similarly, in chapter 41, "The Divine Gift of Prayer," we set forth how and in what manner man must worship the Lord so as to gain salvation in his eternal kingdom. Perfect worship is emulation; there is no better way to worship God than to so live as to become like him. To be like him is to gain eternal life. To gain this greatest of all rewards, the seeker of salvation must be free to choose between the Lord and Lucifer, for without the damnation of the devil, there can be no salvation with the Savior.

Freedom of worship is thus one of the chief identifying characteristics of the true church. Religious freedom is of God; compulsion in religion is of the devil. It was so in pre-existence; it is so now; and it will be so everlastingly. And so, in expounding upon the eleventh Article of Faith, we assert with unshakable surety our belief in and allegiance to the doctrine of freedom of worship. We claim it for ourselves; we allow it to others; nay, more, we encourage others to worship as they choose and pledge ourselves to defend them in so doing.

We have staggered under the iron fist of persecution during our whole latter-day history, and we know that hatred and ill will and death will continue to be spewed out upon us until the coming end of the world. We have been driven and scourged and slain; the blood of our prophets stains Illinois; at Haun's Mill the innocent blood of the martyrs for truth cries unto the Lord of Hosts; and on frozen and desolate hills, across half a continent, lie the lonely graves of suffering saints who chose death in preference to the creeds of compulsion of a decadent Christendom. Our allegiance to freedom of worship has been tested in the refiner's fire, and we know that persecution against any sect or cult today may be turned upon us or any other group tomorrow.

We believe in, sustain, uphold, support, and advocate freedom of worship for all men. And we are bold to declare that any government, political system, church, sect, cult, or group of worshippers that either denies men the freedom to worship as they choose or imposes on them a system or way of worship by force is not of God.

The History of Freedom of Worship

Lucifer utterly failed in the preexistence to destroy agency and force salvation upon all men. Had he succeeded, the salvation he sponsored would in reality have been damnation, for it would not have raised men to the high status enjoyed by the Eternal Father. But with satanic zeal he carries on the same war here on earth. Compulsion, as a way of worship, was proposed, rejected, and died in the premortal life. To envision how religious compulsion and religious persecution have operated and do now operate, let us simply allude to and make a brief recitation of a few of the known and universally recognized facts of history.

1. *The Adamic theocracy.*

When the Lord placed Adam, the first man of all men, and Eve, the mother of all living, upon the earth, he gave them dominion over all things, including their seed after them. He vested in them what we call civil power, by which they governed themselves and their children; and he revealed unto them his own pure religion, through which they could worship their Creator and, if faithful, become like him and gain the type of life he lives, which is eternal life.

There was no separation of church and state; all governmental powers, whether civil or religious, centered in one Supreme Head. They came from God and were administered among men by his legal administrators who were sent and duly commissioned by him. This type of government is a theocracy; it is the government of God. Under it, there is no need for a civil power on the one hand and a religious arm on the other. All the affairs of government are intertwined into one with direction coming from God himself, by revelation, to those whom he commissions to represent him on earth.

A theocracy cannot operate except among righteous people who voluntarily submit to its authority. Under this system of government, which is the Lord's way of ruling on earth, there is and must be absolute freedom of worship. It is, in effect, a system of government in which the Church, which is the kingdom of God on earth, rules over the Lord's people. The Church, being true and being the Lord's, of necessity administers the gospel. The gospel is the plan of salvation presented by the Father in the Grand Council, the chief characteristic of which is agency. Thus, in a theocracy, "men are free according to the flesh; and all things are given them which are expedient unto man. And they are free to choose liberty and eternal life, through the Mediator of all men, or to choose captivity and death, according to the captivity and power of the devil." (2 Nephi 2:27.)

The theocracy of the Adamic age was patriarchal, and from Adam to Noah all the legitimate powers of government, both civil and religious, descended from father to son. That is to say, government in all its forms and with all its powers was centered in the family.

2. *Cain institutes an imitation theocracy.*

As Adam represented the Lord on earth, so Cain acted for and on behalf of Lucifer. Indeed, this first murderer of all murderers is himself Perdition—he was so designated in pre-existence—and he will rule over Satan himself when the devil and his angels are cast out everlastingly. Cain apostatized, left the church, and, as Abel's blood cried out against him, fled from the presence of Adam and the faithful saints. He thereupon set up his own government, both civil and religious, patterned after the Adamic theocracy, except that Cain received no revelation and the Lord gave him no direction. Hence, his government was illegitimate; it imitated the true order but was man-made and Satan-inspired.

From the slivers of information we have, it is apparent that Cain imposed his way of worship upon his seed and that they no longer had the true gospel, the true church, and the true plan of salvation. But, be it noted, their way of worship was mandated by their rulers; they were taught and commanded what to believe. As to the true gospel, "Satan came among them, saying: . . . Believe it not; and they believed it not, and they loved Satan more than God. And men began from that time forth to be carnal, sensual, and devilish." (Moses 5:13.) And thus the pattern was set. Ever thereafter, when evil and carnal men set up governments of compulsion, governments in which the secular arm imposed a way of worship upon men, such governments were not of God and such ways of worship had no divine approval.

3. *Government in Enoch's day.*

By the time of Enoch, the seventh generation from Adam, the population of the earth was great and the governments among men diverse. Adam and his faithful seed gloried in their divine system of government; Cain and his seed, and all who had fallen away, had nations and governments and religions—imposed religions—of their own. Up to this point in time, a separation of church and state had never entered the minds of men. All anyone knew about was a government that controlled both civically and religiously. When Enoch preached among the wicked, made converts, and built his City of Holiness, that original Zion operated so perfectly upon theocratic principles that the Lord of heaven himself came and dwelt with his people. So perfect was the system and so righteous were the people that they received instruction from the Lord in person as well as from his duly constituted servants on earth. What better system of government could there be? Providentially it is one that will differ only in size and complexity from the government that shall prevail over all the earth when the Lord reigns during the Millennial era.

4. *Government after the flood.*

In Enoch's day, all the faithful saints were translated and taken up into heaven. From the taking up of Zion to the coming of the flood, all of the worthy converts were also caught up by the powers of heaven to receive an inheritance in that Zion which had fled from the earth. This left only Noah and his family to build the ark. The masses of men in that day loved Satan more than God and imposed Lucifer's carnal and evil ways of worship upon the hosts of the earth.

After the immersion of the earth in the waters of Noah came a day of new beginning. As in Adam's day, the faithful lived under a theocratic system, and as in the days before the flood, those who chose to live after the manner of the world set up their own governments and their own ways of worship. The seed of Shem, Ham, and Japheth began to populate the earth, and it so continued for more than four hundred years, when Abraham, who received theocratic power from Melchizedek, went down into Egypt. There he found a descendant of Ham, reigning as Pharaoh, whose government was patterned after the patriarchal governments of old, but which was devoid of priesthood and revelation, and hence, as far as worship is concerned—a worship prescribed, mandated, and commanded by Pharaoh—had turned to "idolatry." (Abraham 1:20-27.)

That which prevailed in Egypt was symbolical of false worship among all peoples and races of the day. No one was free to worship as he chose; all people in all nations worshipped as their governments prescribed, and the head of their government was ordinarily the head of their religious system. This is a concept we must understand if we are to put the worship of all people in all ages in its proper perspective. The worship of the world was decreed and required by Satan, who proposed in preexistence to deny men their agency and save all mankind by forcing them to worship as he decreed.

5. *Government among the Jaredites.*

Incident to the confusing of the tongues at the tower of Babel, the Jaredite people were led to America—by theocratic power. State and church were one. As in the days of Adam and Enoch, the Lord governed all things both civic and religious through the heads of his earthly kingdom. Apostate groups that dissented during the long Jaredite history patterned their system after the only way of government known to them, and it included imposing worldly religions upon their citizens.

6. *Government in ancient Israel.*

Israel inherited the patriarchal system from Abraham, Isaac, and Jacob, and, with the exodus from Egypt, it was renewed by revelation given to Moses. Ancient Israel was a theocracy. God governed. He revealed his religion; he called his prophets; he designated the Levites as his priests; he appointed judges and kings; and he defined their foreign policy and directed when they should go to war. Pursuant to his command, they built a temple in Jerusalem, and the king, who was his servant, offered sacrifices therein. Because there was no law but the Lord's law, certain things more closely connected with religious than civil government were enforced by the sword. The penalty for blasphemy and sabbath desecration, for instance, was death.

What happened in the days of wicked and rebellious kings? They simply instituted their own ways of worship, appointed their own priests, and, when it pleased them so to do, commanded the worship of Baal, or Ashtoreth, or Molech, or whatever deity pleased their fancy. The religions of the Canaanites, Hittites, Amorites, Perizzites, Hivites, and Jebusites, and all the nations that inhabited the land before Israel, were state religions. The worship in Assyria, Babylonia, Egypt, and all the nations of the Gentiles was by government edict. People were not free to choose their own gods and to worship according to the dictates of their own conscience. In the minds of the credulous and superstitious Gentiles, the issues of war and peace, life and death, national survival or defeat were all tied in to the proposition of whose god was the greatest—Baal or Jehovah; the god of the Assyrians or the God of Jacob; the gods of the Canaanites or the Lord of Hosts who camped with Joshua; the god of whatever nation or the God of Israel.

7. *Government among the Nephites.*

The Nephite government was a theocracy. It was no different for these descendants of Israel than for the parents from whom they sprang. Worship and civil power came under one head. And when the Lamanites dissented, they exercised their own governmental power and imposed their own false religion upon their seed.

8. *The Jews and their worship.*

Theocracy as a way of government and worship began to fail with the Babylonian captivity. Although there were brief moments of blazing glory when the Jews returned to Palestine to rebuild the temple and serve Jehovah in Jerusalem, the day of direct heavenly rule was soon past. When our Lord made flesh his tabernacle, the Jews in Palestine served Rome and those dispersed in the nations were subject to Egyptian or Grecian or other rulers. Nevertheless, they remained a distinct and a peculiar people even after they were scattered in all nations following the destruction of Jerusalem by Titus in A.D. 70.

At no time since the beginning of the Christian era have they been able to impose their religious system upon nations or peoples as their forebears did. Indeed, considering the persecutions and drivings and mass executions that have followed them in many nations—especially Spain in the days of the Spanish Inquisition, Russia under the tsars, and Germany under Hitler's heel—it is a miracle they have so much as survived as a people. But it is just as well that they have not been a theocracy during these past two thousand years, for they have not accepted Christ and his gospel, which gospel must prevail whenever a divine theocracy operates. If they were a theocracy today—and they do legislate worship to a degree in the modern nation of Israel—it would be as when Jeroboam made Israel sin by mandating the worship of Baal.

9. *The Gentile nations and their worship.*

With the advent of Greece and Rome as world powers, the control of religious thought began to wane in the Western world. It still continued as a national way of life in Asia and among the Islamic peoples. To this day, the law in some nations enforces the death penalty upon Mohammedans who become Christians. But Greek philosophers and Roman political necessities began to turn the tide against forced worship. The Greek thinkers began to unshackle the minds of men. Rome, unable to impose a sole religion upon the diverse nations under her iron hand, adopted a policy of accepting and worshipping all the gods of all the nations of her empire—with one exception. The God of the Christians was excluded. All gods were acceptable except God the Lord. This included even the deifying and worship of the emperor.

As to the so-called barbaric and uncivilized tribes of Britain, Scandinavia, Germany, and Western Europe, all these had their own national religions, which included many good ethical principles and also an outpouring of sacrifice and slaughter that was hellish in design and origin. All of this was government dictated.

10. *Christianity—free or enforced?*

From a few hated and despised souls in the "sect of the Nazarenes" (Acts 24:5), the true believers in Christ became numerous and influential during the first century. Their kingdom was not of this world, and their warfare was with the spiritual forces of evil. Freedom of worship was one of the great cornerstones on which they built their house of faith. Emblazoned on the banners of their souls were the immortal words of their Founder: "Ye shall know the truth, and the truth shall make you free." (John 8:32.) They stood fast "in the liberty wherewith Christ" had made them free. (Galatians 5:1.)

But scarcely more than a hundred years after the King of Freedom proclaimed liberty to the captives and the opening of the prison doors of the mind to sin-enslaved souls, the liberty that was in Christ died an agonizing death. The world won a temporary victory in the war we wage against evil. Apostasy became universal; darkness covered the earth, and gross darkness the minds of the people. Men lost the knowledge of God and his saving laws and created a new and fallen religion that still bore the name of the ancient faith.

By the time of the emperor Constantine, who reigned from A.D. 306 to 337, this fallen faith without saving power had sufficient numerical strength and political power to give it a preeminence over the even more perverse pagan ways of a spiritually decadent empire. In that day, as a historian of world renown has written, we see "its relation to the temporal power, and its social and political position and import, undergo an entire and permanent change." Indeed, "the reign of Constantine the Great marks the transition of the Christian religion from under persecution by the secular government to union with the same; the beginning of the state-church system. The Graeco-Roman heathenism, the most cultivated and powerful form of idolatry, which history knows, surrenders, after three hundred years' struggle, to Christianity [an apostate Christianity, be it remembered], and dies of incurable consumption, with the confession: Galilean, thou hast conquered! The ruler of the civilized world lays his crown at the feet of the crucified Jesus of Nazareth. The successor of Nero, Domitian, and Diocletian [who persecuted the

Christians] appears in the imperial purple at the council of Nice as protector of the church, and takes his golden throne at the nod of bishops, who still bear the scars of persecution. The despised sect, which, like its Founder in the days of His humiliation, had not where to lay its head, is raised to sovereign authority in the state, enters into the prerogatives of the pagan priesthood, grows rich and powerful, builds countless churches out of the stones of idol temples to the honor of Christ and his martyrs, employs the wisdom of Greece and Rome to vindicate the foolishness of the cross, exerts a molding power upon civil legislation, rules the national life, and leads off the history of the world. But at the same time the church, embracing the mass of the population of the empire, from the Caesar to the meanest slave, and living amidst all its institutions, received into her bosom vast deposits of foreign material from the world and from heathenism, exposing herself to new dangers and imposing upon herself new and heavy labors."

As this union of church and state extended its influence, "the lines of orthodoxy were more and more strictly drawn; freedom of inquiry was restricted; and all departure from the state-church system was met not only, as formerly, with spiritual weapons, but also with civil punishments. So early as the fourth century the dominant party, the orthodox as well as the heterodox, with help of the imperial authority practised deposition, confiscation, and banishment upon its opponents. It was but one step thence to the penalties of torture and death, which were ordained in the middle age, and even so lately as the middle of the seventeenth century, by state-church authority, both Protestant and Roman Catholic, and continue in many countries to this day, against religious dissenters of every kind as enemies to the prevailing order of things. Absolute freedom of religion and of worship is in fact logically impossible in the state-church system. It requires the separation of the spiritual and temporal powers."

In this connection, let us say that unless there is absolute freedom of religion and of worship, there is no salvation. Unless men have their agency—given of God in preexistence, given anew in the garden of Eden, and given again after the fall—unless men are free to choose, they cannot gain liberty and eternal life through the great Mediator of all men.

In setting forth the history of freedom of worship, we may well contrast the Lord's theocracy with the imitations and substitutes that have prevailed in all parts of the earth. And it is in this connection that our historian says: "Constantine, the first Christian Caesar, the founder of Constantinople and the Byzantine empire, and one of the most gifted, energetic, and successful of the Roman emperors, was the first representative of the imposing idea of a Christian theocracy, or of that system of policy which assumes all subjects to be Christians, connects civil and religious rights, and regards church and state as the two arms of one and the same divine government on earth. This idea was more fully developed by his successors, it animated the whole middle age, and is yet working under various forms in these latest times; though it has never been fully realized, whether in the Byzantine, the German, or the Russian empire, the Roman church-state, the Calvinistic republic of Geneva, or the early Puritanic colonies of New England. At the same time, however, Constantine stands also as the type of an undiscriminating and harmful conjunction of Christianity with politics, of the holy symbol of peace with the horrors of war, of the spiritual interests of the kingdom of heaven with the earthly interests of the state. . . . As his predecessors were supreme pontiffs of the heathen religion of the empire, so he desired to be looked upon as a sort of bishop, as universal bishop of the external affairs of the church."

That Constantine did not confine his influence to the external affairs of the church is pointed up in this historical summary: "In the year 325, as the patron of the church, he summoned the council of Nice, and himself attended it; banished the Arians, though he afterwards recalled them; and, in his monarchical spirit of uniformity, showed great zeal for the settlement of all theological disputes, while he was blind to their deep significance. He first introduced the practise of subscription to the articles of a written creed and of the infliction of civil punishments for non-conformity." (Philip Schaff, *History of the Christian Church*, Grand Rapids, Mich.: William B. Eerdmans Publishing Company, 1957, 3:4-5, 7, 12-13, 32.)

Such was and is the sad and sorry state of that Christianity which grew out of primitive Christianity, out of the pure and perfect religious liberty of Jesus and the apostles. Knowing what Satan sought to do in preexistence, and knowing that freedom of choice and worship is essential to salvation, shall we not affirm that the union of church and state, the use of force in maintaining a self-chosen orthodoxy, and the civil punishment of supposed heresy are not of God, and that they are the proof positive of the universal apostasy promised in the prophetic word.

CHAPTER 67

The Rebirth of Freedom of Worship

Freedom of Worship—Its Death and Revival

As far as we can tell from the records and revelations available to us, there was no freedom of worship for any people, except the saints, until the glory that was Greece and the grandeur that was Rome. Under those empires the people were free to choose their own types of false worship. It is doubtful if this was true in any of the earlier world empires.

Before the coming of Christ, the Lord's people were always governed by a theocracy except during the Egyptian bondage of Israel, the Assyrian captivity of the Ten Tribes, the Babylonian bondage of the Jews, and the centuries immediately preceding our Lord's birth in Palestine. Those who were blessed with true religion always had the freedom to choose their way of worship. Otherwise they could not have been saved. Nonbelieving nations, kindreds, families, and peoples during the early millenniums worshipped as their rulers mandated. If there was any freedom of choice between divergent false systems before the days of Greece and of Rome, it was so minimal as to be of no moment.

It appears that when Israel was in Egypt, she followed Jehovah, though the civil power rested with those rulers who knew not Joseph and who chose to enslave the Hebrews. It also appears that those in the Kingdom of Israel (the Ten Tribes), though transplanted to Assyria and subject to an iron yoke, worshipped as they chose. At least it is clear they went out of Assyrian bondage with power and under prophetic leadership. And it seems quite clear that the Kingdom of Judah (the Jews) maintained their religious integrity for seventy years in Babylon. Back in their homeland, though they had their own government for a season, they were soon vassals of worldly powers who, however, never suppressed the Jews in their own divine religion.

By the time the Christian faith was restored in the meridian of time by Jesus and his apostles, the day of a true theocracy was no more than a memory from history past. Our early Christian brethren paid a price, than which there is none greater, for the privilege of worshipping as they chose. Theirs was the dispensation of death and martyrdom. They were crucified on Roman crosses; they were slain by gladiatorial swords and torn by ravenous beasts in the arenas of the Caesars; and they were ignited as human torches on the walls of the Eternal City, which spiritually is as Sodom and Egypt. And with the death of the primitive church, freedom of worship died in the world. For the first time in more than four thousand years, the warriors from the nether regions were in complete control. They were of the world, and it was their world.

Let us now trace the revival of freedom of worship, without which there neither is nor can be any salvation. In doing so, we must state plainly and emphatically that the expressions made are not designed to discredit or demean any body of worshippers, whether past or present. They are, rather, a simple summary of historical verities. They may be read in thousands of texts written by Catholic, Protestant, and nonbelieving authors alike. Catholic authors name them, explain how they came into being, and say they underlie the proper and intended divine development of the true church. Protestant authors recount them as proof of departures from the faith once delivered to the saints. Nonbelieving authors simply record them as known historical events and seek to show their effect and influence upon the social and cultural and governmental development of nations and peoples.

The Black Millennium: A Day of Church Degeneracy

Just as surely as the blessed Christ will usher in the Millennium of peace and freedom, so an accursed Constantine gave to the world a Black Millennium, a millennium of blood and horror in which men believed the approved creeds of the day or died amid flaming fagots. For more than a thousand years, from the fore part of the fourth century to the end of the fifteenth, the world lay in darkness. It was a black and abysmal night; the stench of spiritual death poisoned the nostrils of men; and the jaws of hell gaped wide open to welcome the sensual sinners who loved darkness rather than light because their deeds were evil. In our more enlightened day, it is difficult to conceive of the depths to which government and religion and morality, both private and public, sank in what men universally describe as the dark ages.

This is the age in which the worship of Mary, the worship of images and relics, and the invocation of saints became the established order. It is the era in which the traditions of the fathers attained preeminence over the teachings of the apostles as recorded in the Bible. It is the day of the seven sacraments; of monasticism and monastic orders; of convents, celibacy, and clerical immorality; of mass for the living and mass for the salvation of the dead; of purgatory and indulgences for the living and the dead; of penance and simony and decadent morality in papal places; and of a host of other things that are a clear departure from the truth and simplicity that is in Christ. It is also the time of holy wars fought to save souls and slay the heathen who opposed the gospel of the times; of the seven major crusades and numerous minor ones, all fought in the cause of salvation, all supposedly conferring indulgences on those who shed the blood of the enemies of the church.

This also is the age of superficial conversion, if it can be called such. Those in the Roman empire became Christians because the emperor decreed it; tens of thousands among the heathen, defeated in battle, were given the choice of baptism or death. But above all, it is the age of papal supremacy, when the Bishop of Rome placed himself above every human tribunal and made himself accountable to God alone. It is the age when popes chose and crowned kings and emperors and were themselves deposed by emperors and councils. It is the age in which the state-church alliance became a despotism that could and did punish heretics with death, as, for instance, through the Spanish Inquisition. All of this may be read in any Catholic or Protestant history, although the interpretation placed upon it depends upon the religious predilections of the authors. The issue is not the verity of the known history, but what the events mean where pure religion is concerned.

The lesson, relative to freedom of worship, to be learned from all of this is summed up by Philip Schaff in these words: "An inevitable consequence of the union of church and state was restriction of religious freedom in faith and worship, and the civil punishment of departure from the doctrine and discipline of the established church. . . . After the Nicene age all departures from the reigning state-church faith were not only abhorred and excommunicated as religious errors, but were treated also as crimes against the Christian state, and hence were punished with civil penalties; at first with deposition, banishment, confiscation, and, after Theodosius, even with death."

This persecution of heretics was a natural consequence of the union of religious and civil duties and rights, the confusion of the civil and the ecclesiastical, the judicial and the moral, which came to pass since Constantine. . . .

"It was not till the eighteenth century that a radical revolution of views was accomplished in regard to religious toleration; and the progress of toleration and free worship has gone hand in hand with the gradual loosening of the state-church basis and with the clearer separation of civil and religious rights and of the temporal and spiritual power." (*History of the Christian Church* 3:138-40.)

The Renaissance—a Day of Awakening

In the providences of the Almighty, the Black Millennium must end. A few hundred years thereafter, the gospel is to be restored to prepare a people for the Second Coming of the Son of Man; the papal hold over the minds of men must be broken; and the light and truth and inquiry and freedom of former ages must come again. Let the earth spin and the darkness pass, and a few rays of light will soon dawn in the eastern sky.

That there should be a need for a renaissance is one of the ironies of the ages. But the hard facts of history are that the ban placed by the church upon the authors of antiquity, and upon research and inquiry in general, had brought in such a decadent age that man, made in the image of God, was more like an animal than a divine being. Morality, culture, literacy, learning in general, even theological inquiry—all these were at a low ebb. Nations were made up of warring feudal lords, and most men lived and died without contributing to the well-being of their fellowmen.

Then during the fourteenth and fifteenth centuries and the first part of the sixteenth, there came an awakening. It began in Italy, where the darkness was deepest, thus attesting that man, of the race and family of Deity, cannot forever be fed a diet of ignorance, fear, and superstition. There comes a time when the chains of darkness can no longer shackle the free spirit of those whose father is God. It spread throughout Europe and resulted in "achieving freedom from the intellectual bondage to which the individual man had been subjected by the theology and hierarchy of the Church. The intelligence of Italy, and indeed of Western Europe as a whole, had grown weary of the monastic ideal of life, and the one-sided purpose of the scholastic systems to exalt heavenly concerns by ignoring or degrading things terrestrial. The Renaissance insisted upon the rights of the life that now is, and dignified the total sphere for which man's intellect and his aesthetic and social tastes by nature fit him. It sought to give just recognition to man as the proprietor of the earth. It substituted the enlightened observer for the monk; the citizen for the contemplative recluse. It honored human sympathies more than conventual visions and dexterous theological dialetics. It substituted observations for metaphysics. It held forth the achievements of history. It called man to admire his own creations, the masterpieces of classical literature and the monuments of art. It bade him explore the works of nature and delight himself in their excellency. . . .

"It comprehends the revival of literature and art, the development of rational criticism, the transition from feudalism to a new order of social organization, the elevation of the modern languages of Europe as vehicles for the highest thought, the emancipation of intelligence, and the expansion of human interests, the invention of the printing press, the discoveries of navigation and the exploration of America and the East, and the definition of the solar system by Copernicus and Galileo,—in one word, all the progressive developments of the last two centuries of the Middle Ages, developments which have since been the concern of modern civilization." (Schaff, *History of the Christian Church,* 1960, 6:559-61.)

The Protestant Reformation—Its Blessings and Evils

As the fourteenth and fifteenth centuries were the age of the renaissance in learning and in freeing the mind to solve the problems of the day without adopting and building upon the time-worn and weary *ipse dixits* of dogmatic theology, so the sixteenth century was the age of renaissance in religion itself. The time had then come to take another step in preparing men for the coming restoration of pure and perfect Christianity. From the standpoint of those who do not know that the Protestant Reformation was simply a way station on the highway leading to the promised restoration, the following words help put its importance in perspective: "The Reformation of the sixteenth century is, next to the introduction of Christianity, the greatest event in history. It marks the end of the Middle Ages and the beginning of modern times. Starting from religion, it gave, directly or indirectly, a mighty impulse to every forward movement, and made Protestantism the chief propelling force in the history of modern civilization."

Both Christianity itself and the Protestant Reformation, it is said, "were ushered in by a providential concurrence of events and tendencies in thought. The way for Christianity was prepared by Moses and the Prophets, the dispersion of the Jews, the conquests of Alexander the Great, the language and literature of Greece, the arms and laws of Rome, the decay of idolatry, the spread of skepticism, the aspirations after a new revelation, the hopes of a coming Messiah. The Reformation was preceded and necessitated by the corruptions of the papacy, the decline of monasticism and scholastic theology, the growth of mysticism, the revival of letters, the resurrection of the Greek and Roman classics, the invention of the printing press, the discovery of a new world, the publication of the Greek Testament, the general spirit of enquiry, the striving after national independence and personal freedom. In both centuries we hear the creative voice of the Almighty calling light out of darkness."

The Protestant Reformation was a revolt against many of the practices and self-accepted absolutes of Catholicism. It was a cry of anguish, disbelief, and rejection against papal absolutism and the seven Catholic sacraments as the sole means of gaining salvation; against penance and indulgences and purgatory and the mass for both the living and the dead; against the worship of Mary and images and relics and the invocation of saints in general; against monks and monasticism and convents and priestly celibacy; against the corruptions and crimes and immoralities of the clergy at all levels and in all places. All this was to the good.

It was a call to search the scriptures, to turn to Christ rather than the church for salvation, and to be justified by faith. With it came false doctrines about election and predestination, the all-sufficiency of the scriptures, and numerous other matters. It maintained the false and damning doctrines of the creeds relative to God and the Godhead by perpetuating the Trinitarian concepts of Augustine and Athanasius and the theologians of the dark ages. And above all, it did not bring to pass a restoration of the gospel nor a reversion to primitive Christianity. It freed the people from many heresies and evil practices that had become so entrenched during the Black Millennium, but it did not bring in freedom of worship. It simply shifted the church-state alliance from one despot to another.

Thus: "Instead of one organization, we have in Protestantism a number of distinct national churches and confessions or denominations. Rome, the local centre of unity, was replaced by Wittenberg, Zurich, Geneva, Oxford, Cambridge, Edinburgh. The one great pope had to surrender to many little popes of smaller pretensions, yet each claiming and exercising sovereign power in his domain. The hierarchical rule gave way to the caesaropapal or Erastian principle, that the owner of territory is also the owner of its religion, . . . a principle first maintained by the Byzantine Emperors, and held also by the Czar of Russia, but in subjection to the supreme authority of the ecumenical councils. Every king, prince, and magistrate, who adopted the Reformation, assumed the ecclesiastical supremacy or summepiscopate, and established a national church to the exclusion of Dissenters or Nonconformists who were either expelled, or simply tolerated under various restrictions and disabilities.

"Hence there are as many national or state churches as

there are independent Protestant governments; but all acknowledge the supremacy of the Scriptures as a rule of faith and practice, and most of them also the evangelical confessions as a correct summary of Scripture doctrines. Every little principality in monarchical Germany and every canton in republican Switzerland has its own church establishment, and claims sovereign power to regulate its creed, worship, and discipline. And this power culminates not in the clergy, but in the secular ruler who appoints the ministers of religion and the professors of theology. The property of the church which had accumulated by the pious foundations of the Middle Ages, was secularized during the Reformation period and placed under the control of the state, which in turn assumed the temporal support of the church." (Schaff, *History of the Christian Church* 7:1-2, 43-44.)

The Church of England—A Case in Point

The Protestant Reformation had its real beginning in Germany, but it soon spread to other nations. Because the pendulum swung back and forth between Catholicism and Protestantism in England from the reign of one monarch to another, this island kingdom becomes the ideal illustration of religion by kingly fiat as contrasted with divine revelation.

Henry VIII and Thomas Cranmer were the two moving powers in the break with Rome and the setting up of an independent national church in England. The King was embroiled with the Pope in a violent controversy over his marital affairs. The Roman Pontiff had drafted an order directing the King to cast off his concubine, Anne, or face excommunication or even an interdict against the whole kingdom. During the dark ages the threat or enforcement of interdiction—the denial of all church blessings to a whole nation, thereby effectively keeping any of them from being saved—had kept kingdoms and empires in line.

Not so for England in this day of dawning enlightenment. The King forced through Parliament the Annates Bill. In the language of Sir Winston Churchill: "If the Court of Rome, its preamble ran, endeavoured to wield excommunication, interdict, or process compulsory in England, then all manner of sacraments and divine service should continue to be administered, and the interdict should not by any prelate or minister be executed or divulged. If any one named by the King to a bishopric were restrained by Bulls from Rome from accepting office he should be consecrated by the Archbishop, or any one named to an Archbishopric. And the Annates, a mainstay of the Papal finances, were limited to 5 percent of their former amount."

Thereafter Henry forced upon the clergy "articles of his own, making him effective master of the Church in England," and, "Thomas More resigned the Lord Chancellorship as a protest against royal supremacy in spiritual affairs." Nonetheless, "England was wholly independent of administration from Rome."

Next: "Cranmer became Archbishop in the traditional manner. At the King's request Bulls had been obtained from Rome by threatening the Papacy with a rigorous application of the act of Annates. Cranmer swore to obey the Pope with the usual oath, though reservations were made before and afterwards, and he was consecrated with full ceremonial. This was important: the man who was to carry through the ecclesiastical revolution had thus been accepted by the Pope and endowed with full authority. Two days afterwards, however, a Bill was introduced into Parliament vesting in the Archbishop of Canterbury [Cranmer] the power, formerly possessed by the Pope, to hear and determine all appeals from the ecclesiastical courts in England. Future attempts to use any foreign process would involve the drastic penalties of Praemunire. The judgments of the English courts were not to be affected by any Papal verdict or by excommunication, and any priest who refused to celebrate divine service or administer the sacraments was made liable to imprisonment. This momentous Bill, the work of Thomas Cromwell, which abolished what still remained of Papal authority in England, passed through Parliament in due course, and became known as the Act of Appeals. The following month Henry himself wrote a letter describing his position as 'King and Sovereign, recognising no superior in earth but only God, and not subject to the laws of any earthly creature.' The breach between England and Rome was complete."

Then, during the brief reign of Edward VI (1547-1553), the Reformation made decided progress. "The Book of Common

Prayer, in shining English prose," as Churchill expresses it, "was drawn up by Cranmer and accepted by Parliament in 1549." Thereafter Parliament approved the Articles of Religion. England's Bloody Queen, Mary, then ascended the throne. Her mission was to make the nation Catholic, and the religious legislation of her predecessors was repealed. But she probably did as much as any monarch to assure the triumph of Protestantism by burning Cranmer and the other Protestant bishops at the stake at Oxford in 1555. It was the events of these dreadful days that caused Churchill to write: "Nevertheless the doctrinal revolution enforced by Cranmer under Edward VI, and the Counter-Revolution of Gardiner, Pole, and their assistants under Mary, exposed our agitated Islanders in one single decade to a frightful oscillation. Here were the citizens, the peasants, the whole mass of living beings who composed the nation, ordered in the name of King Edward VI to march along one path to salvation, and under Queen Mary to march back again in the opposite direction; and all who would not move on the first order or turn about on the second must prove their convictions, if necessary, at the gibbet or the stake."

Queen Elizabeth was England's next ruler. "England became Protestant by law, Queen Mary's Catholic legislation was repealed, and the sovereign was declared supreme Governor of the English Church." The concept of religious freedom was as yet unborn. "The idea that a man should pick and choose for himself what doctrines he should adhere to was almost as alien to the mind of the age as the idea that he should select what laws he should obey and what magistrates he should respect." Out of it all, the tenor of the times being what they were, there was but one way to solve religious controversies. It was: "All the novel questions agitating the world—the relation of the National Church to Rome on one side and to the national sovereign on the other; its future organisation; its articles of religion; the disposal of its property, and the property of its monasteries—could only be determined in Parliament." (Winston S. Churchill, *A History of the English Speaking Peoples,* New York: Dodd, Mead, and Company, 1956, 2:58-59, 61, 87, 101, 105-7.)

And in Parliament they were determined. The elected Commons and the hereditary Lords, as advised by the clergy and as ordered and influenced by the King, legislated the doctrine, the ordinances, the forms of worship, the financial support, the court system, the relationship with other religious communities, and all else that involved the souls of men. Enactments of Parliament defined God as being "without body, parts, or passions"; they decreed that "Holy Scripture containeth all things necessary to salvation," and named those books of scripture that were to be considered canonical. These enactments declared that the Nicene, Athanasian, and Apostles creeds were true; that men "are justified by Faith only"; that some are predestined to be saved, others to be damned; that there is no purgatory; that the "invocation of Saints, is a fond thing vainly invented, and grounded upon no warranty of Scripture, but rather repugnant to the Word of God"; that infant baptism is required for salvation; that celibacy for priests is contrary to the will of God; and so on and so on and so on. (*Book of Common Prayer*, pp. 685-702.)

Is it amiss to ask: If a church is created by Parliament, receives its doctrines and powers from Parliament, and is forever subject to Parliament, whose church is it? Can Parliament also resurrect a man or create salvation, or, perchance, must the Lord have something to do with these things?

Wars and Persecutions—Born of Union of Church and State

Religious wars and persecutions are of the devil. There is no such thing as a holy war or a heaven-approved crusade. Men cannot be saved by force, Lucifer to the contrary notwithstanding. During the Christian era, hundreds of thousands have been burned and hanged as heretics while millions have been slain in wars fomented, instigated, commanded, and led by religious leaders. We shall make no attempt to recount these deeds of brutality and butchery; libraries are filled with histories that preserve the ugly and revolting details. There are ample accounts of the dark deeds of the Spanish Inquisition, of the papal crusades against the Albigenses, of the unspeakable atrocities wrought upon the Protestants in the Netherlands in the sixteenth century, of the massacre of St. Bartholomew, and so on. For our purposes, it suffices to say that all these things were possible and came to pass because of the union of church and state. They commenced with Constantine, continued through the Black Millennium, and were not abated in the days of the Protestant Reformation.

True: "The Reformation was a grand act of emancipation from spiritual tyranny, and a vindication of the sacred rights of conscience in matters of religious belief." But: "The very men who claimed and exercised the right of protest . . . denied the same right to others, who differed from them. . . . After having secured liberty from the yoke of popery, they acted on the persecuting principles in which they had been brought up. They had no idea of toleration or liberty in our modern sense. . . . The Protestant divines and princes of the sixteenth century felt it to be their duty to God and to themselves to suppress and punish heresy as well as civil crimes. . . . The world and the church were not ripe for a universal reign of liberty, nor are they now."

And further: "Religious persecution arises not only from bigotry and fanaticism, and the base passions of malice, hatred and uncharitableness, but also from mistaken zeal for truth and orthodoxy, from the intensity of religious conviction, and from the alliance of religion with politics or the union of church and state, whereby an offense against the one becomes an offense against the other." (Schaff, *History of the Christian Church* 7:50-51.)

In America—Freedom of Worship Is Born

Freedom of worship was conceived in Italy during the Renaissance; it gestated in Germany and Western Europe during the Protestant Reformation; but it was born in America after the Constitution of the United States became the supreme law of the land. This establishment of freedom of worship in the New World heaps no credit upon the original colonizers. They neither wanted it nor sought it. Rather, it was forced upon them by political necessity. Political necessity? Nay, by a divine providence, all in preparation for the restoration of the gospel in the dispensation of the fulness of times. Jesus told the Nephites that the Lord would set up in America "a free people by the power of the Father." (3 Nephi 21:4.)

Coming to America to escape religious persecution, the original colonists—retaining their various religious persuasions—immediately set up their own separate systems of worship and reached out to condemn and persecute all others. Witches were burned and heretics persecuted as in the Old World. The American colonists had simply transported the traditions of a false and decadent Christendom to new shores. But the Revolutionary War and the need for national survival brought forth the Constitution with this provision: "Congress shall make no law respecting an establishment of religion, or prohibiting the free exercise thereof." Thus, religious freedom was almost thrust upon them by a power beyond their control, and the union of church and state was forever banned in the United States.

That the Lord's hand was in all this is axiomatic. "I established the Constitution of this land," he tells us, "by the hands of wise men whom I raised up unto this very purpose." Why? That laws might be established and "maintained for the rights and protection of all flesh, according to just and holy principles; that every man may act in doctrine and principle pertaining to futurity, according to the moral agency which I have given unto him, that every man may be accountable for his own sins in the day of judgment." (D&C 101:77-80.) We repeat: There can be no salvation without freedom of worship. To be accountable for their own sins, men must be free to act as they choose. And this is not limited to people in the United States alone. "That principle of freedom," the Lord says, which maintains "rights and privileges, belongs to all mankind, and is justifiable before me." All men are entitled to the same guarantees of freedom as those found in America. "And as pertaining to law of man, whatsoever is more or less than this, cometh of evil." The union of church and state is not of God. "I, the Lord God, make you free, therefore ye are free indeed; and the law also maketh you free." (D&C 98:5-8.)

As devout and devoted believers in freedom of worship and the entire separation of church and state, The Church of Jesus Christ of Latter-day Saints includes the following propositions in its declaration of belief regarding governments and laws in general:

"We believe that no government can exist in peace, except such laws are framed and held inviolate as will secure to each individual the free exercise of conscience, the right and control of property, and the protection of life. . . .

"We believe that religion is instituted of God; and that men are amenable to him, and to him only, for the exercise of it, unless their religious opinions prompt them to infringe upon the rights and liberties of others; but we do not believe that human law has a right to interfere in prescribing rules of worship to bind the consciences of men, nor dictate forms for public or private devotion; that the civil magistrate should restrain crime, but never control conscience; should punish guilt, but never suppress the freedom of the soul. . . .

"We believe that rulers, states, and governments have a right, and are bound to enact laws for the protection of all citizens in the free exercise of their religious belief; but we do not believe that they have a right in justice to deprive citizens of this privilege, or proscribe them in their opinions, so long as a regard and reverence are shown to the laws and such religious opinions do not justify sedition nor conspiracy. . . .

"We do not believe it just to mingle religious influence with civil government, whereby one religious society is fostered and another proscribed in its spiritual privileges, and the individual rights of its members, as citizens, denied.

"We believe that all religious societies have a right to deal with their members for disorderly conduct, according to the rules and regulations of such societies; provided that such dealings be for fellowship and good standing; but we do not believe that any religious society has authority to try men on the right of property or life, to take from them this world's goods, or to put them in jeopardy of either life or limb, or to inflict any physical punishment upon them. They can only excommunicate them from their society, and withdraw from them their fellowship." (D&C 134:2-10.)

ARTICLE 12

*We believe
in being subject to kings,
presidents, rulers, and magistrates,
in obeying, honoring, and sustaining
the law.*

CHAPTER 68

The Church and Civil Power

Civil Power in Ages Past

In the whole realm of revealed religion, few things are of such deep concern to the true saints as their relationship with the powers that be. To have saving power, religion must be free from any power on earth and subject only to the powers in heaven. Lucifer sought to compel men to be saved, and for this grievous heresy and wicked rebellion against the plan of the Father, he and his followers were cast out of heaven. Freedom of religion, freedom of worship, freedom to choose one's own course is essential to salvation. The very instant that compulsion takes over in the world of worship is the moment when agency ceases to operate and we are no longer free to make the choices that lead to salvation.

Unless we voluntarily choose good rather than evil, light in preference to darkness, Deity's way in preference to the devil's, it is philosophically impossible to be saved. Salvation is born of freedom of choice. Even if we were forced to believe the truth itself, in all its parts, and were compelled to worship in every proper way, it could not save us, for no agency would be involved. Thus, as we have seen, civil control of religion is Lucifer's way of enforcing an enduring state of apostasy and of darkness upon all who are subject to such control. Thus also, as long as government controls our way of worship, Lucifer is in control, and we have no hope except to await the day when the chains will be broken and the bondage will cease.

Civil power does exist the world over. We have no choice but to live in subjection to the laws of that land upon which we dwell, and our great desire and hope, in the midst of a wicked world, is to maintain freedom of worship. Under these circumstances, what must our course be? It must be one of using all our power and influence to keep church and state separated, to sustain civil power in its proper realm, and to stipulate in constitutions, in legislative enactments, in executive decrees, in judicial determinations, in every possible way, that men are free to worship as they will and not be subject to compulsion.

In some countries freedom of worship is denied outright. In a large part of the Islamic world, men are commanded to worship as Allah is presumed to have decreed. During the long and dreary ages of darkness that preceded the Renaissance and the Reformation, the dominant church imposed its doctrines upon men at the peril of their lives. Even today, in the nations that still maintain national religions, there are powerful pressures to keep citizens within the national religious fold. Only in the United States are there ideal constitutional guarantees of freedom of worship, and these do not always operate as properly as they should.

The ancient scriptures abound in accounts of how the church and the state used their respective powers in days gone by. Except for a few New Testament recitations, these accounts of how things were done anciently do not bear out our expressed doctrine of obeying, honoring, and sustaining the law, and of being subject to kings, presidents, rulers, and magistrates.

When the Lord's people lived out their days in a theocracy of Deity's own making, they all had freedom of choice and were strengthened in their properly ordained ways of worship by the power of the state. Civil and religious powers were one in ancient Israel, and as long as the Lord and his judges and kings and prophets governed, these powers were used to save souls. But when these powers fell into evil hands; when a devilish dominion supplanted the divine power; when kings and rulers worshipped false gods and commanded the people to do likewise—then the civil power became the sword of Satan to destroy the souls of men. Under such circumstances, should the saints submit to their evil kings and bow to Baal? Or were they obligated to throw off the yoke of bondage and to mandate, in the face of all the powers of the world, that men should be free to worship as they chose?

When Jeroboam took the kingship over the Ten Tribes and adopted as a national religion the worship of Baal, were the people bound to follow him? Through all the long and tortuous centuries, even down through the days of their Assyrian captivity, the Lord sent prophets and messengers to call his people back to the standard of Jehovah.

When Ahab "did evil in the sight of the Lord above all that were before him"; when he married Jezebel "and went and served Baal, and worshipped him"; when he, leading Israel into every abomination, "did more to provoke the Lord God of Israel to anger than all the kings of Israel that were before him" (1 Kings 16:30-33), even decreeing that the people should forsake the Lord and worship Jezebel's god—what then? The Lord's answer was delivered by Elijah, who, having first called down fire from heaven to consume the sacrifices and the altar and the water and the dust and the stones, took nine hundred and fifty of the prophets of Baal "down to the brook Kishon, and slew them there." (1 Kings 18.)

When the backsliding Israelites worshipped Molech, was it right for them to obey the law decreeing that their children should be sacrificed in the fires of that pagan idol? When they were overpowered by the worshippers of Ashtoreth, should they submit to the decree commanding carnal intercourse with the temple prostitutes? Shadrach, Meshach, and Abednego, Jewish captives in Babylon, defied Nebuchadnezzar and did not worship his image of gold; thereupon they were thrown into a fiery furnace from which they were saved by divine power. (Daniel 3.) Daniel was cast into a den of lions when he defied the decree of Darius by praying to the true God. (Daniel 6.) Peter and John, being commanded by the Great Sanhedrin "not to speak at all nor teach in the name of Jesus," defied these Jewish overlords. Their inspired decision: "Whether it be right in the sight of God to hearken unto you more than unto God, judge ye. For we cannot but speak the things which we have seen and heard." (Acts 4:18-20.)

To these few illustrations might be added a host of others, all leading to the conclusion that there are times under which the Lord does not require submission to evil secular power. Obviously there is no sure way of knowing the course we should pursue in each instance except by revelation.

685

Civil Power in Our Present Age

All scripture should be studied in context. Any concepts taught will have application in principle whenever the same circumstances prevail, and perhaps above all other verses of holy writ, these principles of interpretation and application have reference to our twelfth Article of Faith. Certainly this inspired statement relative to obedience to law and subjection to secular authority had total application to the conditions in which the saints found themselves in 1842, when the Prophet penned the Wentworth Letter, of which the Articles of Faith are a part. At that time the Church was dominantly an American church with roots in Western Europe. Strictly speaking, and having in mind the historical context in which the inspired declarations on secular authority were made, they had specific application to the areas where the saints then dwelt. But they apply, in principle, to other areas in which church and state are separated and when like conditions prevail.

There are certain guidelines in the New Testament— differing from those in the Old Testament—that let us know how to operate in subjection to secular authority. These concepts apply to us because the primitive saints faced social and governmental conditions similar to the ones that confront us. Theocracies had ceased long before the days of Jesus and Peter. They and all men were subject to secular powers that used religion for their own purposes, or looked upon it as a necessary evil, or viewed it as pious nonsense not worthy of serious consideration. Thus Jesus, fully aware of Roman domination and Jewish political subservience, when taunted with the Pharisaical question, "Is it lawful to give tribute unto Caesar, or not?" said, "Shew me the tribute money." Thereupon he asked, "Whose is this image and superscription?" Their answer, "Caesar's," brought forth the decree: "Render therefore unto Caesar the things which are Caesar's; and unto God the things that are God's." (Matthew 22:17-21.)

In harmony with this concept, Peter counseled the meridian saints in these words: "Submit yourselves to every ordinance of man for the Lord's sake: whether it be to the king, as supreme; or unto governors, as unto them that are sent by him for the punishment of evildoers, and for the praise of them that do well." Such a course, Peter said, "is the will of God." How could it have been otherwise? Had these early saints rebelled against Caesar and claimed Christ alone as their king, they would have been guilty of sedition and the sword of Caesar would have denied them the opportunity to worship as they desired. Hence these words of counsel: "Honour all men. Love the brotherhood. Fear God. Honour the king." (1 Peter 2:13-17.)

Subjection to secular power does not constitute a divine approval of the system of government involved. However evil and autocratic the Roman empire may have been; regardless of the depravity and degeneracy in high places; notwithstanding the fact that human rights meant nothing to the Caesars—yet Rome was there, Rome ruled, Rome wielded the sword, and all who opposed her did so at the peril of their lives. Peter's next words—"Servants, be subject to your masters with all fear" (1 Peter 2:1-18)—carry the implicit meaning that subjection to government is not an endorsement and approval of the governmental system involved. Slavery is contrary to gospel principles. According to the order of heaven, it is not right that one man should be in bondage to another, and yet where this lesser standard exists, the Lord's counsel, as with reference to governments, is obedience and subjection. Here again, rebellion would bring civil penalties that well might preclude true worship itself.

Paul is of one mind with his fellow apostle in counseling the saints "to be subject to principalities and powers, to obey magistrates, to be ready to every good work, to speak evil of no man, to be no brawlers, but gentle, shewing all meekness unto all men." (Titus 3:1-2.) In this connection he exhorts that "supplications, prayers, intercessions, and giving of thanks, be made for all men; for kings, and for all that are in authority." Why? "That we may lead a quiet and peaceable life in all godliness and honesty." That is, so that we may be free to live our religion and work out our salvation. "For this is good and acceptable in the sight of God our Saviour." (1 Timothy 2:1-3.)

In a hard and difficult passage, which as it stands in the King James Version of the Bible is subject to unfortunate interpretations, Paul counseled the Roman saints to be in subjection to both civil and ecclesiastical authorities. We shall quote this entire passage from the Joseph Smith Translation, italicizing the words that have been changed or added and that give an entirely new meaning and emphasis to the difficult problems involved. Paul is using our enforced obedience to secular power as a pattern for our obedience to the higher ecclesiastical power of the church. We have no option but to obey Caesar, by which obedience we gain temporal benefits; ought we not willingly to obey God, through which obedience we gain eternal blessings?

"Let every soul be subject unto the higher powers," our ancient apostolic colleague tells us. The key to an understanding of what follows is in the definition of "higher powers." Are they the earthly powers of men or the heavenly powers of God? Paul answers our question: "For there is no power *in the church* but of God; the powers that be are ordained of God." Though the worldly powers that be are ordained of God in the sense that he approves the formation of governments to maintain law and order and to govern in the secular field, Paul is in reality speaking of the higher powers in the church as the ones that are ordained of God. "Whosoever therefore resisteth the power [in the church], resisteth the ordinance [that is, the law] of God; and they that resist shall receive to themselves punishment." As those who resist temporal power shall be punished for disobedience, so shall it be with the saints who resist the higher power administered by the church.

"For rulers are not a terror to good works, but to the evil." As this is true in the secular field, so it is in the realm of religion. "Wilt thou then not be afraid of the power? do that which is good, and thou shalt have praise of the same; for he is the minister of God to thee for good." God's ministers are in the church; they hold keys and power and authority from on high; they minister for the blessing and benefit of the saints. Those holding secular power are not the ministers of God except in the sense that they enforce a law against murder, or the like, which law is in harmony with gospel teachings. "But if thou do that which is evil, be afraid; for he [the true minister of God, the minister in the Church] beareth not the *rod* in vain; for he is the minister of God, a revenger to execute wrath upon him that doeth evil." The King James translators have the ministers bearing "the sword" rather than "the rod," which blood-shedding weapon the ministers of Christ do not bear. Their commission is to impose ecclesiastical penalties only, all with the hope that erring brethren will bow beneath the gospel rod and gain salvation. Paul is simply teaching that the penalties they impose for disobedience are a manifestation of the wrath of God upon sinners.

"Wherefore ye must needs be subject [to the powers that be in the Church], not only for wrath, but also for conscience sake." That is, do good for the sake of goodness itself; or, if needs be, do good to escape the penalties for sin. "For, for this cause pay ye *your consecrations* also *unto them;* for they are God's ministers, attending continually upon this very thing." Pay your tithes and offerings, the things you have consecrated to the Lord for the building up of his kingdom, not, as the King James Version has it, your tribute, as though you were paying taxes to a worldly power. The analogy is: If worldly powers require tribute, how much more important it is to pay our voluntary consecrations to the Lord's ministers.

"*But first,* render to all their dues, *according to custom,* tribute to whom tribute, custom to whom custom, *that your consecrations may be done* in fear of him to whom fear *belongs, and in honor of him* to whom honor *belongs. Therefore* owe no man anything." (JST, Romans 13:1-8.) Pay taxes and pay tithing. If we fear the secular sword for not paying taxes, ought we not to fear the gospel rod for failing to pay tithing?

Paul's analogy is inspired and sound, but it is not an authorization, as was assumed during the dark ages, to make a temporal ruler God's minister to enforce religion upon others by the power of the sword. The saints are subject to the powers that be, but those powers have no heaven-originated commission to command in the realm of religion.

In latter-day Israel, the Lord has appointed judges in Israel "to judge his people by the testimony of the just, . . . according to the laws of the kingdom which are given by the prophets of God." That these judges do not rule with omnipotent power is well known. "Let no man think he is ruler; but let God rule him that judgeth, according to the counsel of his own will." So also was it in the days of Paul. And as pertaining to the early Latter-day Saints who lived in and were subject to the laws of the United States of America, the Lord said: "Let no man break the laws of the land, for he that keepeth the laws of God hath no need to break the laws of the land." That this is not true with reference to the laws of all nations is axiomatic. "Wherefore, be subject to the powers that be, until he reigns whose right it is to reign, and subdues all enemies under his feet." (D&C 58:17-22.) The application of this divine decree to the laws of other nations is a matter that must be determined by inspiration as events occur.

Civil Power As It Affects the Saints

Until He rules whose right it is and subdues all enemies under his feet; until he makes a full end of all nations in the day of his coming; until the kingdoms of this world become the kingdom of our God and of his Christ—there will be conflicts between church and state that defy solution. Neither the saints nor Lucifer will yield on the issues involved, and a resolution will be found only after the wicked are destroyed by the brightness of His coming. In every nation the saints will use their influence in the Cause of Righteousness, in the cause of truth, the cause of freedom, the gospel cause. In those same nations, Lucifer will seek to enforce his will. Whenever and wherever he can use either a church or a state as an instrument of damnation, he will do it. We may expect greater opposition and a more definite polarization of the people as the great and dreadful day of the Lord draws nearer. Religious influences will cause political kingdoms to engage in the battle of Armageddon, and there will be martyrdom and destruction on all sides as the gospel is preached in those concluding days of the earth's temporal continuance.

From time to time the Church has made and yet will make formal declarations relative to the problems confronting church and state as they exist at any given time and in any specific area. In 1835 the Church issued a formal declaration of belief regarding governments and laws in general. The portions of this document not heretofore quoted in connection with the eleventh Article of Faith are as follows:

"We believe that governments were instituted of God for the benefit of man." This has reference to the existence of governments as such and is not an endorsement that all governments as they then existed had divine approval. "We believe . . . that he holds men accountable for their acts in relation to them, both in making laws and administering them, for the good and safety of society. . . .

"We believe that all governments necessarily require civil officers and magistrates to enforce the laws of the same; and that such as will administer the law in equity and justice should be sought for and upheld by the voice of the people if a republic, or the will of the sovereign. . . .

"We believe that all men are bound to sustain and uphold the respective governments in which they reside, while protected in their inherent and inalienable rights by the laws of such governments; and that sedition and rebellion are unbecoming every citizen thus protected, and should be punished accordingly; and that all governments have a right to enact such laws as in their own judgments are best calculated to secure the public interest; at the same time, however, holding sacred the freedom of conscience.

"We believe that every man should be honored in his station, rulers and magistrates as such, being placed for the protection of the innocent and the punishment of the guilty; and that to the laws all men show respect and deference, as without them peace and harmony would be supplanted by anarchy and terror; human laws being instituted for the express purpose of regulating our interests as individuals and nations, between man and man; and divine laws given of heaven, prescribing rules on spiritual concerns, for faith and worship, both to be answered by man to his Maker. . . .

"We believe that the commission of crime should be punished according to the nature of the offense; that murder, treason, robbery, theft, and the breach of the general peace, in all respects, should be punished according to their criminality and their tendency to evil among men, by the laws of that government in which the offense is committed; and for the public peace and tranquility all men should step forward and use their ability in bringing offenders against good laws to punishment. . . .

"We believe that men should appeal to the civil law for redress of all wrongs and grievances, where personal abuse is inflicted or the right of property or character infringed, where such laws exist as will protect the same; but we believe that all men are justified in defending themselves, their friends, and property, and the government, from the unlawful assaults and encroachments of all persons in times of exigency, where immediate appeal cannot be made to the laws, and relief afforded.

"We believe it just to preach the gospel to the nations of the earth, and warn the righteous to save themselves from the corruption of the world; but we do not believe it right to interfere with bondservants, neither preach the gospel to, nor baptize them contrary to the will and wish of their masters, nor to meddle with or influence them in the least to cause them to be dissatisfied with their situations in this life, thereby jeopardizing the lives of men; such interference we believe to be unlawful and unjust, and dangerous to the peace of every government allowing human beings to be held in servitude." (D&C 134:1-12.)

In 1899 Elder James E. Talmage, having in mind an American church and writing of conditions as they then existed, gave this wise counsel: "In the case of a conflict between the requirements made by the revealed word of God, and those imposed by the secular law, which of these authorities would the members of the Church be bound to obey? In answer, the words of Christ may be applied—it is the duty of the people to render unto Caesar the things that are Caesar's, and unto God the things that are God's. At the present time the kingdom of heaven as an earthly power, with a reigning King exercising direct and personal authority in temporal matters, has not been established upon the earth. The branches of the Church as such, and the members composing the same, are subjects of the several governments within whose separate realms the Church organizations exist. In this day of comparative enlightenment and freedom there is small cause for expecting any direct interference with the rights of private worship and individual devotion; in all civilized nations the people are accorded the right to pray, and this right is assured by what may be properly called a common law of humankind. No earnest soul is cut off from communion with his God; and with such an open channel of communication, relief from burdensome laws and redress for grievances may be sought from the power that holds control of nations.

"Pending the overruling by Providence in favor of religious liberty, it is the duty of the saints to submit themselves to the laws of their country. Nevertheless, they should use every proper method, as citizens or subjects of their several governments, to secure for themselves and for all men the boon of freedom in religious service. It is not required of them to suffer without protest imposition by lawless persecutors, or through the operation of unjust laws; but their protests should be offered in legal and proper order. The saints have practically demonstrated their acceptance of the doctrine that it is better to suffer evil than to do wrong by purely human opposition to unjust authority. And if by thus submitting themselves to the laws of the land, in the event of such laws being unjust and subversive of human freedom, the people be prevented from doing the work appointed them of God, they are not to be held accountable for the failure to act under the higher law." (Talmage, *The Articles of Faith*, pp. 422-23.)

In the midst of World War II the First Presidency of the Church issued this message to the Church:

"We again warn our people in America of the constantly increasing threat against our inspired Constitution and our free institutions set up under it. The same political tenets and philosophies that have brought war and terror in other parts of the world are at work amongst us in America. The proponents thereof are seeking to undermine our own form of government and to set up instead one of the forms of dictatorships now flourishing in other lands. These revolutionists are using a technique that is as old as the human race,—a fervid but false solicitude for the unfortunate over whom they thus gain mastery, and then enslave them.

"They suit their approaches to the particular group they seek to deceive. Among the Latter-day Saints they speak of their philosophy and their plans under it, as an ushering in of the United Order. Communism and all other similar *isms* bear no relationship whatever to the United Order. They are merely the clumsy counterfeits which Satan always devises of the gospel plan. Communism debases the individual and makes him the enslaved tool of the state to whom he must look for sustenance and religion; the United Order exalts the individual, leaves him his property, 'according to his family, according to his circumstances and his wants and needs,' (D&C 51:3) and provides a system by which he helps care for his less fortunate brethren; the United Order leaves every man free to choose his own religion as his conscience directs. Communism destroys man's God-given free agency; the United Order glorifies it. Latter-day Saints cannot be true to their faith and lend aid, encouragement, or sympathy to any of these false philosophies. They will prove snares to their feet. . . .

"The Church stands for the separation of church and State. The church has no civil political functions. As the church may not assume the functions of the state, so the state may not assume the functions of the church. The church is responsible for and must carry on the work of the Lord, directing the conduct of its members, one towards the other, as followers of the lowly Christ, not forgetting the humble, and poor and needy, and those in distress, leading them all to righteous living and a spiritual life that shall bring them to salvation, exaltation, and eternal progression, in wisdom, knowledge, understanding, and power. . . .

"The state is responsible for the civil control of its citizens or subjects, for their political welfare, and for the carrying forward of political policies, domestic and foreign, of the body politic. For these policies, their success or failure, the state is alone responsible, and it must carry its burdens. All these matters involve and directly affect Church members because they are part of the body politic, and members must give allegiance to their sovereign and render it loyal service when called thereto. But the Church, itself, as such, has no responsibility for these policies, as to which it has no means of doing more than urging its members fully to render that loyalty to their country and to free institutions which the loftiest patriotism calls for.

"Nevertheless, as a correlative of the principle of separation of the church and the State, themselves, there is an obligation running from every citizen or subject to the state. . . .

"The members of the Church have always felt under obligation to come to the defense of their country when a call to arms was made; on occasion the Church has prepared to defend its own members.

"In the days of Nauvoo, the Nauvoo Legion was formed, having in view the possible armed defense of the Saints against mob violence. Following our expulsion from Nauvoo, the Mormon Battalion was recruited by the national government for service in the war with Mexico. When Johnston's army was sent to Utah in 1857 as the result of malicious misrepresentations as to the actions and attitude of the territorial officers and the people, we prepared and used measures of force to prevent the entry of the army into the valleys. During the early years in Utah, forces were raised and used to fight the Indians. In the war with Spain, members of the Church served with the armed forces of the United States, with distinction and honor. In the World War, the Saints of America and of European countries served loyally their respective governments, on both sides of the conflict. Likewise in the present war, righteous men of the Church in both camps have died, some with great heroism, for their own country's sake. In all this our people have but served loyally the country of which they were citizens or subjects under the principles we have already stated. We have felt honored that our brethren have died nobly for their country; the Church has been benefited by their service and sacrifice. . . .

"The Church is and must be against war. The Church itself cannot wage war, unless and until the Lord shall issue new commands. It cannot regard war as a righteous means of settling international disputes; these should and could be settled—the nations agreeing—by peaceful negotiation and adjustment.

"But the Church membership are citizens or subjects of sovereignties over which the Church has no control. The Lord Himself has told us to 'befriend that law which is the constitutional law of the land.' . . .

"While by its terms this revealed word related more especially to this land of America, nevertheless the principles announced are worldwide in their application, and they are specifically addressed to 'you' (Joseph Smith), 'and your brethren of my church.' When, therefore, constitutional law, obedient to these principles, calls the manhood of the Church into the armed service of any country to which they owe allegiance, their highest civic duty requires that they meet that call. If, hearkening to that call and obeying those in command over them, they shall take the lives of those who fight against them, that will not make of them murderers, nor subject them to the penalty that God has prescribed for those who kill, beyond the principle to be mentioned shortly. For it would be a cruel God that would punish His children as moral sinners for acts done by them as the innocent instrumentalities of a sovereign whom He had told them to obey and whose will they were powerless to resist.

"The whole world is in the midst of a war that seems the worst of all time. This Church is a worldwide Church. Its devoted members are in both camps. They are the innocent war instrumentalities of their warring sovereignties. On each side they believe they are fighting for home, and country, and freedom. On each side, our brethren pray to the same God, in the same name, for victory. Both sides cannot be wholly right; perhaps neither is without wrong. God will work out in His own due time and in His own sovereign way the justice and right of the conflict, but He will not hold the innocent instrumentalities of the war, our brethren in arms, responsible for the conflict. This is a major crisis in the world-life of man. God is at the helm." (*Conference Report,* April 1942, pp. 90-95.)

ARTICLE 13

We believe in being honest,
true, chaste, benevolent, virtuous,
and in doing good to all men;
indeed, we may say that we follow the
admonition of Paul—
We believe all things,
we hope all things,
we have endured many things,
and hope to be able to endure all things.
If there is anything
virtuous, lovely, or of good report or
praiseworthy,
we seek after these things.

CHAPTER 69

"Pure Religion and Undefiled"

"The Conclusion of the Whole Matter"

Our dissertation on the Articles of Faith of The Church of Jesus Christ of Latter-day Saints—weak, faltering, insufficient though it may be—draws to a close. There is but little more to say. The thirteenth Article of Faith is in effect an addendum to all the others. It differs from them and does not call for an exposition of the various verities announced in it. But it does provide the ideal occasion to show the relationship between the great doctrines of the preceding twelve articles and the ethical principles set forth in this concluding formal statement of belief.

It is one thing to teach ethical principles, quite another to proclaim the great doctrinal verities, which are the foundation of true Christianity and out of which eternal salvation comes. True it is that salvation is limited to those in whose souls the ethical principles abound, but true it is also that Christian ethics, in the full and saving sense, automatically become a part of the lives of those who first believe Christian doctrines.

Ethical principles are born of doctrinal concepts. To say "We believe in being honest" is to testify that because we believe in Christ and his saving truths, we automatically accept honesty as a divine standard to which every true believer must conform. And so it is with all true principles; they inhere in, are part of, and grow out of the saving truths.

It is the word, the everlasting word, the word of salvation —all of which expressions are synonyms for the gospel— that controls and governs the lives of men. Thus in a time of trouble and peril, the prophet Alma, in seeking to bring peace and prosperity into the lives of the people, "thought it was

expedient that they should try the virtue of the word of God."
Why? Because "the preaching of the word had a great tendency to lead the people to do that which was just—yea, it
had had more powerful effect upon the minds of the people
than the sword, or anything else." (Alma 31:5.)

In teaching the gospel, it is far less effective to say "Be
honest, for honesty is the best policy," and then to reason
from a social standpoint why this is so, than to link honesty
with the gospel out of which it grows by teaching: "Wo unto
the liar, for he shall be thrust down to hell." (2 Nephi 9:34.) It
is only when gospel ethics are tied to gospel doctrines that
they rest on a sure and enduring foundation and gain full
operation in the lives of the saints.

In a great pronouncement to the teachers in the Church,
President J. Reuben Clark, Jr., speaks of "the colorless
instruction of the youth of the Church in elementary ethics."
Speaking of students and to teachers, he says: "These students already know that they must be honest, true, chaste,
benevolent, virtuous, and do good to all men, and that 'if
there is anything virtuous, lovely, or of good report or praiseworthy, we seek after these things'—these things they have
been taught from very birth. They should be encouraged in all
proper ways to do these things which they know to be true,
but they do not need to have a year's course of instruction to
make them believe and know them.

"These students fully sense the hollowness of teachings
which would make the Gospel plan a mere system of ethics,
they know that Christ's teachings are in the highest degree
ethical, but they also know they are more than this. They will
see that ethics relate primarily to the doings of this life, and
that to make of the Gospel a mere system of ethics is to confess a lack of faith, if not a disbelief, in the hereafter. They
know that the Gospel teachings not only touch this life, but
the life that is to come, with its salvation and exaltation as
the final goal.

"These students hunger and thirst, as did their fathers
before them, for a testimony of the things of the spirit and of
the hereafter, and knowing that you cannot rationalize
eternity, they seek faith, and the knowledge which follows
faith. They sense by the spirit they have, that the testimony
they seek is engendered and nurtured by the testimony of

others, and that to gain this testimony which they seek for, one living, burning, honest testimony of a righteous God-fearing man that Jesus is the Christ and that Joseph was God's prophet, is worth a thousand books and lectures aimed at debasing the Gospel to a system of ethics or seeking to rationalize infinity. . . .

"There is neither reason nor is there excuse for our Church religious teaching and training facilities and institutions, unless the youth are to be taught and trained in the principles of the Gospel, embracing therein the two great elements that Jesus is the Christ and that Joseph was God's prophet. The teaching of a system of ethics to the students is not a sufficient reason for running our seminaries and institutes. The great public school system teaches ethics. The students of seminaries and institutes should of course be taught the ordinary canons of good and righteous living, for these are part, and an essential part, of the Gospel. But there are the great principles involved in eternal life, the Priesthood, the resurrection, and many like other things, that go way beyond these canons of good living. These great fundamental principles also must be taught to the youth; they are the things the youth wish first to know about." (J. Reuben Clark, Jr., "The Charted Course of the Church in Education," in *J. Reuben Clark: Selected Papers,* ed. David H. Yarn, Jr., Provo: BYU Press, 1984, pp. 248-49.)

Unless revealed religion lives in the lives of men, it has no saving power. Conformity to the highest ethical standards is the natural outgrowth of believing the eternal truths that save. Morality, chastity, virtue, benevolence—all that is "virtuous, lovely, or of good report or praiseworthy"—these are the fruits of the gospel. It follows that the saints of God conform to the Word of Wisdom; honor the Sabbath day and keep it holy; pay their tithes and offerings gladly and not grudgingly; provide for the poor among them (currently through the great Welfare Program of the kingdom); identify their dead ancestors and perform the ordinances of salvation and exaltation for them in the temples of the Most High; labor freely and anxiously in the missionary cause; consecrate their time and talents freely and willingly for the furtherance of the Lord's work; endure persecution without flinching; and face martyrdom without fear—all because they know of the truth and divinity of the doctrines of salvation they have received.

Reciting some of the blessings of the gospel, Paul said: "The fruit of the Spirit is love, joy, peace, longsuffering, gentleness, goodness, faith, meekness, temperance." These come to those who live the gospel. "They that are Christ's have crucified the flesh with the affections and lusts," the ancient apostle continued. "If we live in the Spirit, let us also walk in the Spirit." (Galatians 5:22-25.)

James, our Lord's brother, counseling as the Spirit gave him utterance, spoke also of the operation of practical religion in the lives of men. "Be ye doers of the word, and not hearers only, deceiving your own selves," he said. "For if any be a hearer of the word, and not a doer, he is like unto a man beholding his natural face in a glass: for he beholdeth himself, and goeth his way, and straightway forgetteth what manner of man he was. But whoso looketh into the perfect law of liberty, and continueth therein, he being not a forgetful hearer, but a doer of the work, this man shall be blessed in his deed. If any man among you seem to be religious, and bridleth not his tongue, but deceiveth his own heart, this man's religion is vain. Pure religion and undefiled before God and the Father is this, To visit the fatherless and widows in their affliction, and to keep himself unspotted from the world." (James 1:22-27.)

And how aptly it was said by one of old: "Let us hear the conclusion of the whole matter: Fear God, and keep his commandments: for this is the whole duty of man." (Ecclesiastes 12:13.) Truly, as it is written, "He who doeth the works of righteousness shall receive his reward, even peace in this world, and eternal life in the world to come." (D&C 59:23.)

It is the hope and prayer of this disciple that the doctrines announced and the truths taught in the Articles of Faith may live in the hearts of the Latter-day Saints and of all who will yet join with them in striving to gain that eternal life which is the greatest of all the gifts of God. There is no salvation in an unused truth; it is only when men conform to the truth and make it a part of their very being that they advance and progress and finally qualify to return to the Eternal Presence.

The Articles of Faith are themselves a living, growing, expanding standard of belief and doctrine and practice. That they set forth eternal truths that will not be altered in time or in eternity is clear to all. One of these truths is that revelation is eternal and that there are many things, now unknown, which are yet to be revealed. These revelations of the present and of the future will contain added knowledge about those truths we have already received. Surely there is more for us to learn about Deity and his doings; about faith, repentance, and baptism; about the Second Coming of the Son of Man and his Millennial reign; about the hand-dealings of the Lord with all nations in ages past; about the spirit world and the realms of resurrected beings; about all of the principles of the gospel —more by far about these and ten thousand other things than we now know.

Since Elder James E. Talmage first published his scholarly work on the Articles of Faith in 1899, there have been two revelations of great importance. The first was the Vision of the Redemption of the Dead received by President Joseph F. Smith in October 1918; the second was the revelation on priesthood given to President Spencer W. Kimball in June 1978. This latter revelation, which offers the priesthood and all of its blessings, including celestial marriage, to those of every nation and race and color, solely on the basis of personal worthiness, is one of the great signs of the times. It enables us, for the first time, to take the gospel in its eternal fulness to those of every nation and kindred and tongue and people. It affects the work of the Lord in this sphere and in the realms ahead. We have no doubt that there are other revelations of like surpassing import that will be received before the Second Coming of the Son of Man.

The Seal of Testimony

Having written according to our best knowledge and understanding in all the pages of this work; knowing that such falls short of that excellence which the subject matter deserves; and both realizing and hoping that others in due course will perfect and improve what is here written—yet having done the work as best we can—there remains but one thing more. That is to place the seal of testimony on both the great latter-day work in which we are engaged and upon the doctrines we have taught. Let this then be our witness, our testimony, our knowledge of the truth and divinity of the gospel cause and of the doctrines of salvation that comprise it. Among those things that we of ourselves know are these:

God lives and is and ever shall be. He is the Everlasting Elohim who dwells in heaven above. He is our Father, the father of our spirits; we are his children, the offspring of his begetting. He has a glorified body of flesh and bones; he lives in the family unit; and he possesses all power, all might, all dominion, and all truth. The name of the kind of life he lives is eternal life.

This Almighty God is the Creator of all things from the beginning. His Firstborn Son, the Lord Jehovah, while yet a spirit being, grew in grace and wisdom until he became like the Father in intelligence and power. There were also many other noble and great ones.

This Holy Man, the Father of us all, who reigns supreme and is a saved being, ordained and established a plan of salvation so that his Firstborn and all his spirit children might advance and progress, become like him, have all power, know all things, live in the family unit, having eternal increase of their own—or in other words, that they might gain for themselves immortality and eternal life. This great and eternal plan of salvation is the gospel of God, meaning the Father. It was adopted by the beloved and chosen one who in the councils of eternity was foreordained to be the Savior and Redeemer to put into full operation, through the infinite and eternal atonement, all the terms and conditions of the Father's plan. Since then, to center our attention in the Atoning One by whom salvation comes, the gospel of God became and is and ever shall be the gospel of Jesus Christ.

Our witness of Jesus Christ is that he is the Son of the Living God, the Only Begotten in the flesh, the Lamb of God; that he ransomed fallen men from the spiritual and temporal death brought into the world by the fall of Adam; and that he took upon himself the sins of all men on conditions of repentance. Born of Mary, rejected by his own, a man of sorrows and acquainted with grief, he bowed beneath an infinite burden in Gethsemane, sweating great drops of blood from every pore. He was crucified. He ministered among the righteous in the world of spirits, and on the third day he burst the bands of death, arising from the Arimathean's tomb in glorious immortality as the firstfruits of them that slept. And in some way, incomprehensible to us but glorious and wondrous to contemplate, the effects of his resurrection pass upon all men so that all shall rise from death to life, being physically perfected and without mortal infirmities, and those who have been faithful and true in all things shall inherit eternal life.

We also testify, and it is our witness to all the world, that God has in these last days restored the fulness of his everlasting gospel, so that once again there are legal administrators who walk the dusty paths of Palestine, as it were, and who have power to preach the gospel, perform the ordinances of salvation and exaltation, and seal men up unto eternal life as did the apostles and prophets of old.

We testify with an absolute knowledge, born of the Spirit, that the Father and the Son, the Supreme Rulers of the Universe, appeared personally to Joseph Smith in a grove of trees, now sacred to the memory of that grand theophany, to usher in the dispensation of the fulness of times; that Joseph the Seer, ranking with Abraham and Moses among the prophets, was called from the foundation of the world to prepare the way for the Second Coming of the Son of Man; and that he received revelations, entertained angels, and was given keys and powers from on high.

We attest with words of soberness that this mighty prophet of the restoration translated the Book of Mormon by the gift and power of God, which volume of holy scripture is the voice of God to the Lehites and to those in all nations of every tribe and lineage. It is our witness that, commanded of God, he organized again among men the earthly kingdom of the Lord Jesus Christ, which kingdom is The Church of Jesus Christ of Latter-day Saints. This church administers the gospel, makes salvation available to men, and is the only true and living church upon the face of the whole earth.

It is our witness that this church, whose "foundation beliefs are the laws and principles laid down in the Articles of Faith," is destined to remain forever on earth; that the gospel it administers is the everlasting gospel that never again will slip from the hands of mortals; and that the earthly kingdom of God the Lord is destined to roll forth until, meeting the kingdom coming down from heaven as the Millennium commences, it fills the whole earth.

What more need we say? These are the great verities.

They must "not be overlooked, forgotten, shaded, or discarded." They, "and each of them, together with all things necessarily implied therein or flowing therefrom, must stand, unchanged, unmodified, without dilution, excuse, apology, or avoidance; they may not be explained away or submerged." (J. Reuben Clark, Jr., "The Charted Course of the Church in Education.")

God is true, Christ is true, and the gospel is true. Salvation is in Christ. His is the honor and the power and the glory forever, but we are his agents, his servants, those whom he hath called out of all mankind to speak his words and do his works. We say: Come unto Christ, all ye ends of the earth. Believe his gospel; repent of all your sins; be baptized and receive the gift of the Holy Ghost; and ever thereafter walk in the light and be one with the saints. Such is the way leading to peace in this life and to eternal life in the world to come. So be it.

INDEX

Aaronic Priesthood: restoration of, 321; is appendage to Melchizedek, 346; offices in, 352-53
Abandonment of sin, 235-36
Abel, faith of, 167
Abraham: sees "noble and great ones," 4, 34; God's covenant with, 36-38, 311, 313, 316-17, 504-9; as type of Christ, 118; as dispensation head, 136; faith of, 198-99; as father of faithful, 503. *See also* Abrahamic covenant; Seed of Abraham
Abrahamic covenant, 36-38, 311, 313, 316-17; giving of, 504-5; descent of, 505-9; obedience brings blessings of, 522; in temple, 539
Accountability, personal, 100
Adam: keys held by, 11, 310; received patriarchal government, 35, 657-58; taught generations about God, 47-48; false concepts about, 103-4; gospel was given to, 133, 135; faith of, 197; was commanded to repent, 214-15; baptism of, 250; place of, in eternal hierarchy, 503. *See also* Fall of Adam
Adam-ondi-Ahman, 640
Administration: gift of, 277-78, 372; legal, of God's kingdom, 319
Adultery, 231-32
Advocacy, law of, 126
Agency: inherent in plan of salvation, 89; through fall and atonement, 89-90; requires opposites, 90-91, 655; is eternal principle, 91-92; requires rewards and punishments, 96. *See also* Freedom of worship
Ahman, 60
Alma the younger, 228-29, 283
America: is land of Joseph, 511; New Jerusalem in, 589; establishment

of, to prepare for restoration, 628; freedom of worship in, 678-80
Angels: ministering of, 203; keys restored by, 322-23; beholding, is gift of Spirit, 374
Animal sacrifices, 114-15
Anthon, Professor Charles, 448-49
Apostasy, 53-57, 141, 143; creates false churches, 338; universal, evidences of, 339-40; prophecies of, 341-42; day of, 343, 439-40; miracles cease because of, 363-66, 367-68; great, Bible proves, 398; foreseen by Nephi, 407-10, 435; foreseen by Isaiah, 434-35; lack of revelation during, 477-78; Israel scattered due to, 525-28, 532-35; is sign of times, 623-24
Apostles: twelve, ordained by Christ, 320; office of, 348-49
Ariel, 430-31
Armageddon, 637-38
Articles of Faith: writing of, 15-16; living truths of, 702-3
Ashtoreth, 532-33
Asking, law of, 378-79
Assyria, 532, 534
Atonement of Christ: was dependent on fall, 81-82, 108; mercy depends on, 94-96, 215; definition of, 107; salvation depends on, 109, 128-30; required divine Sonship, 110-12; was voluntary act, 112; through blood of Christ, 112-14; symbols and types of, 114-18; propitiation through, 122-23; reconciliation through, 123-24; mediation through, 124-25; intercession through, 125-26; advocacy through, 126; infinite and eternal, 130-31; transcendence of, 620-21
Attributes of God, 175-80, 181-83

Idols, worship of, 54, 524-28, 532-34
Ignorance, man cannot be saved in, 43
Immortality, 108; Jesus inherited, from his Father, 111; all men receive, 152; is God's work and glory, 264; gift of, 358
Impartiality of God, 173-74
Infant baptism, 100-101, 251-52
Instinct, God is known by, 45-46
Intellect, use of, in knowing God, 46-47
Intercession, law of, 125-26
Interpretation of tongues, 374-75
Isaac, 37, 39; sacrifice of, as type of Christ, 118; Abrahamic covenant descended to, 505-6
Isaiah, 430-31, 442, 450-52; on gathering of Israel, 535-40
Ishmael, 39
Islamic religion, 54, 98-99, 460
Israel: rebellion in, 39-40, 333, 477; theocracy in, 333-34, 660-61; people of, are gathered by Book of Mormon, 420, 454-58; ultimate triumph of, 434-36, 452, 562-64; history of, 453, 515-16; story of, begins with Abraham, 503; Abrahamic covenant descended to, 506-7; are the Lord's people, 510; eternal inheritance of, 511; foreordination of, 513-14; myths concerning, 517-21; captivity of, 525-26, 532, 534; two kingdoms of, 531; the Lord's pleas to, 541-42; new covenant with, 548-49; compared to olive tree, 556; kingdom to be restored to, 641. *See also* Gathering of Israel; Scattering of Israel

Jackson County, Missouri, 589-90, 594-99, 607
Jaredites, 660
Jeremiah, 3-4, 34, 541-45
Jeroboam, king of Israel, 531-32, 685
Jerusalem: woe to, 430-33; redemption of, 583-84, 632; building of temple in, 587, 589; celestial, 588-89; slaying of two prophets in, 636. *See also* New Jerusalem
Jesus Christ: name of, linked with Joseph Smith, 1-2; foreordination of, 3, 110-11; acceptance of, presupposes acceptance of prophets, 11-12, 27; belief in, is fundamental to salvation, 28-30; God the Father is supreme over, 51; physical resurrection of, 60; volunteered to be Redeemer, 65; specific functions of, in Godhead, 66-69; is Firstborn, 66, 73; role of, in creation, 66-67; as Messiah, 67; as God of Israel, 67; is Only Begotten in flesh, 67-68, 75; as Redeemer, 68; manifests and reveals the Father, 68-69; role of, in judgment, 69, 74; as our Father, 69; suffering endured by, 73-74, 109; divine Sonship of, 110-12; blood of, atones for sin, 112-14; types testify of, 114-18; as dispensation head, 137; as prototype of saved being, 148-49; preached in spirit world, 156, 158; faith is centered in, 185-86; possessed perfect faith, 186, 206; showed resurrected body to faithful, 200; being one with, 206-9; baptism of, 247-48; becoming sons and daughters of, 284-87; priesthood held by, 315-18; church of, bears his name, 336; as God's gift to earth, 358; praying in name of, 381-83; Book of Mormon testifies of, 415-16; visited "other sheep," 427-29; seeing, in flesh, 492-99; as Second Comforter, 498-99; Jews will recognize, 564, 584, 638; two comings of, 620-21; personal reign of, on earth, 639-40; coming of, to Adam-ondi-Ahman, 640; author's testimony of, 704-5. *See also* Atonement of Christ; Light of Christ; Second Coming of Christ.

all priesthood is, 345; all offices are appendages to, 345-46; offices in, 348-52; prepares men to see Lord, 495-96
Mental exertion and faith, 191-92
Mercy: cannot rob justice, 94-96, 215; of God, 171-72, 179-80; repentance depends on, 215; praying for, 385
Messiah, 67
Michael, 2
Milk before meat, 396, 397-98, 443
Millennium: gathering of Israel during, 548, 563-64; destruction of wicked at, 563, 582-83, 646-47; preparing for, 576-79; glory of Zion during, 583-85; state of men during, 642-43; worship during, 643; terrestrial law of, 646-47; state of earth during, 649-50
Miracles: are wrought by faith, 199-201, 203-6; ceasing of, 364-66; are gifts of Spirit, 373. *See also* Gifts of the Spirit
Missionary work: in spirit world, 158-59; to gather righteous to Zion, 573
Mormon Battalion, 695
Mortality: brought by fall, 84-86, 213, 648-49; as probationary estate, 87-88, 213-14, 229-30; is continuation of first estate, 512; Millennial, 642-43
Moses, 136-37; faith of, 199; keys restored by, 322, 529-30; Joseph prophesied of, 425; saw God face to face, 494; saw destiny of Israel, 522, 531. *See also* Law of Moses
Moslems, 54
Murder, 231
Mysteries of godliness, 71-77, 443-44

Natural man, 260-61, 282
Nauvoo Legion, 695
Nauvoo Temple, 602
Nephi, 556-66
Nephites: destruction of, 432; Abrahamic covenant descended to, 506-7; government of, 661

New Testament, 392
New Jerusalem, 578; building of, before Second Coming, 587; in Jackson County, 589-90; building of, is sign of times, 591, 632; directions for building, 601
Nicodemus, 282-83
Noah: taught generations about God, 48; ministry of, 140; faith of, 198; place of, in patriarchal chain, 503
"Noble and great ones," in premortal existence, 4, 34

Oath: sworn by God, 313, 317; solemnity of, 317
Oath and covenant of priesthood, 232, 312-14
Obedience, 237-38; following baptism, 249; to laws of land, 686
Old Testament, 391-92
Olive tree, Israel likened to, 556
Omnipotence of God, 52, 176-77, 182
Omipresence of God, 53
Omniscience of God, 52-53, 176, 181
Only Begotten Son, Jesus as, 67-68, 75
Opposition: against Joseph Smith, 8-10; in all things, 90, 406-7; agency requires, 90-91, 655; through evil gifts, 375-77; to Book of Mormon, 459-64; to cause of Zion, 611-12; saints to avoid stirring up, 617
Order, house of, 306, 307, 324-26
Ordinances: sealed by Holy Spirit of Promise, 272-73, 307; performing, with authority, 324-25. *See also* Baptism; Sacrament
Original sin, false doctrines of, 100-101

Palestine, land of, 511, 527
Paradisiacal creation, 84
Partridge, Edward, 597
Patriarchal order, 35-36, 657-58
Patriarchs, 351-52
Perdition, sons of, 119-20, 144-45, 232-33, 652
Perfection: of God's attributes, 181-83; saints seek, 207

claim to mercy, 214; made available through atonement, 214-16; general, or reformation, 216-17; in gospel sense, 217-18; and baptism, 217-18; universal need for, 218-20; commandments concerning, 219-20, 222; saints' need for, 221; lack of, causes suffering, 222-23; this life is time for, 229-30; procrastination, 230; steps of, 234-40

Respecter of persons, God is not, 173-74, 252

Restitution for sin, 237

Restoration of gospel, 7, 139-41, 319-23, 628-29; hinges on Joseph Smith's calling, 12-13; author's testimony of, 16-17, 705; role of Book of Mormon in, 419-20, 450, 453; is marvelous work and wonder, 450-51, 560-61; for last time, 545; is sign of times, 626-27; preparation of world for, 627-28

Resurrection: nature of bodies after, 72-73; denial of, 104; universal nature of, 108, 119, 153-54; baptism and, 291

Revelation: knowing God through, 48-50; comes through Holy Ghost, 266-67, 269; comes to legal administrators, 319; is gift of Spirit, 375; salvation depends on, 475-76; the Lord's people always receive, 477; general and specific, 478; for Church comes through President, 479-80; yet to come, 481-86; testimony comes through, 487-88; personal, 487-91

Rewards, agency requires, 96

Rigdon, Sidney, 598

Romans: gods of, 54, 662; submission to law of, 686-87

Sabbath, law of, 300-302

Sacrament: testifies of Christ, 116-17; partaking of, worthily, 239-40, 297-98; Jesus gave, to disciples, 295; covenant of, 296; is for church members, 296-97; prepares men for Spirit, 298-99; false systems of, 299-300

Sacrifice: infinite and eternal, 111-12; law of, pointed to Christ, 112, 114-16, 294-95; faith requires, 188-91; and sacrament, 294-95

Sacrifices, human, 55, 534

Salvation: Joseph Smith's role in, 1; is in Christ, 2, 109; depends on belief, 23, 25-26; depends on knowing God, 43-44; depends on mortality, 87-88; degrees of, 96, 144; by grace, 99-100, 149-50; predestination to, 102-3; depends on atonement, 109, 128-30; universal, 146-47; process of gaining, 147-49, 221-22; man cannot provide, for himself, 150, 305; for the dead, 155-59, 229-30, 252, 508-9; depends on faith, 196, 202; depends on repentance, 212; baptism leads to, 244-45; covenant of, 293; depends on revelation, 475-76; is of Israel, 510. *See also* Plan of salvation

Sanctification, 239, 244, 265-66, 494

Satan: men loved, more than God, 53, 659; offered to save all mankind, 65, 92, 655-56; church of, 340-42, 408-10, 625; gifts of, 376-77; binding of, 563, 564; government instituted by, 658-59

Scapegoat, 116

Scattering of Israel, 515, 520; Moses foresaw, 523-25; due to apostasy, 528, 532-35; Jeremiah's words concerning, 543; prophesied by Lehi, 555; Nephi's prophecies concerning, 559-60

Schaff, Philip, quotations from, 670-74, 678

Scriptures: reveal little or much, 71-72; are word of gospel, 389-90; searching, is commandment, 390-91; volumes of, support each other, 418-19; proving truth of, 446-48; of different peoples,

632-33; in Jackson County, 601; in
Nauvoo, 602
Temptation, agency requires, 92
Ten Tribes, lost: location of, myths
about, 520; return of, myths about,
520-21; Millennial return of,
529-30, 641-42
Terrestrial kingdom, 146, 652; law of,
during Millennium, 646-47
Testimony: is gift of Spirit, 371;
praying for, 467; is received by
revelation, 487-88; seal of, 703-6
Theocracy, 35, 684; in Israel, 333,
660-61; of Adamic age, 657-58;
imitation, 658-59; in Enoch's day,
659; after flood, 660
Three Nephites, faith of, 200-201
Three Witnesses to Book of Mormon,
447, 467
Tongues, gift of, 374-75
Translation: gift of, 360, 361-62; of
Bible into Greek, 402-3; errors in,
affecting Bible, 403-5
Truth: gospel embraces all, 132; faith
is founded on, 166-67; God of,
173, 180; dispensed through light
of Christ, 259-60; Holy Ghost
teaches, 267-68; self-evident, 305;
of Book of Mormon, determining,
464-67; yet to be revealed, 483-86
Twelve apostles ordained by Christ,
320

United Order, 600, 615, 618, 693-94
Unity: of members of Godhead, 58,
75-76; of Father and Son, 185; of
men with Christ, 206-9
Unpardonable sin, 231-33, 279-80
Urim and Thummim, 476

Visions, 375
Voice from dust, Book of Mormon as,
436-37

War in heaven, 92
Wars: of Nephites and Lamanites, 432;
of Israel against enemies, 434-36;
and rumors of wars, 582, 633;
preceding Second Coming,

638-39; religious, 677-78; Church's
position on, 695-96
Wentworth Letter, 15
Wesley, John, 364
Wicked, destruction of, 563-64,
582-83, 617, 646-47
Wisdom: complete, of God, 52-53; is
gift of Spirit, 372-73; those lacking,
may ask of God, 379
Witnesses: law of, 446; of Book of
Mormon, 447
Whitmer, David, 447
Words: men to be judged by, 25; of
Christ, belief in, 28; of God are
scripture, 389-91
Works: men to be judged by, 25; faith
without, 102; greater than Christ's,
207-8; of flesh, 224-25
Worldly treasures, 188
Worship: eternal law of, 44;
correctness of, shown by actions,
55-57; manner of, during
Millennium, 643. See also
Freedom of worship

Zedekiah, 534
Zenos, 558-59, 563
Zion, 332-33; gathering of Israel to,
420, 567; of Enoch, 568-69; various
locations of, 569-70, 578; glory of,
570-71; exhortations to gather to,
570-75; temples in, 574-75;
building up, before Millennium,
576-79, 582; all is not well in,
580-81; great day of, is Millennial,
582-85, 594; failure of early saints
to build, 586, 591, 603-4, 607-8,
614-16; to live celestial law, 592,
600, 615; saints commanded to
build, 593-94; in Missouri, 595;
purchasing lands for, 595-99, 610,
618; United Order in, 600;
ultimate redemption of, 604-6,
608-9, 612-14; parable of
redemption of, 610; becoming
worthy to build, 618-19. See also
New Jerusalem
Zion's Camp, 614, 617

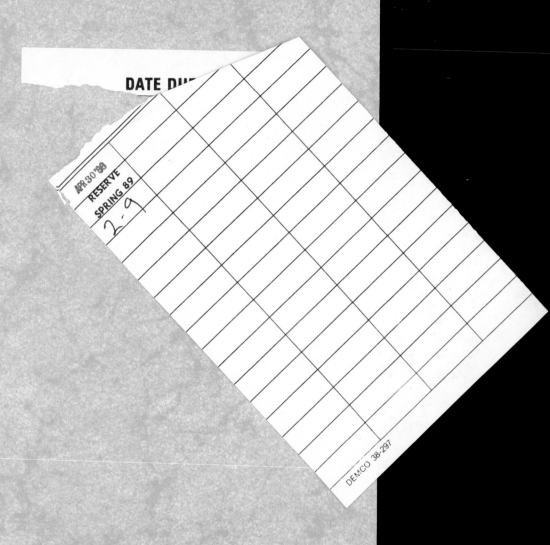